AF894611

Gerd Kohlhepp
The Brazilian Amazonia in Change II

Biblioteca Luso-Afro-Brasileira | Volume 4

Editorial

The Biblioteca Luso-Afro-Brasileira is a publication series of the Ibero-Amerikanischen Instituts Preußischer Kulturbesitz, in which monographs and collections on literature, culture, language, history, economics and politics from the Portuguese-speaking countries are published. The series is multidisciplinary and open to cross-regional and comparative research. The languages of publication are Portuguese, English and German. All publications in this series are subject to a peer-review process.

Gerd Kohlhepp, born in 1940, studied geography, geology, history, prehistory and economics at Universität Heidelberg, where he graduated with a Dr. phil. in 1967. In 1972 he habilitated at the faculty of geosciences at Universität Heidelberg and in the same year became a professor of human geography at Goethe-Universität Frankfurt am Main. In 1978 he was a professor of economic and social geography at Universität Tübingen, where he established a department of Latin American research. He became professor emeritus in 2005. His research in South America focused on human geography and regional socio-economic change, since the 1970s in particular on the social, economic and ecological transformations in the Brazilian Amazon region.

Gerd Kohlhepp

The Brazilian Amazonia in Change II

Five Decades of Exploitation, Deforestation and Attempts at Sustainable Development

[transcript]

Bibliographic information published by the Deutsche Nationalbibliothek
The Deutsche Nationalbibliothek lists this publication in the Deutsche Nationalbibliografie; detailed bibliographic data are available in the Internet at https://dnb.dnb.de

First published in 2025 by transcript Verlag, Bielefeld

transcript Verlag | Hermannstraße 26 | D-33602 Bielefeld | live@transcript-verlag.de

Cover concept: Maria Arndt, Bielefeld
Cover illustration: above: ckybe / Adobe Stock, below: Imago Photo / Adobe Stock
Proofread: Patricia Schulze
Typeset: Patricia Schulze
Printed by Elanders Waiblingen GmbH, Waiblingen
Print-ISBN 978-3-8376-7535-1
PDF-ISBN 978-3-8394-7535-5
https://doi.org/10.14361/9783839475355
ISSN of series: 2752-1990
eISSN of series: 2752-1419

Printed on permanent acid-free text paper.

Contents

II Promising environmental concepts for Amazonia under pressure by economic growth and agrobusiness strategies (1990s–2018)

III Devastation and environmental degradation policies in Amazônia Legal during the Bolsonaro Government (2019–2022)

IV Epilogue

In memory of Orlando Valverde and Hilgard O'Reilly Sternberg,
eminent Brazilian geographers and pioneers in research in the Amazon region.

Preface

In over 50 years, the Brazilian Amazonia has experienced man-made destruction of natural resources and the livelihoods of the Indigenous population. In the 1970s, the Military Government granted private capital almost unlimited access to rain forest areas in the planning region Amazônia Legal with generous financial incentives, after the state-led colonisation of landless people remained unsuccessful. The exploitation of the Amazon's ecosystems for the extraction of mineral resources, large-scale livestock farming and national integration measures was carried out without regard for the Indigenous people and regional socio-ecological vulnerability, contrary to the warnings of scientists and NGOs.

Tropical biodiversity and Indigenous areas were seen as obstacles to economic progress. The government's neglect of sustainable development and the inadequate coordination of state and private projects at federal, regional and local level led to high subsequent costs and robbed the marginalised population of their livelihoods.

Later governments have also implemented administratively inefficient and socio-ecologically damaging mega-programmes (including the Grande Carajás programme and hydropower plants with large reservoirs) with disastrous environmental impacts.

The internationally funded Pilot Programme to conserve the Brazilian tropical rain forests (PPG7) started some significant environmental policy improvements for sustainable development but was not deepened by follow-up programmes. Extensive infrastructure projects (including the Cuiabá–Santarém highway) aimed at a conservative modernisation and attracted southern Brazilian soybean farmers, whose activities also expanded into the humid savannahs in the south-east of the region. The often violent conflicts of interest between the social actors operating on the pioneer front remained unresolved and Indigenous territories, conservation units and protected areas remained at risk.

During the Bolsonaro government, deforestation increased rapidly and environmental institutions were brought to a virtual standstill. Violence and chaos became omnipresent.

Tropical forest ecosystems are a huge CO_2 reservoir. To date, around 20 % of the Brazilian rain forests have been cleared, mostly illegally, and a further 20 % are severely degraded. A socio-ecological transformation process and good local governance are only just beginning to emerge. The elimination of violence, illegality and corruption is still outstanding. The demand from industrialised countries for the supply of cheap raw materials and agricultural commodities is endangering Amazônia Legal without bringing any added value for the majority of its 28 million inhabitants.

The new government of Lula da Silva is facing the great challenge of a fundamental turnaround with the final renunciation of deforestation and the goals of sustainable development and environmental justice in Amazonia.

Large-scale destruction of biodiversity, rising temperatures and instability of precipitation not only pose a threat to the region, but also cause global impacts related to climate change. Over the last two decades, Amazônia Legal has evolved from a CO_2 sink to a source of CO_2 emissions. A deforestation rate of 20–25% marks a tipping point at which rain forests will turn into non-forest ecosystems (humid savannahs). This "point of no return" could be imminent.

The publication *The Brazilian Amazonia in Change* of Jan M.G. Kleinpenning (Professor of Human Geography of Developing Countries at the University of Nijmegen, The Netherlands) and Gerd Kohlhepp (Professor of Economic and Social Geography; formerly Latin American Research Centre at Tübingen University, Germany) is organised in two volumes:

Vol. 1: **Jan M.G. Kleinpenning**: *The Brazilian Amazonia in change I. Opening up and colonisation in the 1970s*

Vol. 2: **Gerd Kohlhepp**: *The Brazilian Amazonia in change II. Five decades of exploitation, deforestation and attempts at sustainable development*

Jan M.G. Kleinpenning and Gerd Kohlhepp

Foreword to Volume 2

When my esteemed Dutch colleague Jan Kleinpenning asked me in the summer of 2021 if I wanted to follow up his volume *The Brazilian Amazonia in change I. Opening up and colonisation in the 1970s,* I was very happy to agree to write about the further developments in the Amazon region until today, which I have studied for five decades. After completing a volume with topics on the economic and social geography of Brazil, I started work on this project at the beginning of 2022.

This has now resulted in the volume *The Brazilian Amazonia in change II. Five decades of exploitation, deforestation and attempts at sustainable development* presented here as Volume 2 in the joint publication Kleinpenning/Kohlhepp *The Brazilian Amazonia in change.* I would like to thank Jan Kleinpenning for his interest and cooperation.

This volume analyses regional development in the Brazilian Amazon region from the beginning of the extensive economic activities of the public and private sectors in the mid-1970s until the renewed assumption of office by President Lula da Silva in 2023.

The following may give a brief insight into the initial impulses and the development process of the author's research on Brazil and Amazonia.

In the 1950s and 1960s, geographical research on Brazil in Germany was strongly concentrated at the University of Heidelberg. The conditions for this were favourable. Gottfried Pfeifer, holder of the Chair of Geography, had benefited greatly from his former professor Leo Waibel's stay in Brazil (1946–1950) as scientific advisor of the Conselho Nacional de Geografia in Rio de Janeiro and his own shorter stay in Brazil in 1950. However, when Pfeifer invited Brazilian colleagues to Heidelberg as visiting professors, the subject of Brazil research became much more vivid and fascinating for the students there.

The author was inspired by Hilgard O'Reilly Sternberg's (Chair of Geography, University of Brazil/UFRJ, Rio de Janeiro) stay in Heidelberg in the summer term of 1961 to conduct field research in Brazil in 1962/63 and write his dissertation on the industrial geography of the state of Santa Catarina. This first research project of the author in Brazil (1962–1967) was followed by economic and social geographic research on agricultural colonisation in northern Paraná (1970–1972), which led to the habilitation thesis.

The visiting professorship of Orlando Valverde (Instituto Brasileiro de Geografia, IBGE, Rio de Janeiro) at the University of Heidelberg in 1967 had already given the author a first impetus for future research on Amazonia. Plans for a Brazilian-German research project in human geography to be carried out with a small research boat in Amazonia had been developed by the research group led by Orlando Valverde and researchers around Gottfried Pfeifer in Heidelberg. In view of the Brazilian government's planned regional development strategies in Amazonia, the timing for the research project seemed favourable.

However, this project could not be realised in the planned form in the early 1970s due to the political restrictions of the Military Government as well as administrative problems at the Brazilian partner organisation. Orlando had tried everything to carry out the joint programme of geographical research in Amazonia and to participate more actively in the discussion on spatial planning and regional development. However, he had underestimated the limitations and complications that existed at the time.

After long negotiations, however, the project topic "Amazonia" was included in the German-Brazilian agreement on scientific and technical cooperation in 1973. Under this umbrella, official permission for research by German scientists in Amazonia was guaranteed and there were further possibilities for spatial access to the Amazon region.

Since 1973, the author had the opportunity to conduct extensive fieldwork in the Amazon region. It initially focused on problems of state regional planning and economic projects, on small-scale agricultural settlement along the Transamazônica and in Rondônia, and on large-scale cattle grazing in south-eastern Pará and Mato Grosso.

In Germany, the author's Amazonian research led to close contact with the working group of Harald Sioli (Max Planck Institute for Limnology, Plön), an expert in tropical ecology highly regarded in Brazil who had lived and researched in Amazonia from 1940 to 1956. In Harald Sioli's succession, Wolfgang J. Junk's working group intensively continued research on tropical ecology in Amazonia.

In the 1980s, conflicts of interest in the Amazonian pioneer zones, migration flows as well as mega-projects, especially the Programa Grande Carajás and the problems of large-scale hydropower plants, were further project topics. In the 1990s, a multidisciplinary research project on the socio-economic structure and dynamics of environmental impacts in the Upper Paraguay River Basin, Mato Grosso, was carried out in close cooperation with the Federal University of Mato Grosso (UFMT) in Cuiabá with numerous colleagues and collaborators as part of the bilateral SHIFT programme.

Participation in the International Advisory Group (IAG) of the International Pilot Programme to conserve the Brazilian tropical rain forests (PPG7) provided in-depth insights into governmental planning and projects that could be greatly expanded through international funding in terms of sustainable development. The collaboration with the IAG group of Brazilian and foreign researchers was an enriching experience that existed many years before and afterwards, especially with Bertha K. Becker (Rio de Janeiro) – including the geography student exchange between Rio de Janeiro (UFRJ) and the author's Department of Geography at the University of Tübingen.

In the following years, it was possible to work on various environmental policy problems concerning the protection of the tropical rain forests in Amazonia and the regional impacts of large-scale projects on the habitat of the Indigenous population.

The author gratefully remembers the enriching cooperation with numerous Brazilian colleagues who were always ready for discussion and unselfishly helpful. Thanks are also due to the institutions and authorities at federal, state and municipal level, to private companies and enterprises. Many of their staff as well as members of NGOs contributed to the success of the research with information, discussions, documents and maps.

A very important role was played by numerous private individuals from all walks of life in Amazonia who were willing to share their knowledge, contacts, experiences and observations with the author. My thanks go to all of them. Special thanks to Prof. Antônio Vizeu da Costa Lima in Belém, whose organisational help made valuable contacts possible.

This also applies to the dedicated German and Brazilian staff, doctoral candidates and student assistants at the Departments of Geography of the universities where the author has been working. Some of them now teach and research as professors in Germany, Austria, Canada and Brazil and continue research on Brazil and Amazonia there.

The author's research in Brazil was almost exclusively funded by German institutions, especially the German Research Foundation (DFG), to which I am particularly grateful.

Thanks are also due to the universities of Heidelberg, Frankfurt and Tübingen, which granted the author leave of absence for research purposes in Amazonia during his activities there between 1965 and 2005.

Dipl. Ing. Richard Szydlak, Tübingen, carried out the cartographic processing of the maps in this volume in a proven manner.

I would like to thank the Ibero American Institute (IAI) in Berlin and its Scientific Director Dr. Peter Birle for including the volume in the publication series "Bibliotheca Luso-Afro-Brasileira." My thanks also go to Patricia Schulze for her technical support in publishing the work.

Tübingen, November 2023 Gerd Kohlhepp

Appreciations of German and Brazilian geographers mentioned in the preface, in publications by Gerd Kohlhepp:

1976. "Der Beitrag Gottfried Pfeifers zur kulturgeographischen Lateinamerika Forschung." *Geographische Zeitschrift* 64, no. 1: 1–12.

1987. "Gottfried Pfeifer (20.1.1901–6.7.1985)." *Geographisches Taschenbuch* 1987/1988: 133–157.

2013. "A importância de Leo Waibel para a geografia brasileira e o início das relações científicas entre o Brasil e a Alemanha no campo da geografia." *Revista Brasileira de Desenvolvimento Regional* 1, no. 2: 29–75.

2015. "Pioneiros brasileiros nas pesquisas geográficas de desenvolvimento regional: Orlando Valverde e Hilgard O'Reilly Sternberg." *Revista Brasileira de Desenvolvimento Regional* 3, no. 1: 27–54.

2017. "Nas trilhas de Leo Waibel: Pesquisas alemãs de Geografia Humana do Brasil – de Heidelberg à Tübingen (1950–2005)." *Revista Brasileira de Geografia* 62, no. 2: 7–24.

2019. "A contribuição de Leo Waibel para o conhecimento da colonizacão agrária no Brasil do séc. XX." *Fronteiras. Journal of Social, Technological and Environmental Science* 8, no. 3: 69–87.

2017. "Orlando Valverde (1917–2006). Um geógrafo brasileiro de renome internacional – entusiasta e entusiasmante." In *Orlando Valverde. O geógrafo e sua obra,* organised by Dirce M. Antunes Suertegaray *et al.*, 157–188. Porto Alegre: Geociências/UFRGS.
2017. "Hilgard O'Reilly Sternberg, um pioneiro nas pesquisas das questões ambientais no Brasil. H. O'Reilly Sternberg, a pioneer in research on environmental issues in Brazil." *Espaço Aberto. Revista do Programa de Pós-Graduação em Geografia da UFRJ* 7, no. 1: 7–21. https://doi.org/10.36403/espacoaberto.2017.11941

I Amazônia Legal in the mid-1970s and 1980s

1. Alternative strategies to the colonisation policy of the Military Government

1.1. The Polamazônia programme as of 1975

At the height of the Brazilian "economic miracle," the prevailing "El Dorado" mentality allowed the private sector to penetrate the Amazônia Legal planning region. Amazônia Legal is the largest regional unit in Brazil. It has an approximate area of 5.2 million km², or about 61 % of Brazil's territory.[1] The region overlaps three distinct biomes: Brazil's Amazon biome, parts of the *cerrado* biome and the northern part of the Pantanal biome.

The scope for private sector activity with economic exploitation and almost unlimited territorial expansion of the Amazonian periphery was greatly expanded and became the new focus of the Military Government's development strategy. The official rationale for this far-reaching decision to switch from state-controlled small-scale agrarian colonisation to the private sector was the first oil price crisis in 1973, when the government was forced to cut back its investments due to the severe financial consequences of expensive oil imports, which accounted for up to 30 % of total import costs. Between 1973 and 1976, the price of oil increased up to five times. 80 % of the national oil demand had to be imported.

By the mid-1970s, it became clear that the failure of agricultural settlement along the Transamazônica between Altamira and Itaituba was due to organisational shortcomings and fundamental ecological problems. *Terra firme* soils are not suitable for agriculture because the lack of inorganic nutrients (nitrogen, phosphorus, etc.), rapid humus decomposition, silting and insufficient colloidal binding of artificial fertilisers, together with the problems of weed infestation and plant diseases, quickly lead to yield losses. Land surveying without knowledge of natural conditions, failure of the selec-

1 Amazônia Legal (Legal Amazon) is formed by the states of Acre, Amapá, Amazonas, Pará, Rondônia, Roraima, Tocantins, and Mato Grosso, and also by the west of the state of Maranhão. The boundaries have been altered several times. In 1977, the state of Mato Grosso became part of the Legal Amazon. Tocantins, after its creation, joined the group in 1988. In 1953, during the second term of President Getulio Vargas, the establishment of the Superintendência do Plano de Valorização Econômica da Amazônia (SPVEA) documented the objectives of valorising the natural resources of the tropical rain forest region with the creation of a targeted planning region, formerly known as Hiléia Amazônica. In 1966, the Superintendence for the Development of the Amazon (SUDAM) was created, responsible for promoting economic initiatives in that region. The planning region Amazônia Legal was established to define the geographical delimitation of the political region in which SUDAM operates. Its purpose was promoting the regional development and the integration of the regional productive base in the national economy.

tion principle in settlement, lack of agricultural extension, inexperience in dealing with the conditions of the humid tropics and unrealistic land use models (crop rotation, rapid conversion to permanent crops) caused initial problems. In addition, overly optimistic official yield forecasts, on which the repayment of government loans was based, unsuitable seeds, lack of cooperative organisation, insufficient marketing opportunities, tropical diseases and inadequate medical care contributed to the desperation of many settlers and to a high percentage of return migration (Kohlhepp 1976a; 1976b).[2]

Since the government was not interested in admitting failures in official planning, the oil price crisis was used to launch a second phase of regional planning strategies with the active participation of the private sector. The Second National Development Plan (1975–1979) focused on the concept of growth poles, which had been discussed in Latin America since the mid-1960s.[3] The "poles of development" were based on separate sectoral priorities, e. g., livestock projects and mineral extraction.

In the Polamazônia programme (SEPLAN 1974; SUDAM 1975; SUDAM/SUDECO 1975), the growth pole concept (Perroux 1950, 1955; Hirschman 1958; Boudeville 1968)[4] was misinterpreted and the result was not a "decentralised concentration" of development, but the widening of the inter- and intra-regional development gap. The periphery became even more dependent on the centre at the national as well as the international level. Instead of growth poles with radiating development impulses, enclaves emerged, artificially maintained (Kohlhepp 1978a; 1978b; 1997b). Conservative modernization "from above" by the military government, incorporating the private sector with the regional and national elites by financial incentives, had to keep up the democratic appearance in order not to endanger international creditworthiness. The military administration saw its leading role as that of the only protagonist capable of realizing modernization through rational planning (Becker and Egler 1992), the regional component often being treated in a superficial manner (Ianni 1979b; Théry and Rivière d'Arc 1980).

1.2. Mentality of "El Dorado": Territorial exploitation by private national and international capital

National and international capital investors were attracted by extremely favourable tax reduction incentives and other benefits. Since the mid-1960s, cattle ranching had increasingly switched from the humid savannahs (*campos cerrados*) of the central Brazilian highlands (Planalto Central) to the peripheral areas of the Amazonian rain forests where a large part of the *cerradão* transition forest had been cleared. As the new roads advanced, ranching constantly expanded into the humid tropical rain forests, higher stock densities being expected. 65 % of the cattle-breeding units acquired their land, before the corridors along the trunk roads – reserved for agrarian colonisation – were established by law in 1971 under INCRA control. This produced conflicts of interest in an area planned for small and medium-sized holdings, mainly with *posseiros*,

2 For a detailed analysis of the agrarian colonisation in the Amazon region see volume 1 of Jan Kleinpenning in the present publication of Kleinpenning/Kohlhepp (cf. Kleinpenning 1975; 1979).

3 See: Hansen (1967), Friedmann (1972), Sandner (1971; 1975).

4 About transferability from industrialized countries to developing countries: Conroy (1973) and Santos (1974).

people without official land title.[5] The ruthless invasion of Indigenous territories was seen as a necessary measure for economic development.

1.2.1. Expansion of cattle ranches in tropical rain forests

The possibility of employing considerable reduction of corporation tax (up to 50 %) as venture capital made it most profitable for Brazilian and foreign companies and financial groups to acquire large tracts of land in Amazônia Legal, gaining additionally from very low land prices. In the beginning, the traditional cattle-breeders from Minas Gerais, Goiás, Mato Grosso do Sul, São Paulo and Rio Grande do Sul, who had less cash available and could employ less tax savings operated largely as managers, administrators, subcontractors or, more rarely, as partners to investors without any experience in the cattle ranching sector.

In 1974, Minister of Agriculture Paulinelli openly stated that it would be foolish to leave Amazonia to those who were not capable of using the land without technical and financial aptitude and efficiency. He only believed in entrepreneurial agriculture to the exclusion of subsistence farming. This statement was in direct contrast to the earlier agricultural colonisation programmes of the Military Government.

National, multinational and foreign banks, insurance companies, real estate companies, mining, transport and road construction companies as well as industrial groups from a wide range of sectors have been attracted to set up livestock projects. On average, 55 % of the capital invested was taken from tax payments. The projects approved by SUDAM were tax-free for 12 years. In addition to tax savings, risk diversification resulting from the range of sectors in which they operated also played a decisive role. For non-Brazilian investors, the focus was on reinvesting profits, as the transfer of profits abroad was prohibited.

Under the law in force in the 1970s, cattle ranchers, like other agricultural enterprises, were only allowed to clear a maximum of 50 % of their property in rain forest areas. Due to the huge area of Amazônia Legal, it was almost impossible to control the extent of the clearing.[6] The size of the cattle farms ranged from 10 000 to several hundred thousand hectares, although SUDAM had set the official maximum area at 60 000 ha since 1973. In 58 % of the farms, investments of DM[7] 5 to 10 million were planned, 15 % wanted to invest more than DM 10 million. Two large projects with investments of more than DM 50 million were carried out by Volkswagen do Brasil in south-eastern Pará with 140 000 ha and by the Liquigas Group (Suiá Missú, 566 000 ha) – with headquarters in Italy and part of its capital owned by the Vatican Bank – in Mato Grosso.

---

5 During Glaser's fieldwork in 1968 (Glaser 1971), land acquisition for cattle ranching projects began in the *cerradão* areas and rain forests east of the Rio Araguaia in northernmost Goiás (now Tocantins State).

6 Initially, the extent of deforestation in the rain forest could only be verified by analysing aerial photographs and ERTS satellite images taken every 18 days when the satellite flew over the area. This meant that the government could only react with a delay when the limits were exceeded, and this was only partially carried out.

7 With the application of projects, SUDAM asked for the scope of the investments planned. According to SUDAM documents, the amount stated was converted by the author in all projects into DM (Deutsche Mark) for a publication in Germany (Kohlhepp 1979). This is the reference mapped in Figs. 1 and 2.

Table 1 shows the volume of project applications for livestock facilities approved up to October 1983.[8] Mato Grosso, with 476 projects, accounted for almost 42 % of the total number and 57.5 % of the total project area,[9] followed by Pará (33 % and 23.5 %). While in 1977 Mato Grosso (340 projects) was by far the leading cattle breeding state in Amazônia Legal with 57 % of all projects and 65 % of the area, the other Amazonian states gained importance in cattle breeding projects at the end of the 1970s (Kohlhepp 1979; 1987a). In all cattle breeding projects, only about 25 000 jobs were planned. On average, only one person was needed as direct labour for 235 ha of pasture.

Table 1: Cattle ranches receiving tax concessions in Amazônia Legal (project applicatons approved before October 1983)

Federal States and Territories (T)	Number of ranches	Number of jobs	Proposed head of cattle		Total area[2)]		Average ranch size in ha[2)]	Average head of cattle per ranch[2)]
			in 1000	in%	in 1000 ha	in%		
Acre	10	372	139.6	2.3	289.9	3.3	28 993	13 966
Amapa (T)	22	521	94.9	1.6	153.4	1.7	6974	4312
Amazonas	20	671	142.8	2.4	290.1	3.3	14 502	7 141
Goiás[1)]	40	1319	359.5	5.9	701.2	8.0	17 531	8976
Maranhão[1)]	17	576	99.0	1.6	139.3	1.6	8193	5821
Mato Grosso[1)]	199	13 725	3733.8	61.6	5063.8	57.5	25 447	18 763
Pará	159	7434	1412.9	23.3	2069.4	23.5	13 015	8886
Rondônia	5	134	40.0	0.6	52.7	0.6	10 534	7992
Roraima (T)	4	139	40.8	0.7	41.1	0.5	10 280	10 206
Total	**476**	**24 891**	**6062.8**	**100.0**	**8800.9**	**100.0**	**18 489**	**12 737**

1) Share of Amazônia Legal

2) Land use limited by law to 50 % of total ranch area

Source: Kohlhepp (1987a, 32), based on projects' statistics in: SUDAM (1983), and author's calculations.

In 1983, the total area of approved cattle projects was 8.8 million ha with a planned cattle population of 6.1 million animals. At that time, cattle population in the Brazilian Amazon was about 2.5 million (1976),[10] including cattle on Marajó Island. The average

8 All the applications for cattle breeding projects approved by SUDAM until October 1983 were evaluated in detail by the author in the SUDAM main office in Belém, according to SUDAM statistics. The results entered in Table 1 with the author's own calculations.

9 Considering the legally fixed percentage of a maximum use of 50 % of the individual project area.

10 The number of bovine livestock in the Legal Amazon region in Brazil surpassed 93 million heads in 2020 (IBGE 2022).

number of cattle per project was up to 12 700, according to information on the application form. A stocking density of 1 to 1.5 cattle/ha was highly optimistically expected. When evaluating the cattle statistics, it should be noted that SUDAM has only recorded cattle farms in Amazonia that are eligible for tax relief. The total number of private cattle ranches operating without incentives and outside the SUDAM conditions was much higher. The amount of land acquired by cattle ranchers could only be estimated. The areas in the rain forest cleared by cattle ranchers up to 1982 were estimated at about 140 000 km², and the total area acquired by cattle ranchers – some of it concealed as land speculation – was probably up to 350 000 km² (Kohlhepp 1987a, 32).

Fig. 1 shows the date of implementation of the livestock projects approved by SUDAM from 1966 onwards, as well as the investment volume. The regional distribution of the projects was concentrated in Mato Grosso and south-eastern Pará. More than 50 % of the total livestock investors were based in São Paulo (Fig. 2).[11] Already at the beginning of the 1980s there were several farm closures.

Fig. 1: Large cattle breeding projects with tax benefits in Amazônia Legal 1983 (> 15 000 ha; year of approval and scope of investments)

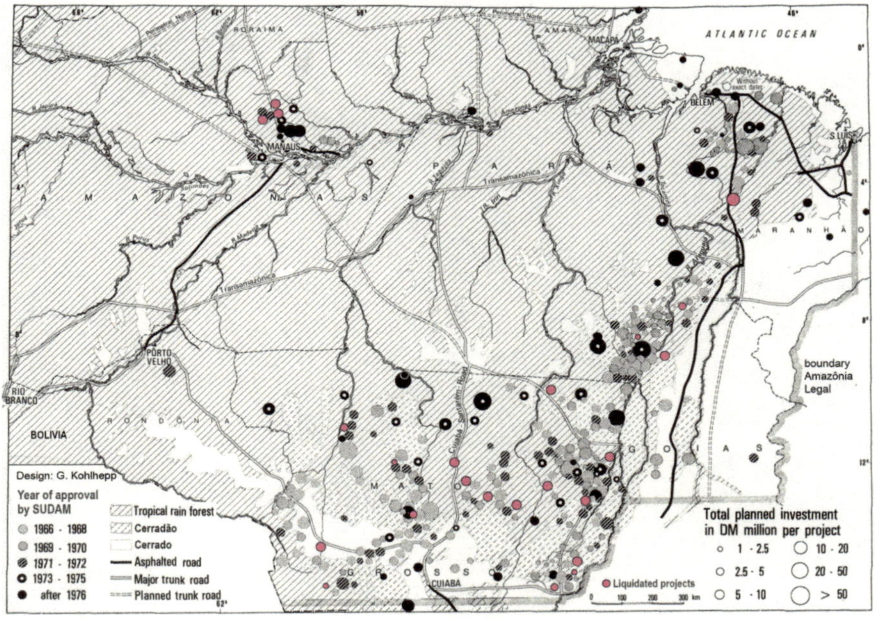

Source: Kohlhepp (1979; 1987a).

The irreversible damage to the very unstable ecological balance in tropical rain forests caused by large-scale slash-and-burn clearing resulted in radical ecological changes, erosion damage, nutrient leaching, surface encrustation and disruption of the water

11 Figs. 1 and 2: Mapping of the location of projects, date of approval, scope of investments, origin of the capital (headquarters of investor's company) was organised by the author according to SUDAM's yearly statistics and documents, and originally published in Kohlhepp (1979) and in an actualized version – data from SUDAM, 1983 – in Kohlhepp (1987a, 29).

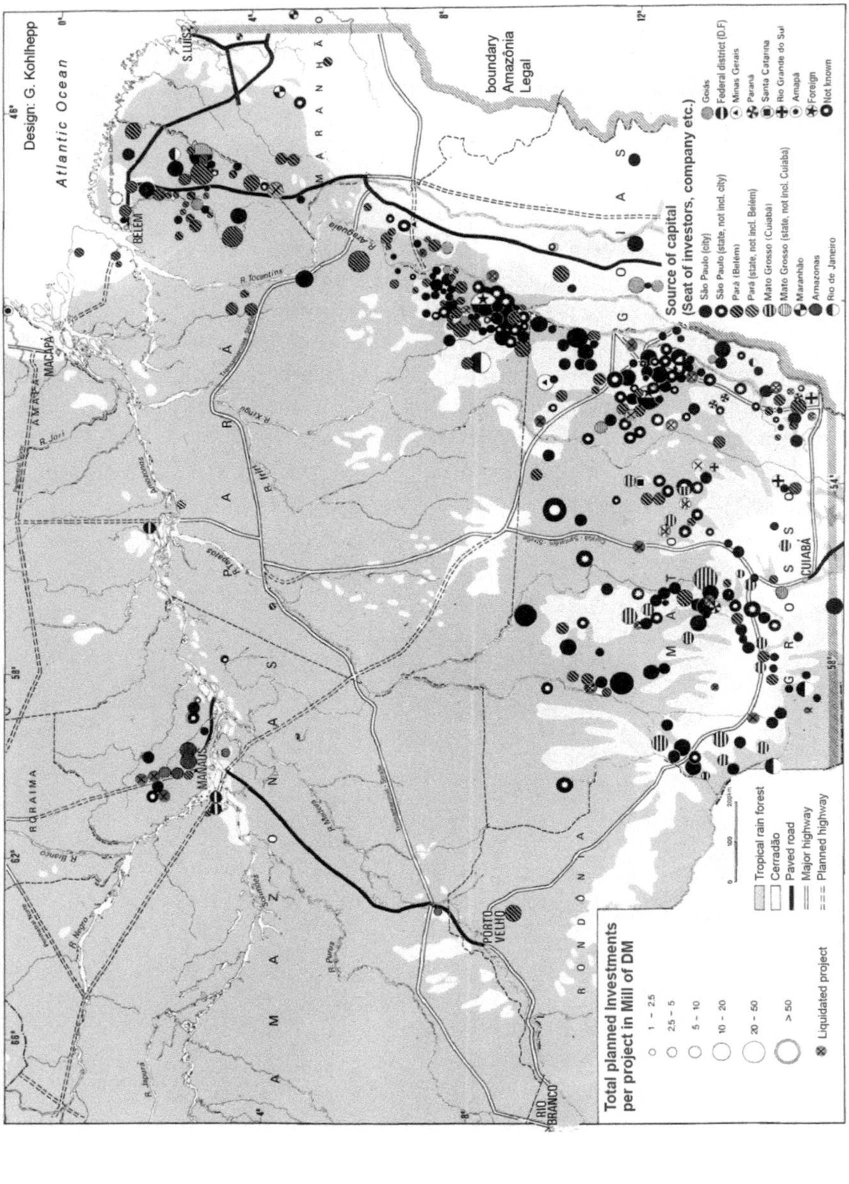

Fig. 2: Regional origin of investors and scope of investments in cattle breeding projects in Amazônia Legal 1983

Source: Kohlhepp (1979; 1987a).

balance, even before the new areas could be sown with grass seed. Other consequences were CO_2 emissions from forest fires, changes in local and regional climate with increasing instability of the annual rainfall cycle. The conversion of large areas of biodiverse tropical rain forests into grass monocultures as pastureland led to controversial disputes in Brazil, with scientists in particular speaking out vehemently against the planned government measures.[12]

12 Goodland and Irwin (1975); Fearnside (1982; 1985); Schmink (1982); Schmink and Wood (1984); Hecht (1983; 1984); Kohlhepp (1979; 1984a). On the conflict constellation and the situation of the tropical timber industry in Pará: Schönenberg (1993); Scholz (1999).

The pasture grass was sown by plane, the cleared pastures were stocked with zebu cattle (Nelore breed) and crosses between zebus, European breeds and *criollo* cattle. Pastures formed after forest cutting and burning (first-cycle pastures) have been established using forage grasses, such as *Panicum maximum* (Guinea grass), *Hyparrhenia rufa* and *Brachiaria decumbens*. New forage grasses such as *Brachiaria humidicula*, among others, replaced the traditional grasses because of better performance in humid tropical areas. The productivity of first-cycle pastures is high during three or four years but declines rapidly with decreasing soil fertility and weed encroachment (Serrão and Nepstad 1996, 222). In advanced stages of degradation, i. e., up to 10 years after pasture establishment, the carrying capacity, which is around 0.7 animals/ha during the lifetime of first-cycle pastures, drops to below 0.3 cattle/ha. With the use of improved pasture technologies and the intensification of cattle production, much degraded first-cycle pastures have been converted to second-cycle pastures (Mattos and Uhl 1994).

In the 1990s, it became already clear that cattle farming, with its ecological and socio-economic constraints, should be only expanded on already deforested land, and that the unsustainable monocultural grazing systems favoured through tax incentives should be transformed into alternative, more sustainable semi-intensive cattle farming models and – much better – into intensive agrosilvipastoral models (Serrão and Nepstad 1996; cf. Hohnwald *et al.* 2010).

The economic prospects were breeding, rearing and fattening and – in some places – meat processing. Brazil had the advantage that the *Trypanosomiasis* disease transmitted by tsetse flies was unknown in the New World tropics. In the 1970s and 1980s, meat from Amazonia served almost exclusively to supply the domestic market, as exports to the European domestic market and the United States were subject to restrictions. With the start of the Polamazônia programme, the export of beef from Amazonia for the world market became a long-term goal that has only become very successful in recent years. [13]

Land speculation and violent conflicts with squatters (*posseiros*) caused serious problems. Several investors only were interested in increasing the value of their estates, favoured by nearby road building, new settlements, and other investments in infrastructure. Cattle breeding served as a suitable means to acquire land using tax incentives. A highly speculative land market emerged, which became more interesting for many investors than cattle breeding itself. "The land itself was the commodity" (Hecht 1985, 680). High profits were made through land speculation which quickly increased the extent of the cleared areas. In times of high inflation, this was a capital safeguard. When productivity of the newly acquired lands played only a secondary role, careful management of the pastures did not take place, leading to the degradation of the deforested areas. For government-subsidized cattle ranching projects, clearing was the hallmark for recognition as "improved land." Overgrazing proved profitable and led to faster forest clearance by shortening grazing per unit area (Hecht *et al.* 1988; Margulis 2004).

In some cases, planned investments were moved back to the company's headquarters, mainly in São Paulo. In the second half of the 1970s, the deforestation of large areas of rain forest had for the first time attracted the attention of scientists and a public interested in the ecological consequences. The vulnerability of the tropical rain

---

13 Cf. chapter III.5.

forest ecosystems to degradation soon became apparent when the integrated cycle of biomass was destroyed.

In the area of podsolic soils in south-eastern Pará, the possibility of permanent grazing seemed very doubtful. The use of artificial fertiliser was hardly conceivable for economic reasons because of the huge areas involved. Due to the overgrazing mentality of the contract managers and the uncontrolled increase in livestock density, which was allowed to many profit-sharing subcontractors, a tendency towards savannah formation was to be feared. The highly speculative tendency to create large-scale landholdings was reinforced by the fact that livestock farming seemed to be economically unviable in the early days, as the carrying capacity was exhausted after only a few years and livestock density decreased sharply (Hecht 1985; Fearnside 1986a; 1986b).

One of the most important private investors in livestock projects was the automobile group Volkswagen do Brasil. The company faced the problem of having to reinvest the non-transferable part of the profits in Brazil. The offer of the Military Government to invest in Amazonia was very gladly accepted by the company management because of the tax advantages. In 1973, with the approval of SUDAM, a 140 000 ha cattle farm was established in south-eastern Pará in the municipality of Santana do Araguaia. VW do Brasil began its project by clearing the rain forest without any experience in agriculture or livestock activities. The regional natural conditions of the remote area were largely unknown and there was no detailed information about the soils. The distance of 2100 km to the headquarters of VW do Brasil in São Bernardo do Campo, S. P., initially proved to be a logistical challenge; aeroplane connections were urgently needed. According to the existing legal regulations, an area of 44 000 ha was cleared by 1984, the livestock amounted to 47 000.[14]

VW do Brasil's Fazenda Vale do Rio Cristalino (CVRC) was very well organised and has been managed by a Swiss agricultural engineer and expert in cattle breeding since 1978. In contrast to many other ranches visited, agrotechnical knowledge was practised here at a high level by an expert who was present almost all the time. Two innovations were realised through this project: Fertilising the pastures (by air) and the production of hay. The regular fertilisation made it possible to increase the dry matter yield per hectare by 2.5 times. Due to a significant dry period of more than three months (June to mid-September), the existing fodder gap was successfully closed by hay and silage. Fattening became successful at a time when cattle in other regions were low in weight. In the initial phase, a rotation system of pastures was practised. In the beginning, the cattle were sold and transported to São Paulo. The planned stocking density of 1.4 animals per ha was achieved and was to be increased by silage. In 1980, the soil quality was examined in detail. The VW ranch proved to be a model farm with excellent management, scientifically based trials with support of the Swiss University of Zurique (ETH), e. g., breeding trials, silage, additional feeding systems, trials on fertilisation and erosion control by avoiding overgrazing.[15] The slopes were not cleared to avoid erosion and landslides.

14 According to CVRC statistics of October 1984. Targets until 1988 had been: 54 000 ha of pastures, 106 000 head of cattle; forest reserve 85 700 ha.

15 Detailed information of the estate manager Friedrich Brügger during the visits of the author at the Fazenda Vale do Rio Cristalino in 1980 and 1982. The first field trip to the Fazenda occurred in 1975 (cf. Kohlhepp 1979; 1987a).

A permanent staff of 230 people (1982)[16] worked within the ranch in a privileged location and under good infrastructural conditions. In stark contrast, subcontractors (*empreiteiras*) were allowed to use hundreds of unskilled workers to cut and burn forests, clear pastures and build fences on the VW do Brasil ranch. These subcontractors, who worked on all the ranches in the region, were unchecked violators of human rights, decent living and working conditions and social standards. The *empreiteiras* were registered companies that were fiscalised by the Ministry of Labour, but it was known that this did not work in the interior of Amazonia.

A slaughterhouse built with a German company and other investors 50 km away was within an area of influence of about 300 km and included ranches with 1.4 million cattle. The target was a slaughter capacity of 150 000 cattle per year. A steam turbine based on wood feed, a cooling system and a water treatment plant allowed additional installations for the production of canned goods, frozen meat, meat extract, packaging material and a tannery – initially only for the domestic market.

During the Military Government, Volkswagen and many other large investors had been invited to participate in the Polamazônia programme and were attracted by the fiscal benefits of the "development model" of exploitation and deforestation of the Amazon. There is no doubt that the initiative to strengthen the "Brazilian miracle" was a support for the repressive political system and guaranteed economic and other benefits, especially for foreign or multinational companies. The activities of large corporations such as Liquigas, VW do Brasil, Villares, Vilela, Mappin, Scarpa, Mendes, Alcântara Machado, Swift, Anglo, Caterpillar, Rank Xerox, Lunardelli, Camargo Corrêa, Finasa, Levy, Bradesco, Codespar, Ometto and others created an "empire" of large landowners. This concentration of powerful groups with huge landholdings obviously helped the Military Government to improve political control in regions with anti-military movements nearby.

It is hard to believe that one of the world's most important car manufacturers overestimated the economic profitability of the ranch but underestimated the costs of the project, the logistical problems in an infrastructurally isolated region and the very complex social situation of hiring workers in the interior of Brazil. The ecological consequences of deforestation were generally not discussed by the decision-makers and the warnings of scientists (Goodland and Irwin 1975; Sioli 1973; 1984) mostly went unheard or were simply not implemented.[17] Protests by environmental movements were ignored. In 1975, a conference of the Brazilian Society for the Advancement of Science (SBPC) discussed scientifically based criticism of forest destruction by CVRC and other cattle ranches. Under the military regime, open protests against government strategies were often interpreted as terrorist or "communist" activities.

Passing on responsibility for the working and living conditions of non-permanent workers by outsourcing contracts to completely uncontrolled subcontractors, which

16 In October 1984, 381 people were employed (880 family members, 205 children in the primary school).

17 On 8 August 1975, the author was invited by the president of VW do Brasil, Wolfgang Sauer, to report on a visit to the CVRC ranch. In this conversation the author addressed the ecological problems of forest destruction, the lack of regional suitability of soils and ecosystems for cattle breeding, conflicts of interest in land use, and regional social inequalities and conflicts with subcontractors. Sauer had an overly optimistic view of cattle ranching as part of the government's development strategies in Amazonia. See also the author's publications on this topic: Kohlhepp (1979; 1987a), among others.

is common in the Brazilian hinterland, was one of the fundamental mistakes made by the top management of VW do Brasil and all other investors. Workers employed by *gatos* to clear forests in groups of a few hundred were exploited by subcontractors who paid very low wages, violated workers' rights, set inhumane labour standards and additionally enriched themselves by selling food at extortionate prices. The conditions in these guarded camps can be described as slave-like. It seems incomprehensible that VW do Brasil did not understand that the ultimate responsibility lay with the owner of the ranch. It was clear to the management that foreign investors – even in their capacity as competitors – were subject to harsher scrutiny.

In the early 1980s, press articles began to focus on the VW do Brasil project. In Brazil, criticism turned from ecological commentary on rain forest destruction to condemnation of foreign capital activities in Amazonia. In Germany, scientists and environmentalists criticised the cattle ranching projects in Amazonia and especially VW's involvement in the highly problematic "development strategy" of the Military Government in Amazonia, which was much appreciated by investors.

In the mid-1980s, press and television reports, newspaper and magazine commentaries, news agency interviews and allegations by the Rural Pastoral Commission (CPT) accumulated into a national and international press campaign against CVRC ("biggest fire of the century," "slave labour") that was devastating for Volkswagen's good standing. Although some reports were journalistic exaggerations with lurid headlines, scientific results were misquoted[18] and the well-known general problems were focused on the VW ranch, the reputation of the largest company and leading car manufacturer in Brazil was at risk. In a time of economic crisis, declining car sales, government price controls on beef, and rising inflation, the VW top management in Germany and Brazil decided to sell the ranch to the Brazilian Matsubara group from Paraná in 1987 at enormous financial loss. Despite, or perhaps because of all the scientific achievements and innovations in veterinary medicine, the project turned out to be a financial disaster.[19] VW could have spared itself the cattle breeding adventure. Despite all the expertise, it was the wrong agricultural activity in the wrong place at the wrong political time, and fortunately ended relatively early, unlike many other large cattle ranches in the region.

With the fiscal incentives of the II National Development Plan, the establishment and expansion of cattle farms in Amazonia began. In summary, the investments were realised in a highly problematic economic sector, in an ecologically vulnerable region, with high investments and state subsidies, very low productivity and with dramatic conflicts of interest and social tensions. In some regions, there were violent conflicts with the Indigenous population and their shifting cultivation, as well as with *posseiros*, who had cleared their land for years without formal title and were deprived of their livelihood. Large landowners who had bought the land "rent-free" tried to force them to vacate, sometimes with small compensation payments. When the *posseiros* refused to move, there were often violent confrontations with the notorious *pistoleiros* of the *fazendeiros*. In the 1970s and early 1980s, about 75 % of rain forest clearing was due to cattle ranching. Later, the area of cattle ranching increased considerably and

18 As an example, the editorial of *Time* (October 18, 1982, no. 42).

19 In recent years two publications reminded of the adventure of cattle ranching by VW do Brasil: Kopper (2017) and Acker (2017).

reached a critical point in the exploitation of the Amazon region with fundamental ecological consequences.[20]

1.2.2. Mineral deposits and mining activities

The knowledge of the Amazonian geology and its mineral deposits had been very scarce at the beginning of the Federal Government's "Amazonian Operation." It was of utmost importance for the Military Government to realise an extensive survey of the existing mineral resources in Amazônia Legal in order to strengthen and to diversify the export sector. The discovery and exploitation of new ore resources made a considerable progress in the 1970s due mainly to aerial and satellite photography and a great deal of technical expenditure in remote sensing as part of the RADAM project. RADAM (Radar in the Amazon), organised in 1970, was the decision of the Military Government to undertake a reconnaissance survey of the Amazon region. The major objective was to collect information on untapped mineral resources, geomorphology, soils, vegetation, and potential land use. In 1975, the programme was expanded to the whole country (RADAMBRASIL). On board of a Caravelle jet was the side-looking airborne radar Goodyear Mapping System 1000 for large-scale mapping and working with high resolution image scanning.[21]

Many prospecting licenses for – in some cases – very large tracts had been issued to Brazilian and foreign companies. However, tin ore mining in Rondônia which had started in 1958, was totally confined to traditional manual procedures of tin washing. Production increased in 1965 with the construction of the Cuiabá-Porto Velho earth road (BR-364). Washing and refining of tin ore (cassiterite) occurred in isolated places under primitive conditions. About 30 000 workers – most of them from the Northeast of Brazil – lived and worked on their own account in a *garimpo* system, which had surpassed the traditional jobs of the regional population as rubber tappers. Cassiterite was transported by small aircrafts to a central location (Ariquemes). Transport to the national consuming industry had to use the only existing road via Cuiabá to Minas Gerais and São Paulo by haulage trucks. At the end of the 1960s, tin mining changed to hydraulic installations on a group basis and the exploitation expanded from alluvial to eluvial deposits (Glaser 1969). As high initial investments in machinery were required, the government asked mining companies to reorganise cassiterite mining. The Billiton group started the first mechanised mine with modern equipment in 1970. Extensive resources were discovered in Rondônia and other locations in Amazonia. Later, a waterway transport of the cassiterite concentrate and the refined tin was shipped from Porto Velho to Santana port in Amapá before being shipped to international clients. From 1975 onwards, Brazil reduced its dependence on Southeast Asian tin imports and supplied the world market as one of the most important tin producers.

Since the mid-1950s, manganese ore has been mined by the Brazilian Icomi company of the Antunes group with the backing of Bethlehem Steel Corp. in the Serra do Navio, 200 km from the coast of Amapá, at that time a Federal Territory. Manganese

20 Cf. chapters II.3 and III.2.1.

21 The National Department of Mineral Production (DNPM) published 26 volumes of the "Survey of natural resources" (Geology, Geomorphology, Pedology, Vegetation, Potential land use) in the RADAMBRASIL project. Volumes 4–20, 22 and 26 concerned Amazônia Legal (DNPM, 1974–1982).

mining was the first industrial mining activity in the Amazon region. Manganese ore deposits of Amapá, in the precambrian part of the Guiana shield, accounted to 30–32 million t (mt) with a Mn content of 48%. The ore was of very high quality, lacking iron and free of phosphate. Commercialisation of manganese is basically allocated to supplying the iron and steel industry. Between 20 to 60 kg of ore were consumed to produce each ton of steel at the technical level of the 1970s.

The deposits were located in an isolated tropical rain forest region. Mining activities started with the 193 km railway construction from the port of Santana to the Serra do Navio mining location. After the northern channel of the Amazon river had been made navigable, exports of manganese ore could be directly transported by larger cargo ships from the port of Santana to the clients, without making the initially necessary detour via the narrow Furos de Breves west of the Island of Marajó and the Rio Pará. Before starting manganese ore exploitation, negotiations of the government with Icomi resulted in agreements of paying royalties and reinvesting in Amapá 20% of the profits of manganese production.

Two residential settlements were constructed by Icomi: one in the vicinity of the Santana port, denominated Vila Amazonas, the other named Vila Serra do Navio, situated close to the mine. According to Brazilian hierarchical norms of company towns, Vila Serra do Navio was divided into a relatively well-equipped workers' settlement and a separated high-standard part for the staff and qualified personal. The settlements became known as "company towns" and for decades set the standard throughout Amazonia for planning, tropical climate housing, health care and malaria control, as well as well-developed infrastructure in other mining and metallurgical companies (Kohlhepp 1977b). Icomi had few outsourced employees, with nearly all activities involving mining and processing of manganese performed by workers directly contracted by the company (Monteiro 2003). Highly qualified employees came from all over Brazil. They had very good salaries and privileges as free flights to visit their families and longer holidays. Workers were contracted mostly in Amapá. Population in Icomi settlements increased to 4200 (1977) with more than 1250 employees.

The most significant change in manganese processing in Icomi's history was the construction of the plant to concentrate the fine fractions of manganese ore from Serra do Navio to a Mn content of 60% and the pelletisation plant at the port of Santana. This enabled increases in ore volume sold, reaching 1.6 mt in 1971, the highest level in the mine's history. In the 1950s and early 1960s, the Soviet Union (USSR) and India were leaders in producing more than 60% of manganese ore worldwide. Later, Australia and South Africa became important producers. With the Icomi activities, Brazil attained the fifth rank in manganese ore production, exporting mainly to the USA and Europe. As part of Icomi's reinvestment process in Amapá, cooperation with the Dutch Bruynzeel Corp. (Brumasa), which dominated the regional timber trade, in the production of plywood and fibreboard was a success during this period.

In the 1970s, mining corporations believed in the capacity of modern techniques and the ability to overcome traditional activities like extractivism to drive regional economic development. However, Icomi's manganese ore mining in Amapá, its financial contributions, royalties, taxes, wages, social benefits and direct or indirect employment have not been able to ensure long-term regional progress and social stability. Despite demonstrating a high-level technology, a successful export strategy and model installations in the company's settlements, the input in Amapá did not gain generalised wide-reaching socio-economic effects. After industrial manganese mining and processing ceased in 1990, environmental damage from contaminated water and inadequate waste disposal remained. A few decades of optimism and export-oriented economic success could not achieve the "industrie motrice" effect (Perroux 1955) of a long-term positive impact on regional development. On the contrary, the development pole problem of reinforcing regional development disparities and creating enclaves and intra-regional socio-economic imbalances in a peripheral region showed the danger of only a temporary cycle of mining extraction.

In 1967, bauxite deposits were discovered by the Canadian Alcan Company in the State of Pará on the Trombetas river, a tributary of the Amazon river. The lateritic bauxite deposits on the southern margin of the precambrian Guiana shield, located in an area of dense tropical rain forests, occur on various plateaux covering an area of more than 2200 km^2 in altitudes varying from 160 to 190 m. The bauxite deposits are high in alumina (43 to 45 % Al_2O_3) and are overlain by 7 to 11 m of unconsolidated sediments. Mineração Rio do Norte (MRN) came to the Trombetas river basin in the 1970s with plans to mine about one billion tons of bauxite deposits. In 1974, an international consortium of Canadian and US companies was founded with Brazilian state participation. Mining operations using open pit mining methods started in 1979. Bauxite ore was crushed, beneficiated, and transported by rail to the near port of Trombetas, where the dried bauxite was loaded on up to 60 000 t ocean going bulk carriers for exports. Later, the national industrial alumina and aluminium industry, 900 km downstream the Amazon river near Belém, was supplied.[22]

In the beginning, open pit mining caused considerable damage by the removal of vegetation and overlying strata before mineral extraction. Degradation of land and enormous water pollution from mine waste were reported by near *quilombo* residents, descendants of runaway slaves. Reforestation started in 1984. Decades later, MRN turned out to be the fourth largest producer of bauxite worldwide.

The iron ore reserves in the Serra dos Carajás in the east of Pará, discovered in 1967, are among the most important deposits (18 billion t of hematite, 66 % Fe) in the world. The extraction of iron ore was the main project of the Programa Grande Carajás (PGC), a regional development programme of enormous proportions. It was combined with large infrastructural investments in new urban centres, railway and port construction, the implementation of a huge hydroelectrical power plant and new industries. The PGC will be analysed in detail in chapter I.4.

Since the 1960s, activities of gold and diamond diggers had increased considerably. According to Brazilian law, landowners do not possess subsoil rights but were given up to 10 % of the mining production value. Wildcat miners working in small-scale gold mining (*garimpo*) in Brazilian Amazonia are known as *garimpeiros*. For landless and unemployed men, *garimpos* became an alternative to find a job. In the Marabá region, the centre of Brazil nut trade, workers left their traditional job of gathering nuts (*castanha do Pará*) and were attracted by the beginning gold rush. Owners of the *castanhais* lost their economic and political power. Some started as entrepreneurs and became claim owners in gold mining (Cleary 1990).

Traditionally, *garimpeiros* worked in small crews of men in alluvial gold deposits with rudimentary pans and shovels as had been done for centuries. The uncontrolled

22 Cf. chapter I.4 on the Grande Carajás Programme.

migration of many thousands of *garimpeiros* to the numerous sites in Amazônia Legal caused environmental degradation and conflicts of interest with local and regional planning authorities, small farmers, large landholders, and disturbances in recently founded rural settlements and even small urban centres. The most problematic incidents were invasions into Indigenous territories with violent clashes by force of arms, assaults, and murder.

Because of the use of mercury in the gold extraction process, large areas around the mines are dangerously contaminated and people eating fish downstream from the mine frequently have elevated mercury levels. Gold mining is responsible for environmental damage like deforestation, damming up of small rivers and sedimentation of vital rivers. Frequently, *garimpeiros* were beyond the reach of the law. Despite the vulnerabilities that the activity implies with hazardous conditions, unhealthy work and failing health services, they do not wish to leave. There was a tradition within families, e. g., in Maranhão, where at least one family member was working as *garimpeiro*. In the mid-1980s, the number of *garimpeiros* in the Brazilian Amazon region increased to about half a million.

1.2.3. Gold boom in Serra Pelada

In 1976, the first occurrence of gold was noticed in Serra Pelada, situated between Marabá, 90 km away, and the near Serra dos Carajás. The Serra Pelada site was part of a concession area of the Cia. Vale do Rio Doce (CVRD), the leading Brazilian mining company. After a false radio message announced the opening of the Serra Pelada to *garimpeiros*, activities quickly expanded. Because of road construction from Marabá to the Serra dos Carajás, in 1980 about 20 000 *garimpeiros* arrived. Considering these dimensions, Serra Pelada was not a typical *garimpo* in Amazonia. In the beginning, gold output was low but was bought up directly without interference of intermediaries. The Ministry of Mining and Energy wanted to stop *garimpo* activities and ordered Docegeo, a subsidiary company of CVRD, to start mechanised gold extraction. In some municipalities in the region, there were protests by the *garimpeiros* and manifestations against Docegeo. People were afraid of mass migration of dismissed *garimpeiros* to their small settlements. The Military Government commanded "Major Curió"[23] of the National Information Service (SNI) to impose order in the chaotic situation and to bring Serra Pelada under government control. He gained public interest later as leader of the *garimpeiro* movement. The *garimpeiros* turned out to become a politically relevant pressure group.

When gold mining became successful, there was a veritable gold rush and Serra Pelada became famous. Huge nuggets were discovered, the largest weighed almost 7 kg. In 1980, 6.6 tons of gold were produced, 40 % of the official national outcome. Even Brazil's President General Figueiredo visited Serra Pelada in 1980. Because of social tensions, manual gold digging was conceded until November 1983. Activities in the open pit mine started at 275 m above sea-level. A social stratification already had

23 The infamous SNI colonel Sebastião de Moura (nickname Curió) had taken part in the "anti-guerrilla" campaign in the early 1970s in the Araguaia region. He organized votes for candidates of the government party PDS in Pará's elections. Later, he was elected mayor of Curionópolis and member of Congress in Brasília for Pará (Kostcho 1984; Valverde 1989).

taken place. Claims were concentrated on a small number of people (2 % with 72 % of the production) and the large majority involved worked as "formigas" (ants), digging away the basic material with pickaxes and removing the dross. In 1983, the peak of gold output was obtained with nearly 14 tons. Curió established a tax office where claim owners had to sell the gold to the Central Bank. An enormous hole – 90 m deep in an area of only 50 ha with a maximum diameter of 1.2 km and 450 000 m^3 of waste rock removed – resulted from digging and removing the brittle material. Sometimes, CVRD was called for contouring work to avoid dangerous slope gliding, which had killed workers frequently. During the rainy season, Serra Pelada remained closed from November to April, causing intense migratory movements of *garimpeiros*.

In 1986,[24] about 65 000 people were working at Serra Pelada without official contracts in a slavery-like system without any social security, living in unhealthy lodgings, suffering from malaria and other tropical infections. Supply of expensive food was controlled by claim owners. Some had more than 50 claims or had a share in a number of other claims and employed up to 850 *formigas*. These poor *garimpeiros* carried 30 kg bags to the processing area, climbing up 80 m on steep slopes and rickety ladders[25] and were paid by claim holders daily according to the number of trips upwards and running down. In long files, these men made up to incredible 50–60 trips per day, earning on the average 1.5 to 2 minimum salaries. In case of illness, they were dismissed. They were not members of the now founded but soon insolvent cooperative and lived without human rights as "bóias frias" of the mining industry (Kohlhepp 1987a; 1987b).

The situation turned dramatic when the authorisation of manual gold extraction ended, and mechanisation – allowing a 70 % higher output – endangered the existence of claim owners and *formigas*. In their despair at losing their jobs and thus seeing their livelihoods threatened, a rebellion ensued with violent actions, burning down public buildings in the neighbourhood, such as the townhall of Parauapebas. Bridges were destroyed, and street barricades stopped road traffic (Guerreiro 1984; Ab'Sáber 1996c). CVRD wanted the *garimpeiros* to be expelled from Serra Pelada.[26] As in many other large-scale projects in Amazonia, it became apparent that the decision-making level had no insight into the structures of traditional communities in the interior and made no effort to take traditional regional conditions into account in their planning. "The *garimpo* was the utmost utopia of the poor in the region" (Ab'Sáber 1996c, 237). The violent uprising of the affected people was the consequence of this situation.

The company feared invasions into the central mining concession area and trouble at the mining site high up in the Serra dos Carajás, as well as considerable impacts in regional planning and economic development. Protests of hundreds of *garimpeiros* commanded by Curió in Brasília made the Congress pass the so called "law Curió," defining Serra Pelada as an open *garimpo*. Thus, the temporary continuation of manual extraction down to a level of 190 m was approved until 1987. From 1980 to 1987, official data stated 38 tons of gold produced at Serra Pelada. The proportion of gold smuggled

24 Field visit of the author at Serra Pelada on September 12, 1986.

25 Sebastião Salgado's impressive photos of the inhuman situation at Serra Pelada became well-known worldwide.

26 Cf. chapter I.4.2.3. Due to the tense situation, CVRD staff did not wear company uniforms during a visit by the author to Serra Pelada in September 1986, and the vehicles were not marked with a company label for security reasons.

to the outside world was significantly lower compared to the Amazon region as a whole (27 %). Some claim owners had started mechanisation of gold extraction and installed fortified camps (in a Wild West manner: "Fort Apache" etc.) where they kept machinery and organised separate private gold output.

Curió had banned arms, alcohol, and women within Serra Pelada. In a distance of 30 km, a rapidly growing settlement – later the town Curionópolis – developed, with a commercial area and a separated red-light district. The government was afraid of violent or even armed conflicts in case of closure of Serra Pelada (Guerreiro 1984). Previous cases showed that claim owners trying to valorise their investments stirred up their *formigas* to fight for their jobs. Heavily armed military police took care of "law and order." Migration of unsettled *garimpeiros* already had caused invasion problems in colonisation projects or Indigenous reservations in other Amazonian regions.[27] In 1986, the admission of families and women in Serra Pelada had intended to reduce social tensions, promoting stabilisation and appeasement.

The wild camp area with incredible hygienic and social conditions changed to a more "urban" situation with increasing infrastructure such as shops and a school. At the end of the 1980s, gold output decreased and Serra Pelada's population was aware of the near exhaustion of gold deposits. In 1992, activities in Serra Pelada came to an end and most of the gold diggers left for other *garimpos* in Amazonia. Today, the Serra Pelada mine is abandoned and the giant crater that was created by hand digging has filled with ground water, forming a small, polluted lake. Finally, CVRD received a government's indemnification because of property rights in the area which had been invaded in the 1980s by thousands of *garimpeiros*.

1.2.4. Strategies of industrial development

A new approach to industrial development in Amazonia was to try to diversify the existing industrial sectors, which had focused on the food industry and the manufacturing products of the area's economy.

Table 2 shows the 187 industrial projects approved by SUDAM up to October 1980 and the diversification of sectors in which new investments were made, which appeared to be balanced.

The maximum investment had been in establishing food, chemical and cement industry. The degree of dependence had increased because of the marked movement away from the preparation and processing of regional raw materials such as rubber and jute. 38 % of the investment planned for the industrialisation of Amazonia had been by basic industries and industries for producer goods, 26 % by food and semi-luxuries industry and 18 % for consumer goods and capital goods each.

Expansion of timber industry had been planned as part of a rational forestry and timber plan promoted by SUDAM (Pandolfo 1974). However, it would have been necessary to define the basic features of a forestry policy in order to control the use of the timber resources in Amazonia according to ecological requirements and the problems of using timber in Indigenous territories and in the forest reserves which had been established by law but were not respected and protected. In view of the great wealth

27 In 1985 *garimpeiros* invaded Yanomami territories in Roraima (Serra dos Surucucús). After an alert of FUNAI, they were expelled by the federal police (Cleary 1990, 206).

of species but the low ratio of individual trees per area which could be used in timber industry, destruction of forests by fire clearance was cheaper than selecting useful timber and transporting it for long distances.

Table 2: Industrial investment in Amazônia Legal (projects approved by October 1980)

Sector	Number of projects	Total investments (in %)	% of tax benefit
Food	35	19.8	62.3
Chemical Industry	15	13.0	44.9
Non-metallic minerals	12	10.7	67.2
Timber	24	9.4	50.2
Textiles	14	6.0	37.6
Metal processing	10	5.1	70.6
Electrical	8	5.0	22.7
Mining Industry	6	4.8	18.6
Drinks	9	3.3	33.0
Others	54	22.9	39.0
Total	**187**	**100.0**	**48.0**

Source: Kohlhepp (1984a, 663); author's calculations from data provided by SUDAM in Belém, November 1980.

The industries planned were concentrated almost entirely in Pará (33 % of the industrial investment planned), Amazonas (32 %) and Mato Grosso (25 %). In Table 3, investments and job-creation of private, non-agricultural enterprises are presented. The 65 000 jobs in industrial and mining companies did not imply a perceptible alleviation of the serious unemployment situation. A high level of automation did not favour job-creation and it was of crucial importance for the ability of industrial firms to compete with other industries in the traditional economic centres of Brazil and abroad. Hardly any of the labour force with the required qualification came from Amazonia but from South and Southeast Brazil. Therefore, there was an urgent need to build labour-intensive industries where more unskilled labour could be trained.

The source of investment funds (Table 4) shows the extreme importance of tax reductions as an incentive for the private sector. As had been stated before, this was particularly the case of cattle-breeding (55 %), agro-industry (52 %) and industrial and mining projects (42 %) in which only between 20 % and 23 % had to be obtained from internal resources.

The Polamazônia programme did not only cause fundamental changes in rural areas but especially in the urban centres of Amazonia. The improvement and functional equipment of state capitals – in their role as "bridgeheads" of a centre-periphery system – resulted in a distinct transition of the town centre with social and spatial structural changes. Manaus, the capital of the state of Amazonas, turned out to be a special type of a development pole.

Table 3: Investments and job-creation by private non-agricultural enterprises in Amazônia Legal (up to August 1982)

Amazônia Legal Federal states and territories (T)	**Industry and mining**		**Tertiary and energy sector**		**Special projects**	
	P.I. (in %)	P.J.	P.I. (in %)	P.J.	P.I. (in %)	P.J.
Acre	0.9	362	1.1	255	-	-
Amapa (T)	0.4	3958	1.3	256	2.9	240
Amazonas	31.9	28 945	3.6	2038	15.3	473
Goiás[1)]	2.3	656	2.3	2396	-	-
Maranhão[1)]	5.2	4695	9.9	1050	-	-
Mato Grosso[1)]	25.2	3551	3.0	1892	-	-
Pará	33.1	21 398	76.8	3715	81.7	3224
Rondônia	0.6	1091	1.3	231	0.1	47
Roraima (T)	0.4	193	0.7	5798	-	-
Total	**100.0**	**64 849**	**100.0**	**17 631**	**100.0**	**3984**
Investments in mill. US$[2)]		56.5		136		29
Investments (%)		48.6		11.7		2.5
Planned jobs (%)		57.8		15.7		3.6
Number of projects		206		28		20
Projects (%)		31.3		4.3		3.0

1) State's share of Amazônia Legal
2) Conversion rate for comparison (August 1982): 1 US Dollar = 189 Cruzeiros
P.I.: Planned investments
P.J.: Planned jobs

Source: Kohlhepp (1984a, 665); author's calculations of data in: SUDAM (1983).

The establishment of a Free Trade Zone in and around Manaus in 1967 with an area of 10 000 km², administered by SUFRAMA, an autarchy with its own legal status controlled by the Ministry of the Interior, anticipated the strategy of development poles, implemented in the II National Development Plan for Amazonia (1975–1979) as a new strategy of regional development planning. The Free Trade Zone of the metropolitan area of Manaus had been developed by concerted efforts to create a pole of industrial development. Tax incentives and exemption of import customs had been implemented to cause a strong economic impetus to the central Amazonian urban centre in order to lift the Amazon region out of an economic isolation that it had fallen into. There was an expectation of very positive spread-effects on the surroundings and all the western region of the Amazon Basin.

Table 4: Source of investment funds in different economic sectors (August 1982)

Sector	Internal	Other	Re-investment	From tax reduction	Total
Cattle-breeding	19.7	24.4	0.4	55.5	100.0
Agro-industry	20.3	21.5	6.5	51.7	100.0
Industry and mining	23.0	33.9	1.9	41.6	100.0
Tertiary sector	14.6	67.9	-	17.5	100.0
Special projects	33.9	24.5	1.5	40.1	100.0
Total	**21.1**	**33.7**	**1.6**	**43.6**	**100.0**
Composition of investment funds (%)					

Source: Kohlhepp (1984a, 665); author's calculations of data in: SUDAM (1983).

With the start of the industrial sector in 1973, many industrial companies accepted the new strategy and the unconventional location using the high state-subsidized allowances. Tax incentives and subsequent complementary legislation created comparative advantages in this area over other Brazilian regions. As a result, the Manaus Free Trade Zone attracted new investment to the area. Mostly subsidiary companies of southeast- and south-Brazilian enterprises initiated their activities almost exclusively as assembly plants of imported foreign semi-finished products. With the opening of a very well established industrial park with a good infrastructure on an area of 16 km^2, Manaus gained a specific quality as industrial site, improved by the existence of many cheap, but unskilled workers.

The number of industries increased rapidly and at the end of 1984[28] a labour force of about 45 000 was employed by 259 companies. In another 44 industries in construction or planned, more than 8000 people waited for a new job. This was an extremely positive situation on the labour market.

The Polamazônia programme was characterized by a shift of the main concentration of development activities to the private sector and the use of tax reductions making Amazonia attractive as an investment region. The periphery became increasingly dependent on the centre. The centre-oriented economic development of Amazonia failed in achieving socio-economically balanced regional development. Particularly since the discovery of numerous deposits of mineral resources, the dynamic progress of Amazonian economic development produced a stratification of regional planning priorities and economic interests proved to be predominant.

Government subsidies enabled the presence of industrial sectors in Manaus, normally producing at this site without any locational advantages. This is especially the case with the electrical and electronics industry with more than 25 % of investments and 38 % of the labour force available. In a labour-intensive operation or assembly of

28 In 1985, the site of the industrial park of Manaus was analysed and mapped by the author evaluating SUFRAMA statistics on individual projects of industrial enterprises approved. Table 5 is based on detailed calculations of the author according to project documents of SUFRAMA in Manaus, 1985 (Kohlhepp 1986, Fig. 12).

electronic entertainment products, colour televisions, video cassettes, magnetic tapes, tape recorders, radios, Hi-Fi-equipment, electronic calculators, and quartz watches were produced. Another range of products concentrated on motorbikes, bicycles and products of plastic and textile industry. Only the timber and food industries as well as construction were mainly based on regional or local raw materials.

In 1985, the capacity of the industrial park of Manaus containing 45 % of all industries of the Free Trade Zone had been exhausted. The implementation of a second industrial park planned had been delayed by the Brazilian economic recession in the beginning of the 1980s. The artificial upturn of this specifically structured and increasing import-oriented industrial sector in Manaus gave rise to a totally new situation on the job market. Suddenly, the job supply not only showed a depletion of the local labour potential, but triggered a significant pull effect that led to an enormous rural exodus from the surrounding areas as well as interurban mobility from the municipalities of central Amazonia that exceeded the job supply in Manaus.

It became clear that cancelling the fiscal locational advantages, guaranteed by law until 1997, would deprive the "extended workbench" of its site-specific right to exist. The consequences of such a situation would have been disastrous for the labour market in Manaus. The subsidiary branches either would automate the production or shut down the manufacturing sector. The working force would hardly find job alternatives because the workers only were trained for a specific manufacturing process and production run in many cases was geared for manual fitting.

In the mid-1980s, the "pole" Manaus achieved only a very limited impulse of positive spread effects in the regional development of central and western Amazonia. Much stronger was the suction effect of an increasing migration in the surroundings to the metropolitan area of Manaus. Another phenomenon bound up with the Free Trade Zone became evident in the city of Manaus. Numerous shops with duty-free goods were concentrated in the city (cf. Kohlhepp 1986, Figs. 12 and 13), offering Brazilian inland tourists to buy some hundred US Dollars' worth of products free of taxes, a very popular urge of spending. This increased returns of hotels and restaurants and made air services to and from Manaus fully booked.

Evaluating the locational quality of the industrial park in Manaus, doubts remained about the continuity of this development. The high degree of dependence of this site on state subsidies may not be able to stand up to a cost-benefit-analysis in the long run.[29]

The priority areas for regional development were fixed in the Polamazônia programme, the demarcation criteria had been very imprecise (Fig. 3). The public and private "development poles" had been so far concentrated on central, eastern, and south-eastern Amazonia. The more extensive lowlands of the Upper Amazonia west of the Madeira river have hardly been incorporated in the regional development plans.

The establishment of development poles, a basic element of the II National Development Plan, had intended to correct the imbalance between centre and periphery. Success of the measure depended on careful planning in the location of industries, on the volume of investment, the extent of regionally polarised development and the pull effect within the region.

29 See chapter II.6.3.1.

Table 5: Number of people employed and investment in industries in the Free trade Zone of Manaus (up to December 1984)

Industrial sector	**Existing Industries**			**Industries under construction and planned**[1)]			**Total industries**			
								Workforce		
	Number	Workforce	Investment share in%	Number	Workforce	Investment share in%	Number	absolute	in%	Investment share in%
Electrical	45	17442	25.8	17	3044	23.2	62	20486	38.6	25.3
Wood	43	5669	14.5	-	-	-	43	5669	10.7	11.6
Vehicle	12	3876	13.4	3	862	7.7	15	4738	8.9	12.3
Metal	18	1389	9.6	7	1526	2.7	25	2915	5.5	8.3
Watch, optical	19	2659	5.6	1	265	0.5	20	2924	5.5	4.6
Textile	8	2542	8.8	-	-	-	8	2542	4.8	7.1
Plastics	16	2538	4.8	-	-	-	16	2538	4.8	3.8
Beverages	7	1879	2.5	-	-	-	7	1879	3.5	2.0
Food	18	1361	2.0	1	232	0.1	19	1593	3.0	1.6
Stone & earth	5	417	0.2	3	931	56.8	8	1348	2.5	11.4
Paper	3	178	0.8	4	734	2.9	7	912	1.7	1.2
Machinery	11	737	2.4	2	129	0.4	13	866	1.6	2.0
Chemical	11	543	3.4	1	77	0.1	12	620	1.2	2.8
Furniture	9	526	0.7	1	40	-	10	566	1.1	0.6
Printing	5	270	0.3	1	152	0.3	6	422	0.8	0.3
Clothing	7	345	0.2	1	12	1.8	8	357	0.7	0.5
Leather	4	315	0.1	-	-	-	4	315	0.6	0.1
Others	18	2263	4.9	2	138	3.5	20	2401	4.5	4.5
Total	**259**	**44949**	**100.0**	**44**	**8142**	**100.0**	**303**	**53091**	**100.0**	**100.0**
			1.213 billion Cruzeiros			0.3 billion Cruzeiros				1.513 billion Cruzeiros
1) Submitted projects proposal										

Source: Kohlhepp (1986, 183, Table 2); author's calculation; data provided by SUFRAMA in Manaus in 1985.

In the mid-1980s, Amazonia faced the threat of a new cycle of exploitation with increasing interregional and intraregional disparities. 15 years of developing programmes for Amazonia resulted in a mentality of unlimited expectations of economic progress without taking in consideration its ecological consequences and the coordination of state and private development projects. Sectoral and regional planning did not meet social needs, nor did it create clear guidelines for the spatial organisation of dynamic development processes in a peripheral frontier region.

Corruption in land title registers (*grilos*) and excessive land speculation, violent conflicts with Indigenous populations, and the military strategy of "security and development" determined this critical phase. The enormous destruction of tropical rain forests by slash-and-burn clearing with irrecoverable damage for ecosystems had started and developmentism of the Military Government had not been willing to hear scientific warnings of a threatening ecological disaster.

1.2.5. The Jarí-Project: The dream of a multi-dimensional mega-project of an US tycoon

The Military Government tried to attract private capital to Amazônia Legal conceding enormous subsidies. Despite the framework conditions granted by the government, the room for manoeuvre of private investors remained very large. However, the Jarí project was an exception in terms of dimension, the establishment of an isolated enclave and the almost uncontrolled activities of the foreign owner in the Amazon region over 15 years.

With official approval in 1967, Daniel K. Ludwig, the US-American owner of National Bulk Carriers, the largest merchant fleet worldwide, and of a ramified economic empire, purchased a huge area at the Jarí river, a tributary of the Amazon river, in Pará and the former Territory of Amapá. Only US$ 3 million were paid for an area of at least 16 000 km², but Jarí claimed 36 500 km² – nearly the area of Switzerland – in an application to SUDAM in 1975.[30] Ludwig had made the biggest land purchase ever registered to a private individual. Controversial data of this estate demonstrate the uncertainty and the dubious quality of land titles in the Amazon region. Land purchase had been realized before passing of a law in 1971, regulating acquisition of land by foreigners. According to this new law, a maximum of 25 % of a municipal area was allowed to be in foreign hands, only 40 % from this to one owner.

The Jarí Forestry and Agricultural Enterprises were a combined enterprise of silvicultural plantations, associated with an industrial complex of cellulose production, a mining project, and an agricultural part with cattle-breeding and mechanised rice cultivation and water buffalo ranching in the floodplain (*várzea*). In the beginning, Jarí had been discussed by planners and politicians to be a "model" of regional economic development with the nationalistic background of having a future solution for the economic exploitation of Amazonia. The lack of information and of published research on the economic and ecological viability of this project as well as "the company's tight access to the area" (Fearnside and Rankin 1980, 146) was a characteristic of Jarí.[31]

30 The area had been covered by 170 land titles of 52 different sellers, in 1976 32 titles had been legalised (Fearnside and Rankin 1980, 155).

31 After two refused attempts to visit the Jarí project during the Ludwig era, the author had only a chance of a field trip to the area in 1986, after the project's taking over of a Brazilian group of large

Fig. 3: The Polamazônia concept and regional priority areas in Amazonia

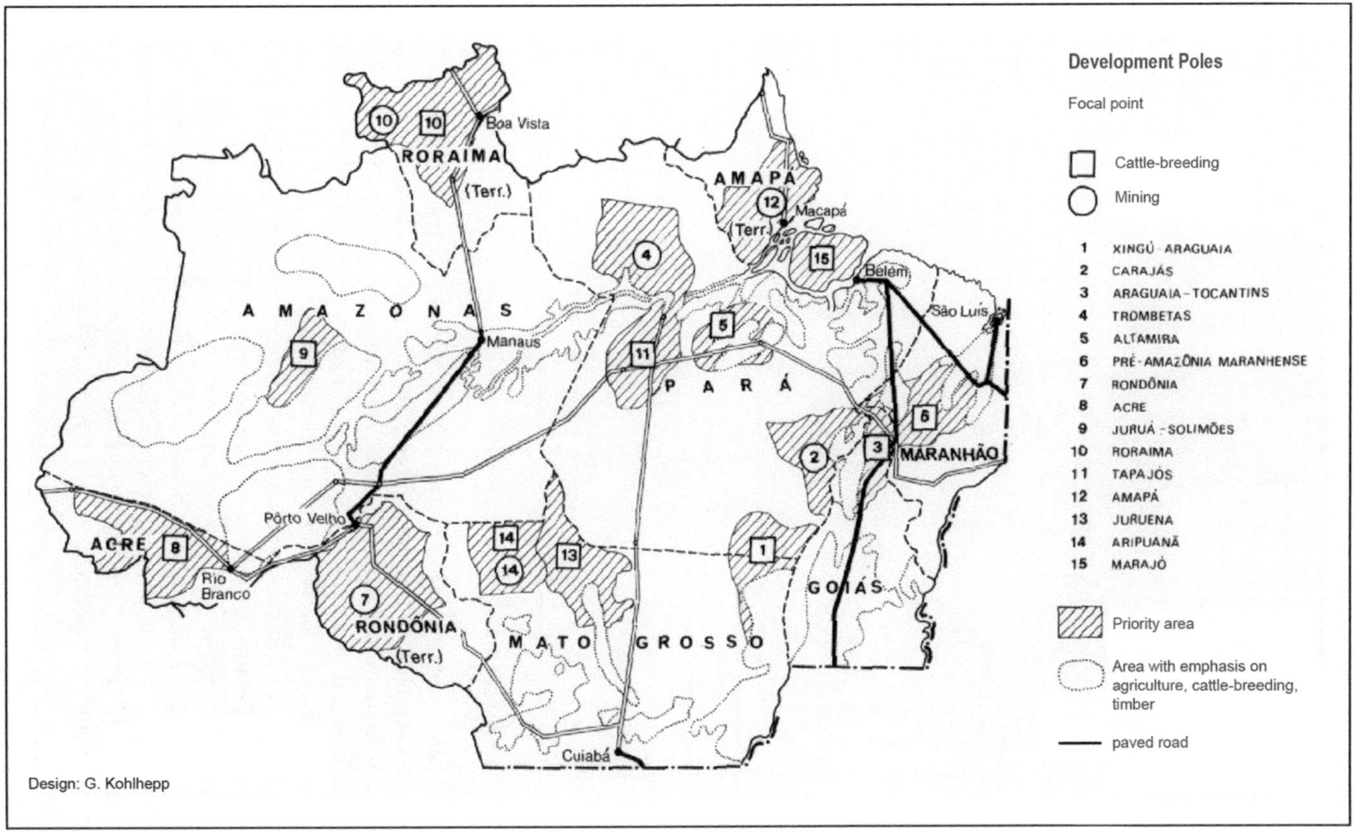

Source: according to documents of SEPLAN (1974) and SUDAM/SUDECO (1975); published in Kohlhepp (1978a, 12).

Fig. 4: The Jarí Project

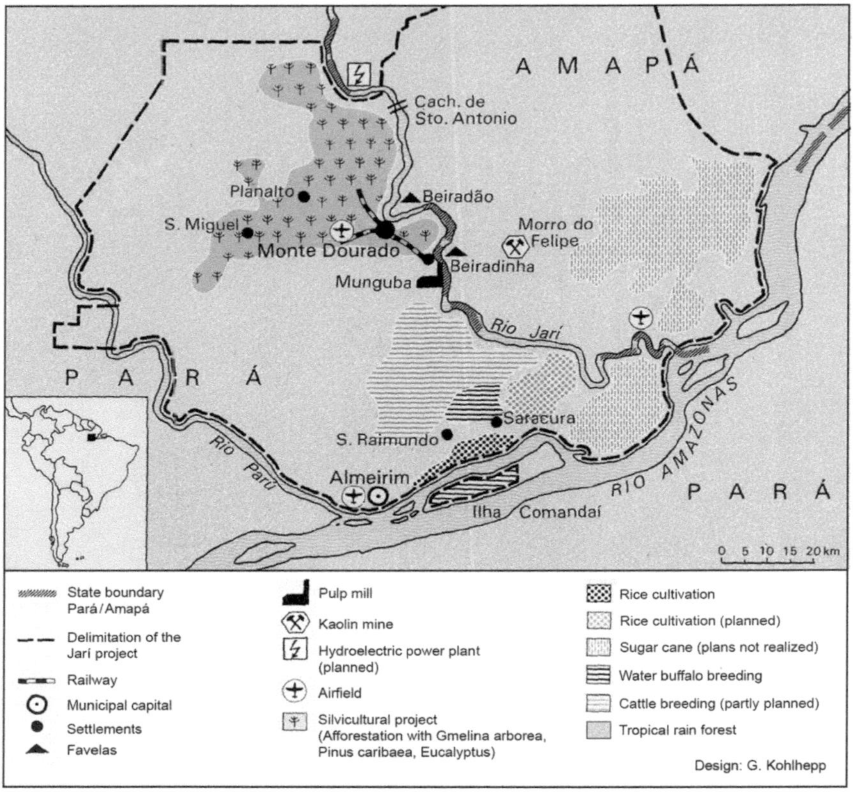

Source: Kohlhepp (1987a, 34).

Jarí had the advantage to be financially and technically very well endowed. Headquarter of the project's administration and technical staff was located at the small town of Monte Dourado on the Jarí river. Basis of Ludwig's Jarí enterprise was the production of cellulose, and silvicultural plantations, necessary to feed the pulp mill planned. Since most of the rain forest timber was not suitable for paper production because of the large number of different species and heterogeneous timber quality, the original forest had been cut down on an area of more than 110 000 ha (= 6 % of Jarí's native forest) and replaced by problematic monoculture tree plantations of non-regional exotic species. Before clearing started, good timber of more than 40 species had been extracted for house construction and manufacture. Forest clearing using heavy bulldozers damaged topsoil and nutrients, removing the forest cover hardened the lateritic soil. Workers from Northeast Brazil recruited by subcontractors for four months became employed for manual land clearing. During felling activities, about 4000 workers lived in camps. Some communities in the project area lost their land to the plantations. About 2000 squatters lived in the Jarí area causing fire problems in the plantations when they

companies. Interviews with different staff members in all projects could be realised, documents on the economic activities, statistics and maps were consulted (cf. Kohlhepp 1987a, 34 f.), cf. Fig. 4.

prepared land for planting. Resettling of squatters had been hindered by lacking legal confirmation of Jarí's land claims. Many families migrated to more remote areas, or to near towns. Afforestation began in 1969 with the rapidly growing *Gmelina arborea*, a species from Southeast Asia, and *Pinus caribaea* from the Caribbean. As growth of *Gmelina* depended very much on soil quality in different locations, the normal time of cutting *Gmelina* trees had to be shortened from 6–7 to 4 years, *Pinus* from 12 to 8 years. Additionally, insect and plant diseases attacked the plantations so that *Pinus caribaea* and later *Eucalyptus deglupta* – frequently with uneven growth – and *Eucalyptus urophylla* became more important. *Eucalyptus* pulp only achieved a lower market price and *Eucalyptus* had been planted to a large extent in other parts of Brazil with lower costs. Fear of shortfall of wood supply for the pulp mill and concern over the growth of newly planted seedlings started fertilizing of *Gmelina* and *Eucalyptus* in 1982 (Fearnside and Rankin 1985). In 1986, the share of the plantations in the replanted area was about one third of each tree species, reafforestation of *Gmelina* had diminished by 50 %. Ludwig made efforts to contract the best professionals for Jarí's forestry staff, but the forestry plantations continued to cause enormous epidemiological problems and costs, not to mention the ecological consequences of the enormous destruction of the native forests and the disastrous effects on biodiversity.

In 1978, Ludwig ordered a pulp mill and power plant built in Japan to be shipped as a floating complex in two sections over 21 000 km to Brazil and towed to the Jarí river port Munguba. Reports in national and international newspapers and magazines flooded the press with sensational stories about this spectacular event.[32] Pulp production with a capacity of 750 t/day required 4000 m^3 of pulpwood per day, using the three replanted species according to the rhythm of wood cutting dependent on annual rainfall distribution. The installation of the pulp mill attracted many people looking for work. The energy problem initially could be solved by burning more than half a million m^3 per year of wood in a steam engine. An urgently needed hydroelectric project was not approved by Eletronorte, the government-owned company holding the monopoly on power supply. Exports of bleached pulp to Europe started in 1979 and a biologically treated sewage disposal was installed.

The Kaolin mine with reserves of 50 mt was a very important deposit. A railway and port facilities made the Jarí open pit mine an excellent site for transport and exports. Kaolin, a fine white clay used to coat paper with the gloss necessary in printing, was important in ceramics, cosmetics, and medicine. There was a great demand for high-grade Kaolin on the world market, 80 % of the production of 240 000 t/a (1986) had been exported to Germany (47 %) and Japan (30 %) during the first years of mining.

The infrastructure included a 65 km railroad, a deep-water river port up to ships of 40 000 tdw, more than 5000 km of roads, and the town Monte Dourado with hundreds of houses for the working force, a well-equipped company town for the staff and qualified employees, shops, schools, a hospital, medical services to all residents, a police station, and three small airports. Heavy construction and harvesting machinery and an enormous number of trucks and cars had been imported. In the beginning of the 1980s, population in Jarí estate rapidly increased. About 8500 people were employed there, only 40 foreigners as staff members. More than 30 000 people were living inside

32 "Jarí: A billion-dollar gamble"; "Ludwig's Amazon empire"; "A giant pulp mill for the Amazon wilderness"; "Ludwig's mystery in the Amazon jungle"; among others McIntyre (1980).

the Jarí territory, many at the border in a shanty town called Beiradão. *Favelas* with houses on stilts along the Jarí river with numerous social problems, widespread prostitution, drugs, violence, and very poor sanitary conditions caused increasing security problems from the point of view of Jarí executives. They did not feel responsible for this problem but blamed the political institutions of Amapá for lacking infrastructural measures and administrative organisation. Security forces were recruited to keep about 3000 *garimpeiros* outside the Jarí borders, according to information of the Jarí staff.

Besides the main projects of afforestation with the pulp mill and the kaolin processing, Jarí started two agricultural initiatives with innovation potential: Rice cultivation and water buffalo ranching in the floodplain. Rice production in the *várzea* near São Raimundo used new rice varieties developed at the famous International Rice Research Institute (IRI) in the Philippines. As natural soil fertility sedimentation in the *várzea* by annual flooding had been interrupted by diking, the nutrients had to be supplied through fertilization, sprayed with herbicides and pesticides by small airplanes. Different high-yielding varieties had prolonged tests in getting resistance to insects and weeds. Highly mechanized cultivation with hydraulic installations was very expensive and economic profitability seemed to be low in the beginning. A very modern rice mill had been imported. The adaptation of large-scale rice production techniques to the *várzea* had been the most far-reaching innovation (Gall 1979). A two-crop cycle per year was expected to yield exceptional 9 t/ha/year. It became difficult to find a second crop for crop rotation in the rice fields of 4000 ha. Plans to expand the cultivated area to 14 000 ha as originally planned depended on solutions for persistent biological problems, special equipment, water management, building of canals, and training of workers for specific control in the fields. The cultivation of sugar cane originally planned was not realised.

In 1986, a herd of more than 9000 water buffalos – very common on Marajó Island – was grazing in the floodplain of the Jarí estate. Buffalos grow faster than cattle and can be slaughtered after 2½ years. In Monte Dourado a slaughterhouse had been installed. Buffalo meat achieved 30 % of daily meat consumption in Jarí. Processing of buffalo cheese was one of the new production lines. Corresponding to 70 000 ha of pastures in the Jarí *várzea*, an extension of the buffalo stock to 30 000 had been considered. Cattle ranching of 3000 nelore bulls on *terra firme* area was of secondary importance. Pastures, mainly with Guinea grass (*Panicum maximum*), were planted to demonstrate Jarí's claim to land against squatters in the region.[33]

The Military Government initially supported Ludwig's plans as a possible "model" to exploit economically the natural resources of the rain forest region by exclusively foreign investing in high-grade modernisation of development projects. The Jarí project was given tax reductions and allowance for tax-free imports, but Ludwig did not use loans of the Brazilian National Development Bank (BNDES) or private Brazilian bank transactions. In the beginning of the 1980s with the first indications of a redemocratization process, government officials began to criticize the extent of land ownership, the exemption of taxes and the lacking communication of the project's management with national and regional authorities. Ludwig became a special enemy of the National Information Service (SNI) under military control, opposed to foreign landowners and

33 All statistical data mentioned had been given to the author by Jari's staff in October 1986.

projects without state-controlled decisions (*Veja*, January 13, 1982, p. 73). Nationalizing Jarí was the central political objective of the military hardliners.

Scientists of different disciplines analysed the Jarí project and evaluated biological problems of reafforestation with monocultures of non-regional species, of soil fertility on *terra firme* areas, and ecological consequences of large-scale rain forest clearing and forest fires. Studies criticised failures in regional development planning, rated the economic viability of the individual projects and working conditions of people, especially those recruited by subcontractors (Fearnside 1987; Fearnside and Rankin 1980; 1985; Garrido Filha 1980; Valverde 1981; Gall 1979; Kohlhepp 1987a).[34] Non-governmental organisations (NGOs), in particular environmentally oriented groups, achieved a scientific level in their critical evaluation of government policies.

Newspaper reports started an intensive nationalist campaign against Jarí, criticising "the US colonisation of the Amazon," "the American invasion," "sell out of Amazonia," the obscurity of the project's activities and the impossibility to visit the area without permission of the project's management. Social tensions and the enormous ecological impact of far-reaching project's procedures, still in a test phase, were open to attack.[35] Some of the accusations were justified, others wrong or exaggerated (slave labour, project-owned army, smuggling of gold, timber etc.), but the anti-foreign public pressure in Brazil increased and the Military Government became extremely worried about the situation. Succeeding the Generals Médici and Geisel, supporters of Jarí, President General Figueiredo (1979–1985) had to organise the transition to democracy, being aware of the public anti-military mood and hostility towards foreign influence in Brazil.

Bureaucratic restrictions, the government's banning of the construction of a hydroelectric plant at the Sto. Antônio falls of Jarí river (Fig. 3), the blocked import of a newsprint industry and incentives refused for reafforestation – granted to Brazilian competitors – and for infrastructure and housing development scheme contributed to Ludwig's decision to stop the Jarí project. The official order to sell pulp, kaolin, and rice with state-controlled "frozen" prices (Plano Cruzado) inside Brazil caused severe financial losses and finally speeded up the end of Jarí. After mutual apportioning of blame, in 1982 Ludwig – at the age of 85 years – frustrated and annoyed handed over his Jarí project to a consortium of 27 Brazilian companies, a "roundtable of the big Brazilian capital" (*Veja*, January 13, 1982, p. 70).[36] After having invested US$ 1.3 billion,

34 National and international scientific conferences discussed the Jarí experiment, e. g., in the multinational event of ADLAF (German Association for Latin American Research) at the Institute of Geography at Tübingen University in 1986, with an important participation of Brazilian scientists (cf. Kohlhepp and Schrader 1987).

35 Pinto (1984); Sautchuk *et al.* (1980), McIntyre (1980), among others.

36 Arranged by Planning Minister Delfim Netto, the powerful and internationally respected entrepreneur Antunes at the age of 75 years was in charge of this complicated agreement. The companies involved in 1982 had property assets of US$ 8 billion and 0.65 million employees. 10 banks, 3 insurance companies, 9 industrial and mining groups, 4 large construction companies and one agro-industrial group formed this unusual conglomeration. The holding of the new Companhia do Jarí controlled three enterprises: The forestry, the mining, and the agro-industrial group. For US$ 40 million, the Antunes group became owner of the Kaolin mine, establishing the Cadam company. In Amapá, manganese mining had also been controlled by Antunes (cf. chapter I. 1.2.2). The idea of a takeover of the Jarí project by the mining giant Cia. Vale do Rio Doce (CVRD) had not been realised because of ongoing planning of the Grande Carajás Programme.

Ludwig did not receive any money, but the consortium took on the company's debts of US$ 280 million. BNDES supported the consortium with a US$ 180 million loan. Ludwig received a gradually diminishing amount of the possible profits of the operations for 40 years. As he had no heirs, the profits were to be transferred to his Swiss-based Daniel Ludwig Foundation for cancer research.

Ludwig was an exceptionally successful entrepreneur, but an egomaniac, stubborn, and controlling the last details. Obviously, he was unwilling to understand the project's huge environmental and social impacts, the political climate for foreign-owned operations in Amazonia, and his increasingly dependent situation in view of democratic governments to be expected. He detested public appearance, avoiding public relations, and causing mythmaking. With his rough treatment of his staff, he had fired 29 directors of the Jarí project and decided everything essential by himself, visiting Jarí several times a year (*Veja*, January 13, 1982; Pinto 1984; 1986). The press campaign against Ludwig and his project reminded of the press reports against Volkswagen's activities in cattle-breeding at the same time in Pará.

The Jarí project was the largest private enterprise ever realised by a single entrepreneur. The Brazilian public never had any influence on what happened in Jarí during the Ludwig era. With the ownership in the hands of Brazilian companies, the government approved projects which had not been granted before to Ludwig. The transition of owners caused dismission of workers.

Finally, it must be emphasised that a large-scale forestry project with a goal of monoculture plantations of non-native species in inner-tropical forest regions was a highly problematic experiment with extremely negative biodiversity impacts. It became clear that it could not serve as a model case for an adequate ecological and socioeconomic use in ecosystems of tropical rain forests. Even with economically optimal prerequisites, a foreign-owned project of this dimension was likely to create problems for internal policy and questions of national sovereignty. An enclave with a total lack of communication with the home country's government easily came under pressure by the Military Government.

The project never had been supervised by state-controlled institutions to evaluate its regional influence. The Brazilian government neither had the funds for this mega-project, nor were the highly qualified experts available in Brazil in the 1970s. The overambitious project without any chance of a regional multiplier effect caused a clash of social structures: Self-confident foreign representatives of modernised exploitation of natural resources and unskilled regional working force, dependent on profit-oriented decisions and lacking impetus or even interest in regional development outside the project's area. Besides the huge Ford rubber plantation in Fordlândia (1928–1945) at the Tapajós river, the Jarí project turned out to be the second US-financed setback in Amazonia.

2. Polonoroeste: A new strategy of integrated rural development

The failure of agrarian colonisation in the 1970s along the Transamazônica[37] with its specific restrictions made Rondônia in southwestern Amazonia the new favourite area for migration from Southeast and South Brazil. While the agricultural measures of the Polamazônia programme had been concentrated on promoting the establishment of large farms, the Polonoroeste programme in Rondônia and in northwestern Mato Grosso in the early 1980's resurrected the idea of agrarian colonisation by small-scale farmers.

In Rondônia, the agrarian colonisation had led to a different approach in regional development planning. With the participation of the World Bank[38] since 1981 – the first activity of the World Bank in the Brazilian agrarian colonisation in Amazonia – an integrated rural development programme was carried out. The new concept for a poverty-oriented integrated development of rural areas based on three premises:

- The rural lower social classes as targets,
- development of strategies for satisfying basic needs,
- participation to be encouraged.

As the constant conflicts between environmental, economic, social, and political interests in the pioneer regions caused ever greater problems, the example of Rondônia was a test case for reconciling these conflicting interests, resulting in a new regional development programme (Théry 1981; Kohlhepp and Coy 1985). Besides economic and political motives ("national security"), socio-political considerations were well to the fore within this regional policy. "Amazonia as a safety valve" has been the slogan and the essential background for the national promotion of the development of the pioneer front in Amazonia at the time of the Military Government. The intention to develop and colonise Amazonia was to reduce the increasing potential for conflict in the Northeast of Brazil – problems of land access and basic drought problems – as well as in the Southeast and South due to transformation processes in the agricultural structure.

37 Cf. Kleinpenning, volume I of this publication; Kohlhepp (1976a; 1976b; 1978a).

38 The total budget of the Polonoroeste programme amounted to US$ 1.5 billion, one third provided by the World Bank.

2.1. Increasing migration activities and agrarian colonisation in Rondônia[39]

Rondônia's position was characterised by the considerable, spontaneous migration of the rural "surplus population," mostly from South and Southeast Brazil, constituting a regional population growth rate of 15.8 % per year during the 1970's, the highest in Brazil. Of special importance was the establishment of government-directed agrarian colonisation projects in small holdings, mainly in central Rondônia along the federal road between Cuiabá and Porto Velho (BR-364) as well as in the southwest and northwest of Rondônia. The programme was organised by the colonisation authority INCRA and based on the distribution of 100 ha lots. The settlers had to preserve 50 % of their land as forest.

The number of migrants arriving in the region in the 1970s was up to 255 000. Migration figures showed a distinct increase from 1981 to June 1985 with more than 438 000 people. Apart from traditional motives of migration and the deterioration of living conditions within the regions of origin because of failing access to land, land use changes combined with dismissal of farm workers and the general economic crisis, the completion of the BR-364 was a main reason for the increase, especially in 1984. This allowed steady access to the region throughout the year, something which had been impossible in previous years during five months in the rainy season. However, absorption and integration of new immigrants in Rondônia still constituted the most important task for regional development planning.

After the end of the coffee cycle, the mechanisation of agriculture and the conversion of crop land into pasture, a high percentage of migrants came from the regions of the older pioneer fronts, especially from the north and northwest of Paraná (Norte Novo, Norte Novissimo) (Kohlhepp 1991b; 2014). Other states of origin were Mato Grosso do Sul, Mato Grosso, Minas Gerais and Espírito Santo with landless people from rural areas or young farmers without inheritance rights. The reasons for the increasing importance of rural migrants from São Paulo were agrarian transformation and urban groups with a rural past who were never integrated into an urban "society" and often became socially marginalised (see Table 6).

In connection with the increase in immigration in Rondônia, structural changes have been noted among migrant groups. A considerable increase could be stated in the urban origin of the last residence of migrants. At the end of the 1970s, about three quarters of the migrants came from rural and only one quarter from urban areas, whereas since 1981 this ratio has been almost reversed. It could be analysed that the continuous decrease in the number of migrants occupied in agriculture, from 58 % in 1979 to only 27 % in 1984, ran parallel with the trend pointed out above. Simultaneously, urban occupations such as trade or construction industry had an increase from 8 % in 1979 to 14 % in 1984.

39 This chapter is based on an evaluation of the Polonoroeste programme by order of the German GTZ (Kohlhepp and Coy 1985), publications of Kohlhepp and Coy (1986); Coy (1986); Kohlhepp (1987a) and especially Coy (1988).

Table 6: State of origin of migrants to Rondônia 1979–1984.

	1979	1980	1981	1982	1983	1984
Number of migrants	36 791	49 205	60 218	58 052	92 723	153 327
Variation in %		33.7	22.3	-3.6	59.7	65.4
State	**1979**	**1980**	**1981**	**1982**	**1983**	**1984**
	in %					
Paraná	37.4	38.9	22.9	23.0	29.3	26.7
Mato Grosso	23.3	17.5	14.6	15.0	11.5	13.0
Mato Grosso do Sul	9.0	9.8	7.6	7.2	8.0	6.6
Espírito Santo	5.5	5.6	5.6	8.2	8.5	6.4
Minas Gerais	4.1	5.5	4.5	10.6	9.2	9.9
São Paulo	6.3	6.7	9.9	9.3	9.4	12.4
Goiás	3.4	3.4	3.4	4.8	3.4	3.9
Ceará	1.6	1.0	1.6	1.5	1.9	1.8
Bahia	1.7	2.0	1.8	3.9	4.8	4.0
Rio de Janeiro	0.9	0.9	1.1	1.3	0.9	1.4
Rio Grande do Sul	0.8	1.1	0.7	0.6	0.7	0.9
Amazonas	-	-	12.8	4.9	2.3	3.3
Pará	-	-	3.6	1.9	1.9	1.4
Roraima (T)	-	-	1.2	0.7	0.4	0.2
Other states	4.6	6.1	7.5	6.2	7.0	7.9
Foreign Countries	1.3	1.4	1.2	0.9	0.8	0.2
Total	**100.0**	**100.0**	**100.0**	**100.0**	**100.0**	**100.0**
T) Federal Territory in 1984						

Source: SEPLAN-RO/NURE (1984; 1985) and calculations by Kohlhepp and Coy (1985, Table 3).

Basic problems of existence or precarious living conditions in the towns of the Southeast had an impact as a "push"-factor, especially for the lower social strata. The increasing economic and social differentiation of the pioneer front and the consolidation of the regional urban-rural structures played a role, since groups of migrants came directly into towns, trying to establish urban economic activities. Besides the mentioned "push"-factor, a number of "pull"-factors played an important role among migration motives. The most decisive of these "pull"-factors was the desire for land in Amazonia, a region with unlimited land capacity in the settlers' imagination, arguing without any detailed knowledge of the real living conditions. Migration and receiving a plot of land for their own use was seen as social advancement, since the bulk of migrants had to be reckoned among the landless people (tenants, agricultural labourers etc.) and *minifundistas* in their region of origin.

The installation of small farmer settlement schemes by INCRA was very important. INCRA retailed lots of 100 ha in the beginning of the migration but changed to 50 ha lots because of the high demand for land. The land use system was expected to be a combination of annual crops, mainly to secure subsistence needs, and perennial crops (coffee, cocoa, rubber) for market production. Up to July 1985, about 44 000 families received land within the INCRA settlement schemes, pushing Rondônia ahead of all governmental colonisation areas in Amazônia Legal.

However, unfortunately only a portion of these migrants could be settled. The largely increasing migration on the one hand and the limited settlement capacity of the projects on the other, led to an ever-increasing disequilibrium between demand for and supply of land. More than 20 000 families registered and selected by INCRA had not received their lot. As a result, an increasing social stratification took place within the older colonisation projects. Many new arrivals derived their income as sharecroppers or so called *agregados* on the farms of other peasants, forming a new class of landless people. Difficulties in settling in Rondônia because of exhausted capacity for settlement in areas favourable to agriculture and low capacity of new projects had negative consequences. Thousands of families "waited" for their chance to get land and lived in bad hygienic conditions in thatched huts without financial means to bridge the uncertain time gap and always fearing problems of marginalisation.

Related to the opening of colonisation areas was the emergence of several new central places. The most important of these settlements had been located along the BR-364 between Cuiabá and Porto Velho. In addition, however, new dynamic settlements have emerged that are far away from the central "development axis" (e. g., Rolim de Moura, Alvorada do Oeste) (see Fig. 5).

Since the beginning of the colonisation process, fundamental problems in rural areas had been caused by a considerable infrastructural deficit, concerning access road construction, agricultural commercialisation, public health, and education. Both, the federal colonisation authority INCRA and later the Rondônian institutions had not been able to keep pace with the rapidly developing rural areas. The permanent pressure upon land reserves in Rondônia was only met by dividing land into new lots and distributing them without establishing the necessary infrastructure. The retrenchment of national support could be seen in the change of settlement forms over the period of the 1970s from the so-called Integrated Colonisation Projects (PIC) to Guided Settlement Projects (PAD) and the Rapid Settlement Projects (PAR) (Fig. 5) (Kohlhepp 1984b, 138; Coy 1985; Kohlhepp and Coy 1986, 63).

The conflict between economic valorisation and colonisation on the one hand and the necessity for ecological conservation of the tropical rain forest on the other became one of the major problems. Conflicts of interest between smallholders and large landowners, between settlers and the Indigenous population[40] and land speculation activities caused increasing problems. The number of families involved in these land conflicts, especially in the Amazonian *frontier* region led to social stratification processes, i. e., the reproduction of unequal social structures in colonisation areas.

Fig. 5: Spatial organisation of Rondônia. Colonisation areas, forest reserves and Indigenous territories

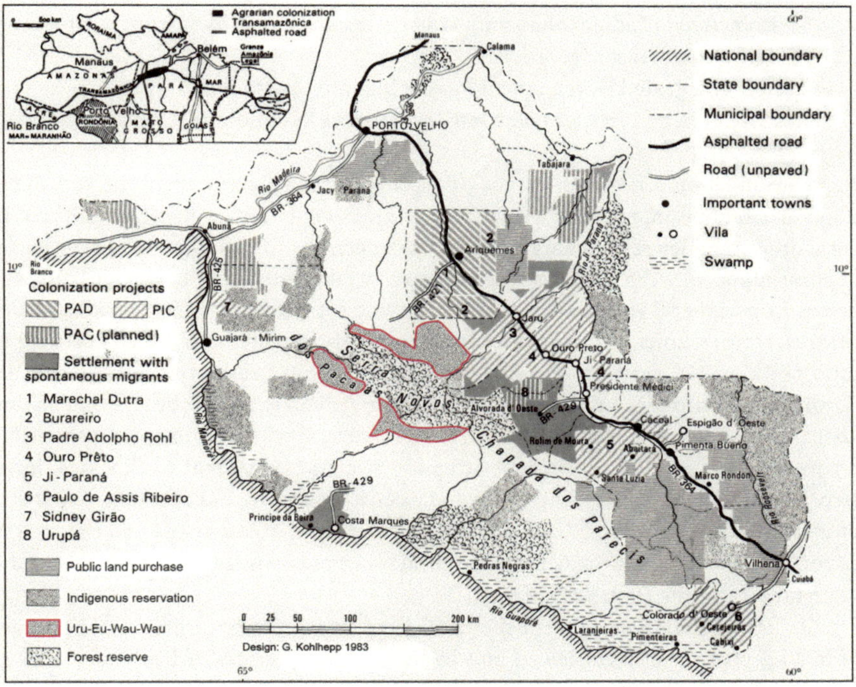

Source: Kohlhepp (1984b).

2.2. Evaluation of the Polonoroeste programme and its modifications

The various national efforts to keep spatial organisation in Rondônia under control and the increasing challenge of the rapid development of Rondônia and 14 municipalities of north-western Mato Grosso finally led to the Polonoroeste programme, announced in 1981. As result of a request of the Military Government, the World Bank financed the asphalting of BR-364, which was completed in September 1984. This road was the backbone of the region and the main access to southwestern Amazonia. Measures to consolidate the existing colonisation areas by "Integrated Rural Development Projects" accompanied the programme. The influence of the World Bank as a financing agency had certainly played an important role in the application of the concept of "Integrat-

40 Cf. chapter I, 3. The settlers' resentment and contesting of the large "reservations" for the Indigenous population became a serious problem.

ed Rural Development." Polonoroeste was seen as a new and more adequate starting point for the Amazon region, needing to be handled with particular sensitivity.[41]

The following issues were of prior significance:

Phase I of Polonoroeste:

- Consolidation of the older settlement areas in Rondônia (Integrated Rural Development Project Rondônia: PDRI-RO),
- problems of public health, especially the defeat of malaria,
- protection of Indigenous groups and their settlements in the programme area,
- environmental conservation.

Phase II: Integrated Development Project in Mato Grosso (PDRI-MT).
Phase III: Determination of new settlement areas in Rondônia.

The consolidation measures of the Integrated Rural Development in the PDRI-Rondônia mainly intended improvement and consolidation of living conditions in rural areas of older settlements. Its focus has been the installation of "Urban nuclei of rural support".[42] The NUAR correspond to central places of the lowest "urban" categories in peripheral rural areas, providing basic infrastructure like schools, health centres, storage units, private trade, and handicraft for a defined *Hinterland* of up to 1000 families. *Colonos* from the *Hinterland* were urged to settle in the NUAR, maintaining their main residence on their rural holdings. Apart from fundamental doubts about the viability of the "urban" NUAR model,[43] several other factors were responsible for its modification: Administrative irregularities and functional weaknesses, infrastructural problems concerning water and electricity supply, and a lack of integration of institutions within the NUAR. Construction of rural access roads and the conservation of these unpaved roads under tropical weather conditions has been one of the main targets for the *Hinterland* of the NUAR.

The local population accused the contracted firms and government supervisors of having plans poorly conceived and badly executed. Contracted teachers worked for several months without being paid. Local officials felt totally isolated and were discriminated by the enormous gap between low-level programme execution and higher-level administration. According to the programme, the settlers are to be involved in local decision-making and in the implementation of projects. To this end, the establishment of "rural development commissions" in the communities, the election of local leaders and "administrators" in each NUAR from the group of settlers was a central task, as they shared the same social background. However, the reality of a dictatorial regime made active participation of those involved extremely difficult. When the new municipalities took over responsibility for the NUAR, the difficult financial and political situation of these municipalities became a problem in a consolidation process. This was the case in conflicts of interest between municipal and state level.

---

41 According to the opinion of representatives of the World Bank: Mahar (1982); Skillings (1985), Goodland (1985).

42 "Núcleos Urbanos de Apoio Rural" (NUAR).

43 This central place model reminded of the concept of *agrovilas* of the Transamazônica colonisation scheme, which failed because of the long distances to the home residence on the farm plots and the failing means of transport (cf. Kohlhepp 1976a; 1978c).

One of the basic problems was the health situation. Health posts in the NUAR were present, but the availability of medical supply was either lacking or totally inadequate. Medicines to combat the most important regional diseases such as the ubiquitous malaria,[44] infections, vitamin deficiency and children's diseases often had been unavailable. Regular visits of doctors did not take place in any of the NUAR. Public health care provision could be described as totally deficient despite of the personal commitment of some employees of the local medical service. The state of health of most of the population has been unsatisfactory.

Agricultural marketing conditions and the agricultural extension service (Emater) had enormous difficulties to be organised. A major problem was the different regional origin of Emater employees and the *colonos*. Due to their lack of detailed local knowledge, the technicians were rarely able to convey information adapted to the ecological conditions of agricultural production, such as regional perennial cultivation of *Guaraná* or agro-silvicultural techniques etc. Success and failure ultimately depended on the acceptance by smallholders. There was often an unbridgeable gap between the Emater technicians and the rural population. For political reasons, the technicians often refused to collaborate with the self-help organisations of rural producers. Agricultural credits, prices of agrarian products (rice and maize) and their marketing were partly hindered by national guidelines, especially in periods of economic crisis. The dependence on intermediaries, the danger of indebtedness, fixed prices etc. persisted as daily problems.

Living conditions of the rural population in the older colonisation areas of Rondônia had not been greatly affected by the introduction of the NUAR due to conceptual deficiencies in the NUAR-model. The originally planned number of 39 NUAR has been reduced to less than 10. Obviously, regional imbalances occurred. The focus on decentralised measures to meet local needs was necessary.

Unfortunately, the measures of PDRI-RO had no decisive influence on the main development trends in rural Rondônia. In the land use sector, a steep increase of pastures could be stated. Annual crops (for subsistence and market) and perennial crops (coffee, cocoa, rubber) remained insignificant. This development was due to plant diseases in perennial crops, strong price fluctuations for some cash crops, low prices for annual crops, especially rice, lack of credit for agricultural investments and excessive interest rates.

In a state-organised colonisation programme, a homogeneous structure of social and land rights aspects was usually created on the basis of an equal distribution of land. The heavy migration flow was responsible for an increasing social stratification of the rural population which was marked by a high rate of farm sales. In some areas, more than 50% of the farms had been sold at least once within 10 years. The rate of abandonment ranged from 10 to 25%. In the project Ouro Preto,[45] the oldest INCRA settlement scheme, only 38% of the families were landowners. Only a small number of lots were in the hands of the original INCRA settlers. The sale of whole or divided plots is a typical change in colonisation projects in Rondônia. The main reasons for selling

44 As a form of protest, people installed a banner in the streets of Ariquemes in Rondônia, calling the town "World capital of malaria" (Observation of the author during field research in 1977).

45 Field studies by Martin Coy in PIC Ouro Preto, Rondônia (Cf. Coy 1988; Kohlhepp and Coy 1985; 1986).

plots were problems of difficult climate adaptation, isolation, lack of infrastructure, yield losses, debts, lack of experience in farm management and diseases.

New migrants equipped with some capital arrived and started purchasing land. The tendency towards land concentration on the one hand and fragmentation of plots on the other, resulting in *minifundios* through the sale of parts of the original agricultural land, was prevalent. Purchasing of some plots occurred with absentee-ownership and the formation of *fazendas* for cattle raising. A new regional urban social class of advocates, businessmen, traders, shopkeepers, doctors, and civil servants turned out to become the winner of this development, increasing social disparities. This was one of the characteristics of "consolidated" frontier regions in Brazil.

The new settlement projects Urupá and Machadinho of Polonoroeste (Phase III) faced the problem that the members of many families selected in 1982, who were waiting for their plots to be allocated, had found other jobs, e. g., in the urban economy, and immediately sold their plots again. The realisation of the new projects with a limited capacity for absorption of settlers became time-consuming and cumbersome, despite of sophisticated planning techniques (aerial photography, soil tests, appropriate survey of the plots). This improvement caused relatively high costs of US$ 7000 per family settled. The INCRA recommendation of cultivation of perennial crops (*Guaraná*, rubber, Brazil nut) could only partly be realised because of high initial costs and lack of credits. Under the prevailing conditions, with the designation of new colonisation areas increasing land conflicts, invasions of *fazendas*, of Indigenous territories and forest reserves were to be expected.

With the planned settlement of about 20 000 families – 15 000 in Rondônia – it became clear that this programme would also involve negative impacts, such as considerable migration flows and growth of population, increasing land conflicts, rise in land prices and intensification of land speculation. A controversial discussion on the national and international scale started after the mid-term evaluation of the programme due to existing problems with the protection of the Indigenous populations and environmental conservation aspects. Pressure of US, Brazilian and European ecological NGOs, scientists, and politicians[46] contributed to a temporary withholding of programme funds. The threat of discontinuation of the Polonoroeste programme in case certain conditions were not met and the redefinition of the programme's priorities led to a detailed work plan with the necessary measures to be implemented in the following years, together with follow-up programmes such as Planafloro.[47] The end of the Military Government in 1985 and a transition period of redemocratisation had played an important role in renewing colonisation strategies in Rondônia. The ostensible strategy for an agrarian reform, unsolid in all details, remained a "declaration of intention."

The aggravation of the agrarian colonisation in Rondônia with the exhausted capacity of projects, continuous and increasing migration with numerous conflicts of

---

46 In the US House of Representatives, the Committee on Science and Technology (Subcommittee on Natural Resources, Agricultural Research and Environment) and in the German Parliament, among others, members of the "Green" party demanded more effective measures for the protection of the Indigenous areas and forest reserves in the programme region (Kohlhepp and Coy 1985).

47 Planafloro was a project of the Federal Government in partnership with the World Bank to implement an improved natural resources management in Rondônia in the 1990s.

interest raised the new problem of the consequences for neighbouring states and regions. With the financial support of the World Bank, existing colonisation projects had been consolidated, but the "development from below" concept could not be successfully realised. Among other improvements needed, providing smallholders with credits at favourable conditions, cooperative organisation, marketing facilities, agricultural extension service and training of technicians in agroforestry systems ought to be realised. Polonoroeste suffered from too optimistic timing of goals.

National agencies like INCRA, FUNAI or IBDF were neither administratively capable nor financially in a position to fulfil the basic requirements of their objectives. Institutional strengthening of the responsible authorities and planning agencies on federal or state level should be given priority by international financing. For the first time in South America, a rural development programme had been given a disbursement moratorium because environmental aspects were neglected. This emphasised a specific problem: If preconditions were created in the environmental sector and it turned out that the partner was not able to finance qualified personnel to protect Indigenous reservations, forest reserves, etc. from encroachment, this problem was to be solved through special loans.

Finally, spontaneous migration to Rondônia increased rapidly to more than 150 000 people per year, leading to a sharp increase in land seized and uncontrolled settlement in areas with limited agricultural carrying capacity. Consequently, large areas of forest were cleared, and even more forest was cut down as numerous small-scale settlers were displaced by land speculators and cattle farmers.

At the same time, a steadily growing stream of settlers poured into the rapidly developing private colonisation projects in northern Mato Grosso and to Acre. The spatial mobility of people remaining landless or trying to survive as *minifundistas* was high and emigration to new pioneer zones in Acre demonstrated that Rondônia had become part of the "moving frontiers," typical for Brazil.

2.3. Impact of migration flows and colonisation activities in Rondônia on the State of Acre

Because of the loan proposal of the Inter-American Development Bank (IDB) for asphalting of the Porto Velho-Rio Branco section of the BR-364, the state of Acre – isolated overland for five to six months every year – became the new focus of interest for migrants. Since Acre, a federal state since 1962, did not have any infrastructural and institutional prerequisites, a threatening migration rush to Acre would cause a chaotic situation and entail serious negative consequences. In 1985, the US representative in the IDB voted against the approval because of failing environmental studies ought to be incorporated into a revised project. An extension of the Polonoroeste programme to Acre was not intended neither by the international financing agencies nor by the Brazilian government (Kohlhepp and Coy 1985).

The historical geopolitical background of Acre's integration from Bolivian into Brazilian territory in 1903 by the Treaty of Petrópolis had caused a complicated situation of land titles in this region. The regional economy was based on immense resources of *Hevea brasiliensis*. Acre became the most important region for rubber production in Amazonia. Export companies financed the trading houses which financed the *se-*

ringalistas, the rural "entrepreneurs" and "owners" of large areas with *Hevea* (*seringais*). In the beginning of the 20th century, immigrants from the drought-struck Brazilian Northeast were contracted to extract *latex* and held in a slave-like dependence on the *seringalistas*. With the end of the rubber boom in 1912 and another short boom during World War II, many *Hevea* areas were abandoned by the former "owners" and the remaining rubber tappers (*seringueiros*) became de-facto-owners, handling the now unimportant *latex* extraction.

This caused an uncertain legal status of landownership in Acre. In the 1970s, three different types of land titles (Bolivian, Acrean, Brazilian) existed, which never had been legalised. Large estates with dubious size concentrated an enormous part of the state area. Incentives for investing capital in SUDAM-controlled projects in Amazônia Legal attracted investors from Southeast Brazil. Some tax-favoured cattle-ranchers basically had land speculation and tax reduction motives. Violent actions against *seringueiros* occurred and pressure on the local population was accompanied by bribery of local and state authorities. The incapacity of INCRA to oppose actions of politically influential groups impeded the installation of colonisation projects in a good location and with adequate infrastructural conditions.

While the population of Rondônia between 1970 and the mid-1980s increased tenfold and exceeded one million in 1985, Acre with a very low immigration rate had an increase of only 65 % (Table 7). The municipality of the state capital Rio Branco concentrated about 40 % of Acre's population.

Table 7: Population in Rondônia and Acre 1950–1985 (Index: 1950 = 100)

	Acre		**Rondônia**	
	Number	in %	Number	in %
1950	114 755	100.0	36 935	100.0
1960	158 184	137.8	69 792	189.0
1970	215 299	187.6	111 064	300.7
1980	301 605	262.8	491 069	1329.5
1985*	356 313	310.5	1 028 429	2784.4
*) Estimation				

Source: IBGE (1984), and author's calculations in: Kohlhepp and Coy (1985).

In the 1970s some Probor programmes of Sudhevea[48] tried to recuperate native *seringais* in Acre, but the problem of the disease of *Microcyclus ulei* in *Hevea* areas retarded the growth of *Hevea* plants. Land speculation, deforestation, and cattle ranches had a fatal influence on most of the rural population and their traditional extractive economy. Sudhevea did not participate in the agricultural planning and in regional development projects.

48 In 1967, the Superintendency of Rubber (Sudhevea), submitted to the Ministry of Industry and Commerce, had been founded to execute the economic policy in favour of rubber in the national territory. Probor (Programme for Rubber Production) was the programme to realise this aim.

When the federal government and the Acre state administration became aware of the social problems caused by the expulsion of workers from the abandoned *seringais*, they tried to start some colonisation projects. Increasing social tensions made the governments think of expropriation because of social interest. An area of about 0,8 million ha was destined for directed colonisation. In 1980, the government decided to create an Integrated Rural Development Project (PDRI) with the central objectives of regulating the land title situation in rural areas and promoting small-scale agriculture for *ex-seringueiros* and small holders. The results did not meet the necessities of the regional population.

The integrated development programme Planacre tried a consolidation of previous plans. In order to improve the knowledge of natural resources and ecological conditions as well as the socio-economic structure and its regional differentiation, the Acre government identified four study projects: Indigenous population (demarcation of areas), defining areas of biological and forest preservation, agro-ecological zoning and control of diseases. The World Bank funded these specific projects, which was a first step for an integrated development plan. The decision to initiate special studies and research activities for the elaboration of Planacre – IDB financed studies on ecological and socio-economic conditions, complementary to the World Bank's financing of pre-studies – was the only possibility of a scientific information basis for all future planning in Acre. The results of these studies of course should have been available before the BR-364 road construction.

Planacre was not able to provide the necessary science-based results for decisions in the Acre regional policy at the time required. The loan proposal for the Porto Velho–Rio Branco road construction had been approved by IDB at a premature moment. The impact of the precipitate prolonging of BR-364 to Acre caused severe problems as had been proved unfortunately in other cases of uncoordinated access to new frontiers of colonisation. As neither the World Bank nor IDB were planning to finance development projects in Acre, the responsibility of a road paving project with well-known consequences of a chaotic future scenario sticked to the financing institution. Considering the beginning of asphalting the BR-364 from Porto Velho to Rio Branco, it was really alarming that hardly anything had been done in regional planning to successfully handle the expected migration waves. Conflicts of interest between immigrants, local peasants, large landholders, cattle ranchers, timber companies, *garimpeiros*, and the Indigenous population as well as the lacking protection of forest reserves characterised the colonisation process in southwestern Amazonia.

3. Conflicts of interest at the Amazonian pioneer fronts in the 1980s

3.1. Land conflicts

The pioneer front areas in Amazônia Legal were characterised by confrontation and clashes between different social actors in a permanent struggle for land access and spatial domination of rain forest areas. The state monopoly of violence was rarely existing in these peripheral regions, or the official institutions were weakened or frequently corruptible. Land use conflicts of varying extent and intensity existed despite state spatial planning, administrative measures and existing legal requirements. Violation of law plays a key role in most conflicts of interest. Unequal balance of power and unequal power of disposition of natural resources lead to indirect "structural violence" (Galtung 1972) or even to direct violent activities between persons or groups involved.

Land conflicts finally mean suppression and driving out of the weakest actors. This happened despite the fact that in many cases huge land reserves were available, often considered inexhaustible. One of the basic problems was the untrustworthiness of land titles, sometimes based on dubious or falsified historical documents, on federal, state or municipal allocations or by forging of the land register through bribery. Demands for ownership of large landholders occupying land in frontier areas frequently were entirely unfounded. Many real estate owners acquired land by illegal procedures (*grilagem*).

Since the 1970s, land reclamation of competing social actors increased rapidly and conflicts of interest expanded and intensified in many Amazonian regions.[49] The strategy of rapid occupation and valorisation of land by exploiting natural resources and gaining economic profits enabled a steadily escalating rivalry concerning land use. Coexistence of competing social groups and their different economic systems was only possible with restrictions. The official authorities responsible for government-controlled spatial organisation of frontier regions neither were financially nor personally well-equipped to resolve the outstanding problems and bringing peace to all the actors in this tense atmosphere.

49 On land conflicts in general in Amazonia cf. Ianni (1979a; 1981); Mahar (1979); Barbira-Scazzochio (1980); Becker (1982); Foweraker (1982); Schmink (1982); Morán (1983); Schmink and Wood (1984); Martins (1982); Bunker (1985); Hecht and Cockburn (1990); Kosinski (1991); Kohlhepp (1977a; 1979); Kohlhepp and Coy (1986); Coy (1988).

There were conflicts between the capitalist frontier and the peasant frontier. Regional smallholders, squatters (*posseiros*) without land titles and migrants from other Brazilian regions settled in state-organised or private colonisation projects, trying to survive by fighting the space-grabbing activities of large landowners. These *fazendeiros* counteracted the peasants' aim to improve their living conditions using slash-and-burn agriculture in a land rotation system to guarantee a subsistence economy. Cattle ranchers burning large forest areas and expanding their pastures, large soybean farmers increasing plantations and using extensive infrastructure or sawmill owners trying to get precious wood regardless of owning the terrain interfered directly or indirectly in the way of life of peasants. Land speculation plays a significant role in realizing pressure on squatters in spontaneous settlement activities. As a rule, there was no understanding between the conflict parties. In case of refusing the displacement, large landholders frequently used their *pistoleiros*, a private militia resolving any problem by acts of violence, very rarely being sentenced.

During the military regime, protests against illegal activities of large landholders had been difficult and frequently could be interpreted as anti-governmental actions and resistance against law and order. In some regions with anti-guerrilla military operations, e. g., in the Araguaia-Tocantins region (Bico de Papagaio), extensive land occupation of some economic groups or *fazendeiros* obtained support of the Military Government.

Government-controlled development planning in pioneer regions and the decision makers of newly founded municipalities frequently exercised a superficial control of the actors' activities and favoured capital holders and their influence on the local economy against interests of smallholders. In an increasing extent in the 1980s, Christian organisations (Comissão Pastoral da Terra, CPT, founded in 1975) struggling for social justice and human rights offered advice and support to small farmers and landless people, addressing land distribution and violence problems. After re-democratization, party affiliation gained importance and had a decisive influence on land conflict problems. At the extractive pioneer front, land conflicts between gold and diamond miners (*garimpeiros*), rubber tappers (*seringueiros*), traditional groups gathering Brazil nuts and on the other hand large-scale mining, timber companies or cattle ranches resulted in violent clashes. Frequently, the conflicting situation remained unsolved during longer periods.

In most cases, no one of the neo-Brazilian social actors was open to discussion with each other and a general characterisation of land conflicts at the frontier was a struggle of everyone being against everyone and every group fighting for its own interest unwilling to make concessions. Sometimes, police had to take action in case of ubiquitous invasions of colonisation projects, *fazendas*, forest reserves, and Indigenous reservations. Frequently, INCRA had to start legal proceedings against the "owners" of *fazendas* without land title or only installed for land speculation purposes, threatening settlers in official projects.

All these groups acted in a shared belief that the Indigenous population in Amazonia and their territories should not impede the space-consuming economic activities of the powerful as well as the weak participants of the exploitation process. Peasants feared attacks by neighbouring Indigenous groups, the large actors were scared by the loss of time and profit by the intervention of the government agency for Indigenous affairs FUNAI to protect Indigenous groups and areas. The different social actors did not show any empathy and understanding for the basic needs of the Indigenous people, their traditional way of life and their land property rights, prescribed by law. Indigenous reservations were ultimately favoured but, in many cases, not respected, and invasions have often ended in massacres with casualties on both sides.

3.2. Situation of the Indigenous people: Violence, displacement, attempts for protection in Indigenous "reservations" and the problem of invasions

The history of integrating the Amazon region into the neo-Brazilian economic system is characterised by violence against the Indigenous population, displacement of tribes, causing socio-cultural fragmentation and even extermination. The attack of modern "civilization" on the Indigenous living space in Amazonia was threatening the existence of dozens of Indigenous tribes. From the disparaging point of view of some Brazilians at the frontier, the Indigenous people were considered *bichos da mata* (forest animals) during the first phase of the Amazonian exploitation.

Focus of the conflicts between the Indigenous groups and the modern Brazilian social actors were land occupation and the rights of disposal of the regional natural resources. In contrast to the logic of economic interest groups trying to "valorise" the natural potential, to the Indigenous population the tropical forest areas are the basis of their physical, social, and cultural survival.[50]

In 1910, the Brazilian government had started a policy to protect the Indigenous population, concentrating on the so-called "pacification" of these groups. The direction of the new Indian Protection Service (SPI) was given to Cândido Mariano da Silva Rondon, who had Bororo origin and decades of experience in expeditions in Amazonia and contacts with Indigenous tribes. The legislation that established the SPI "explicitly stated that it was the obligation of the Brazilian government to protect Indians against the destructive effects of frontier expansion and to defend their lives, liberty, and property against extermination and exploitation" (Davis 1977, 3). The rights of Indigenous people to live on their lands and to continue their ancient and traditional ways of life were recognized by the legislation. Brazilian governments established an orphan-like guardianship for the Indigenous population to defend their legal privileges. Although there have been more than 30 legal statutes demonstrating the consciousness of official obligations as to the Indigenous people, the reality did not prove the implementation of those legal guarantees.

During the first decades, the pacifist ideals of Rondon were successful with the motto "Die if it be necessary but kill never". Indigenous posts in the frontier regions were created. The Indigenous tribes accepted the gifts and overtures of the SPI agents, but later they often suffered from rubber tappers, logging companies and settlers encroaching on their territories. The SPI tried to mediate, but often Indigenous tribes were displaced or killed, died from the transmission of infections or were eventually

50 Among the numerous publications on the Indigenous population in Amazonia and related conflicts of interest cf. Ribeiro (1962; 1970); Lévi-Strauss (1963); Hopper (1967); Meggers (1971); Dostal (1972); Brooks *et al.* (1973); Hanbury-Tenison (1973); Junqueira (1973); Davis (1977); Hemming (1985); Hartmann (1989); Villas-Bôas and Villas-Bôas (1973; 1994).

marginalised. From 1900 to 1957, the Indigenous population dropped from about one million to less than 200 000 and 87 tribes disappeared. The remaining tribes were classified in four categories: Relative isolation, intermittent contact, permanent contact, and integration (Ribeiro 1957). In 1957, over 120 tribes lived in the Amazon region, most of them in small groups between 100 and 500 individuals.

During the *Estado Novo*, the Brazilian government had started a campaign to conquest the "west" of the interior, creating in 1943 the Roncador-Xingu Expedition and the Foundation Central Brasil. The aim of the Roncador-Xingu Expedition was to research the natural conditions and spatial distribution of the Indigenous tribes as a basis for mapping the regional settlement of Central Brazil. Access road construction with the rest of the country, the setting up of some urban nuclei (Aragarças, Xavantina) and the installation of some military bases (Serra do Cachimbo, Jacareacanga) as posts of support to secure air traffic to Manaus by radio contact could be realised (Kohlhepp and Dutra e Silva 2022). As the expedition faced great logistical difficulties, complicated contacts were made with Indigenous tribes, in 1945 with the "hostile" Xavantes and in 1946 with the Kalapalos on the Culuene river in the upper Xingu region (Villas-Bôas and Villas-Bôas 1973; 1994). The Foundation Central Brasil, incorporated into the expedition, had the instruction to organise and coordinate the exploration and colonisation of the Brazilian West, especially the regions of the Araguaia and Xingu rivers.

These two institutions definitely marked the policy of expansion of the agricultural and demographic frontiers of Central Brasil and had a decisive influence on subsequent development policy in this region.

In the late 1950s, new agents were contracted, and the administration of the SPI became deeply infested by corruption. There was little control over the activities of SPI agents and the quality of contacting the Indigenous tribes deteriorated. Economic motives rather than humanitarian considerations began to form the Indigenous policy of the military regime in Brazil. In 1968, the Minister of the Interior commissioned the attorney general Figueiredo to carry out a detailed investigation on corruption and crimes among officials of the SPI. The "Figueiredo Report"[51] – obviously it got "lost" afterwards – "found evidence of widespread corruption and sadism, ranging from the massacre of whole tribes by dynamite, machine guns and sugar laced with arsenic [...]" (Davis 1977, 10). These accusations had worldwide repercussions and caused shocks, protests and a flood of newspaper articles and radio reports. It became clear that SPI agents, landowners and speculators had passed infectious diseases to Indigenous tribes without immunity against influenza, measles, or tuberculosis. Even the Brazilian *Jornal do Brasil* called these crimes genocide and violation of human rights. Nearly half of the 700 SPI employees were charged with crimes or dismissed.

The Military Government closed the Indian Protection Service and in 1967 established a new government agency: the National Indian Foundation (FUNAI), submitted to the Ministry of the Interior. When political hardliners and staunch development supporters like the new President Médici and his Interior Minister Costa Cavalcanti started building the Transamazônica in Amazonia in 1970, the pressure on the Indigenous tribes intensified. Developing the Amazon region and the Brazilian economic "miracle" made new headlines. The official slogans "Land without people for people without land" and "We don't let some Indians hinder our progress" became

51 Comments on the Figueiredo Report (5115 pages) cf. Davis (1977).

well-known and clearly demonstrated that the existence of the Indigenous population and their territories were disrespected. Because of worldwide protests in favour of the Indigenous people in the Amazon region, some international organisations[52] had the opportunity to make investigation trips in Amazonia, the Brazilian government being compelled to give infrastructural support.

During the military governments, Amazônia Legal went through intensive agricultural colonisation with enormous migration waves despite of difficult ecological and poor soil conditions. Spontaneous colonisation activities turned out to be highly problematic for Indigenous territories. *Posseiros* tried to survive at the conflict-ridden Amazonian pioneer fronts and being in trouble they did not respect Indigenous reservations. Until the mid-1980s, the Indigenous population in the Amazon region suffered most from the attacks of "wild capitalism" by large groups with an enormous number of cattle raising farms,[53] mining projects, regional development activities based on the newly installed road network, and huge constructions of hydroelectric power plants. The prospecting boom of mining companies with camps for geological research, heavy machinery, blasting operations, construction of access roads, airfields, helicopter landing strips and aircraft noise caused a permanent molestation of the Indigenous people nearby.

Loggers from timber companies and *garimpeiros* with uncontrolled activities and high spatial mobility, willing to use violence, were extremely difficult to control. In case the Indigenous resisted, cruel "punitive expeditions" were organised in which the tribes were deliberately killed or expelled so that the disputed areas remained "indian-free". The contact of some Indigenous tribes with highway construction workers had negative consequences such as prostitution, alcohol, and forced labour services. Infrastructural and economic projects and FUNAI's low budget prevented organising more contact expeditions to relatively isolated Indigenous areas before the tribes were surprised and shocked by the encroaching modernisation.

In the mid-1980s, the Indigenous population approximately totalled 150–200 000. Two thirds of the Amazonian tribes had less than 500 people. Only very few Indigenous tribes amounted to more than 5000 persons, such as the Ticuna in eastern Amazonia, the Makuxi and the Yanomami in the border region of Roraima with Venezuela (Fig. 6). The number of Indigenous people living in isolation without contacts with the neo-Brazilian world remained unknown.

These tribes obviously lived in the northern, north-western und western parts of Amazonia. Besides the territories at the periphery of Brazilian Amazônia Legal, the distribution of the Indigenous population in Amazonia focussed on the middle and upper courses of southern tributaries of the Amazon river. The reason for this was the danger posed by *seringueiros* invading the forests, starting from the Amazon river towards the south, i. e., upstream of the tributaries. The Indigenous tribes retreated to the non-navigable upper courses of the hydrographic tributary system, which were inaccessible to the invaders (Kohlhepp 1987a).

52 Among others, the Primitive People's Fund (Hanbury-Tenison 1973) and the Aborigines Protection Society (Brooks *et al.* 1973).

53 Cf. chapter I.1.2.1.

Fig. 6: Indigenous population of Amazonian tribal groups

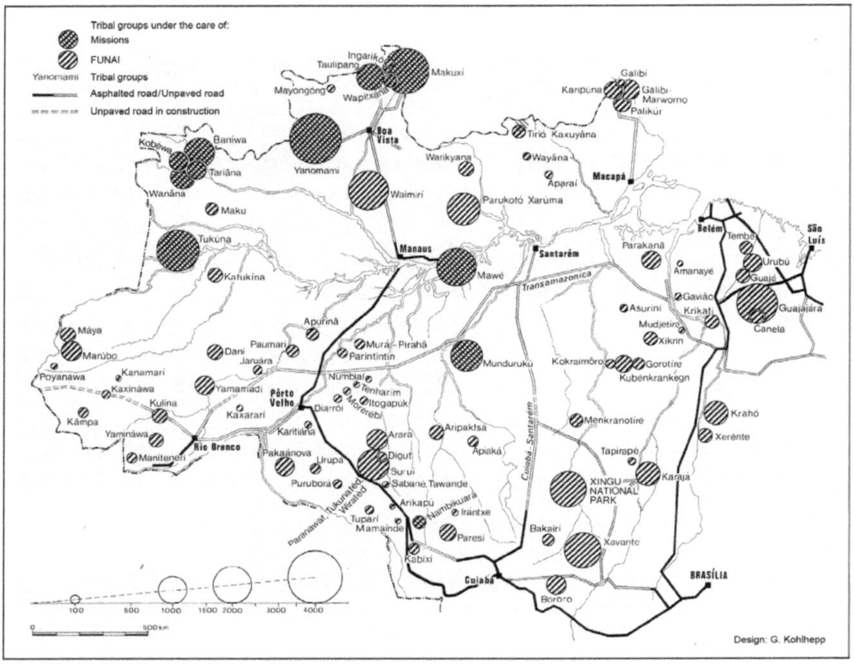

Source: Draft in Kohlhepp (1986, 173; 1987a, 45); data from Dória and Ricardo (1972) and Brooks (1974).

Over the millennia, Indigenous peoples have adapted their economic system of hunting, gathering, shifting cultivation and population growth through birth control to the ecological conditions of the tropical rain forests, the biodiversity and the carrying capacity of the food potential of their territories. They had developed a tradition of extracting medicinal plants in the rain forest. Grasses, herbs, flowers, tree bark, animal secretions etc. were used by shamans to relieve pain, infections, inflammation and to cure a wide variety of illnesses, including malaria and snake bites. The shock of conflicting contacts with "modern civilisation" caused demoralisation, loss of cultural identity and of economic independence. In this apparently hopeless situation at the end of the 1960s, the birth rate of the Indigenous population in many tribes declined nearly to zero as a sign of losing the will to live.

Indigenous lands must be properly demarcated, but in the 1980s demarcation remained in a preliminary phase. Each ecological zone is an integrated system of interactions between plants, animals, soils and shows a predictability of natural resource locations (Posey 1982; 1987). Indigenous villages are located amid the maximum of species diversity because each zone provides natural products and attracts different game species during different seasons. The shifting cultivation systems of the Indigenous populations are more complicated than those used by the *caboclo* population and better adapted to tropical conditions. They prevent exposure to direct sunlight and tropical rainfall, avoiding erosion and leaching (Goodland and Irwin 1975).

3.2.1. Indigenous parks and reservations

Two opposing models of Indigenous policy existed in Brazil: The first was radically protectionist. The Indigenous tribes were to be protected by the government in closed "Indian parks and reservations" from border attacks and gradually prepared as independent ethnic groups to integrate into Brazilian society and economy. In contrast, a second model had been developed during the SPI period and was later assumed by the FUNAI. It was a developmentalist approach, based on the rapid integration of Indigenous groups into the regional economy and rural class structure as a reserve labour force (Davis 1977).

After decades of discussions about the installation of Indigenous reservations, in 1961 the legal protection of National Parks was a first step. The National Parks of Xingu, Araguaia and Tumucumaque, in 1969 Aripuanã was added, were declared forest reserves and Indigenous protection areas (Fig. 7). The three Villas-Bôas brothers played a very important role in organising peaceful contacts with the Indigenous tribes and were named directors of the Xingu National Park. As they noted, in 1946 Indigenous tribes were living in nearly unchanged conditions as described by the German physician and ethnologist Karl von den Steinen during his expeditions in the 1880s.[54]

Fig. 7: Major road construction, national parks, Indigenous reservations, and forest reserves in Legal Amazonia at the end of the 1970s

Source: Documents and maps of SUDAM, FUNAI, DNER, IBDF; cf. Kohlhepp (1977a, 22; 1984a, 651).

To defend Indigenous populations from pressure of pioneer front expansion, some reservations had been legalised. However, only very few successfully realised their function. Indigenous land needs to be properly demarcated, but in the 1980s demar-

54 Karl von den Steinen (1886; 1894) had a great influence in evolving Brazilian ethnology of Amazonian Indigenous tribes. Cf. Villas-Bôas and Villas-Bôas (1973; 1994); Hartmann (1989). Cf. Hemming (2019).

cation was still at a preliminary stage. The main problem of modern exploitation and regional development planning in Amazonia was the need for large areas of land for the shifting cultivation methods of Indigenous tribes, which were on a collision course with the planning ideology of politicians and development technocrats (Kohlhepp 1987a). They criticised the large reservation areas for "some" Indigenous people, were poorly informed and compared the area to the land of a settler family in a colonisation project.

In 1970, the Military Government named General Bandeira de Mello, a military intelligence officer, as the new president of FUNAI. He claimed that the protection of the Indigenous population under FUNAI tutelage would be coordinated with the programme for roadbuilding, occupation, and settlement of Amazonia. In October 1970, a contract between FUNAI and SUDAM was signed to pacify Indigenous tribes along the prospected route of the Transamazônica. FUNAI agents had to prevent Indigenous tribes to be an "obstacle" for the rapid occupation of Amazonia and to provide workers' protection against supposed Indigenous attacks.[55]

In the same year, Brazil's President General Médici announced a new "Indian Statute" with directions for the Indigenous policy in the Amazon region, posing a threat to the territorial integrity of Indigenous tribes urging "to intervene in native areas and physically to relocate Indian tribes" for different purposes like public works of interest to national development or to maintain national security (Davis 1977, 58).

The government of Mato Grosso had made land concession areas available to southern Brazilian colonisation companies, and there was intense speculation on land before the establishment of the Xingu National Park. In northern Mato Grosso, land conflicts turned out to be dangerous for the Villas-Bôas plans of an Indigenous park. By fraud and falsifications, large areas had been stated officially as not inhabited by Indigenous people and were thus freely available for sale. In 1996, the sum of private land titles in Mato Grosso amounted to 120% of the state area (Röper 2001, 177). Protests of the Villas-Bôas brothers forced the state government by pressure of the federal government to annul land titles in the supposed park area. Although the originally planned park area had been strongly reduced, the Xingu National Park was given an area of 22000 km².

Unfortunately, as part of the Amazon road building programme in 1971, the northern part of Xingu Park was cut off by a road (BR-080), which was originally supposed to connect Brasília with Manaus but was never completed. The section of road that runs through the Xingu Park could have been built outside the park, but the pressure from the large livestock groups obviously had a decisive influence. One of the main groups affected was the Txukahamai[56] tribe, which had recently been resettled to the Xingu Park, but was now relocated again to the south to the central area of the park, where another 13 tribes and about 1500 Indigenous people lived (Fig. 8). The area lost in the north of the Xingu National Park was added in the south, with serious ecological consequences, as the *campo cerrado* vegetation there could not be used as habitat for Indigenous groups of forest dwellers. The fights of the Villas-Bôas brothers for survival

55 In September 1973, during the visit of the author in the camps of the Transamazon road workers between Sucundurí and Jacareacanga, they were digging ditches filled with petroleum round the camp, setting fire at night against threatened "attacks of Indigenous tribes or jaguars."

56 The Txukahamai, more specifically Mentuktíre, a northern Kayapó tribe.

of the Indigenous groups were successful in preventing the crossing of the planned BR-242 road. Two Indigenous posts were organised to support the Indigenous groups, giving preventive health measures and medical care. There was a permanent threat of influenza or measles infections during contacts with the official personnel or the staff of the Brazilian Air Force with a small base inside the Park.

Fig. 8: Xingu National Park and settlement areas of Indigenous tribes

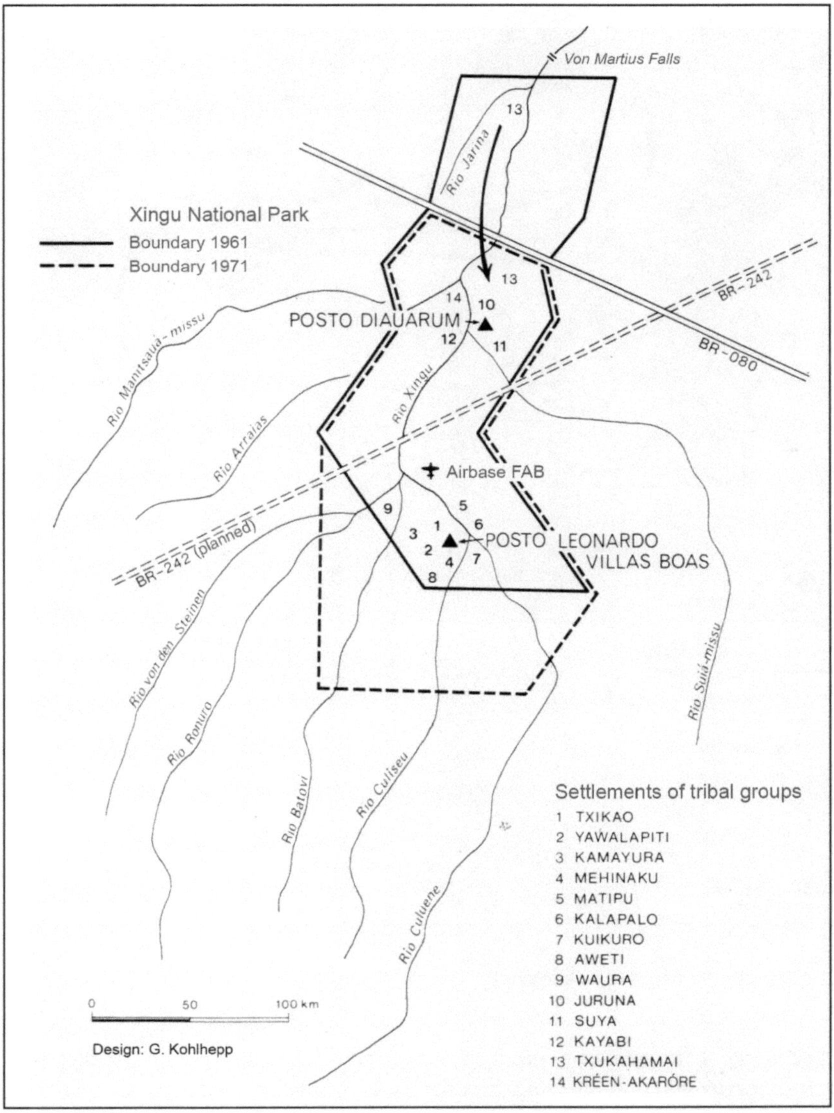

Source: Documents of FUNAI. Cf. Junqueira (1973, 11), Kohlhepp (1986, 178 f.).

With the Indian Statute, the Park was named Xingu Indigenous Park in 1973. The area of the Park was extended in 1984 when the lost region was regained and finally demarcated in 1987. This could only be realised because parts of the Mentuktíre refused to leave their original territory and were unwilling to resettle in the Park (Pasca 2004).

Fig. 9: Displacement, relocation, and resettlement of Indigenous tribes in Mato Grosso

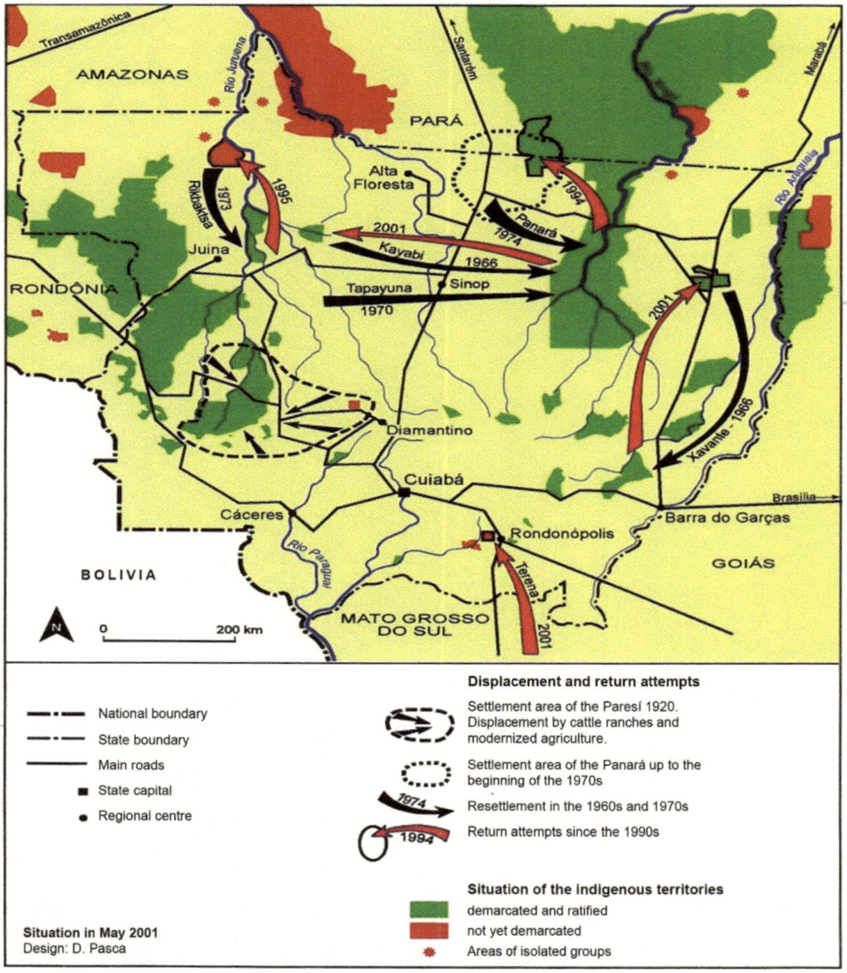

Source: Based on the map of Pasca (2004, 163).

Displacement of Indigenous tribes from their traditional environment to other areas and the resettlement of some tribes into the Xingu Indigenous Park caused enormous problems because of different ecological conditions, a new neighbourhood, loss of cultural identity and difficulties in getting used to new surroundings. Fig. 9 gives an idea of the complicated scenario of displacement and resettlement of Indigenous tribes in Mato Grosso and in some cases their "victories" to return to the original territory.

In the case of the Panará – formerly called Kreen-Akarore – the construction of the Cuiabá–Santarém road (BR-163) destroyed their living area and the Villas-Bôas felt compelled in 1974 to resettle this strongly weakened and humbled group – loss of 90 % of its population by infectious diseases – into the Xingu Indigenous Park. In the 1990s, they regained a part of their original territory with support of some NGOs.[57] The Kayabí and the Tapayuna had to be resettled into the Xingu Park after rubber tappers and colonisation activities (Gleba Arinos) (Kohlhepp and Dutra e Silva 2022) in northern Mato Grosso invaded their territories and permanent violent conflicts occurred. The Rikbáktsa had to leave their territory in 1973 and regained part of it in 1995.

The Villas-Bôas convinced Indigenous groups to remain as an autonomous group until the time of a more direct contact with the neo-Brazilian people. The aim was to preserve the social cohesion in each of the tribal groups. Doubts always remained present about the strategies to protect the Indigenous population against the counterstrategies of government institutions and economic pressure groups.

> But what kind of protection can we offer? Perhaps what we are really interested in is the little bit of land the Indian still possesses. Or perhaps we are seeking a source of cheap labour. This is how you can interpret all the humanity we have been imposing on the Indian.[58]

During the military governments, the newly installed FUNAI was not adequately equipped. Only few newly trained employees were contracted, experienced ethnologists (*sertanistas*) especially lacking, an insufficient number of vehicles and motorboats available. Scarce financial funds prevented medical care and social support. Protection of the borders of reservations could hardly be realised. This proved a restricted room for manoeuvre. However, it should be emphasised that some experienced FUNAI *sertanistas* worked with utmost attention in trying to contact peacefully Indigenous tribes under very difficult circumstances, working totally isolated. While cultural traditions and territorial integrity of the Indigenous tribes should have been protected, FUNAI had to submit to the strategies of the federal government's regional policy, favouring the exploitation of natural resources by private economic companies. The legally defined obligations were ostensibly realised, experienced anthropologists were put aside and discrimination of the Indigenous population hardly hidden.

Obviously, the official FUNAI programme was a camouflage and in the guiding principle of the Military Government the Indigenous people had no importance at all. For most of the military leaders[59] and politicians, Indigenous tribes were a nuisance and spoiled the "Amazonian miracle." The protection of Indigenous territories was accepted until such time as state planning and integration strategies or powerful private economic interests came into conflict with reservation policies. In Brazil, installing of

57 Sources of Fig. 9: Pasca (2004, 163; 2005); Archive of OPAN, Cuiabá; survey of documents by Dan Pasca in the Instituto Socio-Ambiental (ISA) in 2001.

58 Orlando Villas-Bôas, former Director of the Xingu Indigenous Park, cited in: Davis (1977, 47).

59 Fortunately, there were exceptions to this rule: The Commander of the Brazilian Air Force (FAB) in Amazonia, Brigadeiro João Camarão Telles Ribeiro, interested in geographical research, invited the author in October 1975 to join an inspection flight to several Indigenous areas and the National Park Tumucumaque. There was a missionary outpost at the Tiriós tribe and a military station of the FAB on the national border with Surinam.

Indigenous reservations had been a topic for decades and remains controversial until today. Enemies of an adequate Indigenous policy argued in an underhanded manner like supporters of the Indigenous people that reservations for human beings would demonstrate an inhuman "zoo-effect." Experienced *sertanistas* emphasised the need of a slow preparation of native people for contacts with the outside world. They considered well protected reservations including ecologically adequate living space to be inevitably necessary.

The process of installing and legalising Indigenous reservations had been slow and heavily disputed. Even after having been officially announced, reservations always remained under pressure of economic activities in the surroundings. Until the mid-1980s, only in 8 % of the Indigenous reservations the demarcations became legally effective. The exploitation of the Amazon region always was characterised by the invasion of Indigenous areas and even of officially legalised reservations.

3.2.2. Problems of invasions of Indigenous territories

One of the first well documented invasions of Indigenous areas during the period of the military governments was the case of the Cinta Larga tribe in North Mato Grosso and Rondônia. Already in the beginning of the 1960s, a 1.8 million ha forest reserve was established by law between the Juruena and Arinos rivers. In 1969, the Aripuanã National Park was created to the west of the forest reserve and a reserve for the Cinta Larga was established. They had been contacted in 1968 and represented one of the largest Indigenous groups in Amazonia with more than 10 000 people and more than 100 villages. This group and the Suruí tribe had already suffered from the intrusion of rubber tappers and *garimpeiros* into their land in earlier decades. Colonisation companies and cattle ranchers came to the area claiming false, previously "acquired" land titles. A rubber extraction company had attacked a Cinta Larga village by dropping poisoned sugar and firing explosives from the air.[60] Many bloody clashes with Indigenous groups occurred and had a worldwide publicity.

In the 1970s, large cassiterite deposits in the Aripuanã Park were discovered and a frantic activity of national and international mining companies started. Geological investigations on mineral resources with airstrips for researching groups caused stress to the Indigenous people, resettlement projects were discussed, and the area of the Aripuanã Park was reduced. The Cinta Larga were the victims of the new mineral boom in this region. More mineral resources were only supposed to exist, such as titanium and uranium, but never extracted. The Aripuanã Indigenous Park never had a positive effect for the Indigenous people. Many Cinta Larga suffered from infectious diseases (tuberculosis, hepatitis), the FUNAI personnel did not take any precautions (Davis 1977, 87) and only a small group survived. The government declared the region a restricted area because of strategically important mineral resources.

The installation of a scientific centre "Cidade Humboldt" for geological and mineralogical research, studies on the potential of natural resources of the Amazon ecosystems and applied sciences was announced in 1972 (IPEA/IPLAN 1973; Davis 1977; Kohlhepp 1977a). This was supposed to be the Military Government's response to international concern about environmental issues and the future of the Amazon region,

60 This incident in 1963 became known as "Massacre at parallel eleven" (Davis 1977, 79).

referring to the Man and the Biosphere programme of the UNESCO (1971) and the UN Conference on the Environment in Stockholm (1972). After a first effort to build installations and to realise cooperation with federal, regional, and scientific institutions for a scientifically based regional development planning, the Humboldt project – under administration of the National Council for Scientific and Technological Development (CNPq) – did not succeed because of bureaucratic problems. Already in 1975 it was forgotten and during the Polamazônia programme it was not mentioned again.

In central Rondônia, the final demarcation of the reservation of the Uru-Eu-Wau-Wau was part of the reformulation of the Polonoroeste programme.[61] The area was invaded by settlers and gold-prospectors, and other invasions were caused by road construction nearby. The overlapping of the Indigenous reservation and the National Park Pakaas Novos (under the auspices of IBDF) caused administrative and legal problems. A National Park with options of tourism is not compatible with the status of an Indigenous reservation. This has been a constant problem since the reservation policy began in 1961 and has never been resolved. In other Indigenous areas, conflicts increased when invading *posseiros* were taken hostage by Indigenous groups. The FUNAI staff was not well equipped, and no trained anthropologist worked in Rondônia in the 1980s. The staff number was by no means sufficient to control the 16 Indigenous reservations. Additional means for "Indigenous posts," for vaccination measures, and the technical infrastructure of the agency were lacking. In the mid-1980s, 30 % of the state area of Rondônia were declared Indigenous reservations and forest protection areas, but effective control failed to materialise (Kohlhepp and Coy 1985; 1986).

The decision to realise a master plan for a highway network in Amazonia was the most serious problem for a sound planning of Indigenous reservations. Roads drawn straight without detailed topographical knowledge – despite aerial and satellite imagery – crossed numerous Indigenous territories and, a few years later, reservations and forest reserves. The Brazilian Army Corps of Engineers and large private road construction companies with heavy machinery equipment, produced by multinational companies, were the main actors. International loans to finance this programme were available, among others the largest World Bank loan ever for a road project.

About 5000 Indigenous people in 29 tribes were supposed to live along the Transamazônica and the Cuiabá–Santarém road, among them the Kreen-Akarore and the Parakanã. The Parakanã had earlier contacts with the neo-Brazilian world, but when the Transamazon road crossed their territories a so-called "pacification expedition" had a disastrous consequence for the tribe. After contacts with FUNAI staff and road construction workers, the Paracanã were stricken with influenza, infections and veneral diseases. The Kreen-Akarore (Panará) – as mentioned above – had been resettled in 1974 into the Xingu Indigenous Park after the traumatic effect of invasions of their territories. They were in a state of sickness, hunger, and despair. Brooks (1974) called these events "ethnocide in the Amazon".

The territories of the Waimiri-Atroari, located north of Manaus, had been isolated during a long period. The tribe of more than 2000 people was described as "hostile" and contacts ended fatally. A failed attempt of the Italian Father Calleri at "pacification" became known worldwide when in 1968 the Waimiri-Atroari killed all the team members. In 1971, a reservation was decreed, but the construction of the Manaus–BoaVista

61 Cf. Chapter I, 2 and Fig. 5.

road (later extended to Caracas), passing through the Indigenous reservation, started at the same time.[62] The Waimiri-Atroari tried to resist the invasions and showed their fighting strength by shooting arrows against helicopters of the Brazilian Army Corps, responsible for the road construction. Although they had accepted gifts, they killed 15 FUNAI agents who had invaded their territory and destroyed an Indigenous post after confronting them with bulldozers, logging and helicopter noise (Davis 1977; Kohlhepp 1977a). A leading FUNAI agent called for revenge by an armed attack "with dynamite, grenades, tear gas, and bursts of submachine guns to give the Indians a demonstration of the force of our civilization."[63] These events had an extended coverage by the international press. Violent attacks of the Waimiri-Atroari against the use of repressive military force to control the tribe continued and road construction was delayed. Some of the Waimiri-Atroari withdrew inside the reservation, heavily reduced in area because of the reservoir of the hydroelectric power plant Balbina and by cassiterite mining. Other tribe members had contact with road workers, suffered from diseases, and remained in a humiliating situation.

North of the Amazon river, the planned routing of the Perimetral Norte, an east-west axis, touched the southern limit of the Tumucumaque National Park and threatened to cross the huge Yanomami territory in the west of Roraima state. About 10–15 000 Yanomami living in hundreds of isolated Indigenous villages at the border region of Brazil and Venezuela very rarely had contact with Italian catholic and North American evangelical missionaries. In 1975, an Italian Salesian priest tried to make contact with a group of Yanomami at the end of the forest clearance for the Perimetral Norte route.[64] When the discovery of a large uranium deposit in the Surucucus region was announced in 1975, the situation of the Indigenous people seemed to get worse. Brazil had planned to install eight nuclear power plants in an agreement of advanced technology with the Federal Republic of Germany and the extraction of uranium in Roraima was threatening. In an interview, the Governor of Roraima, General Ramos Pereira, commented "that an area as rich as this – with gold, diamonds, and uranium – cannot afford the luxury of conserving half a dozen Indian tribes who are holding back the developing of Brazil."[65]

As is so often the case, the announcement of mineral deposits was used as a strategy to overcome existing planning and legal regulations. The exploitation did not begin when the nuclear programme was delayed and was only realised on a small scale decades later. Finally, the construction of the Perimetral Norte was stopped because of insurmountable difficulties with granite intrusions of the Guiana shield and the perception that this road had no longer priority in Brazil and no connection was planned in Colombia.

In the 1980s, the Yanomami territories were frequently invaded by *garimpeiros*. Airstrips and access roads were often destroyed by military forces but always rapidly reconstructed by the gold prospectors. Fig. 10 shows the distribution of Indigenous ar-

---

62 Cf. Fig. 7.

63 FUNAI agent Amáncio, director of the pacification efforts along the Manaus–Boa Vista road, cited in Davis (1977, 97).

64 Visit of the author at km 211 of the Perimetral Norte, west of the camp of the construction company Camargo Corrêa near Caracaraí, in October 1975. Cf. Fig. 7.

65 *O Estado de São Paulo*, March 1, 1975.

eas, *garimpos* and the high number of airstrips, many inside the Indigenous areas. The Roraima state government was not interested in strict restrictions on the *garimpeiros*, who contributed to a flourishing gold trade and positively influenced the economy in the state capital Boa Vista. Extensive air taxi traffic remained unimpeded. Gold mining activities and massacres against Yanomami people are continuing until today.[66]

Fig. 10: Invasions of garimpeiros *in Yanomami territories in 1989*

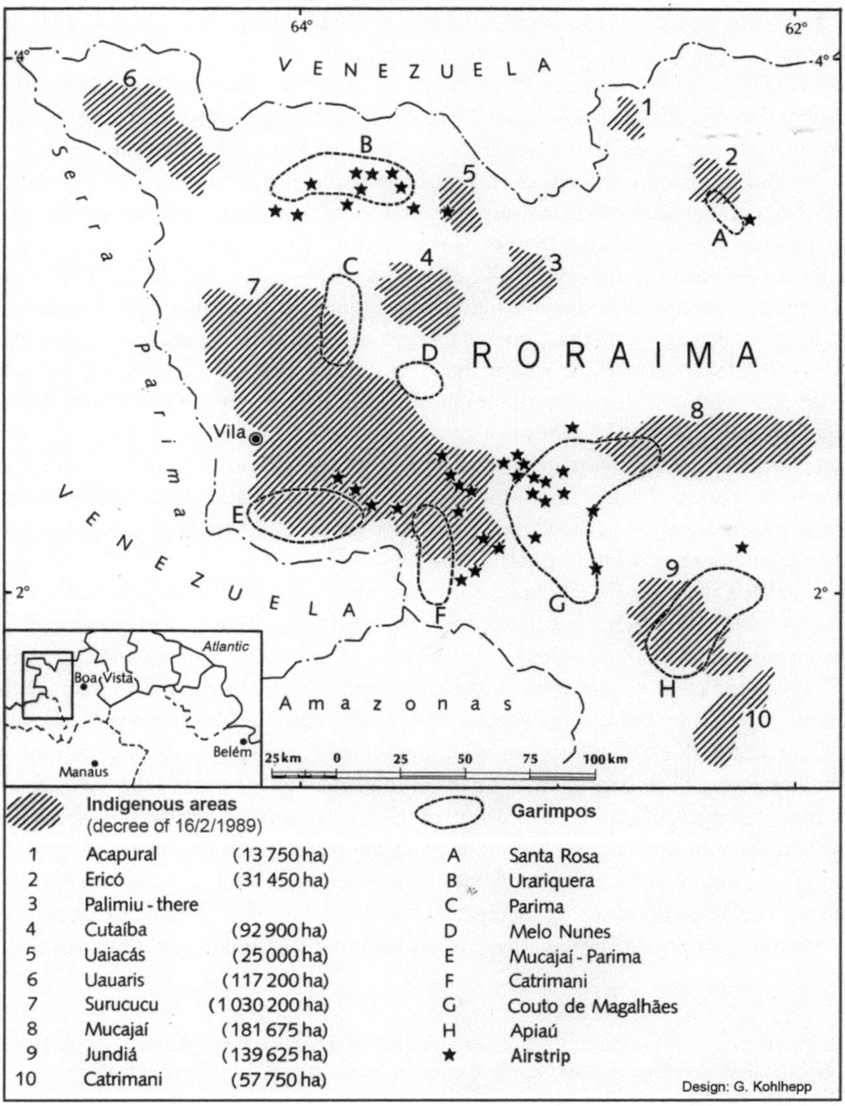

Source: Kohlhepp (1998b); based on: *Jornal do Brasil*, June 25, 1989, p. 14.

66 See chapter III.3.

3.2.3. Missionary activities

In the 1970s and 1980s, the situation in the Tumucumaque National Park,[67] located near the border to Surinam, was relatively calm because of the isolation of the Park area, at that time only superficially demarcated. Access to the Park was only possible by the Brazilian Air Force (FAB). In Tumucumaque, the FAB had a border detachment, an airstrip on a *cerrado* area, and supplied goods and petroleum for the military station and the Franciscan Mission of the Tirió tribe, established on the upper Parú de Oeste. The Tirió – in 1975 about 250 people in Brazil – lived on both sides of the border, in Surinam two protestant missions were set up. Many Tiriós crossed the border. In the mid-1970s no invasions in the Tirió territory occurred. The missionaries organised the construction of a village, the Mission Tiriós. Some Tiriό decided not to live in the Mission but with easy access to the central village and its service infrastructure.

Obviously, a good cooperation of the FAB, mission and the Indigenous people existed.[68] Assistance to the Tiriό in healthcare and education was provided by the priests and air transport by the FAB in case of emergency. The missionaries acted as intermediaries between the state and the Indigenous people, preparing them for a future peaceful coexistence with the non-Indigenous population. Vaccination programmes had been implemented by the Evandro Chagas Institute, among others. Only in the 1980s, FUNAI started working among the Tiriό and supplied additional health service.

Divergent opinions exist on the implications of missionary activities with Indigenous people. It is evident that most catholic and protestant missionaries in recent years have been strongly supportive and protective of the Indigenous population and, with the exception of a few fanatical missions with fundamental evangelical credentials, are more involved in social and medical care than in the tradition of converting the Indigenous population to Christianity. Open-minded missionaries inform tribal groups about the dangers of civilisation, economic exploitation, displacement, and diseases. Efforts are being made to conserve and teach Indigenous languages, elaborating rules of grammar, written documents on Indigenous legends and vocal music.[69] In most cases, missionaries have better control over Indigenous contacts with traders, *garimpeiros* and loggers than state agency personnel. Frequently, missionaries disagreed with FUNAI decisions, and they were not well accepted by government agents because of competing interests in serving. The dependence of the Indigenous tribes on the supply of goods, the problem of selling artifacts outside the boundaries of reservations or missions as well as the appropriate and hygienic use of clothes are topics of divergent opinions. Missionaries try to make a peaceful, slow transition into the modern world possible, helping to impede violent conflicts with neighbouring people. For groups of economic interest, they are the most persistent enemies and frequently

67 Cf. Fig. 7.

68 During the visit of the author at Tumucumaque in October 1975, the military personnel had no access to the Indigenous village and the German Franciscan missionaries had an open communication with the tribe members.

69 In the 1940s, the German ecologist Harald Sioli visited the Franciscan mission at the Cururú river, an affluent of Rio Tapajós, and published his detailed observations on the very positive activities of the missionaries in relation with the Mundurukú. Long before SPI agents came to this isolated place, the missionaries were of great importance for the sound and undisturbed existence of these tribes (Sioli 2007).

they live under constant threat. Some missionaries and priests in urban communities had been assassinated because of their long-term intervening on behalf of the Indigenous survival.

In 1973, the Indigenous Missionary Council (CIMI), created by the National Conference of Bishops, tried to develop an Indigenous consciousness in Brazil by encouraging encounters of representatives of the different ethnic groups. The Indigenous problems had an international repercussion and catholic and protestant welfare organisations began supporting autochthonous Indigenous projects.[70] A serious problem was the danger of splitting different ethnic groups through competing missions, which weakened ethnic survivability. Especially difficult was the attitude of evangelical missions concerning methods of catechisation. They rejected the reformulation of the proclamation of the Gospel and activities to improve the social and material needs of the Indigenous people (Prien 1989).

In 1980, the ecumenical meeting in Manaus for Indigenous pastoral care in Amazonia started a revival in respecting Indigenous culture, ethnic identity, their right of self-determination and to live on their traditional territories prescribed by law. The reality of the last decades concerning "integration" and "acculturation" clearly demonstrated the impossibility of planning a rapid integration of Indigenous people into the neo-Brazilian society. Integration was combined with "justified" fighting and violence against tribal groups, "pacification", numerical decimation, relocation, reservations, sometimes forced working conditions, religious conversion, physical and psychological degeneration, and marginalisation (Kohlhepp 1987a, 47–48). The loss of cultural identity, natural religion, language, tribal relations, norms for sustainable living and self-sufficient economy in a traditionally used ecosystem resulted in complete uprooting and demoralisation.

In the 1980s, Indigenous tribes started to stand up, protesting against lacking justice in cases of murder, violence, invasions, and the danger of forced relocation. They occupied local FUNAI office buildings, blocked roads, airstrips of *garimpos* and demanded a reformulation of the Indigenous policy. Some Indigenous tribes intensified political actions and in 1982 a chief of the Xavante became delegate in the Brazilian Parliament.

The situation of the Indigenous population in the decades after the 1980s will be analysed in the mega-project Programa Grande Carajás, the Pilot Programme to conserve the Brazilian rain forests (PPG7) and during the Bolsonaro Government.[71]

3.3. Deforestation and forest reserves until the end of the 1980s

During the 1980s, deforestation of tropical rain forests in Brazilian Amazonia began to increase rapidly. Lowland rain forests are characterized by a multi-storied structure, comprising three or four stories. Primary forests of the moist tropics are characterised by high biological diversity.

70 In Germany an "Ecumenical Committee for Indigenous Affairs" (ÖAI) was created in 1974 and the ecclesiastical relief organizations "Bread for the world," Misereor and Adveniat became important supporters of the Indigenous people worldwide (Prien 1989).

71 Chapters I. 4.2.; 4.5; II. 2.4.4; III. 3.

Large-scale deforestation was realised by groups of woodcutters (organised by logging firms – *empreiteiros* – with 100–150 workers) cutting trunks with axes or power saw or – in large companies – using bulldozers and chains to pull down shallow-rooted trees, burning afterwards hundreds of hectares to get areas for livestock or arable farming. In projects of roadbuilding, mineral extraction, industrial districts, or flooded reservoirs of large hydroelectric power plants, clear-felling is used to remove all the vegetation in one cutting. This is the case when there are only a few commercially valuable species in the forest, making selective felling uneconomic. Parts of large estates, still tree-covered, were taxed at a rate of 3.5 % of their unimproved property value. By using the land, taxes could be greatly reduced. Use in this context means deforestation. It is therefore in the interest of large landowners to completely clear their land up to the permitted percentage of 50 % at that time, even if they have no intention of using it.

The programme for expanding the generation of hydroelectric power, using the natural hydropower potential of the Amazon region, provided for the establishment of numerous power stations and the creation of immense reservoirs. The Tucuruí reservoir, covering 2430 km², had already shown that clearing areas which are later to be flooded is an extremely expensive procedure that is hardly ever profitable. In view of this fact and the relative lack of relief energy in the Amazon Basin, most of the planned reservoirs and the related infrastructural installations will flood large areas of still intact forest. The Balbina reservoir with 2360 km², located in the northeast of Manaus, required 31 times the surface area per MW of installed capacity compared even with Tucuruí (Fearnside 1989a; Kohlhepp *et al.* 1987). In the 1980s, Eletrobrás still had the basic plan to build 79 reservoirs in the Amazônia Legal planning region, with most of the reservoirs located in the tropical forest area. The area flooded was estimated to be almost 100 000 km². Apart from the destruction of the rainforest, the serious ecological consequences and the irreplaceable loss of species and gene pools, this would endanger territories and living space of some Indigenous tribes.[72]

In small-scale agrarian colonisation, peasants fell and burn only some hectares per year, using a primitive shifting-cultivation system on their plots with a restricted area. Before burning, they sell valuable timber to sawmills. Mass migration of settlers into the rain forests of Amazonia – in state or private colonisation projects or spontaneously – caused an extreme expansion of deforestation by accumulation of thousands of deforesting small-holdings, observed in some regions like Rondônia,[73] Mato Grosso or Pará.

With the 50 % clause in the 1980s, Brazilian law stipulated that 50 % of the land must be preserved as forest to avoid uncontrolled clearing. This clause turned out to be a more theoretical rule, controlling was nearly impracticable. By reselling legally owned land, another 50 % of the remaining forest could be cleared and so on, in effect allowing for complete deforestation.

The use of tropical timber and timber production have a long tradition and correspond to the growing demand in industrialised countries. The extent to which a forest is destroyed by logging operations primarily depends on the felling methods. Selective felling is a procedure in which only a few trees of commercial value are removed, in many cases with high logging and transportation costs. Mahogany (*Swietania macro-*

72 Cf. chapter I, 3.2.

73 Cf. chapter I, 2.

phylla) is one of the highly valorised species and preferentially exported. Damage is often caused by logging roads. When only very few trees are extracted per hectare, at least 10 % of the overall forest is destroyed. Tropical hardwoods are principally used in the construction sector for making windows and doors. Timber from tropical forests is used for furniture, in the form of veneers, plywood, as railway ties or in bridge construction. In the 1980s, the reason for using tropical woods was the low price compared with domestic timber species in non-tropical countries.

Only a portion of the stem wood is used. Roughly 50 % of the wood mass of each felled tree is left in the forest to rot because transport is not economical. A high percentage of the fuelwood cut from trees to be burnt is used domestically or in industrial steam engines.

A new wave of destruction of rain forests was associated with charcoal production used in the manufacture of pig iron. Since the start of the Grande Carajás Programme (PGC) in the mid-1980s, the use of iron ore in smelter sites along the Carajás railroad was planned to develop a regional iron and steel industry. There are no pit-coal deposits in Brazil with an adequate high quality for iron and steel production. For financial reasons, no plans to import pit-coal-based coke existed. As it is economically unprofitable to produce pig iron in electric furnaces, the production of charcoal did in fact form the basis for the Brazilian iron industry. In 1986, 36 % of the iron produced in Brazil were based on charcoal use in blast furnaces. In East Amazonia, an area of 15 000 km^2 was considered necessary for charcoal production. According to Brazilian law, each consumer of charcoal must prepare an afforestation plan which guarantees that 50 % of the need will be met after 10 years. Up to 1987, no one of the pig iron manufacturers had met the target of an own afforestation. Even immediate afforestation carried out for the next 10 years – given the necessary growth period of the trees – the wood will have to be cut from the surrounding rain forests.[74] The wood felling activity increased rapidly, and numerous charcoal kilns arranged in batteries of 10 to 20 units had been built along the highway axes.[75]

Large-scale afforestation in Amazonia with different species was only realised in the Jarí-Project, the felled wood being used for the huge pulp mill installed at the Jarí river.[76]

The *cerradão* transition forests between the *campos cerrados* and the moist tropical forests are especially endangered by fires from pasture preparation in the *cerrado* region. Deforestation fires to clear primary forests through cattle ranching or slash-and-burn agriculture often encroach on standing forests. The vulnerability of the Amazonian rain forests to fires favoured by El Niño droughts and general climate changes with rainfall deficits or changes in the lengthening of the rainy season was increasing sharply. The problem first became apparent in the 1980s.

A high percentage of the occurring deforestation has been and still is illegal. The fundamental problem was the difficulty to control and impose sanctions on illegal deforestation. In the 1980s, the Brazilian Institute of Forest Development (IBDF, created in 1967) was the responsible federal agency until the 1989 creation of the Brazilian Institute of Environment and Renewable Natural Resources (IBAMA) under the Ministry

74 Cf. IDESP (1987); Kohlhepp *et al.* (1987).

75 Cf. chapters I, 4.2.5 and II, 7.

76 Cf. chapter I, 1.2.5.

of Environment. Both institutions were not sufficiently equipped, and their budget did not cope with the challenges of organising an effective deforestation control of the huge tropical rain forests.

It is important to emphasise that already in 1934, the Forest Code was the first Brazilian forest law on a federal level, distinguishing forests as "protected," "reforested" and "productive." This forest code was motivated more by the demand to regulate logging activities than to protect the forests. Although reafforestation of non-Amazonian rain forests had been propagated in the 1950s and early 1960s ("for every tree felled, two must be planted"), devastation of tropical forests continued. The New Forest Code of the Military Government in 1965 described forests as "goods of public interest," facilitating a flexible interpretation of legal disposition. Owners of private forests outside Amazonia had to protect 20 % of the forest. In Amazonian private properties, deforestation was only allowed up to 50 % of the area. Unfortunately, this ecologically sensible law could be circumvented through repeated sales of parts of the land, allowing almost the entire area to be legally cleared. In Brazil, this strategy was called "mathematics of devastation."

The natural rain forest area[77] of Amazônia Legal amounted to 4.1 million km², i. e., 81.3 % of the planning region's area. Until 1975, only 0.6 % of the rain forests had been cleared. By 1978, the clearing rate had increased to 3.7 %. A very alarming increase in the clear-cutting rate to 9.2 % occurred by 1988.[78] In absolute terms, almost 378 000 km² of Amazonian rain forest have been lost (Table 8). This is more than the area of the Federal Republic of Germany today.

Many scientists[79] had pointed out the high rates of increase in deforestation in Amazonia, particularly in some sub-regions of Rondônia, Mato Grosso and Pará and along the major long-distance roads in construction. The high rates of deforestation in Maranhão and Tocantins (in 1988 separated from Goiás) were related to the relatively low proportion of natural rain forests compared to the national area.

A World Bank study (Mahar 1989) heated up the discussion on deforestation. The area of forest cleared was calculated to be 12 % of the total area of Amazônia Legal. The arguments about the deforestation data took on a political dimension when scientific data from INPE (National Space Research Institute) (forest loss: 9.2 %; reference area: natural forest area) were corrected in an official presentation to 5.12 % (reference area: planning region).[80] The sensitivity of the Brazilian government to the issue of deforestation was made clear when President Sarney used the World Bank data as an opportunity to launch a fierce polemic against international "attempts to undermine and influence Brazil's internal affairs." Similar arguments can be observed in the communication of governments until recent years.

---

77 Data from: Skole and Tucker (1993, Table 2, 1906); the rain forest area was calculated by IBDF with 3.878 million km² (cf. Kohlhepp 1987a, 63).

78 Data after: INPE (2000) (absolute data of deforestation), author's own calculations of the share of the natural rain forest area. Data 1978 (January), 1988 (April).

79 Among others Sioli (1956; 1973; 1984); Valverde and Freitas (1980); Sternberg (1981); Fearnside (1982; 1986a; 1989b); Morán (1990; 1993); Bremer (1999); Anhuf (2008; 2010).

80 In the end, the numerical INPE value had to be corrected to 7 %, as the cleared areas before 1975 had not been taken into account.

Table 8: Deforestation in the Brazilian Planning Region Amazônia Legal 1975–1988 (% of the natural rain forest area)

Amazon States	**Natural rain forest area* (1000 km²)**	**% of state area**	**Deforestation** (in %)**			**up to 1988 (1000 km²)**
			1975	1978	1988	
Pará	1183.6	93.8	0.7	4.5	11.1	131.4
Amazonas	1531.1	97.2	0.05	0.1	1.3	19.9
Amapá	137.4	98.4	0.1	0.1	0.6	0.8
Roraima (T)	172.4	76.4	?	0.1	1.6	2.8
Maranhão	145.8	55.7	?	43.8	62.3	90.8
Tocantins[1)]	30.3	10.9	?	10.6	71.2	21.6
Mato Grosso	527.6	58.6	1,1	3.8	13.6	71.8
Rondônia	212.2	89.1	0.3	2.0	14.1	29.9
Acre	152.4	99.7	0.8	1.6	5.8	8.8
Amazônia Legal	**4092.8**	**81.3**	**0.6**	**3.7**	**9.2**	**377.8**

1) Tocatins 1988; = Goiás (northern part) 1975, 1978
*) Data after: Skole and Tucker (1993, 1906, Table 2)
**) Data after: INPE, 2000 (absolute data of deforestation); calculation of % of natural rain forest area: G. Kohlhepp. Data: 1978 (January), 1988 (April)

Source: Kohlhepp (1998a, 54, Table 1).

Notwithstanding the methodological difficulties in interpreting satellite imagery and attempts to exert political influence on published data on deforestation, it was evident that deforestation increased almost exponentially in the 1980s. Repeated demands to put a stop to the deforestation activity in Amazonia remained unsuccessful. Preventive measures would be needed to create a framework of practical action: High taxes should be imposed to reduce land speculation; financial incentives for environmentally incompatible development projects should be stopped; compliance with statutory environmental regulations should be more strictly monitored and offenders should be more severely punished. International assistance in form of the Tropical Forestry Action Plan and the new concept of "debt-for-nature swaps" should be considered. However, the international interference in deforestation in Brazil had to be managed extremely cautious to convince governments of the possibility of alternatives to deforestation and of slowing down this devastating process.

Without an effective implementation, **Forest Reserves** are subject to a wide range of threats and invasions. One of the first forest reserves (Forest Reserve Juruena) in Brazilian Amazonia was created in the 1960s between the Juruena and Arinos rivers in Mato Grosso with a statutory area of 1.8 million hectares. But in the years that followed, financial and institutional constraints, as well as access via navigable rivers and roads, facilitated the illegal activities of colonisation projects, cattle ranches, gold prospectors and tin miners (Kohlhepp 1977a).

In Rondônia, four forest protection areas with a total area of 1.85 million hectares were implemented under the auspices of IBDF. Two "Biological Reserves" did not involve any human interference. In case of the "National Forest" there was a possibility for a limited utilisation, controlled by IBDF (e.g., limited wood-exploration, afforestation, tourism). Limited use was also possible in the "National Park". In all these reserves, invasion problems occurred frequently, especially by a high number of sawmills invading for illegal timber extraction. Control of forest reserves was undertaken by the newly established Forest Police, a peloton of the Military Police of Rondônia. Equipment costs were met by the Polonoroeste programme (Kohlhepp and Coy 1985). Attempts to avoid forest fragmentation on private land by establishing large block reserves to create the minimum areas required for species protection failed due to the lack of protection of forest reserves. The reserves had been misinterpreted by peasants as potential areas for future land use (Coy 1988).

In many other regions, forest reserves in the 1980s existed only on paper.

Indigenous reservations in the Amazon Basin are as effective as uninhabited National Parks in stopping deforestation and forest fires. Preservation of tropical rain forests is of fundamental importance for the Indigenous population in Amazonia, as analysed above. The Indigenous tribes adapted their economic system with hunting, gathering and a highly efficient shifting cultivation to the ecological conditions of the tropical rain forests and their biodiversity. However, Indigenous reservations, which are urgently needed on the pioneer front, must be properly demarcated and their remaining forests protected.

But the Indigenous people were not the only social groups having their living space in rain forest regions. The survival of the autonomous rubber tappers (*seringueiros*) and their families depended on the collection and use of the products native to the forest (fruits, oils, gums, medicinal plants, etc.). They have developed means of ecologically sustainable use. A new concept arose in 1985 in setting up "extractive reserves" (Allegretti 1990), a term for renewable resource use patterns in the tropical rain forests of Amazonia. The concept of reserve areas for extractivism – with renewable forest resources open to economic activities by the traditional local population – was obviously similar to the concept of "Indigenous reservations", which are protected by law for the exclusive use of the respective groups. At the end of the 1980s, the economic feasibility of the extractive reserves was still in question in terms of prices, transport possibilities and market conditions. Doubts remained (Homma 1994) about the future inclination of these groups to stay within this system of traditional economy, when other economic options or alternatives emerge. As will be analysed in chapter II.2., the concept of "extractive reserves" became a new impetus within the International Pilot Programme to Conserve the Brazilian Tropical Rain Forests in the 1990s.

Another group of people who live off the products of the tropical forests are the collectors of the edible fruits of the Brazil nut tree (*Bertholletia excelsa*). The Brazil nut is of high commercial value and put on the market in its trading centre Marabá. Unfortunately, Brazil nut trees, under the largest trees in the Amazon forests with up to 50 m, have been felled for charcoal production in the Grande Carajás Programme.[81]

Deforestation consequences became better known by an intensifying scientific discussion in the 1970s and 1980s.[82] In tropical rain forest ecosystems, a large part of the important nutrients is stored in the vegetation. Three quarters of the carbon are contained in the biomass itself and only a small part of the nutrients in the soil. The ecosystems can maintain themselves even on nutrient-poor soils, since the nutrients circulate in a self-contained system that is well adapted, preventing their loss by soil fungi (*mycorrhizae*). The breakdown of the highly complicated and susceptible ecosystems of tropical rain forests is caused by the destruction of the closed nutrient cycle by slash-and-burn methods of deforestation. Widespread deforestation has had disastrous effects on the loss of genetic diversity, nutrient leaching, decomposition of organic matter, soil degradation and erosion. Humus only accumulates in the topsoil. Ferralitic, strongly weathered and leached soils predominate in the tropics and have one of the lowest storage capacities for nutrients of all soil types. It became clear, that agricultural activities on Amazonian *terra firme* soils will be ecologically limited. Weischet (1980) called this the "ecological handicap" of the inner tropics. Only shifting cultivation methods of small Indigenous groups, tested over a long period, turned out to be adapted to the ecological conditions in Amazonia. They only caused "needle pricks" (Sioli 1983) in the tropical rain forests and worked the slowly regenerating areas only after decades.

In the Amazonian rain forests, about 20 % of the earth's carbon in living biomass is sequestered. Deforestation means high CO_2 emissions contributing to an increase in temperature, a "greenhouse effect" and the problem of regional and global climate change. The dangers of increasing temperature, regional variability of rainfall, changes in the hydrological cycle and problems of dryness – combined with the danger of additional forest fires – were discussed on a scientific level already in the 1980s, but not appreciated by planners and Brazilian politicians. One of the fundamental problems is that many of the effects of climate change impact in ecological systems only are detectable after irreversible processes have been set in motion (Fearnside 1985, 88). The popular discussion about the function of tropical rain forests for the world's oxygen supply as the "lung of the world" was a misinterpretation in a popular periodical in Brazil of an interview of Harald Sioli.[83]

81 See chapter I, 4.2.5; Deforestation of Brazil nut trees was denied officially but could be proved during field work of the author in the region in 1986.

82 Among many others: Sioli (1973; 1983), Salati (1979), Weischet (1980; 1981), Fearnside (1982; 1985), Bremer (1999).

83 Personal communication of Harald Sioli to the author; Sioli (1983), Fearnside (1985), Kohlhepp (1989b). See chapter III.2. in this publication.

4. Mega-projects and their impact on the regional development in East Amazonia: The Grande Carajás programme (PGC)

4.1. Programme concept, implementation, and targets of the PGC in a transition period to the "New Republic"[84]

In October 1980, the Brazilian President General Figueiredo approved an extensive regional development programme called Programa Grande Carajás (PGC). A region with an area of around 900 000 km² was included as the programme area, located to the north of 8° S between the Amazon, Xingu, and Parnaiba rivers, and covering large parts of the states of Pará and Maranhão (96 % of the state area) and the northern part of Goiás (since 1988 state of Tocantins) (Fig. 11). In 1985, 68 % of the PGC region was covered by tropical rain forests.

The Interministerial Council of the PGC within the Secretariat for Planning (SEPLAN) of the Presidency of the Republic was created as the responsible organisational structure. The new institution had superior executive functions and was placed over the regional development agency for Amazonia (SUDAM), and the state governments. The PGC proudly was announced to be the world's major integrated development project. Investments of about US$ 62 billion and annual revenues of US$ 9–10 billion were scheduled by Minister Delfim Neto within the main sectors mine-metallurgy, agriculture, forestry, and infrastructure.

Priority targets of the PGC (CIPGC 1981) according to SEPLAN (1985):

1. Infrastructure:
   - the Serra dos Carajás - Ponta da Madeira railway,
   - the Ponta da Madeira seaport – system,
   - the Carajás export corridors,
   - facilities for the utilization of waterways for transportation of large masses,
   - transportation infrastructure and equipment,
   - the hydroelectric utilization of the hydrographic basins, especially the Tucuruí project on the Tocantins river.

84 This chapter is based on an evaluation of the Programa Grande Carajás for the German Agency of Technical Cooperation (GTZ) by the author (Kohlhepp *et al.* 1987); Kohlhepp (1985; 1987b).

2. Projects in the fields of:
   - prospecting, extraction, processing, and industrialization of minerals,
   - agriculture, cattle ranching, agroindustry, fishery,
   - forestation, reforestation, processing, and industrialization of wood,
   - utilization of energy resources.

In the start phase of PGC, besides the dominating Carajás iron ore project with its extensive infrastructure the aluminium industry, located at São Luís (Alumar) and at Barcarena near Belém (Albrás/Alunorte), the hydroelectric power station at Tucuruí on the Tocantins river and the large-scale agricultural and agro-industrial sectors gained priority.

Due to the export orientation of all PGC projects and the exceptional importance of the Japanese market during this period and previous contacts with Japanese institutions by order of the Brazilian Government, studies on regional economic development of the PGC region were elaborated by the National Development Centre of Japan (IDCJ) and the Japanese International Cooperation Agency (JICA) (IDCJ 1980; JICA/PGC 1985). In particular, the PGC's agricultural planning was initially strongly influenced by the IDCJ studies, but the proposals turned out to be unrealistic and not at all adapted to the ecological and social conditions of the programme region.[85]

A special and very extensive system of tax and financial incentives was granted to all projects approved. Exemptions from income tax for a period of ten years, exemptions of reductions of import duty and industrialised products tax, issue of licenses for import of machines and other equipment were granted. Furthermore, authorisation of foreign loans and guaranty of the National Treasury to these loans and reduced prices for energy were conceded to those undertakings, installing, expanding, or modernising projects in the PGC area.

In 1981, the Military Government stated that the private sector with small and medium enterprises should be supported, and foreign participation was welcomed in the implementation of PGC.

The delimitation of the programme area was based on three premises (see Fig. 11):

1. Including as central part the mineral province of the Serra dos Carajás, 550 km southwest of Belém, with its enormous iron-ore and other ore deposits,
2. including the future "export corridor" along the railway to the port near São Luís in Maranhão,
3. including the waterway Araguaia/Tocantins with its important hydroelectrical potential.

The Interministerial Council (IC) was authorised to give directions to all federal agencies. Regional planning concepts were elaborated by the Executive Secretariate of PGC and approved by the IC (CIPGC 1981)[86] and should be integrated into the development planning of the regional superintendencies SUDAM, SUDENE and SUDECO, which were responsible for the sub-regions concerned.

---

85 See chapter I.4.6.

86 PGC data in this chapter from CIPGC (1985; 1986).

Fig. 11: Mining and industrial sites in the planning region of the Programa Grande Carajás

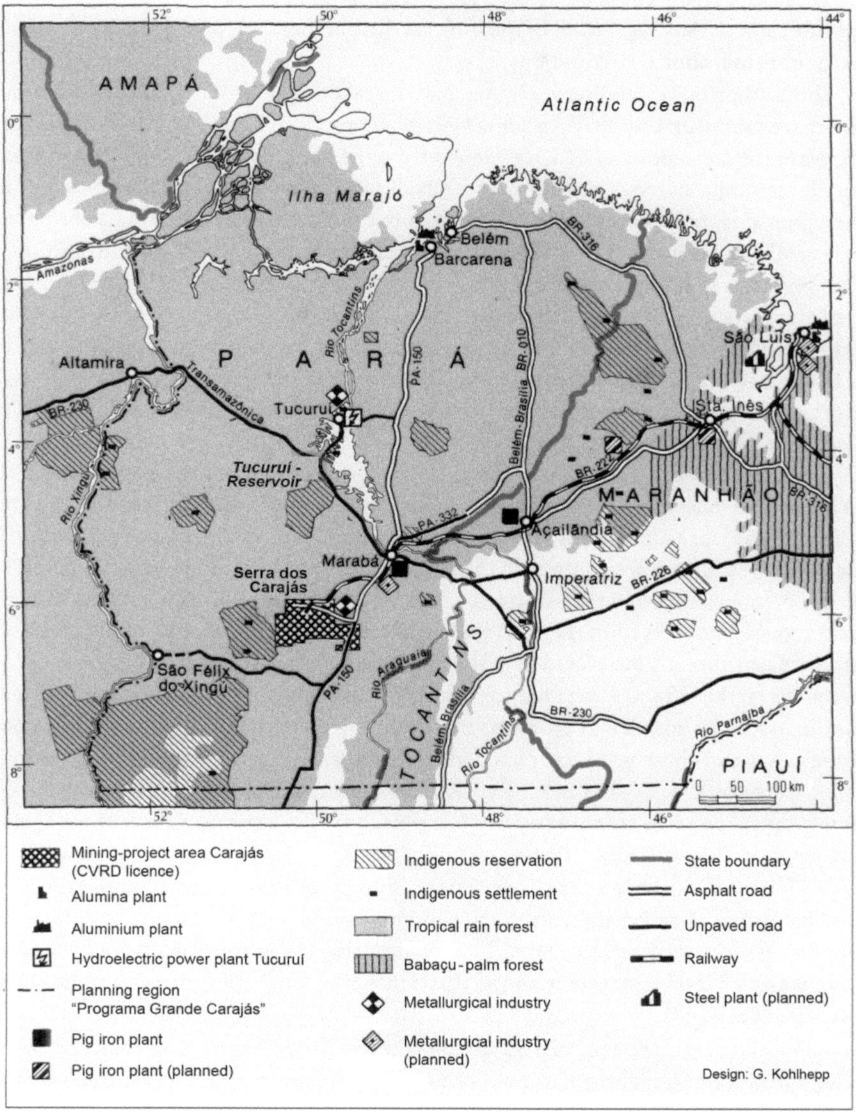

Source: Based on documents of PGC and CVRD; Cf. Kohlhepp (1987b, 217).

Numerous problems of superposition of jurisdiction prevailed in the PGC region. SUDAM and SUDENE areas had an intersection of 246 000 km². Considering the different ecosystems and the difficult socio-economic conditions of the programme area involved, it remained undefined what strategy to be used exactly for the area of intersection. The PGC region was for the most part (92.5 %) in the area of the planning region Amazônia Legal, the sphere of influence and control of SUDAM in Eastern Amazonia. However, SUDAM officials did not participate in the conferences and decisions of the PGC Interministerial Council. SUDAM was deprived of its previous importance but at least partially could be blamed for this situation, because it never developed a specific regional strategy. Most of the projects did not meet regional needs and had no social nor environmental consciousness.

The authoritarian military regime had installed a centralised administration structure subordinating the Amazonian periphery totally under the control of Brasília. The planning conception of PGC developed from the ideology of economic growth-oriented planning without taking into consideration socio-economic or ecological particularities, not to speak of reflections about basic needs of the rural poor population (Martins 1987). As a model of "development from above", PGC planning did not give emphasis to human resources development nor to integrated rural development. Nearly at the same time, the Polonoroeste programme had been announced. This programme of regional development in Rondônia and parts of northwest Mato Grosso based on a World Bank loan was at least planned with an integrated rural development approach.[87] Even if this programme failed on some points, the difference in planning ideology was more than obvious.

The situation was particularly complicated in the rural areas, where INCRA, GETAT, the state jurisdiction and the "special status" of some areas competed with each other. GETAT's executive units, which had been established in the Araguaia-Tocantins region in 1980, could not contribute to calming the land situation.[88] Unclear distribution of responsibilities in planning or even unrealistic solutions of project implementation could be observed in the PGC region. The social and ecological implications of large projects directly interfered with the municipal development of the affected areas. Decisions on the federal government's level regarding large projects were by no means coordinated with municipal problems and planning necessities. Even worse, the consequent costs of these projects remained with the state or municipal administration which were neither prepared nor financially in a position to solve the enormous problems. Marabá and São Luís are two very clear examples of a complete lack of coordination between the vertically different planning levels.[89]

With the end of the Military Government, since April 1985 the new democratic government of the *Nova República* in Brazil was confronted with a regional development programme, planned and executed by the authoritarian regime of its predecessors. There was a chaotic situation with the distribution of land titles, invasions and land conflicts of all kinds.

As for the new directions of PGC, a Consultative Commission of Science and Technology had been established to evaluate the environmental or socio-economic implications of large development projects. The scientific community in Brazil severely complained of lacking consultation, missing fundamental discussions and information regarding PGC sectoral and regional planning. Brazilian scientists deplored unchanged authoritarian structures in decision making in the PGC administration. In fact, there was no structural modification of PGC administration and planning strate-

87 Cf. chapter I.2.

88 GETAT (Grupo Executivo das Terras do Araguaia-Tocantins) was founded in 1980 as land regulation authority. In the mid-1980s, GETAT did land survey and land registration for about 50% of the PGC area. There was a strong connection with the SNI (National Intelligence Service).

89 Cf. Chapter I, 4.4.

gies. The mere participation of the governors of the affected states in the IC conferences of the PGC was the only signal of the new government of an "opening" of the basis of information. But it was an important step, because the regional reaction against the implementation of large-scale projects "from above" with far-reaching negative regional impacts proved to be a constant conflict between federal and state governments or agencies.

The formulation of general statements such as the reduction of regional disparities or socio-economic deficits was followed by the announcement of a necessary improvement of medium-sized structures in all economic sectors. In fact, large infrastructural and export-oriented projects of national interest still played the most important part in the reformulated PGC. However, an internalisation of large projects' benefits within the PGC region was considered to be important. Programmes of social development, democratisation of information, work, and production means and the organisation of communitarian participation were announced to be realised.

It became apparent that the effects of large-scale projects had already caused considerable damage and spatial disorganisation with absurd polarisation processes and intraregional instability since 1980. Most of the large-scale projects had been planned and implemented without detailed pre-studies of impacts on all levels, neither physically nor financially. This had only partially changed when particularly the World Bank and the European Economic Community had combined specific conditions with their loan commitments and therefore interfered indirectly into planning conceptions. At least some modifications and complementary actions could be realised. As these loans concentrated on the Carajas iron ore project, only this part of PGC had been substantially reoriented in close cooperation with the responsible project agency of Cia. Vale do Rio Doce (CVRD).

The PGC was approved at a time when the economic growth rate in Brazil under a high-growth and export-oriented strategy of the Military Government still exceeded 7 % per year (1973–1980), despite the oil price crisis which severely affected the country. External credit was widely available, causing Brazil's external debt to grow rapidly. In the late 1970s, the economic growth had been accompanied by accelerating inflation.

In 1981, the industrial recession had started and severely threatened the economic growth strategy. Thus, the government's goals of increasing export revenues through the valorisation of natural resources, especially in the Amazon region, have been reinforced. Even high investments were accepted in order to increase exports and reduce the burden of foreign debt. According to the government, the PGC seemed to be a way out of the crisis.

The PGC concept was highly risky, as the world market for iron ore in particular had been in overproduction since the decline in iron ore consumption in 1976 and even more so in the 1980s. In the beginning of the 1980s, world-wide iron ore output had been sharply reduced, just at the time when Brazil wanted to increase its production and exports. In 1980, Brazil had reached its maximum iron ore production to that time (95 mt). Between 1979 and 1982, world crude steel production dropped by more than 100 mt to 646 mt (-14 %)[90] due to production cutbacks in western industrialised countries, especially in the United States, but also in Japan.

90 Data: Cf. Kohlhepp (1987b, 221).

This must have been an alarming scenario for the start of a large iron ore mining project in Brazil, being the fundamental part of the PGC. The critical world market situation had a particularly negative impact on Brazil as the second iron ore producing country of the world and the most important exporter (25 % of world iron ore exports). Export prices had increased to a maximum in 1980 and had a sharp downturn thereafter (see Table 9). This was the case with other export-oriented ore and metal products which were of future importance within the PGC projects. Export prices of bauxite constantly decreased from 1980 to 1984, remaining stagnant since then. Aluminium prices had a collapse in 1981/82, continuing very unstable with marked ups (1984) and downs (1986), but remaining always far below the 1980 level.

Table 9: World market commodity prices of iron ore and non-ferrous base metals 1980–1987 (Index 1980 = 100)

Commodity	1982	1984	1986	May 1987
Iron ore	96.2	84.8	80.3	75.6
Manganese	105.7	92.2	90.7	88.6[1)]
Copper	67.8	63.0	62.7	69.5
Bauxite	98.1	77.6	77.3	77.6
Aluminium	55.9	70.5	64.8	79.5
1) March 1987				

Source: IMF (International Monetary Fund): International Financial Statistics, July 1987.

In the planning schedules of PGC and the Carajás iron ore project, increases in real prices had been projected for the second half of the 1980s. Unfortunately, these optimistic forecasts, even of international experts, failed. The decline in iron ore and non-ferrous metal prices on the world market was an extremely poor basis for the PGC, its implementation and its ultimate economic value. As revenues fell short of expectations, export earnings could not compensate for the overall investments and especially the constantly rising financing costs. Due to the prevailing uncertainty and high financial risks, some of the PGC projects, e. g., in the alumina and aluminium sectors, had to be postponed and the budget calculations and loan agreements of the projects had to be reformulated.

When the PGC concept was published, the Brazilian and the international public were at least surprised by the financial dimensions of projected investments. It was particularly emphasised that large-scale capital imports with high interest rates in credit contracts would further accelerate the rapidly rising external debt. Furthermore, critics were worried about optimistic calculations in all programme sectors, considering the extremely tough situation of raw materials on world market level, the decay of the US Dollar and the world-wide economic crisis. Finally, protest arose because the socio-economic and environmental impacts of these large-scale projects and the related social and ecological costs were not duly considered.

As programme planning was neither discussed in public or coordinated with regional entities, nor adapted to the basic needs of the affected regional population, PGC represented a typical example of a "development from above", planned and started by a military government, and afterwards confronted with a strong opposition in the now democratic Brazil.

Table 10: Projects approved within the Programa Grande Carajás in 1986 (until May 31, 1986)

Projects	**Number of projects**	**Investments**		**Proposed number of jobs**		
		million CZ$***	%	direct	%	indirect
Mining*	2	59 714	30.0	7035	15.0	90
Electrical energy	1	68 669	34.6	**22 000	46.9	
Industry Total	35	65 493	33.0	16 562	35.3	32 941
Alumina	1	10 659	5.4	763	1.6	
Aluminium	2	44 585	22.5	5523	11.8	
Pig iron	8	1409	0.7	2099	4.5	15 465
Ferro-manganese alloys	2	626	0.3	754	1.6	3902
Electrolytical manganese	1	505	0.3	321	0.7	
Metallurgical silicium	1	1436	0.7	1251	2.7	
Metallurgical	2	10	0.0	89	0.2	62
Cement	2	1142	0.6	1472	3.1	2900
Timber	2	72	0.0	464	1.0	1132
Charcoal	3	313	0.2	1382	2.9	4700
Fertilizer	1	1838	0.9	404	0.9	2000
Agro-industry	10	2898	1.4	2,040	4.3	2780
Cattle ranching	5	112	0.0	342	0.7	
Agrarian colonization	1	637	0.3	1000	2.1	
Tertiary sector	1	4240	2.1	?	?	
Total	**45**	**198 865**	**100.0**	**46 939**	**100.0**	**33 031**

*) Incl. Transport and export of iron-ore

**) Incl. sub-contractors' companies (with temporary employment)

***) Cruzado (CZ) = From 1986 new Brazilian currency

Source: Kohlhepp (1987b, 244, Table 2). Own compilation by the author, based on individual project data of approved projects; received at CI-PGC in Brasília, September 1986.

Investments of US$ 62 billion were planned in a period of less than 10 years and considering the high interests this sum would amount to more than US$ 100 billion. But that was only the PGC, not to mention other gigantic projects, the Itaipu hydroelectric power plant, the *pró-álcool* programme, the *polos petroquímicos*, the nuclear energy programme and several other mega-projects in other regions of Brazil.

Table 10 shows the situation of the 45 individual projects approved by the PGC by mid-1986. The dominating Carajás iron ore project (Ferro-Carajás), the aluminium industries and the hydroelectric power plant Tucuruí concentrated 92 % of the planned investments and 75 % of the number of direct jobs. The total number of direct jobs given by PGC was 47 000, but since subcontracted construction workers in Tucuruí were included, this number must be reduced by 20 000. Tucuruí had less than 2000 permanent jobs and some other projects had about 4000 jobs less than previously announced The PGC projects approved until May 1986 had only about 23 000 permanent jobs. In view of the number of investments of about US$ 12 billion and high financing costs this was an extremely low number of new jobs. The indirect jobs mentioned in Table 10 refer to contractors and services, e. g., for charcoal supply – nearly half of the total of 33 000 jobs with no official employment contract.

The total investment for the approved projects amounted to US$ 14.2 billion, 35 % for Tucuruí, 33 % for all the industrial projects (28 % aluminium and alumina production) and 30 % for the Carajás iron ore project. 62 % of the investments were internal cash generation by the investors, 51.1 % of the total investments were national capital, 48.9 % foreign capital.[91] Some of the smaller and medium-sized projects were based on tax incentives rather than on long term solid economic planning. Even five cattle ranching projects had been approved, an absurd situation considering the intense discussion in Brazil and internationally on the negative ecological and socio-economic impacts of pasture expansion in tropical forests of East Amazonia.

The Programa Grande Carajás turned out to be *the* extreme mega-project in the Amazon region, established without ecological and social commitment. It was a regional planning strategy to integrate Amazonia into the world market without considering the fragile world market situation of ore and metallurgical commodities. The PGC has been a megalomaniac attempt of the military regime, continued by the democratic governments to demonstrate the potential of Brazil as leading power in the southern hemisphere. Amazonia and its population had no chance to intervene in the government actions.

4.2. The Carajás iron ore project of the Cia. Vale do Rio Doce

4.2.1. CVRD's "northern system" and its importance for the Grande Carajás Region

The Cia. Vale do Rio Doce (CVRD) iron ore project was not only the core project of the PGC, but also the reason for a regional development programme organised as part of the PGC planning.

Founded in 1942, CVRD was a majority state-owned company until its privatisation in 1997. It was traditionally active in iron ore mining but has diversified its activities. CVRD was a very efficient state company, acting with modern management

91 PGC information to the author in September 1986.

characteristics, a holding controlling 86 subsidiary companies and participating in 66 others. Already in 1986, CVRD had been a vast mining and industrial complex producing and selling iron ore, pellets, manganese ore, bauxite, aluminium, gold, titanium ore and wood pulp, and also running railways, ports and ocean transportation (CVRD 1985; 1986). 22 500 people were directly employed, a total of 60 000, counting all the subsidiary companies. CVRD and its activities had been of highest importance to the Brazilian economy and remained at this level (CVRD was renamed in Vale S.A. in 2007). As a carrier of state economic strategies, CVRD implemented and organised an extensive infrastructure network and played an important role not only for economic development but also for regional development.

The traditional centre of mining operations has been the state of Minas Gerais, linked by a highly efficient railway transportation system (Vitória-Minas-railway) with the state of Espírito Santo, where industrial beneficiation plants and large port installations (Tubarão) are located. This "southern system" of CVRD activities, diversified by wood pulp and the reforestation sector, pig iron and ferroalloy industries and a strong cooperation with Japan in the *cerrado* programme[92] was completed by the "northern system" in the Carajás area in East Amazonia.

In 1966, geological survey rights in the Serra dos Carajás region had been granted to CVRD and the Cia. Meridional de Mineração, the Brazilian subsidiary of US Steel. Enormous iron ore and manganese ore deposits were discovered in 1967. In April 1970, a joint venture (AMZA) had been founded between CVRD and US Steel to undertake feasibility studies of the exploration of the iron ore reserves and the implementation of an iron ore project. From the Brazilian point of view this was an excellent possibility to expand the access to the US market, to receive international credits and transfer of know how. In May 1974,[93] a first Carajás project had been conceived and iron ore export planned to start in 1979. The possibility of iron ore transportation by river barges on the Tocantins river was rejected because of missing facilities for a deep-water port at Belém/Pará. Due to the necessary tonnage of large iron ore carriers used in international trade, the port location of Ponta da Madeira near São Luís in the state of Maranhão proved to be the most favourable location. In 1976, AMZA was granted the concession of railway construction between Serra dos Carajás and the port of Ponta da Madeira.

In June 1977, US Steel withdrew from the joint venture in view of project costs, the necessary increase in investments and the difficult situation of the international iron ore market as well as the world crisis in steel production and consumption. Furthermore, the target markets had shifted from the United States to Japan and Western Europe. CVRD acquired the Meridional/US Steel shares in AMZA, US Steel remaining with an option to buy up to 50 % of the iron ore production of Carajás.[94] CVRD's tenta-

92 In the Regional Development Programme in the *cerrado* area of Central Brazil (*Polocentro*), a bilateral agreement with Japan established a development programme for the *cerrado* in Minas Gerais and Goiás. Studies were undertaken by the Japan International Cooperation Agency (JICA). The intense relations with Japan originated from iron ore exports to Japan, and the Japanese demand for grains.

93 During the first visit of the author in July 1974, aircraft landing at Serra dos Carajás occurred on top of the Serra on a roughly graded *cerrado* surface as landing strip. Geological field work, preparation of the mining site and road access for transport of heavy machinery were still in full action. Geologists had to be transported by helicopter to the different locations in the rain forest.

94 Cf. CVRD documents and articles in *Jornal da Vale* (CVRD 1986).

tive to find an adequate counterpart for a new joint venture failed, when Nippon Steel, British Steel and a Spanish Steel Co. desisted from participation due to the high infrastructural investments necessary, particularly for the railway construction.

New studies on optimal production in the Carajás region were completed in 1980. The project scope was substantially reduced in transport capacity from 50 to 35 million t per year and electrification of the railway to the port was no longer included in the project implementation. In October 1980, the Carajás iron ore project was formally approved by the Brazilian President, CVRD being authorised to arrange domestic and international loans. Civil works of railway and port construction already had started. Operations of the beneficiation plant started in 1981 and contracts with 19 clients from Europe and the Far East were signed. Finally, the rights to use the 429 000 ha concession area at Serra dos Carajás were granted to CVRD by the Interministerial Council of PGC. Due to the world economic situation, implementation schedules of the project had to be revised several times, but in 1986 all project parts were in full action according to the revised schedule.

CVRD's "northern system" gained a superior importance within the PGC and the related regional development plans. Diversification was realised by investing in the bauxite and aluminium sectors. The concept of the Rio Doce export corridor of the Vitória-Minas-railway was transferred to the Carajás railway corridor in combination with a regional development programme such as that of the Southeast. But due to financial restrictions, political changes and PGC revisions, particularly in the agricultural sector, the conceptions of JICA could not be realised.

With the Carajás iron ore project, CVRD had strengthened its position as one of the largest mining enterprises worldwide and certainly world's largest iron ore producer and exporter in the second half of the 1980s, combining the two regional systems (1987: 75 mt). The Carajás iron ore project absorbed the bulk of CVRD's investments. Until the end of 1986 direct investments amounted to US$ 2.7 billion. According to the provisional financing plan (1978–1987)[95] for the iron ore project, 38.1 % (US$ 1.79 billion) of the capital investments planned (US$ 4.7 billion) were from CVRD internal cash generation and new capital subscription: 33.5 % (US$ 1.58 billion) from foreign loans (World Bank: US$ 350 million; European Economic Community EEC: 450 million, Japan: 530 million, German KfW: 150 million and US financial institutions: 95 million) and 28.4 % (US$ 1.34 billion) from national sources (BNDES: US$ 700 million, FINAME: 402 million, among others). Nearly half of the direct investments (49.4 %) were absorbed by the railway construction, 13.7 % by the mine, 6.8 % by the port, 4.2 % by townsites and 25.9 % were necessary for administrative and engineering purposes (CVRD 1986).

Environmental and human rights concern rendered the EEC involvement in 1982 more difficult. A World Bank loan was granted with special conditions on Indigenous and environmental protection. Additionally, the effectiveness of the Japanese, the EEC and the German KfW loans were a condition of the proposed World Bank loan. Within foreign loans, the Japanese part was the most important.

Although overproduction, the global economic recession, lower iron ore prices and the specific crisis in the pig iron and crude steel industry made the situation even more

95 Source: Coffey (1985, appendix No. 1); data: Lloyds Bank international; Cf. Kohlhepp *et al.* (1987, Table 10).

difficult, high-grade Carajás iron ore obtained considerable advance contract commitments from steel producers in Western Europe and Japan. As high-grade hematites became depleted in Minas Gerais, CVRD's "northern system" gained high reputation on the iron ore market and extensive contracts were signed.

The installation of the Carajás iron ore project had a considerable influence on the regional employment. During the construction period in the first years of the 1980s, a maximum of over 27 000 workers was employed, in April 1986 still 15 200 employees were engaged in the Carajás iron ore project in construction (43 % employed by contractors), operation, administrative support and maintenance. Finally, there were about 6000 permanent jobs, 60 % for higher, intermediate, and qualified staff. In the end of the 1980s, the annual iron ore production at Carajás was up to 35 million t.[96]

4.2.2. Carajás iron ore reserves and mining

The Serra dos Carajás region is covered by dense tropical rain forests, except for the iron ore bearing *mesa* type *cerrado* clearings above 700 to 900 m above sea level. The *mesas* are of special importance to infrastructural installations like the airport, the townsite and roads. The Serra dos Carajás comprises roughly east-west stretching ranges: Serra Norte, Serra Sul, Serra Leste and Serra de São Félix between 5°50'S and 6°35'S, 49°30'W and 50°45'W. Rock formations exposed in Carajás are of precambrian age. From base to top they include a granite-gneiss basement, a suite of meta-sedimentary and volcanic rocks and sequence of sedimentary clastic rocks. Intrusions are represented by granite plutons. Tectonically, the structure of the Carajás district is a faulted synclinal ridge (Santos 1986, among others). Serra Norte and Serra Sul being respectively the north and south limbs in a distance of about 40 km from one another. There are several large high-grade hematite deposits.

The main iron ore deposits are located in the Serra Norte and Serra Sul. From the five orebodies existing at the end of the 1980s, four were in the Serra Norte with a maximum deposit in the Serra Sul (Table 11 and Fig. 12).[97]

Table 11: Serra dos Carajás: Iron ore reserves (million t = mt)

Sector	Deposit	High-grade		Medium-grade		Total	
		mt	% Fe	mt	in %	mt	% Fe
Serra Norte	N1 - N8	5257	66.7	915	60.8	6172	65.8
Serra Sul	S11	9475	66.8	860	61.1	10 335	66.3
smaller deposits		1019	66.7	359	60.8	1378	65.9
Grand Total		**15 751**	**66.7**	**2134**	**60.9**	**17 885**	**66.0**
High-grade: >64.0 % Fe; Medium-grade: 55.0–63.9 % Fe.							

Source: Research Report AMZA; Santos (1986).

96 In 2021, the Carajás iron ore production at Serra Norte amounted to 110 million t, at the new Serra Sul mining complex (S11D) 73 million t. See details in chapter II.6.3.1.

97 On the development of iron ore mining at Serra Sul, see chapter II.6.3.1.

Fig. 12: Serra dos Carajás. Mineral reserves

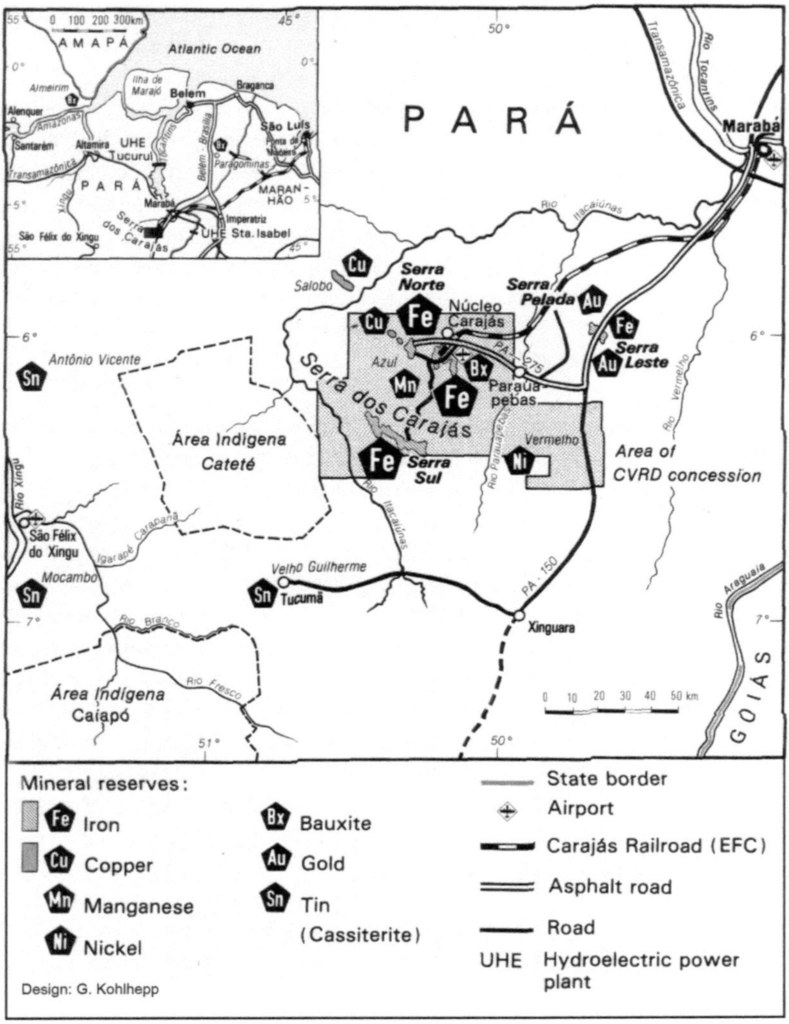

Source: Kohlhepp (1987b, 223); based on documents of CVRD and Ministério das Minas e Energia (1981).

Total high-grade reserves, including smaller deposits, were estimated to 88 % of the reserves, i. e., 15.8 billion t (bt), the grand total of the iron ore reserves being 17.9 bt. In the 1980s, this was the largest iron ore deposit worldwide. It exceeded by far the CVRD iron ore reserves of high-grade hematite in Minas Gerais (2.0 bt), the traditional mining centre of Brazil. The average grade of high-grade ores in Carajás was more than 66 % Fe, even the medium grade ores contain 61 %. Particular attention was paid to the N4-deposit in the central part of the Serra Norte. According to the ore quality and reserve size, but especially because of easier railway accessibility in this part of Serra Norte, N4 was selected as the site for mining start-up in Carajás. Iron ore reserves of 1.28 bt were measured, which corresponds to two-thirds of the total measured reserves. Three basic ore types, classified according to grain-size distribution of "in situ" ore, build up N4 orebody: Friable hematite (84 %), hard hematite (9 %) and soft hematite (7 %). Friable hematite represented the main ore type but did not outcrop. It was covered by *canga*, a crust of ferrous material. Between 1982 and 1986, 12 mt of *canga* had been removed so that open pit mining was possible.[98]

The friable hematite is a natural sinter-feed of excellent quality. A pilot plant at N4 produced one million t of sinter-feed in 1984 and 1985. It was used for quality tests at steel plants in Brazil, Japan, the Federal Republic of Germany and in the US with good results. While sinter-feed nearly exclusively was exported, the natural coarse products were used in the pig iron plants along the railway.

Open pit mining was organised in 15 m high benches. Huge excavators and trucks with a loading capacity of up to 170 t were operating at the mining site, transporting the ore to the near primary crusher. Crushing and screening was organised by computerised techniques at 8000 t/hr. The ore beneficiation area was implanted on the east flank of the N4 reserve with a difference in altitude of about 350 m in an exemplary lay-out with a hydroseeded vegetation cover, contour and draining works as an effective prevention of erosion. The stockpile area had a capacity of 1.6 mt at the beginning. In September 1986, the carloading terminal at the railway loop was working with 8000 t/hr. In between two or three hours an ore train could be loaded.

The implementation schedule for iron ore transport and export had been revised several times from 15 million t per year (mtpy) in the beginning of 1986 to the 35 mtpy-phase at the end of 1987.[99] Mining operations at N4 were scheduled for 303 days per year using three 8 hrs shifts/day. Considering the heavy financial restrictions in Brazil and the extremely difficult infrastructural situation with the railway construction, this was a very good result. Furthermore, the rainy season from November to April with 85 % of the average annual precipitation of 2040 mm (1980–1986) with heavy rainstorms and frequent fog at the altitude of mining caused considerable problems in the beginning of air transport, mining, and export activities.

Besides the huge iron ore reserves, the mineral potential of the Serra dos Carajás mining province is of outstanding diversification (Fig. 11). Large manganese ore deposits (65 mt) were discovered already in 1971. In 1985, a manganese ore beneficiation plant was producing manganese ore (1 mtpy) utilised in ferroalloy plants and battery-grade natural manganese dioxide for the manufacture of electrolytic batteries. The Azul manganese ore mine was used to primarily supply the domestic market. Only about 50 km northwest of the Carajás N4 iron ore mine there exist large copper reserves of about 1.2 bt at Salobo. Brazil urgently needed an increase in copper production, as copper imports in 1986 came up to about US$ 300 million. Although CVRD had planned a master plan for the copper project, including environmental studies, this project was not started until 2004, which led to severe conflicts in the region.

There are also considerable nickel, tin, bauxite, and tungsten deposits in the Serra dos Carajás mining province, prospecting activities were still continuing in the 1980s.

98 Vaz de Melo (1985); Santos (1986); Garrido Filha *et al.* (1988); Ab'Sáber (1996a, b, c); all details according to CVRD information and the Status Reports of CVRD.

99 During the first decade of mining from 1985 to 1996 more than 340 million t of iron ore were transported via the Carajás–Ponta da Madeira railway.

4.2.3. The CVRD concession area in Serra dos Carajás: An "enclave" of well-organised micro-regional planning and development versus a chaotic rural and urban situation "outside"[100]

The CVRD had a very distinct concept of spatial organisation within the 4290 km² concession area in Serra dos Carajás. According to the occurrence of mineral deposits, the geomorphological situation, the ecological conditions and the regional development goals, spatial planning was organised with a focus on the Serra Norte, which initially had the greatest importance. Buffer zones against threatening invasions are clearly documented in Fig. 13. Protection areas were planned along the east border with the colonisation projects (Carajás II and III) outside the concession area and along the Itacaiunas river, the western border in protection of the neighbouring Indigenous reservation Catete. Between Serra Norte and Serra Sul large areas, which were not in use for mining activities, were marked out for natural rain forest and ecological reserves. A future extension of the CVRD concession area to the north was described as fundamentally necessary in view of future mining projects, especially the Salobo copper project, but was denied and only partially used for this project more than two decades later. Huge iron ore mining operations at Serra Sul (S11) started only in the 2010s.[101]

Fig. 13: Spatial organisation in the CVRD concession area in Serra dos Carajás

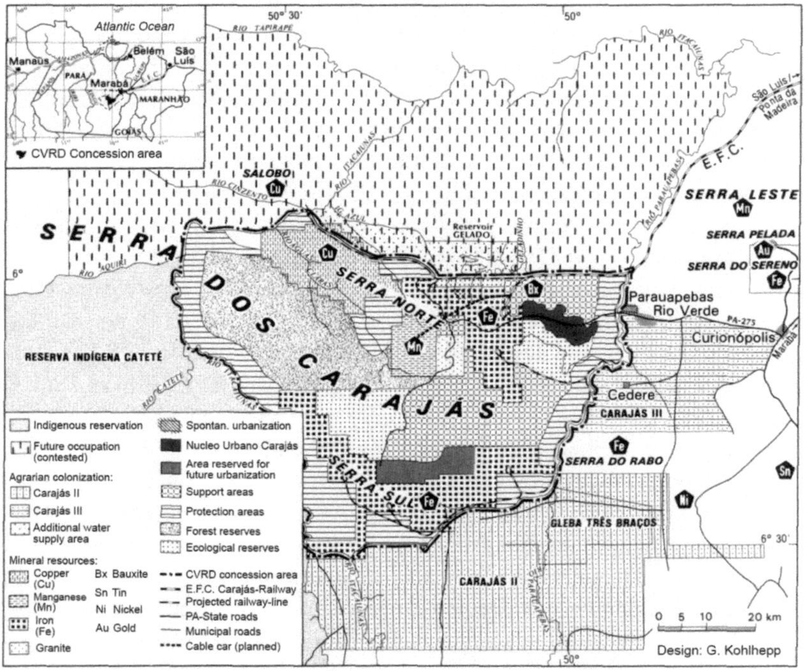

Source: Cf. Kohlhepp (1987b, 228); based on planning documents of the CVRD and additions by the author in Serra dos Carajás in September 1986.

100 This chapter is based on Kohlhepp (1987b; 1987c); Kohlhepp *et al.* (1987).

101 Cf. chapter II.6.3.1.

The main urban nucleus at Serra dos Carajás is located at an altitude of 640 m above sea level on one of the plateaus near the iron-ore mine on the paved PA-275 state highway inside the concession area. The location of the townsite is excellent for climatic reasons, although during the rainy period sometimes there is a problem of fog. The site was located on the prevailing wind side, away from the mining operations and so it is free of dust. The townsite primarily was planned by CVRD for the operational and maintenance staff of the mine and of the railway terminal at Carajás. Non-CVRD people involved in commercial, service, or small industrial activities in the townsite were housed – under protests – outside the concession area at the town of Parauapebas, an originally planned town under severe migration pressure and in 1986 with still chaotic urban characteristics. CVRD had bought the property of a cattle farmer from São Paulo who had ordered the first clearings at the site of today's Parauapebas.

In September 1986,[102] access to Serra dos Carajás was still strictly controlled at the entrance of the CVRD concession area to prevent problems of spontaneous migration invading the area. Only people with a specific charge within CVRD or contractors' operations were allowed to enter this area. The ground-plan of the townsite was a square with a rectangular quadra-pattern. Deforestation for the urban construction and for the airport (opened 1982, a 2 km runway; regular jet air traffic since 1985) was minimized. The functional equipment was exemplary: kindergarten, primary school, secondary school in planning, a large hospital, supermarket, shopping centre, social and sports clubs, cinema, guesthouse, and a hotel were existing, water and electricity supplied from Tucuruí, sewage, garbage collection, and telecommunication working. As there was no reliable regional food supply at the beginning, food for supermarkets and for the workers' restaurants was organised by a contractor with four trucks arriving daily from São Paulo.

The houses in the town belonged to the CVRD and the residents paid only a token amount per month. There were four types of houses according to professional qualification of residents. Urban landscaping, green belts along the peripheral main road and the state highway by-passing outside the townsite made this well-organised urban settlement a model of a typical company town, well known in Brazil.

There was a sharp social segregation between the privileged urban development of the CVRD "enclave" up in the mountains and the tense situation at the foot of the Serra dos Carajás outside the concession area, a conflicted situation severely criticised by the non-CVRD population. Mass migration triggered by large-scale projects, widespread activities of *garimpeiros* and their violent rebellion[103] against CVRD's planned mechanisation of gold mining, as well as spontaneous land occupation in the region made organisational control of access to CVRD's concession area inevitable due to the weakness or absence of state authorities.

Given the extreme isolation of Serra dos Carajás, the townsite was planned to be highly attractive to the new residents. 40 % of the staff came from the Southeast, had experience with CVRD mining in Minas Gerais or iron ore export in Espírito Santo, but were not familiar with the Amazonian reality. The specific age structure of a company town was present in Carajás: 40 % of the urban population were between 26 and

102 Situation during field work of the author in September 1986 in Serra dos Carajás and surroundings.

103 Cf. Serra Pelada, chapter I.1.2.3; Guerreiro (1984); Ab'Sáber (1996c); Becker (1988; 1994).

40 years, 32 % from 18 to 25, only 19 % less than 18 years and 9 % older than 40 years.[104] This indicated a high amount of single young workers or employees and young families.

The CVRD stressed that organisationally it was only responsible for the concession area and a narrow strip along the railway line to the port of Ponta da Madeira. However, in the regional, national, and international discussions about the Grande Carajás programme (PGC), the responsibility for the development problems and failures was given to the CVRD as the main actor.

Outside the CVRD concession area, spontaneously new settlements developed even before the gold rush at Serra Pelada started. This occurred especially along the connection road (PA-275) from the PA-150 to Serra dos Carajás (see Fig. 13). In 1980, Curionópolis emerged from a service centre for various *garimpos* in the vicinity. When Serra Pelada was still a restricted area, the supply of food, building materials and *garimpo* instruments was organised in this new agglomeration where alcohol consumption was abundant and prostitution was economically very important. Later, petrol stations, repair workshops, shops, cheap hotels, etc. were built.

In 1986, 25 000 people lived in Curionópolis, where urban infrastructure remained precarious. No paved roads, no conservation, no water pipes or sewage. Electricity was only supplied by private generators. Removal of garbage was inexistent. Most of the houses were simple wooden constructions, huts were covered with leaves or plastic material. At that time, Curionópolis was a typical pioneer settlement that lost some functions to Serra Pelada. In the beginning of the 1980s, Eldorado (1986: 8000 people) began to develop near the junction of the main roads mentioned. *Garimpeiros* with their families lived there. Commerce increased quickly and work contractors took hands from Eldorado. The admission of women in Serra Pelada relieved Curionópolis and Eldorado of their function as large brothels for the *garimpo* region.

The situation of the extremely bad state of the "asphalt" road from Marabá to Serra dos Carajás proved to be typical for the political conflict between federal, state government and private levels. The Pará state road department was responsible, but because of lacking financial means it wanted PGC or even CVRD taking over the conservation of this road. This made sense because the intensive truck traffic served to supply the CVRD in Serra dos Carajás. At the end of this road, immediately before the gate to Serra dos Carajás, two new settlements emerged: Parauapebas and Rio Verde (cf. Fig. 13).

The appointment of an advisory group (GEAMAM) by CVRD was, on the one hand, due to the conditions imposed by the World Bank, and on the other hand, CVRD's managers in Rio de Janeiro saw that the mining company was unable to solve the regional development tasks it faced in the Carajás region, with all their ecological, social and regional development problems. Especially because the administration of the Programa Grande Carajás (PGC) had not prepared the planning accordingly, this now became a task of CVRD (Ab'Sáber 1996c, 257 f.).[105]

---

104 According to CVRD statistics, evaluated in Serra dos Carajás in September 1986.

105 GEAMAM was an advisory group of outstanding Brazilian scientists who had been invited by the president of the CVRD, Eliezer Batista da Silva, following a new requirement of the World Bank for the granting of loans. GEAMAM played an important role in ordering the environmental and conflictual social situation in regional development and the urban settlements outside the CVRD concession area. GEAMAM, whose members included Warwick Kerr, Aziz N. Ab'Sáber and Herbert O.R. Schubart, made particular efforts to address the situation in the fast-growing, socially conflicted

The basic concept for the origin of Parauapebas was the strategy of CVRD to avoid large *favelas* in the surroundings of the townsite of Serra dos Carajás. However, large projects attracted a mass of construction workers, the majority employed by contracting companies. After termination of construction activities, unskilled workers were dismissed but remained living near the project. This caused considerable problems because they no longer had lodging facilities or a job. *Favelas* normally are the result of this situation. The idea was to instal a planned town – outside the company's borders – with a basic infrastructure in order to settle small industries and craftsmen, providing services to CVRD and the Serra dos Carajás area, offering jobs for the increasing young population.

The foundation of Parauapebas in 1982 was part of the CVRD spatial strategy to implant a belt-like buffer zone east of Serra dos Carajás to protect the concession area against invasions. The other part of this spatial organisation was the installation of the agrarian colonisation projects Carajás II and III south of Parauapebas (cf. Fig. 13). In Parauapebas a large hospital, a primary school, a police station, and a building for the *prefeitura* were constructed by CVRD. As already mentioned, in 1983 some public buildings were burnt during the Serra Pelada *garimpeiro* revolt.

While in Parauapebas official concessions were given to build houses and to instal shops according to the town planning draft, in Rio Verde nothing was planned, but services developed automatically. Numerous brothels opened. A major part of the population were migrants from Maranhão, people escaping from the 1985 flood in the Northeast and dismissed workers from Tucuruí. Many were recruited by subcontractors for jobs in Carajás. Later, peasants from the nearby colonisation projects and *garimpeiros* moved to Rio Verde.

Since 1984, the situation changed distinctly, especially in Parauapebas, where the standards fixed did not meet the basic needs and the previous "image" of a living area for migrants. Population pressure increased and the announcement of the new industrial district attracted even more people. Parauapebas turned from a planned to a spontaneously developing town. As politics changed, CVRD had to transfer the administration of the town to the municipality of Marabá. Immediately, Parauapebas was flooded by invasions. Within two years, the population increased from 2300 (1985) to approximately 25 000 in 1987. A commercial centre developed, and a sharp social segregation could be observed. The administrative change caused another conflict: The state of Pará health service could not finance the hospital. CVRD was urged by the population to maintain the installations but was no longer willing to keep the whole infrastructure of Parauapebas and surroundings going, as this was in state competence. The hospital remained in a desperate state.

In Rio Verde (1985: 9400; 1987: >20 000 inhabitants), a basic spatial reorganisation was realised by GETAT. Despite its character of a pioneer town, a certain consolidation could be observed. The large prostitution area in the centre was transferred to another quarter. The efforts of GEAMAM members have made a significant contribution to the fact that the existing social tensions did not lead to further violent actions, even if not all the sensible suggestions of this group were implemented by CVRD.

---

settlement of Rio Verde, whose integration into the surrounding area was intended to help pacify a tense situation.

It became clear that the CVRD strategies did not address the scale of immigration to this region and that the PGC did not have a sound plan for orderly regional development outside the CVRD concession area. Migration was still increasing in the second half of the 1980s. Most of the migrants came from Maranhão (34 %) and other states of the Northeast (35 %), 11 % from Goiás and only 7 % were people from Pará. Nearly 50 % of the population of Parauapebas and Rio Verde were younger than 18 years, 39 % between 18 and 40 years.[106]

The closure of the outrunning activities in Serra Pelada at the end of the 1980s had a disastrous effect on the increasing social tensions. The state of Pará was not able nor willing to manage the existing and forthcoming problems. One of the fundamental problems was that the PGC did not implement a specific urban development programme in the mass migration regions that were directly affected by the socio-economic impact of the large-scale projects.

CVRD measures to protect the environment and the local population

Unfortunately, the regional development programme for Eastern Amazonia, the PGC, which started in 1980, did not include a specific environmental programme section. This was surprising, considering that the example of the environmentally conscious Polonoroeste programme was prepared by government agencies at almost the same time.

From the four large programme parts of PGC, the Carajás iron ore project was the only one caring of environmental protection. Due to the requirements of the World Bank and – given the size of the projects – the inevitably extensive interventions in the natural and socio-economic conditions, the CVRD assigned responsibility for environmental measures. This was based on the former Minas Gerais experience in 1973 and a research programme was initiated to analyse the environmental impact of the Carajás iron ore project. In 1980, CVRD expanded its activities in environmental research by creating an independent advisory group of outstanding Brazilian scientists and Amazon experts of different disciplines. In 1981/82, this group organised two permanent on-site internal environmental commissions for the mine site and the railway and port areas. They had to identify critical points regarding environment. Ecologists were responsible for monitoring and controlling the environmental aspects of the project (Goodland 1985; Freitas and Shluger 1983; Freitas 1986).

Research projects, symposia, seminars, and discussions were organised in close cooperation with Brazilian and foreign universities, scientific organisations, governmental agencies and international entities like the United Nations Environmental Programme (UNEP), Worldwide Fund for Nature (WWF), among others. Inventories of the regional flora, avifauna, vertebrates, ichthyology and on archaeological sites were carried out in an extensive programme with the renowned Museu Goeldi in Belém. Highest priority was given to projects on socio-economic impacts along the railway line and on water resources in the CVRD's area of influence. Special precautions were taken on the mine site for mine water. Two permanent dams were constructed, one for

106 Data from CVRD statistics and estimates in September 1986. In 2022, the municipality of Parauapebas had a population of 266 400 and a population increase from 2010 to 2022 of 73 %, one of the highest in Brazil (IBGE 2023). Parauapebas and Rio Verde have now grown together and form a conurbation of more than 200 000 inhabitants.

retention of the tailings from the industrial plant and impoundment of water for the industrial process, the other for retention of the fines from the northern dump site at the mine. In the port area of Ponta da Madeira, a pollution control project was carried out.

CVRD installed two large tree nurseries (Serra dos Carajás and São Luís) producing more than 600 000 seeds and sprouts of regional species for reforestation and re-landscaping measures. A botanical and zoological park (for regional species) at Serra dos Carajás supported the environmental education activities for schools and technical personnel.

CVRD mentioned costs of US$ 53.8 million for environmental activities related with the Carajás iron ore project in the period 1981–1985.[107]

The beginning of a new political period was confirmed by a seminar in Belém at the end of September 1986 on "The economic development and environmental impact in areas of the Brazilian humid tropics. The experience of CVRD" with national top-level officials of CVRD and PGC-SEPLAN, other national and international agencies, but especially Brazilian (GEAMAM group) and foreign scientists. This seminar was the first high-ranking event in Amazon affairs in Brazil with open public discussions in impressive frankness. However, this did not eliminate the most critical arguments and problem-oriented awareness of the institutions and agencies involved. It became obvious, that the environmental engagement of the CVRD had already created a highly qualified specialised staff[108] and an active Brazilian advisory group, communicating with many foreign scientists and institutions.

As the government agencies involved in road construction and agricultural colonisation acted without any ecological awareness, CVRD emphasised a necessary social, ecological and economic zoning of its respective territories in Amazonia but remained isolated in the general PGC activities. CVRD had achieved a sort of coordination function between federal, regional, and municipal agencies of the most different functions, NGOs, universities, national research centres and international environmental organisations. It became clear that the CVRD Environment Department's flagship capacity should be strongly supported to promote diffusion of the know-how of an appropriate natural resources management (Kohlhepp *et al.* 1987).

However, CVRD environmental activities did not remain unquestioned. The Lagoa Batata problem at the Trombetas bauxite mining area (CVRD-subsidiary company outside the PGC-region), severe problems along the railroad line, difficulties in spatial planning coordination with unqualified local agencies, the domination of non-Amazonian specialists on the decision-level of management ("Minas Gerais lobby") and on the consultors' level can be mentioned. Universities and scientists in Amazonia reacted negatively to the exclusion of contracts for environmental studies.[109] However, the CVRD could not be held solely responsible for some of these problems, as they were

107 Environmental activities according to Freitas (1986, 24): Studies, consultants, dams, drainage, landscaping, hydrological measures, railway (hydroseeding, laboratory equipment), port (landscaping, purification plant).

108 During the international symposium "Homem e Natureza na Amazônia," organized by the author at the University of Tübingen in May 1986 with the participation of many Brazilian colleagues, the coordinator of the environmental department of CVRD, Maria de Lourdes Davies de Freitas, gave a conference on environmental strategies of CVRD in Carajás (Freitas 1987).

109 Contributions in: Almeida Jr. (1986), among others, in Belém and São Luís.

related to the centre-periphery structures in Brazil and had developed during the authoritarian regime of the previous military governments.

The extent of environmental protection procedures of the CVRD in the Carajás iron ore project went beyond the mere fulfilment of commitments in loan contracts to please the World Bank. However, it was clear to the CVRD management that without environmental measures, international loans could hardly be obtained. In contrast to many other cases in Brazil, CVRD activities in this sector were neither only "cosmetic" nor a pure publicity campaign. It is true that the CVRD used a lot of resources for glossy publications and information on different levels. However, it seemed to be necessary to start a new campaign of information on ongoing controversially discussed projects after two decades of failing information or keeping the public in the dark about problematic development processes. In fact, structural measures with a progressive approach to the problem and a new quality of science-based protection measures were realised.

However, it was obvious that the activities of CVRD's environmental department, which tried to reconcile ecological and economic goals, were also controversial within the company given the amount of money spent. This was to be expected given the very difficult situation on the international iron ore market and the following financial constraints. The support of top management and its room for manoeuvre on environmental issues in a mining company – with the federal government as the main shareholder – was certainly limited by the economic need to export iron ore and support the national budget.

But in the mid-1980s, it became clear that the big corporations had not expected such a well-structured opposition against mega-projects. The activities of NGOs with critical publications and protests in the now democratic Brazil showed that there was a high level of sensitivity and responsibility and a strong public interest in environmental protection in the Amazon region. Examples of this were the Society for the Preservation of Amazonian Natural and Cultural Resources (SOPREN) in Belém, which defined its organisation as "consciousness of the disregarded and oppressed regional population,"[110] or the National Campaign of Defence and Development of Amazonia (CNDDA) in Rio de Janeiro, which had a high scientific claim.[111]

This was a new experience for the decision-makers of large companies and state agencies. Discrimination by PGC officials against some well-informed NGOs as "anti-governmental" or "communist" was totally unjustified and complicated the interrelations.

Although the iron ore project in the Serra dos Carajás did not directly affect an Indigenous area, the CVRD as the responsible and in majority state-owned mining company became involved in the discussion on the future of the Indigenous population when the construction of the Carajás-railway was decided. This decision of the PGC Council – against Pará state interests and against ore transport on the Tocantins river – caused an 890 km traverse of the railway line mostly on Maranhão terri-

110 President of SOPREN, September 1986 in Belém.

111 Since 1967, the CNDDA, founded by Orlando Valverde, as an independent forum published the journal *A Amazônia Brasileira em Foco*. Members of this forum were renowned scientists like Aziz Nacib Ab'Sáber, Darcy Ribeiro, Warwick E. Kerr, Harald Sioli, Philip Fearnside, Irene Garrido Filha, among others. CNDDA organized conferences and protests.

tory and the crossing of some tribal areas. Because of previous alarming news from the Amazon region regarding the impact of development projects on the Indigenous population and in view of the increasing international concern as well as national and regional protests, the railway construction was combined with the recently reformulated strategy of Indigenous protection within the loans of the World Bank, one of the major financing organisations of the Carajás iron ore project. CVRD as holder of an US$ 304.5 million World Bank loan became increasingly confronted with "Indigenous affairs", originally the function of FUNAI.

The World Bank loan granted to the CVRD for the iron ore project came with special conditions for the Indigenous population. A number of US$ 13.6 million was separated to be used within five years in an area influenced by the construction of the railway line between Serra dos Carajás and the port of Ponta da Madeira. The World Bank emphasised the importance of minimising potential adverse impacts, of guaranteeing and protecting land and providing its demarcation to Indigenous areas and reservations. Furthermore, health care programmes, educational support, assistance in staff and infrastructure at the Indigenous posts and economic development projects were recommended. Given the inability of FUNAI, the money had to be directed via CVRD to FUNAI. In June 1982, the company and FUNAI made a special agreement on the World Bank loan.

Although the railway line only affected three Indigenous areas (Mãe-Maria, Caru and Pindaré, cf. Fig. 11) with about 820 inhabitants, the sphere of influence of "CVRD responsibility" was extended to eleven areas with an Indigenous population of 5600 people. The formal criterion of this spatial delimitation was a corridor of 100 km along both sides of the railway axis. This "area of influence" was considered sufficient by all institutions involved. However, in the activities to support the Indigenous communities, the focus on the mentioned areas proved to be impractical, as the inhabitants of other Indigenous areas outside the corridor felt strongly discriminated against. This extended the area of influence to 23 territories and an Indigenous population of about 11 500 people.

FUNAI had elaborated – necessarily in a very short period – a project of assistance to the Indigenous communities in the "railway corridor" without any scientifically based anthropological and ecological concern. The Indigenous tribes and their *caciques* were not informed of the PGC programme and its future consequences, they were not even consulted by FUNAI about the specific projects on their behalf. As FUNAI did not cooperate with renowned Brazilian experts and did not pay attention to the basic needs of the Indigenous groups, CVRD became aware that the financial means were used by FUNAI principally to improve its own infrastructure. FUNAI did not fulfil the basic lines of the agreement.

In view of the aggravating situation, the reactions of the afflicted people, the protests of national and foreign scientists, spontaneous protest movements and the negative international repercussion, the CVRD found itself compelled to intervene in the implementation of the Indigenous project. With scientific support of the Brazilian Association of Anthropology, important field studies were executed, and the real situation of the Indigenous tribes became well known. It was the first systematic analysis of the living conditions and the endangered existence of most of the Indigenous groups of Maranhão and southeastern Pará. The slow or even non-existing delimitation and demarcation process of the Indigenous areas turned out to be the basic problem, urgently necessary to be solved.

Nearly all the well-elaborated proposals of the anthropologists were not taken into consideration by the FUNAI administration. In 1984, the government and CVRD decided to execute a direct supervision on the application of the World Bank financial means within the FUNAI expenses. It became clear that FUNAI was neither able nor qualified to solve the existing problems. For this reason, CVRD had blocked financial resources. As FUNAI had previously informed the Indigenous leaders about its extensive development activities, the Indigenous people protested against the non-fulfilment of promises.

The chaotic FUNAI administrative situation on the federal and regional level – certainly the Military Government had to be blamed for it – made it difficult to consolidate a new indigenist policy. In particular, the approach of participation of the Indigenous population in decision-making structures was never implemented by FUNAI. When FUNAI did not fulfil the contract priorities, CVRD proposed the suspension of the agreement and at least temporarily suspended the transfer of funds during a period of political transition in 1984/85. The situation of the Indigenous population along the railway line and in the PGC region will be discussed in more detail later.[112]

4.2.4. The infrastructural backbone of the CVRD iron ore project: Railway and port facilities

When the Carajás–Ponta da Madeira (EFC) railway line was inaugurated in March 1985, the earthworks and track construction, which were only possible for seven months of the year due to heavy rainfall, had taken more than four years. Extremely difficult natural conditions (Ab'Sáber 1996b) and the track crossing nearly 500 km of tropical rain forests caused enormous logistical problems. Track laying moved from the port to the mine at a rate between 1.1 km/day at the beginning and 1.9 km/day in 1984. Laying of the rails was associated with a tremendous forest devastation of several kilometers on both sides of the line. The railway was single tracked with 1.6 m gauge. About 43 passing turnouts were installed, 60 viaducts and the highly important 2.34 km railway-highway bridge crossing the Tocantins river at Marabá had to be built. The technical state of the railway and its infrastructure was supported by foreign expertise. At the peak of construction works about 20 000 workers were employed. Doubling of the track was planned for the period of an increase in iron ore transports and exports.

The ore trains with 160 cars and 98 t loading capacity each needed three diesel locomotives of 3000 HP each and a fourth at the highest point of the Serra do Gurupí (324 m above sea level). For the round trip mine–port–mine, 52 hours were necessary, i.e., 23 hours for the loaded train with a maximum speed of 65 km/h. Railway activity started with five to six ore trains per day (July 1987) (Kohlhepp 1987b),[113] about half of the Vitoria-Minas railway transport capacity at that period. Modern technical installations were supervising the railway operations, using remote control equipment for signals and line breakdown warning. Large areas at Ponta da Madeira and at Marabá were reserved for main repair and support installations. The railway transportation

112 See chapter I, 4.5.2.

113 For the current situation see chapter II.6.3.1.

system had been the most efficient in Brazil. Electrification was planned but postponed and not realized until today. General cargo transport, including agricultural products, was working as well as passenger service, increasing rapidly in 1987 to 350 000. Passenger transport by rail gained in importance, as fares were 30% of bus fares and journey times were six hours shorter. This was a special CVRD service to the regional population. After initial fierce protests against the construction of the railway, it was accepted by the regional population.

Along the railway line, CVRD installed some small settlements (housing divisions) for permanent personnel stationed at the different railway yards. About 4000 people were living there with a perfect infrastructure, which caused irritation among the traditional local population. As the US$ 1.4 billion Carajás railway was the main transport axis of the state of Maranhão and a major attraction for migrants, a Master Plan of Regional Development was urgently needed. Land speculation, invasions by land grabbers, cattle ranchers, *posseiros* and related violent conflicts were constantly taking place or threatened.[114] Indigenous groups and *quilombolas* demanded that the federal government fulfil requirements related to the demarcation of the remaining lands.

The large maritim terminal was located at Ponta da Madeira on São Marcos Bay. The location on the island of São Luís about 9 km southwest of the capital of Maranhão and near the commercial port of Itaquí was favoured by very good natural conditions such as a deep-water approach. At the quay there was a water depth of 23 m. Tides reach 7 m, but the berthing pier was protected from tide currents by two breakwaters. The São Marcos Bay was wide enough for manoeuvring and anchorages of bulk carriers of 280 000 tdw and two-way simultaneous traffic of the largest vessels.[115] Docenave, the maritim branch of CVRD, operated a fleet of 26 ships, some of them among the most modern vessels. CVRD/Docenave reported numerous contracts by foreign shipping companies, some with ore-oil carriers, to transport Carajás iron ore to Japan, Europe and other destinations. The pier and ship loading equipment was financed by a German KfW loan. The installations at the railway terminal, the unloading capacity (1.30 hrs. for a 160-car train) and the stockpile area were planned for possible future expansion of iron ore mining, transport and exports. A pollution control plan was elaborated, aiming at restoration of vegetable cover, water and residual solids pollution control and landscaping. The ecological and socio-economic impacts of large projects in the municipality of São Luís are analysed in chapters I.4.4. and 4.5.

4.2.5. Pig iron and other metallurgical industries and the charcoal problem

Since the beginning of the PGC, the plan was not only to export the high-quality ores of the Serra dos Carajás, but also to use them in smelter sites along the central transport axis of the Carajás railway for the development of a regional pig iron and steel industry as well as other metallurgical industries. Although some pig iron projects had already been approved in 1986, there were no detailed studies on location factors, no evaluation of industrial sites, not to mention studies on ecological or socio-economic

114 See chapters I.4.5 and 4.6. Cf. SEPLAN (1989); Ab'Sáber (1996b).

115 In January 1987, the record embarkation was by the Norwegian ore carrier "Berge Stahl", at that time the largest worldwide with 365 000 tdw and built in South Korea specifically to transport Carajás iron ore from Ponta da Madeira (CVRD, *Jornal da Vale*, January 1987).

impacts. Even the CVRD complained about a complete lack of coordination and information by the PGC in relation to these projects.

The basic problem was the supply of charcoal, used in large quantities as reduction material in the smelting process. In the mid-1980s it became increasingly clear that the very optimistic calculations and projections for massive afforestation were not feasible, not only for ecological reasons, but also for economic and organisational reasons (Fearnside 1989b and 1989c; Almeida Jr. 1986; Monteiro 1998). As the environmental and social consequences of charcoal production are by far more important than the direct pollution problems, the impacts should have been thoroughly discussed. It was assumed that charcoal production would require an area of about 15 000 km^2, and huge afforestation areas with fast-growing species were planned. This indicated that no transfer of knowledge occurred in view of the well-known ecological problems of large-scale monocultural plantations in the humid tropics. According to previous experience in Amazonia, from the Ford plantations with *Hevea brasiliensis* in the Tapajós region to the large reforestation operations in the Jarí project with *Gmelina arborea, Pinus caribaea* and *Eucalyptus*, reforestation planning in the PGC region was not only superficial but without any scientific approach.

According to PGC information and a report of CODEBAR/SUDAM (1986), 11 projects, incl. seven pig iron plants approved in May 1986, would need 1.1 mt of charcoal. The pig iron plants planned at various locations along the Carajás railway were to produce 1.68 mt of iron annually. Based on a charcoal consumption of 3.2 m^3 per ton of pig iron, the total demand of charcoal in the PGC region would amount to 5.4 million m^3/year. It should be recalled that Brazilian charcoal production through reforestation amounted to 1.61 million m^3 in 1984.

As previous calculations of the reproduction rate per hectare in plantations had been far too optimistic, the *Eucalyptus* area needed for the planned pig iron production would be no less than 26 000 km^2. According to Fearnside (1988), the area potentially needed for reforestation exceeds the Jarí plantations, the largest reforestation area in Amazonia, by a factor of 35, making it almost as large as Belgium. This showed that an afforestation area of this size would be ecologically extremely irresponsible and could not be adequately managed. The PGC afforestation planning had a delusional vision. But even if taken seriously, where in Eastern Amazonia could afforestation areas of this dimension be located for charcoal production in a pig iron industry starting in 1988/89?

A comparison with the state of Minas Gerais, where 84 % of the Brazilian charcoal production (99 % from *Eucalyptus*) from reforested areas were located, proved that this amount was only 25 % of the total consumption of charcoal, the other 75 % being supplied from natural forests with widespread degradation effects. In 1986, reforestation in Minas Gerais covered one million ha. 70 % of the costs of pig iron production came from charcoal production, the range of supply surpassed 500 km, already expanding in neighbouring states. As charcoal supply to the Minas Gerais metallurgical industry would become even more difficult in the near future, industry and large charcoal suppliers were looking for an alternative in the Amazon area (Ab'Sáber 1987). As the transport of charcoal from there to the traditional sites in Minas Gerais was not economically viable, new industries were established in the PGC area based on the regional charcoal supply. Considerable financial interests of Minas entrepreneurs were involved.

As there was no reforestation in the PGC region, the planned industrialisation relied on charcoal production from the tropical rain forests.

Superficial maps – actually sketches – did not refer to natural vegetation conditions or land use. Some of the mapped potential supply areas coincided with *cerrado* areas or even with completely deforested areas with extensive pastures (Valverde 1987). The idea of charcoal supply from strips or corridors along the roads was inviable because forests along the main roads already had been totally destructed, sometimes in "corridors" more than 50 km wide. Furthermore, Indigenous areas and reservations were simply included into the potential supply area. Charcoal production threatened to lead to an onslaught on remaining rain forests, resulting in the ecological collapse of these ecosystems and an alarming increase in conflicts of interest.[116] There was an immediate risk that many industrial projects would organise charcoal supply with subcontractors, as this was the "normal" way to avoid social and environmental implications.

In view of these problems, the use of *babaçu* husks as an alternative for charcoal production was discussed. In the Meio Norte region of Brazil, the natural vegetation of babaçu palm forests (*Orbignya spp.*) was widespread (see Fig. 11), and the use of the husk (*endocarp*) of the *babaçu* fruit was a suitable method to take advantage of the annual regeneration cycle of the fruit. The *endocarp* is composed of nearly 25 % of fixed carbon with excellent quality for charcoal. But there was a restricted know-how of the technical procedure of *babaçu* husk charcoal in smelting. A pilot-plant in Teresina (Piauí) was closed and the Ministry of Mining and Energy had officially desisted from using *babaçu* charcoal. This meant that resuming the use of *babaçu* husk did not guarantee a regular and quantitatively sufficient supply.

However, the most important reasons against large-scale use of *babacu* charcoal in industrial projects were social implications. In Maranhão, *babaçu* palms constitute a very important natural resource, providing cash and subsistence benefits to more than 350 000 peasant families. Traditionally, land for shifting cultivation and *babaçu* palms for extraction activities had been provided by landowners under informal contracts, permitting peasants to live on their property in exchange for in-kind rents and a stable labour supply. Besides cash income from breaking the fruits and selling kernels, *babaçu* palms provide numerous products such as edible oil, feeds, materials for basket-making and finally charcoal, used mostly for private cooking.

In recent years, economic interests of large landholders increasingly changed to mechanized agriculture and expansion of cattle ranching. Both activities severely interfere with the cash and subsistence needs of the landless peasants because *babaçu* stands were eradicated. The public discussion on land reform after the end of the Military Government additionally caused intense pressure on rural families because of limited access to land by fencing of large properties and displacement of peasant families. Violent actions had rapidly increased.[117] In this situation, even tendencies to

116 Charcoal production and its environmental and social impact were a central topic for Brazilian researchers, especially from the Amazon region, and foreign colleagues. Cf. Pinto (1982); IBASE (1983); Almeida Jr. (1986); Castro (1989); Castro and Hébette (1989); Hébette (1991); Andrade (1995); Monteiro (1998) ; Valverde (1987; 1989); Ab'Sáber (1987; 1996b); Fearnside (1988), among others; Fearnside and Rankin (1985); Kohlhepp (1987b); Kohlhepp and Schrader (1987); Kohlhepp *et al.* (1987). See also: IDESP (1987).

117 Cf. chapter I.4.5.

stimulate the use of *babaçu* products for charcoal production would have caused disastrous social consequences.

As a result, the ecologically most favourable alternative, the charcoal production from *babaçu* husks, turned out to be socially irresponsible and politically and even economically impracticable (Kohlhepp 1987b; Kohlhepp *et al.* 1987).

According to forest legislation, every charcoal consumer must own 50 % of the area needed for charcoal production. A reforestation plan had to be prepared for this area, with details of the deforestation cycle. If this was indeed the case – and the doubts were justified – it would create tendencies to enlarge landholdings. Since reforestation was not possible in the short term, charcoal production from natural rain forests remained the only option for supplying the pig iron and metallurgical industries.

Numerous charcoal kilns in batteries of 10 to 20 units had already been built along the highway axis. Although the kilns in the past had been favourably located as far as transportation was concerned, in 1989 they were moving more and more to keep up with the shifting locations of raw materials. As the trees along the main and secondary roads were cleared, the kilns moved deeper into the forests[118] (Fig. 14) and the access roads were widened. In the Marabá region there had already been demonstrations against the destruction of the valuable *castanhais* – self-contained stands of the Brazil nut tree (*Bertholletia excelsa*). For this reason, the sites of the kilns have been relocated also for tactical reasons. Furthermore, landowners perfectly knew about the new environmental legislation and were not keen on being confronted with IBAMA agents. The side roads could not be used without permission from the *castanhais'* owners so that the covert production of charcoal frequently escaped the notice even of government inspectors. Sometimes their mobility had been restricted by direct or indirect intervention of the owners.

According to the estimation of the president of the Syndicate of Rural Workers in 1989, the number of kilns in the micro-region of Marabá was between 2500 and 3000.[119] Due to the uncertainty of how to deal with the charcoal problem, given the conditions of forest legislation and increasing public pressure, some landowners of *castanhais* and rain forests with different vegetation composition behaved aggressively.[120] The syndicate's president, who protested against the conditions of workers in kiln construction and charcoal production, was threatened with death and had to leave the region several times for security reasons. Official information about charcoal production was vague and statistics tried to hide lacking studies. There was an overall need for research. Planning was partly unrealistic and charcoal suppliers were not sure about the success of the approved pig iron projects. In official documents, the use of Brazil nut trees for charcoal production was denied but could be proved at many locations.

118 In October 1989, the author did field work in the region of Marabá with numerous interviews with owners of *castanhais*, workers at charcoal kilns and the president of the Syndicate of Rural Workers of São João do Araguaia, Sr. Almir Ferreira Barros.

119 In March 1994, there were 311 charcoal kilns operating in the municipality of Jacundá/PA alone (Monteiro 1998, Table 8, 140 f.).

120 The author's mapping of charcoal kilns and taking photos of Brazil nut trees felled was not only refused but was violently prevented. The wood was immediately processed into charcoal on site. *Pistoleiros* of landowners stopped interviews and the use of side roads. Fortunately, a detailed photo documentation could be realized by the author.

Fig. 14: Location of charcoal piles in the area Marabá–Tucuruí–Paragominas 1989

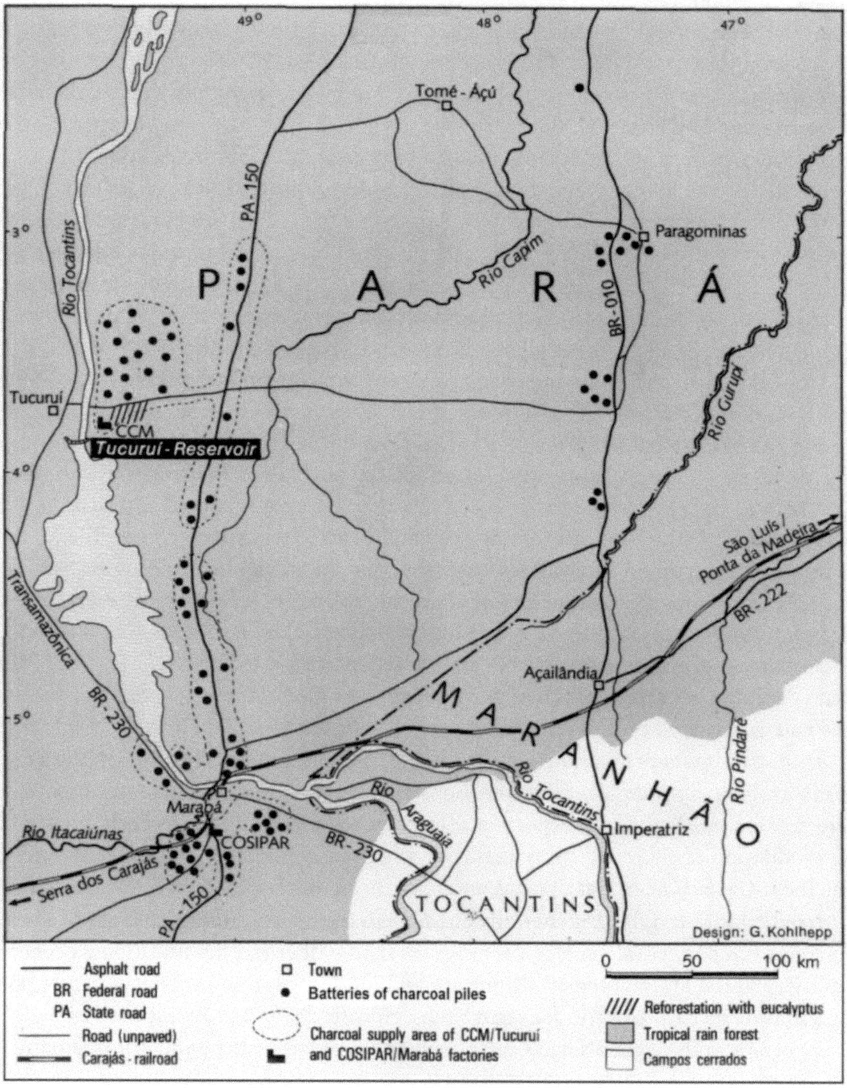

Source: Cf. Kohlhepp (1989a, 96; 1991a, 97); based on IDESP (1988) and own field work information and mapping.

In charcoal kilns mapped in October 1989, high-quality timber was used almost exclusively, frequently including *Bertholletia excelsa* in the immediate surroundings of Marabá. Other species were Jatobá (*Hymenaea courbaril*), Angelim (*Hymenolobium*), and Massaranduba (*Manilkara*). Some of the best trunks were sold to sawmills or bought by timber trade, such as mahogany (*Swietenia macrophylla*). Some *fazendeiros*, who only sold mahogany, burnt down the rest of their forest property and switched to pasture and cattle breeding. Only at a few sites along highway PA-150, mainly wood waste from sawmills was used for charcoal production. Some years later, in 1994, the number of kilns using wood waste from sawmills had increased (Monteiro 1998).

At the beginning of the main charcoal production period, the first kilns were built in 1988 with the know-how of the suppliers in Minas Gerais according to a simple design. Bricks came from Marabá where many brickyards were located. Workers for forest clearing and charcoal production were contracted in Bahia and Espírito Santo. They came in groups of four to eight men and worked under inhuman conditions. Kiln construction was made in one day by four people, earning 10 NCz. (= 2.7 US$)[121] per person/day. Kilns are 2.2 m high with a diameter of 3 m. The workers stayed without any infrastructure in the forest, complaining about lack of water and adequate food, failing social security, lacking support in case of frequent diseases such as malaria and other infections. They were suffering under permanent smoke of the kilns and were responsible for the sequence of all operations until charcoal production.[122]

One kiln filled with timber needed one week for producing 1.5 t of charcoal. Sometimes, working in family groups was realized. They had to attend 16 kilns, i.e., producing 24 t of charcoal per week. With moist wood, the average production per week was about 20 % lower. The example of one battery of kilns: The workers were paid 15 NCz. (= 4 US$) per ton of charcoal. The group of six people earned 360 NCz. (= 97.3 US$) per week.[123] The owners of *castanhais* had lorries to transport the charcoal to the consumer. They gained 230 NCz. (= 62.2 US$) per ton of charcoal, i.e., 5520 NCz. or 1492 US$ for the weekly load of 24 t of charcoal. For an intermediary who organized the work power they paid 25 NCz. per ton of charcoal, i.e., 600 NCz. Net earnings – without considering lorry transport – amounted to weekly 4920 NCz. (= 1330 US$) per battery of kilns. Most of the owners of *castanhais* had several batteries of kilns working. They had a very good profit.

Among the owners of *castanhais* were several members of the Mutran families from Marabá, who had good political connections and were originally from Maranhão. They were traders in Brazil nuts, exporters of precious woods and had recently turned to the production of charcoal, subsequently using their deforested land for cattle breeding. The *castanhais* near Marabá had an area of 5000 to 17 000 ha each. Deforestation occurred rapidly and the destruction of *castanhais* contributed to the collapse of Brazil nut trade and poor rural peoples' earnings for fruit gathering, the traditional economic activity in the Marabá region (Kitamura and Müller 1984). In June 1990, in a region of 1.7 million ha 44.6 % of the area had been deforested (Fig. 15). Forest fires often left a haze over Marabá, schools had been closed and protests by the population remained ineffective.

121 Conversion rate of currencies: 02.10.1989: 1 US$ = 3.7 Cruzado Novo (NCz. official rate; tourist rate: 7.5 NCz.).

122 Some years later in 1994, Monteiro (1998) observed several types of wood supply and charcoal production with specific interrelations between sawmill owners, supply of wood, construction of kilns and delivery to the pig iron industries.

123 Data obtained by interviews in the Marabá region in October 1989. The regional minimum salary per month per person in October,2 1989 was 260 NCz.(= 70.3 US$).

Fig. 15: Deforestation of castanhais *in the Marabá region (Pará) in June 1990*

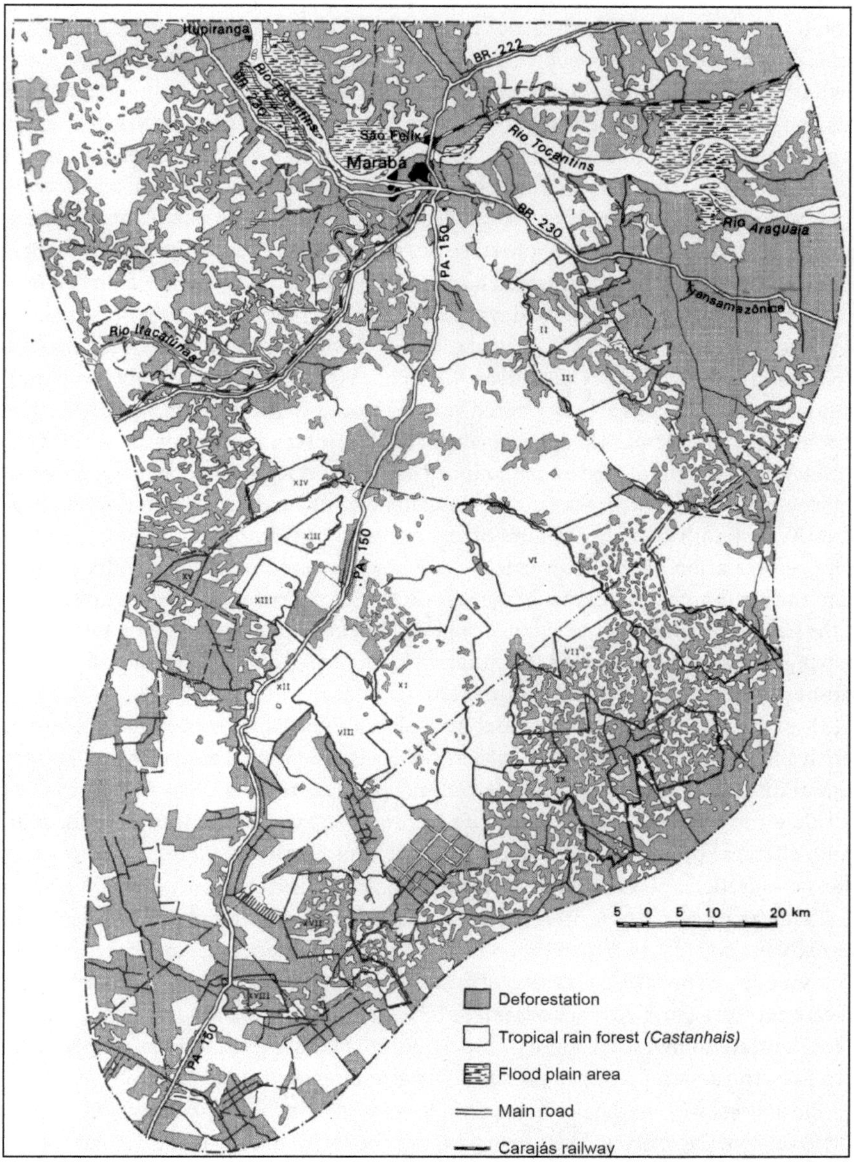

Source: Author's design; Map 1:250 000 elaborated by IDESP, SUDAM, DRN, June 1990: Polígono dos Castanhais: Real estate and forest situation.

As far as the supply of charcoal was concerned, there was complete confusion about the future planning of a quantitatively sufficient and ecologically appropriate supply. Plans to use wood from the Tucuruí reservoir were discussed but could never be realised. It would have been much better to do it before the reservoir had been flooded. Charcoal prices ranged from US$ 40–50 for charcoal made from sawmill waste to over

US$ 80 for charcoal from plantations (probably mainly *Eucalyptus*), which in reality existed only in some small model plantations. As already mentioned, the plantations should have been established earlier to comply with the new environmental regulations. Charcoal from the *roça* of the peasant plots was neither available in large quantities and on a permanent basis, nor was it produced efficiently in the required quality. It was unclear how a permanent supply could be organised during the main rainy season, as many access roads were impassable and the kilns remained inaccessible.

Large areas of tropical rain forests were cleared to meet the charcoal needs of the pig iron industries. The area of forests destroyed depended on the planned scale of industrial production. According to statistics from PGC in October 1989, 5.9 million m^3 of charcoal (= 1.48 mt) per year would be needed to supply the 19 plants which had been approved. The production planned was calculated in 1.36 mt of pig iron and 220 000 t of alloys. The discrepancy in the calculations of the forests to be cleared for charcoal production was enormous. Contrary to PGC data (455 km^2 to clear annually), experts[124] estimated that the annual area cleared would amount to 1000 km^2 or up to 2200 km^2, depending on the biomass and the density of the forest stands, in order to meet a target production of 2.8 mt of pig iron announced earlier by PGC. In October 1989, only four pig iron plants – two at Marabá, two at Açailândia – had already started production. IBAMA's demands that the iron ore plants ensure a consumption of 70 % of charcoal from reforestation by 1992 and reach 100 % by 1995 were systematically disregarded from the beginning. José Lutzenberger, the State Secretary for Environmental Affairs of the new Government of President Collor de Mello, made a clear statement in 1990 to stop pig iron and charcoal production activities in case of disrespected legislation and in order to prevent further expansion (Kohlhepp 1991a).

However, it was clear that charcoal from plantations (*Eucalyptus*) would not be competitive for economic reasons. In 1989,[125] the costs of charcoal amounted to 83 US$/t, with additional transportation costs and handling costs of 15 US$/t of pig iron and 7.5 US$/t iron ore costs. Export prices of pig iron run up to 128–130 US$/t. On the other hand, charcoal produced near the consumer's plant by direct logging of the primary forest was traded at US$ 30.7/t, free smelter, i.e., including transport costs.[126]

This was proof that pig iron production was only profitable through destructive overexploitation of virgin forests and the merciless exploitation of labour force. All the economic actors involved, planning officials, representatives of public authorities and private entrepreneurs, had not considered the environmental and social costs that will force the state to invest far more in the medium and long term to repair the damage caused by the unscrupulous exploitation of natural resources and labour.

The only solution to the problems created by destroying rain forests would be to import coke or using electric blast-furnaces, supplied with energy from the Tucuruí hydroelectrical power station. However, given the world market price for coke (130 US$/t, corresponding in 1989 to the price of one ton of pig iron) these solutions could work only if highly subsidised, probably exclusively from international financial sources,

124 Hearings of international experts in the German Parliament in May/June 1989 (Deutscher Bundestag 1990; Valverde 1989).

125 Information provided by PGC during an interview with one of the managers on October 2, 1989 in Marabá.

126 Interviews of the author on October 4, 1989 near Marabá.

e.g., in the form of "debt-for-nature-swaps". Importing coke would only be worthwhile for the production of ferroalloys, whose retail prices were 10 to 15 times higher than those of pig iron.

The establishment of pig iron industries in Açailândia and the Piquiá railway station there was questioned, as one of the main reasons was the availability of land in Piquiá that was already upgraded by existing infrastructures and owned by the project promoters (Valverde 1989). The hydrographic conditions were not suitable for a high-water demand for the plants mentioned. A direct site at the bank of the Tocantins river, the railway passing nearby, would have been much better.

The economic viability of pig iron projects had been questioned by the National Council of Metallurgy (Consider), classifying pig iron plants with a capacity of less than 1 mtpy as uneconomical. The projects approved had a total production capacity of only 1.1 mtpy, creating 2100 jobs. Five plants had only a capacity of producing between 50 and 55 000 t. This enormous discrepancy in production could not be explained by PGC officials. Pig iron production along the Carajás railway could only be competitive against production in other regions of Brazil (1984: total production of pig iron on charcoal basis 6.2 mt; 92 % in Minas Gerais) with high tax incentives and other benefits granted. FINAM (Investment Fund of Amazonia) funds had been very important.

The number of projects submitted and approved has been very unreliable. Of the 15 pig iron projects planned by the PGC for Maranhão, only 6 were realised and commissioned in 1996, some with long delays. The location of five enterprises was in Açailândia with an individual production capacity between 50 000 and 170 000 t/y, one was located in Rosário (start in 1992) (IDESP 1988; Monteiro 1998). The concentration of pig iron industries and the pollution caused by charcoal kilns in later years led to enormous protests and to the resettlement of a part of the Piquiá population.

Only three projects had been realised in Pará. Two pig iron industries in Marabá (see below) and a metallic silicon production in Breu Branco, 5 km distant from the Tucuruí power plant. Near Tucuruí, Brazil's largest construction company Camargo Corrêa started in 1986 the installation of an industry producing metallic silicon (CCM). The primary location factors were availability of electrical energy, nearby deposits of quartz sands, regional charcoal supply and wood chips from the primary rain forests and own reforestation. A very important factor was the company's infrastructure at Tucuruí, especially heavy machinery, used at the dam and powerhouse or residential areas construction. Tax incentives had been granted to Camargo Corrêa S.A. The company had diversified its activities in the primary and industrial sectors considerably. In the 1980s, the company acquired, among other things, 35 % of the share capital of Alcoa do Brasil.

CCM started with its first blast furnace in April 1988, three other blast furnaces – with support of German industries – were to be installed in the following years with the employment of 600 workers. The total capacity of metallic silicon planned was 36 000 tpy. At that time, this was 12 % of the world's production and 60 % more than the Brazilian output in 1983. 50 % of the charcoal demand (54 000 tpy) were planned to be supplied by company-owned *Eucalyptus* plantations of 35 000 ha, with first results of logging after 6 years. According to CCM staff calculations, 700 charcoal kilns would be needed for supply during the maximum production.[127]

127 Interview of the author with CCM staff on September 15, 1986.

In 1996, 76% of the pig iron production (0.7 mt) along the Carajás-Ponta da Madeira railway was exported. During the first years of production (1988-1995), Açailândia concentrated 66% of the production, Marabá participated with 27% and Rosário (since 1992) with 7% (Monteiro 1998, 99, Table 3; % calculations by the author).

In 2004, the production of pig iron in East Amazonia amounted to 2.96 mt and 3 mt of charcoal were needed for supplying the production. Large areas of tropical rain forests have been destroyed by clearcutting. This process of devastation will continue with the increasing pig iron production, lacking forest management and insignificant reforestation activities. Only 4.6 mt of iron ore (= 6.6% of the iron ore mined at Serra dos Carajás in 2004) were consumed by the regional pig iron production (Monteiro 2005, 160).[128]

Case study: Marabá in the 1980s

The regional centre Marabá (1989: 125 000, 2022: 266 400 inhabitants) at the confluence of the Tocantins and Itacaiúnas rivers started the installation of an industrial district with an area of 3000 ha in 1988. The location had a good infrastructure with railway connection and electricity from the near Tucuruí hydroelectric plant. In 1981, the Itacaiúnas bridge had been built and in 1985 the important bridge over the Tocantins river for railway and road traffic had been inaugurated. Although it was an important transport hub, the road connections to the Belém–Brasília highway via the Transamazônica (BR-230) and the direct connection to Belém (PA-150) were not yet asphalted. Road traffic conditions were very bad. With the construction of the Tucuruí dam, possibilities for river navigation were studied. The transport alternatives of the Carajás railway to São Luís – besides the better port facilities for iron ore shipping and the existing know how in transporting bulk goods by railway – had also a political background because of better relations of the Maranhão state government to the federal decision level.

Marabá was conceivably unsuitable for a heavy industry site from a climatic and ecological point of view. The allocation of rain forest land for the settlement of industrial enterprises was done through non-transparent "donations" without any preliminary studies of the environmental impact and the explosive social situation. The industrial district was established by the state of Pará, financed by CVRD. The local elite of leading families valorised their land by establishing industries (Ab'Sáber 1996b).

In the industrial district of Marabá, the Itaminas Group from Minas Gerais, the largest pig iron producer in Brazil, invested in September 1989 in a pig iron plant (Cosipar) with a capacity of 120 000 tpy (IDESP 1987 and 1988; Monteiro 1998). The company complained about difficulties with local manpower. All specialists came from Minas Gerais. The charcoal problem was dealt with with extreme caution and not discussed in detail. Brazilian producers were the only ones to use charcoal as a reducing agent for ferroalloys and metallic silicon on a large scale. In the mid-1990s, the price of charcoal averaged 44–60% of the price of pig iron (Monteiro 1998, 133).

A second pig iron industry (Simara) in the new industrial district of Marabá was started in 1988 but had to stop production for a few years due to problems with the blast furnace and was only restarted in 1995.[129]

128 For the latest development of the Marabá industrial district, see chapter II.6.3.1.

129 Large project plans of pig iron (1.5 mtpy) with Tjaspromexport of USSR, planned to be located in the industrial district of Marabá, and a ferro manganese production, probably in Parauapebas, were not realized.

At the height of production in Marabá, the pig iron sector employed 8000 direct workers and around 36 000 in the entire production chain. However, the economic crisis of 2008 had a disastrous effect on the industrial district of Marabá, Not even 3000 direct jobs remained. The Cosipar steel plant, the first steel works in Marabá, closed. There were two major unresolved issues. The first was the price of the iron ore supplied by Vale and the second concerned charcoal of legal origin, which remained very difficult to obtain. To date, there is no clear afforestation policy.[130]

Traditionally, Marabá was the centre of trade in Brazilian nuts. Marabá was confronted with modern development strategies when the Transamazônica was built in the early 1970s, passing by Marabá. Camps of road construction workers, agrarian colonisation activities, administrative necessities and SUDAM-sponsored large cattle ranching projects in the surroundings turned Marabá during the 1970s to a sort of basic logistical centre. Marabá also suffered from inundations, the most disastrous in 1980.

The town was divided in three parts: Velha Marabá, the traditional old town, directly at the point of confluence, with the commercial centre and most of the residential quarters, the "cidade do povo". This part was severely affected by flooding, but the population refused to be resettled.

Cidade Nova: Since 1957, some quarters arose on the left bank of the Itacaiúnas river, south of Velha Marabá. This area became the quarter of the social middle and upper class.

Nova Marabá: This was the planned new town, east of Velha Marabá on a *terra firme* site. By order of SUDAM, an ultra-modern urbanisation concept with leaf-like spatial structures has been developed. This large district was very poorly connected to the rest of the town. It was the residential area of the poor population, who also settled on the flood-prone terrain.

Marabá became a prime example of Amazonian urban planning that neither met the needs of the majority of the population nor in any way took into account the social and urban-climatic proposals of Brazilian scientists who considered the specific local environmental conditions, social tensions and urban-rural relations (Ab'Sáber 1996b, 98–102; Kohlhepp 1987b; Kohlhepp *et al.* 1987).

With the construction works of the Carajás iron ore project and *garimpeiro* activities in nearby Serra Pelada in the 1980s, Marabá was overwhelmed by fundamental changes in functional and physiognomic structures. Large construction companies, the CVRD and official agencies, subcontractors and others transferred their subdivisional headquarters to Marabá.

In the 1980s, Marabá suffered from an exceptional migration of mostly unskilled workers, causing increasing population pressure in the infrastructure of all sectors and widespread invasions in Nova Marabá and Cidade Nova with all its negative consequences. Land speculation inside the urban area paralysed systematic urban planning. Rents and living costs exploded. *Garimpeiros* returning from Serra Pelada and other *garimpos* made Marabá a pioneer town with an intensive flow of capital, but extreme poverty of the absolute majority of the population and a high crime rate. After the end of construction work in Tucuruí, thousands of labourers (*barrageiros*) came to Marabá. Huge favelas spread in and around the town. In Marabá there was an adventurous mix of different

130 For today's situation see chapter II.6.3.

social groups with mostly conflicting interests. The new industrial district that emerged at the end of the 1980s attracted a new wave of migrants looking for jobs, directly or indirectly. However, the large majority remained in a desperate situation and unemployed.

As the large municipality of Marabá was very poor, the new industrial projects, including the Parauapebas site, confronted the municipal administration with almost insoluble problems. Town population, budget, infrastructure on all levels were not prepared for the shock to come. Unrealistic structures of administrative competence, lack of coordination and of considering social and environmental costs of development planning were inherent in all large projects. The municipal administration was not integrated in planning and executing procedures. The former authoritarian planning structures were not adapted to the new democratic reality. The ecological and social impacts burdened a development process that, as "development from above", could not be adjusted in time to the regional conditions and the mentality of the local population. As mentioned above, large-scale deforestation of tropical rain forests occurred without any perspective of reafforestation which was not viable ecologically and economically. Illegal logging of remaining primary forests for the production of charcoal for the regional pig iron industry continues to this day (Greenpeace 2013). Today, Marabá is a conurbation with difficult problems of social segregation.

4.3. The hydroelectrical power plant Tucuruí: Environmental and socio-economic impacts

4.3.1. Regional hydroelectric potential and Tucuruí project data

The hydrographic basin of the Tocantins-Araguaia rivers in East Amazonia covers an area of 767 000 km². The hydroelectric potential is estimated at 25 000 MW, i.e., 12 % of the Brazilian total. The two parts of the basin have very different geomorphological characteristics so that the Tocantins with its higher gradient and its higher drainage density concentrates 80 % of the potential and the larger part of the 27 dams proposed to use the total potential of the Tocantins-Araguaia basin.

As the Amazon region is an enormous sedimentary basin with only smooth relief forms, the installation of dams and very large reservoirs was necessary for using the hydroelectrical potential. This meant flooding huge rain forest areas. There was an extremely controversial discussion in Brazil on the government's strategy to implant large powerplants in the Amazon region, particularly because of ecological and socio-economic impacts as well as high financial investments.

Already in 1973, Eletronorte had been created as a regional electric power company, controlled by the head office Eletrobras, to study the hydroelectric potential of the Amazon region and to conduct feasibility studies of implanting power stations in this region. The regional development strategies of the Brazilian Military Government favoured large-scale projects with a high capacity for industrial supply.

Tucuruí was the corner-pillar of this economic development strategy. Located at the Tocantins river, downstream the confluence of the Araguaia and Tocantins rivers, about 200 km north of Marabá and 300 km southwest of Belém, the powerplant Tucuruí was the precondition for all industrialisation programmes, particularly for the decision to concentrate large aluminium producing plants in East Amazonia.[131] As Tucuruí is located in the middle of a tropical rain forest region, there were very few examples that were directly comparable and whose impacts were transferable to the case of Tucuruí, e.g., Brokopondo in tropical Surinam. In Brazilian Amazonia, Tucuruí was only preceded by two small reservoirs: Curuá-Una near Santarém, and Paredo in Amapá.

Construction began in 1975 and an environmental impact analysis was carried out (Goodland 1978). In 1986, Eletronorte published the following data on the project:

The first stage of the project had a final capacity of 4000 MW, with 12 main units of 330 MW and two auxiliary units of 20 MW.[132] In 1986, Tucuruí had the fourth rank world-wide in generating capacity of hydroelectric plants, at that time Itaipú being the leading plant (12 600 MW). The Tocantins river has an average river flow of 11 000 m^3/s, the minimum flow registered was 1511 m^3/s, the maximum flow observed was 68 400 m^3/s. The spillway flow had been prepared for 100 000 m^3/s.

The inundated area of the Tucuruí reservoir at maximum level (72 m above sea-level) is 2430 km^2, the second largest in Brazil (Fig. 16) (as a comparison: Lake Constance/Germany: 538 km^2). The Tocantins river was dammed up nearly 200 km, the length of the reservoir is about 170 km, width on an average 14 km, maximum width 40 km. The total accumulated volume of the reservoir is 46.8 billion m^3, rank three worldwide at that time. Crest level of the dam of about 7 km is 78 m. Concrete structures of about 6 million m^3 had been installed. The first two units were commissioned at the end of 1984. At that time, the cost estimates with financing costs were US$ 5.5 billion for the first stage, including transmission lines.

The information on the cost of installed kW varied considerably in the various Eletronorte publications: US$ 879/kW versus 696/kW for the first stage (June 1986). During the construction of Tucuruí, the possible installation of two locks was considered. Since the decision to transport iron ore to Ponta da Madeira by rail had already been taken some years earlier, in the mid-1980s there were still discussions about transporting agricultural production in the Tocantins-Araguaia Basin to Belém by riverboats. Until 1984, work on the locks progressed normally, but then slowed down due to a lack of funds and finally came to a halt in 1989. However, the possibility of also using the railway connection to São Luís for rural products made the realisation of the lock facilities seem not very likely.

The Tucuruí transmission network is of utmost importance for the industrial development of the region. 500 kV transmission lines were installed for a total length of 1930 km from Tucuruí to Vila do Conde (Albras/Alunorte industries) and Marabá–Imperatriz–São Luís (Alumar), as well as 510 km of 230 kV transmission lines and 11 switching stations. Interconnections with the CHESF grid in the north-east of Brazil were in place.

Compared to other hydropower projects under construction in Amazonia, the ratio of power generation to flooded area in Tucuruí was favourable at 3.3 MW/km^2. In Balbina, north of Manaus, this factor was 0.1 MW/km^2 and some African power plants also had very low values (e.g., Lake Volta, Lake Kariba). On the other hand, Itaipú was proud of a ratio of 9 MW/km^2 due to its unique natural conditions with the Rio Paraná canyon (Kohlhepp 1987c).

131 Cf. chapter I. 4.4.

132 The second stage (Tucuruí II) started in 1998 and the installed capacity today is 8370 MW.

4.3.2. Environmental problems of large reservoirs in the tropics and the Tucuruí situation

Already in the discussion of the 1970s about the importance of hydropower, the licensing authorities and operators often referred to this energy production as "clean energy," in contrast to fossil fuels. It was deliberately concealed that greenhouse gases are emitted on a large scale, especially in tropical forest areas where the forest vegetation in the reservoir area is not cleared before flooding. In an ecological perspective, the main problem was the process of anaerobic decomposition of biomass in the flooded area of the reservoir, the emission of toxic greenhouse gases (CO_2, H_2S, methane – CH_4) from decay of trees left standing in the reservoir. Effects on the pollution of the biomass parts in the turbines, on the water quality and especially on the oxygen content could be observed. With the decomposition of the organic material, the unpleasant smelling gases decreased, but in September 1986 the problem could still be detected in Tucuruí.

In addition to the CO_2 emissions of the reservoirs, the emissions of the construction work must also be included. Extensive earthworks with heavy machinery, deforestation in and around the construction site, enormous heavy goods traffic over years to transport the materials, dam and power plant construction burden the CO_2 balance. In relation to the use of fossil fuels in energy production, this is only compensated for decades later. The Tucuruí dam showed that the actual greenhouse gas emissions were a factor ten higher than its official calculations showed. In 1990, Tucuruí had a global warming impact greater than that of the fuel burned by the city of São Paulo (Fearnside 2002, 21).[133]

Tucuruí was an example of the lack of coordination of measures to remove and use timber in the flooded area. The very different estimates for the total timber volume of the Tucuruí reservoir area varied between 2 and 13.4 million m³. Due to a dispute within the government over the awarding of contracts to companies supported by different ministries, the time available for the start of timber removal was short. Almost 50 % of the wood potential of the reservoir was the valuable Brazil nut tree (*Bertholletia excelsa*). Although the contracted company Capemi was granted the privilege to commercialise these timber stands, deforestation operations remained unsuccessful. The company was not equipped with efficient machinery, had no experience in deforestation and finally went bankrupt in 1983 after clearing only 0.5 % of the submergence area (Fearnside 2001a, 381). Fraud and corruption were strongly suspected. Only 140 000 m³ of timber could be removed in an area of only 30 km² and half of this timber was sold (Kohlhepp *et al.* 1987). In addition to the extraction of construction timber, wood was also to be extracted for the production of charcoal, which was needed in the pig iron works. However, this was not realised. The failure of logging and the inadequate use of the reservoir's timber caused heavy losses of several hundred million US Dollar.

One of the important problems in tropical reservoirs is the mass development of aquatic macrophytes. This causes several problems, e.g., the reduction of the oxygen content of the water and the production of phytoplankton responsible for increased loads of organic material and interference with navigation and fishery. Furthermore,

133 Fearnside has the merit of having pointed out this problem at an early stage and for having explained this in detail in numerous publications, e.g., 1989a; 1997b; 2001a; 2002; 2005, among others.

problems occur with proper flow through turbines and improved living conditions for the vectors of tropical diseases, particularly malaria, schistosomiasis and filariasis.

While in Curuá-Una, the relatively small reservoir of the first hydroelectric plant near Santarém, the macrophyte *Eichhornia crassipes* seriously infected the waters, in Tucuruí because of the low content of nutrients the areas infested have been much smaller than was previously feared (Junk and Mello 1987). Macrophyte areas concentrated on the western bank of the Tucuruí reservoir in an area of approximately 300 km^2.

A favourable situation existed in Tucuruí with the short retention period of water in the reservoir. The water exchange varied from 100 to 120 days between June and October and only 35 to 40 days in the highwater period from November to May. During the peak flow this water retention was only two to three weeks. A quick succession of water renewals leads to better water quality, rapid recovery of oxygen levels and better living conditions for the fish population.

Due to the low content of sedimentary material in clear water rivers, the problem of large sediment deposits did not exist in the Tucuruí reservoir. As deforestation increased, the risk of erosion made protective measures necessary, especially in the peripheral areas of the reservoirs.

Schistosomiasis and Chagas disease occur in the northeast of Brazil, from where there was a massive migration to all projects in Eastern Amazonia. In Tucuruí, a large proportion of the construction workers came from the Northeast, increasing the possibility of the spread of these diseases. The intermediate host of the schistosomiasis disease, the *biomphalaria* water snails, are found in Tucuruí. In the large shore-line areas only periodically flooded, suitable breeding conditions for Anopheles prevail, a high index of malaria infections has been already wide-spread in this region. In Tucuruí, a dramatic impact was caused by mosquitos of the genus *mansonia*. These mosquitoes do not transmit malaria but can transmit several arboviruses. After filling the Tucuruí reservoir, *mansonia* populations, biting night and day, increased tremendously because of breeding grounds in aquatic weeds in the reservoir. This caused a considerable migration of residents to other locations. Especially the settlement area of the Parakanã was affected (Fearnside 1999).

Fishery was a very important subsistence economy in the Tocantins region. The problem of dams is related with the prevention of fish migration to their breeding areas. Fish ladders were not installed at Tucuruí, certainly a negative impact of hindered migration. Parasite infections of fishes did not occur in the first years of the Tucuruí reservoir. Fishermen informed that there were good living conditions for Tucunaré, a commercial fish, in the reservoir. Voracious piscivores live mostly in quiet waters.

The Curupira operation has been widely announced as the largest animal salvage activity ever recorded in the areas to be flooded. Actions of animal salvage were undertaken in cooperation with specialised Brazilian institutes. Although these activities can be interpreted as a signal of environmental awareness – with a lot of public relations propaganda from Eletronorte – it must be stressed that positive effects are doubtful, as the animals invade other habitats and cause environmental pressure.

One of the problems stirring up public discussion was the use of toxic herbicides for clearing rain forest areas for Tucuruí's transmission lines. The use of the herbicide Tordon 101-BR by a contractor in 1981/82 for clearing 300 m wide corridors for the transmission line Tucuruí–Mojú–Belém was proved by a commission of the state of Pará. Cases of animal intoxication and poisoning were related to the use of that herbicide. The Minister of Agriculture of Pará condemned the defoliation activities and initiated legal proceedings against the company. Eletronorte, responsible for the order to clear the corridors, stated in a documentation that there was no scientific proof. As Tordon, which is no longer produced today in Brazil and has a very high dioxin content, was extremely dangerous, its use was banned for defoliation work on large areas. Public discussion had a positive influence.

4.3.3. Resettlement problems and socio-economic impacts of the Tucuruí project

As is well known, the evacuation and resettlement of socially very differentiated large population groups within a short period of time results in fundamental problems. In Tucuruí, Eletronorte put the affected population at 16 637 in November 1982. Two years later this number was fixed at 17 319 due to an accelerating migration process. Eletronorte interpreted this process as a result of "planned invasions" in order to participate in the indemnification process. "Hired occupants" cooperating with land speculators were said to have infiltrated the area, sometimes stirred up by local politicians. Even if this was the case, it was obvious that the resettlement concept in Tucuruí was not much better compared to previous negative experiences in Brazil, such as Sobradinho on the Rio São Francisco or Itaipu on the Rio Paraná (Kohlhepp 1987c).

No planning authority with sufficient executive and financial resources was created, and there was no strategy for comprehensive resettlement and no precise coordination of the corresponding measures (Mougeot 1986). Within four years (1980–1984) about 4000 procedures were carried out. Soon there were complaints against the implementation of compensation, as the procedures did not reflect the reality of regional land ownership and agricultural structures. All the problems known from other projects occurred repeatedly: A large part of the population had squatter status; compensation formalities were based on proof of land titles, and cash compensation for investments by non-landowners was low. The provision of alternative land was slow and uncoordinated, cash payments were devalued by inflation, owners of large farms were supposedly compensated more cheaply, and the resettlement of people was slowed down.

In 1983, a protest movement began, supported by CPT and other NGOs. People refused to move to Nova Jacundá, one of the new urban settlements planned. In fact, the structure and implementation of urban centres for resettled people were significantly changed by the administration and financial constraints of the programme. In 1984, protest actions became more intensive. More than 1000 people camped in Novo Repartimento for weeks, in order to get crop losses indemnified, having been caused by the damming-up of the Tocantins at an earlier date than previously fixed. The protests focused on the period between the expropriation and the provision of new land, as the settlers had stopped their agricultural activities in anticipation of the resettlement, which sometimes took place five years later. Refusal of indemnifications by Eletronorte provoked actions of civil disobedience and was accompanied by blockade actions and military police counteractions.

Fig.16: Tucuruí hydroelectric power plant and reservoir. Relocation of the population

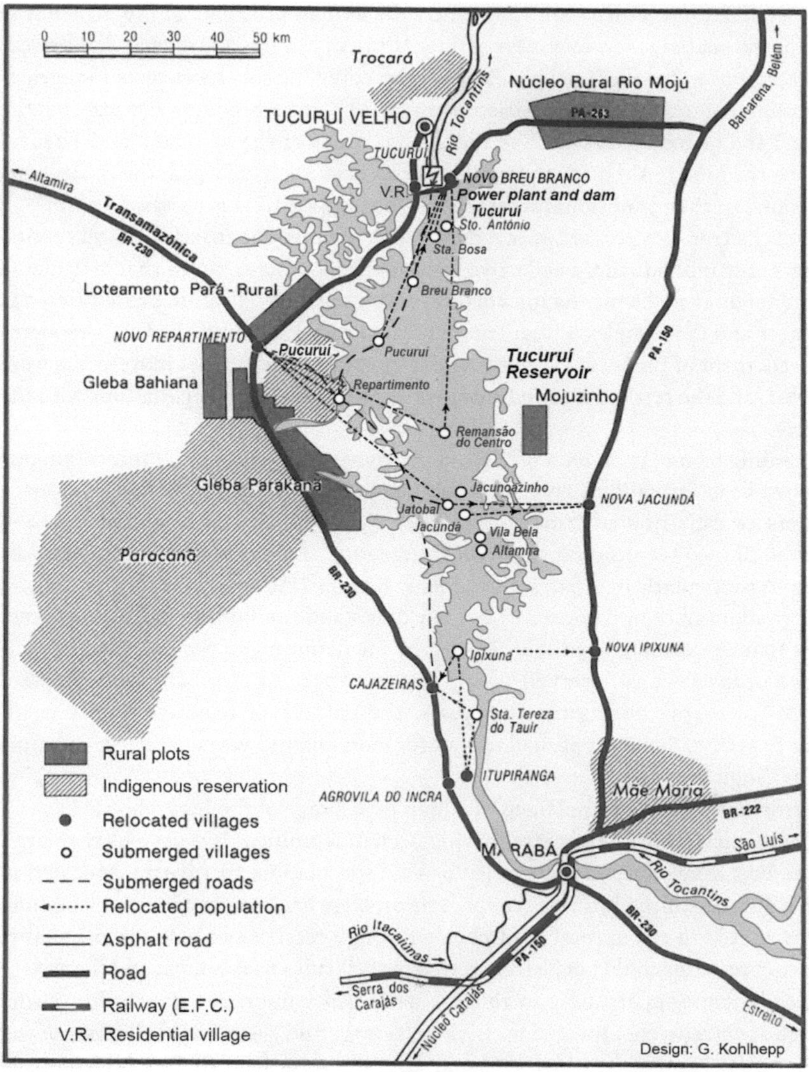

Source: Cf. Kohlhepp (1987b, 237); based on Eletronorte documents.

Fig. 16 gives a detailed survey of the submerged and relocated villages and the directions of the relocation process. Furthermore, the new rural allotments are indicated. There have been many constraints as to a successful rural resettlement: A bad infrastructure for access to land, lack of financial and agrotechnical support as well as of social assistance.

The situation was completely confused in the recently established INCRA agricultural colonisation projects along the Transamazônica near Marabá. Settlement had progressed until 1979, when public authorities already knew that this area would be partially flooded. The Transamazônica had to be partly rerouted north of the Agrovila do INCRA, all investments of the settlers were lost, and institutional and technical investments had no return. Not to mention the human problems of the people who had to be evacuated just a few years after settling in a state-controlled rural project. The compensation for these people did not even cover the transport costs for agricultural equipment to the new destination. The resettlement procedures also affected the Parakanã Indigenous groups.[134] The Indigenous areas of the Parakanã and Pucuruí had to be redefined. Although the total area has been even enlarged, the Indigenous population lost their traditional access to the Tocantins fishing grounds.

When Eletronorte refused to negotiate with groups but insisted on discussing problems only individually, a collective consciousness process began that articulated the fundamental problems. As information about the compensation procedures was very scarce and the complex bureaucracy had created uncertainty, the CPT supported the resettlement of the *posseiros*. Joint solidarity actions and protest movements were organised, and the settlers received advice on how to proceed in negotiations with the company.

According to statistical data of Eletronorte (1986) nearly 4950 indemnification processes had been formalised. 135 000 ha had been acquired for resettlement purposes. 2205 plots were distributed in urban areas (Nova Jacundá 793, Novo Repartimento 669, Novo Breu Branco 568, Itupiranga 75, Cajazeiras 100), 2876 in rural areas. 1222 houses were built, particularly in urban settlements and in the Núcleo Rural Rio Mojú.

The total number of compensation procedures and the number of resettlements suggest that the number of people affected by the damming of the river and the construction of the Tucuruí reservoir was 25 000 to 30 000. As outmigration took place which had occurred during the first years, the number of relocated people could amount to 35 000. Some people had to wait for more than 30 years to receive indemnification (Xingu Vivo 2012).

Eletronorte officials complained of a high percentage of families who sold the urban or rural plots immediately after having been indemnified. It is obvious that large-scale projects were always accompanied by land speculation. In Tucuruí, speculation has been duly organised by some groups. This problem has been known for a long time and was related to the uprooting of people through resettlement. As the original riparian communities could not be transferred in their full social context and there were often no economic opportunities in the new settlements, migration was the result. The new urban centres were provided with water, sewage and electricity facilities, but the situation was characterised by the "usual" disagreement between the big company that builds the settlement and organises the resettlement and the state or municipal bodies that have to bear the related costs.

A visit in October 1986 in one of the "urban" nuclei, Novo Breu Branco, manifested a desolate state of this settlement. Streets were in bad conditions, mounts of garbage piled up without organised deposit, houses already demolished, and the area reserved for expansion was occupied by invasions. This suggests that planners overestimate the self-organisation capacity and private initiative of people who have no experience in this field. The new "ambiente" had been artificially created and the resettled population found no inner bond with it.

134 See chapter I, 4.5.2.

Many problems related to resettlement programmes could be avoided if the organisation started early and made sure to offer people economic alternatives. Indemnification procedures should be duly published and must be transparent to all people affected. Lacking sensibility of large enterprises to the daily problems and to the future existence of the population has been obvious. People have been uprooted and suffer from many physical and psychological problems caused by the shock of modern interference in their lives.

The downstream population on the lower Tocantins river suffered from the radical alteration of the aquatic environment. Fish catch declined by 60 %, which severely restricted the fishermen's ability to survive. The impact of Tucuruí on the Indigenous population[135] was irresponsible. The Tucuruí reservoir flooded parts of three reservations, the Parakanã lost 36 % of their territory. The transmission lines of the Tucuruí power station cut through four Indigenous reservations. The Parakanã tribe was removed five times by FUNAI in the 1970s and finally, in 1982, the remainder of this tribe was transferred by helicopter to a new village (Marudjevara) constructed by Eletronorte. Malaria and other diseases contributed to a high mortality. After a first assistance programme was discontinued in 1979, it was not until years later that a new aid programme was launched, which included health care, primary education, and assistance in securing the reservation's borders. A small amount of compensation was paid to the Gavião tribe for laying the transmission lines through the reservation. However, cash payments of compensation to Indigenous tribes remain problematic because they are not familiar with money and therefore, as in other cases, it is often not put to good use (Fearnside 1999). The allocation of land would have promised more success.

During the peak of civil works in 1982, more than 30 000 workers were contracted, living in four large residential camps near the powerplant site. The number of people employed decreased to 7400 in July 1986. The population directly associated with the Tucuruí project at that time was 22 500.

The Eletronorte company town (*vila residencial*) was very well equipped, and the houses were of good quality. In addition to the efficient "normal" functional inequality, there was a large hospital – probably the best in Pará outside Belém at the time – with excellent facilities, good school equipment, and a large leisure offer with cinemas, sports clubs, and playgrounds. As in many other cases in Brazil, the problem of maintaining a high quality standard after the completion of project implementation was one of the issues discussed by the residents.

Close to the company, the location of the old riparian village of Tucuruí Velho has proven to be extremely problematic. Migrants flooded the village and the population increased dramatically from 4000 (1975) to over 110 000 in 1986. After construction stopped, many of the dismissed workers remained in Tucuruí Velho without the possibility of finding a new job. All the problems that will be described in detail later,[136] occurred: no infrastructural capacity to withstand the existing population pressure, excessive unemployment, deformation of social structures, insecurity, and a high crime rate.

The Tucuruí power plant, which operated with seven main units in April 1986, distributed the electrical energy according to the following scheme: 50 % for the alu-

135 Cf. chapter I.4.5.2.

136 Cf. chapter I.4.5. Cf. Castro and Hébette (1989).

minium industry, 20 % for the state of Pará (17 % Belém), 12 % for Maranhão (São Luís 6 %), 10 % for CHESF (Northeast), 4 % for Goiás and the rest for the construction work in Tucuruí and the operation of CVRD. This shows that the aluminium industry was the dominant consumer.

4.4. Alumina and aluminium industries in the PGC region

4.4.1. General situation and energy prices

Brazilian bauxite deposits in the Amazon were the third largest known deposits in the 1980s. Since the first large bauxite deposits in Amazonia had been discovered in 1966 in the Rio Trombetas area outside the PGC region, these deposits became important for mining in the late 1970s. Within the PGC region, there are significant bauxite reserves in the Paragominas area south of Belém, about 50 % of the known Brazilian deposits. However, the Trombetas deposits were favoured at the beginning of industrial activities.

The international interest in expanding aluminium production in Brazil had political reasons. Due to the – at the time – unstable situation in Jamaica, Guyana and Surinam, the large bauxite producers and the dominant multinationals controlling global aluminium production were looking for new location options. In view of the large raw material deposits in the Amazon region and Brazilian plans for the eastern Amazon, including large hydroelectric power plants, the PGC region became increasingly interesting. The PGC aluminium industry projects began construction when an alarming decline in global aluminium production reflected the extremely difficult situation of economic recession, bauxite surplus and subsequent price collapse. Even in this highly problematic situation, Amazonia was integrated into the volatile world market under the pressure of multinational interests and geopolitical misplanning by the Brazilian government, without taking into account financial, economic and environmental uncertainties.

The shift of aluminium production to developing countries can be seen in the Japanese companies, which reached a production peak of 1.2 mt in 1977, which abruptly declined in 1981 and amounted to only 0.23 mt in 1985. In 1983, Brazil already surpassed Japan in aluminium production, even before the PGC aluminium plants came on stream. In 1986, Brazil reached fifth place in the world ranking of aluminium production with 0.757 mt. The USA reduced its production by 25 % between 1980 and 1985. The decline in aluminium production in the leading industrialised countries was also caused by strict new environmental legislation, which required heavy investment in pollution control equipment.

The most important location factor in aluminium production is a high availability of electrical energy at low prices. On average, electrical energy covers one third of the aluminium production costs. According to Albras/Alunorte industries, 15 400 kwh were needed to produce one ton of aluminium in September 1986, and 1250 kwh for one ton of alumina. High energy prices and, on the other hand, environmental concerns about aluminium plants in industrialised countries – especially in Japan – led to a relocation to developing countries.

With the construction of Tucuruí, Brazil enabled a direct and permanent supply of large amounts of energy to nearby consumers. All over the world, large consumers in the industrial sector received significant price discounts. However, in the case of Tucuruí energy for Alumar and Albras/Alunorte aluminium production prices were exceptionally low. Tucuruí energy prices were US$ 0.032/kwh in September 1986.

In 1986, Albras alone consumed 63 % of Tucuruí's energy production. According to a decree issued by the Ministry of Mines and Energy in August 1979, energy prices for the aluminium plants were to be reduced by 15 %. However, in 1986 the industries paid far less. The figures varied between US$ 0.016 and US$ 0.0075/kwh, i.e., the aluminium industry received a reduction of at least 47 %, but more likely 77 % (Kohlhepp 1987b). If the financing costs of all loans for Tucuruí are taken into account, the rates for electrical energy amounted to only 23 % of the effective energy production costs (Altvater1987b).

Thus, enormous public subsidies of well over a hundred million US Dollar per year were granted to satisfy the aluminium producers. Despite these high subsidies, the production costs for aluminium were higher than the world market prices. This explained the high pressure that the aluminium producers put on the electricity company Eletronorte. The prices for electrical energy had been agreed for a period of 20 years. All attempts to negotiate prices failed because of the aluminium sales crisis, which forced a reduction in production costs to a level that could not be compensated.

When planning the aluminium industries, energy costs had been set at a maximum of 20 % of the world market price for aluminium. Based on the reduced Tucuruí rates, the share of energy costs in the PGC aluminium projects was only between 9.4 and 18.8 %. The subsidisation of energy prices allowed rates of only 37.6 to 75 % of the average energy prices in global aluminium production. In the United States, energy prices in aluminium production were 4.5 times and in Japan even more than 6 times higher than the average Tucuruí price (Kohlhepp 1987b).[137]

4.4.2. Locations of alumina and aluminium plants and status of projects in the second half of the 1980s

4.4.2.1. Albras/Alunorte at Barcarena, Pará

Alumina or aluminium oxide is the biggest cost factor in aluminium production. High quality alumina is required to produce high quality aluminium metal with low environmental impact. The location of the large industrial complex for alumina and aluminium production was determined 40 km south of Belém in the municipality of Barcarena at the port of Vila do Conde (Fig. 11). The decisive factors were the relatively close power generation of Tucuruí (330 km away), which is connected with 500 kV, and the bauxite deposits of the Rio Trombetas, a northern tributary of the Amazon, 1100 km upstream.

CVRD has been active in the bauxite and aluminium sector since 1974. Since the Canadian company Alcan, which had discovered the excellent bauxite in the Trombetas region, was not interested in setting up a bauxite project, CVRD decided to become the main shareholder in the mining company Mineração Rio de Norte (MRN) (46 %;

137 All data based on informations by Eletronorte (Brasília, 24.09.1986), Albras/Alunorte (Barcarena, 25./26.09.1986).

Alcan 19 %; Cia. Bras. de Alumínio 10 %; Billiton-Shell 10 %; Norsk Hydro 10 %; Reynolds 5 %; Alcan Aluminium Ltd. 5 %). A mining project with a capacity of 3.3 mtpy had been planned and the project became profitable when aluminium prices started to rise in the mid-1970s.

Since bauxite export to Japan was not possible at the time for cost reasons – only ships with up to 35 000 tdw could navigate the Trombetas river – a Brazilian-Japanese joint venture in the alumina sector with a plant location in the Amazon region was envisaged. In 1976, the first bilateral contracts were signed and in 1977 the Nippon Amazon Aluminium Co. (Nalco, later Naac) was founded in Japan. CVRD founded Valenorte Alumínio Ltda. as a subsidiary.

Two plants had been planned:

Alumina production: Alunorte (Alumina do Norte do Brasil Ltda.) (Shareholders: CVRD 61 %; Naac 39 %)
Aluminium production: Albras (Alumínio Brasileiro S.A.) (Shareholders: CVRD 51 %; Naac 49 %)

The Japanese involvement in Albras and Alunorte was based on efficient infrastructure, fully financed by Brazil, in particular electric power from Tucuruí, ports and access canals, urban development, roads, etc. Tax incentives were also granted. As the Japanese aluminium production had growth rates of 20 % until 1977 (maximum 1977: 1193 mt), Albras' initial production plan called for 0.64 mtpy of aluminium and 1.3 mtpy of alumina.

In 1981, the financing contract was signed when international prices had passed their peak and the aluminium crisis became obvious. The Japanese contract partners insisted on a production of only 50 % of the earlier plans. Alunorte and Albrás production was scheduled to start in June 1984. The complex was and is one of the largest in the world and the largest in this sector in Latin America. The investment costs for Albrás were US$ 1.3 billion and for Alunorte US$ 0.62 billion. 70 % of the total investment was loans, 30 % was cash from the shareholders. An area of 26 000 ha was acquired in Barcarena for the siting of the facilities. The natural conditions of the port site in Vila do Conde on the banks of the Rio Pará were favourable and allowed access to vessels of 35 000 tdw, as well as in the Rio Trombetas.

Albras commissioned the first production stage (160 000 tpy) in 1985. Alunorte slowed down the implementation of the project due to unfavourable conditions in the world alumina market. CVRD's own bauxite deposit at Rio Trombetas was not used for Albras' aluminium production, as Alunorte's construction did not proceed in the face of low world alumina market prices that could not compensate for its own alumina production. This was the reason officially given by Albras in October 1986, but certainly not the only one, as its competitor Alumar (Alcoa/Shell/Billiton) in São Luís was supplied by MRN (main shareholder CVRD) with bauxite for its integrated alumina industrial complex in São Luís. In contrast, Albras – as Alunorte was not yet completed – imported alumina at compensation prices from Surinam, Venezuela and Jamaica.

In December 1986, Naac announced its withdrawal from the Alunorte project. The Japanese counterparty refrained from further participation in view of the price development and a disagreement with CVRD about the further implementation and financing of the project. The plants, which were only about 50 % completed, were temporarily shut down.[138] In 1987, the president of Albras described the Alunorte project as "paralysed but not dead" (CVRD 1987, *Jornal da Vale* 13: 107).

In the meantime, MRN had increased bauxite production and sales to 4.4 mt, 75 % of which was for export and 25 % for the domestic market, i.e., to supply Alumar in Maranhão. The excellent raw material and the modern port facilities on the Rio Trombetas were therefore not used for CVRD operation in Barcarena.

Albras reached a production of 160 000 t in 1987, which was exported to Japan as well as to Europe and the USA. In the same year, CVRD announced the start of preparations for stage 2 in October 1987, which envisaged a production of 0.32 mtpy of aluminium in 1991. The CVRD-Naac joint venture in Albras remained unaffected by the Alunorte situation. The total investment for Albras had been calculated at US$ 1.369 billion.

There was a long and complicated discussion between the partners on the implementation of stage 2, with the problems being the low aluminium prices on the world market and the appreciation of the yen, which made it necessary for Brazil to negotiate on a US Dollar basis. As Brazil's debt to the Japanese had increased from US$ 3 60million to over US$ 600 million due to the appreciation of the Japanese currency on the international market, a refinancing of US$ 560 million was negotiated with a grace period extended to 8 years and repayment extended to 20 years.

Due to project delays and financial constraints in federal government programmes, the construction and implementation of Barcarena townsite, the project's planned urban centre (*Vila dos Cabanos*), also remained in a precarious state.[139]

4.4.2.2. Alumar at São Luís

The Alumar industrial complex, an alumina refinery and aluminium plant in the southwest of the capital of the state of Maranhão São Luís, was the largest private investment ever registered in Brazil. The total planned investment was US$ 1.5 billion. Alumar's shareholders were Alcoa do Brasil (60 %) and Billiton (40 %). Alcoa do Brasil was a subsidiary of Alcoa, the world's leading aluminium company, which had started operations in Brazil in 1965. Billiton was part of the Royal Dutch Shell group, which was involved in bauxite mining in Trombetas.

Plans to install huge alumina and aluminium industries had already led to protests in advance. There were fears from scientists that environmental impacts such as water pollution, air pollution and damage to ecological conditions would negatively affect the Baixada Maranhense (Ab'Sáber 1996b). This was especially true since the expansion of the metropolitan region of São Luís had already led to major environmental damage, which would be exacerbated by the coming heavy immigration.

The start-up phase of the integrated production of alumina and aluminium began in August 1984 with 500 000 tpy of alumina and 100 000 tpy of aluminium. The second phase was opened at the end of 1986, when aluminium production reached 245 000 tpy. In 1984, the Brazilian consortium Camargo Corrêa, originally a construction company with commitments to major projects throughout Brazil and now systematically diversifying its activities, acquired 35 % of the shares of Alcoa do Brasil.

---

138 During the visit of the author in August 1987 (cf. Kohlhepp 1987b).

139 See chapter 4.4.4.

Alumar's site was located in the port area and allowed for the unloading of bauxite from Trombetas. The port was used exclusively by Alumar and was equipped to unload vessels up to 40 000 tdw. An area of 1700 ha was set aside for the construction of the plant in the industrial area of São Luís, 25 km from the city centre. Another large area was reserved for the deposit of red mud and for an environmental buffer zone. In mid-1986, Tucuruí supplied the Alumar company with one third of its production of 5 turbines. The power grid of Tucuruí transported electrical energy via Marabá–Imperatriz to São Luís with a transmission line of 500 kV over a distance of 1030 km.

Unlike Albras, Alumar was supplied by MRN with bauxite from Trombetas. As MRN's prices were five to six times higher than Australian bauxite (excluding transport costs), Alcoa planned to open mining in its own deposits in the Trombetas region. The very modern facilities of Alumar, the leader in Brazilian aluminium production, allowed for integrated industrial processing of bauxite–alumina–aluminium. In the late 1980s, there were even discussions about expanding Alumar's production from 0.5 mtpy of alumina to 3 mtpy and from 245 000 to 380 000 tpy of aluminium. Alumar's calculations depended on the multinational strategies of Alcoa and Billiton, and it was difficult to compare their raw material policies with those of Albras/Alunorte.

4.4.3. Environmental problems at the alumina-aluminium projects of the PGC-region

During the construction of the Alumar industrial complex, environmental movements protested against the huge, land-intensive plants for the production of alumina and aluminium, which had been built without prior public discussion or detailed information. Apart from the impacts of the construction with deforestation, destruction of mangrove areas and resettlement of settlers, the problems of retention and dumping of the highly toxic red mud produced in the refining process of alumina production were particularly alarming. The ratio is: 1000 kg of alumina = 830 kg of red mud. These residues, which contain very toxic and corrosive substances, are the reason for the pollution of the groundwater (Kohlhepp 1987b; Kohlhepp *et al.* 1987).

The initial confusion was compounded when the Secretary of Natural Resources, Technology and Environment, responsible for the control of industrial activities in Maranhão, declared that his agency was unable to carry out this task because of a lack of qualified technicians. The public distrusted not only the monitoring capabilities, but also the pressure capacity of the national authorities towards the multinationals. NGOs and government representatives were convinced that public protests contributed significantly to environmental protection measures.

Alumar had 1800 ha of land for its huge facilities and conveyor belts. 2000 ha were officially ceded to Alumar and used for the ponds to deposit red mud. Each pond had an area of 15 ha and was sealed at the bottom with a 40 cm layer of compacted clay, covered with a protective PVC sheet to prevent groundwater intrusion. The solids settled while the liquids were returned to the refinery's tanks by pumps. This water recycling process allowed the company to significantly reduce water consumption, which had originally been a critical point in the evaluation of the plant site and in the public discussion.

The area of 2000 ha has to be transformed after the soil is reprocessed and new green areas must be created. The PVC layer under the red mud remained unless this material could be reused in the ceramic or cement industry. At that time, in Japan red mud was still deposited in the sea.

To retain the residues, a drainage system and a rainwater control system were installed. The wastewater was treated in a sewage plant, the only one in Maranhão. Air pollution was greatly reduced by meeting the filtering conditions of highly industrialised countries. A green buffer zone of 5000 ha was acquired and ceded to the government on the condition that Alumar take responsibility for this area. Obviously, this area served more for the plant's own safety and to avoid compensation payments to adjacent residential areas in case of emissions than for the protection of natural vegetation. Cooperation with universities and specialised institutes was carried out with monitoring programmes regarding soil, vegetation, water quality and special projects (e.g., marine biology).

In the 1980s, alumina and aluminium production in industrialised countries faced extensive environmental regulations and protests against the traditional locations of these industries. In Japan in particular, relocating these plants to developing countries was therefore one of the solutions. Among many foreign investors in this industrial sector, the idea of installing industries with lower environmental standards prevailed. The Amazon and the PGC development programme with subsidies and tax benefits from the Brazilian government was one of the most attractive options. While the Military Government was initially very keen on high investment and approved a weak control system for environmental damage, re-democratisation in the second half of the 1980s allowed for public discussion and protest movements and helped to introduce ecologically appropriate production conditions. The activities of some well-organised NGOs contributed to the improvement of environmental protection measures in industrial production.

The Albras/Alunorte plants in Barcarena were only partially operational in the mid-1980s. As the construction of the alumina power plant was considerably delayed and partly cancelled, there were no problems with red mud at that time. Ecological studies were only carried out after construction had already begun. According to the company, Albras' environmental protection measures met Japanese standards.

Due to the difficult economic situation of the aluminium industry, the administrative problems with Japanese colleagues and the political conflict of competence between federal and regional state authorities, it remained questionable whether the environmental protection measures would be maintained at all levels. This was already the case with the construction of the new townsite of Barcarena and its environmental impact.

4.4.4. Socio-economic impacts of large projects

The spatial impact of large-scale projects directly affects the local or regional population. In fact, large areas of land were expropriated and most settlers – as is common in Brazil – did not have land titles for the rural or urban properties they used or occupied. Since information about the planned projects was always sparse and usually arrived late, rumours increased the uncertainty of the affected population. Without consideration of the vital needs of the population, usually without economic alternatives, the resettlement programmes were often – sometimes intentionally – not planned in advance but were carried out unexpectedly and had catastrophic effects on the population. The affected people were often blamed for standing in the way of planners. They were terrified of the coming problems, in many cases unable to articulate themselves, unresponsive to the logic of the planners, trying to escape their despair on an emotional level and completely confused by the discussions that were incomprehensible to them. The breakdown of social interactions of those to be resettled can never be compensated.

The implementation of large-scale projects was not coordinated in any way with regional or local administrations and – even worse – no financial provision was made for the socio-economic and spatial design of the emerging scenarios. This was not the fault of the municipal urban planning departments – if they existed at all at that time – but the problem of higher-level decisions and the lack of responsibility to pragmatically analyse and remedy the consequences. Given the poor situation of most of those directly affected, it was not surprising that they sometimes believed dubious consultants or lawyers, which complicated their situation.

The initial high attraction of large-scale projects can be explained in most cases by the employment capacity of construction companies. The possibility to get a job even without special professional qualifications, to eat and live in the contractors' camps led to a high rate of migration to the project areas. The socio-economic structures of the project suddenly changed. New patterns of organisation were "imported". Prices for goods and services rose rapidly. New neighbourhoods emerged with expanding prostitution around the construction workers' camps. Immediately after the completion of parts of the project or the end of project work, most of the temporary migrants working at the site faced economic collapse as their employment contracts ended. Often, workers were treated very badly by the subcontractors and there were even fraudulent contracts.

Very often there was no alternative employment or continuation of contracts in other projects. On the other hand, many of the workers were socially uprooted, so there was no return to the region of origin. Without wages, food and housing, they contributed to the mass of people without a livelihood, which led to the extremely high growth rates in the urban centres. Large favelas emerged, invasions of urban properties were commonplace, and crime rates increased significantly. Left alone to deal with these problems, the local administration was overwhelmed and helpless in view of the scarce budgetary resources and the extent of the extremely serious problems. The infrastructural capacities were exhausted at all levels and in all areas.

Large-scale projects often lead to enclaves with artificial structures that are spatially isolated. Access to the company towns is strongly controlled and socially segregated from the surrounding area. Polarisation effects prevail and intra-regional disparities steadily increase. Spreading effects, as expected in theoretical conceptions, rarely occurred and when they did, interactions were again segregated. Social contacts could not be realised in the informal sector either. The supply of food could not be provided regionally, and the supply of the company towns was organised from outside the region.

Since participation in economic progress has been reserved for a relatively small number of people with permanent jobs, – workers with higher qualifications are often not of regional origin – resentment and envy are widespread and social tensions and conflicts of interest with the excluded majority are rapidly increasing. Lack of perspectives further restrict the scope of life and action of those people who could actually be called "victims of the planners." It is not only a financial problem to look for solutions, but a fundamental question of human dignity to deal decently with the problems of those affected. Special attention needs to be paid to the subcontractors' employment contracts and the treatment of the workers.

This socio-economic situation of large-scale projects of the 1980s has unfortunately not changed in recent years and can still be observed today in many of the state-organised or private projects in Amazonia and throughout Brazil. Appropriate parts of the project costs should be reserved for accompanying measures to minimise the social and ecological impacts.

Case study: São Luís/Maranhão in the 1980s

São Luís had an urban population of 124 000 in 1960, which increased through natural growth to 168 000 (1970) and 183 000 (1980). The district of Anil in the municipality of São Luís, on the other hand, increased its urban population from 38 000 (1970) to 222 000 (1980). This quarter of the São Luís urban area received most of the high immigration to São Luís in the second half of the 1970s, when the PGC projects were announced.

In 1987, the urban population of the São Luís conurbation was more than 650 000 people. The capital of the state of Maranhão, which became one of the cornerstones of the PGC, was literally overrun by a completely uncontrollable wave of migration from the neighbouring states of the Northeast and from the interior of Maranhão. The average growth rate of the São Luís population was 8 % per year between 1980 and 1985.[140]

In PGC project planning, the municipality of São Luís lost 190 km^2 for large project areas, especially for the CVRD and Alumar projects and an area reserved for a planned steel industry (Siderbras). The construction of Alumar resulted in the resettlement of more than 20 000 people. CVRD reported that 700 squatters were living on the company's land. They were compensated and resettled in a 44 ha area ("hill of hope"), which was acquired by the company and equipped with basic infrastructure measures: water and electricity supply, school, social centre, recreation area. A special housing programme was implemented by the CVRD for low-income workers.

There was no coordination with the town planning department during the construction work. The urban planners of São Luís shared that enormous migration at the beginning of the 1980s had disastrous effects on the urban infrastructure. In addition, federal interference occurred in the activities of the National Housing Bank (BNH). Large areas of land were acquired from private landowners, in some cases far outside the urban core area. The BNH started to build its standard houses in drab neighbourhoods without social infrastructure. The BNH settlements for more than 25 000 people did not meet the needs of the lowest social strata. But even for families earning a regular minimum wage, only transport costs from the SAB area to the city's tertiary sector or to school for three people per family amounted to the minimum wage.

All transport facilities for this population had to be organised by the municipality and had to be subsidised. The enormous social costs of the population increase could not be compensated by tax income of the municipal administration, as tax exemption and reductions were conceded to large projects and other taxes were not on the

140 Demographic data according to the municipal administration of São Luís. In 2022, the São Luís metropolitan area had a population of 1.63 million (IBGE 2023).

municipal level. Land speculation has been unimaginable. Prices for ground, houses and apartments have increased to such an extent that industries and even CVRD were building houses for their staff.

The permanent employment effect of the projects in São Luís after the end of construction works was no more than 2500 jobs. However, for the higher-ranking jobholders working conditions, professional training, and social facilities, even for their families, were very good.

About 30 % of the city area had been "invaded". The city administration had no financial means to implement an alternative housing concept for the *favela* population. Only less than 55 % of the city's population had a regular water supply, 39 % had sewage systems, and only 18 % were picked up by the rubbish collection. According to a São Luís city planning officer, urban planning was reduced to a mere and inefficient management of a mess caused by the inappropriate and uncoordinated approach to major projects.

Case study: Barcarena/Pará

A department of urban development (Codebar) had been established as part of a federal agency to build the urban area for the Albras/Alunorte industrial complex. In contrast to São Luís, all urban facilities had to be created in Barcarena, 40 km south of Belém. An area of 26 000 ha was acquired. The resettlement of the 482 squatter families living in this area was organised by setting up an "agricultural colony" on a very small area of only 1200 ha with plots of 2.5 ha per family. Because of the good market access in the new town or in nearby Belém, an intensive agricultural production model with horticulture was planned. Since the resettled population was not used to horticulture and the natural conditions in the area were also poor, this project failed. It was a typical example of the dreams of irresponsible planners who completely lacked local expertise. The shock of the construction of an industrial macro-project had driven away many settlers who had previously practised subsistence farming and fishing. Some migrated to Belém or the surrounding area when they were compensated and sold their rural properties.

In September 1986, despite the activities of a small working group of Albras in the social sector and some agricultural projects with the University of Pará (fishpond, etc.), the "colony" was in a desolate state (Kohlhepp *et al.* 1987; Castro and Carmo 2019): isolated, insufficient water supply, extremely poor central facilities, no school equipment, no medical care, no medicines. The children rarely attended classes as they had to walk long distances. This situation was caused by the political struggle between Albras (federal level) and the Pará state authorities. The large-scale Barcarena project was set up without prior consultation with the community and the state administration. However, the latter had to pay for the sudden costs incurred by the municipality. In view of an investment volume for the industrial complex of almost US$ 2 billion, it was hard to believe that there were no funds available to secure the existence of the resettled population.

More than 50 subcontracting companies occupied the area with 12 000 workers. Conditions were precarious and workers protested about food quality. The suppliers' camps extended to the small village of Vila do Conde. Traditional social relations and small-scale economic structures were completely deformed by the impact of the camps and the spread of prostitution. As in many other cases, the superficial economic boom collapsed after the construction work was completed. The unskilled workers were laid off and the flow of money collapsed.

The main task for Codebar was the planning and implementation of a town with about 50 000 inhabitants. An excellent plan had been prepared in the early 1980s, but by 1986 this project was in a precarious situation. Delays and partial paralysis of the projects did not attract many migrants to Barcarena. At the time of the author's visit, only 800 families were living there. Due to the slow development of the "town," no shop owners were interested in setting up shops. The few shops had a range of low quality and high prices. Some of the establishments were already dilapidated. The residents of Barcarena were annoyed by the inadequate water supply and the lack of sewage facilities, as the sewage flowed directly into the Rio Murucupí, which was planned as a recreational area. The population protested because of the poor infrastructure and an open rubbish dump that was constantly burning. Codebar claimed that the difficulties were caused by the poor execution of the work by the contractors. However, the reason was the aforementioned problem of disagreement between the federal and state/municipal levels on all details of project implementation.

Besides these problems, there were the "usual" conflicts between the people from outside, the "arrogant *mineiros*" – in the eyes of the people of Pará – with better education and their "expert" status, and the local population, mostly made up of unskilled people. The *mineiros*, engineers and technicians from Minas Gerais with an industrial background, were full of prejudice against the population of Pará. They considered them lazy and unreliable. Sometimes social conflicts broke out. 62 % of workers in a higher position came from Minas Gerais (32 %), Rio de Janeiro and São Paulo, only 14 % were born in Pará. At the middle level, 35 % are from the Southeast of Brazil, 46 % from Pará. At the lowest level of employment, 80 % are from the Amazon and only 7 % from the Southeast.

The technicians of the different companies and of Codebar often lived in Belém, or when the opportunity arose, they fled from Barcarena to Belém. Most of the employees in the company town lived in a ghetto situation with little leisure time. The transport links to Belém were poor. One bus company monopolised transport by bus and ferry. Since direct shipping to Belém and back cost up to 10 % of the minimum wage, people felt trapped. This situation led to enormous problems and tensions as well as high job mobility.

4.5. Problems of regional development and conflicts in the PGC region

4.5.1. Deforestation in East Amazonia

Compared to the very rapidly increasing and alarming forest destruction during the agricultural colonisation process in Rondônia through cattle ranching projects and the mostly careless activities and impacts of road construction networks, even the large-scale projects such as Tucuruí and the Serra dos Carajás iron ore project had a relatively low rate of deforestation. However, since the construction of the Brasília–Belém road (BR-010), rain forest destruction has been a pervasive phenomenon in Pará, east of the Rio Tocantins, in the southeast of the state and in large-scale projects in Maranhão. Deforestation was no longer concentrated in corridor-like zones along the main roads (Transamazônica, BR-230; BR-222, etc.) (cf. Fig. 11), but expanded to areas further inland, such as remote Gurupí and the central Rio Pindaré region.

One of the most affected PGC regions in the 1980s was the municipality of Marabá, the PA-150 state road south of Marabá and the PA-275 (cf. Figs. 12 and 13) to the border of the CVRD concession area. Charcoal production for the pig iron industry was the most important and devastating factor. Fig. 17 clearly shows the spatial impact of this clearing process, especially between 1977 and 1985. Since 1985, the forests along the road between Marabá and Parauapebas on the edge of the Serra dos Carajás, the main axis of migration, have been almost completely destroyed. In the 1980s, the pioneer fronts moved far beyond the Rio Tocantins to the west and approached the Rio Xingu. Economic interests and excessive land speculation increasingly focused on the region between these two river systems.

Fig. 17: Deforestation in the Carajás region: Marabá–Xinguara 1972–1985

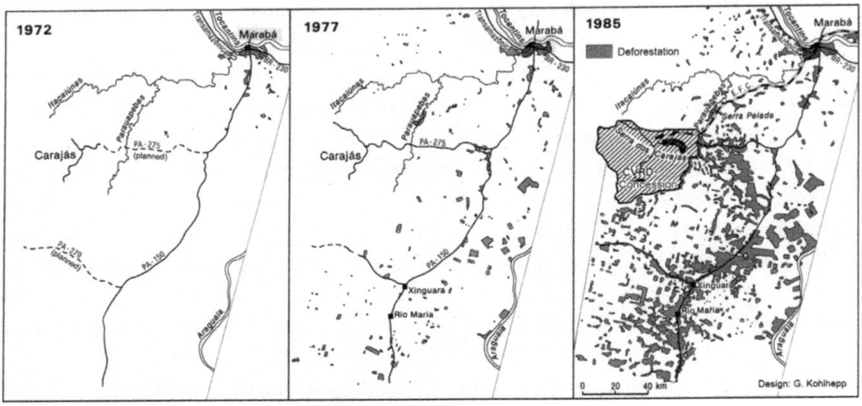

Source: Cf. Kohlhepp (1987b); based on *Jornal do Brasil*, August 3, 1986.

The evaluation of Landsat satellite images for a region of 280 000 km² (= 31 % of the PGC region) in eastern Pará and western Maranhão made it possible to quantify deforestation. In 1979, almost 10 % of the forest area had been cleared. In the large municipalities of Paragominas and Imperatriz, this factor was 16 % and 32 % respectively. There were municipalities where more than 60 % of the area had been cleared, most of them in a short period of less than 10 years. By the mid-1980s, according to INPE, forest destruction in the PGC region, originally two-thirds covered by rain forest, had expanded to 28–30 %, with an annual growth rate of 3–4 %. In the state of Maranhão, with a natural rain forest cover of only 56 %, deforestation had already reached 62 % of the forest area by 1988.

As the IBDF regulations with the 50 % clause to protect the forest were generally not respected, there was neither a management structure nor the political intention to effectively control deforestation activities. Afforestation planning was not scientifically sound. The law that was supposed to encourage charcoal producers to reforest could not be implemented from the beginning. Official bodies did not provide any impetus through information campaigns or active support.

Not even the majority of the livestock projects officially approved by SUDAM complied with the Forest Code. Monitoring was extremely difficult due to the poor IBDF infrastructure. But even when violations of the Code were uncovered, fines were small and there was ample scope for evading official prosecution. The forest clearing activities of the large landowners had turned to modern technology. Power saws were widespread, and even the use of huge chains – 80 to 100 m long, weighing 10 t – pulled by tractors or caterpillars was common in regions where the trees had shallow roots, i.e., in forest areas with *cerradão* vegetation.

As for the extent of the acceleration of deforestation, some figures might illustrate recent trends in the 1980s:

It took the following number of man-days to clear one hectare of rainforest (Valverde 1987):

- using axis in the traditional method of wood-cutting without technological input and the availability of cheap manpower: 42 man/days
- using motor saw: 2 man/days
- using tractors and chains: 0.1 man/days

Specialised subcontractors (*empreiteiras*) carried out this "modern" version of deforestation and tried to fulfil their contracts as quickly as possible. They cared neither about the ecological nor the social impacts.

Thus, in addition to the already known ecological impacts of deforestation such as increased solar radiation, erosion problems, catastrophic changes in evapotranspiration and the entire water cycle, regional climatic impacts were observed for the first time: changes in the periodicity and length of the rainy season and dry sub-periods, reduction in rainfall. The use of heavy machinery had serious consequences, such as the compaction of soils or the complete tangling of the upper soil horizons due to the uprooting of trunks and roots.

In some cases, it was even possible to prove the use of "Agent Orange" for defoliation, which may have been smuggled in via the Manaus free trade zone. This was the case with a company in the municipality of Tailândia/Pará that laid high-voltage power lines from Tucuruí.[141] Fieldwork of the author in 1974 revealed two – isolated – cases of cattle farms near Paragominas that had conducted experiments with highly toxic chemicals to defoliate and increase the rate of burning.

Timber industry concentrated in Açailândia, Imperatriz, Marabá or Paragominas contributed to the extinction of many highly rated precious wood species, such as: mahogany (*Swietenia macrophylla*), rose wood (*Aniba roseodora*), maçaranduba (*Manilkara huberi*), ipê (*Tabebuia sp.*), jatobá (*Hymenaea martiana*), sucupira (*Diplotropia purpurea*), cedro-rosa (*Cedrela sp.*), angelim pedra (*Hymenolobium excelsum*), copaiba (*Copaifera multijuga*), piquiá (*Caryocar villosum*), tatajuba (*Bagassa guianensis*) etc. As the road network has been constantly expanded and improved, logging has increased excessively.

The already mentioned destruction of *Bertholletia excelsa* in the regions of Marabá, Ituporanga, Jacundá, Tucuruí and São João do Araguaia led to a 55 % decline in Brazil nut production (in Marabá from 1979–1985: 85 %). However, the most important reason was not the loss of Brazil nut area (1979–1983: 11 %), but a significant decline in the pro-

141 Cf. chapter I, 4.3.2.

ductivity of the *Bertholletia* stocks, the *castanhais*. During the period mentioned, productivity dropped by 49 %, probably due to the dry fog after burning, which paralyses insect pollination activity.

The acceleration of deforestation was often related to the indiscriminate use of fire. Due to very remote locations and lack of access, timber transport was sometimes impossible and even rare timber was destroyed. Land speculation purposes, which attempted to prove continuous land use, made burning an economic activity with a claim to land titles. The economy of the collectors was affected by the destruction of Brazil nut, *Hevea brasiliensis, Castilloa ulei* and other medicinal plants used mainly by the Indigenous population. Deforestation has destroyed their knowledge of natural resources and threatened the livelihood of Indigenous people in the PGC region.

The announcement of agrarian reform in the post-military period accelerated deforestation. Large areas of forest were cleared to demonstrate effectively organised land use – mostly defined as pasture – to secure land titles, improve credit opportunities and eventually prevent encroachment by land squatters, especially along roads. The flawed structures of the federal and state governments had permanently allowed overexploitation of forests, sometimes even involving public officials in dubious logging operations and questionable environmental impact assessments. By the late 1980s, the acceleration of tropical forest destruction in the PGC region was alarming.

4.5.2. Problems of the Indigenous population in the PGC region

As already mentioned,[142] the new agency FUNAI (National Indian Foundation) was unfortunately not able to fulfil the expectations for the protection of Indigenous groups. Subordinated to the Ministry of the Interior, FUNAI had to operate within the strict limits of the national guidelines for the development of the Amazon region. Under these conditions, its main task was to accelerate the so-called integration of Indigenous groups and to create a "free space" for the undisturbed implementation of projects in accordance with the decisions of the National Security Council of the Military Government.

In the 1970s, church organisations began a new phase of altruistic direct and indirect support for the Indigenous population. The CIMI (Conselho Indigenista Missionário) promoted the first Indigenous assemblies at regional and national level with groups that had been contacted decades before. This created an awareness of a common destiny among the tribes. The involvement of religious institutions was observed with restraint and sometimes rejection and obstruction by the Military Government. Especially in Eastern Amazonia, Indigenous groups began to free themselves from exploitation under the economic tutelage of FUNAI. The Gaviões, for example, began to directly market the products of their collective economy, especially the Brazil nut.

Starting from the discussion on human rights, in 1979 some Indigenous groups gained new allies in the urban sphere, especially intellectuals and certain professional organisations. The Brazilian Association of Anthropology, in commentaries, strongly criticised the government's planning in the Amazon and the abolition of FUNAI as the coordinating body for Indigenous affairs at the level of decision-making. In 1980, the Union of Indigenous Peoples was founded but not officially recognised. In 1982,

142 Cf. chapter I, 3.2.

when the Xavante *cacique* Mário Juruna was sensationally elected as a member of parliament, a permanent parliamentary commission on Indigenous problems was set up. This commission had to examine every law relating to Indigenous peoples that was presented to Congress. It was also decided to restructure FUNAI. Although 10 presidents replaced each other within only four years, this goal was by no means achieved. Despite the beginning of public discussion and the direct participation of Indigenous leaders in politics, some laws passed Congress that significantly restricted the Indigenous rights guaranteed in the Federal Constitution.

Once again, it became clear that economic interests far outweighed the fundamental interests of those Indigenous groups who, in the official language, "were not economically active but occupied large areas." This statement showed a complete lack of understanding and sympathy for an ethnic group threatened with extinction.

Despite the political commitment to demarcate all Indigenous territories, only 14 % of these territories were regulated at the beginning of 1982. In 1983 (Decree 88.118), the demarcation procedure was provocatively changed by setting up a working group with representatives of some ministries and other federal and regional authorities, defined as "expedient." In the same year, the government released access to mechanised mining by public or private companies in all Indigenous territories. Even the Geological Society of Brazil published a document in November 1984 that classified the known mineral deposits in Indigenous reservations as unnecessary. Furthermore, the attempt to legally prohibit the execution of all public works in Indigenous territories without the consent of the National Congress failed.

When the PGC intensified its activities in Eastern Amazonia in the early 1980s, the prevailing situation was characterised by increasing social tensions (Schmink 1982; Schmink and Wood 1984; 1992; Hall 1989) and an alarming number of encroachments on Indigenous territories in the area and – despite legal obligations – total insecurity towards Indigenous groups. There was no concrete concept for the future of the Indigenous population, which was severely affected by the large-scale projects planned and partly under construction in the eastern regions of Amazônia Legal. In the PGC region, an Indigenous population of more than 13 000 people lived in scattered so-called "Indigenous areas" or "Indigenous reservations," which were mostly endangered by road construction and invasions.

There were 32 of these areas in south-eastern Pará, in Maranhão and – exceptionally – in northern Goiás (today's state of Tocantins) (cf. Fig. 11). Several different Indigenous groups lived in the PGC region with completely different conditions of contact with the non-Indigenous population. While the Guajajara of Maranhão, the largest tribe with more than 6000 people, could look back on a long tradition of more than 300 years of contacts, there lived several Parakanã groups that were only identified and contacted in the early 1980s. The fact that more than 75 000 km^2 were classified as "Indigenous territories," i.e., 8 % of the PGC region, does not show the problems that the Indigenous population faced in the mid-1980s.

As mentioned above,[143] the CVRD, as the main actor in the PGC region, was involved in the decisions about the future of the Indigenous population, in particular in the World Bank loan and the agreement with FUNAI.

143 Cf. chapter I,4.3.2.1.

The Indigenous population of Maranhão (85 % of the total Indigenous population of the CVRD area of influence) belonged to the following language groups and tribes:

Tupi: Guajajara ,Guajá, Urubu-caapor, Tembé
They were living mostly in rainforest areas.
Gê: Gavião, Cricati, Timbira, Pucobié, Rancocamecra, Apeniecra, Canela
These tribes were living in forest regions and/or in *campo cerrado* areas.

The forest tribes of Pará (11% of CVRD+s area of influence) belonged to:

Tupi: Paracanã, Assurini, Suruí, Anambé
Gê: Kayapó, Xicrin, Cararaô, Gavião

In 1986, 12 territories had been demarcated in Maranhão, 6 in Pará and one in Goiás. The terminology and definition of the legal status of Indigenous territories may be resumed shortly:

"identified": technical reports had been approved by FUNAI; delimitation forthcoming
"delimited": proposed by FUNAI; homologated by a decree of the President of Brazil
"demarcated": land survey executed; demarcation work homologated
"homologated and registered at SPU": areas defined by a presidential act and duly registered as an inalienable estate of the Republic (SPU: Serviço do Patrimônio da União).

It is important to emphasise that even the majority of demarcated and homologated Indigenous territories were still not registered with the SPU.

Even the highest legal guarantee did not mean that the status and boundaries of Indigenous territories were respected by groups with conflicting economic interests. Since the boundaries were often drawn without anthropological knowledge, the borders were sometimes at odds with the basic needs of the Indigenous population. Therefore, occasionally even the Indigenous tribes ignored the "artificial" boundaries of their territories, which led to additional conflicts.

The ecological knowledge of Indigenous tribes was not respected and their land use, which contributes to the protection of biodiversity, was not appreciated (Posey 1982; 1985a, b). Posey's (1987) research on the Kayapó, among others, emphasised that irretrievable knowledge of ethnoecology, ethnopedology, ethnopharmacology and ethno-agronomy had been lost.

In the 1980s, there was a multitude of highly urgent problems related to Indigenous territories (Schmink 1982; Schmink and Wood 1984; Hall 1989), only a few of which can be addressed here:

Lack of demarcation: This was the case in the Cricatí area near Imperatriz in Maranhão. They assumed a fraudulent delimitation of their territory. The high voltage line of Eletronorte from Tucuruí crossed the area of the Cricatí. They were compensated for clearing a 100 m corridor, but according to the tribe's *cacique*, this was not done properly. The Cricatí (325 people) refused to double the Eletronorte line, which led to a dangerous situation.

The Guajá were hunter-gatherers and used a wide range of shifting. The 250 people lived outside the officially recognised territories, and some of them remained unknown until September 1985. Their territories in Maranhão, parts of the Gurupí Forest Reserve established in 1961, were divided by a large corridor planned for a future railway line from the Paragominas bauxite deposit to São Luís. Two "points of attraction" were established in the valley of the Rio Gurupí, but the Guajá refused contact and occasionally attacked prospecting teams and road workers. As the Gurupí forest reserve had been badly affected, the problem proved to be extremely complicated.

Invasion problems: In eight Indigenous territories in Eastern Pará and Maranhão, the worsening invasion problems should have been urgently addressed. Squatters, logging companies, Brazil nut collectors, cattle ranching projects, *garimpeiros* and mining companies were identified as the "usual" invaders.

The Kayapó reservation (population of 1400), located far to the southwest of the CVRD concession area, gained notoriety in a tragic way when the Indigenous population desperately resisted the activities of a *fazendeiro* who illegally invaded their territory and killed 21 workers.

The presence of *garimpeiros* in Indigenous territories either led to violent clashes such as attacks or the occupation of airstrips, or the contacts had dire consequences, as they spread disease, alcohol and prostitution.

One of the most complicated problems was the eviction of squatters from Indigenous areas. Since the solutions took a long time, the affected Indigenous tribes used the strategy of putting pressure on the institutions. Road connections were disrupted, bridges destroyed and even hostages taken. Due to the high population pressure on "unoccupied" land in Maranhão, the invasion problems could only be solved through land reform measures, which did not take place.

4.5.2.1. Consequences of PGC projects affecting the Indigenous population

The Carajás railway line caused an overlap in the Indigenous territories of Mãe-Maria, Caru and Pindaré (Fig. 11). The example of the Gavião (173 people) in Mãe-Maria (Figs. 16, 17), 40 km northeast of Marabá, was only the culmination of a long period of forced encroachment on Gavião territories. Traditionally, the Gavião exploited Brazil nuts. In competition with the non-Indigenous population in the region, the Gavião became cheap labour as Brazil nut collectors and eventually came under the control of FUNAI. In 1976, they decided to market their products directly. When the Eletronorte transmission lines cut 150 m wide corridors into their territory and some groups were additionally affected by the damming of the Rio Tocantins, the Gavião agreed to relocate the new village of Mãe-Maria in 1979. The basis of the settlement was the payment of compensation for the loss of their Brazil nut areas, large timber reserves, hunting grounds, fields and villages. It was one of the first examples of compensation agreements with planned cash payments in advance. However, the Gavião had to defend themselves with blockades and protests against a fraudulent calculation by the regional FUNAI authority and only received the money after four years, which in the meantime had been devalued by inflation (Vidal 1986).

That is why they were warned when the construction of the Carajás railway began in 1982, which was cut through their reserve over a length of 27 km and passed by their new village at a distance of only 3 km. Since sale of Brazil nuts had dropped to less than 5 % of the previous quantities and the daily passage of up to 15 iron ore and passenger trains[144] significantly reduced their hunting opportunities, the compensation payments had to be used to strengthen educational institutions and support their agricultural activities. They insisted that compensation payments be advanced by the CVRD, which was responsible for railway construction. With the help of blockades of the construction work, they finally succeeded in obtaining fair compensation, which was, however, extremely difficult to determine. The CVRD contracts were regularly executed. This could be confirmed through site visits and discussions with lawyers from both sides.

The situation of the two other Indigenous territories Caru (312 members of the Guajajara and Guajá tribes) and Pindaré (337 Guajajara) along the railway line was already highly endangered before railway construction began. Large landowners, with the support of the Maranhão state government, "bought" land also within the Gurupí forest reserve. *Fazendeiros*, squatters and road construction companies had to reduce their areas considerably. Land conflicts and invasions led to an obvious degeneration of Indigenous communities, which was exacerbated by the influence of railway traffic.

As mentioned earlier, charcoal production for pig iron factories increased the pressure of deforestation by sawmills on Indigenous areas, causing fear and unrest. The attacks on the rain forest areas of the Indigenous reservations could hardly be controlled and threatened the fatal collapse of Indigenous communities. In 1986, the number of uprooted Indigenous people migrating to neighbouring towns increased, causing significant problems. In Marabá, the Casa do Indio was overcrowded, maintained to care for and protect migrant Indigenous people from negative influences in the urban area. Dozens of Suruí came here because living conditions in their area were deteriorating. In São Luís, the problems were even worse.

Case study: Cateté (Kayapó-Xicrim)

Initially, mining activities in the Serra dos Carajás had no impact on the Cateté reservation, which lies to the west of the CVRD concession area. The migration from Marabá to the southwest was blocked, the CVRD set up observation posts and maintained a protection zone between the Serra dos Carajás and Cateté. During the author's visit in September 1986, the danger was much greater due to numerous *garimpeiros* and squatters entering the area via the newly opened road to São Félix do Xingu (cf. Figs. 11, 12, 13 and 15).

The Xicrim of Cateté were still isolated and could only be reached by air, with access strictly controlled. The central village of Xicrim Cateté (312 inhabitants) was surrounded by intact tropical rain forest. The village still had the traditional layout. 16 large houses stood in a circle 80 m in diameter. While the shape of the houses was built in the old style, the building materials were partly modern, i.e., the palm leaf roof was reinforced with plastic.

The Xicrim population was obviously healthy, with many children running around. They were good-looking, funny, curious, active and attentive. This was a big difference from other areas where there was a general apathy. The health facilities were complete, rooms for counselling, treatment, including dental care, a well-stocked medicine store. A nurse was not yet available. Influenza and colds were treated frequently. Tropical

144 The situation has deteriorated extremely until today, with more than 60 trains/day in 2022. See chapter II.6.3.

diseases were very rare and even malaria could be reduced by disinfecting the houses. There were index cards of each resident with detailed information about diseases etc. In a few critical cases, the local patients and their accompanying family members were taken to the modern hospital of Serra dos Carajás.

The good health of the tribal population in Xicrim Cateté was reflected in the increase in population. Shortly after the first contact (164 people in 1962), the number dropped to 94 in 1967. Since then, there has been a steady increase, reaching 286 people in 1984. At the time of the visit, the population had 312 members. The Xicrim were still very well adapted to traditional ways of using natural resources. Hunting, fishing, gathering and shifting cultivation were practised to a sufficient extent. The result was a healthy diet.

The school was adequately equipped, but lessons in Portuguese were given by a teacher who did not know the Kayapó language. The cacique's son was well aware of the opportunity to criticise: he mentioned the leaking roof of the school building and demanded a new school made of bricks "like in the Serra dos Carajás." The Xicrim knew the borders of their reservation well and checked daily to see if there were any intruders. They wanted to earn money and asked for their motorboat to be repaired because they wanted to sell Brazil nuts directly in Marabá to avoid the intermediate trade and thus the interference of FUNAI.

This situation differed considerably from that of other Indigenous groups, e.g., the Urubu-caapor (494 people) in Alto Turiaçu, the Guajajara in Pindaré or the Assurini do Xingu (53 people) in Coatinemo, who had a high mortality rate and at times a zero-birth rate. Transmission of infections and tropical diseases were the most common reasons. Low birth rates were result of a no-future mentality, which was common in areas with many conflicts and invasions or in cases of multiple resettlements.

Case study: Parakanã (village of Marudjevara)

The village of Parakanã was located 180 km northeast of Serra Norte/ CVRD concession area (Figs. 11, 16, 17). In the 1970s, their territory was cut through by the construction of the Transamazônica. Their deplorable history continued. Although the Tucuruí plans were already fixed, their new territory was in the region that was flooded by the Tucuruí reservoir in 1984. After another resettlement, they were cut off from their traditional fishing grounds along the Rio Tocantins. They reacted desperately to this and violent confrontations ensued.

The inhabitants of the village of Marudjevara were contacted for the first time in 1977, some family groups only in 1983. Due to the exemplary organisation – there were index cards – it could be ascertained that the population increased from 61 (1983; Vidal 1986) to 82 in September 1986, 9 Indigenous people came to the village from another Parakanã group. The facilities of the Indigenous post were in good order. The men and older boys were absent during the visit because of a hunting trip. The women were very shy and did not speak Portuguese. The village was recently built, the shape and types of houses were different from the original ones.

The population lived mainly from hunting and shifting cultivation, which was organised with a long fallow period every three years. They were probably not used to clothes because of the recent contact and the women still seemed to have problems using them. There is a scientifically based discussion that it is nonsensical to give them non-native clothes. However, in other cases they asked for "modern" clothes. The health and nutrition situation seemed to be good. Diseases were properly treated. The Parakanã carefully controlled the artificial boundaries of their territory, which fortunately was still large enough for their needs.

The Parakanã reservation was surrounded by large farms and *garimpos*. Deforestation was widespread and there was much slash-and-burn agriculture. The proximity to alluvial gold deposits made the protection of the Indigenous land extremely difficult. CVRD proposed a large buffer zone. Considering the intense activities of various social actors in the region, a conservation corridor should be established along the southern border of the reservation. Unfortunately, this could not be realised due to the small number of FUNAI and IBDF staff.

4.5.2.2. Final evaluation of the Indigenous situation in the PGC region in the 1980s

It must be emphasised that the mega-programme PGC had no specific strategy on how to organise the living conditions and protection of the territories of the Indigenous population in eastern Amazonia. FUNAI, as the responsible agency, was not able to adequately solve the problems of the Indigenous people. This agency was dependent on political strategies, worked with a small budget, misuse of financial resources, persistent corruption, lack of qualified anthropologists and an incredible administrative chaos. In its 18 years of existence, FUNAI had 14 presidents. At least some of them asked to be dismissed because they became fully aware of their extreme limitations of action and the impossibility of achieving the goal of their work.

However, FUNAI faced a problem at a higher level. Neither the Military Government nor the subsequent democratic governments were willing to invest in Indigenous affairs, and they did not admit their indifference, lack of appreciation and understanding for the Indigenous people. Some of the activities were only carried out "para inglês ver," i.e., to satisfy the international public and to facilitate further foreign funding for development programmes. In the existing conflicts of interest, economic progress was much more important than social or environmental criteria. At the decision-making level, the Indigenous population in their regionally dispersed territories was still seen as an obstacle to the economic exploitation of Amazonia.

CVRD, as the main actor in the PGC programme, interfered in Indigenous affairs because the World Bank granted a loan to the CVRD that was tied to an agreement with FUNAI, which controlled the budget for a separate loan component for Indigenous people.[145] CVRD was blamed by FUNAI for the limited access to this budget. In fact, CVRD did not tolerate the financial resources being used to improve FUNAI's technical infrastructure, thereby neglecting the basic objectives of the loan. On the other hand, payments from the contract in 1985 represented only one third of the meagre total budget of this agency, which had to be used for the benefit of 6.5% of the Indigenous population of Brazil.

The CVRD found itself in a very difficult situation. There were a number of obstacles due to FUNAI's organisational and management structures. Fieldwork of a group of consultants (anthropologists, medical doctors and a lawyer) and CVRD staff was hampered by obstructive FUNAI procedures and conflicting working concepts. The CVRD administration felt that the responsibility assumed for the Indigenous people

145 Cf. chapter I. 4.2.3.1

went far beyond the obligations of a mining company and the impact of its own project on a few Indigenous areas. In fact, since the 1982 contract agreement, *garimpeiro* activities, timber exploitation, waves of migration, chaotic land distribution in INCRA and GETAT projects, serious conflicts of interest between social groups, instability of federal and regional government agencies, uncoordinated PGC regional planning objectives and incredible land speculation had significantly altered the original contract terms.

Aware that CVRD was the only constant factor in "Indigenous policy" within the PGC region, there was a fundamental intention to resolve the ongoing problems. This was a matter of CVRD's high national and international reputation. CVRD officials felt that the constant disputes with FUNAI and the negative news about the development problems in East Amazonia became more and more associated with its activities. The involvement in the agreement became a burden on CVRD's image.

CVRD's environmental department dealt with the issues of the agreement with FUNAI, especially the financial transactions and monitoring. A small, competent team of very reliable people managed the various problems with a great sense of responsibility. This was not an easy task even within the company, because CVRD's basic objectives were mining and the export of mineral products.

Some Indigenous groups were no longer cooperative as they were confused by too many and divergent suggestions of how to protect them against the impact of PGC projects. Furthermore, they were disappointed by long administrative procedures and FUNAI promises still unfulfilled. The reactions of the Indigenous tribes changed significantly in view of projects, often undefined and implanted without previous consultation of the affected groups. Different stages of contact with the non-Indigenous population, attempts from outside to influence the decisions of the *caciques*, new leadership structures and consequences of "integration" caused complex problems. Especially bad "advisors" and dubious lawyers trying to gain money by "defending" the rights of the Indigenous people provoked reactions which were contrary to the traditional isolation and protection approach. The new "cash cycle" made tribal people tempted to sell timber or Brazil nuts and leasing land within the reservation to non-Indigenous tenants. This was illegal, but only on the condition of Indigenous people having no disposing capacity. Justified indemnification payments sometimes were used to buy absurd and expensive objects, such as a small airplane.

By 1986, only 40 % of Indigenous territories had been demarcated in the PGC region, but 31 % of the areas were invaded and 55 % of Indigenous territories were still not registered with the SPU.

In conclusion, there was a fundamental conflict at the moral-ethical level in addressing Indigenous problems within a regional development programme: the positivist mentality of granting financial compensation for the deprivation of habitat and the destruction of the cultural identity and self-determined economic existence of a minority that was the government's protégé under the Brazilian Constitution.

4.6. The PGC-Agrícola plan

The natural vegetation of most of the PGC region was rain forest with various forest ecosystems. The composition of the forests changed in the east and southeast with the increase of dry months. In the east, the occurrence of the *babaçu* oil palm (*Orbygnia martiana*) increased, resulting in extensive palm forests in Maranhão and northern Piauí. South of 8°S, the tropical rain forests very soon changed to the *cerradão* formation, a transitional forest vegetation with about 4 months of aridity and the *cerrado*, the savannah with 5 to 6 arid months.

As already mentioned, the immense biomass of the tropical rain forests is not an indication of good soils with high crop production. The region's soils are very poor and – in line with regional differentiation – there are severe limitations to sustainable agricultural production.

In the 1980s, most agricultural units were managed by sharecroppers (almost 45 %) and by squatters (up to 40 %). Landowners constituted a very small minority, but almost 90 % of the land belonged to them. Estates of 10 000 hectares and more grew considerably in the course of land upgrading. The unequal distribution of land in Maranhão was extreme (Gini index 0.927; Brazil: 0.86). The regions with the highest land concentration were those of traditional land tenure – semi-feudal *fazendas* – while the pioneer front regions of Mearim, Pindaré and Imperatriz still had lower land concentration. But as land values increased, so did the demand and pressure of the large landowners on the squatters.

The basic idea of the PGC agricultural planning in 1983 was to use the existing Carajás railway as a starting point for a broader development of regional agricultural production.[146] Three years earlier, a report had been submitted by a Japanese advisory group invited by the CVRD to assess the export opportunities that would be created by the coming railway infrastructure in the PGC region. This report called for an "export corridor" in which 300 livestock farms, each covering 10 000 ha, would be established. The level of investment proposed in official publications for the agricultural sector dropped from US$ 8.1 billion to US$ 1.8 billion in later revisions of the PGC Agrícola Plan.

The programme area was to be divided into seven "development poles": Castanhal, Bacabal, Marabá, Araguaina, Imperatriz, São Felix do Xingu and Balsas. The objectives of the plan were defined very superficially as follows (Ministério da Agricultura 1983, vol. 3, p. IV, 16–17):

- to contribute to increasing the agricultural productivity of the region,
- to stop the trend of forest devastation and degradation of natural resources,
- to make the agricultural sector economically viable and promote a full employment economy,
- to reverse the trend towards concentration of land ownership and promote the formation and consolidation of a layer of economically sound family farms.

In addition to the official objectives, there were other important reasons for the PGC-Agrícola that were not articulated in the plan's documentation: The establish-

146 Cf. Ministério da Agricultura (1983; 6 volumes).

ment of highly profitable enterprises in the most desirable locations for agribusiness interests, and the containment of discontent and violence that could disrupt projects contributing to the national economy (Fearnside 1986b). CVRD was undoubtedly interested in protecting its concession area from possible encroachment by squatters from nearby areas of land conflict.

The PGC-Agrícola plan served as an initiative for negotiating loans from the Inter-American Development Bank. The plan proposed different cropping systems for small, medium and large farms (80 – >500 ha). Planners believed that livestock farming was suitable for the region. Although the planners accurately described the land tenure problems and social tensions in the region, they were convinced that with the envisaged selection of more than 10 000 small production units and technical and financial support, the regional situation could be calmed down.

The government's strategy has always been to present the PGC Agrícola as a provisional version in order to be able to react as flexibly as possible to new land conflicts and protests by the rural population. At the institutional level, there was no clear responsibility for the implementation of the plan. The PGC-Agrícola plan never received its own budget. In 1986, the new head of the inter-ministerial PGC programme declared that he no longer felt attached to the PGC-Agrícola plan,[147] as it had been adopted by the previous government.

It was alarming that some parts of the plan had already been realised through sectoral planning activities using generally available credit lines. These projects include:

- subsidies to capital-intensive cattle raising, credits for rain forest clearing, investment in cattle and marketing,
- research in charcoal production,
- soybean or rice production in medium and big estates,
- an isolated irrigation project in the Mearim valley,
- subsidies in agroindustrial projects (e.g., *babaçu*-oil processing).

The lack of coherence of these projects, which were not targeted at the regional population but at companies from outside, certainly did not contribute to pacifying existing social tensions, but reinforced the process of uneven development and increasing socio-economic inequalities.

Smallholders live in better conditions than tenants or sharecroppers, who have to deliver 30–50 % of the value of their production to the *fazendeiro*. Most tenants suffer from additional dependencies, such as the need to sell their produce and buy the necessary staple products from the farm owner's local shop. Tenants were increasingly threatened by farm modernisation or the transition from arable to livestock farming, where most labour was no longer needed.

The fundamental problem in the PGC region was land tenure. Unfortunately, as in most rural areas of Brazil, many land titles must be considered semi-legal or illegal. This situation was familiar from Brazilian settlement history, in particular from the pioneer areas. The seizure of land was rarely accompanied by an official land register.

Neither the State Land Regulatory Authority nor INCRA were able to establish a functioning land registry in the region. There was a real need for a land regulatory

---

147 Interview with the author on 2 September 1986; cf. Kohlhepp *et al.* (1987, 186).

authority that was able to calm violent land conflicts and that could provide a basis for legal and equitable land distribution and registration.

For this reason, GETAT (land authority of the Araguaia-Tocantins region) was created in 1980, responsible for about 50 % of the PGC region, mainly in the south-east of Pará and the west of Maranhão. GETAT's main tasks were land surveying, registration and the establishment of colonisation projects such as Carajás II and III or expropriation for land regulation. In the first half of the 1980s, the military regime made the last effort to reorganise the economic, social and political structures in Amazônia Legal by concentrating all decision-making power in the National Security Council (SNI). GETAT – completely independent of the PGC administration – was entrusted with three overarching tasks (Branford and Glock 1985, 156): 1) creating a new order of legal land access, 2) creating a new regional political base and 3) undermining the influence of the church in the region.

The first long-term goal could not be achieved, as national, sectoral and regional development policies were at odds with regional needs. The second objective was successful because the political "climate" has changed since GETAT tried to intervene. The third objective was temporarily achieved. The power of GETAT, its cooperation with the SNI and the state's policy of repression and intimidation created a situation of constant surveillance and fear, especially until the end of 1983.

Since 1952, the Catholic Church of Maranhão has been involved in programmes to support the rural population in order to reduce social conflicts between landowners and farm workers and tenants. In 1960, the Archdiocese of São Luís launched a pilot land reform programme. The Church purchased an area of 130 km² and distributed land to rural families without sufficient arable land. The Church supported the creation of unions of independent peasants in 1963, although the local political power and the government tried to prevent any form of social protest. At the end of 1963, the National Federation of Agricultural Workers (Confederação Nacional dos Trabalhadores na Agricultura, CONTAG) was formed to represent all agricultural workers' unions.

After the 1964 military coup, the government retained the organisational structure of CONTAG, but intervened and eliminated its political functions. The leaders of the local union representatives were appointed by the state and thus no longer represented the rural poor. Despite the state repression, the autonomous underground unions continued their activities. In Maranhão, the bishops did not publicly support formal demands for social change until 1973. However, the priests in the parishes, often young men from Europe, tried to convince the rural population to defend their rights and organise. The development policy of SUDAM in the 1970s, with large-scale land ownership, enormous actions of illegal land occupation, increase of land prices and forcible eviction of land squatters, led to a renewal of social commitment by the official church representatives in Maranhão.[148]

In 1975, the Amazonian bishops founded the Comissão Pastoral da Terra (CPT), an ecclesiastical support service for the rural population that helped them obtain land titles or defended their rights against oppression and eviction. Soon, the government regarded the clergy as a leading component of the social movements in the rural areas, arguing with the accusation of "communist" infiltration. The CPT in Maranhão documented land conflicts, murders and violent actions against land squatters and small

148 Kohlhepp *et al.* (1987); the part about Maranhão has been elaborated by Reinhold Lücker. Cf. Almeida (1982); Asselin (1982).

farmers. Several foreign priests had to leave the country, some were attacked or killed. Although repression against active local priests increased, the government could not diminish the important political influence of the church in the region.

Fig. 18: Land ownership in the Southwest of the PGC region

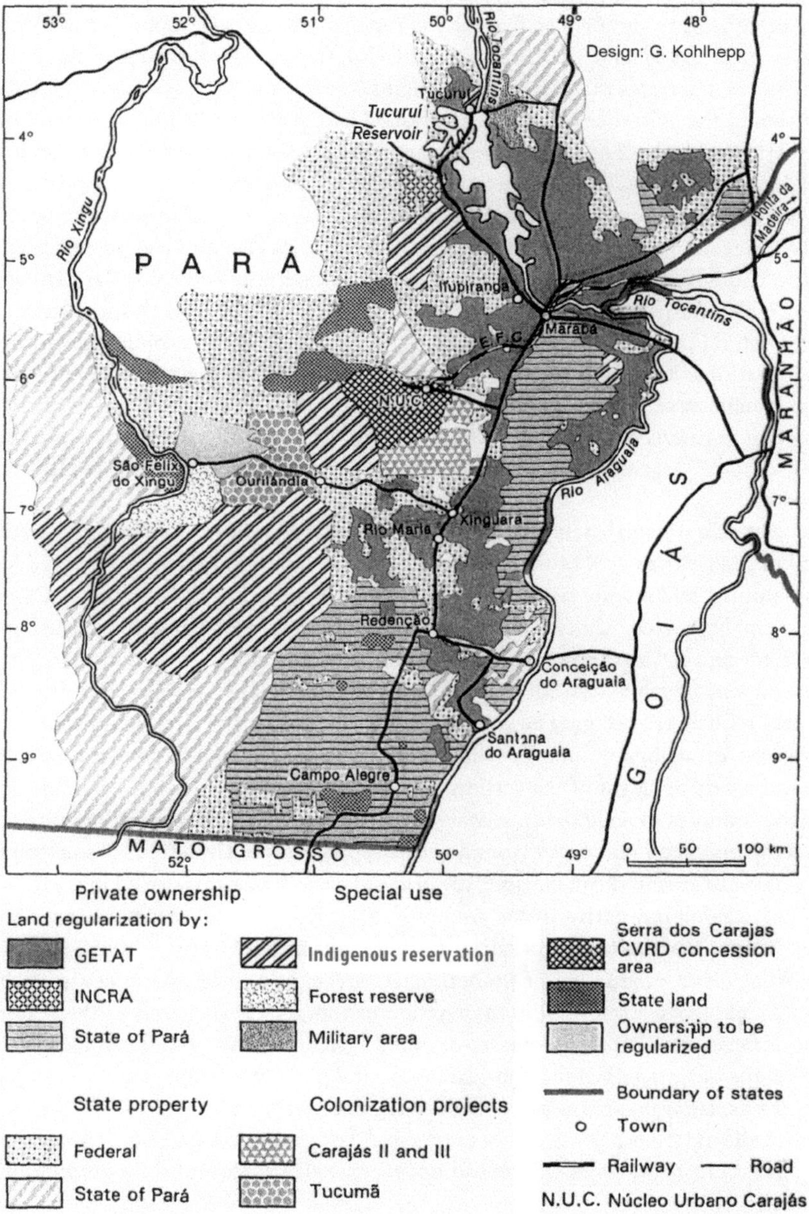

Source: Cf. Kohlhepp (1987b, 230); based on documents and maps of CVRD and GETAT.

Police or SNI violence against priests, lay brothers, and trade union leaders had decreased since 1984. In the regions most affected by social tensions, the priests not only fulfilled their religious duty, but also worked as agricultural advisors or directed social defence. The open conflict between the church and the state culminated in the formal excommunication of the former governor of Maranhão in March 1986.

Land tenure in the PGC region was an extremely complex problem due to the interference of numerous authorities, federal and regional entities and a number of divergent laws on access to land and land titles. The situation in the southwest of the PGC region in Pará illustrates the prevailing problems (see Fig. 18).
In addition to the existence of land titles granted by INCRA, GETAT and the state of Pará, or land owned by the federal government (*terra devoluta*) or the state government of Pará, there were areas of special use: Indigenous reservations or areas not yet registered, forest reserves and military areas. There were also special colonisation projects of GETAT (Carajás II and III) and areas given to companies (Tucumã) for colonisation. CVRD had a high-ranking position in land ownership with its Serra dos Carajás concession area for the iron ore project as the core project of the Programa Grande Carajás.

The predominant problem on the pioneer front is always the rapidly expanding land occupation without any regard for existing land titles and boundaries of properties, Indigenous reservations or projects. An example of the advancing pioneer front was the region between Marabá and Xinguara (Fig. 17), which showed the inability of official bodies to organise this settlement process accompanied by uncontrolled deforestation.

The largest municipality in the GETAT study area was São Félix do Xingu with 116 500 km². More than 25 % of this area was allocated to large companies involved in logging, mining and private settlement. 29 companies owned 1.3 million ha, or 11 % of the municipality's area (Almeida 1986). A large area (0.4 million ha) was awarded by INCRA after an auction to the construction company Andrade Gutierrez in the Gleba Tucumã (Morán 1987) between São Félix do Xingu and Xinguara (see Fig. 18) for private settlement with plots averaging 86 ha and better soils than in the Carajás II and III GETAT projects. The company built the village of Tucumã and provided a good infrastructure of access roads. Most of the settlers came from Rio Grande do Sul and had left their home families of *minifundistas*. Many of them had no experience in agriculture. As the company's economic expectations were disappointed and hundreds of squatters had invaded the area in the meantime, the original project was abandoned in 1987.

GETAT was mainly active in the area of the "agricultural poles" Araguaina, São Félix do Xingu, Marabá and Imperatriz. In these areas, GETAT created the basis for an export-oriented production of timber, meat, soybeans and cereals in accordance with JICA's planning strategy. The valorisation of this region was seen as the result of large-scale, capital-intensive, market-oriented agriculture, which was completely at odds with the basic needs of the poor, landless rural population. This population was seen by the decision-makers as an obstacle to regional progress.

72 % of all land titles belonged to peasants with less than 100 ha, i.e., only 5 % of the land in question. Many plots of land did not reach a size sufficient for a production unit of a family.

With the Carajás II (1983) and III (1982) projects, east and south of the CVRD concession area (see Figs. 13 and 18), GETAT established two peasant settlements which offered less infrastructure and services compared to INCRA's colonisation projects on the Transamazônica. The regional development centres (Cedere) with state administration, primary school and health centre had a simpler structure than those of the Polonoroeste programme in Rondônia. The settlement was realised with a minimum of costs and as quickly as possible, as the pressure from the large landowners in the region increased.

In Carajás III, the number of plots sold was reduced from 4000 to 2000, and the size from 50 to 25 ha. The upgrading of the land through the construction of the road from Marabá to Serra dos Carajás increased the pressure of land speculators. The idea of settling farmers from southern Brazil with technical training in agriculture as trainers for the other farmers had no positive effect. Their knowledge did not work in the Amazonian region, and they were disappointed by the restrictions to focus on annual crops. Moreover, the intention to give advice to the other farmers was not accepted (Fearnside 1986b). The situation in Carajás II was strongly influenced by the greater distance to the road and especially transport problems occurred during the rainy season.

In the PGC region, land conflicts prevailed to such an extent that violence and pressure from the large landowners decisively influenced the decision-making level of strategic planning. The needs of smallholders were not translated into viable and politically implementable solutions even after re-democratisation.

In the PGC region, the reasons for land conflicts were as follows:

- Very unequal agricultural structures with a growing proportion of rural families without access to land tenure;
- Traditional forms of land ownership in large landholdings (*latifundios*) with a paternalistic role of the landowner towards his tenants and farm workers and with the role of the landowner changing to a capitalist entrepreneur;
- *Grilagem*: The illegal occupation of state land or occupied land by large landowners, merchants, politicians or corporations, mainly for purposes of expansion or speculation, with the resident population threatened and forced to leave the land or surrender up to 50 % of their crops. Land titles were often obtained by presenting forged documents, forgery, bribery and other forms of corruption. Illegal land occupation was often defended by the new landowners with violence and the help of *pistoleiros*;
- In the *cartórios*, the offices where land titles are granted, these titles could sometimes be illegally prepared, "bought" and registered, leading to confusion and counteractions by the defrauded population;
- Demographic increase in the rural population with no chance of land ownership;
- Immigration of migrant groups from other states, especially from Ceará, Rio Grande do Norte and Bahia;
- National development policies that favour the establishment of large-scale landholdings in cattle breeding or arable farming, especially by migrant companies from the South or Southeast of Brazil. In many cases, landowners organised their lands in absentia and appointed administrators to oversee the work on the *fazendas*;
- Invasions and appropriation of tribal lands by squatters, prospectors or large landowners.

The regions with the most violent conflicts had shifted from Araguaia river and southern Maranhão to south Pará and the rain forest area in western Maranhão in the early 1980s. In 1985, there were 140 murders in land conflicts in Pará (97, mainly in the Xingu region) and Maranhão (43) (Kohlhepp *et al.* 1987, 182).[149]

The increase in violent conflicts is certainly also related to the agrarian reform (PNRA law) promulgated in 1985 (MIRAD 1985). *Grileiros* and large landowners feared that the existing squatters would claim their own property rights on their land if the land reform was implemented, and therefore tried to get their land "clean," as they called it.

On the other hand, the squatters became better informed about their rights and the process of eviction through information campaigns by the church and rural associations. New forms of cooperation developed among squatters, which could be described as mutual assistance in self-defence. There was a tendency for squatters to arm themselves, and some were enlisted as *pistoleiros* to defend rural communities (MIRAD 1986, 51ff.) against *pistoleiros* of *grileiros* or other large landowners. These vigilante measures became increasingly common. One reason for these illegal conditions was the lack of help from the local police or official courts to defend the human rights of the affected land squatters and small landowners.

Along the Carajás railway line to Ponta da Madeira/São Luís, the smallholders had no official support. Permanent pressure from large landowners, no political interest in securing the smallholders' land titles, "accidental" forest fires, and delays in the construction of roads to transport agricultural goods to the railway station made life difficult for the settlers. The settlement of farmers in the areas along the railway line was prevented with many political tricks and the threat of *pistoleiros*. The resistance and resilience of the rural population had already weakened in recent years and resignation spread.[150]

The rural atmosphere in the regions of São João do Araguaia, Marabá, Vizeu (PA) and Imperatriz was more than tense. Land conflicts were recognised as a kind of civil war in a documentary annex to MIRAD (1986). This unbearable situation led to an exodus from areas of social tension. The share of the rural population in Maranhão stagnated, and in several municipalities, there was a net decrease in absolute numbers. Most of the rural exodus was directed to the urban centres.

The Military Government (1964–1985) had obstructed open discussion of agrarian reform and persecuted its protagonists. Instead of an agrarian reform, it formulated the alternatives of modernising agriculture and colonising Amazonia. The covert discussion on agrarian reform increased from 1983 onwards, essentially determined by the grassroots church communities that formulated and stimulated the protests of the peasants and landless rural population.

The 1963 Agrarian Reform Act was transformed into regional agrarian reform programmes in 1985, which identified priority projects within the states. The aim of these projects was to settle squatters and agricultural workers on expropriated, unused land,

149 Data from the Ministry of Agrarian Reform and Agrarian Development (MIRAD 1986, 83-84) and reports of CPT.

150 Interview with Frans Gistelinck, in São Luís, September 23, 1986 (cf. Gistelinck 1988). Brazilian President José Sarney, as governor of Maranhão (1966–1970), had also mentioned years ago that the problem of squatters and small farmers could be solved by migration.

especially on large plots where there had been repeated serious land conflicts. Landowners were to be compensated in the sense of a conservative land reform. For the majority of the Brazilian population, it seemed clear that the agrarian reform (Ianni 1979a) should be carried out. However, a strong opposition soon formed within the centre and the right wing of the PMDB political party. The UDR, a newly formed and growing group of large landowners, concentrated its protest against the consequences of the planned agrarian reform. Most of the MPs in Brazil belonged to the urban bourgeoisie and were open to the big landowner groups. After the November 1986 elections, the agrarian reform programmes were considered secondary, and the political discussion focused on the Constituent Assembly. In 1987, the political majority for agrarian reform was lost and it became clear that the existing social structure of rural areas would not be fundamentally changed in the near future. The legal possibility of expropriating underused large estates remained very limited due to the lack of financial means for compensation.

Development policies in Amazonia have increased the demand for land, unfortunately also for speculative purposes. Capital groups from South and Southeast Brazil used the unique opportunity of tax incentives to seize very large areas at very low land prices in relation to their home regions. Apart from some state-controlled colonisation projects, small landowners could not withstand the enormous pressure of legal and illegal land acquisition. The land problem took on a new dimension and social tensions and violent conflicts of interest dominated the rural scenario (J. Martins 1982 and 1983; Hébette 1986). Land in Amazônia Legal was offered on the national and international land market, excluding most of the region's inhabitants who were not fully integrated into the cash economy.

The PGC-Agrícola plan missed an invaluable opportunity to orient agricultural development towards socially and culturally appropriate and sustainable forms of production in order to meet social needs of the regional rural population and to achieve socially balanced regional development.

4.7. Final considerations about the Grande Carajás programme (PGC)

In analysing the PGC, it must be emphasised that, as a regional development programme for eastern Amazonia, it can be characterised as an administratively and functionally inefficient, institutionally uncoordinated and vertically incoherent mega-programme. The objective of verticalising regional planning, i.e., decentralising spatial planning decisions and involving the affected population of the region, was not achieved. The Grande Carajás programme was perceived by the regional population as an "attack on the heart of Amazonia" (Pinto 1982). A new integrated regional planning approach, which would have been urgently needed, was not realised after the political change in the mid-1980s.

The PGC was not a "precisely defined development plan, instead taking the form of a legal framework for the granting of state subsidies to promote projects specifically aimed at achieving integration of Brazil into the world markets" (cf. Deutscher Bundestag 1990, 316). As a large-scale development programme in the Brazilian planning region Amazônia Legal, the PGC had been implemented without its own budget, without sufficient technical staff and without taking into account the needs of a large part of the regional population. It represented the pattern of a "development from above" with numerous negative social and environmental consequences. The follow-up costs of large-scale projects and the coordination of planning at the municipal level had been neglected financially and operationally. Tax incentives for large-scale projects had reduced tax revenues flowing into the municipalities (Binswanger 1987; Mahar 1989).

After a multitude of macro-planning – and in certain cases "pseudo-planning" (Ab'Sáber 1989) – and predatory proposals for the Amazon region, there had been several proposals and scientifically sound studies on ecological, economic and agro-ecological zoning. The concept of ecological and economic zoning required a multidisciplinary analysis to determine the specific possibilities of priority objectives for each sub-area of the territory concerned, in accordance with the criteria of ecological development (Sachs 1980; Kohlhepp 1983b; 1987c; 1991c). "The simplistic idea that certain ecological spaces should be matched by economic spaces, in a totally adjustable overlapping set-up" (Ab'Sáber 1989, 5) is not acceptable. There is a risk of misuse or misinterpretation by the administration. The basic problem is that land use planning as a provisional measure has only a theoretical value. It must serve as a "guideline" for future development, but the reality of current land use may completely contradict the results of zoning or at least differ significantly from them. The crucial issue lies in the methods and policies for rezoning space – and land tenure – in line with the ecological and socio-economic "vocation" of the respective sub-areas (Kohlhepp and Schrader 1987).

There was a lack of clear definition of the intended spatial organisation based on studies of environmental and socio-economic conditions and their intra-regional differentiation. Major projects should only have been put into operation after studies on environmental impacts had been completed. The cost of protection against environmental degradation should be included as an integral part of the project cost. Information of the Amazonian population affected by these projects was inadequate and delayed. The resettlement and compensation measures were carried out without the right of objection and co-determination of those affected and without consultation with the respective competent regional and local authorities.

The programme region did not receive an adequate share of the profits from the exploitation of mineral resources in large-scale projects. Small and medium-sized projects of social relevance that are ecologically and regionally adapted were urgently lacking. Although there was already an awareness of the social and economic consequences of large-scale projects in other Brazilian regions, integrated planning measures were very rarely implemented in Amazonia.

The Programa Grande Carajás (PGC), with its enormous volume of investment and the government's old style of "development propaganda," attracted large masses of migrants. The iron ore project as "the heart of the PGC" occupied only a limited concession area in the Serra dos Carajás and was organised by CVRD in an environmentally sustainable way. Nevertheless, the associated projects and the almost uncontrollable spontaneous development processes, especially outside the spatially limited projects, have led to an almost chaotic situation in the PGC region (Almeida Jr. 1986; Kohlhepp 1987b; 1987c). The construction of paved roads, the Carajás ore railway, the new deep-sea port Ponta da Madeira near São Luís, the construction of the reservoir and the large-scale power plant in Tucuruí with its widely ramified electricity distribution network, as well as the huge aluminium smelters in Barcarena near Belém and in São

Luís have triggered a massive influx of people. The danger of enclave formation was inherent in these mega-projects (Kohlhepp 1991c; 1997b).

The pig iron and other metallurgical projects in the PGC region, using charcoal as an energy source and reducing agent, led to a new wave of tropical forest destruction. There were divergent opinions in the CVRD administration[151] when evaluating charcoal-based pig iron projects. Considering the environmental costs, it would have been advisable to resort to non-predatory alternatives such as importing coke, even using international loans. The costs of social and environmental impacts of large-scale projects must be adequately considered in the long run.

The overlaying of the region's traditional, social and economic structures by new spatial structures and the socio-economic disparities within the region, exacerbated by polarisation effects of mega-projects, contributed even more to regional disintegration and widespread spatial and social segregation (Hébette 1985; Hemming 1985; Kohlhepp *et al.* 1987; Hall 1987, 1989; Fearnside 1989d; Kohlhepp 1991c).

The lack of regional participation in all sectors reinforced the "syndrome of the periphery of the periphery", i.e., the surrender of affairs to decisions from outside, both at the national and international level: the so-called "integration" into the world market under extremely unfavourable trade conditions (Altvater 1987a; Kohlhepp and Schrader 1987; Nitsch 1989; Kohlhepp 1995).

The PGC-Agrícola appeared as a kind of "appendix" of the PGC and almost excluded the fundamental problems of smallholder agriculture. It lacked a new strategy of integrated rural development, which could not be achieved without an agro-social structural change and a concomitant appeasement of rural violence (Ianni 1981; J. Martins 1982 and 1983; Hébette 1986). Unfortunately, priority was given to the large landowners. The problem of land ownership with forged land titles could not be solved. Sustainable land use models were disregarded, and livestock and soybean cultivation became predominant. Private colonisation projects favoured migrants, especially from southern Brazil. In the PGC, appropriate infrastructure and extension services were not provided by GETAT and INCRA to small farmers. The landless rural population of the PGC region had very difficult access to land and remained marginalised. Smallholder agriculture projects should have been accompanied by intensive advisory services on a cooperative basis and integrated into communal development programmes. There was a lack of political will to support the participation of the local rural population and to respect intellectual property rights with regard to strategies of helping people to help themselves.

Numerous conflicts of interest on the pioneer front, spontaneous land occupation, disregard for Indigenous reservation boundaries, dangerous legal uncertainty, the constant intensification of land use conflicts and ever scarcer land meant that the coexistence of competing social groups and their economic goals created almost insoluble problems of coordination. This underlined the lack of common development goals for Amazonia.

Obviously, the meaning of the PGC-Agrícola plan was purely a political strategy under the conditions of the last "abertura" period at the end of military governments. The theoretical background and the strategies chosen were not significantly different

151 Interview of the author with the CVRD Vice-president and the Superintendent of Planning at Serra dos Carajás, September 1./2., 1986.

from those of the 1970s, when the growth pole strategy and general economic growth policies prevailed. There was no sign of a serious regional development strategy.

For a long time, Amazonia was seen, both in Brazil and abroad, as a source of natural resource exploitation, often mistakenly considered as "unlimited." Spatial organisation took the form of the misuse of Amazonia in terms of unconditional valorisation in the sense of an "inland colony," without regard to environmental and social conditions and without the regional population having opportunities to satisfy their basic needs. The geopolitical concept of Amazonia as a vast empty space, as reflected in the regional planning of the last decades, was a fundamental mistake.

Amazonia must not be made the object of speculation and investment for the purpose of tax advantages in the interest of companies outside Amazonia. The tropical forests of Amazonia must no longer be a field of experimentation for so-called "development models" that are ecologically and socially unsustainable and a field of manoeuvre for different groups of non-Amazonian interests.

In Brazilian history, many politicians and social actors on the pioneer front considered Indigenous tribes in the rain forests as enemies that prevented economic progress. To this day, parts of the neo-Brazilian population fundamentally do not respect the rights of the Indigenous population to their own living space as guaranteed in the Constitution. Indigenous groups were identified as obstacles to social advancement or to the profit maximisation of the invaders of their territories. There was a lack of awareness of the unjustified persecution of a vulnerable ethnic minority, a lack of understanding of their need for space to hunt, gather and for their shifting cultivation. This was the situation at the beginning of the Grande Carajás programme in the 1980s during a military regime convinced that it had a unique opportunity to solve the "Indigenous problem" in its own authoritarian way without the slightest ethnic, social and environmental scruples.

Considering the Indigenous population of Central and East Amazonia, it was a fatal mistake not to provide protecting measures in all parts of the PGC region. Regarding the institutional weakness of FUNAI, after re-democratisation the new government did not succeed in effectively reorganising this public institution and improving the financial conditions and the qualification of the staff. Donations from international organisations for projects to protect Indigenous peoples, as well as support for local and regional NGOs, should have been welcomed and not rejected because of nationalist or political reservations.

An urgent demarcation of Indigenous territories, demarcation and – if necessary – control and re-demarcation taking into account the basic ecological, socio-cultural and economic needs of Indigenous groups did not take place. Territorial integrity should have been ensured by spatially contiguous territories for related tribal groups. Much too late and only partially, the full participation of Indigenous representatives was included in all operational arrangements. An institutionalised advisory group of renowned Brazilian anthropologists should have been established in cooperation with official bodies. The Indigenous population must decide on the objectives of further actions in favour of an undisturbed Indigenous way of life. Regional information campaigns to strengthen public understanding of basic Indigenous needs were completely lacking.

In case of unavoidable impacts of development projects, the amount and use of compensation for Indigenous groups should be determined and monitored by a special commission consisting of Indigenous representatives, their legal advisor (non-turnover lawyer), specialised anthropologists, a FUNAI officer and members of local/regional non-profit NGOs.

The PGC used CVRD's highly qualified staff and national as well as international reputation to achieve important political goals without taking care of the social and environmental issues. This raised the question of for whom in Amazonia the mega-programme and its "development" was ultimately planned.

As a "warning shot," the Grande Carajás programme had a significant influence on the situation in Amazonia in later decades. It was the starting point for considerations on an urgently needed sustainable development of Amazonia, which was then attempted to be realised in the International Pilot Programme to conserve the Brazilian rain forests (PPG7).[152]

152 See chapter II.1.2.

5. The energy-related Plano 2010 and its possible impacts on Amazonia

The Plano 2010 developed by Eletrobras, the Brazilian umbrella organisation of the national electricity industry, was a threatening regional plan in Amazônia Legal in 1987. The programme to expand hydropower generation using the natural hydropower potential of the Amazon envisaged the construction of numerous power plants and thus the creation of large reservoirs (Eletrobras 1987a; 1987b).

The 2430 km² Tucuruí reservoir had already shown that clearing forest areas to be flooded later was an extremely costly procedure that was hardly profitable, depending on the location. The organisational problems were enormous due to the peripheral location.[153] In view of this fact and the lack of relief energy in the Amazon basin, most of the planned reservoirs flood large areas of still intact rain forest.

For example, the 2360 km² Balbina reservoir, located 150 km northeast of Manaus, required 31 times the area per MW of installed capacity compared to Tucuruí (Fearnside 1989a; Kohlhepp 1998c). Originally, this project, which started producing electricity in 1989, was planned to supply the regional conurbation of Manaus with 250 MW. However, due to the relatively small catchment area of the Rio Uatumã and the extremely low gradient of the river, only a secured capacity of 110 MW could be realised. More than a third of the reservoir area with 1500 islands was covered by rain forest and was less than 4 m deep, the water exchange extremely slow at 14 months. High acidity, low oxygen content, toxic gases and the rapid spread of macrophytes characterised the environmental impacts in the reservoir. The loss of rainforest and the displacement of about one third of the Waimiri-Atroari, one of the most persecuted tribes, were the tragic consequences.[154] Balbina was probably the most glaring example of the misplanning of hydropower strategies for the Amazon region.

The planned reservoirs flood the habitats of Indigenous tribes that are naturally located near the rivers. In the case of Tucuruí on the Rio Tocantins, the Paracanã were affected. The planned damming of the Rio Xingu for the construction of the huge Babaquara power plant with a huge reservoir of more than 6100 km² was discussed, which would drive the Arara and Kararaô tribes out of their traditional settlement areas (Comissão Pro-Indio 1988).[155]

According to the framework plans of Eletrobras, the financing of which was still completely open, a total of 79 reservoirs were to be built in Amazônia Legal by 2010

153 Cf. chapter I.4.3; Kohlhepp (1987b; 1991a).

154 Cf. chapter I.3.2.2.

155 Cf. Kohlhepp (1991a, Fig. 7: Flooding planned along the Xingu and Irirí rivers).

with an installed capacity of around 86 000 MW (Fig. 19). In 1985, the total capacity of Brazil was 44 000 MW! All but one of the planned reservoirs were to be located in the tropical rain forest. The exaggerated vision of the regional electricity company Eletronorte for the Tocantins-Araguaia Basin can be seen in Fig. 20.[156]

Fortunately, this programme was unrealistic and financially unfeasible. However, its existence shows the strategy of "modernisation" supported by the powerful lobby of construction companies, without taking into account environmental or social criteria. In the meantime, however, some power plant projects have been realised. In total, there are five dams on the Rio Tocantins, besides the Tucuruí dam and reservoir: Estreito, Luiz Eduardo Magalhães (Lajeado), on the upper Rio Tocantins Peixe Angical as well as Cana Brava and the Serra da Mesa dam in the state of Goiás (Fearnside 2015a). These power plants are located in the *cerrado* region, some have run-of-river reservoirs.

All the estimates of the total area to be flooded in rain forest areas remained largely speculative, but the eight largest reservoirs are likely to cover about 20 000 km². An overall planning figure of almost incredible 100 000 km² had been mentioned (Fearnside 1989a).

Figure 19. Hydroelectric power plants and reservoirs planned in Amazonia in 1988

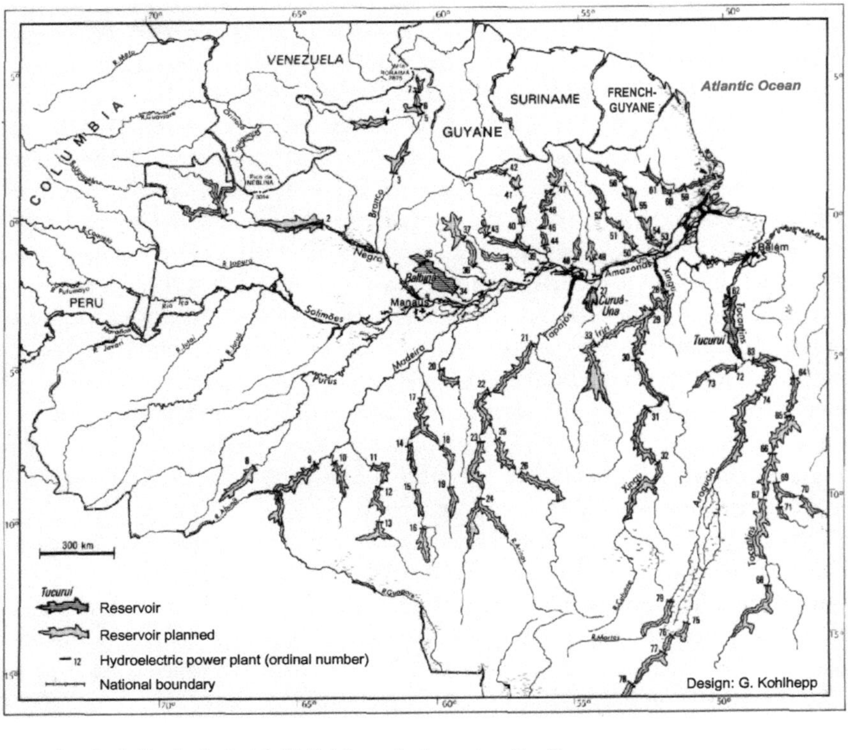

Source: Comissão Pro-Indio (1988); Cf. Kohlhepp (1989a; 1991a, Fig. 6).

156 The energy potential in the Tocantins-Araguaia- Basin was estimated at 19 430 MW, with Tucuruí alone accounting for 38 %.

Figure 20. Eletronorte's vision of hydroelectric power plants and reservoirs in the Tocantins-Araguaia river basin

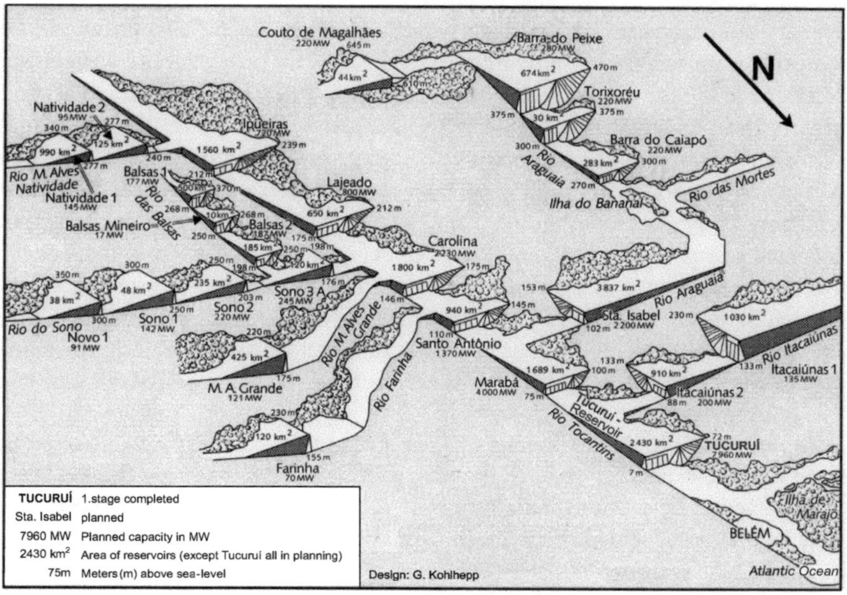

Source: Eletronorte (1986) and additional information of Eletrobras (1987a).

In addition to the destruction of vast areas of rain forest and the irreplaceable loss of species and gene pools, the realisation of these projects would result in an accumulation of severe ecological and regional climate impacts, which have already been empirically documented in the reservoirs under construction or recently completed. These irresponsible and megalomaniac visions of the planners not only led to the end of the biodiversity of tropical forests in the floodplains, but also threatened the existence of endangered Indigenous tribes through the associated infrastructural facilities. These included construction workers' camps, roads, airfields, company towns, power transmission lines, settlement of industrial plants as well as spontaneous and planned waves of migration.

The strong protests of the regional population, also at national and international level, against the possible granting of the second loan for the energy sector by the World Bank to Brazil had shown that the public was increasingly against the plans to build the reservoirs. Scientists, NGOs and even some technicians and engineers stressed that Amazonia should not simply become a power supplier for the industrial centres in the Southeast, as this would not be economically viable even in the long term (Sternberg 1988). The demand for electrical energy in the Southeast must be met from other sources. For local and micro-regional power supply in the Amazon, there are alternative solutions such as the construction of small-scale power plants, but the underlying technology is of no interest to the powerful hydropower and dam lobbies.

In 1989, the World Bank announced a new official policy on dams and reservoirs (Goodland 1989; 1990a). "The overall aim of this policy parallels economic least cost: That is to ensure that borrowers promote their environmentally and socially low-cost project investment options and exclude environmentally and socially high-cost projects, while maintaining optimal environmental and social standards" (Goodland 1989, 7). Other Bank policies had to be considered, such as resettlement, tribal groups, biodiversity, cultural assets, riparian rights and dam safety. The cost-benefit analyses had to include estimates for all mitigation measures and for quantifiable environmental losses due to the project. The new policy required a systematic environmental assessment by independent experts selected and approved by the Bank. The environmental impact assessment had to be completed before project implementation. This was particularly important in Brazil, where the consequences of sometimes dubious environmental impact assessments (EIA/RIMA) were very destructive processes and prevented highly problematic projects from being stopped. The World Bank encouraged the participation of community organisations of the project-affected population, research institutes and NGOs in consultations with project authorities and – often non-existent in the 1980s – public hearings. In Brazil, government authorities interested in World Bank loans for hydropower projects must have perceived this new Bank policy as a "revolution."

In 1989, massive demonstrations by the Kayapó in Altamira had convinced the World Bank to cancel funding for the Babaquara/Kararaô project on the Rio Xingu, which came to a halt. Unfortunately, this project was later resurrected under the new name Belo Monte,[157] but without a loan from the World Bank for the construction of the dam.

157 See chapter II.6.

6. The Significance of the New Constitution of 1988 for environmental policy in Amazonia

6.1. Steps in the development of Brazilian Environmental Policy on the way to integration into the New Constitution by "Nossa Natureza"

As already mentioned,[158] Brazil had its first federal forest law (Código Florestal) in 1934, combined with laws for fishing, hunting and water protection. With the takeover of power by the military regime, a long prepared new forest law (Novo Código Florestal) was passed in 1965. Forests became "goods of public interest," from which legal restrictions on private property could be derived. In addition, it was decided to establish national, state, and municipal parks as well as biological reserves. In pristine forest areas, logging of up to 50 % of private property was allowed.

For the first time, the exploitation of primary forests in Amazonia without consistent land use plans was prohibited. Not only did the legal provisions offer many opportunities for flexibility – increased clearing through repeated sale of parts of the property ("mathematics of devastation") – but the Military Government's development strategies for Amazonia pushed environmental and especially forest laws into the background. When demands for a national environmental protection policy arose in Parliament in the second half of the 1960s, the Military Government took them up only indirectly in 1967 by establishing a National Council for Combating Environmental Pollution (Calcagnotto 1990).

At the first United Nations Conference on the Human Environment in Stockholm in 1972, environmental protection was described by many developing countries, including Brazil, as a luxury of the rich industrialised countries and an obstacle to development. Despite the vehement reaction of the developing countries, however, Stockholm provided the first decisive impetus to create the conditions for a national environmental policy, including in Brazil.

Official environmental policy in Brazil began with the establishment of an Environmental Protection Agency (SEMA), created in October 1973 by a decree of the then Brazilian President General Médici. In this most repressive phase of the military dictatorship, where environmental issues were dealt with by the National Security Council (SNI) (Guimarães 1989), this step was initially surprising.

Two reasons were crucial for the creation of SEMA (Kohlhepp 1991a; 1991d; 2020a):

158 Cf. chapter I.3.3.

1. SEMA was intended as a response to international criticism of Brazil's stance in Stockholm and had both tactical and pragmatic reasons. It was foreseeable that environmental protection requirements were to be expected in the future when granting international loans, especially by the World Bank (Goodland 1985; 1989).
2. A nationally publicised case of environmental poisoning by a cellulose factory near Porto Alegre had led to considerable unrest among the population and to initial protest actions for better environmental protection. A citizens' initiative had demanded the establishment of an environmental authority.

Although there were authorities responsible for environmental issues in the broadest sense, they were assigned to nine different ministries and were embroiled in jurisdictional disputes. The solution was seen in a central federal authority with subordinate state authorities.

However, SEMA proved to be institutionally weak and politically wanting from the beginning. Although it met the formal requirements of international organisations and their loan conditions (Viola 1988), it only had a marginal position in the Ministry of the Interior, to which it was assigned. Ecological problems in the exploitation of Amazonia were not taken seriously by the government and there was no political will to equip SEMA according to its necessary tasks. SEMA's area of work in the 1970s was the control of environmental pollution and contamination. The problems of natural resource degradation, including the tropical rain forests of Amazonia, were subordinated and politically negated because of the government's national development strategy for Amazonia. The majority of SEMA's staff were natural scientists, and the agency could be described as "depoliticised" (Guimarães 1986, 321).

The head of SEMA, Paulo Nogueira Neto, an internationally renowned scientist, had repeatedly pointed out the existing environmental problems during the Military Government, despite difficult political conditions and poor facilities, and held his office for 12 years with great personal commitment.

In 1981, the national environmental policy was redefined (PNMA), positively influenced by the 1st United Nations Conference on the Human Environment in Stockholm in 1972. During the slow political opening, responsibilities were hierarchically structured in the National Environmental System (SISNAMA). Its highest body, the National Environment Council (CONAMA), had the task of formulating environmental policy guidelines, but did not meet for the first time until 1984. CONAMA included representatives of state institutions, but civil organisations were far underrepresented. The military treated CONAMA and its activities with the greatest suspicion (Melo-Reiners 2009, 151). CONAMA's most important resolution concerned the performance of environmental impact studies prior to the official approval of projects with a major impact on the environment (road and railway construction, dams, power plants, high-voltage transmission lines, industry, etc.). A distinction was made between a detailed study of the environmental impact (EIA) and a summary of the results of the EIA, a report (RIMA).

SEMA's marginal position remained even after the end of military rule in the New Republic after 1985. In the case of SEMA, for example, the "ecology programme" ("paquote ecológico") announced with great propaganda effort by the new Sarney government in June 1986 comprised only one sixth of the budget of the environmental agency of the state of São Paulo. The new head of SEMA resigned in 1988 after two years, pointing out that the agency was unable to fulfil its tasks and was not fit for work.

At least since the 2nd United Nations Conference on the Environment in Nairobi in 1982, it was clear to many developing countries that preventing environmental damage was cheaper than mitigating the damage afterwards. However, this self-knowledge was apparently less important than the fact that the World Bank had been demanding environmental impact assessments when granting loans for development projects since the second half of the 1970s.

In the meantime, public interest in increased environmental protection had been articulated in Brazil. And not only in the urban areas, but also in the rural regions with the problems of modernising agriculture with over-fertilisation, excessive use of insecticides, pesticides and so on. But this was especially the case in the Amazon region due to the exploitation of the natural potential and the large-scale destruction of the tropical rain forests.

The 1988 Federal Constitution was the first Brazilian law to dedicate a separate chapter to environmental protection, thus accepting and strengthening the environmental legislation of the time and promoting the creation of new regulations.[159] The Constitution of 1988 is a 245-clause charter that was drafted in 17 months by the Constituent Assembly. The 1988 Constitution can be seen as an attempt to replace the constitutional order and the military's strategy of economic growth over any social improvement with the suppression of civil liberties and the presence of an all-powerful central government.

In chapter VI, Article 225 of the Constitution (Consitution 1988), the topic of the environment was dealt with:

> Everyone has the right to an ecologically balanced environment, which is a public good for the people's use and is essential for a healthy life. The government and the community have a duty to defend and to preserve the environment for present and future generations.

Paragraph 1 set out the government's responsibility to obtain these rights:

1. preserve and restore essential ecological processes and provide for ecological treatment of species and ecosystems,
2. preserve the diversity and integrity of the genetic patrimony of the country and to control entities engaged in research and manipulation of genetic material,
3. define, in all units of the Federation, territorial spaces and their components that are to be specially protected, prohibiting any use that compromises the integrity of the characteristics that justify their protection,
4. require, as provided by law, a prior environmental impact study, which shall be made public, for installation of works or activities that may cause significant degradation of the environment,
5. control production, commercialisation and employment of techniques, methods and substances that carry a risk to life, the quality of life and the environment,

159 The eighth Constitution in the history of Brazil entered into force on October 5, 1988.

6. promote environmental education at all levels of teaching and public awareness of the need to preserve the environment,
7. protect the fauna and the flora, prohibiting, as provided by law, all practices that jeopardize their ecological functions, cause extinction of species or subject animals to cruelty.

§2 of Art. 225 provides that those who undertake mining activities shall restore any environmental degradation to its previous condition, according to the technical standards issued by the competent public authority.

One of the most important legal regulations (§ 1,4) requires that the competent authority requires in advance a written assessment of the impact that any potentially harmful activity could have on the environment. Permission to start construction of the installation or to commence the activity is made conditional on the submission of this study (Rocha 1989).

- §3: Procedures and activities found to be harmful to the environment shall entail criminal and administrative sanctions against the polluters – natural or legal persons – without prejudice to the obligation to remedy the damage caused.
- §4: The Brazilian Amazonian Forest, the Atlantic Forest, the Serra do Mar, the Pantanal Mato-Grossense and the coastal zone are part of the national patrimony, and they shall be used, as provided by law, under conditions which ensure the preservation of the environment, therein included the use of mineral resources.
- §5: The unoccupied lands or lands seized by the states through discriminatory actions which are necessary to protect the natural ecosystems are inalienable.

Although these statements were kept in a very general form and the nature of the measures was completely open, Article 225 was only included in the Constitution after tough debates in the Constituent Assembly. The Brazilian environmental movements played a major role in the first inclusion of an environmental chapter in the Federal Constitution.[160] Fábio Feldmann, member of Parliament of the Green Party (Partido Verde), coordinated the environmental activities and acted as mediator between the ecological movement and the Constituent Assembly. Environmental protection had been successfully incorporated into the Federal Constitution in an adequate form. In 1988/89, environmentalists engaged with strong commitment in anchoring environmental protection in the constitution of federal states.

Overall, it can be stated that "the Federal Constitution of 1988 represented a milestone in the Brazilian environmental legal system" (Silva and Lages 2020, 24) and included significant advances for environmental protection. An environmental dimension of fundamental rights was added to the social dimension (Melo-Reiners 2009, 165). Thus, the full extent of the worsening ecological problems of the Amazon region was officially recognised in Brazil (Vieira 1988; 1993, 113). The environmental legislation also included effective resource protection in the Amazon area. The environment was recognised as a constitutional right "since its violation encompassed risks that included political, legal and social insecurity, standing out for the rapid trajectory of transformation and incorporation in the law" (Silva and Lages 2020, 22).

160 Cf. Chapter I.6.2

The concept of "national patrimony" (§4) meant for the Amazonian rain forests that they are protected and that land use in these regions is carried out under the legal conditions that guarantee the preservation of the environment. However, the term "national natural heritage" is not clearly defined, the spatial boundaries of the large-scale division of the natural area are not clearly established and no land use plans are drawn up. Specific legislation on ecologically compatible land use did not exist.

The previous approaches to a natural or economic differentiation of large areas, e.g., for spatial planning in Amazonia, had been based on different criteria (agro-ecological zoning, economic-ecological zoning), which were often completely incompatible with reality.

After the dissolution of the former authorities IBDF (forestry), SUDEPE (fisheries), SUDHEVEA (rubber extraction) and SEMA, IBAMA was founded in February 1989 as the new central authority for the environment and renewable natural resources. As an independent organisation, IBAMA was initially attached to the Ministry of the Interior and was responsible for formulating, coordinating, executing (including by delegation) and monitoring national environmental policy. IBAMA thus took over the tasks of the former SEMA and was now responsible for the implementation of the new National Environmental Programme (PNMA), which was financed with US$ 200 million in international funds (World Bank 1990).

Against the background of increasing internal disputes over non-compliance with environmental laws and strong external pressure on the Brazilian government for better protection of the Amazon rain forest, IBAMA's task was to devote more attention to monitoring natural resources and controlling economic activities. This concerned in particular the detection and prosecution of illegal logging and the prevention of illegal trade in wildlife, hides and skins.

As part of the reformulation of numerous legal provisions, it was also stipulated that the legally binding forest reserves of each plot of land must be registered in the land register in order to prevent sale and subsequent clearing. CONAMA had to cede the political function of advising the president to the Supreme Council for the Environment (CSMA), which led to competence problems.

As a new substantive version of environmental policy, the programme Our Nature (Nossa Natureza) was implemented in the last phase of the Sarney government in 1989, which was greatly enhanced by political propaganda (a catalogue of environmental measures unique in the world). The objectives of the programme, the main points of which were incorporated into the Constitution, were the protection of large ecosystem complexes, the systematic organisation of environmental protection, strategies to prevent environmentally harmful activities, environmental education and the development of public awareness for nature conservation. In addition, the organisation of settlement and exploration of the Amazon region, the appropriate use of renewable natural resources, the regeneration of damaged ecosystems and the protection of Indigenous tribal groups and their collective economy were mentioned as objectives (Constituinte 1989).

Within the framework of the Nossa Natureza programme, numerous laws and ordinances were passed that were intended to restrict the existing scope of action of economic actors in the Amazonian rain forest for environmental reasons. For example, all tax incentives for cattle grazing projects in the planning region Amazônia Legal were cancelled, initially limited to 90 days. In addition, all companies involved in the industrial processing and trade of raw materials had to register with IBAMA. The conditions for charcoal production were also detailed, and producers were obliged to carry out reforestation. Six inter-ministerial working groups were set up to propose solutions.

Finally, in July 1989, the National Environmental Fund (FNMA), one of the components of Nossa Natureza, was established. The future resources of the fund were to be used for the development of projects that took into account the environment and natural resources.

Like the establishment of SEMA and IBAMA, Nossa Natureza should be seen as a reaction to the vehement criticism of international institutions, foreign governments and NGOs rather than an independent concept. Before the announcement of the Nossa Natureza programme, there was – once again – a highly polemical discussion in the media by senior military officials about the threatening internationalisation of Amazonia and the endangerment of national security. Even civilian members of the government, such as the IBAMA president, were not fully informed about the content of Nossa Natureza until the programme was announced.[161]

The establishment of environmental agencies and the passing of corresponding laws were by no means a guarantee that the issues discussed were put into practice and that the legal requirements were fulfilled. Due to its size – the planning region Amazônia Legal covers an area of more than 5 million km² – and the natural conditions, the Amazon region was difficult to fit into the state regulatory framework. In particular, it was a major problem to monitor the implementation of the necessary measures and their impact. On the other hand, the administrative apparatus was in a constant process of reorganisation and development projects were underway or being planned. Apart from the existing difficult coordination problems, the effectiveness of the measures was also hampered by pervasive corruption (Kohlhepp 1991a).[162]

When in 1988 and 1989 government agencies and even President Sarney overreacted and described the justified criticism of deforestation as harassment and attempts to internationalise Amazonia, this was certainly not the best way to convince domestic and foreign observers or even international lenders that the problems were being discussed soberly and objectively or that the political will existed to enforce the new environmental legislation (Schipulle 1989). In the new Constitution, clear-cutting was still seen as evidence of economic activity, even though the destruction of rain forests often did nothing but fuel speculation, which led to an increase in land values.

The new Constitution addressed two other fundamental problems of Amazonia: Land reform and Indigenous problems.

Land reform gave rise to heated debates, but the final text showed the domination of the interests of the landowning class, especially in the National Union of Landowners (UDR). Art. 184, in principle allowed the central government to expropriate rural landholdings that did not fulfil their social function. However, expropriations for the purpose of land reform were not supposed to affect productive property and were "in a sufficiently vague manner so as to block effective redistribution of land" (Rocha 1989, 77). Agrarian reform was postponed. In the preference for the economic constitution and the lack of a forward-looking development concept, the problematic relationship

161 Cf. *Jornal do Brasil*, April 7, 1989.

162 Today, the Sarney government is considered disastrous by Brazilian experts. Clientelism was widespread, with long-lasting consequences for the Brazilian Republic after the military dictatorship.

of the new Constitution to the reality of the country found its most obvious expression (Paul 1990; 1994, 204).

Article 231 of the Constitution recognised the social organisation, customs, languages, beliefs and traditions of the Indigenous peoples, as well as their original rights to the lands they had traditionally inhabited. Formal ownership and demarcation of their lands rested with the central government. The Indigenous population was granted exclusive extraction of resources from soils, rivers and lakes. However, there was an important exception: in the case of exploitation by third parties,

> the exploitation of resources from rivers, including the generation of energy, as well as mineral extraction and research in the lands inhabited by Indigenous tribes, shall be made conditional upon a prior authorisation from Congress, which can only be granted after consultation with the interested Indigenous communities (Rocha 1989, 82).

These communities must share in the profits from exploitation. The problems of natural resource exploitation in Indigenous territories have not been solved to this day and the laws are repeatedly circumvented through exemptions.

According to Rocha (1989, 82), "it is clear that the Constitution stopped far short of a clearcut solution of this highly controversial issue," and the prohibition of all mineral exploitation on Indigenous lands would be the best solution. Art. 232 states that Indigenous individuals and communities have legal capacity and are represented by a public defender (Ministério Público). FUNAI remained the official body entrusted with the task of representing the interests of Indigenous communities.

Brazil's quite progressive environmental legislation was unfortunately in stark contrast to actual practice, which was characterised by disregard for environmental regulations, especially in Amazonia (Melo-Reiners 2009, 165). The 1988 Constitution "failed due to the real conditions of implementation, remained in many parts symbolic external representation of the political system without chances of normative integration into the social process" (Paul 1994, 204).

The discrepancy between the claim to protect the tropical rain forests with the new environmental legislation and the reality in Amazonia could not have been greater. Despite the commitment of some employees of the environmental authorities, scientists, and NGOs, and despite the increasing awareness of the media, individual and group interests in combination with organisational deficits had so far managed to prevent a general breakthrough in the protection of the forests of the Amazon region. Conflicts of interest over land settlement and land use in Amazonia have escalated to the point of violent confrontations.

Against this backdrop, and given the disastrous financial situation of the country, the fact that in 1989 only one third of the US$ 180 million earmarked for investment in Nossa Natureza was available was proof that the attempts to halt the progressive destruction of biodiversity in Amazonia with innovative laws in the new Constitution were in jeopardy. During the Sarney government, there was a lack of political will to implement the environmental protection measures enshrined in law in the Constitution. This was especially true for the protection of the tropical rain forests, for which external funding was offered but still rejected by the government.

6.2. The emergence of environmental movements and their active political role[163]

As early as the most repressive phase of the military regime in the early 1970s, the first cautious statements on environmental policy were made, pointing to the ecological consequences of the uncompromising economic development model. Criticism of the development strategy of the time was interpreted by the military as subversive behaviour and identified as anti-government with accusations of communist infiltration. Thus, it is understandable that criticism dared to be voiced mainly in scientific circles and on certain technical issues.

Although the Fundação Brasileira de Conservação para a Natureza (FBCN) had been founded in Rio de Janeiro in 1958 as the first nongovernmental organization (NGO), the group was recruited from the elite of traditional conservationists and did not achieve prominence. In addition, regional efforts by conservationists and naturalists to establish nature reserves became known.[164] All these approaches had no environmental significance.

In 1971, with the founding of AGAPAN, the first NGO in environmental protection and an important movement in Porto Alegre/Rio Grande do Sul, environmental problems were put into a development policy context for the first time. José Lutzenberger, an agricultural engineer who had previously worked in the chemical industry in the area of crop protection, initiated the discussion about the consequences of the rapid modernisation of agriculture with aggressive statements against the use of agrochemical products. He began a vigorous campaign against pesticides and in favour of organic farming. In his Brazilian *manifesto*, provocatively titled "The end of the future?" (Lutzenberger 1977), he vehemently criticised Brazil's economic development model and the power structures behind it. His commitment to an ecological society soon brought him contacts with European environmental groups and thus an international reputation as a particularly militant environmental activist.[165]

At the end of the 1970s, the first signs of a political-ideological approach linking social reforms and ecological goals began to emerge. Despite some courageous actions by individual campaigners, the environmental movement had not yet succeeded in influencing the political debate (Viola 1988).

This changed quickly, however, when the 1979 amnesty allowed numerous exiles to return to Brazil, helping to spread European environmental ideas. Militant leftists associated with "green" ideas during their exile in Western Europe became leaders of the Brazilian environmental movements and also played a crucial role in the founding of the Green Party (Partido Verde, PV). After the military regime, these informa-

163 This chapter is based on Kohlhepp (1991d).

164 Regional activities took place in Santa Catarina (Raulino Reitz), Espírito Santo (Augusto Ruschi) and Rio Grande do Sul (Henrique Rössler) as well as of the well-known landscape architect Roberto Burle Marx.

165 During the Collor de Mello government (1990–1992), Lutzenberger was appointed the first special Secretary of the Environment in 1990. He used his position to reverse policies that favoured large corporations to destroy Amazonian rain forests and played an important role in the recognition of Indigenous territories. Permanent attacks by powerful interest groups hindered his activities. After a sharp confrontation with a vice-president of the World Bank and his provocation against IBAMA, which he called a 100 % subsidiary of timber trade, he had to resign in March 1992.

tion streams met the youth of a new middle class that, after a long period of political repression, sharply attacked the military's earlier decisions in the economic and socio-political spheres.

In Brazil, the development of the Green Party and its electoral potential was linked to the emergence of this new middle class, whose youth wanted to articulate their protest in social and environmental policies. Environmental groups succeeded for the first time in 1982 in electing three deputies at the state level in Rio de Janeiro, São Paulo and Rio Grande do Sul. The decisive year of the environmental movement's political participation was 1986, when various meetings produced the environmental organizations' guidelines for the new federal Constitution, as well as non-partisan "green lists."

When the environmental movement could not agree on the formation of a Green Party, the leading "Greens" Fernando Gabeira, Carlos Minc[166] and Liszt Vieira entered into a coalition with the Workers' Party (Partido dos Trabalhadores, PT) in Rio de Janeiro in 1987. Finally, in 1988, the Green Party (PV) was founded with the goal of implementing "socialist and ecological policies." Because of the prevailing problems, close ties had to be forged with leftist groups.

For the non-partisan Green Parliamentary Front that emerged in 1986, the lawyer Fábio Feldmann (São Paulo), already known as president of the NGO Oikos, represented the environmental movements in the Constituent Assembly and did much to introduce the environmental chapter into the Federal Constitution.

For the overall understanding of the Brazilian environmental movement, it is important to emphasise that the autochthonous groups distinguished themselves from the PV, since the founders of the PV did not come from the ecology movement but lived in exile as representatives of the leftist resistance against the military regime in various European countries and had little involvement in the self-discovery of the environmental movement in Brazil.

In the early 1990s, the programmatic statements of the new president Collor de Mello,[167] the emphasised openness towards NGOs and the involvement of some groups in the field of environmental planning and implementation created an overall positive climate for NGO activities in environmental issues. In view of the extraordinary financial bottlenecks of state institutions and the continuing administrative sluggishness, private environmental organisations saw an almost unlimited field of action for the implementation of environmental protection measures. Possibilities of tax deductibility for the establishment of environmental foundations as well as the expectation of internal and external donations and the use of tax funds for environmental projects led to a founding boom of environmentally oriented NGOs. While in 1983 SEMA put the number of active environmental groups in Brazil at 563, in September 1989 around 1500 were counted.

After the phase of protest actions and targeted public relations work, NGOs became increasingly involved in the development of solution concepts and against envi-

166 Carlos Minc became Minister of Environment in 2008–2010.

167 Collor de Mello defeated the leftist politician Luiz Inácio Lula da Silva in 1989 and in 1990 became Brazil's first popularly elected president in nearly 30 years. The country's economic decline, a staggering foreign debt and hyperinflation, failed to improve. Moreover, Collor de Mello was accused of corruption, and he resigned in December 1992 as his trial was about to begin. He was convicted in 1993 and barred from holding public office for a period of eight years.

ronmentally harmful development projects, organised seminars and workshops with specific problem-oriented environmental topics.

Admittedly, it must be borne in mind that only a few environmental organisations had the technical capacities, the organisational structure and the national and international contacts to carry out sound and continuous work in the environmental field. Many new environmental NGOs tried to participate in environmental projects of government agencies, especially in the run-up to UNCED 1992 in Rio de Janeiro and because of the expected funding from external sources. Aziz Ab'Sáber (1989) saw less the problem of administrative inexperience or opportunistic free riders among NGOs, but rather the lack of ecological expertise among many of those involved.

At the beginning of the 1990s, there was a wide spectrum of impressive environmental activities shortly after re-democratisation:

- professionally managed large organisations, which had a special lobby with state environmental entities, performing a kind of consulting function, with technically and politically experienced leaders and competent collaborators (e.g., SOS Mata Atlântica, São Paulo, founded in 1986);
- smaller, tightly managed NGOs, whose high level of factual competence was concentrated in a specialized leader (e.g., IEA, Mary Allegretti, Curitiba; 1986; Ecotrópica – Foundation for support of life in the tropics, Adalberto Eberhard, Cuiabá; 1989);
- organisations close to political parties that had political influence through well-known personalities and integrated environmental activities into economic and socio-political objectives (e.g., NGO Oikos, Fábio Feldmann, São Paulo; 1982);
- groups that had constituted themselves as NGOs with a regional reference (e.g., Amazonia) or sectoral goals (e.g., environmental education) on a scientific basis and due to many years of ecological research beyond day-to-day political events. They were led by scientists with an international reputation without a large administrative apparatus and worked voluntarily on a multiplier basis with publications or TV-presence (e.g., CNDDA, 1967, with Orlando Valverde and colleagues in Rio de Janeiro; ADEA, 1974, with João José Bigarella in Curitiba);
- nature conservation groups of traditional orientation, which without elaborate organisation in the beginning focused on local or micro-regional environmental problems, starting their activities on a voluntary basis and contributed with their public relations work to the strengthening of the environmental awareness of the population (e.g., APREMAVI, Miriam Prochnow, Wigold Schäffer, Alto Vale do Itajaí, Santa Catarina; 1987), among others;
- groups with an idealistically philosophical view of nature conservation, at that time especially in Southeast and South Brazil;
- groups that were increasingly or exclusively activist and wanted to raise awareness in demonstrations or special actions in the environmental field or were using environmental issues in a specific party-political way but did not strike for concrete project activities.

Some of the smaller NGOs have been particularly active in Amazonia, where they have contributed a lot to the analysis of problems of exploitation in this region and have developed approaches to solving unsolved problems.[168] In addition, they even succeeded in raising international funding through extensive applications.

In 1992, the UNCED conference also led to the founding of a so-called "consórcio," an association of 13 environmental organisations that sought to allocate foreign debt and use this money for environmental projects ("debt-for-nature swaps"). A debt-for-nature swap is an agreement in which an indebted developing country, in exchange for the cancellation of part of its foreign debt, seeks to create funds in local currency that will be used to finance a specific conservation programme. Debt-for-nature swaps are not part of World Bank lending. However, the objectives of debt-for-nature swaps fit with the Bank's support for conservation and debt reduction, and such arrangements have been facilitated by the World Bank.

Project proposals included the establishment of "Unidades de conservação" (protected areas: parks, biological and ecological reserves) at federal, state and municipal levels, environmental education and ecotourism, establishment of databases, and institutional strengthening of NGOs and research institutes. The total amount of projects submitted up to June 1990 was US$ 265 million (Kohlhepp 1991d).

It became apparent that the favourable situation in the implementation of the UNCED findings in 1992 was exploited in Brazil, sometimes leading to generous cost calculations for project proposals and raising suspicions of a bidding mentality out of self-interest (staff positions). In view of the advantageous upswing in the environmental sector, considerable expertise in the field of application was deployed and competition for funding developed. Major multinational environmental organisations (including WWF) had close links with Brazilian NGOs and were already quite generous in co-financing projects.

By networking environmental activities, conservation organisations increasingly received support from Indigenous organisations, from the independent rubber tapping movement and from church circles.

The 1990s showed an impressive development of NGOs, which increasingly became involved with meaningful ideas in public discussions, in the environmental impact assessment of major projects, and in the critical analysis of official environmental policies. This was especially true for their activities regarding Amazonia.

---

168 CNDDA, founded early in 1967, with its publication "A Amazônia Brasileira em Foco;" IEA (Institute of Amazonian Studies), founded in 1986 in Curitiba, with research in Acre on extractive reserves and *seringueiros* (Allegretti 1990); among others, SOPREN (Belém), ECOTRÓPICA (1989, Cuiabá), ECOPORÉ (1988, Ação Ecológica Vale do Guaporé, Rolim de Moura, Rondônia), FBCN (1958, Rio) and Fundação GAIA (founded in 1988 by Lutzenberger) had projects in Amazonia in 1990. In 1990, IMAZON (Amazon Institute of People and the Environment), later on one of the most active NGOs, started its activities in Belém.

II Promising environmental concepts for Amazonia under pressure by economic growth and agrobusiness strategies (1990s–2018)

1. Previous international initiatives for the protection of tropical rain forests

First warnings from scientists about the consequences of the destruction of tropical rain forests were already expressed in the early 1970s. The report to the US-president in 1980 entitled "Global 2000" also showed serious consequences of rain forest destruction. The topic became a key international issue when the effects of large-scale slash-and-burn operations on the global climate and the emergence of a dangerous greenhouse effect were predicted.

International activities to protect tropical rain forests had been wide-ranging, from a global plan to individual projects. Participants were international governmental organisations, national governments, and NGOs at an international and national level.[169]

1.1. Tropical Forestry Action Plan (TFAP)

The Tropical Forestry Action Plan was the most important concept at the international level with the aim to use and protect the tropical forests, respecting the national sovereignty of the rain forest countries. The TFAP had been submitted on the initiative of the FAO in 1985 and in 1986/87 presented to the public by the FAO together with the World Bank, the UN Development Programme (UNEP) and the World Resources Institute.

The TFAP was an international non-binding global framework plan that served as a guideline for the development and implementation of protection and use strategies and was intended to form the basis for the coordination of international development aid and for forest protection and forest development in the tropics.[170]

The aim has been to draw up and implement national action plans for as many tropical forest countries as possible in a concerted action of all interested states and organisations.

Focus of the TFAP had been the following topics, among others:

- integration of forestry and land use,
- development of the forestry and timber industry through measures to promote adapted forestry and wood-processing industries,

169 This chapter is based on Kohlhepp (1991d); Kolk (1998).

170 Cf. Deutscher Bundestag (1990); results of the Enquete-Commission with experts' hearings in 1988 and 1989.

- conservation of tropical forest ecosystems,
- strengthening of the participating state and private institutions (NGOs).

By 1990, 23 countries had drawn up plans, forestry sector studies had been carried out in 35 countries, and 11 countries had requested support from donors. The Brazilian government under President Sarney (1985–1990) had been opposed to the TFAP.

In the international discussion of experts, the evaluation of the TFAP was extremely controversial and disparate.

The arguments of the proponents had been:

- Sustainable management of rain forests will have positive consequences (jobs, income, social facilities);
- Increased exports of forestry production will – in addition to increasing local added value – also improve the foreign exchange situation;
- The population will only show a self-interest in the preservation of the forests through a certain economic use.

Critics questioned whether these advantages could be really achieved, and the following criticisms were emphasized:

- The TFAP is too focused on forestry aspects, in particular in the industrial use of forests;
- Due to the use of financial resources associated with the implementation of the TFAP, there would be an increased negative impact;
- The people living in and from the forest being given too little consideration;
- The local population and NGOs were not sufficiently involved;
- The existing power structures would be consolidated by the influx of financial resources.

These justified doubts about the effectiveness of the TFAP were raised by both the design of the plan and the negative experience with the previous national plans. The main argument of the critics had been doubts about the concept of sustainability which would itself contribute to the destruction of rain forests through the planned forestry exploitation. In addition, it was criticised that the TFAP was not linked to other measures such as agrarian reform or debt problems.

1.2. International Tropical Timber Agreement (ITTA)

The ITTA was a primary commodity convention which was negotiated in 1983 by 36 producer and 34 consumer countries of tropical timber under the aegis of the UN Conference on Trade and Development (UNCTAD). The objectives were basically economic, but ecological aspects should also be taken into account. As an instrument of international economic policy, the convention aimed at stabilising the markets for certain primary commodities and creating a framework of international cooperation between the participating countries to solve the problems of tropical timber trade.

The aim should also be, among other topics, to ensure the use and conservation of tropical forests and their genetic resources in order to maintain the ecological balance in the affected regions. The 44 member countries, including Brazil, represented 75 % of the total tropical forest stands and more than 95 % of the international tropical timber trade.

The value of the ITTA and the activities of the International Tropical Timber Organisation (ITTO) were judged very differently. Positive views argued that the ITTA was the only UNCTAD agreement which considered the conservation of tropical rain forests. Furthermore, ITTA had been supported by trade and environmental organisations and producer and consumer countries had equal rights. Critics saw the main importing countries of tropical timber favoured. For nature conservation organisations, conservation measures should have been improved in the ITTA.

The ITTA certainly was not suitable as a basis for a global tropical forest protection policy.

1.3. Activities of international governmental organisations

Of particular note is the Man and the Biosphere (MAB) programme, launched by UNESCO in 1971, which initiated research activities on the impact of human activities on various ecosystems. Tropical and subtropical forest ecosystems had become the focus of interest.

UNESCO was mainly about developing sustainable land use concepts, which were compatible with the traditional know-how and the living conditions of the population and the ecosystems, as well as reforestation and regeneration of degraded ecosystems in the humid tropics.

The concept of biosphere reserves provided the creation of an international network of protected regions, demonstrating the value of conservation measures. Innovative in this concept was the network character linking nature conservation with research, land use planning, environmental monitoring, training, environmental education and participation of the local population. The application for recognition of a region as a biosphere reserve had to be submitted via the national MAB committee to the UNESCO-MAB secretariat.

Another UNESCO activity for the protection of tropical forests was the World Heritage Trust Fund. The legal basis for the Fund was the Convention for Protection of the World Cultural and National Heritage, adopted by UNESCO in 1973. The aim of the Fund was the protection of landscapes and ecosystems of outstanding universal significance which were already subject to nature conservation regulations and had been classified as national parks. UNESCO funds have been made available for this protection.

There was a difference between world heritage site and biosphere reserves: "nature and species conservation figure most prominently in the first, while in the second the emphasis is on human beings and the harmonious integration of their needs into the natural environment" (Deutscher Bundestag 1990, 610).

In this context, it had been discussed to make high compensation payments to the tropical forest countries in return for the abandonment of the use of forests.

As already mentioned, the UN Environmental Programme (UNEP) gave assistance – together with the FAO, among others – for the implementation of the TFAP. The activities of UNEP are combined with strategies to ward off climate change and its consequences. Based on the premise that tropical forest countries need their forest products to feed their population and to reduce foreign debt, in 1988 UNEP proposed the establishment of a global tropical rain forest conservation fund. A worldwide forest inventory, realized by the FAO in certain periods of time was of great importance.

The objectives of UNEP had been the coordination of conservation activities and improving analysis of the destruction, while also verifying the extent to which the Environment Programme could mobilize financial and technical aid within the UN system. Furthermore, to develop a global, regional and national awareness of the impact of the destruction of the tropical forests and to find ways and means for the Environmental Programme to strengthen the national capability of managing and conserving the tropical forests in six selected developing countries (UNEP 1989, 29). UNEP and the World Meteorological Organisation founded in 1988 the Intergovernmental Panel on Climate Change (IPCC) with the objective to prepare internationally coordinated scientific studies of the effect of climatic changes. The main aims for its working groups concentrated on ascertaining "the contribution made by forests to the carbon dioxide balance in the earth's atmosphere, to determine the impact of deforestation on the increased concentration of greenhouse gases in the atmosphere and to investigate the extent to which forests counteract climatic changes" (Deutscher Bundestag 1990, 612).

1.4. International government initiatives

The destruction of tropical rain forests and its consequences had increasingly caused attention in international conferences on the highest levels, particularly the Economic Summits.

The Economic Summit held in Toronto in June 1988 was the first attempt in international government initiatives with a declaration of the need of conservation of the tropical forests, among other topics of climate change.

During the Paris Economic Summit in July 1989, at the level of the heads of governments, environmental policy issues, especially the conservation of tropical rain forests, were given the highest priority. The participating countries agreed to provide financial and technical support to the efforts of states with tropical forests. The initiative of the Federal Republic of Germany had been especially accepted as the basis for joint action in this field. A fundamental message of the Paris Summit was also that in future economic decisions should take greater account of environmental concerns. In this context, there has been a discussion on reducing the foreign debt of heavily indebted countries in favour of environmental measures.

The Economic Summit of Houston in July 1990 has been setting the course decisively. Germany confirmed its pioneering role in the protection of tropical rain forests. The World Bank, the EC-Commission, and the Heads of State of the seven most important industrialized countries (G7) offered Brazil a Pilot Programme to protect the tropical forests (PPG7), which was accepted by the new Collor de Mello government under the pressure of the upcoming global UNCED meeting in Rio de Janeiro in June 1992. This meeting, called in Brazil Eco-92, which in addition to a great challenge for the host should also bring completely new possibilities for environmental agreements offered chances for the implementation of extensive and regionally concentrated tropical rain forest programmes, such as the PPG7.[171] The active participation of international and Brazilian NGOs has been considered as very important for the discussion of environmental and Indigenous issues in relation to tropical forests.

The 4th Action Programme of the European Community (EC) for environmental protection had spoken out in favour of placing even greater emphasis on the importance of forests in the EC's development and cooperation agreements. In bilateral cooperation between EC member countries and developing countries large sums of money (1988: US$ 434 million) were allocated to forestry, with forestry being included in general agricultural programmes in particular.

From 1976 to 1986, the EC had supported 206 projects of NGOs in developing countries with over DM 450 million (Latin America: 28.5%), some of which were also invested in projects for the conservation of tropical forests. However, except for general forestry projects, EC's efforts in the direct area of tropical rain forest protection had not progressed beyond the design stage (cf. Deutscher Bundestag 1990, 632).

1.5. The German contribution to the protection of tropical rain forests in Brazil until 1990

At the end of 1989, the Brazilian government, the World Bank, and the German government agreed to jointly finance the Brazilian National Programme for the Protection of the Environment (PNMA).

The objectives of this programme were:

- Securing the forest protection zones, in particular in the Amazon region: National Parks, biological and ecological reserves etc. (Unidades de Conservação);
- Conservation of endangered ecosystems: Atlantic forests, mangrove areas, Pantanal;
- Strengthening of federal and state environmental authorities.

In planning the programme, Brazilian and international NGOs had been actively involved (e.g., Funatura, SOS Mata Atlântica, WWF). During the first PNMA period of three years US$ 200 million had been available (World Bank 58%, Brazil 23%, Germany 19%).

In addition to securing forest protection zones, extractive reserves for rubber tappers, etc., strengthening of IBAMA had been a main issue. Until 1993, Germany made DM 250 million available for the protection of tropical rain forests in Brazil, for reforestation of degraded former forest areas and for productive forest management and the creation of sustainable forms of forest management.

Furthermore, some bilateral environmental projects with Brazil had been implemented, including cooperation with political foundations and churches, with NGOs in Brazil as well as environmental projects in non-Amazon regions (Serra do Mar in São Paulo, Pantanal). These support measures and concrete proposals should encour-

171 Cf. Chapter II.2

age Brazil to continue improving the necessary framework conditions in legal, institutional, social, and economic terms, as well as to include important environmental aspects in structural adjustment programmes.

The findings of the Brundtland Commission (Commission on Environment and Development 1987) in 1987 has shown that there is a direct correlation between environment and development. Without massive outside help, developing countries will not be able to break out of the vicious circle of poverty and environmental degradation. As part of internationally coordinated measures, Germany participated in the development of concepts to support Brazil (Schipulle 1992, 152; Bundespresseamt 1990). This also included the exchange of debts for rain forest conservation measures (debt-for-nature-swaps) and regulations for the tropical timber importing industry.

The Enquete Commission Preventive Measures to Protect the Earth's Atmosphere of the German Parliament, which was composed of members of parliament and invited scientists, presented the 2nd report in 1989 after three hearings with numerous international and national experts, one year of deliberations and the inclusion of scientific research results, focusing on "[p]rotecting the tropical forests: a high-priority international task."[172]

Based on a detailed inventory of the extent and causes of tropical rain forest destruction, a far-reaching concept of measures with numerous coordinated and timed policies of national, European, and international level was recommended. These recommendations for action had been submitted to parliamentary decision-making. The goal was to bring about the widest possible and fast-acting protection of the tropical rain forests and the Indigenous population living in them.

In contrast to the Sarney government (1985–1990), the Collor de Mello government, the first democratically elected President in 30 years, who had come in office in 1990, had expressly welcomed those initiatives and its willingness to cooperate.

This was evident both at the UNCED meeting in Rio de Janeiro in 1992 and in the preparation and implementation of the International Pilot Programme for the conservation of Brazil's tropical rain forests (PPG7),[173] which started immediately afterwards.

1.6. UN Conference on Environment and Development (UNCED) in Rio de Janeiro in 1992

The United Nations Conference on Environment and Development (UNCED), also known as the Earth Summit, was held in Rio de Janeiro in June 1992. This global conference, held 20 years after the first Human Environment Conference in Stockholm in 1972, had worldwide repercussion and brought together political leaders, diplomats, scientists, representatives of the media and NGOs from 179 countries, focusing on the impact of human socio-economic activities on the environment and measures for defence of the environment. A "Global Forum" of NGOs was also held in Rio de Janeiro at the same time, bringing together numerous NGO representatives, who presented their specific vision of the world's future in relation to environment and socio-economic development.

172 Deutscher Bundestag (1990); statement: Kohlhepp (1989c), among others.

173 See chapter II.2.

The primary objective of the Rio Summit was to produce a broad agenda for international action on environmental and development issues that would help to guide international cooperation and development policy. The conference was an extremely relevant event for the consolidation of environmental law on a global level and especially in Brazil.

The Earth Summit concluded that the concept of sustainable development[174] was an attainable global goal at the local, national, regional or international level. It also recognised that integrating and balancing economic, social and environmental concerns in meeting our needs is vital for sustaining human life and that such an integrated approach had to be realised. This required new perceptions of the way making decisions for production and consumption. This concept caused a lively debate within governments and between governments and their citizens on how to ensure sustainability for development.

Five major documents[175] had been produced in the UNCED event:

- Declaration of Rio de Janeiro on Environment and Development,
- Declaration on Forests' Principles,
- Convention on Biodiversity,
- Convention on the Climate,
- Agenda 21.

The Rio Declaration proclaimed 27 principles, referring to the "integral and interdependent nature of the Earth". The first principle stated that sustainable development primarily concerns human beings, who are entitled to live healthy and productive lives in harmony with nature. Principle 11 created an expectation that states will enact environmental legislation. Further articles include formulations of the precautionary principle, which should be "widely applied by states according to their capabilities" (principle 15). National authorities should endeavour to promote the internalisation of environmental costs (pr. 16).

Very clear statements appeared in principle 22:

> Indigenous people and their communities [...] have a vital role in environmental management and development because of their knowledge and traditional practices. States should recognise and duly support their identity, culture and interests and enable their effective participation in the achievement of sustainable development.

Even in this relatively modest form, this was of extraordinary importance for the situation in the Amazon region of Brazil, as for the first time the Indigenous population was seen in a larger overall context.

The Declaration on Forests' Principles (formally the Authoritative Statement of Principles for a Global Consensus on the Management, Conservation and Sustain-

---

174 A vast number of publications on this subject appeared, showing the multiple dimensions of sustainable development (Browder 1989; Goodland (1990b); Adams 1991; Goodman and Redclift 1991; Sachs 1992; Clüsener-Godt and Sachs 1995; among others). Cf. Sachs (1980) on ecodevelopment. The Earth Summit also led to the creation of the Commission on Sustainable Development (CSD).

175 Published by the UN Department of Economic and Social Affairs (DESA), New York, 1992.

able Development of all Types of Forests) was another 1992 statement produced at the Earth Summit. It is a non-legally binding document that makes several recommendations for conservation and sustainable development forestry. The negotiation of the document was complicated by demands by developing nations in the Group of 77 for increased foreign aid in order to invest for the setting aside of forest reserves. Industrialised nations resisted those demands, and the final document was a compromise.

The purpose of this document was to provide a framework for national action and international cooperation and:

- strengthening political commitment and action at all levels to implement effectively sustainable management of forests,
- enhancing the contribution of forests to the achievement of the internationally agreed development goals.

It was recognised that sustainable forest management, as a dynamic and evolving concept, is intended to maintain the economic, social and environmental value of all types of forests, for the benefit of present and future generations. Its effective implementation is needed at all levels, dependent upon adequate financial resources and the transfer of environmentally sound technologies.

The document expressed utmost concern about continued deforestation and forest degradation, as well as the slow rate of afforestation and forest cover recovery, about the resulting adverse impact on economies, the environment, including biological diversity, and "the livelihoods of at least a billion people and their cultural heritage." Although the goal of the forest convention, bound by international law, had not been achieved, the Forest Declaration signed by 172 states and the forest-related chapters of Agenda 21 (chapter 11: "Combating deforestation") have nevertheless set out fundamental guidelines and approaches for conservation and sustainable forest management. As Brazil owns 30 % of the world's tropical rain forests, the development processes in Brazil played a strategic role in the fight for forest conservation, decisive for the future. The impacts of climate change on forests and sustainable forest management and the contribution of forests to coping with climate change were highlighted. The document tried to convince member states that the implementation of sustainable forest management is dependent on good governance at all levels.

The Convention on Biological Diversity (CBD) was a multilateral treaty. The convention had three main goals: the conservation of biodiversity, the sustainable use of its components, and the fair sharing of benefits arising from genetic resources. Its objective was the development of national strategies for conservation and sustainable use of biodiversity. The CBD was often seen as the key document regarding sustainable development.

The UN Framework Convention on Climate Change,[176] (UNFCCC) or Global Warming Convention, is a binding treaty that requires nations to reduce their emissions of

176 "Climate change means a change of climate which is attributed directly or indirectly to human activity that alters the composition of the global atmosphere and which is in addition to natural climate variability observed over comparable time periods" (UNFCCC document, Article 1, Definitions, No. 2).

carbon dioxide, methane, and other "greenhouse"[177] gases thought to be responsible for global warming. Emissions define the release of greenhouse gases into the atmosphere over a specified area and period of time. Unfortunately, the treaty failed to set binding targets for emission reductions. Such targets were only set later in the Kyoto Protocol (1997).

Industrialised countries had to report regularly on their climate change policies and measures. They must submit an annual inventory of their greenhouse gas emissions (base year: 1990). Developing countries report in more general terms on their actions both to address climate change and to adapt to its impacts. They got funds for the preparation of the reports.

For scientists and climate activists the convention was a disappointment. It did not contribute to stabilize or even reduce emissions of greenhouse gases by industrialised countries but contained no commitment at all on reductions.

The Agenda 21[178] was a "daring programme of action", supported by 180 countries, calling for a global partnership with new strategies to achieve overall sustainable development. "The essence of human sustainability is the balance between ecological, social and economic progress. This necessitates an adequate economic development which is both socially equitable and environmentally friendly." Its recommendations provided for new methods of education and new ways of preserving natural resources. Agenda 21 was a world-wide participation programme ("our common future") and a comprehensive plan of action on global, national and local levels by UN organisations, governments, and major groups in every area with human impacts on the environment.

The Commission on Sustainable Development (CSD), created in December 1992, should monitor the implementation of the agreements. A five-year review of the progress of the Rio summit was planned for 1997 by the UN General Assembly.

177 "Greenhouse gases" means those gaseous constituents of the atmosphere, both natural and anthropogenic, that absorb and re-emit infrared radiation" (Article 1, No. 5).

178 http://www.un.org/esa/sustdev/agenda21.htm.

2. The International Pilot Programme to Conserve the Brazilian Rain Forests (PPG7: 1993–2009): An approach to sustainable regional development[1]

2.1. Introductory note

From a Brazilian point of view, the exertion of international influence and the phrase "common heritage of mankind" for the Amazonian tropical forests naturally were interpreted as conflict prone. These areas are, of course, subject to Brazilian jurisdiction. National sovereignty and the issue of the danger of a possible internationalisation of the Amazon region – sometimes played up politically in Brazil – have always been decisive factors for all Brazilian governments against international interference in the internal affairs of the country (Melo-Reiners 2009, 142 f.).

In the Amazon region, discourse dominated by international considerations and interests, the Brazilian and especially the Amazonian regional view and needs must of course be given special attention (Paul and Vieira 1993). The conservation or use of rain forests and their resources are part of national sovereignty. However, the protection of the Amazonian rain forests cannot be the sole task of Brazil but is a human task (Melo-Reiners 2009, 144) due to the magnitude and the consequences of destruction for climate change issues.

For the Brazilian population and the governments from the 1990s onwards, the search for sustainable development was of particular importance for the future viability of the country (Goodman and Hall 1990).

2.2. Situation in the Brazilian Amazon region at the beginning of the Pilot Programme

2.2.1. Inventory of the causes of rain forest destruction and necessary measures to solve the problems

The national and international discussion on the increasing deforestation in Amazônia Legal focused on the problematic development programmes of the government, the almost uncontrolled activities of private economic interest groups, the problems of the

179 This overview is based on Kohlhepp (1991e; 1992; 1995).

affected regional population, in particular the struggle for survival of the Indigenous people. Overall, environmental legislation was hardly respected and state control was still very patchy or skilfully circumvented.

The destruction of tropical rain forests and environmental damage in Amazonia was caused by mostly planned state and private activities in the following sectors:

- infrastructural measures (e.g., network of road construction; power lines),
- rapidly increasing deforestation by cattle ranches of large estate holders, combined with aggressive land speculation,
- mainly illegal wood cutting activities of sawmills and timber trade,
- extraction of mineral resources with its basic infrastructure (iron ore, manganese, bauxite),
- construction of large hydroelectric power plants with enormous reservoirs,
- large industrial complexes (alumina and aluminium industries, pig iron works etc.),
- energy production from biomass: charcoal production,
- uncontrolled spatial mobility of gold and diamond diggers (*garimpeiros*) with pollution and poisoning of rivers by using mercury in gold extraction,
- agrarian colonisation with large numbers of small-holders with slash-and-burn agriculture,
- continuous increase in spontaneous land occupation of small-holders,
- invasion of soybean cultivation into the ecosystems of Southern Amazonia, caused by the world-market oriented agribusiness,
- large agricultural and forestry projects (Jarí project),
- rapid development of urban expansion of pioneer towns and their infrastructure.

Summarizing possible measures to bring a positive influence into environmental policy, socially relevant to regional planning and to territorial organisation in Amazonia, the following direct and indirect actions for the protection of the Amazonian rain forests ought to be done:[180]

- Discourage speculative interests completely by cancellation of fiscal incentives in environmentally predatory projects, which had already been done;
- Prohibit the installation of major extensive stockbreeding projects (Hecht 1984; 1985);
- Discourage and minimize internal migration into Amazonia through special programmes, providing alternatives in the extra-Amazonian regions;
- Consolidate existing land settlement projects preventing the advance of the agricultural frontier and starting methods of ecodevelopment and agroforestry (Goodland 1989; Brünig 1989; Anderson 1990), trying to learn from the Indigenous non-predatory knowledge and methods of using natural resources (Posey 1985a);
- Stop planning of new agrarian colonisation projects;
- Provide concepts for the organisation and control of the pan-mining operations and the spatial mobility of the *garimpeiros* (Garrido Filha *et al.* 1988);

---

180 Cf. chapters I.1.–5.

- Evaluate the environmental compatibility of major projects and determine their social relevance to the regional populations (Binswanger 1987; Goodland 1989). This should involve the instrumentalisation of objective criteria. A new type of cost-benefit analysis should fit within the context of the "new rationality" (Sachs 1980), which covers both economic efficiency and ecological effectiveness. Regarding projects thought to be economically indispensable (e.g., industry and mining) there must be a new, properly considered scale of evaluation of costs. The ecological and social costs of economic growth, both direct and indirect, need to be calculated and, as far as possible, minimised (Kohlhepp 1989b; 1990);
- The positive effectiveness of these projects must be seen on both the medium- and long-term basis. All this meant going beyond the traditional approaches of pillage, exploitation, and use, which were devoid of any commitment to the true potential. This called for a political will to make its clout felt over and above the economic lobbies (Kohlhepp 1991e, 155 f.);
- Install and protect areas for permanent preservation or preferential conservation, such as conservation units and Indigenous reservations (Constituinte 1989). This concept already existed but the reservations will undoubtedly need to be protected in a more efficient manner;
- Realize a new concept that arose in 1985 in setting up "extractive reserves," a term for renewable resource use patterns in the tropical rain forests of Amazonia, in the areas of autonomous wild rubber tapping operations. These areas are occupied by social groups, whose survival depends on the gathering and use of products native to the forest (fruits, oils, gums, medicinal plants etc) and who have developed means of ecologically sustainable use (Allegretti 1990, 1994; Nepstad and Schwartzman 1993);
- The concept of reservation areas for extractivism – with renewable forest resources open to economic activities by traditional local populations – resembled the concept of "Indigenous reservations," that are also protected by law for the exclusive use of the respective groups. The economic feasibility of the extractive reserves has been questioned (Homma 1994) as regards to prices, transport facilities and market conditions, and there remained doubts about the future inclination of these groups to stay within this system of traditional economy if other economic options or alternatives appear;
- Reforest degraded areas with native species, although it was well known that this is difficult to achieve (Valverde and Freitas 1980; Fearnside 1989b), using the *Floram* suggestions (IEA/USP 1990). Without suitable reforestation, charcoal production for pig iron plants along the Carajás railway was a highly predatory activity and needed fundamental revision in terms of energy supply;[181]
- Decentralise research on Amazon environmental problems to the Amazon region itself, strengthening of the regional research and environmental institutions (Lourenço 1995);
- Focusing efforts on urban planning and the reorganisation of urbanisation in order to improve the quality of life for urban populations and create new urban development models with an environmental and social basis and find solutions to adapt them to their role in a sustainable development pattern (Becker 1985 and 1995; Coy 1992; Silveira 1993).

181 See chapter I.4.2.5; Muntingh (1988); Sternberg (1988); Mahar (1989); Kohlhepp (1989a).

2.2.2. The situation of deforestation

The development programmes of the Brazilian Military Governments for the planning region Amazônia Legal in the 1970s and 1980s had led to a quickly increasing destruction of the Amazonian rain forests. The Operation Amazonia (1966–1970), the Programme of National Integration (PIN, 1970–1974), the Polamazônia programme (1974–1980) with the starting activities of the private sector, the "Integrated rural development programmes" of the beginning 1980s and the "mega-programmes" of the later 1980s had disastrous consequences.[182] Numerous scientists had already pointed out the dangerously rapid increase in deforestation rates at an early stage.[183] Deforestation in Amazonia had already destroyed more than 10 % (1975: 0.6 %) of the rain forest area within 15 years, by 1990, i.e., about 410 000 km² (more than the area of Germany and Switzerland) of the 4.093 million km² total area of natural rain forests (81.3 % of the area of Amazônia Legal) in the Brazilian Amazon region.[184]

Figure 21. Deforestation in the Brazilian Amazon region 1975–1998

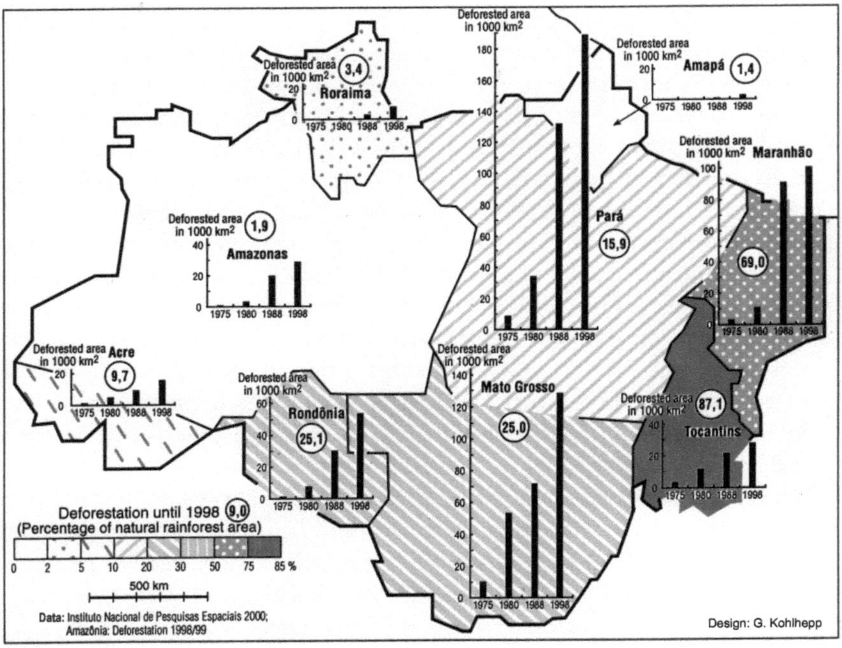

Source: Data of deforestation: INPE (1998). Regional data: calculations by the author in: Kohlhepp (1998a, Fig. 2).

182 See Volume 1 (Jan Kleinpenning) of this publication and volume 2 (Gerd Kohlhepp) chapters I.1–5.

183 Sioli (1973; 1984; 1985); Mahar (1989); Fearnside (1989b; 1990), among others.

184 Kohlhepp (1998a, Table 1): based on Skole and Tucker's (1993) calculation of the natural rain forest area of Amazonia and calculations of the author about the proportion of the deforested rain forest areas on the respective area of the Brazilian federal states in Amazonia. Data of absolute deforestation until 1990: INPE (1998).

In 1990, regional disparities in deforestation in the different states of Amazonia were extraordinarily large. While only 1.4 % of the forest area had been cleared in the almost completely forest-covered huge state of Amazonas, the federal states Mato Grosso and Rondônia, suffering greatly from development pressure, already showed forest losses of 15.8 % each. Pará and Mato Grosso had the highest absolute forest destruction (Fig. 21). Maranhão (64.1 %) and Tocantins (75.5 %) showed the highest percentage of forest losses because of relatively small rain forest areas and a high proportion of humid savannahs (*campos cerrados*: MA: 44.3 % of the state area; TO: 89.1 %).

The average annual forest losses in Amazônia Legal between 1978 and 1988 amounted to unimaginably 21 130 km² (area of the state of El Salvador). From 1988 to 1991 this average annual deforestation decreased to 11 130 km² (size of Jamaica), because the fiscal incentives for Amazonian investments had been eliminated. Unfortunately, this tendency to reduce deforestation could not be maintained, since the budget of the MMA had been cut in half because of the financial crisis. During the two-year period from 1992–1994, the average annual deforestation rate was 14 900 km².

According to INPE, in 1994–1995 deforested areas in Amazônia Legal reached a dizzying magnitude of more than 29 000 km² (about the area of Belgium). During the government of President Franco (1992–1994) environmental issues played only a minor role and environmental and forest protection were completely inefficient. An explanatory approach for this "explosive" increase could be found in the attempt of the main actors to clear as large forest areas as possible before and immediately after President Cardoso took office. This meant that it should be done before a reorganisation of IBAMA, feared by these interest groups as announced new laws on forest protection could be realized and lead to stronger control and severe restrictions of deforestation (Kohlhepp 1998a, 55). In the following years, deforestation decreased rapidly (1996–1997: 13 037 km²). In 1996, a series of measures was implemented by the MMA to protect rain forests. IBAMA also re-examined the forest management plans (Scholz 2002; 2007). The Cardoso government increased the protected forest share per area from 50 to 80 %. The total devastation of the natural forest cover in Amazonia until 1998 was up to 13.5 %. 83 % of this total deforestation occurred in Mato Grosso, Pará and Rondônia.

However, not only direct forest destruction, but also the indirect consequences of human influences and measures damage the forest ecosystem. Not only has selective logging destroyed more than half of the forest vegetation per unit area, but larger clearings dry out the edges of the surrounding forest areas and lead to a sharp increase in fire risk. The same problem occurred when forest remnants in clearing areas were too fragmented, which was also relevant to the question of the critical minimum size of protected forest areas (Laurance 1998).

Production of timber in logs in Amazonia increased rapidly and in 1997 amounted to 28 million m³, 75 % were extracted in Pará and Mato Grosso. Timber exports to foreign markets accounted for only 14 % of the total volume, while 56 % of the consumption of Amazonian timber was concentrated on the Southeast and South of Brazil (Smeraldi and Veríssimo 1999). The contribution of timber from Amazonia to Brazil's overall wood production had rapidly increased from 14 to 85 % in just two decades. With the destruction of Southeast Asian tropical forests, the Amazon region was targeted by transnational corporations to be the key resource area for tropical timber in the future (Cotton and Romine 1999). Asian, in particular Malaysian companies were entering in an aggressive manner trying to get concessions for large-scale-logging. Illegal timber extraction spread everywhere (Greenpeace 1997; Amigos da Terra 1997). Logging crews severely damaged 10 000 to 15 000 km² of forest per year that were not included in deforestation statistics (Nepstad *et al.* 1999). As logging was spreading across large parts of Amazonia in an unregulated manner, zoning of timber extraction should be organised according to ecological criteria and protection from logging in specific areas must be strictly controlled (Veríssimo *et al.* 1998).

Landsat satellite images were taken on a scale of 1:250 000 and evaluated in an ambitious programme by the renowned National Institute for Space Research (INPE).[185] The satellite images used by the PRODES project only recorded changes in vegetation cover from a size of 6.25 ha (Kirchhoff 1992; Miranda *et al.* 1994; Krug *et al.* 1997). The forest area affected by human activities was much larger than the figures shown in the INPE deforestation monitoring programme. This was caused by forest surface fires, getting out of control. These ground-level fires that occur underneath the canopy of rain forests could not be detected by satellite, but due to their effect of drying out the vegetation they caused later larger fires.

These fires could arise when – after a drought of five months – the drought tolerance of tropical rain forests with their natural shady, moist microclimate is exhausted, the absorbed soil water is depleted and leaf fall begins due to drought stress, which leads to a layer of foliage drying out by sunlight. As a result, and due to selective logging, which is particularly exposed to the vulnerability of the forest ecosystems, the risk of unintentional forest fires increased excessively.

The fires close to the ground, which initially leave the treetops untouched, lead to the drying out of the trunks and – a little later – to a strong fire hazard of the entire biomass. The ground-level fires enlarged the rain forest areas affected by fires up to 60 % and destroyed a high percentage of aboveground biomass, in a regionally different manner (Nepstad 1999; Nepstad *et al.* 1999). Extreme droughts in some regions of Amazonia, such as those observed in Roraima in 1998, combined with huge wildfires, will be discussed later.[186]

The detailed evaluation of satellite images by INPE and the implementation of the results in the activities of MMA and IBAMA showed very clearly the tendency of intensified fires in the east and southeast of Amazônia Legal, particularly in the Grande Carajás region, and in the north of Mato Grosso. The fire activities along the Transamazônica, the Cuiabá–Santarém road (BR-163) and the BR-364 in central Rondônia are also emerging (Fig. 22). The concentration of fires, photographed by the NOAA satellite in 1998, gives an idea of the magnitude of burning in large sub-regions of Amazonia. The "arc of deforestation" was extending from Rondônia, via northern Mato Grosso, Southeast Pará to Maranhão, causing huge emissions of CO_2 (Fearnside 1997a, b).

185 For more than 30 years, INPE analysed deforestation in the Amazon region with its monitoring systems. Brazil began to record deforestation rates in detail annually in 1988. Landsat satellite images were initially printed on paper and the size of clearings were calculated by photo evaluation. The PRODES (Measurement of Deforestation by Remote Sensing) project was based on Landsat satellite images and later by NOAA satellite and others. Today, INPE's programmes are internationally recognised. The systems were digitised in 2003. The modernisation process of INPE and the interference of the Bolsonaro Government will be described in chapter III.1.

186 See chapter II.3.2.

Figure 22. Areas of concentration of fires in Amazônia Legal in 1998

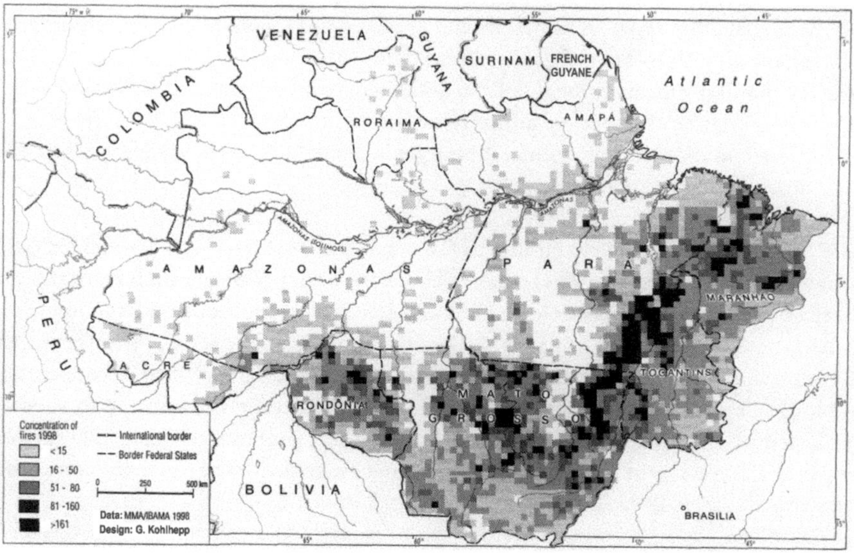

Source: INPE (1998) (map prepared by MMA/IBAMA); published in Kohlhepp (2001b, Fig. 5).

The satellite-based radar surveillance of Amazonia, which was provided for by the much-discussed SIVAM project of the Secretaria de Assuntos Estratégicos and the military, established during the Franco Government, could also be of utmost importance for the environmental authorities if the data collected were appropriately accessible. This, especially since illegal activities of logging and slash-and-burn operations could be quickly verified, and perpetrators could be identified and punished.

2.3. Creation and main objectives of the Pilot Programme

In view of this given situation, there was an urgent need of looking for new strategies of sustainable regional development. The objective of sustainable regional development proved to be highly complex and not easy to implement in accordance with the given political and social conditions:[187]

- The base factor of a "development from below" meant participation of all regional/local actors of the civil society in regional planning and development;
- An adjustment of land use to the local/regional ecological conditions has to be done according to the limitations of the carrying capacity of ecosystems;
- Permanent control of the process of realizing sustainable development with "popular monitoring" by the civil society would be essential;

187 Sustainable regional development: Cf. Sachs (1992); Clüsener-Godt and Sachs (1995); Coy (2001; 2005).

- A stronger orientation towards endogenous potentials and "milieus" of regional/ local production will be of decisive importance;
- Strengthening regional networks and local/regional economic cycles and improving the situation of social groups fighting for survival;
- Harmonizing local/regional politics with policies on other administrative levels;
- Improving the efficiency of administration;
- A re-evaluation of the regional identity will contribute to the awareness of a sustainable use of regional resources.

The International Pilot Programme to Conserve the Brazilian Rain Forests (PPG7)[188] was a result of the international concern about the destruction of rain forests and was based on the initiative of the German Chancellor Kohl at the Houston Economic Summit of the G7 countries in July 1990. Following the request of the G7 governments, the Commission of the European Community and the World Bank joined in cooperation with the Brazilian government to prepare a comprehensive programme to substantially reduce the deforestation rate in Brazil. The G7's proposal to financially support the Brazilian review of new regional development models for the Amazon region, that had already started, was accepted by Brazilian authorities.

Despite all counteracting activities, new discussions on the national sovereignty and the resistance of Brazilian nationalists and economic lobbies against foreign interference in Brazilian domestic policies, the Collor de Mello government[189] submitted a programme proposal to the G7 countries at the London Summit in July 1991. This was just on the eve of the Rio UNCED, focused on the spotlight of the international public.

In December 1991, the programme was approved by all the countries and institutions involved, and the G7 countries, the European Union, together with the Netherlands, renewed their commitment to provide financial and technical assistance for about US$ 250 million initially, which was later greatly increased. The objectives of the so called PPG7 programme were endorsed, the World Bank was commissioned to coordinate the programme and a Rain Forest Trust Fund (RFT) with about US$ 60 million was established under World Bank trusteeship. In terms of project financing, the G7 countries acted as donor countries. The financial benefits were gifts and were not based on the usual lending. Germany contributed with about 50 % of the costs.

The PPG7 applied to all tropical forests of the country, i.e., also to the Atlantic rain forests (Mata Atlântica), already largely destroyed (Dean 1997), but the absolute focus was on the Amazon region. It consisted of a set of projects that should contribute to the sustainable development of natural and human resources. The overall objective was "to maximise the environmental benefits of Brazil's rain forests consistent with Brazil's development goals" (World Bank 1994). This had to be achieved through the implementation of a sustainable development approach.

Referring to the strategy of sustainable development, Sachs (1992) who elaborated the ecodevelopment concept (Sachs 1980; Glaeser 1984), included five dimensions of sustainability (social, economic, ecological, spatial, cultural), which go much beyond

188 The PPG7 analysis in this chapter is based on publications of Kohlhepp (1995; 1998a; 2001a; 2005; 2018).

189 With José Lutzenberger as special Secretary of the Environment in a period of transition until the establishment of the Ministry of Environment in December 1992.

the vague definition of the Brundtland Commission (1987) "development which meets the needs of the present without compromising the ability of future generations to meet their own needs." The key issue of sustainability can be defined as "improving the living conditions of human communities, while keeping within the limits of the carrying capacity of the ecosystem" (Sachs 1992).

The goals and approaches of the regional development policies of the World Bank have changed since the 1960's. Modernisation theory and aims to catch up with the development level of industrial countries characterised the projects of the 1960's and 1970's. Growth poles, which proved their negative consequences in increasing regional disparities were replaced at the beginning of the 1980's by the poverty-oriented concept of integrated rural development, considering basic needs, participation and development from below. The environmental concept, in addition to the social relevance of projects, became predominant during the 1980's, and just before the beginning of the 1990 decade, the new paradigm of sustainable development prevailed.

Through the attainment of the PPG7 objectives, there was a possibility to provide a model of North-South cooperation on global environmental issues – global actors as the World Bank, G7 countries and the European Community with national, regional, and local Brazilian actors – and to prove the feasibility of harmonising economic and ecological objectives in tropical rain forests. Moreover, it helped to preserve biodiversity and the immense genetic resources of the tropical rain forests, as well as to reduce Brazilian carbon emissions by reducing the deforestation rate (World Bank 1994).

The Pilot Programme has been conceived as an experimental programme with the goal to introduce the sustainable use of resources and to make the results transferable to other tropical rain forest regions. It was a unique opportunity to realize the principles of sustainable development, established at the Agenda 21 of the UNCED Summit in Rio de Janeiro, in 1992.

The basic insight of the Rio Summit laid above all in the fact that the protection of tropical forests could not be limited to the spatial segregation of large forest areas. In the beginning, this had been demanded in the "puristic" ecological and nature conservation debate. With sustainable forest management and resource use, socio-economic and socio-cultural factors for the benefit of local/regional forest dwellers gained greater attention.

Protecting all forest areas without any use was and is until today an unrealistic and politically unenforceable idea in the countries concerned. However, the objective must be a resource-conserving national development policy in which the measures for the conservation and sustainable management of tropical forests are embedded. This was the goal in the preparation and implementation of the PPG7.

With the explicit emphasis on national sovereignty and the determination not to regard tropical forests as a "global good," the traditional reservations of Brazil and other emerging and developing countries against the "global allocation" of tropical forests and against international initiatives for tropical forest protection were dismantled. This opened the way for the PPG7 to be realised in Brazil with the prospect of success.

The coordination structure of the PPG7 emphasised the central function of the new Ministry of Environment (MMA) on the Brazilian side, which prepared the projects in cooperation with some ministries (Justice, Science and Technology) and specific authorities (IBAMA, FUNAI). The World Bank had decentralised programme governance, coordination, and auditing of the process with a new department in Brasília – at the special request of the International Advisory Group (IAG)[190] – where some donor countries and the EU also had their own project coordinators on the ground. In the years of preparation of PPG7, the Brazilian government had fundamentally changed the structure of its environmental policy. After many years of experimentation, a fully functional Ministry of Environment with a special focus on the Amazon region (SCA) had emerged at the federal level only in December 1992.[191] At the regional level of the federal states, a first basis of environmental authorities had been laid in Amazonia, which were specifically improved by the PPG7 as part of decentralisation strategies (Becker 2001; 2010).

The increasing willingness of institutional actors in the national and global spheres to be flexible and to consider regional challenges with increased networking of activities in terms of content and space, had resulted in a programme that tested indicators for sustainable development under the improved framework conditions of an integrated regional policy.

Numerous innovative statements, the reduction of regional conflicts through articulation and participation of those affected, involving a wide range of local actors in a bottom-up approach, were positive features of this pilot phase. Furthermore, the focus was laid on a coordinated action of the federal government, the regional and local level and on the embedding of projects in a targeted accompanying programme of applied research.

The main objectives of PPG7 can be summarized as follows (World Bank 1993, 1994; MMA/SCA 1996; MMA/World Bank 1998):[192]

- Preserving biodiversity and genetic resources of tropical rain forest ecosystems;
- Serving as a model of North–South cooperation to resolve global environmental issues;
- Proving the compatibility of ecological, economic, social objectives and environmental policy in the protection and use of the natural resources of tropical rain forests;
- Contributing to decrease emissions of CO_2 by reducing the rate of deforestation;
- Changing development strategies to a sound environmental and social concept;
- Keeping economic growth within the limits of the carrying capacity of the ecosystems;
- Protecting the living space of Indigenous populations.

190 The International Advisory Group (IAG) had been installed in 1993 as an independent international scientific commission, whose 11 members had been proposed by the World Bank, the G7 countries and the Brazilian Government for their expertise on Amazonia. There were experts from seven scientific disciplines (Forestry, Ecology, Biology, Human Geography, Sociology, Agronomy and Anthropology) and from seven countries (4 Brazilian scientists). The IAG exercised an advising role throughout the Programme, with its members being replaced after one or two 4-year periods. In numerous working sessions in Brasília and many excursions in different regions of Amazonia with detailed project analysis, proposals had been made for improving the PPG7 and the content of the projects. The author of this publication, as a Human Geographer, had been a chairman (1993–1997) and member of the IAG (1993–2001).

191 In the same month, President Collor de Mello was accused of corruption, and he resigned in December 1992 as his trial was about to begin. He was convicted in 1993 and barred from holding public office for a period of eight years. His successor was Vice-president Itamar Franco (1992–1994).

192 Ministério do Meio Ambiente, dos Recursos Hídricos e da Amazônia Legal (Ministry of Environment, MMA); Secretaria de Coordenação da Amazônia (SCA); cf. Kohlhepp (1998a).

To achieve these very ambitious objectives, the following sets of measures were implemented, which were reflected in the various projects of the PPG7:

- Strengthening federal authorities in the implementation of sustainable environmental policies, including local knowledge, with the participation of NGOs and the private sector;
- Improving the management of natural resources and of protected areas;
- Promotion of small projects of regional NGOs and dissemination of knowledge;
- Goal-oriented promotion of applied research on sustainable management.

2.4. Structure, subprogrammes and components of the Pilot Programme

In contrast to the lack of a stable concept of the military governments for the regional development of Amazonia,[193] the guiding objectives of the Pilot Programme were now in line with the declared development goals of the new democratic government (MMA/SCA 1995) and with a declaration of consensus by the affected federal states in Amazonia, which were of crucial importance in the context of the planned decentralisation of the Brazilian development policy.

The PPG7 comprised four subprogrammes which helped strengthening the institutional capacity of the public sector, consolidating, and enforcing the implementation of a sound environmental policy as well as improving the management of natural resources and protected areas, by encouraging ecologically appropriate investments, and by monitoring and controlling the environmental impacts. The first projects were approved in 1994 and implemented in 1995:[194]

- Demonstration Projects (project proposals of NGOs),
- Applied Science and Technology,
- Natural Resources Policy Project,
- Management of Natural Resources.

2.4.1. Demonstration Projects

The so-called "Demonstration Projects" were key elements of PPG7, which had generated high expectations at the NGO level, regarding the possibilities of financial resources to promote small-scale development initiatives and direct benefit to the regional population. For the first time, an attempt has been made to approach a "development from below," in which the local and regional population (smallholders, rubber tappers, Indigenous tribal groups, environmental protection groups) received grants and could articulate proposals in low-impact use of native forest resources (agroforestry, rehabilitation of degraded land, medicinal plants) tailored to their needs and to implement them at the municipal level. The importance of creating knowledge in agroforestry (Anderson 1990; Smith *et al.* 1996; 1998) and the dissemination of the results cannot be

193 See chapter I.1-5; cf. Kohlhepp (1987a).

194 In 1995, President Fernando Henrique Cardoso took office (1995–2002).

emphasised more strongly. The focus was on testing alternative solutions to local environmental problems.

In view of numerous previous attempts to carry out nature conservation with government-controlled initiatives, the demonstration projects were based on the granting of the necessary leeway for the projects themselves by the affected groups and special attention was placed on the feasibility of small projects.

The MMA and the NGO umbrella organisation for Amazonia GTA decided together on the allocation of funds. The financial resources – relatively small sums of an average of US$ 140 000 per project – went directly to the NGOs through a special funding channel set up by the Bank of Brazil. Fortunately, one of the most serious impasses of the project, the formal guarantee-requirement of donor countries for the proper application of funds, could be also solved. This was absolutely new in an international cooperation.

Furthermore, a network of NGOs was supported in the project areas (Hall 1997a). About 300 NGOs are coordinated in Amazonia by the GTA which tried to build up organisational capacity, essential for the effective execution of this high-risk project. More than 600 community groups, associations of rubber tappers and environmental organisations had been key partners of the project. Fortunately, the projects had developed extremely favourably and had very positive diffusion effects. Promising initiatives such as environmental education, projects at small community level and proposals from Indigenous groups were implemented in numerous municipalities and sub-regions of Amazonia (Théry 1997a; 1997b). Workshops for the exchange of experience in different regions of Amazonia as well as training courses were particularly successful.

The appropriate marketing of products manufactured in sustainable use will become increasingly important in the future to strengthen the motivation and economic ability to survive of the groups involved, as was demonstrated in the extractive reserves. To this end, the private sector needed to be involved in a much greater extent. Germany not only contributed more than 60 % to the financing of the demonstration projects, but also in this special case exceptionally waived the false use guarantee by the Brazilian government. This was realised to implement the project, which could not give it to NGOs.

The Demonstration Projects offered a unique and innovative opportunity for a partnership between governmental and non-governmental organisations with positive spread effects for the regional population.

2.4.2. Applied Science and Technology

This subprogramme combined the need to improve scientific research on Amazon ecosystems and the sustainable use of their resources, as well as to promote the dissemination of scientific knowledge. Two well-known centres of excellence, the INPA (Instituto Nacional de Pesquisas da Amazônia, Manaus) and the Museu Paraense Emílio Goeldi (Belém), were selected to receive extra support, in order to substantially improve the regional research basis and to help recruiting and retaining researchers of the highest scientific level.

The "direct research" component for problem-oriented research enabled highly qualified scientists of the Amazon region to apply for funding, the projects being selected by a Brazilian Scientific Evaluation Commission on a transparent competitive basis. More than 100 projects with a specific innovative approach had been approved in the first period of the subprogramme. There were three research priorities: Amazonian ecosystems' structure and function, sustainable natural resource management, combined with the recuperation of degraded areas and socio-economic as well as cultural systems in man-environment relations. An attempt was made to achieve an even more direct orientation of research projects towards the needs of the affected regional target groups and the region-specific challenges to strengthen the long-demanded scientific contribution to sustainable regional development in Amazonia (Kohlhepp 1987e).

Several G7 countries participated in this subprogramme with associated bilateral projects, which were concentrated on tropical ecology and environmental research. Projects of the German-Brazilian scientific and technical cooperation within the framework of the SHIFT programme (Studies on Human Impact on Tropical Forests and Floodplains in the Brazilian Tropics) (Kohlhepp 1997a; BMBF 1998)[195] were understood as a German contribution[196] to this subprogramme and were closely tied to the objectives of PPG7 in terms of content. It was focused "on the assessment of the impact of human activities on tropical ecosystems and should contribute to the development of sustainable land use systems in tropical regions, in which progressive destruction of the environment and, as a consequence, disturbances of large-scale climate occurred" (Lieberei and Salati 1998). Furthermore, it contributed to the aims of the UNESCO research programme Man and the Biosphere. SHIFT was an interdisciplinary, multi-institutional programme pretending to link basic and applied research to contribute to the solution of major environmental problems in the tropical forests and floodplains of Brazil. In a series of intensive SHIFT workshops in Brazil and Germany, research results were presented and discussed. Representatives of the politically responsible authorities of the Brazilian Ministry of Environment and project coordinators of some of the donor countries also participated. German and Brazilian scientists wanted to transfer the results to the PPG7 projects, which were in preparation at the time.

195 The SHIFT programme (CNPq/MMA/IBAMA – BMFT/BMBF, 1990–2002) was the largest bilateral research programme of the two countries. Focus was on the Amazon Basin (Eastern and Central Amazonia, Várzea), the floodplain of the Pantanal and the catchment area of the Upper Rio Paraguai in Mato Grosso. A wide range of scientific disciplines and dozens of Brazilian and German universities and research centres were involved. Many scientists on both sides owed their career to SHIFT. Outside the Amazon region, the forests of the Mata Atlântica had been part of this research programme in tropical ecology. SHIFT's scientific yield was exceptionally good, as evidenced by numerous publications, including high-ranking research results. One example is the successful cooperation between the UFMT in Cuiabá and the chair of Human Geography at the Latin America Research Centre of the Institute of Geography at the University of Tübingen, which has resulted in numerous dissertations (cf. Kohlhepp 2017b; see chapter II.8.2). Scientific programme coordinators of SHIFT were Eneas Salati (São Paulo) and Wolfgang J. Junk (MPI-Plön/Germany). Another German-Brazilian research programme in the Amazon region dealt with Mangrove Dynamics and Management (MADAM 1995–2005), i.e., sustainable management of mangrove forests and its resources in the Belém coastal region.

196 See the publications of the German Ministries BMBF (1995) and BMZ (1998).

2.4.3. The Natural Resources Policy Project (NRPP)

This subprogramme integrated four projects dealing with national resources policy: institutional strengthening of the state environmental entities in the nine states of Amazonia, zoning, monitoring, and control activities. The project had the objectives to strengthen the policy analysis and the implementation capabilities of the entities, dealing with environmental management, at the federal government, state, and municipal level. The active participation opportunities of the regional and local population played a special role. The aim was the permanent resolution of conflicts of interests and the coordination of PPG7 with the regional and environmental policy planned for Amazonia.

In addition, the concept of the so-called "zoning" was put to the test. To this end, an extensive methodological discussion took place,[197] with doubts remaining on the methodological approach. The priority of drawing up an information system on the basics of spatial planning in the sense of strategic planning proved necessary. The zoning project consolidated the results of the ecological-economic zoning study, carried out by the Brazilian Institute of Geography and Statistics (IBGE), in order to establish a system of territorial information for critical areas in the Amazon region. Existing land tenure and land use problems made the transfer of the results of zoning an emergency case and an important political instrument. Zoning and legislative measures have to be linked, in order to establish a clear basis for state and municipal authority actions, as to what purpose such zoning should be used for. The risk of misuse and the risk of being ecologically and socially counterproductive has to be seriously considered.

Integrated environmental management projects were based on a governmental environmental plan that must define problems and carry out strategic actions in priority regions to solve the problems. Only in a further step, land use planning can be carried out for critical regions with the participation of all stakeholders. This certainly entailed risks in the implementation but was indispensable for the realisation of spatial planning measures. The ministries of environment of the Amazonian states Acre, Pará, and Amazonas were supported in the implementation of the projects by experts from the German Society for Technical Cooperation (GTZ).

2.4.4. Management of Natural Resources and Conservation Units

The very ambitious, comprehensive, and complex subprogramme consisted of a group of important basic projects that should contribute to the sustainable use of natural resources and thus to consolidate Brazil's environmental policy. Conservation units are areas legally established by the government, in order to meet the needs of protection and sustainable exploitation of biodiversity.

This subprogramme covered the following components:

- Demarcation and protection of Indigenous people and territories (PPTAL);
- Establishment of Extractive Reserves (Resex);

197 Ab'Sáber (1989; 1995); SAE (1991); Schubart (1994); Kohlhepp (1995); Nitsch (1996); Becker and Egler (1997); MMA/SCA (1997); Mahar and Ducrot (1998); Mahar (2000); Mello (1997; 2000); Mello and Théry (2001).

- Sustainable management of forests and support measures for forest administration (Promanejo);
- Management of natural resources in floodplain areas (ProVárzea);
- Establishment of "ecological corridors" (parks and reserves);
- Monitoring and control of slash-and-burn operations (Prodesque).

The demarcation and protection of Indigenous people and territories was one of the long-planned projects, controversially discussed in domestic politics and highly sensitive (Kasburg and Gramkow 1999).[198] Priority was given to the survival and protection of the Indigenous people living in rain forests and the safeguarding of their habitat, cultural identity, and ecologically adapted forms of economy. When the project was started, the number of Indigenous people living in the Amazonian forests was estimated of about 300 000. The key programme components were the identification, demarcation, official recognition, and registration of Indigenous territories, securing the Indigenous peoples legal rights to their land, accompanying studies and training measures as well as support of the implementing agency FUNAI.

The Integrated Project for the Protection of Indigenous Peoples and Lands in the Legal Amazon (PPTAL), implemented by FUNAI, was the result of a partnership between the Brazilian government, the German government, and international technical and financial support agencies, such as the United Nations Programme for Development (UNDP) and the World Bank. The project was designed as an open programme in cooperation with the German GTZ and largely financed by Germany.

The PPTAL encouraged the participation of Indigenous communities and organisations through support for monitoring projects for demarcations in progress and surveillance plans for lands already demarcated. It also provided support for training actions related to territorial management and protection by the Indigenous peoples.

When the project was included in the PPG7 in 1994/95, only about half of the 416 Indigenous territories recognised by FUNAI had been legally secured. The total area of the Indigenous reservations officially covered about 21 % of the area of Amazônia Legal, often hardly protected. Since the beginning, the legislation of Indigenous territories has been extraordinarily complicated and required the formal steps of identification, definition of boundaries, demarcation, and homologation (official registration).

In the PPG7, 115 areas of about 47 million ha were demarcated with funds from the PPTAL. The work included the opening of aisles in the forests, the setting of border markers and finally the preparation of the entire process of legislation. In addition, identification and studies of cartographic determination were carried out in 70 new areas and the identification was completed.

The implementation of the project was in the hands of FUNAI, which could count on the support of GTZ and some NGOs. Since the appeals filed under Decree No. 1775 of 1996 against the recognition of Indigenous reservations had been rejected by the Ministry of Justice, it was hoped that further delays in the project could be avoided (Kohlhepp 1998b). In November 1997, another 8.7 million ha were registered as Indigenous reservations.

The identification and demarcation (May 1998) of the Indigenous territory Javarí on the border of Peru, with 8.3 million ha the largest and perhaps least known Indigenous

198 See chapter I.3.2.

area in the west of Amazonia, was very important for securing this area. The participation of tribal groups in the border markings of the Indigenous areas made the demarcation procedures more efficient and cost effective. The monitoring of the control of the reservations contributed to a higher success rate. The Indigenous people had used the natural resources of the tropical forest ecosystems for a long time without causing environmental degradation. The tribal groups' special knowledge of the regional natural resources (Posey 2000) was considered fundamental for the sustainable use and management of forest resources.

Fig. 23 shows the legal situation in 1998 of all Indigenous territories within the PPTAL. Very large Indigenous areas are located in the north and west, on the borders with Surinam, Columbia, and Peru, which were – as many other similar areas – decisively promoted in the PPG7 programme and looked forward to final demarcation or homologation. However, this map does not yet say anything about the state of border security of the reservations and about the conditions of the increasing expansion pressure of the economic actors in Amazonia.

Despite conservation of natural resources in the Indigenous territories and thus the protection of the living space of these groups, the dangers of degradation and loss of native knowledge could not be completely ruled out. Added to this were the modern goals of commercialisation of natural resources (e.g., the sale of wood) by the younger Indigenous generation.

The protection of Indigenous territories and their inhabitants was extremely necessary in order not to continue exposing the vulnerable groups to the development pressures of modern Brazil. The project was a milestone in the never-ending story of discussions on the need of reservations or questioning their demarcation, or even the recurring ideas of a hasty integration of the Indigenous tribes into the world of neo-Brazilian economic interest groups.

The PPG7 tried to help the Brazilian government financially and technically to demarcate the Indigenous areas and to protect them with the active participation of the Indigenous population. The necessity to include a boundary enforcement component in this project was based upon the fact, that the spatial, physical, and cultural integrity of the Indigenous groups was threatened (Kohlhepp 1998b; Pasca 2004; Heck *et al.* 2005). Since the demarcation of these reservations is anchored in the Brazilian Constitution and half of the Indigenous territories had not yet been demarcated, there was an urgent need to speed up this process. One of the most serious problems was the resettlement of non-Indigenous squatters and the prevention of invasions by large landholders, *garimpeiros*, and timber companies, as the information of the planned activities could encourage the invasion of the areas to be demarcated. To clarify the situation, studies were undertaken of more clearly defining the scale and nature of the non-Indigenous occupation of reservation areas and thus also to ensure that isolated tribes that had not yet been contacted could continue to be protected.

The international financial resources available made it more difficult for objections of state governments and private actors to disrupt and for fiscal arguments to cancel or postpone this project. The PPTAL contributed decisively to the rapid identification and demarcation and for a better knowledge of the areas inhabited by Indigenous tribes. Field work in more than 180 Indigenous areas was executed and the project could be completed very successfully (Gramkow 2002).

Figure 23. Legal situation of Indigenous reservations in 1998 in the PPG7 project Indigenous Lands (PPTAL)

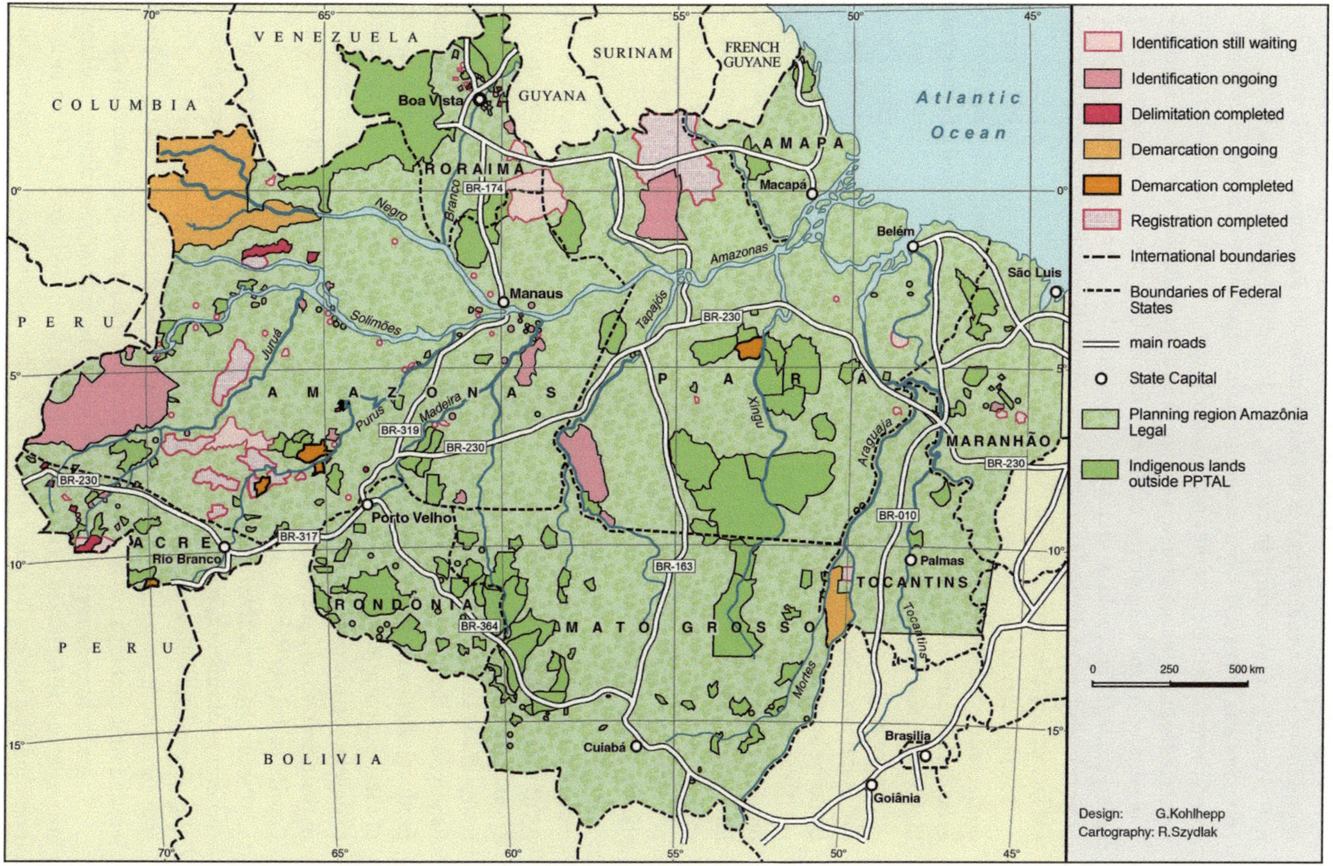

Source: Maps and documents of FUNAI and GTZ; published in Kohlhepp (1998a, Fig. 5).

The project demarcated 50 % more Indigenous territories and registered 40 % more than originally planned. While deforestation in Amazônia Legal had increased rapidly and in the forest-covered states of Mato Grosso and Rondônia already amounted to well over 20 % of the natural forest area, the degree of deforestation in Indigenous reservations was only 1.5 %, which underlined the importance of protected regions. This strengthened the hope that the prevention of forest destruction would then continue in protected regions without foreign support and without delays. The efficiency of PPTAL was reduced by the long period of 15 years for implementation, originally 6 years had been planned. This could be attributed to logistical problems in the execution of this project in regions of difficult access in Amazonia, the cumbersome bureaucracy, and the lack of qualified employees at FUNAI.[199]

The project was extremely sensitive to nationalistic political trends, but progress in demarcating and protecting Indigenous reserves could no longer be postponed. However, the allocation of land for Indigenous reservations has remained a permanent and highly controversial topic to this day.[200]

Improving the management and the conservation of the rain forest by "promoting sustainable social, economic and environmental management methods based on the knowledge and traditional practices of the local Amazon population" (World Bank 1994) was the main objective of the establishment of the "Extractive Reserves" (Resex) project. An extractive reserve is an area used by traditional populations whose livelihood is based on extraction and subsistence agriculture. The establishment of extractive reserves intended to grant the non-Indigenous population of the rain forest a permanent collection right of use, without felling trees. The families have been living there since the rubber boom in the late 19th century for over 120 years.

Despite their official name, extractive reserves are multiple-use areas that included extractive as well as small-scale agricultural activities. The economic viability of these groups could not be assured by rubber extraction alone. The forest dwellers extracted different non-timber forest products (latex, fruits, palm pulp and fibres, resins, nuts) and engaged in subsistence agriculture (in a very limited area), hunting, fishing, and the processing and hopefully a well-prepared marketing of non-timber products (Assies 1997). The basic objectives are to protect the livelihoods and culture of these people and to ensure sustainable use of natural resources. The new approach to developing the concept of extractive reserves[201] aimed to realise an intensification in the direction of agroforestry (Fearnside 1989e), an idea developed by the National Council of Rubber Tappers and its advisors.

The idea of extractive reserves is said to have originated in 1985 at the first national conference of rubber tappers in Brasília. This meeting formally united tappers and environmentalists who were interested in saving the Amazonian rain forest. The rubber tappers' movement was led by Chico Mendes, who faced death threats by cattle ranchers and timber companies and was ultimately murdered in Xapuri (Acre) in 1988.

In extractive reserves, the land is owned by the federal government, the land and its resources being leased to traditional dwellers. The land cannot be sold or used for non-forest activities. The administration of these areas was in the responsibility of

199 Information by KfW in Ex-Post Evaluation Brief of PPTAL in 2013.

200 See chapters II.7.2 and III.3.

201 Allegretti (1990; 1994), among others; Clüsener-Godt and Sachs (1994); Emperaire (1996).

IBAMA, together with local communities. The objective of such a partitioning of land ownership was to eliminate land speculation and conflicts as destabilising factors for extractivists.

Rubber tappers and Pará nut collectors should be enabled to an ecologically sustainable, socially acceptable, and economically viable use of resources. Protection against forest destruction, legal safeguarding of their living and economically used area, strengthening of local communities and conservation of biodiversity were key objectives. Already in 1980, about 68 000 rubber tapper families had been counted but the number may have been much greater. They occupied 4–7 % of the area of Amazônia Legal at a density of 300 to 500 ha per family, i.e., 1.0–1.7 persons/km^2. Families have the right to tap in their traditional collecting areas within the reserves (Fearnside 1989e).

The main components were land regularisation according to the legal basis of the Constitution of 1988 and organisational requirements for implementation, community organisation, improvement of productive activities and training for project management. The main problems were lack of sufficient land for the reserves and the need of migration to urban settlements, as had been the case in Rondônia.

The concept of extractive reserves and settlements has been subject of active debates. Extractive reserves are only one more element for rain forest conservation and development, but one of the few in which local communities have played a major role. In 1990, four extractive reserves had been established: in Acre Chico Mendes and Alto Juruá, in Rondônia Rio Ouro Preto and in Amapá Alto Cajarí, with a total area of 2.2 million ha. In the Resex project the implementation was organised and in the remaining 1990s some smaller reserves were installed in Rondônia and more reserves in Mato Grosso, Pará and Maranhão. Until 2004, about 60 federal and state extractive reserves were created and the regularisation and demarcation of 2.1 million ha of land destined for extractive reserves had begun (MMA/PPG7 2009).

The Chico Mendes extractive reserve (0.97 million ha) was the first and largest reserve, created in 1990 and today administered by the Chico Mendes Institute for Biodiversity Conservation.[202] The reserve is named after the assassinated rubber tapper and environmentalist Chico Mendes. Struggling to protect their livelihood against cattle ranchers, miners, and land-hungry settlers, the tappers had formed cooperatives.

The idea helped to consolidate support for rain forest protection in Brazil and abroad. NGOs embraced the idea, as did politicians, human and cultural rights groups, and ecologists. In other Latin American countries, where tropical forests formerly had been preserved as national parks and Indigenous reservations, new campaigns were inspired by the Brazilian model.

The project of sustainable management of forests and support measures for forest administration ((Projeto de Apoio ao Manejo Florestal Sustentável na Amazonia, Promanejo) was a pioneer project which aimed to promote the sustainable production of timber and non-timber forest products as a contribution to regional development. This project component, financed mainly by Germany, only started at the end of the 1990s. It was planned to use a broad concept of sustainable forest management, considering

202 The objective of the Chico Mendes Institute is to protect the Brazilian natural heritage and promote the environmental development. The Chico Mendes Institute of Biodiversity Conservation (ICMBio) is an autarchy and was created in 2007.

social, economic, and ecological benefits with a large diversity and scope of productive activities.

After the failure of government initiatives to diminish predatory forms of forest exploitation, forest certification based on environmental and social standards emerged in 1997, promoting sustainable forest management. Among the certification initiatives, the Forest Stewardship Council (FSC) gained significant recognition.[203] At that time, only a very small number of companies had received the FSC seal of certification in Brazil. Only one was an Amazon timber producer, a Swiss-owned company in the state of Amazonas, operating with management of natural forests (Smeraldi and Veríssimo 1999). The demand for certification depended on the awareness of the final timber consumer and the international trading and market regulations.

In view of the increase in Amazonia's participation in world hardwood trade from 2 % in 1989 to 8 % in 1995 and a boosting international pressure on timber resources, the promotion of innovative methods in the forestry sector were of greatest importance. Reforms in forest management and forest policy, the testing of techniques for careful and participating forest management in the Tapajós National Forest with the involvement of NGOs and the implementation of "social forestry" (IEA/USP 1990; Ab'Sáber 1995) activities were planned to be realised with actively involving the local communities.

Selective wood-cutting in connection with the term sustainability is a highly controversial conflict in forestry (Burger 1991; Brünig and Poker 1991). Moreover, it is highly doubtful whether this type of use will be possible in the long run under pressure of economic interests, as secondary forest destruction is high and there was only little knowledge about growth rates of tropical timber. It was clear that in future export of tropical timber certification will be a fundamental condition.

Of the other components of the project, the management of natural resources in floodplain areas (Projeto Manejo dos Recursos Naturais da Várzea, ProVárzea), which aimed at the sustainable use of the natural resources of the *várzea* areas (Sioli 1968; 1973; 1983; 1984; Sternberg 1998 [1956]; Junk 1989; Junk *et al.* 2000) with a focus on fishery, deserved special attention. This has given economically viable alternatives to slash-and-burn farming to the riverside population. The initial project proposal was submitted by IBAMA. With this project, the PPG7 enabled the training of community leaders to develop the management of lakes and training in monitoring agreements on fishing. These experiences of environmental management originated from social pacts on the use of natural resources with local communities and representatives of civil society organisations. One of the most important components was support for promising initiatives for the sustainable management of *várzea* resources.

In order to secure forest protection zones, the ecological corridors project was another key component which started in 2001. An ecological corridor is a large geographical area where coordinated biodiversity conservation measures are implemented in priority areas. Focus was given to two corridors: five large areas in Amazonia and two in the Atlantic Forest. In Amazonia, the project was carried out to integrate existing protected areas (conservation units, private reserves, Indigenous reservations) into a concept of ecological corridors and thus to create a regional network of

203 The Forest Stewardship Council (FSC) is an international coalition of environmental, social, and private-sector organisations for the promotion of sustainable forest management through voluntary certification (http://www.fsc.org).

larger areas for the protection of biodiversity, overcoming natural or man-induced barriers, enabling the dispersal of animal and plant species. The central corridor of Amazonia (52 million ha) was located mainly in the state of Amazonas, connecting the hydrographic basins of Rio Negro, Rio Solimões and other large rivers and integrating 55 protected areas (federal, state and municipal conservation units and private reserves) and 65 Indigenous reservations. From the scientific point of view this was an intact, biologically important, and high-priority corridor (MMA/PPG7 2009), covering theoretically 75 % of the region's biodiversity within one third of the forested area (Hall 2000, 102).

The ecological corridors included a variety of protected areas, the buffer zones and linkages between the areas. Effective conservation of biodiversity in protected areas within the corridors should contribute to strengthening the protected areas and stimulating natural resources management by local populations. The complex project was planned to be implemented in two phases. Conservation policies in Amazonia[204] were confronted with a series of problems in allocating scarce resources, but a new legislation, approved in 2000, created a broad range of conservation options in the National System of Conservation Units (SNUC) with the intention to ensure the consolidation of protected areas. The existence of these areas generated benefits for the society through "environmental services": good water quality, protection of soil and mitigation of the consequences of climate change. The contribution of PPG7 to the setting up of a new conservation policy has been significant.

The situation of slash-and-burn operations at the time had prompted the MMA and the World Bank to focus an originally planned project for the reuse of degraded areas on a project of measures to control slash-and-burn and forest fires (PRODESQUE). The focus should be on monitoring and, at local level, on the development and application of methods to monitor illegal logging, forest destruction and fires (Nepstad *et al.* 1999) in the priority zones of the National Resources Policy Project. The project was designed to assist federal, state, and municipal environmental agencies to develop a unified system of monitoring and surveillance for deforestation and illegal fires.[205]

In mid-1998, a project for monitoring and analysis (AMA) of the PPG7 was started, in which a systematic study of each project was carried out in order to evaluate the results and promote the diffusion of knowledge acquired. With fast feedback, the Pilot Programme and its subprogrammes and components became more transparent and, at the same time, the ability to implement the "lessons learned" and the extensive circulation of results obtained by the project were subject to critical analysis by all actors. This was carried out in cooperation with the International Advisory Group (IAG), which for the first time in this form and on behalf of all participants analysed the concept, progress in the programme, and evaluation of projects in an international environmental programme.

---

204 In addition to the Pilot Programme, the World Bank mobilized grant funding for conservation activities through the Global Environmental Facility (GEF), i.e., the National Biodiversity Project (Probio) and the Brazilian Biodiversity Fund project (Fundo Brasileiro para a Biodiversidade, Funbio), approved in 1996 (Redwood III 2002, 19).

205 In 1998, the World Bank assisted IBAMA and other state and municipal environmental agencies and local communities through a Programme for Prevention and Control of Forest Fires in the Deforestation Arc (Proarco) through a loan of US$ 15 million and a parallel US$ 2 million grant for the Prodesque project of the PPG7 (Redwood III, 2002).

Figure 24. Pilot Programme (PPG7): Approved projects in Amazônia Legal in 1996

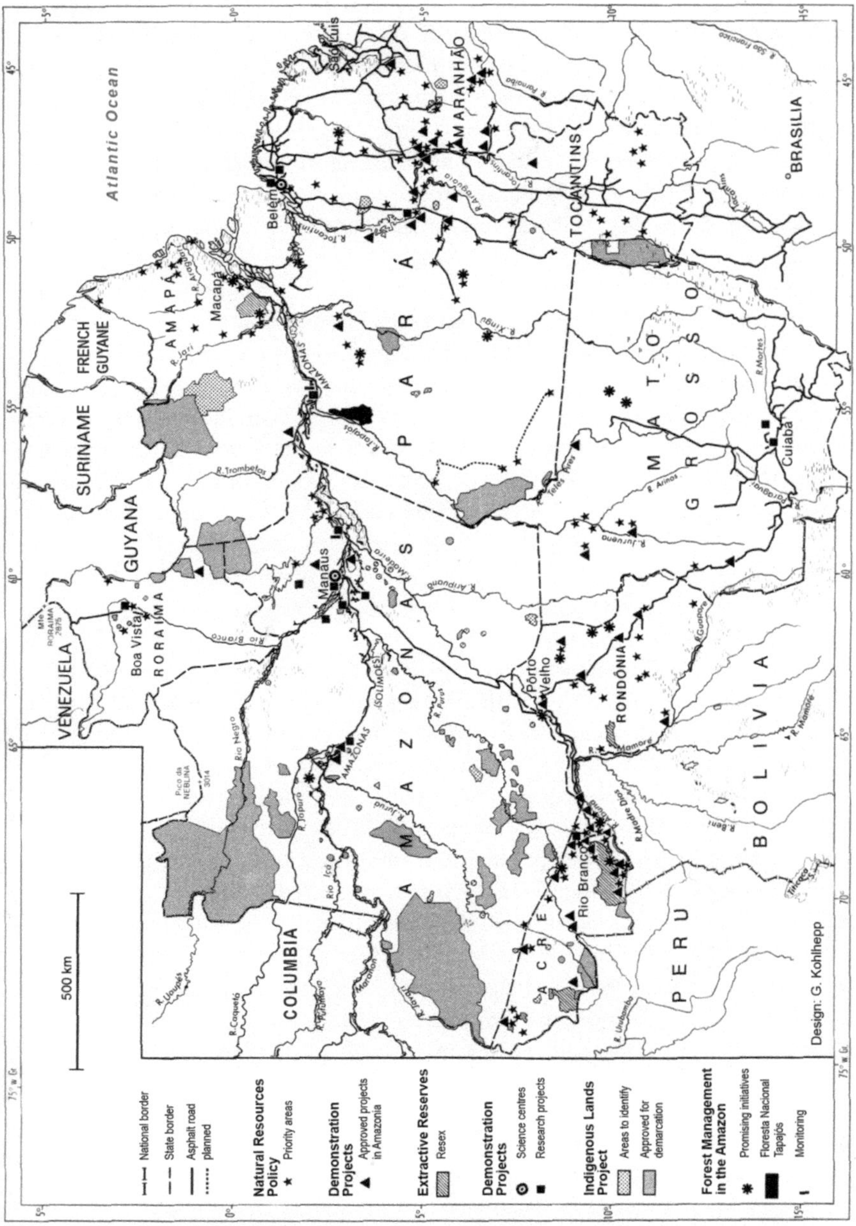

Source: MMA/SCA (1996); Théry (1997a); published in Kohlhepp (1998a, Fig. 6).

The PPG7 subprogrammes and component projects were located in all the states of Amazonia, so that there were favourable conditions for the establishment of a network of projects regionally, ecologically and socially adapted and linked with the local and regional actors of the Amazonian population.

Investments in the Pilot Programme (PPG7) totalled US$ 463 million. Germany had taken over 50 % of the total costs, the EU (excluding Germany) 12 %, Brazil took over

11 %, mainly costs of personnel. NGOs contributed with 7 % to the financing and the Rain Forest Trust Fund with 20 %.[206]

2.5. Evaluation of the PPG7: the most important results and deficiencies

The PPG7 was an extremely complex programme, and its experimental nature gave an exemplary stimulus to a learning process in sustainable development at international, national, regional, and local levels (Becker 2001). It showed a unique possibility to stimulate the authentic participation of local communities in decision-making in the resource management strategies. "The PPG7 acted as a catalysing force for sustainable development processes" (Scholz and Schönenberg 2007, 115).

During the 1990's, Brazilian governments after long inner struggles with economic lobbies made up their mind to realise the Pilot Programme to Conserve the Tropical Forests of Brazil and to install the Ministry of Environment and the Legal Amazon (MMA). The change in development strategies had been one of the basic guidelines of a hopefully announced new regional policy for Amazonia, after ecological and social disorder having prevailed in some Amazon regions over the past 30 years.

In a difficult beginning, the various actors of the PPG7, the Brazilian Government, the representatives of the donor countries and their financing and technical authorities and a new department of the World Bank, transferred to Brasília, first had to get to know each other. The exchange of different arguments resulted in an intensive and fruitful cooperation in the projects' complex preparation.

The enormous administrative difficulties with coordination problems of different legal systems, complicated approval procedures on all sides of the partners and a new process of financial transactions[207] were greatly underestimated at the beginning. This was then reflected in the running times of preparation and execution of the projects. In addition, the realisation of the projects had to be carried out with enormous preparatory work in a huge region that was hardly known in detail and difficult to access. A few years earlier, such cooperation between Brazilian government authorities and co-deciding foreign institutions would have been unthinkable.

It would have been better to install the independent multidisciplinary scientific International Advisory Group (IAG) at the moment of the political approval of the PPG7, in order to discuss the project mixture at the very beginning and to give some advice to the selection process of projects and to specific regional, ecological, and social priorities. Thanks to the excellent cooperation of Brazilian and foreign scientists in the IAG and their expertise and empirical experience through many years of research in Amazonia, respected by all participants, the responsible actors of the coordination unit for

206 Information of MMA and World Bank in: MMA/PPG7 (2009, 56).

207 Here an example: Payments are subject to budgetary obligations for a given financial year. The fear, that in the case of controversial projects (e.g., the Indigenous project) deliberately delayed planning and execution would expire funding from donor countries, could be solved positively. The German Minister of Finance, having been informed by the IAG, exceptionally unlocked appropriations committed to the financial year. As a result, these funds now were permanently available and increased the pressure on the Brazilian side of implementing the project.

Amazonia of the MMA, of donor countries and the World Bank frequently could be convinced by IAG's proposals.

Unfortunately, some important ministries, agencies, and institutions, dealing with the problems of the Amazon region, did not participate in the programme (Ministry of National Integration, Ministry of Agrarian Development, etc.).

There was no close interaction between the PPG7 and the Brazilian policy of investments in the sectors of agriculture, transport, mining, energy, and urban development. There was a lack of specific impulses to a poverty-oriented regional policy for Amazonia. The private sector – except for the NGOs – at the beginning was not integrated into the programme planning and implementing structures.

There was a wide range of possible topics within the scope of sustainable development proposals for the PPG7. Unfortunately, some complex problems were not or not sufficiently considered, such as the urban problems in an "urbanized forest region" (Becker 1995; Coy 1992; Browder and Godfrey 1997). The same applied to the nutrient potential, land use and natural resource management in the *várzea* areas or the economic activities of some regional population groups, such as gold diggers, small-scale farmers, the riverine population, fishermen and workers in commercial homework.

Conceptual weaknesses remained, such as the exclusion of smallholders' problems, those of urban environment, the issues of poverty-stricken people and the findings of scientific research in the SHIFT programme. NGOs were more likely to do pioneering work (Hall 1997a; GTA/FOE 1994; 1996), such as Poema with the help of the Daimler Benz AG in the surroundings of Belém and on Marajó Island (POEMA 1994).[208]

It turned out to be extremely important, that the overall programme concept should have interactions of sustainability components, a strategic vision of integration of the various projects with each other and into a clearly defined regional development strategy. The new regional policy of the Brazilian government for Amazonia (MMA/SCA 1995; MMA/CONAMAZ 1998) would have to reduce the previous shortcomings in the coordination of the PPG7 with important sectors of agriculture, among other sectors already mentioned and with the real political-economic framework conditions (Scholz and Schönenberg 2007). The traditional colonisation schemes of INCRA with the settlement of people in precarious conditions was counterproductive to the efforts of PPG7. In particular, the explosive problem of landless people (MST) could not be resolved with a disorganised settlement in Amazonia.

The regional state governments did not participate in the initial planning process and the information policy on the PPG7 came only very slowly to the regional and municipal levels. Parallel planning measures to solve problems affecting Amazonia outside the Amazon region did not exist.

208 Poema stands for Poverty and Environment in Amazonia Research and Development Programme. In the beginning of the 1990s, the University of Pará launched Poema on the island of Marajó with the aim of combining measures to protect the Amazonian ecosystem with initiatives to combat poverty. Among other projects, the uses of coconut fibres for the head restraints of the drivers' seats in trucks were realised. The university's venture was supported by Daimler Benz. Willi Hoss was works council at Daimler Benz in Stuttgart, member of the German Parliament and later active as an environmental activist. He contributed to the success of this cooperation.

Progress with the execution of the programme had been considerably slower than was originally hoped and caused criticism.[209] The main challenge was the need of a maximum of administrative flexibility on all parts and appropriate funding mechanisms. Approvals for international financing for PPG7 projects had been severely delayed during the Franco government. The credibility of this innovative programme depended on all the participants making a concerted effort in concentrating on key issues.

Although the PPG7 comprised an amount of nearly half a billion US Dollar, this was only a small percentage of the "normal" official investments in Amazonia. Furthermore, some of the G7 countries – especially the US – had only contributed to a very small extent to the RFT and the total costs of PPG7.

Since decentralisation allowed Amazon state governments to shape environmental policy at least partly according to their own goals, the activities and statements of the Amazon state governor caused considerable unease. While his "strategic plan to develop Amazonas" (Planamazonas) in 1994 still concentrated on major projects, the "Carta dos governadores da Amazônia", signed in March 1995 by the new governors, emphasised the new development paradigm of a sustainable development and was related to an action plan. This document demonstrated a strong political will for a national dialogue and a national consensus in environmental policy.

The implementation of sustainable development projects will be impossible without a strong effort for recuperation of popular local knowledge, accumulated by Indigenous people and *caboclo* riverine population. It has been a challenge for the Brazilian government to prove that the resolutions of the 1992 UNCED Conference are reflected by a new pattern of regional development and that their integration into the framework of the Pilot Programme is socially and environmentally sustainable.

Summarizing the most important positive results of the PPG7:

- The PPG7 was oriented to maximise the cooperation between government institutions and civil society – completely non-existing during more than 20 years of military dictatorship – and improving the public awareness of environmental consciousness;
- One of the main PPG7 contributions was strengthening the environmental institutions and building up social capital interactions from public agencies to civil society, and the private sector (Jordão 2022);
- Decentralisation of environmental management in priority areas of Amazonian states with capacity to elaborate state-controlled environmental policies;
- Evolution of a concept of joint management, with public-private-partnership between government entities and the different groups of civil society (active networks of NGOs);
- So far unknown negotiations between government, civil society and the private sector were enabled, aiming at the formation of political deals for the benefit of sustainable development ("Agendas positivas");

209 Critical programme analysis only makes sense after a certain period of time and in knowledge of all programme and project levels with regard to monitoring success. The assessments of FASE/IBASE (1993), Fatheuer (1993); Hagemann (1994) were published when the first five projects – after the signing of grant agreements – were entering the implementation phase or were still in preparation.

- Implementation of "Demonstration Projects", with the intention to generate income, strengthening of a basis of subsistence for the affected regional population, sustainable use and conservation of natural resources. This enabled creating management ability in local communities, that had been completely forgotten by the government for a long time;
- Improvement of the security of the habitat of the Indigenous population, demarcation and protection of their territories and a dissemination of the traditional knowledge of these groups;
- Development of innovative methodologies of monitoring and control of deforestation.

The obvious deficiencies of the PPG7:

- The elaboration of a group of individualised projects – according to sectoral demands of government institutions – made it difficult to prepare and implement a consistent strategy of the PPG7. This shortcoming was criticised right at the beginning by the IAG, as well as the non-participation of some important ministries, which was justified by the government with initial organisational problems;
- The articulation between the components of the PPG7 and other government programmes was fragile, including with other MMA programmes (Scholz and Schönenberg 2007);
- Some important ministries were not directly involved in the first phase (Ministry of Agrarian Development, Ministry of National Integration etc.), without this being convincingly justified;
- Urban problems were excluded in PPG7, although Amazonia was considered an urbanised forest region;
- Most of the problems of small farmers, tenants, and settlers without land title (*posseiros*) were not considered (land issues, technical assistance in small-scale agriculture, infrastructure for small-scale production). The potential for reapplication of demonstration projects of sustainable production through rural credit programmes (e.g., the National programme to strengthen family farming, PRONAF) has been little used;
- Results of the scientific SHIFT programme have only been directly incorporated to a relatively small extent into the projects to be carried out;
- The reduction of deforestation rates has not been achieved during the first phase of PPG7.

The pilot phase of PPG7 (1993–2001) aimed at maximising environmental conditions in the Amazon by intensifying cooperation between and among government institutions and the civil society. Reflections on the continuation of the programme in a second phase were strengthened in 2001. Donor countries and the World Bank attached particular importance to the inclusion of other ministries in the programming. As there was still sufficient uncalled funding, after the mid-term review the participants agreed to extend the Programme until 2009. This decision was linked to the aim of reducing excessive administration costs, ensuring faster execution of projects, and increasing the share of funding for "grass roots actions."[210]

Despite all deficits or organisational and implementation obstacles, the PPG7 has been the most extensive example of an international environmental cooperation programme, realised in the Brazilian Amazon region with the express participation of the Brazilian government. Some industrialised countries demonstrated their credibility by making their financial commitment to support the Brazilian efforts with a pilot programme in favour of an approach of sustainable development for the benefit of all inhabitants of the region and a responsible use of natural resources of the tropical rain forest ecosystems of Amazonia.

Despite start-up difficulties, the Pilot Programme had a framework that could not bring about a short-term halt of rain forest destruction but created the environmental conditions for participating action in terms of sustainability. However, the opening of economic alternatives with economically friendly management methods for the regional population in the sense of "productive conservation" (Hall 1997b), together with the awareness of the need for forest protection, will be able to slow down deforestation. This requires the political implementation of the necessary measures and the continuity of activities. Public pressure on the government increased by small farmers, trade unions and environmental activists who argued in favour of a bottom-up strategy for the Amazon based on environmental concerns (Scholz and Schönenberg 2007).

210 After six years, "the overall rate of disbursement stood at only around 30 %, suggesting poor executing capacity on the part of the government" (Redwood III 2002, 19).

3. Extensive infrastructure programmes as an extreme contrast to concurrent environmental policy measures

3.1. Brasil em Ação (Brazil in Action) (1996-1999) and Avança Brasil (Let's go, Brazil) (2000-2003/07)[211]

Since the installation of the Pilot Programme to Conserve the Brazilian Rain Forests" (PPG7) in the 1990s, state activities in the Amazon region developed in a disparate manner. On the one hand, because of UNCED 1992 and PPG7 there was the commitment to realise sustainable development, protection of the living space of the local and regional population as well as the environment as objective of regional policy. On the other hand, government's goals for the next years concentrated on intense improvement in infrastructure, regional economic growth and global market integration, a large part in the Amazon region.

The new integrated national policy for Amazônia Legal (MMA/SCA 1995; MMA/CONAMAZ 1998; BNDES 1998) aimed at consolidating the situation in Amazonia and planned, at least in the official version, to take decisive steps towards sustainable resource use oriented towards the interests and welfare of the Amazonian population through decentralisation measures and the participation of civil society. This formed a fundamental contrast to the new programme Brazil in Action and its extension in the mega-programme Let's go, Brazil, the government's new development programme, which started after the turn of the century with planning perspectives until 2007 (MPBM 1999; MPOG 2000; BNDES 2000).

The donor countries of the PPG7, which had supported Brazil with great commitment and high financial outlay and had awakened a strong environmental awareness in the regional rural population of the Amazon region, were disappointed about these highly problematic development programmes. These programmes were counterproductive to the previous environmental guidelines and associated with a high potential of forest destruction. Enormous private economic interests were involved in the strengthening of the infrastructure.

Conflicts in many sub-areas and partly of a marked regional significance were foreseeable and destroyed some of the best efforts of PPG7. These new programmes also dampened donor countries' willingness to invest more heavily in the extension of

211 This chapter is based on Kohlhepp (2001b; 2001c).

a second part of PPG7. Since in some countries press publications appeared against the investments in PPG7, which were futile from a journalistic point of view, the governments had to answer to their own population for the financing that had taken place.

As a step to improve infrastructure, "the Brazilian government commissioned a major study of integrated national development regions, identifying and evaluating hundreds of projects that offered the potential to accelerate economic and social development in coming years" (MPBM 1999, 5). Many of these infrastructure projects offered investment opportunities for private companies via privatisation, joint ventures, and other forms of participation. Specific "development structures for investment" were focussing on regional or sectorial topics.

Projects were assessed in groups in order to identify potential synergies and were analysed within the context of nine major development regions, the so-called "national axes of integration and development." These "development regions" had a certain identity, a distinct "economic vocation" and were part of a long-term geostrategic vision of national development. The terminology of the Ministry of Planning in Avança Brasil with "national axes of integration and development," "economic corridors" and the regional progress seen only in terms of economic growth reminded of the Military Governments' approach of exploitation and valorisation of the Amazonian periphery in the 1970s with the National Integration Programme (PIN).

The projects prioritised and officially mentioned, represented a potential of US$ 43 billion of total investment in Amazônia Legal from 2000 to 2007. The Brazilian government made major investments in developing projects throughout Brazil and especially in the Amazon region through the Avança Brasil programme. There, the government's goals included doubling of paved roads, the construction of waterways, ports, railways, and hydroelectric power plants.

The basic guidelines of the Avança Brasil programme (Cardoso 1998) of President Cardoso's government were:

- consolidation of economic stability,
- promotion of sustained economic growth, generating jobs and income opportunities,
- elimination of hunger, fighting poverty and social exclusion, improving income distribution,
- consolidation of democracy, promoting human rights.

As to the Amazon region, there were four bundles of projects (MPBM 1999):

1. Northern international integration,
2. logistics in the Madeira-Amazonas region,
3. logistics in Central Brazil,
4. hydroelectric generation and transmission lines.

1. The two northern Amazon states, Roraima and Amapá, should be linked with neighbouring countries by paved highways. This redrew the map for a new geopolitical scenario. Caracas could be reached by trucks from Manaus via BR-174. Besides the considerable smuggling of timber to Venezuela, the regional trade – the Manaus Free Trade Zone was a major producer of household electronics – could be expanded. It seemed

doubtful whether the government's goal to facilitate eco-tourism would be successful. The paved road connection from Macapá (Amapá) to Cayenne (French Guyana) will be complemented by a road from Boa Vista (Roraima) to Georgetown (Guyana).

Despite the military control over this northern border region, drug traffic, ubiquitous in the Amazon region, was imminent also to the Caribbean and Atlantic ports and airports (Machado 1996). The 200 km transmission line (230 KV) Venezuela–Brazil from the huge hydroelectric power plant Guri to Boa Vista, the first major cross-border energy project in northern Brazil, completed in 2000, will greatly improve energy supply in Boa Vista. Roraima had been previously excluded from Brazil's energy supply because there were no long-distance lines to the north over the Rio Amazonas.

2. The main objective of infrastructural planning in this group of projects was to allow transport of agricultural production, connecting waterway and road transport systems. Since 1997, after works to improve navigability of the Rio Madeira and the installation of river ports in Porto Velho (Rondônia) and Itacoatiara (Amazonas) by private investors, shipment was possible year-round with modern barges mainly with soybeans from Mato Grosso and Rondônia downriver by barge tows of up to 6000 tons to Itacoatiara, east of Manaus, on the Amazon river. This new transhipment terminal enabled soybean transport directly to the European market by ocean-going freighters of up to 80 000 GRT, reducing considerably transport time and reduced transport costs by half in relation to the grain ports of Paranaguá (Paraná) and Santos (São Paulo) in South and Southeast Brazil which were distant up to 2000 km by road and had a much wider sea route to Europe.[212]

Together with the extension of BR-364 from Cuiabá to Porto Velho and the Mato Grosso section of BR-163 from Cuiabá to Alta Floresta, increasing waterway transport of the production of the rapidly increasing soybean and ranching area of Mato Grosso was northbound. In 2000, the regional production of soybeans was estimated at 6.5 mt and a livestock of 18 million head (Kohlhepp 2001b; 2001c). The agribusiness boom turned Porto Velho to a new port centre with 1.8 mt (1998) and a container terminal in construction.

With the improvement of the highway system in Mato Grosso and Rondônia, overland traffic between South Brazil and the Manaus free trade zone was gradually shifting from the Belém–Brasília route (BR-153) to Porto Velho. This enabled return freight, such as household electronics, from Manaus to the South and Southeast. Paving 490 km of the BR-364 in Acre to Cruzeiro do Sul – with the futurist plan to reach the Pacific via the overland route – and the reconstruction of the totally impassable BR-319 stretch from Porto Velho to Manaus were main points of interest in this infrastructure project. The highly questionable reopening of the road link to Manaus – a hot topic again today – seemed unnecessary in view of the Madeira waterway. Miscellaneous highway improvements were connecting road and river transport also in the region of the Purús river.

It was noteworthy that Avança Brasil initially had no detailed plans for the continuation of the paving of the Cuiabá–Santarém road (BR-163). But it was already clear at that time that economic and regional pressure groups, especially timber trade companies, would achieve this priority goal between the Mato Grosso–Pará border and Santarém at the mouth of the Rio Tapajós into the Rio Amazonas. Sawmills were already

212 See chapter II.4.4.

advancing along the road axis of the BR-163 in Mato Grosso (Schneider *et al.* 2000a, 19). Traffic conditions on the northern section of the route in Pará remained extremely precarious.

A new topic was the gas pipeline project (5 million m³) from the Rio Urucu natural gas field, Brazil's largest onshore natural gas reserve, to Porto Velho (500 km) and from Coari to Manaus (420 km) to supply the planned thermoelectric plants in Porto Velho and Manaus. The gas pipeline to Manaus, planned to be ready in 2000, was inaugurated in 2009.

3. Although some development projects of Avança Brasil in Central Brazil were realised outside the planning region of Amazônia Legal, the consequences directly and indirectly affected the situation of the southern fringe of Amazonia. As agriculture spread rapidly in the Planalto Central, the transport infrastructure to the main national markets and seaports was complicated and needed to be improved. The Ferronorte, a railway project of continental dimensions, was planned to link southwestern and central Amazonia with the existing rail network running to the coast. Ferronorte, a federal concession, was funded privately by one of the "soybean kings," Olacyr de Moraes, and the first 410 km of the track from the Rio Paraná in north-western direction were built in 1999. This should complete a multimodal system which is executed for the long haul by an alternative either by waterway or by railroad.

4. The main projects in the northern part of Central Brazil were hydro-electric power plants on the Tocantins river and the transmission line completed in 1999, linking the hydro-power system of the North – including Tucuruí extension, doubling the capacity to 8325 MW and installation of locks planned – with the system of the Centre-West region by a 1300 km power grid connection of 500 kV. A series of hydro-electric plants equipped with locks was under construction or planned along the Tocantins river (Fearnside 2015b; Oliveira and Oliveira 2021), e.g., the Lajeado project (850 MW), giving an additional 5000 MW capacity for the regional development of the state of Tocantins, created in 1988 and turning into a new "El Dorado" of agribusiness activities. Ongoing privatisation of the electricity sector will offer the construction of new plants to private investments on long-term concessions.

For the Araguaia–Tocantins waterway with a dozen terminals, only the construction of the Santa Isabel Canal and locks to bypass rapids were included in the Avança Brasil budget. The construction works of the planned waterways Araguaia–Tocantins and Teles Pires–Tapajós had to be stopped by IBAMA because of high environmental risk, irregularities in the studies presented by the Ministry of Transport (Carvalho 1999) and multiple failings in the environmental impact statement (Fearnside 2001c). The official conflict with these projects was accompanied by extensive protests of affected Indigenous groups.

In times of "bottom-up" development efforts and decentralisation in all sectors, it was a strange experience to accompany more "top-down" strategies, absolutely not adapted ecologically and to the basic needs of the regional population. There was a wide gap between planning ideology of the politically strong Ministry of Planning on the one hand and the Ministry of Environment on the other.

The regional development authority SUDAM has never carried out self-determined or even participatory regional planning and development according to the endogenous regional potentials. Rather, under the military governments, national goals of economic growth were implemented in the sense of a centre-oriented upgrading of

Amazonia. Later, SUDAM was more and more degraded to an instrument of regional interest groups. As already mentioned, SUDAM – like the other regional development authorities – has lost much of its importance since the 1980s. Some years later, SUDAM was drowning by fraudulence and corruption, the case being investigated by the Federal Police (*Veja*, April 11, 2001). Even high-ranking politicians were involved in the "rombo amazônico" (Amazon withholding) of some billion reais. In May 2001, SUDAM was abolished and replaced by a new entity, the so-called Agency of Development of Amazonia (ADA).

The second multi-year investment plan did not take into account the needs of the governments of the Amazon states, but favoured national logistical requirements with export corridors to intensify foreign trade with the Northern Hemisphere and with Mercosur partners in South America.

The G7 countries were funders of an innovative environmental programme linked to rainforest protection, and at the same time – at least the European G7 members and Japan – indirectly and directly promoted soybean expansion on the northern pioneer front in Central Brazil, advancing from the *campos cerrados* into the Amazon rain forest areas, supported by huge public and private financial investments in infrastructure and agricultural research. At the end of the 1990s, soybean cultivation could be observed in Pará state in Paragominas and the Santarém area. In the state of Amazonas, it had penetrated into the surroundings of Humaitá.

When the European market needed more protein-rich fattening feed to replace animal waste after the BSE crisis, the export of genetically unmodified soybeans from Brazil experienced a new boom. The new "soybean king" Blairo Maggi in Mato Grosso was in a superior position, being the largest private investor in soybean cultivation and one of the defenders of soybean expansion in rain forest areas. As owner of the Amaggi Group, a large company that harvests, processes and exports soybeans, and owns soybean terminals and highways, he benefitted greatly from Avança Brasil which provided the appropriate infrastructural basis for his economic activities. In 2003, he became Governor (2003–2010) of the state of Mato Grosso and was now also politically able to determine the agribusiness development in the central Amazonian region. "To me, a 40 percent increase in deforestation doesn't mean anything at all, and I don't feel the slightest guilt over what we are doing here [...]."[213]

Large landowners who grew soybeans were able, through the forces of the world market, to convert cleared land of smallholders who were displaced to new pioneer areas into more soybean plantations. Because of massive infrastructure development needed to provide transportation for harvest and agrochemical inputs, the environmental impacts of soybean expansion were threatening tropical biodiversity. The social parameters were also extremely problematic. According to EMBRAPA research in Maranhão, only one worker is needed for a cultivation area of 167 ha of soybeans (Carvalho 1999; Fearnside 2001c). This meant that the expansion of soybean production offered no prospects for the rural labour market, especially as the remaining smallholders were displaced and forced to migrate to the urban centres where they didn't have any job opportunities.

The Avança Brasil programme was an undertaking of conservative modernisation, without any environmental component or social relevance for the mass of the Ama-

213 Blairo Maggi in an interview in *The New York Times*, September 13, 2003.

zonian population (Becker 1999; Nepstad *et al.* 2000). Wide-ranging negative consequences occurred and there was a lack of rigid measures of checking the environmental compatibility of the projects in preparation and in monitoring ongoing projects.

It was not the first time that justified doubts arose regarding the seriousness of environmental impact assessments. In these assessments (EIA/RIMA) only direct impacts, e.g., quality of the road surface and bed, were considered, however, the associated economic side effects of the implementation of the projects, causing environmental damage, were not assessed at all. In many cases, consulting companies prepared reports favourable to the approved projects, because they were contracted by the proponents of the projects, interested in the positive assessment of EIA/RIMA due to strong financial investment in the project (Fearnside 2001b).

Unfortunately, it could often be stated that a positive assessment of projects within government development programmes increased the chances of the reviewers to be considered again. This was especially the case at a time when only a few specialised consultants existed and some of the consulting firms also involved former employees of environmental authorities.

Environmental impacts of the Avança Brasil programme had been studied very carefully by several groups of scientists. One of the main problems was that powerful interest groups with direct financial involvement and in favour of realising a project were mobilized before environmental impacts were assessed. Only shortly before the beginning of construction works of a project, environmental studies and the assessment of possible impacts happened. Even international funding was attracted before environmental consequences of a project were studied (Fearnside 2001b).

The planned infrastructure would provoke an additional deforestation of 120 000–270 000 km^2 within 20 to 30 years (0.4–1.35 million ha/year) which would liberate 6–11 Gt C (200–550 million t C/year) in the period of deforestation (Barros, Nepstad, and Capobianco *et al.* 2001). Forest loss and loss of biodiversity, in particular the lost possibilities for sustainable use of forests, were irresponsible. In addition, the huge emissions of CO_2 will have a considerable negative impact on climate change which was also becoming increasingly noticeable in this period in Amazonia.

3.2. New challenges regarding forest destruction: El Niño events and forest fires in Roraima

After the extensive infrastructure measures in the development programmes Brasil em ação and Avança Brasil had already contributed greatly to further deforestation, the El Niño phenomenon now brought further challenges – for the first time with major regional consequences and the certainty that this will occur repeatedly.

During El Niño, the system of the Walker Circulation of air and water breaks down. This is caused by a warming of the ocean surface to above-average sea surface temperatures, in the eastern tropical Pacific Ocean. While El Niño brings rainfall to the west coast of North America, South America tends to experience drought during El Niño. Dry climatic conditions that occur because of El Niño and burning to clear rain forest for agriculture are the perfect situation to cause forest fires all over the Amazon. These fires can spread out of control and cause even more forest loss than would "normally" occur.

The El Niño dryness reduces tree growth and trees store less carbon. The Amazon basin plays an important role in the global carbon budget as the Amazon is one of the most important regions of the world for the storage of CO_2 from the atmosphere. Interannual climate variability associated with El Niño can affect the Amazon ecosystem carbon balance. In addition, dry weather causes the soil to release carbon.

El Niño events have been known during the past 2000 years in Amazonia (Meggers 1994), but became more frequent in the last decades. Long drought periods affect huge areas of Amazonia. Moreover, rainfall reductions are a result of deforestation in the Amazon region (Nobre *et al.* 1991). It increased – together with selected logging – the inflammability of intact tropical rain forests, which in years of average precipitation are hardly vulnerable to burning.

During the severe drought from July/August of 1997 to April/May of 1998 rainfall reduction in locations far away from each other caused an enormous deficit in precipitation, compared with the cumulative amount of rainfall in "average" years. The nine months' deficit ranged from 500 mm in Belém and 900 mm in Marabá to 1200 mm in Belterra on the Rio Tapajós in Central Amazonia (Nepstad *et al.* 1999; cf. Kohlhepp 2001b, Fig. 4).[214]

Case study: Roraima

After a nine-month drought, in the first quarter of 1998 extensive fires in the northernmost state of Brazilian Amazonia had catastrophic consequences. Fires for pasture preparation in the *campos cerrados* areas of Roraima and fires to clear-cut primary forest by slash-and-burn agriculture escaped to standing forests, dried by the El Niño phenomenon. A fire frontline of 115 km extension at the end of March 1998 even threatened dense rain forests near the Yanomami reservation. In Roraima, an area of 33 000 km² (larger than the area of Belgium) was destroyed by fires, nearly 10 000 km² of rain forest (Kohlhepp 1998a). Roraima declared a state of emergency. About 12 000 people, including 7000 Indigenous people, needed immediate support. The loss of houses, plantations, seeds, and about 14 000 cattle, the sharp increase of health problems, in particular respiratory diseases, and water shortage required national and international relief efforts (Estado de Roraima/SEPLAN 1998).

As a result of this disaster, the actions of the PPG7-Prodesque project were accelerated to improve fire risk prediction, reduce the occurrence of accidental fires and the techniques to fight them, and improve fire management and organisational structures for firefighting, including training programmes.

The vulnerability of Amazonian rain forests regarding fires favoured by El Niño droughts was highly increasing. According to a very meritorious map on fire risks in Amazonia (IPAM *et al.* 1998), in 1998 about 400 000 km² of intact forests, i.e., 11.5 % of the forest area of Amazônia Legal, were at risk of fire. Nearly 50 % were classified as forest regions "with high risk." Among them, large parts of the municipalities of São Félix do Xingu, Marabá, Altamira, Santarém in Pará or Boa Vista in Roraima were very much endangered.

214 Another example from Paragominas in East Pará 1997: For 200 days a precipitation of only 88 mm, but an evapotranspiration of 800 mm.

Figure 25. Fires in the state of Roraima (Northern Amazonia) in 1998

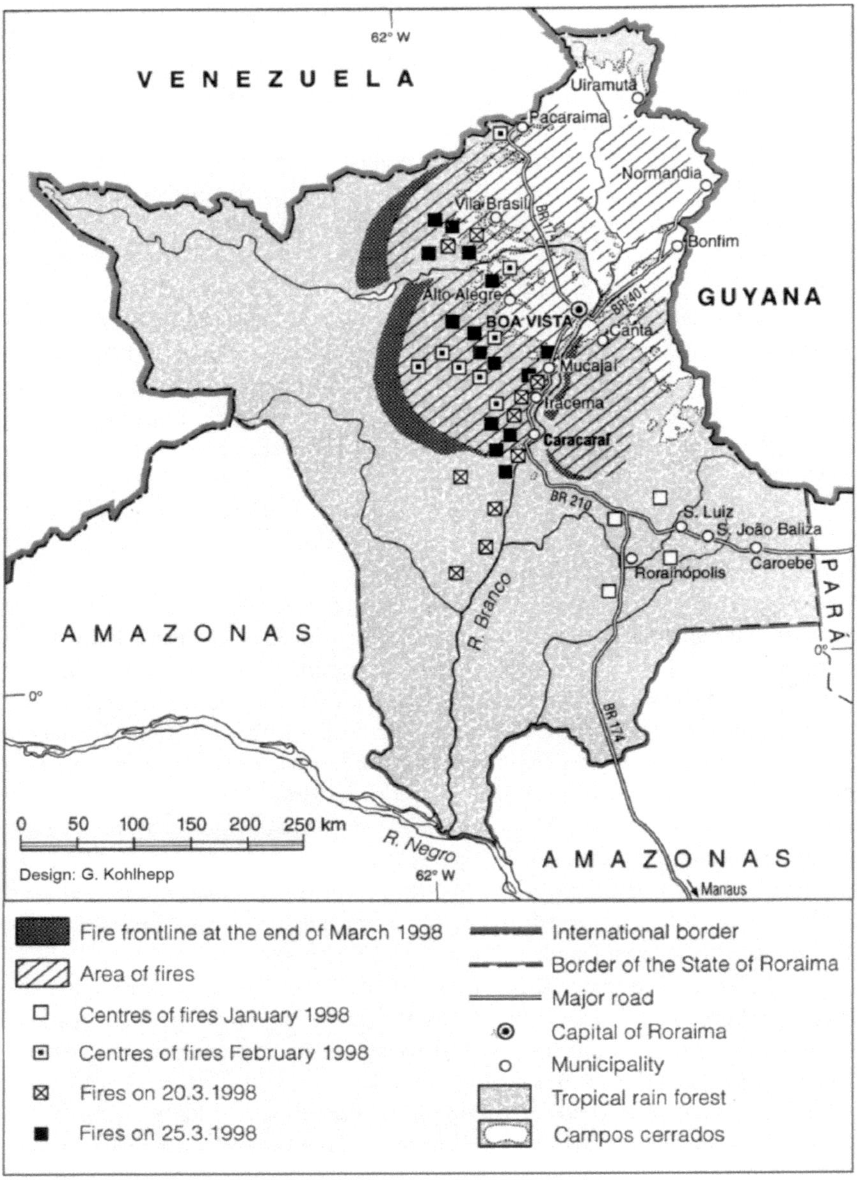

Source: Estado de Roraima/SEPLAN (1998); published in Kohlhepp (1998a, Fig. 8 and 2001b, Fig. 6).

3.3. Amazonia: an "urbanised forest"

In 2000, about 20.1 million people were living in the planning region of Amazônia Legal, 71.4 % in urban settlements and 28.6 % belonged to the rural population (IBGE 2001).[215] About 380 000 people referred to themselves as Indigenous, 40 % living in the rain forest.[216] There was a number of tribes that had not yet been contacted.

From the point of view of the distribution of the population, Amazonia was called "an urbanised forest" (Becker 1995) with "rain forest cities" (Machado 1982; Browder and Godfrey 1997) and pioneer towns with an extremely rapid growth (Volbeda 1986; Coy 1992; 2001). Since the second half of the 1970s, urbanisation in Amazônia Legal had brought about fundamental changes. The Amazonian towns attracted migration from the riverside population of the surroundings and in some cases also Indigenous people. The vast majority were people who had been expelled from colonisation projects. Others were displaced from the pioneer front or *garimpeiros* who lost their job. Waves of migrants came from Brazilian regions outside Amazonia.

Unfortunately, the hope of finding a job in the urban sphere was very often disappointed. The huge development projects with large construction works such as dams and hydroelectric power plants, mining projects or infrastructure constructions attracted a large number of workers who found employment only at the beginning and had no follow-up employment after the project was completed. In the larger cities, slums were created by displaced people for whom the urban labour market offered hardly any opportunities. A "new urban poverty" emerged (Ab'Sáber 2005, 23).

The two outstanding metropolitan areas of Manaus (2019: 2.68 million inhabitants [IBGE estimate]) and Belém (2.51 million) are dominating Amazônia Legal.

Manaus with the Free Trade Zone, managed by SUFRAMA, the river port, and an important industrial district[217] is the main administrative centre in Central Amazonia. The capital of the huge state of Amazonas, situated near the confluence of the Rio Negro and Rio Solimões, owns universities and the renowned research institute INPA (National Institute for Amazon Research). In addition to the strong pull effect of the city and the associated migration, Manaus has a touristic significance. Manaus is a transport hub for shipping and air traffic.

The Free Trade Zone of Manaus (FTZM) had three different phases[218]:

1. The first phase from 1967 to 1980 was characterised by a policy of subsidies for the industrial sectors. Some industrial goods could only be imported by retailers located in Manaus. The city of Manaus received many Brazilian tourists who had the possibility to buy tax-free and cheap imported goods. Numerous shops with duty-free goods were concentrated in downtown Manaus and offered a popular buying pleasure up to a few hundred dollars' worth. At the same time, this increased the turnover of hotels and restaurants and increased the occupancy rates of flight connections to and from Manaus.[219]

---

215 Total population of Amazônia Legal in 2022: 27.8 million (IBGE 2023).

216 Data of the Instituto SocioAmbiental.

217 Cf. chapter I.1.2.4

218 Cf. https://www.suframa.gov.br/zfm_historia.cfm (accessed August 20, 2022).

219 A map of the functional structure of shops in downtown Manaus see Kohlhepp (1986, Fig. 13).

2. The second phase ran from 1975/80 to 1990 and consisted of even larger subsidies to the industrial and services sectors. To receive the fiscal benefits associated with the Free Trade Zone, companies should not only be located in Manaus, but also use at least a minimum percentage of national products as inputs.
3. The third phase (1991–1996) coincided with the opening of the Brazilian economy. Since import tariffs were reduced in Brazil, the relative subsidy received by firms located in Manaus – compared to firms in other parts of the country – was reduced and the FTZM lost part of its relevance.

Today more than 60 % of all trading within the Free Trade Zone is related to electronics and motorcycles, with chemicals and metallurgy as two other significant industries. Companies within the FTZM enjoy up to an 88 % reduction in import duties on the inputs of industrial goods and an exclusive 75 % reduction on income tax for reinvestments. The industrial zone directly employs more than 80 000 people and generates annual revenue of R$ 120 billion.

Belém is situated on the Guajará Bay, part of the vast delta of the Amazon river, about 130 km up the Pará river from the Atlantic Ocean, separated from the larger part of the Amazon delta by the huge Marajo Island. Belém is the gateway to the Amazon river, its river navigation is connected to the extra-Amazonian regions of the country by main roads. The intense migration caused severe problems for the urban infrastructure and led to the spread of suburban slums.

Belém had been the headquarters of the Brazilian agency SUDAM, the Superintendency for the Development of Amazonia. After a massive corruption scandal involving high-ranking politicians, the Brazilian government closed the agency in 2002. Belém is also home of important research institutes and universities. The Museu Paraense Emílio Goeldi is a Brazilian research institution and museum. The institution is well known for researching and analysing the biological and sociocultural diversity of the Amazon Basin, contributing to its cultural memory. It has also the aim of increasing public awareness of science in the Amazon by means of its museums, botanical garden, and zoological park. A famous centre of agricultural and agroforestry research and an institute for research on tropical diseases are located in Belém.

São Luís (metropolitan area 2019: 1.63 million) and the booming Mato Grosso capital **Cuiabá** (metropolitan area 2019: 1.04 million) are very important urban centres. São Luís, capital of the poor state of Maranhão, had been greatly upgraded economically by the Carajás railway, the important port for the booming iron ore export and the alumina and aluminium industries, but suffered from increasing migration and excessive demands on urban infrastructure.[220] Since 1960, Cuiabá has been the door to the new colonisation regions of North Mato Grosso and became the starting point for the economic and urban development along the BR-163 through the expanding agribusiness with soybean cultivation, timber industry and cattle breeding. Capital concentration of the regional economic elite and large migration flows changed the cityscape (Coy 1992; 1995).[221]

In the state capitals of Rondônia, **Porto Velho** (municipality 2022: 0.45 million), of Amapá, **Macapá** (0.44 m.), of Acre, **Rio Branco** (0,36 m.) and Roraima, **Boa Vista** (0,41 m.) the population increased rapidly. Decentralised state entities gained influ-

220 Cf. chapter I.4.4.4

221 Cf. chapter II.4.1.

ence and tried to organise economic activities in these states. Some state capitals have multiplied their population since 1970, Boa Vista, Porto Velho, Manaus and Cuiabá have more than quadrupled. After the founding of the state of Tocantins, the former northern part of the state of Goiás, the new capital Palmas, founded in 1990 on the Rio Tocantins, had already grown to over 300 000 inhabitants today.

The traditional location of urban settlements along the Solimões and Amazon river and some main tributaries was completed by an increasing population in medium-sized and small towns along the different development axis. This was obvious along the BR-364 in Rondônia, along the BR-163 northwards of Cuiabá in Mato Grosso, the BR-010 (Brasília–Belém) and the central part of the Transamazônica (BR-230).

Marabá (PA) and **Imperatriz** (MA) and their sub-region, which is strongly influenced by the Grande Carajás programme, as well as the east of Maranhão have a concentration of small towns. Santarém, the port city on the Rio Amazon, at the mouth of the Rio Tapajós, already had a special significance as the terminus of the BR-163. Its significance increased greatly after the asphalting of this main road, which is very important for soybean transports for export via river ports on the Rio Amazon or the Rio Tapajós. **Altamira** (PA), which had already grown strongly through the construction of the Transamazônica, and **Tucuruí** (PA) have grown enormously due to the construction of the large hydroelectric power plants – Tucuruí on the Rio Tocantins and later Belo Monte on the Rio Xingu. Due to high migration, there are numerous problems of urban social fragmentation.

Figure 26. Population in the Brazilian Amazon region in 1996 (without Indigenous population)

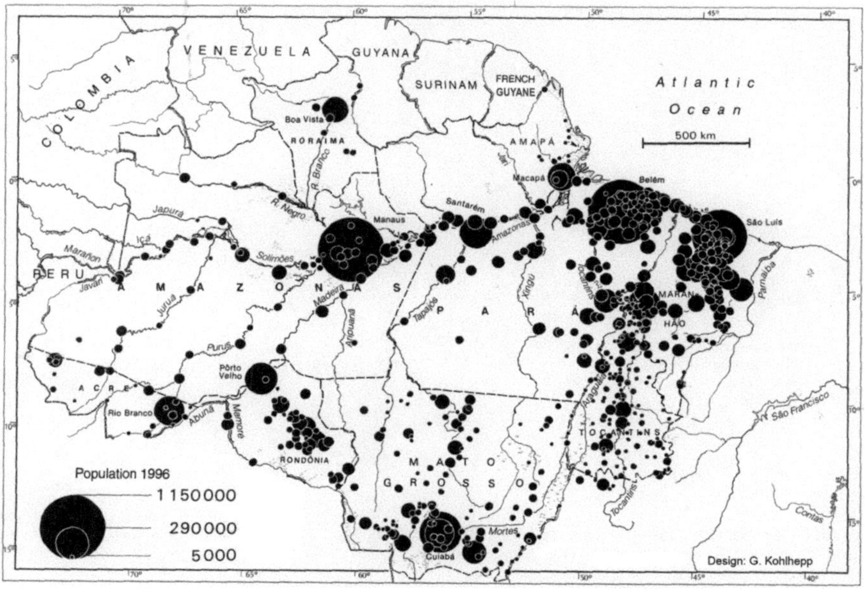

Source: Théry (1997a; 1997b); map published in Kohlhepp (1998a, Fig. 4 and 2001b, Fig. 2).

Because of the extensive migration, frontiers advance rapidly, and towns try to concentrate efforts to reorganise urbanisation and to establish new urban development models with a sustainable social and ecological basis (Coy 1992).[222]

3.4. Situation in 2000: A new macro-zoning of Amazonia as result of development programmes in the 1980s and 1990s

In the Avança Brasil programme the planning region Amazônia Legal was cut up in sub-regions. A new macro-zoning developed, which was formed by the current axes. It was obvious that cattle ranching, subsistence agriculture and logging activities would not remain concentrated on a strip of 50 km on both sides of the roads (Nepstad *et al.* 2000), but will cause wide-spread environmental impacts by deforestation and an increase in accidental fires.

In southern and eastern Amazonia, infrastructure, settlement systems, agricultural production and cattle ranching with large holdings prevail, causing a conflicting situation for small-scale agriculture and squatters. In those sub-regions of Amazônia, production dominated conservation and social measures were strongly needed.

In the new macro-zoning, there remained two core regions (Fig. 27) (Becker 1999):[223]

Figure 27. Amazônia Legal. Scheme of the new macro-zoning

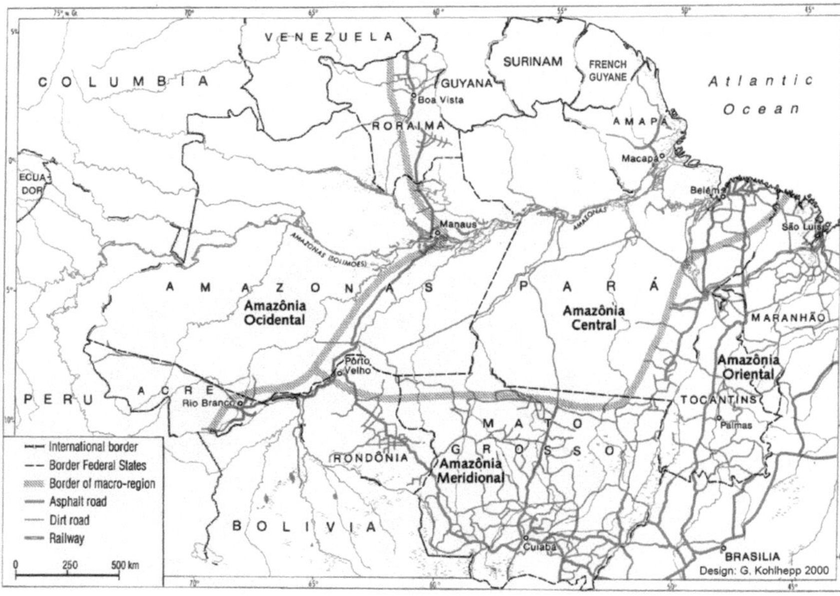

Sources: Becker (1999); map published in Kohlhepp (2001b, Fig. 10 and 2007a, Fig. 10).

222 See chapter II.4.1.

223 Chapter II.3.4.; based on Kohlhepp (2001b).

1. **Central Amazônia**, mostly the state of Pará and the east of Amazonia, cut through by transport axes south of the Rio Amazonas and containing numerous Indigenous lands and conservation units. This was a highly vulnerable region under very strong pressure, caused by the invading agribusiness frontier and Avança Brasil infrastructural projects. The goal for the future must be to reconcile production and conservation, with the part of the subregion north of the Amazon river reserved for conservation units.
2. **Amazônia Ocidental**, the huge region west of the central axis Rio Branco–Porto Velho–Manaus–Boa Vista, with a very low rate of deforestation – in 2000 – should be destined for conservation issues. Large Indigenous territories, the creation of the so-called "Central Ecological Corridor" along the Rio Solimões, new conservation units, such as the "reserves of sustainable development" (Becker 1999; 2001; 2005) should be protected against any "development" euphoria. This could be realised with support of SIVAN, the military-based satellite monitoring programme in Amazonia, given the specific need of vigilance and control in view of increasing drug trafficking activities. No road construction and no large-scale project should be permitted in this region.

The traditional geopolitical vision of Amazonia as a vast empty space, reflected in regional planning of the past decades, has been a fundamental error. The sustainability approach as the only acceptable alternative of future development[224] and the concept of productive conservation (Hall 1997a) compete with the mostly destructive development ideology of mega-programmes in Para and Mato Grosso (Dubreuil, Bariou, and Passos 2004; Kohlhepp 2005).

In addition, the proposal by the "bancada ruralista", which represents large landowners in the Brazilian Congress, to change the forestry law, which still requires private farms in Amazonia to keep 80 % of their land forested, threatened Amazonia's forests. In contrast to the CONAMA and the Brazilian Ministry of Environment, the *fazendeiros*' lobby was trying to reduce land use restrictions to a 20 % or at least 50 % rate of forest cover, opening the Amazon region to a large-scale expansion of the agricultural frontier. As the Congress decision was postponed several times and discussions continued, the struggle between the traditional exploitation model of regional development based on deforestation and the new goal of sustainable use of forest resources was still prevalent.

As scientific research increasingly focused on the problem of greenhouse gas emissions from deforestation, it became clear that mega-programmes such as the Grande Carajás programme and its follow-up programmes Brasil em Ação and Avança Brasil were no longer justified in a sustainability-oriented strategy for the future. The destruction of each hectare of forest causes a net release of nearly 200 metric tons of CO_2-equivalent carbon (Fearnside 2001d). Carbon-offset funds to be paid to developing countries and discussed in the Kyoto Protocol could become an important mechanism for promoting forest conservation (Laurance *et al.* 2001; Fearnside 1997a, 2000, 2001d).

224 Anderson (1990); Clüsener-Godt and Sachs (1995); Castro and Pinton (1997); Schneider *et al.* (2000a; 2000b); Hall (2000); Haddad and Resende (2002); Coy and Kohlhepp (2005); Mello-Théry (2006).

At the turn of the century, Amazonia was at the crossroads (Hall 2000). It is hoped that political decisions and regional self-determination will support sustainable resource management and become of great importance for improving the living conditions of the regional population, especially all survival-oriented social groups. The government's previous goals focused on improving infrastructure, growing the regional economy and strengthening integration into global markets. Traditional planning terminology like regional "economic vocation" led to projects of conservative modernisation without any environmental and social responsibility. Preventing processes of rapid ecological and socio-economic degradation for the benefit of the Amazonian people and preserving Amazonia's rich biodiversity must be the new guiding principles.

4. Private colonisation in Mato Grosso and expansion of agribusiness into the *cerradão* and tropical forest ecosystems

4.1. Migration flows and private colonisation from 1970 onwards

In the humid savannah (*campos cerrados*) of Mato Grosso, large-scale extensive livestock farming was traditionally the predominant form of economy. Subsistence-oriented peasant agriculture or – since the 18th century – artisanal gold and diamond mining (*garimpagem*) existed in niches or extremely peripheral areas. Mato Grosso was a very isolated part of the Brazilian Midwest (Centro Oeste) due to the lack of transport links with only a few roads passable all year round and the enormous distances to the urban centres. The only railway connection from the Southeast ended in Anápolis in the state of Goiás.

In the decades after World War II, this changed fundamentally. The new capital Brasília, inaugurated in 1960, contributed to the development of Central Brazil and set strong impulses towards the incorporation (Kleinpenning 1986; 1991) of the "interior" with a functional orientation of the periphery towards the centre of national markets or the world market, as the later soybean boom clearly showed.

Initial attempts by a group of entrepreneurs from Rio Grande do Sul (Mayer brothers from Santa Rosa) to buy land without state support and start private agricultural colonisation in the mid-1950s met with almost insurmountable difficulties in developing land (eventually 220 000 ha) on the Rio Arinos, 700 km north of Cuiabá in the rain forests of northern Mato Grosso. The plots of 25–50 ha were mainly bought by Brazilian settlers of German origin from southern Brazil, who were forced to migrate to new pioneer fronts due to increasing population pressure in the old colonisation areas of Rio Grande do Sul and the impossibility to continue the traditional inheritance sharing in small properties in their home region. The colonisation company Conomali as well as the investments of the rubber planter groups from Germany operating in the neighbourhood had very little success (Kohlhepp and Dutra e Silva 2022; Pfeifer 1966).

For the development of private colonisation in North Mato Grosso, the *Estatuto da Terra*, adopted in 1964, was important, which for the first time officially provided the possibility of private initiatives for land development. Although state colonisation by INCRA had reached a peak in the early 1970s with its agrarian colonisation projects along the eastern section of the Transamazônica,[225] low-interest loans made it possible to buy private land from 1971 onwards. When state colonisation proved to be unsuccessful and the costs too high (Kohlhepp 1976a), the Polamazônia programme[226] brought special support and tax incentives for private enterprises and development projects from the mid-1970s.

In addition to the large-scale private companies strongly supported by SUDAM in the field of cattle breeding, the owners of private colonisation companies, as well as the landowners with dubious land titles, were now also active in the Association of Amazon Entrepreneurs, who promised themselves a lucrative business through the sale of land. Land acquisition in Mato Grosso was often carried out without respect for the settlement areas of Indigenous groups or traditional Brazilian smallholders, squatters (*posseiros*) who often had not achieved land titles. Land grabbing at the Amazon frontier of Mato Grosso was associated with *grilagem*, corruption, and violence (Oliveira 2016).

The absolute majority of colonisation companies came from South and Southeast Brazil. Between 1970 and 1987, 86 colonisation projects were registered with the INCRA licensing authority (Coy and Lücker 1993).

Three groups of settlers in the new private colonisation projects in Mato Grosso could be distinguished:

1. The first migrants came from North Paraná, where the coffee cultivation boom had come to a premature end. The occurring frosts in the years 1969, 1975, 1979 and 1981 – often only a single night frost, but with the consequence of up to three years of crop failure or total loss of plants – from the mid-1970s finally heralded the end of the coffee cycle and the beginning of the fundamental structural changes in agriculture in northern Paraná. Those who were involved in coffee cultivation in northern Paraná as landowners or tenants were mostly from São Paulo, sometimes also from Minas Gerais. Many of those who became owners through an activity as subcontractors (*empreiteiro*) or tenants were descendants of Italian coffee plantation workers from São Paulo.

However, the structural changes in agriculture had serious social consequences for small farmers and tenants as well as for the rural workforce. In contrast to coffee cultivation, highly mechanised agriculture with rapidly increasing soybean cultivation and even more so expansion of extensive stock raising had only a very low labour requirement. In the 1970s and 1980s, there were numerous operational closures of small holdings and dismissal of farm workers, especially in north-western Paraná, and catastrophic rural unemployment. In the decade 1970–1980, the rural population in North Paraná declined by almost one million people (Kohlhepp 2014; 1991b; 2020b).

Since the pioneer front in North Paraná had reached the national and ecological borders, a first migration of new land seekers and agricultural workers occurred to the neighbouring areas of the state of Mato Grosso do Sul, which had been created in 1977 by separation from Mato Grosso, as well as to the subtropical rain forests of eastern Paraguay. From the beginning of the 1970s, rural exodus took aim at new pioneer fronts, in particular the new colonisation projects in Amazonian Rondônia and in the

225 Cf. Kleinpenning, vol. 1 of this publication.

226 Cf. chapter I.1.1.

cerradão[227] and the rain forests of North Mato Grosso, where private colonisation companies from Paraná initiated a dynamic development.

For this purpose, after the end of coffee cultivation, especially in the Norte Novissimo of Paraná, numerous former owners of small farms or tenants were recruited via real-estate offices as settlers, attracted by very low land prices and the prospect of much larger land holdings. Among them, many so-called *empreiteiros*, a special form of subcontractor in the rural social scheme, which was important in coffee cultivation. They were specialised in the initial planting of larger coffee plantations for landowners. They brought the coffee planting to production maturity and were also called *formadores*. By selling the small first and second coffee harvests – determined by the 4 to 6 year contract – and selling the one-year harvests that were allowed as intermediate plantings, they came to capital and were then able to acquire land in Mato Grosso themselves (Kohlhepp 2014, Fig. 3a, Table 11).

In the initial phase, know how from Paraná was used to promote coffee cultivation (*coffea robusta*), which was soon abandoned due to low soil fertility and high transport costs (Coy and Lücker 1993). However, capital, colonisation model and pioneering spirit of leaders and settlers from North Paraná found new perspectives in Mato Grosso. For the colonisation companies, the sale of urban land in the fast-growing pioneer towns proved to be an additional lucrative business (Coy 1992).

2. The second group of migrants to the colonisation areas of Mato Grosso came from Rio Grande do Sul, Santa Catarina and West Paraná. These southern Brazilian migrants were mostly descendants of 19th century German and Italian immigrants, peasants from the land-deprived colonisation areas. They had nothing to do with coffee cultivation in North Paraná. Since the 1960s, a first wave had bought land in the subtropical forests south of the Rio Piquirí, which formed a border in western Paraná for the expansion of coffee cultivation due to the risk of frost. In West Paraná, they first continued their traditional agricultural system, an "improved land-rotation system" (Waibel 1950, 533) with the cultivation of staple foods and maize refinement by pig fattening in mostly 25 ha farms. Due to traditional inheritance sharing of the small plots, the sons were forced to buy land in East Paraguay and Rondônia. The emigration of young people from small and small medium-sized family farms in southern Brazil often meant a kind of "land consolidation," as the plot size of those remaining on site was expanded and thus the economic viability of the farm was ensured. For settling in North Mato Grosso, they had been successfully recruited by agents of the colonisation companies. For these land buyers, West Paraná had remained only another stage hike on the way from northern Rio Grande do Sul via the west of Santa Catarina to West Paraná and finally to Rondônia and North Mato Grosso.

A special sub-group of migrants to North Mato Grosso was the smaller part of a total of about 8000 families who lost their land because of the expropriations during the construction of the large hydroelectric power plant and the reservoir of Itaipu. They received too little compensation payments, most of them with a long delay. In Paraná, they had

227 *Cerradão* is a drought-resistant type of transition forest, with relatively sparse trees. It includes species of the humid savannah (*campos cerrados*) and others of rain forests. Tree coverage is of 50 % to 90 %. Waibel (1948) mentioned the *cerradão* in the Planalto Central of Goiás as a transitional forest with narrower or broader zones between forest and *campo cerrado*, based on Gonzaga de Campos: Mappa florestal do Brasil. Rio de Janeiro, 1926, 48. See footnote 229. Cf. Dutra e Silva (2020).

no chance to acquire land because of the excessive land prices. Among those affected by the relocation were also settlers without a land title (*posseiros*), who received no compensation. The power plant company Itaipu Binacional recommended to everyone the migration to North Mato Grosso. Some of the colonisation companies, in the "hunt" for land buyers, took advantage of the inexperience of the resettlers and especially of those with capital from compensation payments (Kohlhepp 1987d; Kohlhepp and Karp 1987).[228]

Later, migrants already had support of well-managed service-oriented cooperatives of West Paraná, where soybean-wheat crop rotation known from the farmers' areas of origin gained importance. Furthermore, they had experience with service-providing agricultural cooperatives, which not only provided the technological package of a production and marketing structure, but also the mediation of agricultural loans, training, consulting, medical care, agricultural broadcasting programmes and cultural offerings (Karp 1986, 1987; Kohlhepp 2020b).

3. Since the mid-1970s, migrants from Rio Grande do Sul and Santa Catarina had come directly to the *campos cerrados* and *cerradão* areas in Mato Grosso. Their land purchase was increasingly carried out without the mediation of colonisation companies. Frequently, they were well-funded investors, especially from the northern Rio Grande do Sul highland, who had experience in modernised but too small farms. They were supported by well-organised cooperatives and were characterised by a cohesion shaped by their origins, a higher level of education, neighbourly help, a willingness to experiment and a consolidated church and community life. In the following decades, they dominated the medium and large-scale soybean cultivation in Mato Grosso.

By 1987, a total of 3.1 million hectares of land had been offered by private colonisation companies and over 18 000 plots of various sizes had been sold. State controlled colonisation provided only about 20 % of this area (Coy and Lücker 1993).

Colonisation in North Mato Grosso was based on the large biomes of the region. In the northernmost rain forest in the Aripuanã region, private colonisation companies with very large estates were active. Small farmers of south Brazilian origin who traditionally cultivated basic foodstuffs in slash-and-burn agriculture without mechanisation in family farms with little starting capital have been settled on plots of mostly 25–50 ha of land in the areas of Alta Floresta, Guarantã do Norte, Colíder and others. The state colonisation company Codemat was an exception, as the state of Mato Grosso was otherwise completely restrained in colonisation, leaving surveying, road construction, spatial planning and the construction of pioneer towns to private companies. Initially, besides basic food, coffee (*coffea robusta*) was grown, later also permanent crops such as cocoa, guaraná (*Paullinia cupana*) and rubber. Gold mining also attracted thousands of *garimpeiros* in northern Mato Grosso, mostly from the Northeast and North of Brazil, to the newly opened *garimpos*.

In the *cerradão* areas, colonisation began in 1972 around Sinop, which became an important pioneer town. In the second half of the 1970s, the purchase of land in this region intensified, which became an important guideline for the development of other pioneer towns through the beginning of the construction of the Cuiabá–Santarém road axis (BR-163) in Mato Grosso. Sinop (Sociedade Imobiliária Noroeste do Paraná) was one of the oldest colonisation enterprises in northern Mato Grosso which sold in the Gleba Celeste

228 Among the colonisation companies that sold land to Itaipu victims were Sinop, Colider, Brasnorte, Mutum-Eldorado, Indeco, etc.

about 650 000 ha of land in 6200 plots (25–50 ha) to settlers and tenants who previously worked on coffee cultivation in northern Paraná and who were now unemployed.

After the failure of coffee cultivation, which had almost completely disappeared by 1980, the future of colonisation was posed by major problems due to the unresolved question of land use through new cash crops. Many settlers sold their land and emigrated, partly to the surrounding pioneer towns. Against the background of the Brazilian energy crisis and the Proálcool programme since 1975/76, a major agro-industrial project in biofuel production based on manioc brought a temporary upswing in Sinop, which, however, forced the smallholder farms to grow manioc for the most part. In the 1980s, after structural changes in the rural sector with new south Brazilian actors, soybean cultivation and cattle breeding became increasingly important in the region.

Figure 28. Spatial organisation of private colonisation and pioneer towns in North Mato Grosso

Source: Coy (1992, 14, Fig. 1).

For the settlers of some colonisation regions in northern Mato Grosso, Paraná remained their place of origin and reference, with many intense family and cultural connections, finally the region of success and the "place of longing" ("local da saudade"). Bus companies like the Expresso Maringá connected the old and new pioneer fronts, whose names of the new border villages in Mato Grosso as well as in eastern Paraguay resembled the old land in Paraná (Nova Esperança, Novo Eldorado etc.) (Coy, Klingler, and Kohlhepp 2017, 14, 25, 37; cf. Coy 1992).

In the *campos cerrados*, land acquisition developed on the basis of larger plots (200–500 ha). Here, well-funded southern Brazilian farmers emerged who decisively influenced the development of soybean cultivation by agricultural modernisation. They formed a new social class of independent farmers who built new networks in the region. In Sorriso, development began in 1976/77, where over 500 000 hectares were sold to about 1000 land buyers from southern Brazil.

In the Araguaia-Xingu region of south-eastern Mato Grosso, the Lutheran pastor Norberto Schwantes, son of small farmers in Carazinho, Rio Grande do Sul, founded a new private colonisation company, but with a distinct difference to the companies that sold land for profit. He was one of the first to enter the *campos cerrados* with the aim of promoting a cooperative spirit in agricultural colonisation.[229] With about 400 members of the "Colonisation Cooperative 31 de Março" from the region of Tenente Portela, Rio Grande do Sul, he came to Barra do Garças in 1972, where the Canarana project meant an "escape gate" for landless and small farmers (Silva *et al.* 2022). The cooperative's activities against the backdrop of deliberations on agrarian reform were viewed with great scepticism during the military governments, when this issue was still sensitive (Schwantes 1989).

With 400 to 500 ha of land, the members of the cooperative had to cultivate up to 40 times as large land areas as in their areas of origin. As in the rest of Brazil, the goal of agriculture in Mato Grosso was initially discriminated against as impractical in the *campos cerrados*, where extensive cattle grazing traditionally predominated. After the granting of land titles in 1975 and the initial cultivation of rice, agricultural credits enabled the development of modernised agriculture with a high degree of mechanisation, so that soybean cultivation became prevalent in the 1980s. Farm size increased, the ownership changed and more and more land buyers from southern Brazil came to the region. This was the beginning of regional development along a new road axis from Barra do Garças to the border of Pará (BR-158). Conflicts with cattle farming and with *posseiros* occurred frequently.

The owners of the colonisation companies were decisive as leaders for the development of pioneer towns. This applies, for example, to Alta Floresta and Sinop, where

229 The German geographer Leo Waibel, scientific advisor to the Conselho Nacional de Geografia in Rio de Janeiro (1946–1950), in the second half of the 1940s was convinced during his research on the Planalto Central that in the near future, the best types of soil in the *cerrado* would be cultivated by permanent agriculture with crop rotation and the cultivation of more sophisticated plants (Waibel 1948, 373; cf. Kohlhepp 2021a). Already in the beginning of the 20th century, the *campos limpos* in South Brazil, e.g., the *Campos Gerais* in Paraná, had become innovation centres of successful agrarian colonisation in regions outside forest areas (e.g., Carambeí: Waibel 1950). The fugitive settlement Entre Rios near Guarapuava in Central Paraná, founded in 1952 with people of an ethnic German-speaking population (Danube Swabians), who lived in various countries of south-eastern Europe in the Danube river valley and had been expelled after World War II, became another highlight of the *campos* colonisation (Cf. Kohlhepp 1989d).

a personality cult developed around the local leaders Ariosto da Riva or Enio Pepino (Coy 1992). Among these personalities in Mato Grosso may also be counted the – later no longer successful – early founder of Porto dos Gaúchos, Guilherme "Willy" Mayer, and Norberto Schwantes (Canarana) (Kohlhepp and Dutra e Silva 2022). The frontier narrative of the successful conquest at the pioneer front is still existing for the "winners" who care about the myths of "unlimited" economic progress and optimistic future visions.

Southern Brazilian migrants initially remained isolated, were alien to the region and remained for a long time without contact with the traditional social groups in Mato Grosso. In some colonisation areas in northern Mato Grosso, "south Brazilian enclaves" were formed, initially almost homogeneous territories of mostly southern Brazilians of German and Italian descendance with the same regional, often even micro-regional origin and with a comparable economic starting state. Kinship networks were formed, from which a stabilising continuity between the region of origin and the target region emanated. Relations with the home region did not break off and often the migrant acted as the first outpost in the new homeland, followed by other family members. Clusters of families of common ethno-social and regional origin were often encountered (Kohlhepp and Blumenschein 2000).

In the *campos cerrados*, the farms of modernised agriculture distinguished themselves from the traditional farms of the traditional population of Mato Grosso due to their participation in specific credit and infrastructure programmes. The creation of a "South Brazilian diaspora" in the Mid-West also revealed socio-cultural differences with the traditional population, even beyond the borders of the Midwest, e.g., also in Rondônia and in East Paraguay (Kohlhepp 1984c; 1999). This could be observed in cultural conflicts with an exaggerated emphasis of one's own regional identity (traditional population versus "gaúcho"/"sulista") and in Mato Grosso also on a political level with the emancipation of newly founded municipalities with a predominant southern Brazilian population.

The narrative of a traditional settler of Barra do Garças in south-eastern Mato Grosso clearly illustrates the contemplative spirit of the "old frontier" and, at the same time, inner anger and finally acceptance in relation to the capacity of the "new frontier" "to establish itself in an arrogant and absolute way":

> The southern people arrived and dominated everything: they bought the best land, obtained the best funding from Banco do Brasil, built the best houses of the town, made noise everywhere with their trucks and stereos, are arrogant to the local people, already have the political dominance of the county and they will dominate the state as well [...].[230]

In an interview with Dom Pedro Casaldáliga, Bishop of the Prelature of São Félix do Araguaia, the same problem was mentioned:

230 Statement of Valdón Varjão, cited in: Passos (2019, 47).

> From 1960, the big landowners arrived from São Paulo and the South, arrogant people, went on acquiring land, deforesting, forming pasture areas, introducing cattle, expelling people – indians, north-eastern people – those who arrived before.[231]

In the following years, the political influence of the south Brazilian migrants also grew beyond the local municipal council (Camara Municipal) and the mayor and was also shaped by members of parliament, ministers, governor of the state and federal senators at the supra-regional level. The legacy of south Brazilian migrants is also expressed in the "centros de tradições gaúchas" (Haesbaert 1997, 1994; Kohlhepp and Blumenschein 2000, Fig. 1), the evangelical-Lutheran churches, as well as the radio stations with *gaúcho* music, which diffused with the migration of south Brazilians to the Midwest.

Like in other large colonisation projects in Brazil, e.g., the Cia. Terras Norte do Paraná project in North Paraná,[232] planned pioneer urban settlements were founded as a condition of the colonisation company or in later periods of the licensing authority INCRA. In case of a favourable development of a colonisation project, selling of urban plots was an additional lucrative business for the owners of the colonisation companies, who always reserved expansion areas in the new towns. Sinop was one of the first pioneer towns in northern Mato Grosso (1974). With more than 196 000 inhabitants today and a population increase of 73.4 % between 2010 and 2022, Sinop is the "urban centre of agribusiness" (Coy, Töpfer and Zirkl 2020; Coy *et al.* 2022; IBGE 2023).

Since the rural population had to be supplied with a variety of products, shopkeepers were often persuaded to set up shops by the allocation of free urban land. In pioneer towns in forest areas, a new urban middle class soon developed with merchants, transport companies, administrative employees of the colonisation companies and other service providers. In *cerrado* towns, the owners of larger farms became part of the urban population, where contacts with banks, insurance companies, urban commerce, trading enterprises of agricultural machinery, companies for the marketing of

231 Interview during field work of Messias Passos (2015, 91) on September 7, 1991 with one of the best-known exponents of liberation theology.

232 The originally British private colonisation company Cia. Terras Norte do Paraná (CTNP) was nationalised in 1944 and continued under the leadership of a group of entrepreneurs from São Paulo under the name CMNP (Cia. Melhoramentos Norte do Paraná). The exemplary company envisaged the creation of town squares in the individual glebas when allocating land in North Paraná. The systematically planned urban settlements arranged along the guiding axis of the railway line were laid out at certain intervals according to criteria of central locations. This structure showed the successful coordination of colonisation model, traffic development with its own railway line and integration of urban settlement cores at the pioneer front. In the case of the towns, a rigid chessboard floor plan was only initially used in Londrina (1930). Later founded larger towns (e.g., Maringá: 1947) received very flexible floor plans according to modern town planning (cf. Kohlhepp 2014/1975). The Paraná-born owners of colonisation companies in Mato Grosso were well informed about this urban system. In São Paulo and in the colonisation areas of 19th century European immigrants in Rio Grande do Sul and Santa Catarina town squares were also founded as central places within the rural colonisation areas. From 1951 to 1955, CMNP founded 22 pioneer towns. Until 1970, a total of 62 towns had appeared on CMNP land, of which 35 were the headquarters of municipalities and 27 of district seats. The names of the urban settlements founded throughout northern Paraná emphasised the optimism and pioneering spirit of all participants: Bela Vista do Paraíso, Terra Rica, Pérola, Diamante do Norte, Bom Sucesso, Nova Esperança among others, some of these names were transferred to Mato Grosso (Kohlhepp 2020b).

agricultural products and the service sector were necessary and schools for the children and hospitals and medical care were available. These farmers left their farms in the care of administrators and a few employees.

The elevation to a municipality gave the pioneer town a special position as the seat of the municipal administration and the emergence of new local elites, who politically and economically – often both together – determined the fate of the town and the surrounding area. However, many of the former pioneer towns – as examined in detail for Sinop (Coy 1991; 1992; 1995; Coy, Töpfer and Zirkl 2020) – experienced several economic cycles that determined economic rise, immigration, temporary stagnation, and social segregation that began within a decade. But in the self-perception of its successful inhabitants, the town is one of the Brazilian "metropolises of the future" due to its "pioneering spirit" and growth dynamics. Frontier discourses in Brazil were often only related to one's own success and lack any differentiated evaluation, especially regarding social and environmental degradation.

In these towns, far-reaching changes began after only a few years through socio-spatial differentiation. This was evident in the townscape with an incipient social segregation. The successful colonisation projects have formed a new middle class and new local elites who call the shots in urban politics and economic life. In addition to the neighbourhoods of the successful, marginal areas with failed settlers, immigrants without capital and residents who fed on daily relief services increasingly appeared.

In addition to the socio-spatial changes, a fundamental functional and physiognomic structural change of towns has also taken place during the soybean boom. Large silos and industries of national and multinational corporations for the processing of agricultural products, concessionaires for agricultural machinery, trucks and off-road vehicles, shops for the sale of agrochemical products, transport and export companies, repair shops, consulting offices, banks and insurance companies characterise the townscape. A new urban attitude to life fills the middle and upper classes. School facilities and the establishment of state and private universities show the interest in a solid education, which has a special focus in the field of agricultural science.

With the urban social fragmentation dependent on the soybean boom, a verticalisation in the town centre developed and new separated "gated communities" for the urban upper class were created. This also showed that social conflicts had increased sharply. World market dependency and increasing international competition in agricultural production and the labour market dependent on commodities have a precarious potential vulnerability. These dependencies, together with the long-overlooked ecological consequences of monocultures, make it difficult to predict the future development of these towns.

Cuiabá, the capital of the state of Mato Grosso, had been an isolated stagnant provincial town with a traditional urban and economic structure until the 1960s. The population increase in Cuiabá of just over 100 000 inhabitants (1960) to more than 650 000 today (2020: Metropolitan Region Vale do Rio Cuiabá with Cuiabá/Várzea Grande: >1 million) caused almost revolutionary structural changes in functional equipment and urban physiognomy. Today, Cuiabá is an important regional metropolis in Amazônia Legal, one of the most important centres of soybean processing in the Brazilian Midwest.

In Cuiabá, uncontrolled urban expansion, land speculation in urban plots, lack of low-cost housing, invasions and illegally developing marginal quarters characterise the urban scenery. On the other hand, the dynamic verticalisation of the new town centre, the diversification of local trade and a wide range of high-end goods, new shopping centres, imposing buildings of national and multinational agro-industrial companies, banks, transport companies and modern neighbourhoods of the middle and upper classes bear witness to the new era. All this is linked to the agribusiness boom.

A new urban lifestyle of the successful is prevailing, demonstrated in "gated communities", the most modern fleet of cars and off-road vehicles, trendy restaurants, country clubs, etc. The urban infrastructure underlines the socio-spatial fragmentation. In some areas the absence of any infrastructural installations and environmental impacts as water pollution and lacking sewage purification plants are the reason for social conflicts. The degradation of the peri-urban environment was obvious as the municipal garbage (in 1990: 250 t/day) was dumped without any control on a waste disposal (Coy 1995; Coy *et al.* 1997).

The state of Mato Grosso, which had just 600 000 people in 1970, today has a population of 3.66 million.[233] Overall, net migration of about one million families can be assumed for the period 1975–1996 alone, taking into account all southern Brazilian migrants to Mato Grosso and neighbouring states in the Midwest, from smallholder settlers to agricultural entrepreneurs.

4.2. Regional development and boom of soybean cultivation in Mato Grosso

Soybeans are used in animal feed and food. Soybeans are processed in the form of meal and pellets into the highly demanded soybean meal, which is the most common animal feed due to the combination of high protein content and relatively low prices. Soybeans are now an important product for the mass production of high priced beef, pork and chicken and one of the most successful cash crops in the agricultural world market. The smaller part of production goes into the production of soybean oil, which is used for both edible (e.g., soy sauce, tofu) and non-edible products (cosmetics, soaps and detergents) and as a base for diesel fuels.

Brazilian soybean cultivation began in southern Brazil in the northern highland of Rio Grande do Sul in smallholder farms with polyculture before 1940, expanded with wheat-soybean crop rotation in the 1960s[234] and then gradually took possession of parts of the west of Santa Catarina, of North Paraná and of Brazil's Midwest over the past 50 years.

Carriers of large-scale agricultural development of the humid savannahs (*campos cerrados*) in the central Brazilian highlands were the *sulistas*, farmers who have migrated from the southern states since the mid-1970s and who created modern land management after a difficult initial phase. With the migration of southern Brazilian actors, the plateaus (*chapadões*) of the Planalto Central, traditionally used extensively through cattle grazing and extraction economy, were for the first time fed into large-scale, modernised and export-oriented agriculture. The extensive *campos cerrados* are

233 See chapter II.7.1. Data 2022: IBGE (2023).

234 As for the development of soybean cultivation in the Alto Uruguai region cf. Pfeifer and Kohlhepp (1967); Lücker (1986).

usually endowed with infertile dark red to reddish-yellow latosols and an extended dry period exists from June to September. In contrast, in southern Brazil, on the other hand, agriculture had been carried out all year round on relatively fertile forest soils and on relatively small plots.

Not only have the migrants brought about a paradigm shift in the land use of the *campos cerrados* and carried the expansion of soybean cultivation into the humid savannahs of the Planalto Central, but – as a result of this development – in Mato Grosso, in addition to an increasing economic power in rural and urban areas, they have also considerably expanded their political influence in the region at all levels. It is precisely the socio-cultural conflict with the traditional population of the state that has contributed to a unifying identity among the south Brazilians (e.g., the Centros de tradições gaúchas), although they were of different regional and social origins.

This development, which required a capital- and energy-intensive input of external resources, would not have been possible without special state-organised programmes (Proterra: 1972–1978; Polocentro: 1975–1982; Prodecer: 1980s) for land redistribution and stimulation of agroindustry in a development process of the *campos cerrados*.

However, the dream of growing soybean on a large scale was not easy to implement, because one was neither familiar with large agricultural machinery nor with professional farm management (cultivation methods, market information, personnel management, etc.). Reproduction of practical knowledge in the target region was limited, e.g., in the case of the no-till method, since in Mato Grosso the dry "winter" did not allow crop rotation with an intercrop in a usual manner.

A south Brazilian pioneer from the *cerrado* area of Nova Mutum, who arrived in the region in the 1970s, expressed very well this situation:

> I am stressed out, I have to be a farmer, mechanic, master the computer, know how to purchase, know how to sell, know how to use chemical fertilizers… there are too many things on my mind; and, even worse, I started feeling afraid of not being able to hold my 400-hectare property that is becoming too small for all that, for the costs of the machinery, for the bargain power with the banks, for the companies that buy and sell what we need here in the crops […] (cited in Passos 2015, 87).

After dry rice cultivation in the initial phase, which suffered particularly from the rice crisis and the credit bottlenecks in the context of the world debt crisis, from 1982 soybean cultivation in particular proved to be an effective form of land use to cover the government's foreign exchange needs through export-oriented production and to counteract the current production costs through price increases, since from that time onwards the interest-subsidised loans ceased to exist. The rapid expansion of cultivation was also facilitated by the possibility of extensive mechanical clearing of the *cerrado* vegetation and highly mechanised cultivation on the plateaus. The biodiverse humid savannah ecosystem was perceived by the farmers as a worthless obstacle.

The expansion of soybean cultivation in Mato Grosso was related to the following factors (Kohlhepp and Blumenschein 2000; Coy *et al.* 2017):

- availability of large land reserves with much lower land prices compared to South Brazil,
- immigration of south Brazilian farmers, who mostly were forced leaving their home because of lack of land in traditional inheritance sharing and were able to acquire many times more land in Mato Grosso,
- favourable conditions for mechanised agriculture because of low relief energy,
- use of new varieties adapted to regional climatic conditions,
- introduction of the no-till method, based on the use of high pesticide levels (glyphosate) and genetically modified seeds.

Migration was usually accompanied by social advancement, as former tenants also became landowners. The subsidised loans of the government's special programmes and the minimum price policy of the 1980s, which favoured soybean cultivation in the Midwest, also contributed to this. But land prices, which were up to six times cheaper than in southern Brazil, also made it possible to acquire much larger agricultural areas in the Midwest, ranging from 500 to several tens of thousands of hectares. In addition to family farms with family workers living on the farm and medium-sized farms whose owners live in the municipal towns, speculation-oriented large-scale farms have also settled. The owners of large farms were absentees who lived in Rio Grande do Sul and especially in Paraná and managed larger consortia, and some were also politically active in these states.

The introduction of site-appropriate and knowledge-intensive land use procedures also required flexible farm management and a qualified workforce. It is precisely these characteristics that were seldom present in large companies, where they led to the cessation of operations to a particularly high degree. This took place regardless of the size of the farm and could also cover mega-farms, as was demonstrated by the abandonment of the 100 000-hectare Fazenda Itamaratí Norte (municipality of Campo Novo do Parecis) of the former "rei da soja" (soybean king) Olacyr de Moraes in 1996.

The unprecedented decline in government credit financing for soybean cultivation and other government interventions in the wake of agricultural policy deregulation, as well as the increasing agro-ecological degradation caused by soybean monoculture, also contributed to a severe crisis in soybean cultivation in Mato Grosso in the 1990s.

South Brazilian agricultural entrepreneurs preferred to employ rural workers from their own area of origin who already had experience in mechanised agriculture, including former small landowners and tenants. The short-term employment of unskilled workers for grubbing-up work, etc., which takes place via employment agencies (*gatos*) in a *bóia fria* system, is still characterised by daily commuting from the peripheral urban areas to the frequently changing short-term workplaces. Despite a strategy of agrarian modernisation, the agrarian social conditions in the *cerrado* region remain tied to family relationships.

Unlike the cultivation of dry rice in monoculture, which lost productivity after the third year of harvest, soybean cultivation in monoculture proved to be viable in the medium term, albeit with a considerably higher use of external inputs (artificial fertilizers, lime, pesticides, high fuel consumption). The modernised soybean production in Mato Grosso thus grew considerably, reaching 7.2 million t in 1997/98. In just a few years, Mato Grosso has thus become one of the most important soybean producers in Brazil and has been in second place after Paraná (7.3 million t) at that time.

Brazil launched its "Green Revolution" in a modernised form with the promotion of agricultural research, consulting, technical assistance, high mechanisation and a specific price and credit policy. A major factor was the process of world market integration of the periphery based on soybean monoculture and agro-industrialisation and the commissioning of the first agro-industrial complex (industrial processing, soybean oil refinery, pellet production, agricultural trade, transport and storage capacities) (Kohlhepp and Blumenschein 2000). Agribusiness is integrated into global value chains with agricultural production, marketing, logistics, financing, agricultural machinery, and trade strategies. In addition, with numerous agricultural machinery, trucks and car concessionaires, with agrochemical trade, consultancies, banks, etc., there is an ever-larger urban service sector, as an important part of a local/regional value chain (Coy *et al.* 2017; Coy, Töpfer, and Zirkl 2020).

Agricultural trading corporations (the big four: ADM, Bunge, Cargill, Dreyfuss) and the national Amaggi company,[235] one of the largest companies exporting commodities in Latin America, are controlling 75 % of the worldwide trading of grains.

Transnational input companies with about the same share on the world market were trying to introduce new technology packages and have had a targeted influence on the exchange of agricultural information. All the global players in the agricultural machinery, seeds and agrochemical sector are present in the new regional urban centres with sales offices and consulting agencies. "Agro towns" such as Sinop or Tangará da Serra exert the function of powerful multi-purpose "command centres" whereas the countryside is more and more reduced to serve as a "production machine" (Coy, Töpfer, and Zirkl 2020, 59). Networks in agricultural consulting, credit financing, supply of inputs and market relations created a new techno-economist paradigm (Blumenschein 2001).

The exponential increase in soybean production in Mato Grosso, which has amounted to up to one million tons per year in the late 1990s was mainly achieved through the development of new land in the Médio Norte of Mato Grosso (Chapada dos Parecis). This region, notably the stretch between Tangará da Serra and Sapezal on the axis of the BR-364, with huge contiguous plateaus, which were extremely good to manage with a modern machine park, developed into a large new production centre. However, the high price of soybean – partly favoured by the exchange rate – led these producers to expand soybean cultivation in the so-called "marginal areas," where the pedological and hydrological conditions are not suitable for crop cultivation. Another "producers' front" is located along the MT-242 that links the federal road axis BR-163 and 158. "250 km from 'landless men' to 'manless land' along dirty roads, where the signs indicate only names of farms and distances" (Passos 2019, 48 f.). There is a climate of social exclusion, much stronger than in the phase of the colonising companies. Today, the rural habitat in these regions is depopulated.

The later land use dynamics in the *cerrado* were characterised by the change from a soybean monoculture to a more diversified and verticalised land use pattern. New crops and forms of land use are strongly influenced by local, regional and supra-re-

235 The company of the Maggi family began in São Miguel do Iguaçu (PR) with seeds Maggi. Later, the family migrated to Mato Grosso, where the son Blairo started with large-scale soybean cultivation and is today head of the huge trading corporation and the largest private producer of soybeans in the world. He acted as federal Minister of Agriculture and Governor of Mato Grosso.

gional networks. Part of these networks are, for example, private-public research institutions with the direct participation of agricultural entrepreneurs, common silos, collective exchange of information, farm management and agricultural marketing in so-called *condomínios* and credit cooperatives. The cooperation between these networks with face-to-face contacts, e.g., in the agro town of Tangará da Serra, results in an innovative milieu (Blumenschein 2001). Some of these towns – just like Sorriso and Sinop as well – belong now to the most economically successful municipalities in Brazil.

The operational monostructure and the uniform orientation of the agricultural regions, which were geared to a specific use of resources, became a major obstacle to future regional development in the *cerrado*. While capital-weak and heavily indebted farms were forced to lease or sell their land or leave arable land open and also to strive for grassland, others were trying to counter the crisis with a diversification of land use, gentle tillage (no-till, green manure) and with the help of alternative sources of finance and sales channels.

The path of success of the south Brazilian farmers to a new rural elite in Mato Grosso in large-scale soybean cultivation was particularly favourable from 1982 to 2005, which made its extensive and rapid spread possible (Fig. 31). The specific regional fit into an export-oriented market economy has made its susceptibility to crises apparent in recent years. The presence of the southern Brazilians in the *cerrado*, which was often described in Brazil as a "model of success," must therefore be put into perspective. The comprehensive use of resources, which stood out from the traditional subsistence economy of the traditional population, enabled for the first time the formal, capitalist "valorisation" of the once extensive and earlier only sporadically used *cerrado* plateaus (Kohlhepp and Blumenschein 2000).

In Mato Grosso, only 2 % of people employed in agriculture are active in soybean cultivation, although soybean dominates 80 % of the arable area in this state. This proves the agro-social problems of the extraordinary development boom (Coy *et al.* 2017). In addition, it is precisely the low employment rate of workers and the strong division of labour among seasonal workers that have led to the short-term unqualified labour being pushed into marginalised social niches, which remained largely without trade union organisation.

The ruthless expansion of large soybean farms and the concentration of ownership led to the displacement of smallholders (mostly *posseiros*) who had been traditionally engaged in subsistence agriculture in this region. The increasing "capitalisation" of regional agriculture, with which the "family farms" – once the target group of colonisation activity – could not keep up has now been largely replaced by "agricultural entrepreneurs" as the most important group of actors.

In addition to the social consequences mentioned above, the increase in production and export success also cause severe environmental damage: compaction of the soils through the use of large machines, severe soil erosion, which could be significantly reduced by no-till, expansion of monocultures with destruction of natural biodiversity and increasing susceptibility to plant diseases, contamination of the soil and contamination of groundwater. Due to over-fertilisation and excessive application of plant protection products and, in the case of soybeans, a significant proportion of rain forest destruction was caused by farms invading the southern Amazon biome.

The reform of the Biosafety Act in 2005 led to the liberalisation of genetic engineering in the agricultural sector. A controversial emergency decree had already made it possible in 2003 to officially release of transgenic soybean cultivation, initially planned for only one year, under pressure from the agribusiness lobby, despite the protest of the Minister of Environment (Kohlhepp 2010a).

Today, multinational agricultural corporations operate with increasing supply of genetically modified seeds, such as the herbicide-tolerant Roundup Ready of the contested monopolist Monsanto, as well as coordinated agrochemicals and their own marketing strategies with high royalties. Brazil has thus lost its special position that distinguished it from the almost exclusively transgenic cultivation in the United States, Argentina and Paraguay, but it continues to dominate the world soybean market after the US.

Unstable soybean prices, deregulation of national agricultural policy and ecological degradation have led to the diversification of land use with cotton in addition to soybean-maize crop rotation. Cotton cultivation in the *cerrado* was regarded as a second economic mainstay after the first phase of decades of soybean monoculture, but initially had problems due to the regionally too high rainfall and humidity. Today, cotton is grown on large farms over 500 hectares with high mechanisation. New networks of knowledge exchange with the direct participation of farmers, credit cooperatives and agricultural innovations (e.g., no-till) as well as fruit and vegetable cultivation and poultry farming close to the market led to the above-mentioned innovative milieu (Blumenschein 2004; cf. 1995). There are efforts to "incorporate" pasture use as a third phase to combine cattle farming with modernised agriculture. In addition, there is a tendency to "refine" local feed production in large chicken farms or in large feedlots, mostly in direct connection with slaughterhouses, to further increase regional added value (Coy *et al.* 2017).

The regional economic success is highly fragile. It is determined by the price quotation of globally marketed commodities on the stock exchanges in Chicago. Furthermore, it depends on the prices of agricultural machinery, seeds, fertilisers and pesticides as well as on the all-important development of transport and export costs, because the distance factor is still the decisive location disadvantage of the Midwest. The lower limit of profitable farms is likely to be over 500 ha today. The ecological and social costs of the extraordinary soybean boom are enormous. However, a consolidation of a new social area in the Midwest in the next generation also presupposes that global market-oriented soybean cultivation in conjunction with a diversification of land use could reduce the socio-economic vulnerability and also the ecological consequences of agricultural modernisation. The dependence on multinational companies, whose rules and regulations dominate planting, fertilisation and marketing, makes it increasingly clear that the increased use of agrochemicals is destroying regional biodiversity and that at least a partial conversion to organic products should be sought, which has already begun slowly in Mato Grosso do Sul and Goiás in recent times.

The northern migration of soybean cultivation had begun in the mid-1970s and reached the state of Mato Grosso in the southeast in the Rondonópolis region. In 1994, two priority regions emerged: the *cerrado* in the southeast of the state and the *cerrado/cerradão* region around Sinop and Sorriso on the south-north road axis BR-163 and the plateaus of the Chapada dos Parecis (Médio Norte). By 2004, production activities intensified and by 2014 soybean production reached a maximum in the Médio Norte as well as an expansion in the east, even near the Xingu Indigenous Park (Fig. 29).

Figure 29. Municipal soybean production in Mato Grosso 1994–2004–2014

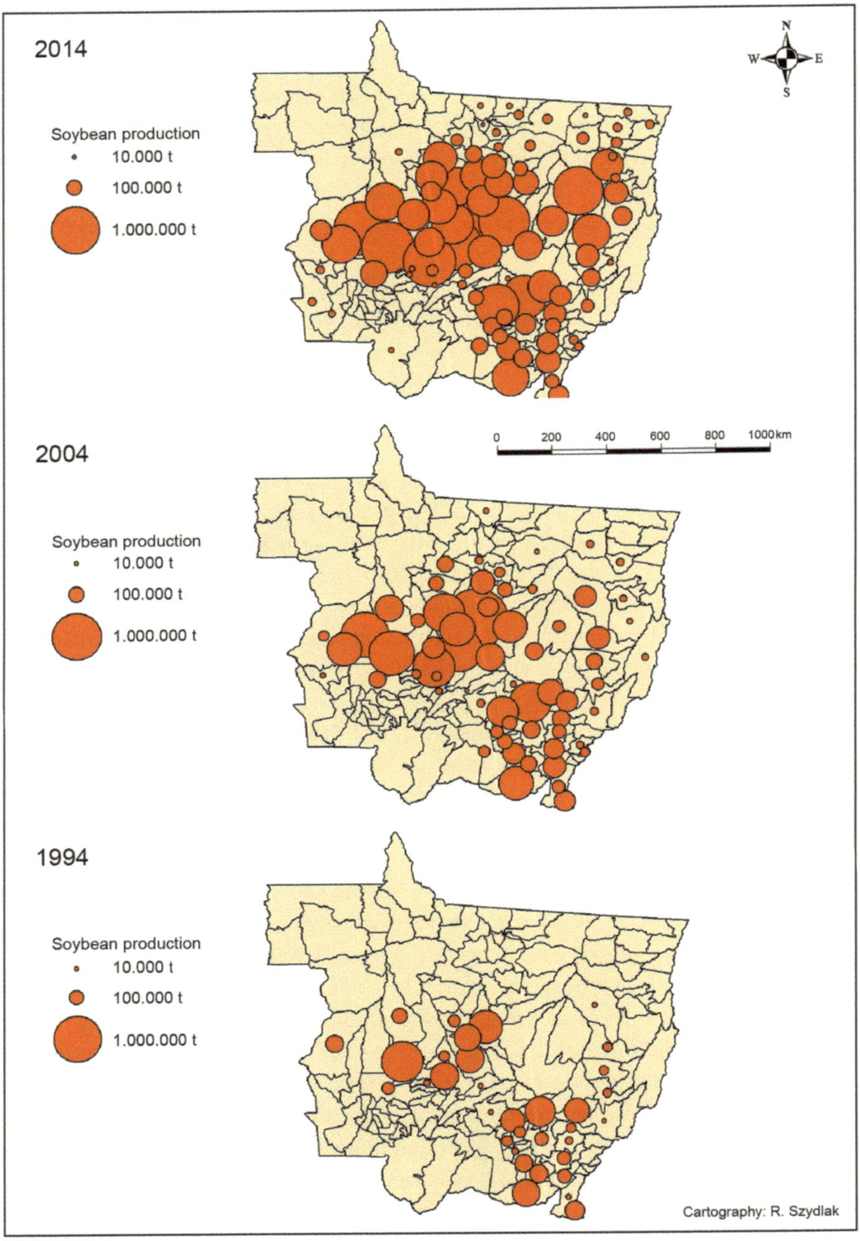

Source: Author+s design, according to: Lima and Penna (2016, Fig. 1); data from IBGE (1994; 2004); IMEA 2014.

In the last decade, further expansion of soybean cultivation and encroachment into the tropical rain forests of northern Mato Grosso has been evident. There were also former left open cleared pastures in the Amazon biome used for soybean cultivation (Fig. 30).

Figure 30. Soybean cultivation and pastureland in Mato Grosso in 2020

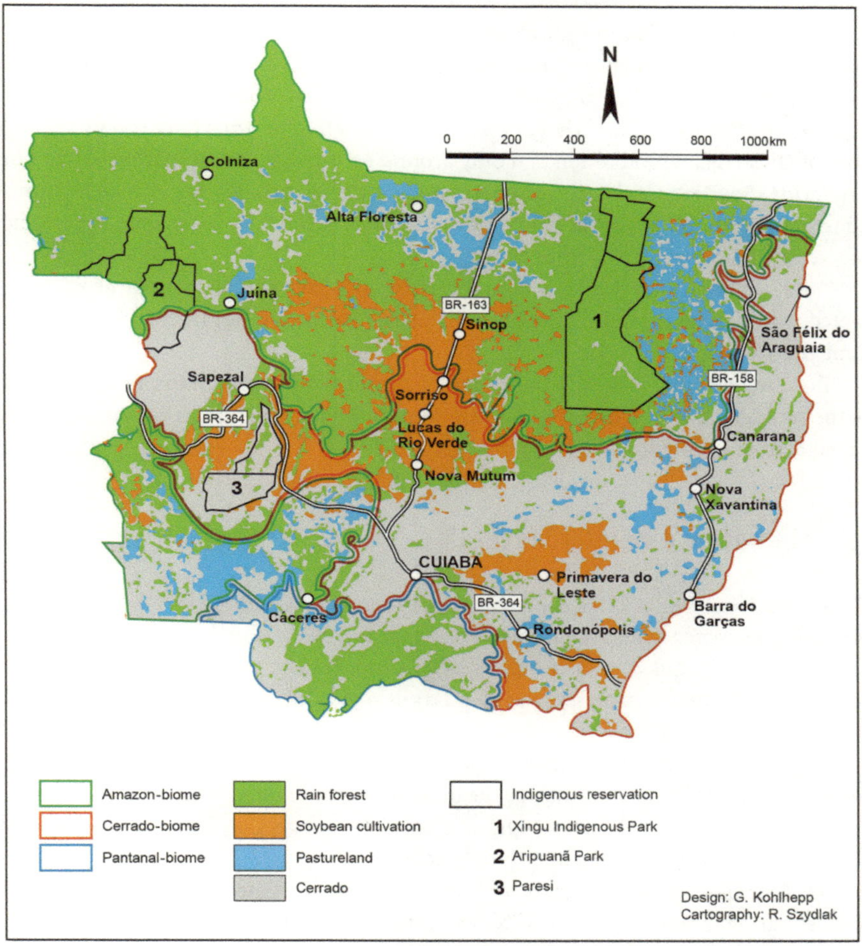

Source: Author's design, according to: Mapeamento SojaMaps 2019 (Universidade do Estado de Mato Grosso), pesquisa.unemat.br/gaaf/sojamaps; Cassol *et al.* (2020, Fig. 8).

In Mato Grosso, the area under soybean cultivation increased in 2018/19 by 225 400 ha, 64 % of the new areas were located in the Amazon biome. Between 1985 and 2019, a conversion of native vegetation of 22.1 million ha or 28 % loss occurred. Pasture grew 165 % with an area of 12.8 million ha. The area of agricultural crops increased by 349 % (9 million ha) (Information SEDEC-Mato Grosso in 2019; Canto *et al.* 2020). These were the driving factors of an excessive deforestation in Mato Grosso (Simões *et al.* 2020). In 2020, Mato Grosso produced not only 28.7 % of soybeans, 35 % of maize and 71 % of cotton grown in Brazil but had additionally 15 % of Brazil's large cattle herd. Very large clearings for pastures occurred until 2005, especially in North Mato Grosso (Fig. 30).

Since 2003, Brazil has been the largest beef exporter. 40 % of Brazil's cattle are kept in Amazônia Legal, where they occupy 79.5 % of the land used. Already in 2006, the pastures in Amazonia covered 55.4 million hectares, of which 60 % are in Mato Grosso and Pará (Greenpeace 2009a).

Soybean production in Amazônia Legal is far more lucrative than cattle production, the profitability averages about US$ 300 per hectare versus roughly US$ 50 to 100 per hectare per year for cattle production (Vera-Diaz *et al.* 2009). However, it must be emphasised that the productivity of soybean cultivation in Amazonia is only around 50 % of US soybean production and only around 60 % compared to southern Brazil or Argentina. Soybean cultivation requires soil and climatic conditions, which are limited to approximately 3 % of the remaining Amazonian forest. Soybeans are expanding onto cattle pastures cleared prior to 2008.

Today, in the Amazon biome of Mato Grosso 64 % are rain forests, a large part protected by Indigenous lands (Xingu and Aripuanã Parks, Fig. 30, 1, 2), 26 % is pastureland and 3 % cropland.

The danger of the further penetration of soybean cultivation into the rain forests of the southern Amazon had already been recognised earlier and was combated with a special measure, the so-called "soy moratorium."

4.3. The soybean moratorium

High rates of deforestation in the Amazon between 2002 and 2004 and the connection between this increase and the expansion of soybean cultivation led to considerations of intervening in this development, especially in circles of the environmental movement. In 2006, public protests over the Cargill soybean terminal in Santarém and a campaign by Greenpeace called international attention to deforestation associated with soybean production in the Brazilian Amazon region. The campaign was treated as a serious crisis by the Brazilian soybean sector – under intense international scrutiny – as well as by international traders such as ADM, Bunge, Cargill, and Dreyfuss that operated in Brazil (Nepstad and Shimada 2018).

The Brazilian Soybean Moratorium (BSM) was an agreement among trading companies, national and international NGOs, retailers, and banks to not purchase or finance soybean grown in fields that were deforested after 2006, later changed to 2008, in the Brazilian Amazon biome. The BSM had been considered as the establishment of simple rules to eliminate deforestation from soybean supply chains, an agreement, easily to monitor, with a deforestation "cut-off date." 95 % of soybean production in the Amazon biome is grown in Mato Grosso. 80 % of the soybean producers participated in the moratorium (Gibbs *et al.* 2014; Nepstad and Shimada 2018).

The Brazilian Association of Vegetable Oil Industries, represented by the Amaggi group,[236] and the Association of Cereal Exporters in Brazil, which purchase 90 % of the soybean produced in the Amazon, signed the zero-deforestation soybean agreement. The moratorium operated as a "market exclusion" policy. Since soybean farmers rely on tradings to finance their production, they are complying with the moratorium. Producers violating the moratorium lose market access for their soybean production.

---

236 The Amaggi group had already established a monitoring system for its suppliers as a requirement for the IFC loan of 2002.

The BSM resulted in the formation of the Soybean Working Group (Grupo de Trabalho da Soja, GTS) to oversee the implementation and monitoring of the agreement. The Ministry of the Environment in 2008 officially joined the GTS and INPE was brought in to lead the monitoring efforts to identify places where soybean was being grown on land deforested after the cut-off date (Gibbs *et al.* 2014). If a violation was confirmed, the property was placed on the "black list" maintained by the GTS and checked by the soybean traders before purchase. The soybean moratorium was renewed every one or two years until 2016, when it was implemented "indefinitely." A well-controlled longer-term commitment could help maintain deforestation-free soybean supply chains.

The economic potential of soybean cultivation caused increasing deforestation rates both through the direct conversion of forests to soybean fields and through the effects of soybean on land prices. Amazon soybean expansion has not been suppressed by the BSM, because of the abundance of suitable cattle pastures for conversion to soybean. Cattle pastures that had been acquired at very low prices were now worth two or three thousand US Dollar per hectare. Cattle ranchers who decided to sell their land to soybean producers suddenly were in a strong financial position to acquire new landholdings on the rapidly advancing agricultural frontier (Nepstad and Shimada 2018).

The dynamics of soybean replacing forests are complex because soybean is often planted several years after the clearance of tree cover. During the interim period land can be used for other purposes, typically as pasture for grazing cattle.

There is a general consensus that the moratorium has been successful. Only one percent of soybean production in Brazilian Amazonia sold to participants in the BSM is associated with forest clearing after the cut-off date. In the two years preceding the agreement, nearly 30 % of soybean expansion occurred through deforestation rather than by replacement of pasture or other previously cleared lands (Gibbs *et al.* 2014).

The soybean moratorium was the world's first major regional decline in tropical deforestation, beginning in 2005. The BSM has achieved a nearly zero deforestation free soybean sector in the Amazon region. The moratorium was an initiative that complemented the Prevention and Control Programme for Deforestation in Amazonia (PPCDAm) that was launched during the government of President Lula da Silva. The BSM could have been better harmonized with the PPCDAm if it had made specific linkages to the implementation of the Rural Environmental Registry of private properties (CAR) and the Forest Code (Nepstad and Shimada 2018; Gibbs *et al.* 2014).

However, since 2012 deforestation has increased again as the control measures used to slow deforestation have begun to weaken. Increasing soybean prices caused a resurgence of direct soybean-related deforestation without passing an initial period as cattle pasture. Recently a report by Global Forest Watch estimated this deforestation in 2019 as an area of 29 000 ha (Schneider *et al.* 2021), another study calculated the direct deforestation by new soybean plantings in Mato Grosso as of at least 42 000 ha since 2020 (Finer and Ariñez 2022).

From the perspective of corporate risk management, the BSM is probably the world's most successful value chain intervention for addressing tropical deforestation. Certainly, the effectiveness of this intervention and its contribution to regional solutions to tropical deforestation would be greater if they were designed to reinforce land-use regulations and public policies and programmes for successful transitions to sustainable development (Nepstad and Shimada 2018). However, BSM measures were insufficient for solving tropical deforestation in large areas.

The soybean moratorium was restricted to the Amazon rain forest biome where only 10 % of national soybean production is taking place and soybeans are frequently being planted on former pastures. During the 1980s and 1990s, the humid savannah (*cerrado*) ecosystem has been transformed into a high-production region for soybeans and other commodities with the loss of a large part of the natural tree and shrub vegetation,[237] which could be legally cleared. Environmental protection measures in the *cerrado* were much weaker than in the Amazon region. Over the last 20 years, the extent of soybean production in this biome has more than doubled, direct vegetation conversion to soybean was almost twice as high as in the Amazon biome. In 2019, a third of the entire South American soybean planted area was located in the *cerrado* (Schneider *et al.* 2021).

The expansion of the Brazilian soybean production was motivated by the high degree of absorption capacity of the European Union market. The intervention of the soybean moratorium was mainly due to the severe environmental requirements imposed by the Europeans. China, with 32.4 % the most important market for Brazilian exports, in 2021 was the leading importer of soybeans worldwide and by far the largest sales market for Brazilian soybeans with 70 % of the soybean export value share (quoted from de.statista.com in 2021). This could mean that the much lower importance that China devotes to environmental policy issues could also facilitate the expansion of soybean cultivation in Brazil into the Amazon biome. Since 2020, Brazil has been the world's leading producer and exporter of this oilseed ahead of the US and has recently benefited from the escalating trade war between China and the US. The competitive situation between the US and Brazil in soybean exports shows that transport costs can be of decisive importance.[238]

4.4. Soybean production in Mato Grosso and the impact of logistical optimisation of export-oriented soybean transport in Amazônia Legal

Soybean cultivation in Mato Grosso showed a steady increase until the year 2000 and an extreme expansion between 2000 and 2005, whereby the cultivation area was doubled. Between 2010 and 2015 another increase in the cultivated area by about 50 % brought the soybean area to 9 million ha and reached a volume of 10 million ha in 2020 (Fig. 31). With 645 000 hectares, the municipality of Sorriso on the BR-163 road has the largest area under soybean cultivation in Mato Grosso.

Soybean production has continued to reach new records over the past two decades, with a very strong increase until 2015 and further significant annual increases. In 2020, Mato Grosso reached a harvest quantity of 33.8 million t of soybeans (Fig. 31)., i.e., 28.7 %

237 From August 2020 to July 2021 deforestation of the Brazilian *cerrado* amounted to 8531 km² (WWF).

238 Brazil's transport costs are much higher than those in the United States. In the US, the cost of transporting a ton of soybean from farms to the export port averages US$ 15. Brazilian farmers pay an average of US$ 37 per ton (cf. Vera-Diaz *et al.* 2009, 15). According to IMEA data of 2018, one t of soybean from Sorriso/MT via Santos to China: US$ 117. From Iowa /US via New Orleans to China: US$ 58 and from Córdoba (Argentina) to China: US$ 52 (Coy, Töpfer and Zirkl 2020, 53).

of the Brazilian soybean production. Rio Grande do Sul and Paraná followed by a long way with 15 % each. In Brazilian soybean export, Mato Grosso also holds first place with 23.7 million t (27.5 %), ahead of Rio Grande do Sul (14.6 %) and Paraná (12.3 %) (Fig. 32).

Figure 31. Soybean harvest area and production in Mato Grosso 1975–2020

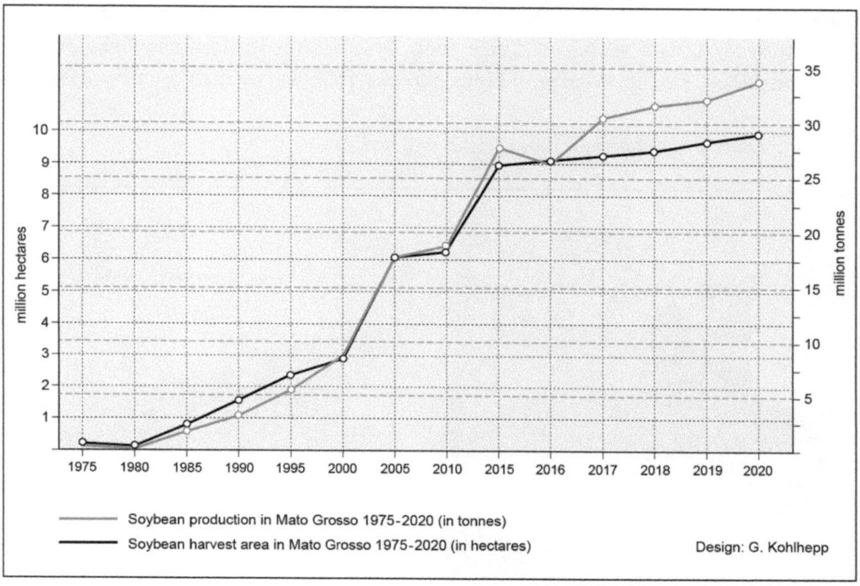

Source: Data provieded by Sérgio Leal, SEDEC- Mato Grosso, in 2021.

Figure 32. Brazilian soybean exports in 2021 (by State; in millions of t)

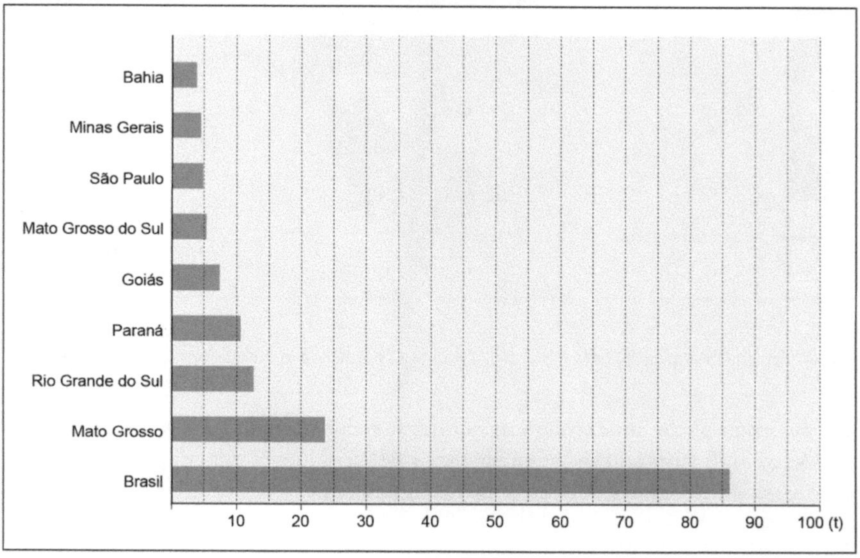

Source: CONAB data 05/2021: harvest 2020/21.

Due to mechanisation of cultivation and high input of fertilisers and pesticides, productivity (1975: 1400 kg/ha) has risen to 3492 kg/ha by 2021, which in addition to ecological consequences also caused enormously high operating costs. The importance of soybean cultivation in Mato Grosso is underlined by the fact that this state in 2021 made a decisive contribution to Brazil's leading position on the world market with a production of 135.4 million t, that is 37.3 % of the world's soybean production. The US holds the second place with 31 %. Since 2020, Brazil is the leader in soybean exports with 86 million t, i.e., 50.3 % of worldwide exports, followed by the US with 36.3 %.

Figure 33. Human Development Index (HDI) in Brazil

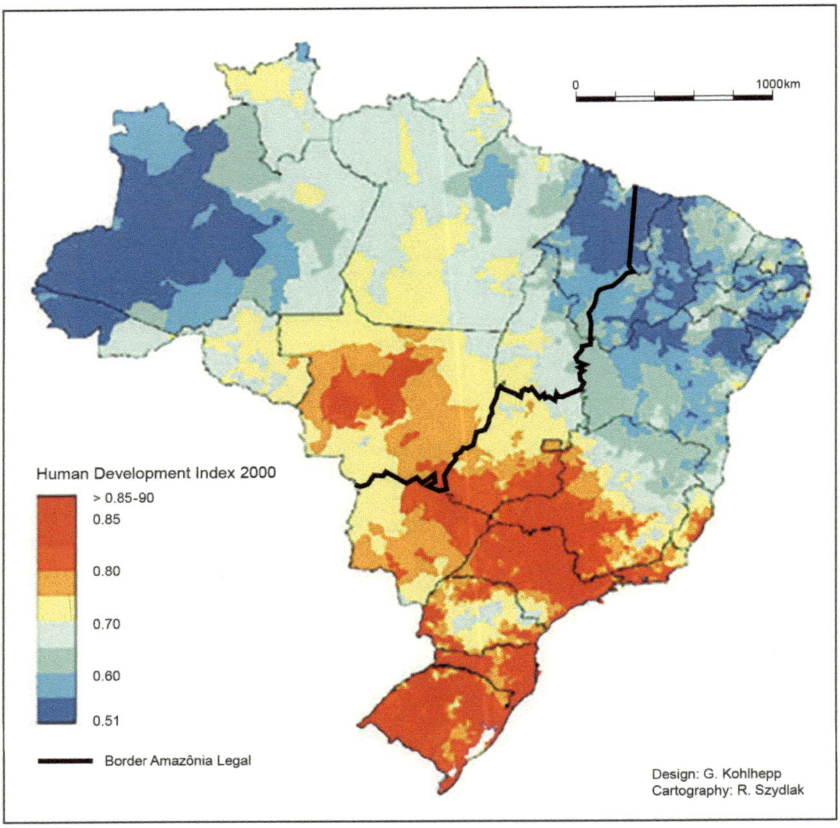

Source: Bertrand, Mello, and Théry (2007, 25); data IPEA.; published in: Kohlhepp (2010b, 99).

The expansion of the modernised agricultural economy led to a wedge-shaped penetration of high Human Development Index (HDI) values[239] inland, especially in the core areas of soybean cultivation with young, dynamic pioneer towns and immigra-

239 Although the HDI indicators (life expectancy, literacy rate, purchasing power) certainly do not allow for a comprehensive analysis of the level of development, the values give a very clear picture of the regional disparities in the sum of the areas for the general standard of living.

tion from the South in the state of Mato Grosso (Fig. 33). Economically successful agro towns, such as the self-proclaimed "soybean world capital" Sorriso in northern Mato Grosso with a good infrastructure, stand out but also emphasise the disparities of "winners" and "losers" of this path of development within the state. Due to the relatively small population of 3.5 million inhabitants in Mato Grosso, the factor "purchasing power" of the "winners" is increasingly noticeable in HDI values. Since the data of Fig. 33 are based on the year 2000, the disparities certainly have increased.

The huge production of the agricultural commodities soybean and maize in Mato Grosso required a more complex logistical network and expansion of transport routes and export ports in order to supply the world market with these agricultural goods by more efficient logistics for the Brazilian agribusiness. The ever-increasing penetrating of the cultivation areas inland and thus into the tropical rain forests increased the distances to the traditional soybean exporting seaports of Santos (SP), Paranaguá (PR) and São Francisco do Sul (SC) in Southeast and South Brazil to more than 2000 km. Especially in the first two ports, which were already heavily congested and where truck queues of tens of kilometres often formed in the high season after the soybean harvest, the ports in Amazonia have become a good option for this grain flow.

Initially, from Mato Grosso to São Paulo and Paraná there were precarious road connections, which were then supplemented by asphalt roads and railways. In order to shorten the distances to the customer countries in Europe and East Asia and thus the transport costs, the agricultural goods of Mato Grosso were transported via the road axis BR-163 (Cuiabá–Santarém: 1732 km) to be exported via the Santarém port in the Amazon region. The reduction of transport costs also played an important role in the competition with the US, the other large soybean and maize producer and exporter.

After an early announcement of the construction project of the BR-163 in the mid-1960s, the road construction began in 1971. While the highway in Mato Grosso to the border with the state of Pará was asphalted in the 1980s, it had been proposed to pave the road entirely as part of the Avança Brasil project (2000–2007). However, the section in Pará[240] remained as an earth road that led through dense tropical rain forests, with a high threat potential for Indigenous territories and enormous environmental destructions. In 2019, the long-disputed asphalting[241] was completed with a 51 km long stretch of the highway until Miritituba, a new port at the Rio Tapajos.

Until a few years ago, the unpaved sections of BR-163 in Pará were the nightmare of all trading and transport companies as well as truck drivers, because in the rainy season – especially from December to June – trucks with up to 40 t of cargo got stuck for days due to the extremely bad conditions of the earth road with mud holes, impassable runs and precarious wooden bridges. Huge queues of heavy trucks caused enormous delays in transports, hindering the flow of agricultural crops from the region.

Santarém, the end point of highway BR-163 – on the right edge of the Tapajós river, about three kilometres from the confluence with the Amazon River – is a strategic port between the road and waterway modes for the transport of goods via the BR-163 and the Tapajós and Teles-Pires rivers. On a leased area with the loading facility of Car-

240 In Pará, asphalt was only available from Santarém to the small town of Rurópolis on the Transamazônica.

241 The details of the Plan of Regional Sustainable Development of the Area of Influence of the Highway BR-163 (Cuiabá–Santarém) are dealt with in chapter II.5.

gill, Santarém initially was the main export port for grains in the north. Due to public protests in Santarém against the expansion of soybean cultivation and the activities of trading companies, some large companies have concentrated their activities to Miritituba, making this port the main transshipment point of the so-called "Arco Norte" (Northern Arch). The Arco Norte system also meant the establishment and privatisation of new loading and transshipment stations in Amazonia, combined with a transport realignment of the export system for agricultural commodities, started during the Avança Brasil programme and continued in the Growth Acceleration Programme.

The term Arco Norte is defined as a logistic strategy that refers to ports and stations of transshipment north of the 16th parallel south, in the states of Rondônia, Amazonas, Pará, Amapá and Maranhão. The Arco Norte system is formed by transshipment ports: Itacoatiara in the state of Amazonas; Santarém, Barcarena, and Vila do Conde in Pará; São Luís and Itaquí in Maranhão, and Santana in Amapá, from where the agricultural products proceed for export overseas (Fig. 34). Two stations of transshipment of cargo are operational support for the multimodal corridors: Porto Velho in Rondônia and Miritituba in Pará, among others (Russo *et al.* 2022).

Since 1997, the terminal of Porto Velho had been used as a private terminal of the Amaggi group for soybean transhipment using bulk bin barges via the Madeira river to Itacoatiara, in a distance of 1060 km. The BR-364 to Rondônia, opened in the 1960s and asphalted in the 1980s, brought a significant transport and freight cost advantage for the soybean growing areas in the mid-west of Mato Grosso around Sapezal (850 km to Porto Velho) and the Chapada dos Parecis. At that time, large road sections to Santarém were not asphalted. Using the highway to Porto Velho, transport costs decreased by one third and transport time by three days from 11 to 8 days on average (river transport: Porto Velho–Itacoatiara: 4 days) in relation to transport via Paranaguá in South Brazil (Blumenschein 2001, 69). The Cargill company has been operating in Porto Velho since 2003 and considered it a strategic location for transportation of grains produced in Rondônia and in the mid-western region of Mato Grosso. The transshipment with convoys of bulk bin barges (40 000 t) is destined for Itacoatiara or directly to Santarém. Between July and November there can be problems on the Rio Madeira due to low water and sandbanks.

The port of Itacoatiara is located in the state of Amazonas, on the left margin of the Rio Negro, near of its affluence to the Solimões/Amazon river. This port has a profoundness of 11 meters. The main product exported in this port is soybean through a bulk carrier terminal.

The transshipment terminal of Miritituba in the municipality of Itaituba in Pará, located on the Rio Tapajós, began operating in 2016. The transshipment operation consists of the reception of trucks and the loading of bulk bin barges. Miritituba stands out for allowing the distribution of grains produced in the Midwest, using the BR-163 road for transports from the central region of Mato Grosso (Sinop, Sorriso among others) to the transshipment terminal of Miritituba at a distance of about 1000 km. Miritituba is "a bottleneck in the infrastructure of the country."[242] Five large trading companies are present, dominated by a joint venture of the national giant Amaggi and Bunge, one of the leading transnational tradings worldwide. River transport with barges allows freight cost savings of up to 40 % compared to ports in the South and

242 According to the Minister of infrastructure Tarcísio de Freitas in 2021.

Southeast, which can only be made by trailer. Transporting grains between Miritituba and Vila do Conde/PA (1100 km) for export, vessels load fertilisers on the return trip.

Figure 34. The new transportation network "Arco Norte" for agrobusiness commodities in Mato Grosso

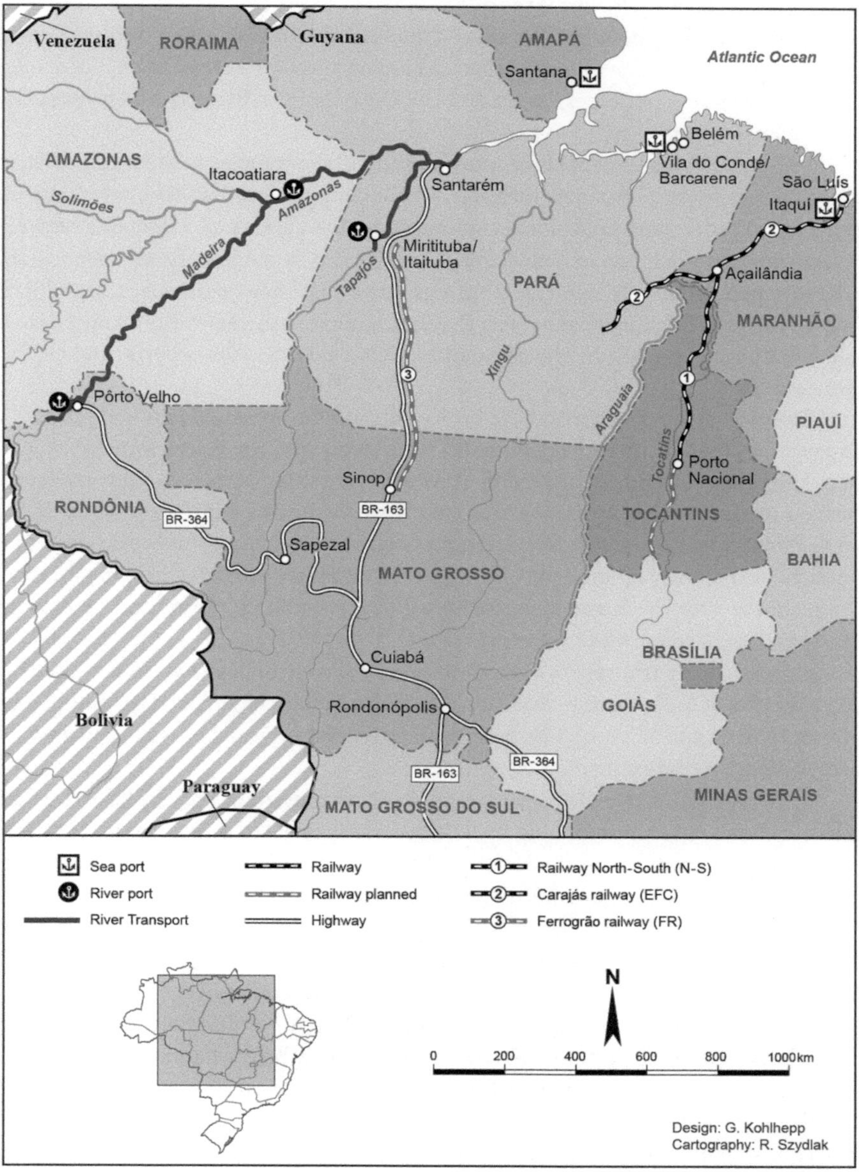

Source: Author's design, according to Lima and Penna (2016, Fig. 5); Russo *et al.* (2022, Figs .3, 6); Souza-Higa and Gatti (2020) and own additions.

The great economic success of soybean farmers, trading groups and also of international financial institutions is offset by the problems of the local and regional population caused by transport and transshipment activities. Taking Miritituba as an example, this small district of Itaituba is a very poor location with a high level of poverty: its GDP per capita is almost half the index of the state of Pará (INESC 2021). The main impact on daily life in Miritituba is the traffic of up to 1500 trucks per day in the period of high harvest causing noise, pollution, and dust clouds. In addition to the disturbance of a never-ending queue of heavy vehicles passing through a small town, obstructed access to livelihood resources, increases in violence, drug trafficking, and prostitution were reported.

Local Indigenous leaders of the Munduruku call the complex in Miritituba district "illegal" because the companies involved did not comply with Brazilian law, requiring prior consultation with traditional communities. The absence of a dialogue between companies and the affected communities has been lamented by the Indigenous and riverside populations. In contrast, tradings claim that they operate legally and have met all the licensing requirements by the environmental secretariat of Pará. Licenses approved were contested by the population, public institutions, experts, and civil society groups.

Waterway and port projects have been a concern for the Munduruku of the Médio Tapajós for decades. Artisanal fishing for subsistence and the boat traffic of the local population was severely disturbed by the intensive traffic of bulk carriers transporting commodities. Access to many areas in the riverside area has been banned. In the environmental impact assessment of projects planned, ecological and socio-economic impacts were mostly ignored, or only vague actions were proposed to mitigate them. Compensation for the forced insertion into global production chains and for obvious losses and impairments was never granted.[243]

The commodity transport companies took total control of the river. Hundreds of communities of Indigenous or traditional fishing populations suffered from reduction of fishing stock and of fish quality because of water pollution and protested against the great damage to the entire environment.

The port of Vila do Conde in Barcarena, Pará, an important port for loading of alumina, hydrate and aluminium ingots,[244] is becoming very attractive also for the draining of soybean produced in the North and Northeast regions to the external market, consolidating itself as a new alternative of maritime transport.

The Itaqui port in Maranhão is directly connected to the Carajás railroad operated by the Vale company, transporting iron ore from the Serra dos Carajás mines.[245] From Açailândia/MA, there is a connection by the North–South railroad until Porto National in Tocantins (720 km). The North–South railway (EF-151) was designed 40 years ago to be the backbone of the national railway system, integrating the national territory, and contributing to reduce the logistical cost of freight transport of agribusiness production like soybeans and maize as well as fertilisers and fuels. After long start-up difficulties and temporary standstill, the continuation from Porto Nacional in southern

243 Cf. https://www.tapajosdefato.com.br/noticia/288/arco-norte-um-projeto-de-destruicao-para-a-amazonia (accessed September 12, 2022).

244 Cf. chapter I.4.4.2.

245 Cf. chapter I.4.2.4.

direction via Ouro Verde/Anápolis (Goiás) and Estrela d'Oeste (São Paulo) (1540 km) was completed in June 2023, allowing a connection with the Paulista railway network in the Southeast, giving access to the port of Santos. In Rio Verde (Goiás), a large multimodal terminal was built for soybeans and fertilisers with the capacity to move 11 million tons per year. Another terminal is working in São Simão (GO/MG) with a capacity to handle 5.5 million tons of soybeans, maize and soybean meal per year.

In the north, the broad gauge North–South railway connects with the Carajás railway in Açailândia (MA), from where the port of Itaqui can be reached. A 480 km railway connection from Açailândia to the important port of Barcarena/Vila de Conde (Pará) is planned.

The port of Itaquí has a strategic location in relation to the Asian market whose route is via the Panamá canal. In addition, compared to the ports in Southeast and South Brazil, this port shortens the shipping time by about 7 days, which favours competition for Arco Norte. The biggest demand, related to the increase of grains production in the states of Maranhão, Tocantins, Piauí, and Bahia[246] is the amplification of the operational capacity of the Itaquí port (Russo *et al.* 2022).

The terminal of Porto Nacional is localised on the Rio Tocantins, 60 km from Palmas, the capital of Tocantins. Transhipment of the soybean production of Mato Grosso is carried out through the highway (BR-158) to the North–South railroad destined to the Itaqui port in Maranhão.

Besides the Rio Madeira corridor (Porto Velho–Itacoatiara) and the Tapajós–Amazonas corridor (Miritituba–Vila do Conde, among others) there is a projected corridor of the Ferrogrão, the grain railway. This railway project, a nine-year-old strategic project of the largest multinational agribusiness companies, was designed to be implanted parallelly to the BR-163 between Sinop in central Mato Grosso and Miritituba on the Tapajós river in Pará (935 km). The aim is to replace a significant part of truck transport and reduce CO_2 emissions by up to 1 million t[247] and to cut back transport costs for the export of agrarian commodities by 30 to 40 %. The project is already controversial in the planning phase. On the one hand, it is intended to prevent deforestation due to the route along the BR-163, on the other hand, strong interventions in the socio-economic situation of the regional population and an additional deforestation potential are feared. So, the project is constantly objected by Indigenous peoples and communities in the region (Russo *et al.* 2022; INESC 2021).[248] Legal hurdles still stand in the way of the project, as both Indigenous territories and the Jamanxim National Park would be affected by the construction.

Not only the well-known big transnational traders are trying to influence the development decisively, but also China is taking action. China is increasingly trying to invest in domestic companies, logistics, warehousing, transport (interest in the Ferro-

---

246 In recent years, soybean cultivation in Mato Grosso has expanded into the outskirts of the Amazon biome. More recently, also in Northeast Brazil soybean production increased in the states of Maranhão, Tocantins, Piauí and Bahia, the so-called MATOPIBA region.

247 According to the Ministry of Infrastructure; cf. https://www.germanwatch.org/en/eu-regulation-deforestation-free-products (accessed September 12, 2022).

248 According to Tapajós de Fato the logistical processes for the construction of these projects are already ready, regardless of popular opinion. This is disrespectful to social movements, Indigenous council unions and other entities who live there or who take their livelihood from this territory (cf. link in footnote 243).

grão railway [Abdenur *et al.* 2021]) and trading. China has also invested heavily in the traditional export ports of Santos and Paranaguá (Coy *et al.* 2020, 37 f.).

Now the Amazon ports have exporting capacity, the challenge is transporting the soybeans to the transshipment terminals and ports. The round trip has been reduced from 10 to 4 or 6 days on an average. Given the production and export growth forecast for the next decade, it is crucial to avoid a shortage of port capacity to meet regional export needs.

The volume of soybean and maize handled in Brazilian ports between 2010 and 2019 increased by 350 %. In 2020, 104 million t of soybean exports left Brazilian ports. In 2010, the Arco Norte ports participated with 23 % in handling Brazilian soybean and maize, increasing to 31 % in 2015. In 2020, the ports of Amazônia Legal came up to 50 % of transhipment into grain freighters to overseas. This means that the ports of Amazonia have already caught up with the competitors in Southeast and South Brazil and will probably soon have overtaken them. In exports of soybean and maize, after the still leading port of Santos the port of Vila do Conde/Barcarena is already in second place, followed by Santarém. Freight costs have roughly halved and due to the asphalting of BR-163, which was completed in 2019, freight costs in Mato Grosso have also fallen significantly (Sorriso–Miritituba 2020 to 2021: 16 %) (Borges 2021; Souza-Higa and Gatti 2020). Due to the new export corridors, some towns that have gained importance as hubs of soybean handling to the Southeast will also lose importance in the coming years. This applies, for example, to Rondonópolis, a regional centre in southeastern Mato Grosso, up to now the control centre of regional soybean trade (Friedrich 1999).

The boom in soybean cultivation in Amazônia Legal is strongly encouraged by reductions in transport costs. About 30 % of the cost of producing soybeans is associated with transportation; therefore, high transport costs are the main constraint on the expansion of agriculture in Amazonia. Investments by the Brazilian Government's Pluriannual Plans have improved transportation networks. Paving of highways means promoting the expansion of a globalised agricultural frontier, strongly dominated by external decisions, and – consequently – leads to an ever-faster deforestation of large areas for cattle ranching, soybean expansion and logging activities with extremely high environmental and social costs. Between 1978 and 1994, approximately 318 000 km^2 of rain forest were eliminated within 50 km of major paved highways, accounting for more than two-thirds of the total Amazon deforestation. Paving the Cuiabá–Santarém road (BR-163) expanded the area where growing soybeans is economically feasible by about 70 percent, from 120 000 to 205 000 km^2. Most of this new area is in the state of Pará and is covered largely by forests (Vera-Diaz *et al.* 2009).

The Brazilian government considered paving the BR-163 to be a priority for regional and national integration. Its completion in 2019, originally planned for 2008, in reality reduced the cost of transporting soybeans. In North Mato Grosso, the expansion of the soybean agribusiness caused deep transformations of economic, social and territorial structures. This is especially true for the BR-163 corridor.[249] Under the influence of a highly modernised and globalised production system, regional and local actor constellations, social and power relations, have been subject to profound changes (Coy, Töpfer, and Zirkl 2020; Coy and Huber 2020; Coy *et al.* 2021).

249 The specific problems will be analysed in chapter II.5.2.

5. The new regional policy of the Plan of Sustainable Amazonia (PAS)

5.1. Political initiatives during the government of President Lula da Silva

At the beginning of the administration of President Lula da Silva (2003–2010), two political initiatives decisively redefined the context in which the Pilot Programme was included that seemed to have fallen by the wayside.

In May 2003, the president and the governors of the states of Amazônia Legal decided to install the Plan of Sustainable Amazonia (PAS), coordinated by the Ministry of National Integration in partnership with the Ministry of the Environment (MIN/MMA 2004).

In view of the increasing rates of deforestation,[250] the federal government created an inter-ministerial working group with 14 ministries, in order to install the Action Plan for the Prevention and Control of Deforestation in the Legal Amazon(PPCDAm), launched in July 2003. These activities motivated the political decision to reconfigure a second phase of the PPG7, including institutional arrangements. According to the government, there was a historical opportunity to take advantage of the accumulated knowledge and the social capital of PPG7 in the construction of structuring public policies, aimed at the implementation of new models of sustainable development in the country.

It was planned to integrate the various dimensions of sustainability – social, cultural, economic, political, and environmental. Some potential topics for new innovative initiatives include land policy (new agrarian reform model, land regularisation, fight against land grabbing), pasture management, recovery of degraded areas, technical assistance and rural extension for sustainable production, alternatives for forest concession and management of natural resources on Indigenous lands. There was a broad consensus that cooperation with other countries in the Amazon basin could be developed in a second phase of the PPG7.

The still high deforestation rates showed that the inter-ministerial working group did not achieve its main objective in the first years of existence. The PAS, with a view to minimising environmental degradation and conflicts in the Amazon Region, had five thematic axes (MIN/MMA 2004):

250 2001: 18165 km^2, 2003: 25396 km^2 (data: INPE)

1. Environmental management and spatial planning,
2. sustainable production with innovation and competitiveness,
3. social inclusion and citizenship,
4. infrastructure for development,
5. new funding standard.

According to the government, environmental management and territorial planning are the decisive factors of a strategic role of the state in promoting sustainable development (MIN 2003; Capobianco 2017). The fundamental instruments for this were: land regularisation, economic and ecological zoning, environmental licensing in rural properties and consolidation of the protected areas system. However, it is important to realize that 24 % of the Amazonian territory are private property, 45 % (23 % conservation units; 22 % Indigenous territories) are areas legally protected. It is a huge challenge for any government to maintain and secure the officially protected areas of Amazônia Legal according to the legal principles.

The creation of new conservation units of about 16 million hectares by the Amazon Region Protected Areas (ARPA) programme was a very positive initiative (Fig. 35). ARPA was a programme of the Federal Government, planned for ten years, with the objective of protecting biological diversity in the Amazon biome and creating and consolidating 60 million hectares of conservation units and promoting sustainable development in the region (Silva 2005).[251]

Protected areas (PAs) include conservation units (UCs) and Indigenous territories covering 45 % of the area of Amazônia Legal (Santos *et al.* 2021).[252] UCs range from strict protection (7.9 %) to those that allow the sustainable use of resources (10.6 %). Conservation units are areas considered essential from an economic point of view, as they conserve socio-biodiversity, in addition to being providers of environmental services and generators of business opportunities.

Ecological corridors are not political or administrative units but important for the conservation of biodiversity. They are defined as

> portions of natural or semi-natural ecosystems connecting PAs, which allow gene flow and biota movements among them, facilitating species dispersion and the recolonisation of degraded areas, as well as the maintenance of populations that require, for their survival, greater area sizes than those protected in individual protected areas.[253]

---

251 In 2000, the National System of Protected Areas (SNUC) was established comprising federal, state, municipal and district protected areas (PAs), with different specific objectives regarding the form of protection and allowed uses. Attempts were made to optimise the role of PAs with regard to integrated planning and to ensure that significant and ecologically viable samples of the Brazilian ecosystems are properly represented within the protected areas (MIN/MMA 2004; https://www.mma.gov.br/). A good example of the planning and establishment of protected areas and the associated environmental problems and conflicting interests of various social actors in the Upper River Paraguay Basin in Mato Grosso is provided by Röper (2001).

252 Areas of environmental protection (APA: 3.7%) are included in the UCs.

253 http://www.mma.gov.br/areasprotegidas/cadastro-nacional-de-ucs/dados-consolidados (accessed April 20, 2021).

Figure 35. Protected areas in Amazônia Legal in 2020

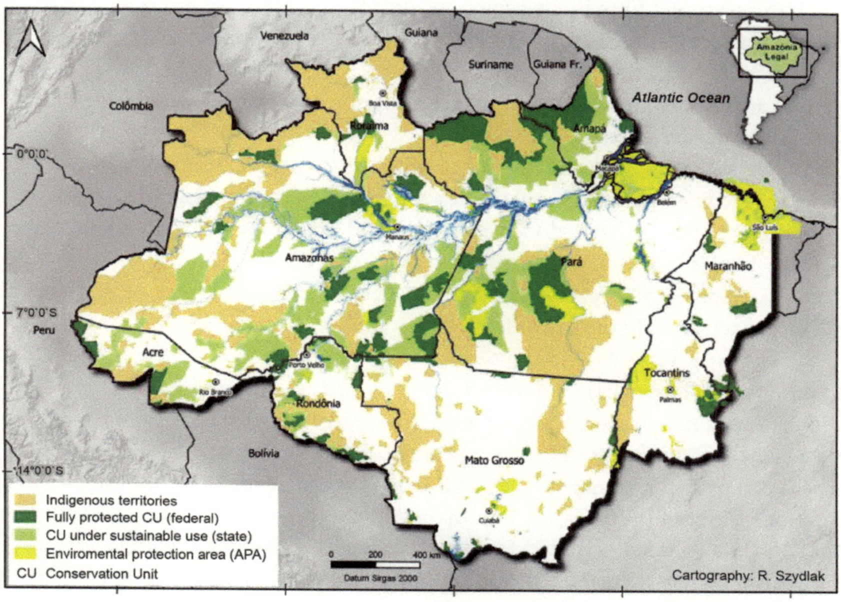

Sources: Celentano and Veríssimo (2007, Fig. 19); IMAZON (2021, Fig. 24); ISA (2020).

Half of the federal PAs are of sustainable use,[254] covering a total area of over 40 million ha.

The ARPA programme was implemented in partnership with state and municipal governments and had the support of the World Bank, the German Government Cooperation Bank (KfW), the German Technical Cooperation Agency (GTZ) and WWF Brazil (Kohlhepp 2007a).

The inclusion and citizenship were conceived in the conception that the Amazon is "an urbanised forest" (Becker 1995). The absence of public policies had left much of the urban population marginalised. The social inclusion strategy intended to disseminate universal policies regarding education, health, and public security, accelerate the fight against poverty, community development, etc. Another objective was to prevent poor rural populations from being chased away from their territories (UNEP 2006).

The permanent inter-ministerial working group proposed measures and had to coordinate actions for the reduction of deforestation rates through the following instruments (GTI 2006; UNEP 2006):

254 They are divided into five main categories (Melo-Reiners 2009, 153 f.): Environmental Protection Area (*Área de Proteção Ambiental*, APA), Area of Relevant Ecological Interest (*Área de Relevante Interesse Ecológico*, ARIE), National Forest (*Floresta Nacional*, Flona), Extractive Reserve (*Reserva Extrativista*, Resex), Sustainable Development Reserve (*Reserva de Desenvolvimento Sustentável*, RDS). Among the PAs of sustainable use extractive reserves comprise over 12 million ha. The Flonas are also designated for the maintenance of traditional peoples, and Brazil holds 67 protected areas under this category, distributed in four biomes: Amazon, Cerrado, Caatinga and Atlantic Forest.

- Land use planning and legalisation of land tenure in the municipalities in the "Arc of Deforestation." This is the region where the agricultural border advances towards the forest and where the highest rates of deforestation of the Amazon region are found;
- Fiscal and credit incentives to expand economic efficiency and sustainability of areas already deforested;
- Procedures for environmentally sustainable infrastructure works;
- Job and income generation in activities with rehabilitation of degraded areas;
- Addition of open and abandoned areas to the production chain, and management of forest areas;
- Integrated performance of federal agencies responsible for monitoring and control of illegal activities in the Arc of Deforestation.

The Pluriannual Plans (PPA) 1996–1999 and 2000–2003 were part of a strategy of integration of Amazonia to the Brazilian productive space. The Avança Brasil Programme invested US$ 3.5 billion in four transport corridors (Théry 2005). Due to impacts in untouched regions so far, Avança Brasil had become the centre of numerous protests and discussions. Some of the mega-projects in the Amazon region were not carried out due to dubious "Environmental Impact Studies" (EIA) and "Environmental Impact Reports" (RIMA). Others, however, were carried out after lengthy negotiations and modifications to the projects.

In view of the highly problematic infrastructural programmes of the former Cardoso government, the strategies of the new Lula da Silva government, contained in the multiannual plan 2004–2007 ("Brazil for all"), were anxiously expected. Within the first few months, all of IBAMA's office managers had been replaced, which was associated with the hope that the action scope of civil society groups would be expanded, and a cooperative environmental policy could contribute to solving corruption problems (Melo-Reiners 2009; Scholz *et al.* 2003). Despite insufficient integration of objectives of the Pilot Programme (PPG7) in the environmental policies of the successor programmes, it had been possible – this had already started in the PPG7 – to involve the most important stakeholders such as public authorities, civil society actors and the private sector in a dialogue in some programmes, which had a positive impact on political decisions on the use of natural resources (Scholz 2007; Kohlhepp and Coy 2010). Opportunities for a sustainable use of the natural potential, e.g., in biologically favourable areas such as the *várzea* of the white water rivers (Junk *et al.* 2000; Junk 2003), sustainable regional development (Coy and Neuburger 2002; Kohlhepp 2005) and good local governance in sustainable municipal development were available and had been used at least partially. "Good governance is based on policy-advising on the national level, institutional development on the regional level and empowerment of civil society on the local level" (Segebart 2007, 367).[255] Participation and monitoring are important factors for good local governance. The challenge is to organise frontier expansion so that most forests remain standing and "government and civil society are gradually developing the policies, technology and institutional capacity to meet this challenge" (Nepstad *et al.* 2002, 629).

---

255 Action research on the implementation of participatory monitoring of sustainable municipal development plans was realised in municipalities in the northeast of Pará.

Although the Pilot Programme's demonstration projects successfully involved local neo-Brazilian and Indigenous populations in sustainable use projects, in the shadow of international climate and environmental protection programmes, local groups whose survival was at risk were excluded from support from national and international state actors and NGOs, as in the case of the *cabocla* communities on the lower Rio Negro (Neuburger 2008). This applies in general to smallholder agriculture in Amazonia, which for a long time was almost completely ignored in all project planning and ran the risk of being marginalised as an excluded group. Poverty, displacement and socio-economic and ecological degradation led to a high degree of vulnerability but gave rise to new forms of organisation and specific survival strategies at local level.[256] The smallholders' expectations of the Lula da Silva government were therefore very high.

The Action Plan for Prevention and Control of the Legal Amazon Deforestation (PPCDAm) was a governmental effort which significantly contributed to the decrease of deforestation rates. In 2003, most of the deforestation, mainly illegal, spanned an arc between southeast Maranhão, southern Pará, northern Tocantins, south of Mato Grosso, Rondônia, southern Amazonas, and southeast Acre – the "Arc of Deforestation." Livestock ranching was responsible for 80 % of deforestation, followed by soybean crop expansion, logging, infrastructure projects, the setting of bush fires, and the illegal occupation of public lands. The implementation of the PPCDAm programme began in 2005 and was twice revised (2008 and 2011).

The results of the PPCDAm were the creation of more than 50 million ha of protected areas at federal and state level, especially in regions under heavy deforestation pressure, and the ratification of more than 10 million hectares of Indigenous territories. Furthermore, the inhibition of more than 60 000 irregular land titles for rural properties was realised and 25 600 rural landholdings in the Terra Legal programme had been awarded.

There are also other examples of Brazilian efforts aimed at discouraging illegal deforestation in the Amazonian forests, such as the implementation of frameworks for management of public forests, which were introduced in Brazil's legal system in 2006. Besides this, the Brazilian government intended to invest around US$ 500 million in initiatives connected to the PPCDAm over the 2008–2011 period, under its Pluriannual Plan (PPA). This signalled to all agencies that deforestation had received the highest level of priority. In order to promote a continuous and consistent deforestation reduction, the PPCDAm has been updated for the periods 2012–2015 and 2016–2020.

Law enforcement efforts successfully tried to uncover illegal activities and organised land- and timber-grabbing groups; "blacklists" of high deforestation municipalities were established. Farmers involved in illegal deforestation lost their access to public farm credit programmes (Nepstad *et al.* 2014; Nepstad and Shimada 2018).[257]

The president's decision to appoint Marina Silva as Minister of Environment was an extremely clever move and led to the strengthening of the credibility of the Brazilian government internationally. She descended from a rubber tapper family in Acre and led the Association of Rubber Tappers with Chico Mendes, a pioneer of the Brazil-

256 A good example is the study by Neuburger (2002) on pioneer frontier development in the hinterland of Cáceres, Mato Grosso.

257 Regarding the actions of government territorial control and planning and the successful measures implemented to reduce deforestation, see also: Capobianco (2017).

ian environmental movement who was murdered in 1988. As a native Amazonian and member of Brazil's Federal Senate (1994–2002), she built support for environmental protection of the forest reserves as well as for social justice and sustainable development in the Amazon region.

Her appointing was associated with high expectations (Mello *et al.* 2004; 2005). Numerous prominent NGO representatives had been invited to join the staff of the Ministry. Her conviction as a defender of the rain forest's traditional dwellers against the encroachment of ranchers and loggers and the drastic measures to protect the Amazon forest, clamping down on illegal forest devastation activities made her the main enemy of all opponents of state controls in the environmental sector. However, she managed to reduce deforestation by almost 60 % from 2004 to 2007. She instituted "a sophisticated system to root out corruption within IBAMA" (Tollefson 2015). However, Marina Silva "did not need to start from scratch" (Nepstad and Shimada 2018, 16) because tools for controlling Amazon deforestation were already in place, initiated under President Cardoso.

In 2006, Marina Silva announced a proposal to establish a tropical forest fund for receiving performance-based donations to help Brazil advance the strategies to greatly decrease deforestation. In 2007, the government of Norway responded with a major commitment to the Amazon Fund, established to prevent greenhouse gas emissions through rain forest conservation. It provides funding for measures to prevent, control and combat deforestation and for the conservation and sustainable use of resources in the Brazilian Amazon. The Amazon Fund was based on a Brazilian target of reducing Amazon deforestation by 70 % by 2017.[258]

The Amazon Fund investment has supported state-level programmes to encourage farmer participation in the Rural Environmental Registry (CAR), mandatory for all rural properties in the country, and projects led by NGOs. The projects have been most relevant to small-scale producers. The combination of the PPCDAm, the establishment of the Amazon Fund, and support from the Ministry of Environment created the basis for state governments to elaborate state level plans for prevention and control of deforestation and an efficient socio-environmental governance.

In May 2008, Marina Silva resigned after losing political influence and self-assertion for control of environmental policies within the Federal Government. She had become increasingly isolated and was involved in struggles between developmentalists and environmentalists in the administration. In Lula da Silva's second term, there were frictions with other ministers, who accused her of blocking the environmental licensing of projects. One of the main clashes was with the then Minister of the Civil House, Dilma Rousseff, responsible for the Growth Acceleration Programme (PAC). The main reason was that Marina Silva opposed approval of new hydroelectric dams in Amazônia Legal, especially in the Rio Madeira,[259] and criticised the president's biofuels programme. She also lost the fight against the planting of genetically modified crops.

---

258 This target was subsequently increased to 80 % by 2020 as Norway finalized its pledge of one billion dollars to the Amazon Fund. Cf. chapter III.4.

259 São Paulo (Reuters) 05.03.2007: President Lula da Silva said that nuclear energy will be the alternative for Brazil if obstacles to building new hydroelectric dams cannot be overcome in time. This was a clear political threat to Environment Minister Marina Silva and environmental movements in the region.

President Lula da Silva reduced the power of the Minister of Environment by splitting IBAMA into two agencies and separating environmental protection from the issuance of environmental licenses. The resignation of Marina Silva is believed to have been prompted by the president's decision to withdraw the highly praised PAS from the auspices of the Ministry of Environment and give it in the hands of the Minister of Strategic Affairs, Mangabeira Unger, a Harvard law professor with limited experience with Amazon affairs, and a declared "developmentalist," certainly not a representative of sensitive environment and resource protection. It had been central for Marina Silva to drawing up the Plan of Sustainable Amazonia and believed she would oversee its implementation.[260]

According to a statement of the vice president of Conservation International South America in 2008 "her resignation is a disaster for the Lula administration. If the government had any global credibility in environmental issues, it was because of minister Marina."[261] Lula da Silva had called Marina Silva the "mother of the Sustainable Amazon Plan (PAS)", finally launched by the government in 2008. It was a setback for Brazil's ambitions to become a major voice in global environmental debates, exposed the shortcomings of Brazil's Amazon policy and damaged Brazil's international reputation.

This event made it abundantly clear that President Lula da Silva, under intense pressure from agribusiness, was more concerned with economic development than with conservation as a commodity export boom fuelled Brazil's economic growth, the "golden years" of Brazilian foreign trade. The Lula da Silva government benefited in particular from China's huge absorption capacity for soybeans, iron ore, meat and mineral oil. Enormous tensions between the promotion of modernisation-oriented regional development on the one hand and the strengthening of protection and sustainability made a balance between the two options extremely difficult.

The Growth Acceleration Programme (PAC) was another major infrastructure programme of the Federal Government, launched in 2007. Consisting of a set of economic policies and investment projects with the objective of accelerating economic growth in Brazil, the programme had a huge budget for the 2007–2010 period. The continuation of the asphalting of the BR-163 had been expressly confirmed. The successor government of Dilma Rousseff (2011–2016) has continued the PAC programme under the name PAC-2.

Numerous innovative programme ideas, such as the Proambiente programme, which aimed to compensate for environmental services, were crushed in the mills of the ministerial bureaucracy. However, innovative approaches to rain forest protection have been launched by individual states in Amazonia. Particularly noteworthy is the so-called Bolsa Floresta programme in the state of Amazonas, which was initially limited to federal protected areas and financially compensated the renunciation of de-

260 After resigning, she left the Workers' Party (PT) after 30 years of affiliation, became member of the Green Party (PV) and ran for president in 2010, 2014 and in 2018. In 2007, she was awarded by the Champions of the Earth award, the UN's top environmental award. On the start of a renewed career as Environment Minister, see chapter IV.2.

261 https://news.mongabay.com/2008/05/brazils-environmental-minister-resigns-after-losing-amazon-fight/ (accessed September 4, 2024).

forestation as an environmental benefit and combined it with other social transfers (Kohlhepp and Coy 2010).

To the great irritation of environmentalists, disappointment of members of the Workers' Party (PT) itself and great surprise for many people, some of the newly initiated infrastructure projects gained special attention. The national development plan PAC strongly overshadowed the sustainability goals with its infrastructure projects. This mainly referred to the construction of roads and of hydroelectric power plants and dams with large reservoirs.

The Plan of Sustainable Amazonia (PAS) was realised without resolving the severe conflicts between the convinced supporters of infrastructure development and the engaged and well-prepared environmental groups with the aim of regional sustainability. "Environmental" policies were frequently realized without direct participation of the Ministry of Environment and with a total lack of consideration of the most important environmental factors. The government was unwilling or unable to implement the sustainability approach in its programmes after the departure of Marina Silva. The extensive activities of ranching projects could not be reduced, and the agribusiness was specially supported. Deforestation fell sharply, but the proportion of illegal logging remained high.

The PAS initiated the Operation "Green Arc" ("Arco Verde") as a reaction to the command-and-control operations to finance projects of reafforestation and recuperation of degraded areas in Amazônia Legal. The governance arrangement brought together municipal, state, and federal administrations with the objectives of legalising land tenure and creating positive incentives to promote sustainable activities, helping rural landowners to clarify and legalise land tenure. The "Arco Verde" region is composed of the municipalities having the highest deforestation rates. The government tried to establish its presence in these municipalities and to strengthen the sustainable development's strategies. Only a modest part of the government's sustainability goals in the PAS programme was achieved.

Due to the chaotic situation in the BR-163 region, the Federal Government decided to implement a special regional development programme in an area where the government had increasingly lost control.

5.2. The Sustainable Regional Development Plan for the area under the influence of the BR-163 (Cuiabá-Santarém)

This plan, implemented to cushion possible negative consequences of the major infrastructure project, was based on the assumption that it must be possible to achieve economic growth and national integration goals with social justice and preservation as well as the sustainable use of natural resources. It aimed at combating the illegal occupation of public lands, the creation and consolidation of conservation units and Indigenous lands, the provision of services in urban centres (treated water, basic sanitation), increased food security, the valorisation of traditional knowledge about biodiversity, among others. This could only succeed if the participation of all social actors in the design and implementation, but also in the monitoring and evaluation of the plan was guaranteed.

The plan met the demands of the civil society for sustainability of the region, consolidated in the *Carta de Santarém* of April 2004.[262] It included demands related to basic services, land planning and combating violence, management of natural resources, social and cultural strengthening of local populations, environmental management, and monitoring. The first public hearings on the environmental impacts (EIA/RIMA) of the planned asphalting of the BR-163 took place in April 2004. Fearnside criticised very clearly that the key problem was "that environmental impact assessment and licensing procedures are subject to pressure from those interested in speedy and obstacle-free construction of the infrastructure" (2007, 608). In addition, it must be emphasised that the most important environmental damage was not intensively incorporated into the assessments, either intentionally or due to a lack of expertise.

The severity of the problems linked to this project, a mere transport corridor for agricultural commodities, had led to a broad mobilisation of social movement organisations – Indigenous people, smallholders, rubber tappers, NGOs – as well as private institutions specialised in environmental research. The latter tried to bring in the expertise of those not directly involved in the projects.

In particular, the asphalting of the 950 km section of the BR-163 (Cuiabá–Santarém) in Pará triggered strong criticism and fears that it could cause major ecological damage and impact on Indigenous lands. Many small landowners working on a subsistence basis were expelled from their land as a result of the preparations of the highway construction. Property rights of these landowners were poorly protected, and they were vulnerable to the activities of speculators and developers. Grabbing of Indigenous lands had been explicitly a component of the land occupation process in the north of Mato Grosso and in southwest Pará, receiving support from agricultural projects encouraged and funded by the Federal Government.

In addition, Indigenous land was forcibly seized by speculators who relied on forged documents certifying that the people were not Indigenous or even land squatters (UNEP 2006). "A climate of generalized lawlessness and impunity prevails, and matters related to environment and to land tenure are especially unregulated" (Fearnside 2007, 601). Deforestation and illegal logging had accelerated in anticipation of highway paving. In the course of deregulation and flexibilisation, the Federal Government withdrew from many areas of action on the regional scene and left the field to private capital and various global players as new actors. The high potential of conflicts led to a rapid increase of clashes of different social actors, which, without any state control or mediation, often manifested themselves in violent actions and unpunished murders.

The BR-163 plan was under the responsibility of the inter-ministerial working group (GTI 2006), decreed by a President's Act in May 2004. The sphere of influence covered 73 municipalities (28 in Pará, 39 in Mato Grosso and 6 in Amazonas) and an area of 1.2 million km².

Two rounds of public consultations were held in the region to identify the demands and expectations of local participants of the plan and to collect suggestions from the different social groups likely to be interested, such as state governments, municipalities, entrepreneurs and workers representative entities, civil society forums, etc. A

262 Cf. https://ipam.org.br/wp-content/uploads/2004/03/plano_de_desenvolvimento_territorial_int.pdf (August 18, 2004).

public consultation was held in Brasília on the request of NGOs and the civil society. The objective was to bring about a more balanced scenario, such as sustainable exploration of natural resources and to foster increasing levels of governance. In the second round, the Indigenous populations were absent, because of travel problems to the meeting venues and because of the non-adherence to the promise to organise an own round of meetings for them.

The development on the central Amazonian pioneer front is an example of the socio-economic and political complexity of environmental problems, its influencing factors and its wide-ranging consequences. The most diverse conflicts of interest between the actors in Amazonia led to a constantly escalating competition in the use of space associated with illegal actions and often violence. From the perspective of political ecology, Amazonia is to be understood as a politicised environment and thus as an area of conflicting interests of actors (Coy and Neuburger 2008; Fearnside 2008; Kohlhepp and Coy 2010). There is a wide variety of stakeholder groups. On the one hand, so-called place-based actors, i.e., those anchored at the local level, and on the other hand, non-place-based actors, who have a much wider radius of action (Kohlhepp and Coy 2010).

Regional policy in Amazonia takes place under global influences and dependencies. This applies in particular to the economic interests and globally networked value chains of the agribusiness.

Since modernisation goals and economic development ideology met irreconcilably with a new environmental discourse and goals of social justice, the negotiation of a common basis for regional development within the framework of the BR-163 plan seemed almost hopeless.

Soybean farmers, sawmills, timber trade, transport companies, representatives of the municipalities concerned, urban businessmen, land speculators, often with fake ownership documents, but also land-hungry settlers are place-based actors expecting economic upswing from the asphalted long-distance road connection. Their hopes are faced by parts of the civil society, such as small farmers' unions, rubber tappers, Indigenous groups, who fear displacement and are supported by environmental groups on the ground.

In the conflict of the opposing interests of the actors, the powerful actors had so far steered the planning and its implementation almost without contradiction or at least decisively influenced it. The majority of the marginalised local actors had only a very limited right to be heard.

This local conflict-laden situation was overshadowed by the influence of the large non-place-based actors. These include certain federal ministries (transport, planning, integration), the governments of the states concerned, private investors as well as the transnational agribusiness, which markets local/regional production and its export globally.

As a counterpart, regional and national environmental agencies as well as national and international NGOs, strengthened in recent decades, appeared on the scene, committed to ecological and social sustainability and ethical economic behaviour. The NGOs are often scientifically and administratively very well networked, have been tested in discussions and the organisation of public meetings of the persons concerned and support the regional actors of civil society on a broad basis. In the case of environmental protection, some NGOs, and socio-environmental institutes (such as Isa,

Imazon, and Ipam) have acted by producing extremely relevant technical information for mapping demands and for proposing solutions, as in the case of the polygons of the conservation units (Pereira, A. *et al.* 2022).

The basic problem of the discourse on regional development in the area of BR-163 was the decisive question of an export corridor or a sustainable development for the protection of vulnerable groups because of socio-ecological reasons. Rain forest destruction has increasingly taken place out of profit or speculative interest. On the other hand, the struggle for survival is the goal and the everlasting hope for a better living. These groups saw the need to implement basic requirements and poverty-oriented strategies that are geared to the model of regional sustainability.

Despite the well-known consequences, the Lula da Silva government – especially after the resigning of Marina Silva as Minister of Environment – was still sticking to its major infrastructure projects in Amazonia, such as the asphalting of the Cuiabá–Santarém long-distance road (BR-163). The road was the backbone of one of the most important export corridors in the Brazilian Amazon. In the energy sector, the Belo Monte hydroelectric power plant[263] at the Xingu river had priority, whose construction – under the project name Babaquara – was denied in 1988 (Kohlhepp 1989a; 1998c). Hydroelectric dams on the Madeira river and a planned waterway connecting Guaporé and Beni rivers now had priority as well. In view of the large number of conflicts of interest, a new dynamic of regional constellations of actors had emerged (Scholz *et al.* 2003; Alencar 2005; Coy and Neuburger 2008).

The activities of social actors increasingly shifted northwards to south-western Pará. The road ran in southern Pará near the Serra do Cachimbo, a mountain range (250–750 m above sea level), where a support facility to the operation of aircraft flying on a straight route between the north and the southeast of Brazil had been established by the Brazilian Air Force in 1950. In the 1970s, a centre for testing weapons and training of the Brazilian Armed Forces had been set up.[264]

The paving of BR-163 in Pará had mobilised new actors and activities from Mato Grosso to Novo Progresso, Castelo dos Sonhos, among other new settlements in the state of Pará, with an increase of tensions and conflicts. Illegal land grabbing, land speculation, displacement of small farmers, threats to Indigenous groups determined the scene. Novo Progresso became the new regional centre. The area, originally intended as farmland, experienced a major expansion of large-scale livestock farming, selective logging and timber trading after the gold boom. Cattle population in the municipality of Novo Progresso increased sixfold between 2000 and 2014 to over 600 000 animals (Klingler in Coy, Klingler, and Kohlhepp 2017, 29).

Under pressure from agribusiness, the state had assumed a strategic role in the implementation of the BR-163 plan by expanding infrastructure and establishing de-

---

263 Cf. chapter II.6.

264 In the 1970s and 1980s, during the military regime, Brazil had a secret programme to develop nuclear weapons. In the beginning of the 1980s, evidence surfaced in the press of the existence of two major shafts in the Air Force base in the Serra do Cachimbo. These raised suspicions over nuclear activities, as the shafts had been possibly designed as testing sites for nuclear explosives – which has always been officially denied – or for the storage of nuclear waste from nuclear power plants. Although extremely remote at that time, the location was relatively close to Indigenous settlement areas. The programme could not be realized and was dismantled in 1990, five years after the military regime ended.

velopment poles. In addition, environmental and institutional factors have gained influence in the form of the establishment of protected areas, control, and monitoring of illegal land grabbing. The demand for environmental protection was a historical concern, as opening the road could allow access for loggers and land grabbers, creating an "aisle of devastation" (Coy and Klingler 2014; Pereira, A. *et al.* 2022). Faced with the very pressing but completely unresolved issue of legally secured land access, the state blocked itself with the aim of preventing illegal logging and land speculation in the land grabbing process in the long term.

In addition, globally controlled discourses on rain forest destruction, CO_2 emissions, threats to Indigenous habitats or sustainable value chains were becoming increasingly important in the negotiation process of land use at the frontier. At the local level, more than ever, actors were simultaneously squeezed into the global logics of international value chains on the one hand and the sustainability discourse on the other and are increasingly unable to make self-determined and responsible decisions due to the restricted rights of disposal over land (Klingler 2022).

Farmers in the region had heeded the government's call to develop land in Amazonia since the 1980s. They cling to the frontier myth of having successfully achieved their goal and fulfilled their duty but are now complaining about rapidly changing laws and the new environmental and global climate dialogue and its direct and indirect repercussions. From their point of view, areas in which they had established farms with official approval were suddenly designated as protected areas (Jamanxim National Park etc.). "We are not the bad guys" was the reaction of one of the affected farmers,[265] who felt overwhelmed by national requirements and international demands for sustainability.

As a conclusion of the Sustainable Plan BR-163, which envisaged the legalisation of land titles along the road and the delimitation of protection and sustainable use areas such as conservation units and extractive reserves, it must be stated that the plan was not properly implemented by the government. The BR-163 plan did not have its own resources, which meant that each ministry had to fit the plan's actions into its budget. Low use of resources, insufficient inspection, lack of INCRA and IBAMA personnel, improper implementation of the protected areas were some of the most important failures which resulted in the advance of the agricultural frontier opening new areas.

People took possession of land by means of false deeds (*grileiros*), submitting applications to INCRA to regularise huge areas over which they did not have any legal right, using local people who act as false applicants ("laranjas"). To obtain contiguous plots of land larger than 2500 ha, the maximum limit for disposal of individual plots of public land, frequently some applications of "relatives" were presented.

As a key measure, the government turned huge areas of land along the road into conservation units, removing them from the land speculation market, but no appropriate precautions have been taken to protect them adequately.

When the road project was retaken after the standstill caused by the 2008 crisis, many leaders of the government agencies responsible for the articulation around the plan had moved to other agencies. This could have contributed to the governmental

---

265 Interview by Stefanie Nolen, January 26, 2018, in Novo Progresso, https://www.theglobeandmail.com/news/world/amazon-rainforest-deforestation-crisis/article37722932/ (accessed October 20, 2022).

demobilisation regarding the sustainable and territorial aspects of the road-paving project (Oliveira 2015; Pereira, A. *et al.* 2022). Although a majority favoured the participation process promoted, a mix of trust and disbelief prevailed over the governmental policy (UNEP 2006). The lack of trust in the state's ability to act sometimes led to civil disobedience.

The PPG7 International Advisory Group (IAG) presented clearly formulated critiques and detailed recommendations for better organisation of public land registration and for monitoring and clarifying the problems that the government had been slow to address, despite the accelerating land occupation process. There was a lack of clear indications on how to connect the licensing procedure of the BR-163 and the Sustainable BR-163 plan. The transversality of policies and practices was not occurring on the expansion fronts of the Amazon region. The recognition of the value of environmental services in Amazonia was necessary, with the accelerated creation of knowledge chains that become production chains, such as the bio-industry.[266]

NGOs most frequently raised contentions against state and local governments, loggers, urban entrepreneurs and urban workers. Migration, the increase of violence and crime, environmental devastation, and the difficulties of access to land were the issues most frequently seen as important.

Referring to federative coordination, most of the region's mayors favoured the road but opposed the plan, particularly the command-and-control actions and land-use planning in the context of the demand for environmental protection. The mayors especially defended the interests of the local elite related to mining, agriculture, timber extraction, and timber trade. Unlike sectoral coordination, there was no institutional arrangement to promote this coordination between federal, state, and municipal governments (Pereira, A. *et al.* 2022). The organisation of an effective participation in the region could be expected from the Federal Government as the responsible actor. However, its agencies INCRA and IBAMA were often described as inoperative, ineffective, bureaucratic, and corrupt (UNEP 2006). There was also considerable tension between the Ministry of Environment (MMA) and IBAMA, the federal agency under the MMA, which has to exercise the environmental police role.

The local civil society in Novo Progresso criticised alternative regional development strategies due to negative experiences in the implementation of the participatory development goals of the Sustainable Regional Development Plan of BR-163 as well as the low proportion of definitive land titles in the land regulation programme Terra Legal (Klingler 2022).

As a result, it must be noted that the BR-163 plan can only be seen positively for those who already had the advantages of the asphalting of the road. The new highway benefits the economic elite of Mato Grosso, the largest soybean producer and exporter in the country, and to some extent in southwest Pará. Electronic products from the Free Trade Zone of Manaus, meat, timber, and agroforest products, in addition to soybeans, are the main cargo. Those who lived in the towns located along the highway in particular gave more importance to economic expansion than to the environmental features included in the plan.

Participation of all in the benefit of the new corridor did not work as planned. Social disparities between the actors alongside the BR-163 increased excessively as did

266 IAG Relatórios XX–XXII (2003; 2004a; b).

the vulnerability of the urban and the rural poor as well as the Indigenous people. The "winners" of the BR-163 try to defend their position against all interference by all means, including against environmental laws. As a result of displacement processes in rural areas, intraregional migration to regional centres and new pioneer towns was increasing, leading to impoverishment growth and very conspicuous fragmentation processes.

Violence is omnipresent. In 2019, the Pastoral Land Commission denounced that in all municipalities in Pará around the highway (Trairão, Itaituba and Novo Progresso) there are small farmers, settlers, extractivists and Indigenous peoples threatened with death. The concession of the Amazon section of the BR-163 highway for a period of 10 years in 2022 transformed it into a privatized highway for corporate use and increased conflicts.

The reason for this overall situation is clear: The highway should not have been paved until after a state of law had been established. Furthermore, it should have been independently certified that sufficient governance arrangements prevails to secure and finance protected areas and enforce environmental legislation (Fearnside 2007; Rodrigues and Nahum 2023). This, of course, before making de facto decisions on the implementation of infrastructure projects at the expense of a large part of the regional population for whom the state has a duty of care. Improvement of governance in the Amazon failed widely.

Public and private sector strategies of valorisation led to a continuous transformation of social relations with nature. Due to the resulting dependencies, this transformation represents a socio-ecological challenge. The concept of post-frontier shows the narrative shift that discusses the frontier-governance between modernisation-oriented development and valorisation towards socio-ecological protection modalities of "sustainable development" (Klingler in Coy *et al.* 2017; Klingler 2022).[267] In the post-frontier phase, the Amazonian rain forests have long since become "political forests" (Vandergeest and Peluso 2015, 162).

267 Klingler's research of the example of Novo Progresso shows how new peripheries develop into spaces of global significance in the course of the expansion of resource frontiers.

6. The hydroelectric power plant Belo Monte and its environmental and socio-ecological impacts

6.1. The struggle of operators and opponents of the construction of Belo Monte, the confusion of judgements and political entanglements

Already at the end of the 1960s, a project study by the American Hudson Institute had shown a scenario of huge reservoirs for energy production in Amazonia. Two decades later, after vigorous Brazilian protests against this foreign interference, the reservoir ideas appeared in a modified form in the national energy plan.

Since the possibilities of using hydropower have been exhausted in large parts of the country, Amazonia became the new target area of the energy programme Plano 2010 at the end of the 1980s. Due to the ecological and social problems of large reservoirs already built during the 1980s on the Rio Tocantins (Tucuruí) and Rio Uatumã (Balbina), there were violent protests against the construction of reservoir chains on the tributaries of the Amazon and the plan was abandoned (Kohlhepp 1998c; 2010c).[268] The low natural gradient in Amazonia leads to extensive reservoirs during the construction of hydroelectric power plants, which flood large areas of rainforest and thus destroy parts of the habitat of the riverine and the Indigenous populations.

Lack of resettlement management, low and delayed compensation payments, and unwillingness to resolve conflicts of interest characterise all power plant constructions with large reservoirs since Itaipu and Sobradinho. In the case of the earlier large-scale projects, there was no detailed environmental impact assessment, the scientific know-how to assess the ecological consequences was lacking and project development during the military dictatorship lacked any sensitivity to the socio-economic consequences, which manifested itself in a complete underestimation of the social needs and the related costs.

Brazil's democratic opening with the new environmental legislation and regulations on environmental impact assessment (EIA) had initially led to a turn away from excessive planning of ambitious "mammoth projects." This decision stood until 20 years ago, despite excessive lobbying by the construction companies and the hydroelectric power plants.

The strong overall industrial development, the implementation of large aluminium smelters in East Amazonia, the agricultural boom in Central Brazil as well as the ex-

268 See chapters I.4.3 and I.5 in this volume.

pansion of urban centres have led in the first decade of the 21st century to the resumption of power plants and reservoir plans in a modified form. This was favoured by the international climate debate and hydropower as so-called "clean" or "green" energy. The reservoirs with flooded biomass and their enormous release of CO_2 and methane have often been forgotten in the life cycle assessment of hydropower.

The construction of the large power plant Tucuruì (8400 MW) was carried out within the framework of the regional development programme Grande Carajas (PGC),[269] in particular for the subsidised energy supply of the regional alumina and aluminium industries. A particular example of the absurdity of some projects was the Balbina power plant, which was built to supply the regional metropolis of Manaus. However, due to the natural conditions and the large environmental degradation caused by the 2360 km² reservoir, the energy production is barely sufficient to supply an urban quarter. Due to the serious environmental and social consequences of such projects, the World Bank denied Brazil the second energy sector loan.

The Altamira complex (Babaquara/Kararaô) on the Rio Xingu, which was rejected in its earlier form in 1989, was revitalised and came back on the agenda during the Lula da Silva government in 2003. It was renamed the new Belo Monte mega-project, even without prior consultation with the Indigenous people of the region. This project with a planned installed capacity of 11 000 MW was one of the largest hydroelectric power plants in the world. The government had offered little transparency to the people affected by the hydroelectric project, as has been unfortunately always the case in Brazil. Fierce protests occurred, especially by the Indigenous population[270] because of their endangered reservations and an area of 6150 km² planned to be flooded.

Between 1989 and 2002, the project had been redesigned. The reservoir's surface area was scaled down to 480 km² by moving the dam further upstream to reduce flooding of the Bacajá Indigenous area. The new environmental impact assessment contained the introduction of a run-of-river model, in contrast to the large reservoirs which were characteristic of previous projects.

In 2007, at the beginning of Lula da Silva's second term, the Growth Acceleration Programme (PAC) was introduced with enormous investments. The Belo Monte power plant complex figured as an anchor project of the new investment plans. In 2010, the environmental agency IBAMA granted a provisional environmental license for the construction of the dam despite critics from within the agency about pressure to approve the project and incomplete information in the EIA, presented by Eletrobras and participating construction enterprises. Independent Brazilian experts had issued a report on the EIA, identifying problems such as the project's uncertain cost, deforestation, uncertainties in generation capacity, high amount of greenhouse gas emissions and in particular the lack of consideration for those affected along the river's 100 km long southern "big bend" (Volta Grande). 140 Brazilian and international human rights organisations and environmental movements complained about the decision-making

---

269 See chapter I.4

270 Indigenous tribes of the region had organised the "First Encounter of the Indigenous Nations of the Xingu" in 1989. The encounter, symbolised by the provocation of the Indigenous woman leader Tuíra holding her machete against the face of the responsible manager, was leading to intensive disputes both in Brazil and internationally over the consequences of the planned six dams. As a result, five dams were removed from planning.

process in granting the environmental license for the project in a letter to President Lula da Silva in 2010.[271]

In April 2010, the Federal Attorney General suspended the project and cancelled the provisional environmental license as unconstitutional because of the lack of identifying the activities taking place in Indigenous territories, in particular in the Volta Grande region at the southern loop of the Xingu river. In August 2010, Lula da Silva signed the contract with Norte Energia S.A., in charge of and operating the Belo Monte hydroelectric power plant, a consortium mostly owned by the government, and funded primarily by the Brazilian Development Bank (BNDES). However, the construction was not permitted to begin on the Belo Monte dam complex until IBAMA granted the second of the federally required environmental licenses, the installation license. At least more than 20 conditions had not been met. FUNAI staff members expressed concerns about the location of the project, its impact on Indigenous territories, and the lack of attention to Indigenous people and opposed the operation license.

In 2011, however, the FUNAI management surprisingly stated that there was no reason to deny a limited construction license. The newly elected President Dilma Rousseff in 2011 strongly advocated rapid construction progress. As the Belo Monte licensing process neared full installation approval, international groups (Amazon Watch and International Rivers) made renewed appeals to President Dilma Rousseff: a petition signed by 500 000 people in February 2011 and a Brazilian petition with 1.3 million signatures (Fearnside 2017b).

The president of the environmental agency IBAMA resigned in dissent and because of political pressure to grant a license for the Belo Monte dam.[272] He was rapidly replaced and in June 2011 IBAMA granted the full license to construct the dam after – according to official information – additional studies had been carried out and costs paid to address relevant social and environmental problems. The only remaining license concerned the operation of the power plant.

Despite numerous lawsuits against Belo Monte construction and judgements to stop the project, construction works continued with partial permits. In February 2011, a federal judge had blocked the project citing environmental reasons. Construction received permission to resume work in November 2011, after another federal judge ruled that Indigenous people did not have to be consulted by law before work approval. In August 2012, work on the dam was stopped again by order of the Brazilian Federal Court, with the argument that the Indigenous peoples had not been consulted. The Supreme Federal Court overturned the decision of a lower court that had suspended the dam's operating license and ordered construction to recommence. The lower court suspension was due to allegations of human rights violations.

The Federal Public Ministry in Belém described the "valid operating license" for Belo Monte as "totally illegal." "The dam forced its way past multiple legal challenges by means of "security suspensions," a relic of Brazil's military dictatorship that allows

---

271 Compilation of information based on Brazilian and international press reports and statements from environmental organizations, e.g., *O Globo*, *Folha de São Paulo*, *O Estado de São Paulo*, *The Times*, *Financial Times*, *The Guardian*, BBC News, *FAZ*, *NZZ*, *Handelsblatt*, *The New York Times*, *The Washington Post*, Bloomberg Businessweek, Reuters; Greenpeace, International Rivers, Indigenous Peoples Issues and Resources, Rainforest Foundation, Amazon Watch, Mongabay, among others.

272 https://news.mongabay.com/2011/01/brazils-environment-chief-resigns-over-controversial-amazon-dam/ (accessed September 4, 2024).

projects to go forward despite any number of illegalities if they are needed to avoid "damage to the public economy" (Fearnside 2021a).

The showdown of the granting of the three-step environmental license and the repeatedly contradictory court decisions of different federal and regional court levels at short intervals led to uncertainty, disappointment, and anger as well as to ongoing protests of the affected population, in particular the Indigenous groups, but also of NGOs and environmental organisations. On the other side, the constant objections and accusations by environmental groups and the back and forth in licensing and the respective judgements annoyed the energy company Norte Energia as well as the timing, work organisation and financial management of the engineering and construction companies or consulting firms involved.

Belo Monte caused immense popular resistance and was highly questioned for lack of qualified environmental impact assessments prior to the start of the construction works. The project has been facing strong opposition from scientists, environmentalists, and local residents. Even an anti-Belo Monte film was produced. Celebrities publicly criticised the expected environmental impact of the Belo Monte power plant. Local people, including members of the local Indigenous tribes, several times occupied one of the dam's construction sites. The protestors demanded that the consortium responsible for the construction should ensure that the Indigenous lands be demarcated before starting work.

The politically very tense situation was characterised by the fact that President Dilma Rousseff in 2011 recalled the Brazilian ambassador to the Organization of American States (OAS), when the Inter-American Commission on Human Rights of the OAS officially requested that the licensing process for Belo Monte be suspended because the human rights of the traditional peoples to be affected had not been considered (Hall and Branford 2012).

Public hearings on the construction and on the environmental and social impacts of Belo Monte became particularly important due to the severe conflicts between the social actors involved and the number of participants. The public hearing, in the scope of environmental licensing, has been made compulsory in Brazil in 1986.

> It consists of an administrative procedure provoked by the public power through a licensing agency but paid by the entrepreneur and it aims at informing the population about the project which is under licensing. The public hearings are part of the licensing of those activities which may cause a significant environmental impact (Tagliani *et al.* 2020, 5).

As has long been criticised by many scientists, most environmental impact studies lack a focus on core issues and sometimes shift their focus to less relevant issues to divert attention from important points.[273] Transparency as to the criteria employed in assessing the significance of impacts is generally lacking. EIA and licensing procedures frequently are subject of political and economic pressure, interested in trouble-free progress of construction works.

Sometimes, NGOs successfully tried to exert pressure on the authorities with the threat of larger gatherings of people affected, even outside public hearings, in order to

273 Especially Fearnside (2007), among others.

achieve improvements for the local population. Informal knowledge of the local population and their perception of risk and cultural impact were often disregarded. The common practice of selecting comments only after decisions have been made has always been a cause of discontent and protests in society. The public hearings obviously did not adequately fulfil the role of promoting public participation, being an overly formal, bureaucratic, and inhibiting process. The recommendation for improving this situation could be a board of certified and independent environmental analysts and a closer cooperation with scientists and independent specialised entities. Environmental authorities must be provided with adequate material conditions and human resources to promote sustainable development through efficient inspection and monitoring capacities (Tagliani *et al.* 2020).

During the construction of the Belo Monte complex, it became apparent that the conflicts of interest between the operators and their supporters on the one hand and the opponents, i.e., the population affected by the construction work and its impacts and the supporting active environmental groups on the other, were almost insoluble.

The pro-dam actors were represented by the government agencies Eletrobrás and the National Agency for Electrical Energy (ANEEL), the powerful and influential construction companies that were specialised in dam construction, the aluminium and electro-intensive metallic silicon producing industries as well as the iron ore giant CVRD (Vale) and related industries. Additionally, groups of professionals, who were connected and dependent on the construction of Belo Monte, supported the dam construction, such as engineers, technicians, construction workers and other employees, consulting firms, professionals of different service providers, lawyers, security companies etc. as well as commercial interests from outside and from the near urban centre Altamira to supply the construction site and its work force. Local businessmen founded the Regional Forum for Economic and Socio-Environmental Development of the Transamazônica and Xingu. Politicians on the local and regional level supported all the activities of regional development and tried to use this for themselves and their municipalities. Even some federal judges could be counted as pro-dam key actors (Millikan and Hurwitz 2011; Fearnside 2017a, 18).

Indigenous groups were the most important opponents of dam construction, leading the anti-dam campaign. Indigenous Juruna and Arara people, as well as those of sixteen other ethnic groups were severely impacted by the construction works. They have maintained protests and demonstrations against Belo Monte during many years, occupied construction sites and government offices. Another group on the anti-dam side were the non-Indigenous riverside dwellers (*ribeirinhos*), living from fishing at the southern loop of the Xingu, now with reduced flow and in an area flooded by the Belo Monte main reservoir. Residents of Altamira, who were affected by the impacts of the construction work and the partial flooding of their residential area have also joined the protests.

An important organisation of the non-Indigenous opponents was the Movement for the Development of the Transamazon Highway and the Xingu, having contacts with a large group of social organisations. The catholic church in Altamira has been another important actor supporting the people threatened and endangered by Belo Monte. In particular, the bishop of the diocese of Xingu, Dom Erwin Kräutler, who had to live with bodyguards and a bulletproof vest due to threats, was one of the open eminent critics of the Belo Monte complex. President Lula da Silva had promised that

"Belo Monte will not be shoved down anyone's throat" (Hurwitz 2010, n. p.). However, Bishop Kräutler later stated that "none of Lula's promises have been kept."[274]

Brazilian environmental research organisations and NGOs contributed commendably to the detailed examination of the information provided by Norte Energia about the measures carried out for environmental protection. Their harsh criticism of the construction work and its ecological and social implications was supported by scientific expertise and mapping. These organisations include, among others: Instituto Socio Ambiental (ISA), Amigos da Terra Amazônia Brasileira, Comissão Pró-Índio de São Paulo, Comissão Pastoral da Terra (CPT) and the Movement of People Affected by Dams (Movimento dos Atingidos por Barragens, MAB). International support came from Cultural Survival, International Rivers and Amazon Watch.

Norte Energia has managed, in a very clever but now well-known way, to divide the Indigenous anti-dam groups by giving the chiefs very practical gifts such as motorboats, vehicles, petrol or food (Heurich 2013) in order to reduce or even to end their actions against the project. This led to many quarrels, envy and resentment within the tribes and their villages. This strategy was also successfully applied to some non-Indigenous groups who were subsequently swept into their activities and lost members who switched to the dam supporters. The awarding of smaller contracts for studies on environmental issues served to involve NGOs and was also intended to mitigate criticism. Some lawyers and consultants worked on both sides or changed sides.

After the disappointment of the Lula da Silva government's continued promotion of Belo Monte, overlapping interests with stress and disagreements arose in groups close to the president's Workers' Party (PT) (Scholz *et al.* 2003; Fearnside 2017a). The government gave funds for social and environmental projects to NGOs hoping they would refrain as much as possible from aggressive comments to Belo Monte. The same occurred with the Movement of People Affected by Dams. They dropped their opposition to Belo Monte when the PT won the election (Bratman 2014; 2015).

In Brazil's "lava jato" ("car wash") corruption scandal,[275] initially focused on the Petrobras corporation,[276] the state-owned flagship in the Brazilian oil business, chief executives admitted that bribes paid by large construction companies to the petroleum sector also applied to the electrical sector and the construction contracts for Belo Monte. Brazilian prosecutors uncovered a parallel scheme of massive fraud in the construction of mega-dam projects in Amazonia such as Belo Monte and Jirau on the Madeira river, involving a cartel of Brazil's largest construction companies, powerful

274 Interview by Bruno Calixto, Época Blog do Planeta, May 13, 2014, https://epoca.globo.com/colunas-e-blogs/blog-do-planeta/noticia/2014/05/bdom-erwin-krautlerb-do-que-lula-prometeu-nada-foi-cumprido.html (accessed September 4, 2024).

275 The "operation car wash" ("lava jato") was a criminal investigation by the Federal Police. Originally, it was a money laundering investigation, first uncovered at a car wash in Brasília, what led to this specific name. It began in 2014 and expanded to cover allegations of corruption at the Petrobras corporation, where executives accepted bribes in return for awarding contracts to construction firms at inflated prices. Investigations incriminated members of Petrobras, managers of large Brazilian construction companies, such as the Odebrecht Group, politicians from Brazil's largest parties, presidents of the Chamber of Deputies and the Federal Senate, state governors, and finally President Lula da Silva. The Federal Police considered it the largest corruption investigation in the country's history.

276 In March 2015, Brazil's Supreme Court disclosed an initial list of 54 top politicians approved for formal investigations in connection with Petrobras corruption.

politicians, and high-level government officials (Millikan and Poirier 2015; Watts 2019). CEOs of the who's who in the powerful construction business faced charges from federal prosecutors for "corruption, money laundering and participation in a criminal organization."[277]

In 2013, it was revealed that the four largest donors to election campaigns in Brazil in the first decade of the 21st century were construction companies building dams and power plants in Amazonia.[278] In Dilma Rousseff's 2010 election campaign, three of the four largest donors were also construction companies.[279] The leading political parties obtained financial support from construction enterprises "whether this is obtained as legal political donations, as illegal donations to secret slush funds ('caixa dois'), or as bribes to key politicians" (Fearnside 2017a, 17). The ruling Workers Party (PT)[280] and its former coalition partner, the Brazilian Democratic Movement Party (PMDB), were allegedly paid US$ 20 million each by the three construction companies.

Over 150 chief executives and leading politicians have been convicted in relation to the investigation since 2014, dozens were jailed, among them former Brazilian President Lula da Silva, the former president of congress, and former top ministers in Brazil's Workers' Party. Lula da Silva has always proclaimed his innocence and argued the case against him was politically motivated. He served 18 months of a 12-year term "for corruption and money-laundering" before being released from prison in November 2019. Due to his imprisonment, Lula da Silva could not run as a presidential candidate in 2018. The Supreme Court justice ordered that the charges against the ex-president were dropped, because of irregularities in the conduct of the proceedings by Judge Moro had put a strain on the process.

This scandal made it clear why Belo Monte was built despite all ecological, hydrological, social, financial, and economic counterarguments. The "lava jato" scandal exposed a culture of systemic graft, mutual dependencies and corruption in Brazilian politics and business life. All this led to serious damage to the reputation of the political and economic system of the country and to Brazil's international standing.

---

277 Fearnside (2017a, 17) according to *Folha de São Paulo*, February 6, 2016.

278 During the 2003–2010 presidency of Lula da Silva, executive posts in Petrobras were offered to his political allies. The criminal conspiracy ran after 2003, during a period when Dilma Rousseff, successor of Lula da Silva as President of the Republic in 2011, chaired the company's board of directors as Minister of Mines and Energy and later as chief of staff of the Lula da Silva administration. Though Dilma Rousseff was not directly implicated in the scandal, "lava jato" played a role in her impeachment in 2016.

279 *Folha de São Paulo*, 21 January 2013; Agência Brasil, 30 November 2010. The construction giant Odebrecht Group, in 2010 with 181 000 employees in 21 countries, was involved in the construction of many hydroelectric power plants and dams. The company was one of the biggest donors to politicians in Brazil and offered bribes in exchange for contracts in Brazil and in at least eleven other countries, mostly in Latin America. The Odebrecht Group made a leniency deal with US and Swiss authorities, in which it confessed to corruption and paid US$ 2.6 billion in fines for its criminal activities – the largest sum of its kind ever paid worldwide. About US$ 800 million returned to Brazilian state coffers (Summary of newspapers reports).

280 In March 2016, the former PT leader in the Senate confessed to federal prosecutors in exchange for leniency in the "lava jato" corruption probes that "the Belo Monte bribe served as a decisive contribution to the election campaign of 2010 and 2014" (Fearnside 2017a, 17).

6.2. The hydroelectric power plant Belo Monte and its environmental and social impacts

The Belo Monte hydroelectric dam complex on the Xingu river was completed in November 2019. The total installed capacity of the power plant is 11 233 MW, which makes it the second largest hydroelectric complex in Brazil behind the binational Brazilian-Paraguayan Itaipu dam (14 000 MW) and the fourth largest in the world by installed capacity. This, behind the Three Gorges dam (22 500 MW), the Itaipu dam and the Xiluodu dam (13 860 MW) in China.

The Belo Monte hydroelectric project comprises three components: the main dam (36 m high, 6.25 km long) on the Xingu river at Pimental site with a supplemental powerhouse (233 MW) and spillway, creating the Xingu river reservoir; the main powerhouse at Belo Monte (11 000 MW; Belo Monte dam 90 m, 3,5 km) and the Belo Monte reservoir (main reservoir: 478 km²) with the water retained by over a dozen large dikes. The Pimental dam diverts the Xingu river's natural flow into a constructed channel, then into a reservoir and towards the main electricity-producing Belo Monte powerhouse. The total project area is about 1500 km², direct forest clearing was 400 km². The new design diverted the water away from Indigenous territories (Fig. 36).

Figure 36. Belo Monte hydro-electric power plant and reservoirs in the Xingu region

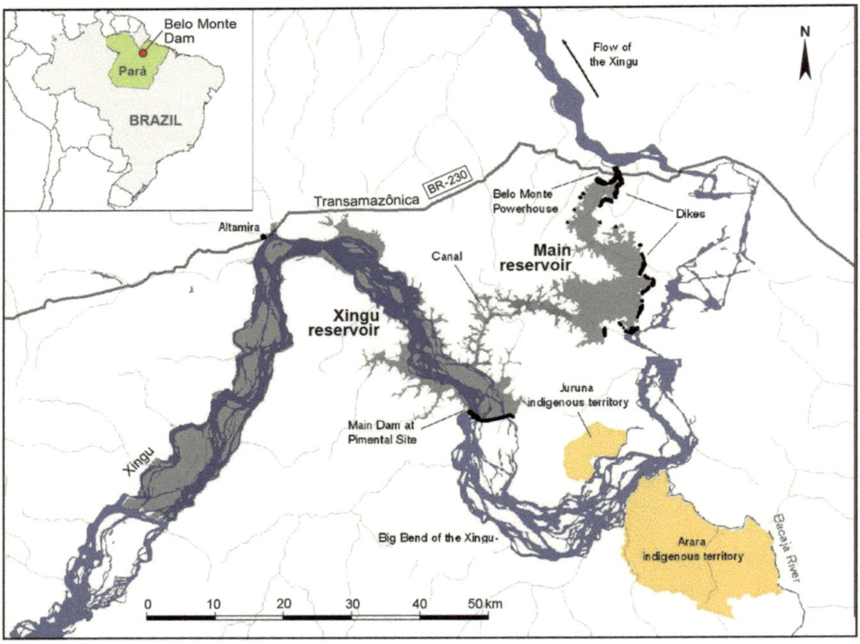

Source: Own elaboration, based on International Rivers and Instituto SocioAmbiental (ISA).

Belo Monte is not a hydro-electric power plant with a storage dam like Tucuruí and others, but a run-of-river plant depending on the river's flow. Belo Monte was planned to operate at an average level of "firm energy" generating 4571 MW throughout the year

(Higgins 2020). Experts had already pointed out early that – according to precipitation conditions in Central Brazil – the extreme differences in the water flow of the Xingu would greatly affect the operational capacity. The former Minister of the Environment of the state of São Paulo argued that Belo Monte would be one of the least efficient hydro-power projects of Brazil, producing only 10 % of its 11 233 MW potential capacity between July and October (1123 MW; an average of only 4419 MW throughout the year, or a 39 % capacity factor) (Antunes 2010).

In 2019, during the dry season in Central Brazil from July to November the flow of the Xingu dropped to an extremely low electrical energy production level of less than 600 MW (Maximum in 2019: 6882 MW in February; Minimum: 276 MW in October) (Higgins 2020). Norte Energia was forced to shut down the turbines frequently to prevent damage. For three months, the Xingu river has not sufficient water "to turn even one of the 20 turbines in the dam's main 11 000 MW main powerhouse" (Fearnside 2017a, 15,16; 2017b, Fig. 1) leaving only the auxiliary powerhouse at Pimental site (233 MW) in operation.

As was well known, the Xingu river has one of the greatest annual variations in water flow of all Amazon tributaries, with high-water season flows up to 60 times those of the low water season (Fearnside 2006; 2017a, 15).[281] In 2010, the statement of Eletronorte – based on President Lula da Silva's resolution – was not convincing that the construction would be possible even without another additional dam and reservoir for river regulation (Kohlhepp 2010c).

It became clear that the new project, which had only been approved without additional dams and reservoirs at the Xingu river, due to the problem of flooding of Indigenous territories, in fact could not be economically viable. Critics claimed that the project only makes financial sense if the Brazilian government builds additional dam reservoirs upstream to guarantee a year-round flow of water. At Belo Monte, the "institutional lie" (Fearnside 2017b, 177) concerning plans for upstream dams was deliberately left out of the discussion in Brazil. According to all known hydrological data, the project should not have been approved due to lacking capacity for the planned energy production. The fear of many observers that the political pressure to build more dams upstream on the Xingu to guarantee a sufficient flow of water soon would increase, seems to be confirmed.

In October 2019, Norte Energia declared "water emergency," as the water level in one reservoir had dropped so much that an unreinforced dam's earthen base could be damaged (Watts 2019). However, the fundamental problem was obvious: Norte Energia needs a total of 1000 m^3/s in Xingu river flow to meet its government agreed requirements, supplying sufficient water to the reservoirs and powerhouses, and to the huge bend (Volta Grande) in the Xingu river bypassed by the Belo Monte project. There is a shoreline populated by *ribeirinhos* and Indigenous people who rely on the water for their fishery and livelihood. When the water flow dipped down to 750 m^3/sec., the company reduced the amount flowing through the channel to the main reservoir to 100 m^3/sec.

---

281 The historic average discharge of the Xingu river in the sector of the Belo Monte hydropower complex for the period from 2004 to 2014 was 1408 ± 513 m^3/s during the low-water season and 18 983 ± 9228 m^3/s in the high-water season, according to the National Water and Sanitation Agency (ANA) in 2017.

The remaining outflow to Volta Grande was extremely low and endangered not only the fishing but also the basic supply of the local residents. The "big bend" is a 100-km stretch of the Xingu river from which 80 % of the water flow has been diverted (Fig. 36). Fish that sustained the populations of the Arara and Juruna along this southern loop of the Xingu river and a third group located on the Bacajá tributary largely disappeared. The fish fauna of the Xingu river is extremely rich, with a high degree of endemism. According to experts, the extremely reduced flow through the "big bend" will not be capable of maintaining species diversity. Further problems loom on the horizon. A new mega-project called Volta Grande Project, led by a Canadian gold mining company, will be situated adjacent to the same stretch of the Xingu that is dewatered by the Belo Monte complex.[282]

Even the navigability of this river stretch is endangered. The Xingu and its tributaries have their sources in Mato Grosso and depend on forest cover for dependable water flow. Deforestation in the Xingu basin increased 81% from 2018 to 2019. Dramatic increases in regional deforestation in Mato Grosso and southern Pará by soybean plantations and cattle ranches caused less precipitation and climate change reduces river flow, which will be dwindled by 20–30% in the Xingu basin in the next 30 years.[283] This will getting worse in the future.

In November 2019, Norte Energia formally asked Brazil's National Electric Energy Agency for authorization to build thermoelectric plants alongside the Belo Monte dams, what would probably mean the use of fossil fuels. "The company denied it was trying to make up for the hydro project's electricity shortfalls" (Higgins 2020).

If allowed to build thermoelectric plants, Norte Energia could at least make more use of its two US$ 3.6 billion 800 kV ultra-high-voltage direct current transmission lines, owned by the Chinese State Grid corporation, which transmit electricity from the Xingu substation to Rio de Janeiro and Minas Gerais states and to the Belo Monte–Estreito line. These power lines are underused for five months of the year. The electric energy produced in Belo Monte is used first for the electro-intensive alumina, aluminium, iron, and other smelting industries in Pará and Maranhão, owned by global players such as Alcoa, Alcan, Norsk Hydro and Vale. The export of these products creates little employment in Brazil. A significant proportion of the energy goes to the powerful industrial sector in Southeast Brazil, mainly in São Paulo and Minas Gerais.

Norte Energia violated national and international laws by not sufficiently consulting Indigenous peoples impacted by Belo Monte. Broken promises in dam construction in the Amazon region since Balbina and Tucurui have a long tradition. The Indigenous protests attracted regional attention and international moral support but were ultimately unsuccessful as construction continued ruthlessly. Since the operator of the power plant continued to make untruthful claims, the Arara responded with a call for help to the international press:

---

282 The mining company was accused of acquiring public lands illegally and mining operations would be about 10 km from Indigenous lands. Impacts of impoundment and mining operations could dramatically alter the Xingu's biodiversity and ecosystem services that support Indigenous people and riverine populations. Tons of toxic waste would be stored in a high-risk tailings dam (Tófoli *et al.* 2017).

283 Data cited in Higgins (2020).

> Letter from the Arara People to the world: We, the Arara Indigenous People of the Iriri river, are tired of being deceived by Norte Energia. We want respect! Ever since the Belo Monte dam arrived, our situation has only worsened. Our territory has become the business counter of the world. Our forest is suffering a lot. With each passing day we hear more noise from chainsaws eating our territory. Our river is growing sadder and weaker every day. This is not normal. We are being attacked from all sides. We have never been in such need. We are very concerned about the future of our children and grandchildren. How long will Norte Energia continue to deceive us? Why hasn't the removal of invaders of our Cachoeira Seca Indigenous Land been carried out until today? We ask everyone to help us build a great campaign for the defense of our territory.[284]

The Indigenous communities suffered from the denial of their fundamental human rights, from loss of biodiversity, landscape degradation, air, noise, and water pollution of construction works, excessive migration pressure, violence, and destruction of living conditions (hunting, fishing). Indigenous tribes reported attacks and harassment, and even the death of Indigenous persons as a result from aggressive illegal activities in their territory.

While the Indigenous groups were sometimes very vocal and were also considered in the suggestions for improvement and partial indemnification during the construction phase, the riverine population (*ribeirinhos*) was initially hardly considered in their needs. They lived on the shores and islands in what is now the Belo Monte main reservoir and along the "big bend". About 18 000 to 20 000 people were affected by the Belo Monte procedures. The urban residents of Altamira who were displaced amounted to 25 000 (Fearnside 2017a, 20). The relocation and the compensation of more than 43 000 people proved to be extremely complicated and could not satisfy the needs of the people concerned, especially since the promises about the amount of compensation payments were not kept. Without the support of social movements, an articulation of those affected would not have been possible (Weißermel 2019). Unfortunately, this is in line with the tradition of unsatisfactory resettlement and precarious compensation payments for earlier large-scale power plant projects.[285]

At Belo Monte, the *ribeirinhos* suffered from involuntary displacement, loss of traditional practices and material losses. Logging activities, soil contamination, erosion problems and decreasing water quality additionally threatened their existence. The river diversion negatively affects fishing, the stability of the groundwater horizon, ability to transport on the river and stagnant water is a risk of water-borne diseases. Options for rural resettlement were located far away from the river so that most people preferred urban resettlement.

Incomprehension of the problems of those affected, unwillingness to give solid treatment of the specific rights of the settlers as well as the non-recognition of interdependent urban and rural life forms caused precarity (Weißermel 2020). The expul-

---

284 Letter from the Arara people, dated 17 November 2020, (signed by Timbektodem Arara, President of the Arara People's Association KOWIT, and Mobu Odo Arara, Chief), translated from Portuguese, cited by Fearnside (2021a). This letter is in response to a letter from Norte Energia to the New York Times, dated 10 October 2020, claiming "that Belo Monte has been guided by respect for the local Indigenous populations and by laws, ratified protocols and conventions." The New York Times declined to publish the Arara response.

285 As in the case of Itaipu, cf. Kohlhepp (1987d), Kohlhepp and Karp (1987).

sion of people who have lived for generations in traditional community structures with mutual support and whose skills, such as fishing, does not make them suitable for other contexts led to a heavy social impact. The disruption of an integrated co-existence with the Xingu river and its ecosystems, lacking social and economic exchange and the process of deterritorialisation affected the riverine people psychologically. At the beginning of the compensation negotiations, the *ribeirinhos* were not recognised as a traditional people by Norte Energia. However, the *ribeirinhos* have a constitutionally guaranteed right to their way of life. They have organised a resistance movement, demanded the creation of a "*ribeirinho* territory" and refused to continue as forced "urban poor" in precarious settlement conditions (Brum 2018) without an adequate infrastructure and a profoundly disrupted social structure.

The urban population of Altamira (1970: 4700; 1974: 13 000, estimates; 2022: 126 000) has grown significantly due to numerous migrants in the last decades.[286] 25 000 workers were temporarily occupied in the Belo Monte construction, only 2000 permanent jobs were retained – the majority of trained employees. Thus, after construction, many thousands of workers remained unemployed in Altamira, leading to increased social tensions and a chaotic situation in precarious neighbourhoods with high rates of crime, violence, drug trafficking and prostitution. In 2017, the Atlas of Violence[287] ranked Altamira as Brazil's most violent large city with an annual murder rate of 125 deaths per 100 000 people (Brum 2018).[288]

However, most urban businesspeople who had supplied the construction site with services and goods have benefited greatly and are still in a very good economic position despite a somewhat declining order situation.

The Brazilian Society for the Advancement of Science (SBPC)[289] authored a 400-page report on the dam's social impacts which claims that Norte Energia has de facto ended the *ribeirinhos*' way of life and means of subsistence. The unpublished report stated:

> With the forced displacement of the *ribeirinho* communities, they lost their territory, access to the natural environment and resources that they relied on for their livelihood and income, which means that they were robbed of the conditions that guaranteed their social and cultural reproduction [...] When they were displaced, they began to buy practically all foodstuffs, living in a situation (of) food insecurity (Anderson 2017, n. p.).

286 At the beginning of the 1970s, Altamira played a key role in the construction of the central part of the Transamazônica (Altamira–Rurópolis–Itaituba). Due to numerous workers and migration, the small town was nearly overwhelmed in its urban functions and experienced a short boom in its commercial activities and as a stronghold for government authorities entrusted with the development programme for Amazonia. However, social tensions were rapidly increasing, the population, which had increased two-and-a-half times to 13 000 within three years, declined and trade stagnated. Cf. Kohlhepp (1976a; 1978c), based on field work in 1973 and 1975. Cf. details about Altamira in Vol. 1, part 2 by Jan Kleinpenning and Vol 1, part 3, chapter by Ron Milder.

287 Published in 2017 by the Institute for Applied Economic Research, a public thinktank.

288 The murder rate in Rio de Janeiro in 2017 was 22 per 100 000 people.

289 SBPC is a non-profit organization, focused on promoting scientific and technological advances and has been playing a key role in expanding and enhancing Brazil's science and technology system, in addition to making science public and more popular.

The excessive costs of the construction of Belo Monte are estimated at around US$ 16 billion upwards, and the transmission lines US$ 3.5 billion. 80 % of the financing came from the Brazilian National Bank for Economic and Social Development (BNDES), including substantial amounts of funding from Brazilian pension funds and tax revenues (Bratman 2014).

It is also revealing that some of Brazil's big construction companies, including Odebrecht and Camargo Corrêa, never invested their money in the Norte Energia consortium at Belo Monte and remained protected from the speculative risk the electric company posed. As a result, only public sector entity investments – from Brazilian pension funds and the state-owned Eletrobras energy company – vouched for Norte Energia (Higgins 2020). As for the consequences of the impact of the mega-project on the environment, the Brazilian government countered the criticism by assuring a spending of US$ 800 million by the consortium to protect the environment.

The fundamental problem of lacking environmental justice in Brazil's Amazonian dam building has not changed. Hydroelectric projects in Amazônia Legal have shown a consistent pattern of human rights violations, actions without consideration of social and environmental concerns in general. Political pressure on individual technical staff members in the licensing department of IBAMA to approve high-priority hydroelectric projects had been common. Amazonia and its people are paying the environmental price for the national corruption in licensing procedures and for the economic progress of countries importing products from Amazonia, countries that would themselves no longer accept the impacts of the kind unleashed by these power plants (Fearnside 2019).

6.3. Political decisions of the Rousseff and Temer governments concerning Amazonia during the decade of the construction of Belo Monte

After President Lula da Silva gave the go-ahead for the Belo Monte power plant complex in 2010, this plan was fully adopted under his successor Dilma Rousseff (PT: 2011–2016). other major infrastructure projects under the Growth Acceleration Programme (PAC-II) were continued or started. During the 2010 presidential campaign her advertising feature was "mother of the PAC" (Fearnside 2017a, 18). She favoured dams with big reservoirs and vetoed all funding for "non-hydraulic renewable energy" in Brazil's Pluriannual Plan (2016–2019).[290] As mentioned earlier, renewed appeals to President Dilma Rousseff with several petitions by international environmental organisations with more than one million signatures to stop the licensing process of Belo Monte remained unheard. As could also be observed later, Rousseff had poor communication with the environmental movements and NGOs.

In addition to the construction of Belo Monte, which filled the headlines, other large hydroelectric power plants, which had already been approved at the end of Lula da Silva's term, were built and came into operation during the presidency of Dilma Rousseff. This mainly concerns the large power plants Jirau and Santo Antônio in Rondônia on the Madeira river, a large tributary of the Amazon river. As in Belo Monte,

290 *Notícias Socioambientais*, January 27, 2016 (ISA).

decision-making and environmental licensing measures were taken against the objections of the technical staff of IBAMA. The decision to build the dams was made before the impacts were thoroughly evaluated and the licensing continued under political pressure (Fearnside 2015b; Souza 2023).[291]

The huge projects based on transnational South American infrastructure integration programmes for power generation were not geared towards the socio-economic, ecological and ethical sustainability of the riverside population. The dynamics of the globalisation of space collide with the way of life of these local traditional communities. Due to the impact of the construction and operation of hydroelectric power plants, the traditional riverside communities living on the banks of the Madeira river were exposed to the effects of globalisation with deterritorialisation, fragmentation of their territory and loss of collective identity. Most of these people suffered from inexistent environmental justice, had to leave their territories, migrated to rural or urban marginalised areas and were plagued by poverty (Souza 2023).[292]

Jirau (installed capacity 3750 MW) and downstream Santo Antônio (3580 MW) are among the largest power plants in Brazil. Both dams are run-of-river projects without large reservoirs (110 and 138 km^2). They are part of a planned four power plant Madeira river hydroelectric complex, which will consist of the two dams in Brazil, a third on the border of Brazil and Bolivia, and a fourth power station inside Bolivia, still in planning. The Madeira river carries very high sediment loads which originate primarily in the Beni sub-catchment region in Bolivia, making sediment data monitoring difficult.

Dam builders at Jirau, the French multinational GDF Suez and Brazilian construction company Camargo Corrêa, failed to adequately consult with Indigenous peoples, as required by law. Despite the environmental re-mediation efforts highlighted by the operators, the construction caused destructive impacts on the rich inland fishery – blockage of fish migration, among others – and conflicts with thousands of displaced fishing people. At both power plants, protests occurred against increasing violence of workers during the construction period. The relocation of the dam at Santo Antônio led to the flooding of lands of resettled population due to the increased level of the reservoir. In addition, there were road closures and temporary power plant occupation due to unfulfilled promises to displaced residents of the use of residential buildings in Nova Mutum built during the construction works.[293] On the other hand, there were riots and strikes by workers against working conditions.

The generated electrical energy of the two Rondonian power plants goes mainly to the Araraquara substation in the state of São Paulo by transmission lines about a distance of 2375 km.

291 Cf. chapter II.5.1.

292 The outspoken leader of one of the fishing cooperatives was murdered in 2016. She was known in the region as Nicinha, denouncing human rights violations committed by the consortium responsible for the Jirau power plant. Her complaints generated two civil investigations being conducted by the Federal Prosecutor's and the State Prosecutor's Office. The assassin escaped from prison in Porto Velho.

293 In 2016, the Movement of People Affected by Dams (MAB) organised a film documentary with numerous interviews of affected people: "Jirau e Santo Antônio: relatos de uma guerra amazônica" ("reports of an Amazon war") (https://www.youtube.com/watch?v=ZFQ11fri3vs, accessed November 26, 2022).

In 2013, the Jirau hydroelectric power plant earned the plant registration under the Clean Development Mechanism (CDM) programme of the United Nations. Jirau is the largest renewable energy plant project to date in terms of tons of carbon dioxide equivalent (CO_2-e) potentially mitigated.[294] The CDM is awarded to innovative projects that help to solve environmental problems such as climate change.

An important feature of the Kyoto Protocol is the CDM

> providing a means by which projects in developing countries can be funded through the sale of carbon credits to developed countries (Annex I countries); thus, allowing the developed countries to meet their Kyoto Protocol emission quotas (assigned amounts) more economically, while at the same time helping the developing countries (non-Annex I countries) to achieve 'sustainable development' (Fearnside 2013b, 682 f.).

For example, the CDM allowed carbon credits to be sold to the European Union Emissions Trading Scheme. Projects for hydroelectric power plants are among the most controversial parts of the CDM, especially in tropical areas such as the Brazilian Amazonia.

The assumption that hydroelectricity is clean energy has been contested, especially for Amazonian dams. In general, Fearnside (2013b, 683) clearly pointed to the doubtful use of emission allowances granted and analysed the rationale for the current CDM rules for granting carbon credit to hydroelectric dams. The Kyoto Protocol[295] required that all CDM projects must contribute to sustainable development. This requirement has been effectively neutralised by the decision that each country decides for itself what sustainable development is, and any project submitted to the CDM by the host country's national authority is automatically assumed to represent sustainable development. This means that three basic criteria must be met: social, environmental, and economic. It is quite obvious that in most cases these criteria are not sufficiently fulfilled. The main problems include underestimation of greenhouse gases (GHG) emis-

294 "Brazil's Jirau hydro project world's largest CDM-registered renewable plant" in *Hydro World*, 6 May 2013.

295 The Kyoto Protocol was adopted in 1997 and entered into force in 2005. It is an international treaty which extended the 1992 United Nations Framework Convention on Climate Change in Rio de Janeiro by committing industrialised countries and economies in transition to limit and reduce greenhouse gases (GHG) emissions in accordance with agreed individual targets. The Protocol based on the scientific consensus that global warming is occurring and that human-made CO_2 emissions are driving it. The Kyoto Protocol only referred to developed countries because it recognised that they are largely responsible for the current high levels of GHG emissions in the atmosphere. The Kyoto Protocol sets binding emission reduction targets for 37 industrialised countries and economies in transition and the European Union. Overall, these targets add up to an average 5% emission reduction compared to 1990 levels over the five-year period 2008–2012. In the Doha Amendment 2012, the Kyoto Protocol was adopted for a second commitment period, lasting until 2020. One important element of the Kyoto Protocol was the establishment of flexible market mechanisms, which are based on the trade of emissions permits. Under the Protocol, countries must meet their targets primarily through national measures. However, the Protocol also offers them an additional means to meet their targets by way of three market-based mechanisms: International Emissions Trading, Clean Development Mechanism (CDM) and Joint implementation (JI). The Protocol also established a rigorous monitoring and verification system, as well as a compliance system to ensure transparency and hold participating countries (Parties) to account.Cf. https://unfccc.int/kyoto_protocol (accessed November 29, 2022).

sions by the reservoir and the construction of the power plant itself, emissions from deforestation induced by the dam construction, and many noncarbon environmental and especially social impacts.

6.3.1. New mega-projects in the Carajás region and Chinese investment in Amazônia Legal

Apart from the construction of large new hydropower plants, attempts were also made in the 2010s to revive Marabá as an industrial location[296] which was severely weakened by the closure of steel plants during the economic crisis in 2008/09. More recently, there have been new project plans.

Brazilian mining giant Vale S.A.[297] and local steel manufacturer Siderúrgica Norte Brasil (Sinobras) signed an agreement to create a new steel unit. The plant will be based in Marabá and focus on the production of steel billets from pig iron. Sinobras was one of the only companies in the industrial district of Marabá that did not stop operations in 2008. Sinobras is the largest operating steel industry in Amazonia and is part of the Belo Monte Hydroelectric Plant consortium. Its current estimated production is 380 000 t of rolled steel per year. It has a staff of 1700 employees. The plant's production is aimed at the domestic market, mainly civil construction.[298]

Vale has started construction of a new US$ 340 million plant to produce "green" pig iron in Marabá. Pig iron is used in steel production. The plant will be built by Vale subsidiary Tecnored, which is focused on developing a low-carbon pig iron process by substituting metallurgical coal with biomass as an energy source. The unit will have an initial capacity to produce 250 000 tpy of "green" pig iron. The start-up is scheduled for 2025.[299]

The big problem remains the supply of biomass, i.e., charcoal. Sinobras has a reforestation project with 16 own *Eucalyptus* plantations in an area of 35 500 ha. However, the company is facing strong criticism and is described as "one of the largest deforesters in the Amazon."[300]

As envisaged since the beginning of iron ore mining at Serra Norte in Carajás, Vale began work on iron ore mining at Serra Sul, some 60 km to the southwest, in the last decade. This project, the largest in Vale's history to date, is the largest such project in the world. The project, called S11D (S: Serra Sul; S11: ore body; block D), has a mining potential of 10 billion t of iron ore, block D on its own contains 2.8 billion t of high

---

296 See chapter I.4.2.5.

297 Formerly Cia. Vale do Rio Doce, privatised in 1997 and renamed in Vale S.A. in 2007. Today, Vale has 55 000 employees and invoices of more than US$ 36 billion/year.

298 https://vale.com, April 15, 2022; https://mining.com, June 4, 2022; https://www.bnamericas.com, June 4, 2022 (accessed August, 28, 2023).

299 https://steelorbis.com, April 13, 2023 (accessed August 28, 2023). State-controlled China Communications Construction Co (CCCC) and Vale have agreed to set up a steel mill with a US$ 450 million investment (https://www.reuters.com/article/markets/currencies/brazils-vale-chinas-cccc-to-co-invest-in-steel-plant-idUSKCN1ST1OR/; accessed September 4, 2024).

300 Steel mills are among the "largest deforesters" because they use wood for charcoal production. For these industries, it is cheaper to buy wood from rain forest areas than to respect environmental protection. The fines were generally not paid (https://www.intercept.com.br/2020/01/31/maiores-desmatadores-amazonia/; accessed 28.08.2023).

quality iron ore reserves to be mined. Production started in 2016, the estimated production capacity is 90 mtpy with a high iron content of 66.7%. An increase to 120 mtpy production at site is planned, so that the Northern System's total mining capacity will be 260 mtpy.

S11D will use truckless mining, trucks are replaced by conveyor belts. Shovels and mobile crushers feed directly onto conveyor belts, which take the ore to processing facilities. This lowers environmental impact. Start of the overall project is expected in the first half of 2024. The project includes the opening of new mining areas and the duplication of the long-distance belt conveyor, among other measures. Vale has been investing heavily in this project (US$ 6,4 billion for the mine and about US$ 8 billion in the railroad and port) to intensify the iron ore extraction and export.[301]

To enable export expansion, Vale had to carry out a doubling of around 570 km of the existing Carajás railway line (EFC: today, more than 980 km) and the expansion of the Ponta da Madeira terminal in São Luís. A 101 km rail spur linking to the S11 mining complex in the municipality of Canaã dos Carajás had to be added. Around 35 trains run simultaneously and the EFC operates trains with a length of 3.5 km with 330 cars transporting more than 40 000 t. On average, 55 iron ore trains, 8 general cargo trains and one passenger train run per day going from the mine to the port and back. The total EFC transport capacity is 230 mtpy of iron ore.[302]

Environmentalists and social movements have complained about human rights violations, land confiscation and lack of compensation. About 5000 ha of land claimed for the Vale project was designated as state public land, occupied by *posseiros* or claimed by landless families to create settlements. Vale ignored the claims of dozens of landless families. Since work began in 2016, there have been several widespread protests and about 600 families from seven camps of landless agricultural workers occupied the access road to the S11D project area. The environmental license was fragmented in many parts so that the cumulative environmental and social impacts of the whole project were not considered. "With the approval of S11D, the other licenses (railroad and port) were only a formal matter, there was no real possibility of rejection."[303]

The duplication of the EFC caused numerous protests by the affected population alongside the railway line in Pará and Maranhão. The permanent traffic of huge iron ore trains with noise and air pollution as well as the vibration caused by the trains led to severe health impairment of the population of settlements, the crossed Indigenous territories and numerous *quilombos*. The communities' main complaints include lack of viable ways to cross the tracks, such as overpasses for goods and cattle and footbridges. According to Vale, significant investments have been made along the entire Carajás railway, totalling 48 new viaducts, 80 level crossings, 15 footbridges, 44 automatic gates, among other protective measures. Obviously, however, according to the

301 https://saladeimprensa.vale.com/press-releases, Augus 13, 2020; Vale (2012). https://www.bloomberglinea.com/english/vale-moves-invests-27-billion-amazon-mining-project-to-expand-iron-output, May 19, 2023 (accessed August 28, 2023).

302 https://im-mining.com/2020/08/14/vale-looks-for-increased-operational-flexibility-with-s11d-iron-ore-expansion-plan/ (accessed August 28, 2023). https://saladeimprensa.vale.com/press-releases, August 13, 2020 (accessed August 28, 2023).

303 https://ejatlas.org/conflict/vales-giant-s11d-iron-ore-project-in-carajas-para-brazil (accessed August 28, 2023).

people many of these investments have often not arrived, probably due to corruption of local institutions.[304]

In 2021, 63 % of Vale's iron ore export was sold to China. About half of the new installations in and around S11D were supplied from China. Brazil's leading export partner is China, whose share has increased extraordinarily in the last two decades (2000: 2 % ; 2021: 32.4 %). China is also the main export destination for Brazilian agricultural commodities, e.g., with 70 % of the Brazilian total soybean exports in 2021.[305]

In 2001, after China joined the World Trade Organisation (WTO), Baosteel, a Chinese state-owned company, made its first major direct investment in the Brazilian Amazon region by investing US$ 650 million in the then recently privatised Vale.

Chinese President Xi Jinping's "Belt and Road" Initiative – a 21st Century "Silk Road" – was launched in 2014 to strengthen China's global strategies to improve the world's transport and other infrastructure and provide China with needed raw materials.

In Brazil, economic actors see the construction of railways as the best solution to the logistical nightmare in the Amazon region. Today, many entrepreneurs in Brazil's interior are pinning their hopes for new infrastructure on Chinese investment and construction. The *Ferrogrão* (grain-railway) in Mato Grosso and Pará has attracted particular interest from China, although its construction is still controversial.[306] China is pushing into commodity trade and transport infrastructure construction and is applying its "Belt and Road" strategy to the Brazilian Amazonia and the *cerrado* in particular. Environmentalists have reacted with great concern to the unrestrained "Belt and Road" activities and their presumed negative impact on Brazil.

During President Temer's visit to China for the 2017 BRICS summit, 22 agreements were signed, including approval for phase 2 of the high-voltage transmission line for the Belo Monte hydropower plant and a financing agreement with China Communication and Construction Company (CCCC) for a US$ 700 million investment in the construction of a private terminal at the port of São Luís (Branford and Torres 2018).

In 2017, a US$ 20 billion investment agreement between China and Brazil allowed Chinese state-owned companies – notably State Grid and China Three Gorges – greater control in strategic sectors such as hydropower in Brazil. State Grid Brazil Holding acquired seven national power transmission companies in Brazil, and China Three Gorges Corporation invested in consortia of hydropower plants in the Amazon basin. China purchased a leading Brazilian engineering company, which now operates as a subsidiary of the state-owned Chinese company CCCC, one of the world's largest builders of railways and industrial waterways. In the last decade, 11 out of the 14 Chinese investments in Brazil's Amazon region were made by state-owned companies.[307]

Chinese interests are mainly focused on the supply chains due to the dependence on Brazilian soybeans. Through state-owned COFCO, China's largest food and agricul-

304 https://observatoriodamineracao.com.br/alongside-the-railroad, August 30, 2023 (accessed August 30, 2023).

305 https://www.datamarnews.com/pt/noticias/china-compra-70-da-soja-e-63-do-minerio-de-ferro-exportado-pelo-brasil/ (accessed August 28, 2023).

306 See chapter II.4.4.; Abdenur *et al.* (2021).

307 https://dialogochino.net/en/trade-investment/53558-china-amazon-footprint-evolve-greener-partnership, May 9, 2022 (accessed August 29, 2023). Garcia *et al.* (2023).

tural company, several trading companies have been bought to reduce dependence on the dominant western tradings ABCD (ADM, Bunge, Cargill and Dreyfus) (Branford and Torres 2018).

Land purchases in Maranhão, Tocantins, Piauí and Bahia (MATOPIBA) have also been made. However, many details in this area remain rather hidden so far.

The Manaus Industrial Park,[308] whose special tax legislation has been repeatedly challenged in Brazil in recent decades, has also increasingly attracted Chinese interest in investing in Latin America since the early 2000s. In contrast to the rest of Brazil, in the Manaus Free Trade Zone the main federal tax incentives include a reduction of up to 88 % of the import tax on inputs, an exemption from the tax on industrial products, a 75 % reduction in the corporate income tax and land for the construction of factories at extremely favourable prices (Garcia *et al.* 2023, 38).

The location of the industrial park in the Manaus Free Trade Zone, with numerous companies building televisions, laptops, smartphones, air conditioners, motorbikes and watches, among others, has long been dominated by companies from the US, Europe, as well as Japan and South Korea (Hiratuka 2022).

As early as the 1990s, China was supplying inputs for the factories in Manaus. In 2004, the situation had changed and China was the main supplier of 28 % of all inputs purchased abroad by the state of Amazonas. In 2015, China's share increased to 47 %. In a second phase, the government and business associations of the state of Amazonas have made efforts to attract Chinese investment to the Manaus Industrial Park, with its specialised workforce, low labour costs and tax incentives. China's average investment share increased between 2008 to 2017 from 2 % to 10 %. China became the most important investor in Manaus, surpassing Germany, Japan, France, Finland and Canada, acquiring companies previously owned by enterprises of these countries.

In 2017, Chinese investors – state-owned, semi-public and private companies – owned 22 factories in Manaus: 13 in the electronics sector (televisions, laptops, smartphones), three in the mechanics sector (air conditioners, watches, household appliances), two in the thermoplastics sector (packaging, car parts, adhesive tape) and four in the two-wheeler sector (motorbikes, bicycles). In 2017, these Chinese companies employed about 10 000 workers (direct employees), or about 10 % of the total labour force in the Manaus Industrial Park.[309]

Initially, there were major difficulties for the unions in getting Chinese companies to comply with Brazilian labour standards. Chinese companies preferred to pay a fine rather than complying with a labour court ruling. They generally pay less than the other global players in the manufacturing sector in Manaus, refusing all the additional benefits that used to be granted, such as the provision of childcare places for employees who needed them for their children. "Chinese companies tend to adjust to the Brazilian legislation, but they do not offer any more than what the law stipulates" (Garcia *et al.* 2023, 54).

The working atmosphere is reported to be bad, local managers have no say, everything is decided in China. When factories were taken over by Chinese companies, almost all the workers were dismissed at first, but recruited again a little later, but at a much lower salary. All high-level positions are filled by Chinese, worker training is

---

308 See chapter I.1.2.4

309 Data and detailed information according to Garcia *et al.* (2023).

almost non-existent (Garcia *et al.* 2023, 54). In Brazil, it is reported that 42% of the employees of Chinese companies quit their jobs within their first year of employment.

The Shenzhen-based Chinese company BYD with manufacturing operations in Brazil since 2015, opened its third factory in Brazil in Manaus, producing lithium iron phosphate batteries for the electric buses assembled in Campinas: "BYD is quite representative of a new phase of the Chinese economy, which has been increasingly concerned with environmental sustainability and moving toward more knowledge-based and technology-intensive sectors" (Hiratuka 2022, n. p.).

This trend would be a good sign in times of planned future closer cooperation between the two states in a new world order as envisaged by BRICS, which would then, however, also have to affect the respective investment and manufacturing activities.

6.3.2. Forest Code – National Plan on Climate Change – Low-Carbon Agriculture Plan – REDD+ strategy

Shortly after President Rousseff came into office, the struggle over the Forest Code brought a first difficult political situation. "The Brazilian Forest Code (BFC) is one of the only laws in the world with restrictions on how much forest landholders must maintain or restore on their private properties" (Nepstad and Shimada 2018, 17). The part of the property that must be maintained under forest is the so-called "legal reserve," ranging from 80% in the Amazon rain forest biome, 35% for *cerradão* in Amazônia Legal, and 20% for *campos cerrados* outside Amazonia. The Forest Code also requires – in addition to the legal reserve – conservation of permanently protected areas (hilltops, mountain slopes, mangroves, and riparian forests) to preserve biodiversity, maintain water quality, and stabilise soils.

In 1996, the Cardoso Government had raised through a Provisional Measure (*Medida Provisoria*) the percentage of the remaining forest area from 50% to 80% due to a massive surge in deforestation in 1995. Farmers can buy land in Amazonia but can only farm 20% of it. This was followed by five years of fierce disputes with the *ruralistas*[310] until it became federal law in 2001. However, in 2000 the state of Mato Grosso decided that the transition forest (*cerradão*) – about half of the forest area in Mato Grosso – is not counted as an Amazonian forest biome. Farmers in the forest transition area of this state only had to leave 50% forest, i.e., they could clear half of their forest area. The federal government overturned this decision in 2005. Under the Bolsonaro government, another attempt was launched in 2022 to circumvent the Forest Code for Amazônia Legal.[311]

In 2011, the powerful agribusiness lobby launched a campaign to fundamentally change the BFC. Although the restrictions on forest clearing contained in the BFC remained largely intact, amnesty was given to farmers who had cleared forest illegally prior to 2008. The Forest Code reduced the legal reserve requirement in Legal Amazonia from 80 to 50%, provided that at least 65% of a state's territory is allocated as either conservation units or as Indigenous reservations. The Brazilian Academy of Science, the Catholic Church, and environmental organisations (WWF, Greenpeace)

---

310 The União Democrática Ruralista (UDR) is the association of large landholders and farmers who are opposed to land reform.

311 Cf. chapter III.2.

urged Rousseff to completely veto the bill. In view of Brazil as host of the Rio+20 Earth Summit, the approval of the bill would have set a poor example of sustainability ahead of a conference for setting new aims for the global environment.

In May 2012, President Rousseff partially vetoed the bill that would have weakened the country's efforts to protect the Amazonian rain forests. However, she received much criticism by environmentalists when the congress approved the changes to the Forest Code and the protection for forests along the rivers. Under the Rousseff administration, there was "a marked shift away from environmental protection in an effort to further spur development and economic growth" (Hurwitz 2012, 17). When the Brazilian Supreme Court decided in March 2018 that the revision of the Forest Code was constitutional, a 22-year period of uncertainty ended (Nepstad and Shimada 2018, 17).

It has been nearly impossible to implement and monitor the Forest Code. Clear ownership titles existed for only 10 percent of private land in Amazônia Legal. Therefore, in 2010 the federal government promoted the environmental regularisation of private rural areas and made it mandatory for all rural properties to be mapped and registered through a system known as Rural Environmental Registry (Cadastro Ambiental Rural, CAR). This is a key component of Brazil's strategy to keep deforestation under control.

Although it is a federal law, the Forest Code is implemented at state level. This means that its success depends on government action to regulate and operate its complex rules and instruments, such as environmental compliance procedures, setting up information systems, acquiring technical resources such as satellites and cartographic databases as well as training human resources.[312]

Because of the failure of state agencies to implement the measures designed to support farmers to comply with the higher legal reserve requirement, farmers were frustrated being "vilified as forest clearing criminals" when the role of the state failed (Nepstad and Shimada 2018, 17). Farmers complained that first the government wanted them to deforest in order to promote agricultural productivity, and then told these same farmers to reforest. A large majority of landowners were not actively restoring patches of their land after too many changes of the law over the years. As those that deforested before 2008 were forgiven of environmental crimes, the farmers that invested in restoration felt cheated by the government for following the law, as they could not convert restored forests to other land uses.[313] Finally, it must be noted that it is difficult to put the law into practice, as about 70 % of the deforestation in Amazônia Legal is done illegally.

Towards the end of the government of Lula da Silva, Brazil had started actions in collaborating with the global effort to combat climate change. As part of the emerging countries, Brazil was in favour of common actions but still without commitment to international law. In 2009, the National Plan on Climate Change (PNMC) was launched through federal law. The 2020 deforestation reduction target was formalised, and the

312 https://www.nature.org/en-us/about-us/where-we-work/latin-america/brazil/stories-in-brazil/brazils-forest-code/ (accessed September 4, 2024). The Nature Conservancy, a global environmental non-profit organisation, was working with the states of Pará and Mato Grosso to support implementation of the CAR, as this is the first step toward successfully complying with the Forest Code requirements.

313 https://www.weforest.org/blog/wildlife-corridors/brazilian-forest-code/ (accessed November 30, 2022).

legal and programmatic framework established for achieving it. Under this law, Brazil should take action to reduce between 36 and 39% of its projected emissions by 2020 (equivalent to a 17% reduction compared to 2005 levels). This objective included 80% reduction in deforestation in the Amazon region (target: 3900 km^2/year, in relation to the average value of the years 1996–2005: 19400 km^2/year) and 40% reduction in deforestation in the *cerrado* biome.[314]

One of the most ambitious features of this new legislation was the Low-Carbon Agriculture Plan (ABC Plan), designed in 2010 to provide resources and incentives for farmers to adopt sustainable agricultural techniques. The objective is to reduce emissions of carbon dioxide (CO_2), methane (CH_4), and nitrous oxide (N_2O) from agriculture, while generating income for vulnerable rural communities. The Plan includes a credit initiative, which provides low-interest loans for sustainable agricultural practices such as no-till agriculture; restoration of degraded pasture; crop-livestock-forestry integration and agroforestry systems; planting of commercial forests; biological nitrogen fixation; and treatment of animal wastes. Efforts are supported to reduce the role livestock farming expansion and other factors play as drivers of deforestation. The target was reducing annual GHG emissions by 133 to 166 million tons of CO_2eq relative to projected future levels by the year 2020.[315]

Since the Lula da Silva government – as alleged by Brazilian environmental organisations – had delayed the national laws on climate change, the implementation of these new comprehensive projects was reserved for the Rousseff government and represented a great burden due to the complexity of the execution necessities.

At the UN climate conference (COP 21) in Paris in 2015, President Rousseff stressed that climate change resulting from human action is one of the biggest global challenges of current times. Brazil submitted its new climate action plan to the UN Framework Convention on Climate Change in advance of the new universal climate change agreement reached in Paris in December 2015.[316]

Brazil reduced its forest cover clearance in the Amazon region by impressive 84% between 2004 and 2012. Amazon deforestation achieved a record low of 4571 km^2 in the year 2011/12 (August 2011–July 2012). A more effective law enforcement through command-and-control measures led to a dramatic drop in deforestation, especially in the "deforestation arc" around southern and south-eastern Amazônia Legal. Illegal logging had fallen, but critics claimed that Brazil had weakened protection measures by revising the Forest Code. However, since 2013 official deforestation rates have been on an upward trend.

By 2013, registered CAR properties covered roughly 32% (23 million ha) of the areas eligible for registration in Mato Grosso and 57% (34 million ha) in Pará. Regis-

314 Deforestation data: INPE/PRODES.

315 http://redd.mma.gov.br/en/component/content/article/160-central-content/top-news/616-measuring-reporting-and-verifying-mrv-redd-results?Itemid=0 (accessed December 2, 2022) and https://climatepolicydatebase.org/policies/ (accessed December 2, 2022).

316 https://unfccc.int/process-and-meetings/the-paris-agreement; https://www.gov.br/mre/pt-br/centrais-de-conteudo/publicacoes/discursos-artigos-e-entrevistas/presidente-da-republica/presidente-da-republica-federativa-do-brasil-discursos/discurso-da-presidenta-da-republica-dilma-rousseff-durante-sessao-de-abertura-da-21-conferencia-das-partes-da-convencao-quadro-das-nacoes-unidas-sobre-a-mudanca-do-clima-cop21-paris-30-de-novembro-de-2015 (accessed December 2, 2022).

tered properties in both states suggested that a good part of the producers have joined. This was positive news, but in times of a declining economic export boom it became increasingly clear that the manifold tasks in the environmental sector of Amazonia could not be solved promptly by the far too small number of employees in government authorities on the federal and state side. Due to the social and economic problems in other regions of Brazil, especially in the Northeast, the possibilities to expand the staff for official affairs in Amazônia Legal remained limited.

By the start of Rousseff's second term in 2015, little of the new Amazon objectives had been achieved. The Forest Law, passed in 2012, had granted amnesty to landowners who deforested illegally before 2008. Meanwhile, a measure requiring farmers to register rural properties and restore or provide compensation for illegally deforested areas has been delayed twice.[317] In view of the impunity for illegal logging before 2008, many farmers waited to comply with the requirements of the Forest Code.

In December 2015, Brazil submitted its REDD+ strategy[318] (Reducing Emissions from Deforestation and Forest Degradation) to the UN Framework Convention on Climate Change. The *plus* is referring to the role of conservation, sustainable management of forests and enhancement of forest carbon stocks. Its overall objective is to contribute to global climate change mitigation by eliminating illegal deforestation, promoting conservation and restoration of forest ecosystems, and fostering a low-carbon and sustainable forest economy, delivering environmental, social, and economic benefits. As the first country worldwide, Brazil achieved full compliance with the UN Framework Convention on Climate Change requirements to receive results-based payments within the REDD+ 2013 Warsaw (COP 19) framework (KfW 2017).

The REDD+ function is to provide financial incentives to developing countries for their results achieved in combating deforestation and forest degradation and in enhancing forest cover. Through this instrument, countries that produce verified results of forest-related greenhouse gas emission reductions and enhancement of forest carbon stocks become eligible to receive results-based payments from various international sources, in particular the Green Climate Fund (GCF). In order to achieve the overall objective, integration of the governance structures of climate change, forest and biodiversity related policies is indispensable, seeking to promote consistency and synergies among them at the federal, state, and municipal levels (Gebara 2017).[319]

In 2017, the ENREDD+ strategy was completed with an Amazon Forest Reference Level approved by the UN Framework Convention on Climate Change, a national registry of emissions reductions, and an agreement for the distribution of emissions reductions among the national governments and state governments of Amazônia Legal.

ENREDD+ will be guided by the National Policy for Climate Change and the Forest Code. It identifies three sectoral plans for implementing ENREDD+: the Action Plans to prevent and control deforestation and fire in the Brazilian Amazon (PPCDAm) and in the *cerrado* (PPCerrado) and the Plan for Low-Carbon Agriculture (ABC) (Gallo *et al.* 2020).

---

317 https://www.foreststreesagroforestry.org/tag/enredd/ (accessed December 2, 2022).

318 Brazilian national version: ENREDD+ strategy.

319 http://redd.mma.gov.br/en/component/content/article/160-central-content/top-news/644-newsletters?Itemid=0; https://unfccc.int/news/forest-protection-in-brazil-boosted-through-redd-plus (accessed December 3, 2022).

In practice, REDD+ projects subsidise the conservation of forest areas. In addition to preserving the carbon stored in these areas, they lead to the conservation of biodiversity and bring social benefits to the region. Although the ENREDD+ programme was at an early stage, a promising agreement between the German government and the government of Acre, in alignment with national Brazilian policies, may be discussed briefly.[320] Acre's particular distinction as an "early mover" lies in its long-term experience of integrating intersectoral policies and programmes within a pro-forest land-use planning approach. Recognizing Acre's environmental achievements in reducing deforestation, Germany provided funding for emission reductions. As a key component of this partnership, the two governments agreed to pilot a results-based REDD+ system in the context of the Official Development Assistance.

Already in 2010, Acre's state government established the System of Incentives to Environmental Services (SISA) with the objective to conserve and recover a broad array of environmental services as a policy framework for sustainable development. In 2012, Germany committed € 16 million in results-based finance to be implemented through the German REDD Early Movers (REM) programme from 2012–2016 and strengthened the programme with an additional € 9 million. The REM programme rewards pioneers of forest protection and climate change mitigation. In 2015, Acre was the first jurisdiction that developed and applied a REDD+ Social and Environmental Standards (REDD+ SES) initiative, following a multi-stakeholder process. Sub-programmes like sustainable smallholder agriculture, Indigenous communities, extractive reserves, and sustainable and diversified animal farming are financed and promising results could be expected. The challenge for Acre will be further continuation of the downward trend in deforestation and providing positive incentives for this process. As the remaining deforestation is more dispersed among very many mid- and small-scale farms, which are more difficult to monitor and to reach, this initiative becomes increasingly difficult, independent of political uncertainties (KfW 2017).

In Brazil, REDD+ promoted changes in the political articulation, funding possibilities and mobilisation of civil society, and brought more visibility to the importance of combating deforestation and forest degradation. However, "lack of political commitment, inefficient forest resource governance, insufficient enforcement of the environmental legislation, social inequalities and land use conflicts remain" (Gallo *et al.* 2020, 5). The early criticism about the limitations of environmental policies considering the potential of REDD+ to contribute to sustainable local development is still justified, as the environmental and social initiatives frequently disregard the capacities of smallholders (Pokorny *et al.* 2013). The legal regulatory policy still is based on the conflict of interests between a national legislation that fosters trade and commercialisation of agricultural commodities, but also promotes exploitation of natural resources, and ignores sustainable use and conservation principles. The growing national and international demand for forest and agricultural commodities, and subsidies that encourage the production of such commodities drive deforestation and the evolving issues of the different actors, especially the private sector (Gebara 2017).

There is a need to align institutional discourse with actions executed and a strong political will for generating sound regulatory frameworks. Brazil was a pioneer in its initial efforts to reduce deforestation. However, the scenario has drastically changed,

320 Based on a report of KfW (2017).

and all efforts made so far will not be sustained without political reforms and the implementation of a sustainable forest management.

At the beginning of her second term in 2015, President Rousseff's decision to appoint an outspoken sceptic of climate change, Aldo Rebelo, as Minister of Science and Technology caused controversial reactions, after a decade in which Brazil had reduced Amazon deforestation and claimed a leadership role in international climate policy. However, this was not the only appointment to cause surprise and dismay in the PT and environmentalist circles. Rousseff named Kátia Abreu, often referred to as "chainsaw queen" in the popular press, as Minister of Agriculture, an assertive agribusiness lobbyist and opponent of environmental circles or Indigenous peoples' land rights in the Brazilian Senate. These appointments indicated political constraints and coalition necessities and no particular interest in attracting support from the environmental movement by pro-Amazon initiatives while pushing for major dams that will only increase pressure on forests. The Rousseff administration spent 72 % less money on anti-deforestation measures than her predecessor Lula da Silva.[321]

The country's disappointing economic performance as well as the poor delivery of public services became obvious, especially in light of the billions spent by the government on infrastructure in major sporting events, agreed during the presidency of Lula da Silva: the World Football Championship in 2014 and the Olympic Games in Rio de Janeiro in 2016. This led to sustained protests by large sections of the population. Rousseff's approval rating was at just 10.8 %. Of course, the financing of social and environmental programmes in Amazonia suffered and the political interest in this region faded into the background.

President Dilma Rousseff was impeached in August 2016 and the Senate removed her from office after six years in power. She was charged with criminal administrative misconduct and disregard for the federal budget in violation of article 85 of the Constitution of Brazil and the Fiscal Responsibility Law. The petition also accused Rousseff of criminal responsibility for failing to act on the scandal at the Brazilian national petroleum company. However, she was not denied political rights.

Rousseff's supporters called the impeachment a *coup*, though it had been approved by the Supreme Court, as well as by large majorities in both houses. Secretly recorded phone conversations confirmed that Rousseff had been ousted because she would not call off the "car wash" investigation (Watts 2017). Vice-President "Temer played a central role in the impeachment of Dilma Rousseff, who was impeached for illegally using money from state banks to bankroll public spending" (Kaiser 2019, n. p.). In 2018, the PT officially launched Rousseff's candidacy for a seat in the Federal Senate from the state of Minas Gerais, but she was defeated for her Senate run.

6.3.3. Amazônia Legal under the Temer government: Change of political party without change of strategies for Amazonia

Michel Temer (Brazilian Democratic Movement Party, PMDB) served as Rousseff's Vice President for six years. He became president in 2016, taking office after the impeachment of Rousseff, even though he was mentioned multiple times in the "car

321 InfoAmazonia, March 31, 2015. https://desmatamento.infoamazonia.org/analise/ (accessed December 3, 2022).

wash" investigation.[322] Temer has moved rapidly to unravel environmental protections to please the powerful agricultural and mining lobbies (Watts 2019). He ensured his survival by proposing to ease restrictions on everything from mining to ranching in protected forests. Dams like Belo Monte were confirmed by the Temer presidential administration in 2016, which, like the PT predecessors, was committed to the regional development in Amazônia Legal by means of large hydroelectric power plants with reservoirs.

Temer has stepped back from Brazil's commitment to protect the Amazon region and his government appeared to be unwilling to take the necessary measures to combat deforestation which increased rapidly. This neglect had negative consequences as the government of Norway, main sponsor of the Amazon Fund, announced a cutback in funding due to the rise in forest destruction. Norway had invested more than US$ 1.1 billion since 2008 to help Brazil protect the forests. The Temer government prepared a new law that opened up the Jamanxim national forest in the state of Pará to the private sector, even though Temer vetoed earlier legislation that would have reduced national forests by 600 000 ha (Poirier and Millikan 2017).

In August 2017, Temer issued a rain forest decree to dissolve the Reserva Nacional do Cobre e Associados, an Amazonian reserve in the states of Pará and Amapá, measuring four million ha to allow mining by private companies and the conversion of forest into crops for agribusiness companies. The decree was revoked after widespread criticism because this would open the door for mining companies to enter the reserve which was set up in 1984 (Watts 2019).

National and multinational firms had expressed an interest in the region, which most probably contains deposits of gold, copper, tantalum, iron ore, nickel, and manganese. Commercial exploitation by big companies in the past has been followed by illegal land grabbers, *garimpeiros*, and road construction workers. Temer's decision threatened to reduce protected areas, to weaken environmental licensing, and diminish Indigenous rights in the interests of the small group of economically powerful companies which were keeping Temer in power.

President Temer signed a legal opinion that directs his government's administration to paralyse all Indigenous land demarcations in the country.

> The move continues a string of devastating assaults on human rights and environmental protections that blatantly cater to Brazil's regressive "ruralista" agribusiness lobby, which Temer is courting in the run-up to a congressional vote [...] that could remove him from office to face charges of rampant corruption (Poirier and Millikan 2017).

This measure was an illegal attempt to strip Indigenous peoples of their rights since Brazil's 1988 Constitution to permanent and exclusive use of their territories, claiming these rights cannot overrule "national interests" such as military operations, road construction, communications infrastructure, and hydroelectric dams. Temer wanted to keep his job at any cost, which required the votes of the *ruralista* bloc.

Temer had appointed senator Blairo Maggi, Brazil's new "soybean king," as Minister of Agriculture. Maggi, a prominent member of the *ruralistas*, supported arguments for a "land reform" in their sense so that protected forests for both the environment

322 Cf. chapter II.6.1.

and Indigenous communities could be cleared for farming, cattle ranching, and mining to create jobs and spur growth.

As investigations referring to the operation "car wash" intensified and after some failed attempts to start impeachment processes against Temer, in June 2016 the president received an eight-year ban from running for office in the presidential campaign for the 2019–2022 period, after being convicted of violating election laws.

In May 2017, secretly taped recordings leaked by *O Globo*, a leading national newspaper, revealed the president discussing to keep up hush money payoffs to a politician convicted of taking bribes with Joesley Batista, the boss of the country's biggest meat-packing firm JBS, the world's leading beef exporter. The Batista family is one of the most influential lobbyists of an expansion of cattle grazing in Amazonia. The firm was investigated over accusations of paying kickbacks to a former speaker of the lower house of Congress who is serving a 15-year sentence for his role in the Petrobras scandal.[323] Thousands of angry demonstrators marched towards the Congress demanding Temer's resignation and immediate direct presidential elections. As president, he was shielded by the immunity of office.

In 2017, Brazil's federal police said that investigators had found evidence President Temer received bribes to help businesses. Prosecutors alleged that Temer was the leader of a "criminal organisation" that took in US$ 472 million in bribes or pending future kickbacks as part of numerous schemes, including the Angra nuclear power plant complex and other state firms. The president's party PMDB long controlled key appointments in Brazil's largely state-run energy sector, including nuclear power plants. Temer was hit with separate corruption charges during his presidency that were blocked by his allies in the Congress, which must authorise charges against an acting president. Additionally, Temer was formally accused of conspiracy against corruption inquiry. He had been a part of schemes diverting public funds since the 1980s said the federal prosecutor.[324] "Temer was more worried about his own job, than the Amazon and the people who live there" (Poirier and Millikan 2017, n. p.).

He completed Rousseff's term until the end of 2018 and, like Lula da Silva, was banned from participating as candidate in the presidential election in October 2018. In March 2019, Temer was arrested during the investigation into operation "car wash." Temer was the second former president – after Lula da Silva[325] – to be arrested in the anti-corruption investigations. In March 2019, a *habeas corpus* was issued on behalf of Temer, who had left office with an approval rating of 7 %.

323 *The Economist*, May 20, 2017, https://www.economist.com/the-americas/2017/05/20/leaked-recordings-are-trouble-for-michel-temer (accessed December 13, 2022).

324 CNBC, Reuters, June 27, 2017, https://www.cnbc.com/2017/06/26/brazil-president-michel-temer-charged-with-corruption.html?&qsearchterm=Temer (accessed 13.12.2022).

325 Lula da Silva was imprisoned in April 2018 after a sentence over 12 years for corruption handed down by the controversial judge Moro. In November 2019, Lula da Silva was released from prison after 19 months. The Supreme Federal Court annulled all convictions against Lula da Silva on March 2021, ruling that the court in Curitiba, which convicted him, lacked jurisdiction to do so. Thus, he was able to run for the presidential elections in October 2022 and he won the election for the 2023–2026 term.

7. Population in Amazônia Legal 1970–2022

7.1. Regional population growth of urban and rural population

The population in Amazônia Legal quadrupled since the 1970s. In 1970, this region had a population of 7.13 million, i.e., 7.7 % of Brazil's total population. In 2020, Amazonia was already inhabited by 28.1 million people (IBGE, estimate), equivalent to 13.3 % of the Brazilian total (Table 12).[326] This means that one in eight Brazilians lives in Amazonia. About 3.3 % of the Amazonian population is Indigenous.

The regional population has developed very differently over time and in terms of its regional impact. In the 1970s and 1980s, there was a very strong immigration to the states of Rondônia, Mato Grosso and along the Transamazônica in Pará. In Rondônia, this was linked to the Polonoroeste programme, which brought with it high migration flows of peasant settlers, especially from southern Brazil, within the framework of state controlled agrarian colonisation.[327] This also applied to the settlement along the central part of the newly opened Transamazônica. In Mato Grosso, increased immigration took place until the early 1990s on the basis of private-sector development by medium-sized and large holdings, especially of south Brazilians farmers.

Today, the most populous states of Amazonia are Pará (30.8 % of the population of Amazônia Legal), Maranhão (21.0 %), Amazonas (15.0 %) and Mato Grosso (12.5 %). The population density of 5.6 inhabitants per km² for the entire region is still low due to the enormous area of the states (Table 13). In Maranhão, due to traditional dense rural settlement in the eastern part of the state density is higher with 22.6 inhabitants per km². Of course, the overall population density says relatively little, especially since the concentration of the population takes place in the few urban centres of Amazonia.

Data on the share of the urban population is only available up to 2010 (IBGE 2011a; 2012).[328] With almost 80 %, the urban population has a very high share – Amazonia was called an "urbanised forest" (Becker 1995).[329] The share of the urban population

326 According to the 2022 Census (IBGE 2023), the population of Amazônia Legal is 27.8 million.

327 Cf. chapter I.2 and Tables 6 and 7.

328 Originally, the census, being carried out decennially, was supposed to take place in mid-2020. However, due to the COVID-19 pandemic, the Brazilian Institute of Geography and Statistics (IBGE) changed the date to 2021. In early 2021, the budget of the Census was cut to only 12 % of the original value, so that the Census was moved again. Brazil's Supreme Court decided that the government had to perform the Census in 2022.

329 cf. chapter II.3.3.

will continue to increase to the present day. Maranhão is an exception with an urban population of only 63.1 %.

Table 12. Population in Amazônia Legal, 1970–2020

Federal states	1970	1980	1991	2000	2010	2020
Acre (AC)	215 299	301 276	417 718	557 526	733 559	894 470
Amapá (AP)	114 230	175 258	289 397	477 032	669 526	861 773
Amazonas (AM)	955 203	1 430 528	2 103 243	2 812 557	3 483 985	4 207 714
Maranhão (MA)	2 401 586	3 254 305	4 088 272	4 730 016	5 475 829	5 914 375
Mato Grosso (MT)	598 849	1 138 918	2 027 231	2 504 353	3 035 122	3 526 220
Pará (PA)	2 166 998	3 403 498	4 950 060	6 192 307	7 581 051	8 690 745
Rondônia (RO)	111 064	491 025	1 132 692	1 379 787	1 562 409	1 796 460
Roraima (RR)	40 885	79 121	217 583	324 397	450 479	631 181
Tocantins (TO)	521 139	739 049	919 863	1 157 098	1 383 445	1 590 248
Amazônia Legal (AL)	**7 125 253**	**11 012 978**	**16 146 059**	**20 135 073**	**24 375 405**	**28 113 186**
Brazil	**93 134 846**	**119011052**	**146825475**	**169799170**	**190755799**	**211755692**

Source: IBGE, Censos Demográficos 1970–2010 (2020: IBGE estimations).

Table 13. Amazônia Legal in 2020: Area and population data

Federal states	Area (in 1000 km²)	Population in 2020 (in 1000 inhabitants)	Population density (people/km²)	Urban population in 2010 (in %)
Acre	164.1	894.5	5.5	72.6
Amapá	142.5	861.8	6.1	89.8
Amazonas	1559.2	4207.7	2.7	79.1
Maranhão	261.9	5,914.4	22.6	63.1
Mato Grosso	903.2	3526.2	3.9	81.8
Pará	1245.8	8690.7	7.0	68.5
Rondônia	237.8	1796.5	7.6	73.6
Roraima	224.3	631.2	2.8	76.6
Tocantins	277.7	1590.2	5.7	78.8
Amazônia Legal	**5016.5**	**28 113.2**	**5.6**	**79.5**
Brazil	**8510.3**	**211 755.7**	**24.9**	**86.8**

Source: IBGE: Censo Demográfico 2010; 2020: IBGE: estimations. Accessed in IMAZON (2021, Table 2), and own calculations.

In recent decades, the large urban centres,[330] i.e., above all the capitals[331] of the Amazonian states, have experienced strong immigration. The traditional centres of Manaus (2019: metropolitan area: 2.68 million) and Belém (m. a.: 2.51) stand out as dominating cities. São Luís (m. a.: 1.63) has experienced a strong population influx, mainly due to the Grande Carajás Programme as terminus of the iron ore railway, as major export port and as an industrial location, especially of an important alumina refinery and an aluminium smelter. Cuiabá has also exceeded the one million mark with its metropolitan area.[332]

In most states of Amazonia, the capitals exert a particular pull effect due to the potential labour market. In all major cities of Amazonia, a strong social fragmentation has developed, with "gated communities" for the local elites and no-go areas in marginal neighbourhoods with omnipresent social segregation. Even in the sparsely populated states such as Roraima, Amapá and Acre, the growth of the urban population of the main cities Boa Vista, Macapá and Rio Branco continues unabated, especially since there is a lack of other larger urban centres as an alternative. Along the main federal roads, in Pará (BR-010, BR-230), Mato Grosso (BR-163, BR-364), Rondônia (BR-364) and Maranhão (BR-010, BR-230, BR-226) there is a network of functionally relatively well equipped middle-sized and small towns.[333] In Tocantins (BR-010), the capital Palmas, which was only founded in 1990 in the *cerrado* region, has developed rapidly (1990: 24 200 inhabitants; 2021: 313 300) (Table 14).

*Table 14. Population increase in the capitals** of the states of Amazônia Legal, 1970–2021*

State capital	1970/80 in %	1980/91 in %	1991/2000 in %	2000/10 in %	2010/21 in %	Population2021* in 1000 inhab.
Rio Branco (AC)	41.2	64.1	28.5	32.9	24.8	419.5
Macapá (AP)	60.2	27.5	57.5	40.8	31,1	522.4
Manaus (AM)	104.5	57.3	38.9	28.4	25.2	2255.9
São Luís (MA)	70.1	51.0	24.9	16.9	10.0	1115.9
Cuiabá (MT)	112.2	82.8	20.3	14.1	13.2	623.6
Belém (PA)	47.8	31.1	2.8	8.9	8.1	1506.4
Porto Velho (RO)	55.6	107.2	16.8	28.1	28.0	548.9
Boa Vista (RR)	87.9	105.2	40.2	42.1	53.6	436.6
Palmas (TO)	-	637.9	464.9	66.6	37.2	313.3
*) Estimation IBGE, 2022						
**) Municipalities						

Source: IBGE: Censos Demográficos 1970–2010 (2021: IBGE estimation). Own calculation of population increase, based on data IBGE.

330 Cf. chapters I.4.2 and I.4.4.; II.3.3. and II.4.1., 4.2.

331 Data based on municipalities in Table 14.

332 Metropolitan region Vale do Rio Cuiabá with Cuiabá and Várzea Grande. Metropolitan areas: IBGE estimate in 2019.

333 Cf. chapters II.3.3 and II.4.2 referring to Mato Grosso and Pará and Fig. 26.

In addition to the four cities with over a million inhabitants (Cuiabá: m.a. 1.04 million), there are another 17 cities in Amazônia Legal with over 100 000 inhabitants (IBGE 2023).

Since immigration to the main cities and the larger urban centres exceeds the capacity of the urban labour market, large marginal neighbourhoods have emerged in the cities with an urban population characterised by high levels of vulnerability. Problems, such as land speculation, invasions and illegally developing quarters with violent social conflicts characterise the urban climate.

The strong population growth in Amazônia Legal means that unchecked urban expansion is exerting increasing pressure on the environment in the surrounding area to supply the cities with goods of daily needs and their functional equipment. Not only the nearby urban surroundings are needed, but the differentiated infrastructural equipment in the transport, industry, trade, and energy sector requires additional use of space. In view of the climatic conditions, the construction of paved roads is the basis for undisturbed transport connections; on the other hand, the region is naturally open to uncontrolled immigration.

Urban development exacerbates the latent conflicts of interest between economic growth with success at all costs and sustainable development with protection of the environment and the region's natural resources. Today, the functional elites of Amazonian cities compare their facilities with the modern functional facilities of cities in other parts of the country, given the information possibilities in social media, and strictly reject disadvantages due to their regional location.

Governors of the states of Amazônia Legal and mayors of emerging municipalities are committed to economic progress. Local NGOs, with the support of national and foreign environmental organisations, are highly critical or even hostile to many development projects in Amazonia that are carried out without feedback with the majority of the affected local or regional population, without regard to neighbouring Indigenous groups or ecological conditions. These groups exercise the activity to be carried out by state authorities of – at least indirect – control of private economic activities.

However, it is becoming increasingly clear that the urban and rural winners of economic development in Amazônia Legal reject restrictions for environmental reasons and also the zero-deforestation strategy or are very critical of it. Environmental protection in Amazonia was at least officially announced by the governments of the 1990s and 2000s, although not always adequately implemented. The Bolsonaro government supported the demands of Amazonia's economic elites in every way, scaled back state control measures to a large extent and thus significantly expanded the room for manoeuvre of the leading economic actors.

The rural population is concentrated mainly in the regions of state-controlled agricultural colonisation in Rondônia, along the Transamazônica in Pará and in some areas with land allocations from INCRA, often without adequate transport connections. Parts of the rural population living along small riverbanks, the riverine population, have often been forgotten in support measures. In the agribusiness areas of Mato Grosso, a permanent migration of farmers to the nearby, often functionally well-equipped towns can be observed. Due to the high mechanisation of field work, relatively few farm workers are employed, and the mobility of landowners allows commuting from the family's urban residence to the fields, especially during sowing and harvest times.

Although one cannot yet speak of an emptying of the rural area, even in the agricultural colonisation areas with relatively large plots, there is a migration of peasants to small central settlements. This was already observed in the 1970s with the *agrovilas* near Altamira. The agricultural activity is carried out during the week on the countryside but the local settlers spend the weekend in small central places where families with schoolchildren live.

In cattle farms, the absentee-ownership is very common. The young generation of ranch landowners frequently has a non-agricultural urban occupation, often outside Amazonia in the family's regions of origin, e.g., as a lawyer, doctor, broker or trader in agricultural machinery, vehicles or agricultural goods. The cattle grazing areas are very sparsely populated, as very little labour is needed on the ranches.[334] The mobile, non-Indigenous and non-agricultural rural population is composed of *garimpeiros*, loggers and transport workers, among others.

7.2. Indigenous population in territories or urban areas and today's situation of Indigenous peoples

The Indigenous peoples of Brazil belong to four large ethnic trunks: Aruak, Karib, Macro-Jê and Tupi. In Brazil, the Indigenous population was first recorded in the 1991 census.[335] In the 2010 census, new questions were asked for the first time, e.g., on self-declared Indigenous peoples, including ethnicity, and on languages spoken.[336] The general data of the 2010 Census recorded 817 963 people (0.44 % of the Brazilian population) who declared themselves Indigenous in Brazil,[337] distributed among 305 ethnic groups. An inventory of the Socio-environmental Institute (ISA) indicates that 252 Indigenous peoples live in Brazil, 48 of them have their habitat across borders with members of the tribe living in neighbouring countries.[338] 274 languages were spoken, with 37.4 % of Indigenous people over the age of five speaking an Indigenous language

334 On average, only one worker is required as direct working force for a pasture of about 230 ha; cf. chapter I.1.2.1.

335 According to Santos *et al.* (2019,n. p.) "the 1991 Census was the first to include the category Indigenous as a response option to the question 'What is your colour or race?'. Prior to that, the national Census, conducted since 1872, instructed enumerators to include the Indigenous population in a category of colour that represented some degree of 'miscegenation,' such as 'pardo' (brown), 'caboclo' or 'mestiça'."

336 Since the beginning of the 2000s, possibilities for improving Census information systems had been discussed at various conferences on population studies and specific seminars on Indigenous demography. In 2008, the IBGE created a working group to discuss the methodology of the 2010 Census regarding Indigenous peoples (Azevedo 2011).

337 According to IBGE (2011b): In all, 896 900 Indigenous people were registered. However, 78 900 people who lived in Indigenous lands declared themselves of another colour or race (mainly "brown", 67.5 %), but considered themselves "Indigenous" according to aspects such as traditions. In 2010, 63.8 % were living in rural areas, most of them in Indigenous territories.

338 Inventory of the Socioenvironmental Institute (ISA) in 2011; cf. Ricardo and Ricardo (2011).

at home while 76.9 % speak Portuguese.[339] 502 783 (61.5 %) lived in rural areas, presumably in Indigenous territories, 315 180 (38.5 %) lived in urban areas.

In 2010, the Indigenous population in Amazônia Legal[340] was 383 683 people (IBGE 2011b). On August 8, 2023, the first data of the Census 2022 for the Indigenous population of Brazil were published (IBGE 2023).[341] In 2022, 1 693 535 Indigenous people lived in Brazil, representing 0.83 % of the total population. 36.7 % of the Indigenous population are living in Indigenous lands. The new figure of the Indigenous population in Brazil, increased by 89 % since the 2010 Census (896 900), is mainly a consequence of methodological changes effected to improve the survey of this population. According to the Minister of Indigenous Peoples Sonia Guajajara, "more Indigenous people felt comfortable identifying themselves us thus" (Cabral and Gomes 2023, n. p.).[342]

In 2022, 867 900 Indigenous people lived in Amazônia Legal, i.e., 51.3 % of the total Indigenous population of Brazil. In Amazônia Legal, the proportion of Indigenous persons living in Indigenous territories is 46.5 %, exceeding the national average (36.7 %). With 490 900 people (= 56.6 % of Amazônia Legal), the state of Amazonas has the biggest Indigenous population, 97 300 (= 11.2 %) are living in Roraima. In Roraima, 15.3 % of the residents of this state are Indigenous people. Manaus is the municipality with the highest number of Indigenous people (71 700), followed by São Gabriel da Cachoeira (AM, 48 300). In some municipalities of the state of Amazonas, the percentage of Indigenous population in the total population is higher than 90 % (Uiramutã: 96.6 %; Santa Isabel do Rio Negro: 96.2 %; São Gabriel da Cachoeira: 93,2 %) (IBGE 2023).

According to data from ISA, the main Indigenous tribes in Amazônia Legal in terms of the number of inhabitants are:[343]

Ticuna: from the Ticuna linguistic family; they are considered the largest Indigenous group living in the region with about 46 000 people, especially on the banks of the Solimões river.
Macuxi: from the Karib linguistic family; the Macuxis are largely found in the state of Roraima. About 30 000 Indigenous people live in isolated villages and small dwellings.
Yanomami: from the Yanomami linguistic family; this group comprises about 27 000 people in the states of Amazonas and Roraima. The Yanomami land is the biggest Indigenous area with 9.5 million ha.

339 The Census revealed that 17.5 % of the Indigenous people do not speak Portuguese (IWGIA 2022).

340 Cf. chapters I.3.2; I.4.5.2; II.2.4.4 in this volume.

341 In the Census 2022, the self-declaration method was used to determine Indigenous identity.

342 The 2022 Census was carried out with an extremely large amount of personnel and labour, with the participation of Indigenous persons, using their specific local knowledge. All possible means of transport were used to get to all the hard-to-reach areas with Indigenous population. In 2022, the question "do you see yourself as an Indigenous person?" was additionally asked in the Census even out of officially delimited Indigenous territories. 15.3 % of the population in Indigenous lands who answered that question affirmatively did it because of this item (Boadle 2023).

343 https://pib.socioambiental.org/en/Table_of_Indigenous_Peoples (accessed December 30, 2022); Ricardo and Ricardo (2011); IBGE (2011b). Data according to the Census of 2010 and IBGE (2023). Outside the Amazon region live the Guarani (85 000 people; Tupi-Guarani linguistic family) and the Caingangue (45 000 people; Macro-Jê). Updated data of the Indigenous tribes will be provided by the 2022 Census, the detailed evaluation of which is to take place before the end of 2023.

Guajajara: from the trunk of the Tupi-Guarani family; the 27 000 existing Guajajaras live in the state of Maranhão.
Terena: from the Aruak linguistic family; there are about 26 000 people of this ethnic group in Brazilian territory. They live in the states of Mato Grosso and outside the Amazon region in Mato Grosso do Sul and São Paulo.
Xavante: from the Macro-Jê linguistic family; the Xavante have a population of 18 000, who are concentrated in Indigenous reservations in the state of Mato Grosso.

With a population increase of about 1.1 %/year[344] the total number of Indigenous people in Amazônia Legal today is 868 000, which is 3.3 % of the total population of this area.[345] Indigenous neighbourhoods are common in large cities such as Manaus. Data from the 2010 Census show that a large number (43.1 %) of the Indigenous population living in urban areas consider themselves descendants of Indigenous peoples, without referring to specific Indigenous groups (Santos *et al.* 2019).

To this day, there are still a number of isolated Indigenous groups that have no contact with the neo-Brazilian population in the region. These are Indigenous groups that have avoided, or even violently rejected, contact with the outside world.[346] 115 records of Indigenous peoples living in isolation are mentioned, 28 of which were confirmed, another 87 remain under investigation. The reference "confirmed" by FUNAI refers to the records whose information was confirmed through overflights, which identified the territories occupied by these peoples. The FUNAI listing is the main source of information for recording the presence of isolated Indigenous peoples. However, ISA has also carried out permanent monitoring of the records of isolated Indigenous peoples for decades (Ricardo and Ricardo 2011).

For a long time, there has been an intensive scientific discussion about the number of inhabitants of Amazonia in pre-Columbian times. The Amazon has been occupied by Indigenous people for over 12 000 years. The Spanish conquistador Francisco de Orellana, who – starting in Ecuador – sailed the Amazon river to the mouth in the Atlantic Ocean on his expedition in 1542, reported large settlements with numerous inhabitants, female warriors ("Amazons") and large richly painted ceramic vessels. Since later expeditions of the Portuguese colonial power made no similar observations, Orellana's descriptions were not believed.

While initial anthropological and archaeological research came to a relatively low number of inhabitants of about 2 million (Meggers and Evans 1957; Meggers 1971), modern research methods estimate pre-Columbian populations of Amazonia to have been 5 to 6 or even up to 10 million.[347] In view of the generally low soil fertility of Amazonian

344 Fertility rates of Indigenous women were substantially higher than the rate observed for the Brazilian population in general (2010–2022: 0.5 %/a). However, there are significantly higher infant mortality rates for the Indigenous population (27.3 per thousand according to the 2010 Census) when compared to the figures for the Brazilian population overall (15.9 per thousand, in 2010) (Santos *et al.* 2019).

345 First results of the Demographic Census of 2022 (IBGE, 2023).

346 FUNAI used to conduct "first contact" expeditions to find these tribes. Nowadays, the strategy is to localise these uncontacted tribes with infrequent flyovers, checking to see if they have moved locations or if non-Indigenous people like loggers or *garimpeiros* are threatening these groups or are illegally invading their lands (Azevedo 2011).

347 Denevan (1966; 2014), among others.

terra firme soils, such a large population can only be explained by the sophisticated use of anthropogenic dark earth (ADE, *terra preta*)[348] soils for an agriculture highly adapted to the Amazonian climatic conditions without over-exploitation of natural resources. It is estimated that between 0.1–10 % of the Amazon Basin can be attributed to the *terra preta* areas (Butler 2005).

Thanks to the findings through numerous cross-disciplinary studies with the aid of satellite imagery and Lidar laser scanner technology over the last two decades,[349] it became clear that the early Indigenous history of the region was characterised by complex societies and cultural as well as agro-biological diversity. The new technological skills made it possible to "eliminate" forest vegetation and to see through the canopy revealing ancient civilisations up to now hidden beneath the trees. Over 6500 archaeological sites have been identified in Brazilian Amazonia with earth work constructions, geoglyphs, ditches, ceramic artifacts, vessels, and urns with zoomorphic and anthropomorphic ornaments.[350] Platform burial mounds, geometric designs and channels are found and mapped in settings that mostly lack stone structures which are today covered by dense forest vegetation in many areas of Amazonia, e.g., in Acre, the Tapajós river, the Xingu Basin and Amapá (Lombardo *et al.* 2018; Pivetta 2018; Neves *et al.* 2021).

Settlements were constructed of wood, clay, bone, and other materials that deteriorate rapidly in the humid tropical climate of the rain forest (Butler 2005). There were either small semi-permanent settlements or clusters of large permanent villages of over 50 ha, such as in the upper Rio Xingu region. At the end of the 19th century, some Kayapó villages had up to several thousand inhabitants (Posey 1985a; 2000). The pre-Columbian Indigenous societies developed technologies such as the production and use of *terra preta*, raised fields, and agroforestry, which optimised development and the expansion of food production systems. Practises of plant cultivation transformed the Amazon region as one of the independent centres of plant domestication (Neves *et al.* 2021, 31).

The collapse of these Indigenous societies immediately after the arrival of the Europeans is almost inconceivable in this catastrophic form. The Amerindian population in the Amazon region decreased by 90 to 95 % within the first one hundred years of European contact. This enormous population decrease resulted in the abandonment of cultivated areas and the overgrowth of those areas by natural vegetation (Denevan 2014). The main reason for this situation was disease, especially smallpox as the first

348 Anthropogenic Dark Earths (ADEs) are black to brown, organic-rich fertile soils with higher pH and nutrient content (P, N, Ca, Mg) that are maintained even under the intense lixiviation of the Amazonian conditions. ADEs are found in many archaeological sites in the Amazon region, dating from ca. 2500 years BP onwards (Neves *et al.* 2021, 17). This mineral-rich soil was purposely created by the pre-Columbian people through processes involving decomposition of domestic refuse products and charcoal as an essential ingredient of terra preta. Today, local inhabitants – e.g., on the Belterra plateau between the Tapajós and the Curuá-Una rivers – recognise the value of *terra preta*. The earth is excavated and sold as potting soil known for its extraordinary productivity. People use it in gardening for years with only minimal additional fertilisation.

349 Lehmann *et al.* (2003); Hecht (2003); Woods *et al.* (2009); Golińska (2014); Lombardo *et al.* (2018); Pivetta (2018), Neves *et al.* (2021), among many other publications.

350 The Marajoara culture with sophisticated large pottery, elaborately painted, flourished on Marajó island at the mouth of the Amazon river. It was the first evidence that a complex society existed with large settlements and major earthworks as mound building. It can only be briefly pointed out here to other cultures in Amazonia, e.g., the Palikur culture in Amapá and the Tefé culture in the middle Amazon river (Solimões).

introduced epidemic and subsequent outbreaks of infectious and devastating diseases such as typhoid, flu, measles, and sexually transmitted diseases against which the Indigenous population had no defensive power at all. In addition, there was the hunt and the enslavement which contributed to further eradication of Indigenous people.

The surviving parts of the Indigenous population were expelled from their fertile and sustainably farmed habitats near the rivers and fled to the remote middle and upper reaches of the tributaries of the Amazon river. As a result of this forced flight, the larger tribes were split into smaller groups who now had to look for new areas for their essential shifting cultivation system. The smaller groups were much more vulnerable to attacks by neo-Brazilian invasions which increasingly restricted the necessary habitat. Prejudice, contempt, neglect, and disadvantage by Brazilian governments at the federal and state levels have also contributed to marginalisation. As mentioned before,[351] the Indigenous population dropped from about one million in 1900 to less than 200 000 in 1957 and 87 tribes disappeared (Ribeiro 1957). To date, the Indigenous population has recovered somewhat from this low point.

There is a predominance of groups containing a few hundred individuals, given that 22.7 % were composed of less than 100 people; 29.2 % between 100 and 499; 27.9 % between 500 and 1999; and only 20.1 % over 2000. While almost all people in Indigenous lands referred to a specific Indigenous ethnic group, outside the Indigenous territories the proportion was 61.4 % (Santos *et al.* 2019). The largest ethnic group is the Ticuna (46 100 people) accounting for 5.3 % of the Indigenous population in Amazônia Legal (IBGE 2011b; 2023). Only six territories have more than 10 000 Indigenous people, 107 have between more than 1000 and 10 000. The Indigenous territory with the largest Indigenous population is the Yanomami area, in Amazonas and Roraima, with 27 000 Indigenous people in an area of 9.5 million ha (Cabral and Gomes 2023).

In 2010, 61.1 % of the population in Indigenous territories spoke Portuguese, 28.8 % did not and 10.1 % made no declaration. 57.3 % spoke an Indigenous language, 32.7 % did not. Outside the Indigenous territories only 3.5 % did not speak Portuguese and 12.7 % used an Indigenous language.[352]

In the Federal Constitution of 1988, a new perspective to the native population had been laid down by law: the issue of original rights to land, a right due to all native peoples.[353] The process of demarcating Indigenous territories was finally established in 1996. Demarcating an Indigenous territory is to guarantee the Indigenous right to the land. It must establish the real extent of Indigenous possession, ensuring the protection of the demarcated limits and preventing occupation by third parties. The largest Indigenous territories which play a very important role in protecting the tropical rain forests are located in Amazonia. 30 % of the transition forests (*cerradão*) and 21 % of the rain forest areas are within their borders (Capobianco 2001). The establishment of these areas for Indigenous protection to consider the demands of the Indigenous population on their ancestral habitat, at least approximately, is one of the most complicated and domestically extremely explosive tasks to this day (Kasburg and Gramkow 1999; Gramkow 2002).

---

351 Cf. chapter I.3.2.

352 IBGE (2011b): people over the age of 5 years. Detailed data of the 2022 Census are not yet available on these points.

353 Cf. chapter I.6.1.

The complicated and long-term process of registration of Indigenous territories takes place in five different phases:[354]

1. Identification and delimitation: During this process, an ethno-historical, sociological, legal, cartographic, environmental study is carried out, as well as a land survey coordinated by an anthropologist of recognised qualification. When finalised and approved by FUNAI, the report – which includes the land to be demarcated – is published in official media, such as the *Diário Oficial.*
   Up to 90 days after the publication of the report, any interested party may present their reasons, accompanied by relevant evidence, to FUNAI, in order to claim compensation or demonstrate existing defects in the report. FUNAI must evaluate all the arguments and submit the procedure to the Minister of Justice within 60 days.
2. Declaration of the boundaries: The Minister will declare the limits of the area and determine physical demarcation or disapprove the identification.
3. Demarcation: When the boundaries have been declared, FUNAI promotes their physical demarcation.[355] Since the PPG7 Programme, demarcation often has been carried out with the active participation of the Indigenous people involved. This has strengthened their control over their territories and capacity building of Indigenous organisations (Kohlhepp 2001b, 374). INCRA has to proceed with the resettlement of eventual non-Indigenous occupants.
4. Approval: The demarcation procedure must be submitted to the president of the Republic for homologation.
5. Registration: The demarcated and homologated territory will be registered in the regional real estate office and in the Union Heritage Secretariate (SPU).

Table 15. Recognition stage of Indigenous territories (ITs) in Amazônia Legal

Status	No. of ITs	Area (in 1000 ha)
Identification still waiting	49 (11.6 %)	1083.7 (0.9 %)
Identified	11 (2.6 %)	1662.5 (1.4 %)
Declared	32 (7.5 %)	6982.5 (6.1 %)
Registered/ Approved	332 (78.3 %)	105 615.7 (91.6 %)
Total	**424 (100.0 %)**	**115 344.4(100.0%)**

Source: https://pib.socioambiental.org/pt/TIs_no_Brasil_hoje (accessed December 28, 2022).

Of the 726 Indigenous territories in Brazil (117.4 million ha = 13.8 % of the area of Brazil) 424 with an area of 115.3 million ha are localised in Amazônia Legal,[356] representing 22.3 % of the area of the Amazonian region and 98.3 % of the extension of all Indigenous territories in Brazil.

354 http://www.funai.gov.br/; IWGIA (2020); https://pib.socioambiental.org/pt (accessed December 29, 2022).

355 Physical demarcation by FUNAI is done by clearing a strip through the forest, placing markers along the entire perimeter and signs warning non-Indigenous people not to enter (cf. Rabben 2010).

356 Cf. Figs. 8, 9 and especially Fig. 23 in this volume.

78 % of the Indigenous territories (ITs) are officially approved and registered, with more than 91 % of the IT area (Table 15). However, unfortunately this does not mean that all the problems of the Indigenous population are fixed, as could be analysed in the previous chapters in this volume.[357] Invasions by mining companies, *garimpeiros*, land grabbers, large hydroelectric projects, loggers, timber companies, cattle-ranchers, road construction and other infrastructural promotion projects frequently had a fatal impact on the security and existence of Indigenous territories.

To quote but one example, in 2009, the case of the Indigenous territory Raposa Serra do Sol in Roraima,[358] an area of 17 400 km² where 26 000 Indigenous people of 17 tribes live in 164 villages (*aldeias*), aroused in particular the national and international public. Even after the approval of the Indigenous territory there were raids and burning down of Indigenous settlements. They were fought by rice farmers whose *fazendas* were established in the immediate vicinity and sometimes even in the middle of the reservation area. The resettlement of the more than 500 non-Indigenous inhabitants of Raposa Serra do Sol should have been completed by mid-2006.

Table 16. Indigenous territories by state in Amazônia Legal (on 22.10.2014)

State	Indigenous land (in 1000 ha)	% of state area
Acre	2459.8	14.9
Amapá	1191.3	8.1
Amazonas	45 232.2	28.5
Maranhão*)	2285.3	8.6
Mato Grosso	15 022.8	16.6
Pará	28 687.4	22.9
Rondônia	5022.8	21.1
Roraima	10 370.7	46.2
Tocantins	2597.6	9.3
Total	**112 869.9**	**22.3**
*) area calculated by SIG/ISA		

Source: https://pib.socioambiental.org/pt/TIs_no_Brasil_hoje (accessed December 28, 2022).

In Brazil, there is an ongoing discussion about the size of the Indigenous territories in Amazônia Legal. Landowners with farms of any size complain that large areas of land

357 Cf. chapters I.3.2; I.4.5.2; II.2.4.4.

358 *Brasil indígena* (FUNAI) 3, no. 1: n. p. March/April 2006. The final judgment of the rumoured case by the supreme court in March 2009 was the most emblematic case referring to the collective Indigenous territorial rights inscribed in the Federal Constitution of 1988. It "mobilized the Indigenous and indigenist movements and relied on the federal executive power in favour of Indigenous rights directly including President Lula da Silva. It was almost a year of tension until the final decision of the supreme court reaffirmed the demarcation of the land in continuous area and determined the removal of non-Indian occupants" (Ricardo and Ricardo 2011, n. p.).

are reserved for relatively few Indigenous people who – in the opinion of the neo-Brazilian population – also do not cultivate the land intensively. This is an often-heard accusation that makes it clear that this part of the non-Indigenous population does not understand or neither accepts shifting cultivation and space-consuming hunting and collectors' needs of the Indigenous people nor traditional sustainable land use with forest protection. Indigenous tribes play a crucial role in conserving biodiversity and their territories are the most important barriers to Amazon deforestation.

Taking the federal states of Amazonia as an example of decision-making in regional planning and development, there exist many levels of conflicts regarding land issues. The main conflict between federal versus state governments concerns public land (*terra devoluta*). Amazonian states claim these lands to be transferred to the regional government. The share of land by Indigenous territories in the state area is more than 20 % in some states of Amazonia (Amazonas, Pará, Rondônia). In Roraima however, a federal territory until 1988, the present-day state government only has a jurisdiction over 48 % of its own state's area, Indigenous lands under FUNAI tutelage representing 46 % (Table 16; cf. Kohlhepp 2001b, 392, Fig. 7). The registration of Indigenous territories by the federal government is therefore often seen by the state governments as a negative influence on the economic development opportunities of the respective Amazonian state. In the case of Roraima, the governor did not accept the federal decision and constantly protested against this situation.[359] Exaggerated proposals by foreign NGOs to establish an Indigenous nation in this northernmost region of Brazil were rather counterproductive to solve the problem.

The Brazilian governments in office since 1985 have approved Indigenous territories in very different ways and intensities:

*Table 17. Approved Indigenous Territories**)

President	No.	Extension (in km²)
Jair Bolsonaro (2019–2022)	0	0
Michel Temer (5/2016–9/2018)	1	192.2
Dilma Rousseff (2011–4/2016)	20	32 661.8
Luís I. Lula da Silva (2003–2010)	65	186 791.7
Fernando H. Cardoso (1995–2002)	99	403 519.9
Itamar Franco (10/1992–1994)	10	54 997.8
Fernando Collor (3/1990–9/1992)	74	257 950.0
José Sarney (4/1985–3/1990)	21	94 528.1
*) The numbers and extension areas cannot be summed up, as many Indigenous territories approved during a government were redefined and approved again.		

Source: https://pib.socioambiental.org/pt/Situação_jurídica_das_TIs_no_Brasil_hoje (accessed December 28, 2022).

359 Cf. the case of Raposa Serra do Sol. At the same time, the expulsion of the gold prospectors after serious conflicts with the Indigenous population in the Yanomami territory was interpreted as an economic weakening of the gold trade and thus the economic power in the capital Boa Vista where some of the officials were significantly involved in the profits.

The governments of the Presidents Collor, Cardoso and Lula da Silva approved a major number of Indigenous territories. During the two terms of office of President Cardoso, nearly 100 Indigenous lands with more than 400 000 km² were designated as Indigenous territories in Amazônia Legal. After 2010, the number of approvals decreased very quickly, under the government of President Bolsonaro no area was approved.

Even with legal recognition, the de facto safeguarding of Indigenous territories and their resources due to regional conflicts of interest and invasions by neo-Brazilian actors is often jeopardised by the lack of state presence on the ground and the administrative weakness of FUNAI. Symbolic barriers cannot protect Indigenous territories from invasions and violent conflicts which occurred in many subregions of Amazônia Legal.[360] The example of the Xingu Indigenous park[361] shows that even the best protected Indigenous territories are suffering more and more from the pressure of the advancing pioneer fronts.

Figure 37. Deforestation in the Xingu River Basin 1994–2010 and the Xingu Indigenous Park

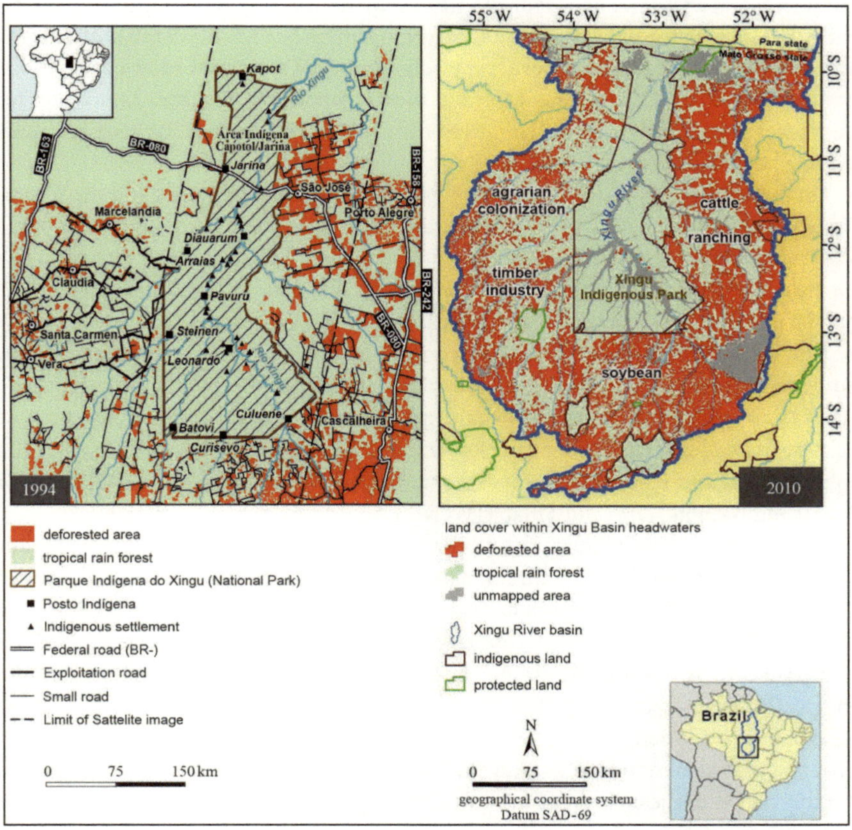

Source: Deforestation in map 1994: cf. Kohlhepp (2001b, Fig. 9); deforestation in map 2010: Durigan *et al.* (2013, Fig. 1).

360 Cf. chapter I.3.2.2.

361 Details of the history and the problems of establishment of the Xingu Indigenous Park see chapter I.3.2.1.

A comparison of deforestation in the Xingu river basin between 1994 and 2010, for example, shows that deforestation has increased dramatically in this relatively short period. From the Cuiabá-Santarém highway (BR-163), agricultural settlement spread from the west along secondary roads in small and medium-sized farms; further south, the timber industry penetrated the adjacent forest areas with expanding clearings. East of the Xingu Indigenous Park, cattle ranches play the most important role in deforestation. From the south, soybean cultivation in large farms, driven by high world market prices, penetrated from the *campos cerrados* into the *cerradão* and the tropical rain forests of the Xingu basin and led to an extensive clearing until the borders of the Park (Fig. 37). Intensive deforestation at the headwaters of the Xingu river and its tributaries are threatening the hydrological conditions and the water quantity and quality downstream. Violent protests of the Indigenous people – about 5000 Indigenous people of 16 ethnicities are living in the Xingu Park – oppose the construction of dams and hydroelectric power stations in the region.

The self-confidence of the Indigenous population (Pasca 2002; Kohlhepp 2007b) that now exists was demonstrated with the occupation of a construction site of a small hydroelectric power plant at the Culuene river, the main headstream of the Xingu river, 120 km upstream of the Park border, by some hundred members of the Indigenous groups of the Xingu Indigenous Park and the neighbouring Xavante. The reason for the protest action was the feared negative impact of the dam on the river's water supply and fish population.

On the other hand, the Indigenous people claimed for public action and the Y Ikatu Xingu campaign was launched in 2004. Objectives of the campaign aimed to reverse deforestation and degradation, to create a new model of development "that respects the environment and socio-cultural diversity of local populations" and as main demand a forest restoration initiative (Durigan *et al.* 2013; ISA 2004; 2012).

Not all the Indigenous territories are as much in the public gaze as the Xingu Indigenous Park. In many of these territories, formally approved and registered, the continuous border violations for illegal exploitation of natural resources and the attacks by force of arms are often little known. This was the case, for example, with the violent spatial and resource use conflicts with external social actors in Mato Grosso (Paresi and Nambikwara) and Amapá (Waiapi).

An example is the Indigenous territory Sararé, approved in 1985 with 1150 Nambikwara living in the tropical rain forests of northwestern Mato Grosso on an area of 67 420 ha in 2001. They lived from hunting, fishing, gathering as well as shifting cultivation and horticulture-like land use. In the 1990s, about 8000 *garimpeiros* invaded the reservation. Their mining operations and the use of mercury in washing out the gold led to pollution and poisoning of the waters. In addition to the environmental damage, the social degradation through prostitution, contagious diseases and lack of future prospects was also catastrophic. The additional intrusion of loggers in the mahogany-rich forests led to the collapse of a traditional resource use (Pasca 2004, Fig. 30; Kohlhepp 2007b, Fig. 5).

The authorities of Mato Grosso only reacted when the World Bank cancelled a loan for the regional development programme Prodeagro after massive protests by national and international NGOs. The hesitation becomes understandable when one considers the involvement of regional political leaders in the timber and gold trading scene. Indigenous groups involved in illegal activities are often played off against each other and corrupted by gifts of profit. The perpetrators have rarely been convicted by the courts.

Given the conflicts over the use of space and resources due to the expansion of modern infrastructure, land grabbing, agribusiness, mining, *garimpeiro* activities, logging, agricultural colonisation, squatters, drug trafficking, biopiracy and environmental degradation, the vulnerability of Indigenous societies in Amazonia remains highly problematic today.

Vulnerability of Indigenous societies (Pasca 2004, 334) is still one of the fundamental problems:

- Socio-cultural vulnerability manifested itself in a cultural shock and alienation, loss of community elements and neglect of traditional knowledge;
- Economic vulnerability is evident in the change in traditional economic methods, the dominance of the market economy over common property and monetisation;
- Physical vulnerability was caused by direct violence, stress by persistent threats, transmitted infectious diseases, lack of nutrition, malnutrition, alcoholism, and suicide.

Generally speaking, Indigenous people are still the losers in regional policy for Amazonia. In recent decades, they have lost the natural base of their habitat due to the extensive destruction of rain forests and are trapped in a network of numerous conflicts of interest. From an ethical point of view, the destruction of Indigenous habitat and its resources for the benefit of ecologically and socially as well as economically questionable development projects in the long term must not be regulated by compensation payments or royalties as well as profit sharing, as has been done (Kohlhepp 2007b).

Due to the extraordinary ethnic diversity, the organisation of Indigenous people's representation and political articulation is very often carried out on a local basis (village, riparians, tribal community), rarer at regional level (e.g., Union of Indigenous Nations of Acre). In 1992, the COIAB, responsible for Amazonia, had developed into the CAPOIB (Conselho de Articulação dos Povos e Organizações Indígenas do Brasil), supported by CIMI (Conselho Indigenista Missionário), an organ of the Brazilian Catholic Bishops' Conference. However, very often there were protests by small Indigenous tribal groups who themselves wanted to solve their problems or even wanted to receive shares in possible royalties. Even within the Indigenous communities, opinions differ greatly about the advantages and disadvantages of contacts and cooperation with neo-Brazilian partners.

The integrative power of tribal affiliation is often no longer present in the traditional way. Conflicts between tribal elders and the younger Indigenous population often concern the nature of contacts and integration into the neo-Brazilian population. The younger tribal members are open to integration into the "modern" society and frequently are strongly interested in economic participation as well as in environmental protection of their local habitat.

It is impressive that in the face of this situation, which still exists among many Indigenous peoples, numerous Indigenous NGOs have been founded since the 1990s. With the background of the Constitution of 1988, bilateral and multilateral development cooperation and international environmental organisations have provided considerable financial resources. The mobilisation of Indigenous organisations and the support of civil society actors as well as their increasing networking with institutions of development cooperation are successes even if there is a risk of new dependencies. Political and territorial strategies have been developed through the increasing pressure of Indigenous NGOs on the government, through participation in the demarcation and guarding of Indigenous territories,[362] through the support of national and international NGOs and through the International Convention for the Protection of Indigenous Societies. Unfortunately, sometimes self-defence was only possible by armed resistance.

In Brazil, the government has transferred more and more tasks to the civil society sector. The Indigenous NGOs have purposefully taken over tasks that the state no longer carried out directly. The outsourcing of projects to secure the economic independence of Indigenous societies to the level of transnational NGOs or multilateral development cooperation is seen with controversy in Brazil (Pasca 2004; Kohlhepp 2007b).

Today, many Indigenous peoples know how to articulate themselves in defence of their rights. Some Indigenous peoples and conservation organisations in Brazilian Amazonia have formed alliances. In the meantime, a number of alliances have emerged, of which only a few examples can be mentioned here.

The Kayapó Indigenous territories of Pará and Mato Grosso and the Xingu Indigenous Park form a kind of barrier against deforestation and prove that the presence and the participation of Indigenous peoples in protection activities have stopped the extermination of tropical rain forest ecosystems.

After decades of violent conflicts with ranchers and *garimpeiros* to protect their territory, "the Kayapó have drawn on their social institutions and collective organisation to forge their own forms of resistance and accommodation to Brazilian society" (Schwartzman and Zimmerman 2005, n. p.) They tried to become familiar with Brazilian administrative and economic institutions and started to organise associations to get support for the needs of the community. Conservation International of Brazil (CI-Brasil) is a non-profit organisation, created in 1990, which contributes to the creation, execution or monitoring and implementation of new policies related to the environment and development. CI-Brasil started its cooperation with a single Kayapó community, A'Ukre, in 1992 and provided technical, administrative, and financial support for the two main Kayapó NGOs.[363] The original objective was giving the Indigenous community an economic alternative to selling mahogany. The Kayapó who had not lost their traditional ecological knowledge (Posey 1982; 1985a; 1985b) and had younger leaders as intercultural mediators, have been politically most successful and were the strongest defenders of Indigenous rights in Brazilian Amazônia Legal. The collective organisation of Kayapó communities remained strong (Schwartzman and Zimmerman 2005).

---

362 The involvement of Indigenous actors in the demarcation and surveillance of the borders of their territories was promoted during the PPG7 programme already in the 1990s. In 2014, the Munduruku did the physical part of demarcation, cutting a border around their territory through the tropical forest. However, they did not get legal rights to the land.

363 Associacão Floresta Protegida (AFP) in Pará and Instituto Raoní (IR) of Mato Grosso (cf. Pasca 2004).

The Instituto SocioAmbiental (ISA) is a non-governmental organisation, working since 1994 with Indigenous, *quilombo*[364] and extractivist communities to develop solutions that protect their territories and the environmental conditions, their culture and traditional knowledge, strengthen their social and political profile, and develop sustainable agriculture. Since 2001, ISA is a civil society organisation of public interest. ISA works with experienced multidisciplinary experts in Indigenous rights and environmental issues, carries out research projects and problem analyses with partner organisations and has also distinguished itself by developing programmatic drafts essential for environmental legislation. They have teams and permanent offices in São Paulo, the Federal District and in four Amazonian states, where they have long-term commitments with partners in the Rio Xingu and Rio Negro regions. Additionally, they instituted a bilingual education programme.

In the 1990s, ISA started a project in the Xingu Indigenous Park and helped the Xingu peoples organise the Xingu Lands Indigenous Association (ATIX), in an effort to achieve greater political and economic autonomy. The ISA–ATIX partnership had developed into an important example of frontier governance (Nepstad *et al.* 2002). Together, they organised territorial monitoring and control, patrolling borders, and maintaining the demarcation of park boundaries which the Xinguanos had defended for many years against neighbouring ranchers (Schwartzman and Zimmerman 2005).

Since the restoration and protection of riparian forest was a very important issue of common interest (ISA 2004; 2012), ISA organised a meeting of ranchers, soybean farmers, peasants, environmentalists, and Indigenous peoples in Canarana, Mato Grosso, in 2004. The positive result was an "unprecedented agreement" of the participants in favour of seeking subsidised official credit for landowners to restore and protect riparian forest in the Xingu headwaters. "The innovative negotiation brokered by ISA and ATIX with regional and national agribusiness promised to achieve a precedent-setting, regional-level resource management process" (Schwartzman and Zimmerman 2005, n. p.).

The Xingu programme acted in partnership with associations and communities of the Xingu Indigenous Park and the Indigenous lands of the Panará in the construction of long-term conservationist and Indigenous alliances and participatory mechanisms of management of its territory through environmental and territorial management plans, valuing the socio-environmental ecosystem services of the Xingu peoples and their organisations (ISA 2013).

Amazon Watch is another non-profit organization founded in 1996 to protect the rain forest and advance the rights of Indigenous peoples in the Amazon Basin. Associations with Indigenous and environmental organisations in campaigns for human rights are supported for preservation of the Amazonian biodiversity and ecosystems. In the meantime, further cooperations with Indigenous associations have been established in Amazonia.

In the last decades, members of the Indigenous society have taken advantage of opportunities for an urban education and work in professions such as civil servants,

364 *Quilombo* is a settlement of Afro-Brazilians, who escaped from slave plantations until abolition of slavery in 1888. They also settled in some regions of Amazonia. In 2003, President Lula da Silva passed a decree recognising *quilombo* communities, descendants of Afro-Brazilian slaves, and their claims to the land they inhabited and the titling and demarcation of their land.

environmental activists, heads of NGOs, city councillors, as lawyers and even in political elective functions as deputies and senators. In his courageous struggle for the rights of Indigenous peoples, the Xavante chief Mário Juruna who had his first contact with non-amerindian people in 1958, was the first Indigenous person to gain a seat in the Brazilian Parliament in 1982. Recently, five Indigenous people were appointed as deputies. The current situation of Indigenous success in political functions is discussed in chapter IV.2.

8. Scientific research centres, research cooperation programmes and NGO activities in the Amazon region

8.1. Brazilian state research centres in Amazonia

Brazil has some excellent research centres in Amazonia that have rendered outstanding services to the scientific exploration of the different Amazon regions for many decades with a wide range of topics. They have made intensive efforts to exchange ideas with national and international partner institutions, invited numerous foreign researchers as guest stays, and trained Brazilian researchers who have devoted themselves to the central topics of basic research and empirical field research. The scientific results have been published in national and international journals. These results have contributed to the fact that within a short period of time the knowledge about Amazonia has greatly improved. Decisive insights into the life of the regional amerindian population as well as the natural resources of Amazonia were gained.

New research results on Amazonian biodiversity, tropical ecosystems and their vulnerability, the importance of tropical forests as carbon storage, consequences of deforestation and land use change with increasing greenhouse gas emissions, and problems of climate change can be mentioned. Improved mapping by satellite imagery contributed to a better understanding of the regional differentiation of specific situations and also made it possible to better localise protected areas and Indigenous territories as well as economic and social conflicts of interest. Many scientific studies brought positive insights into agroforestry and sustainable development and thus gave perspectives for an environmental policy adapted to the natural and social conditions of the region. Brazilian universities and research centres outside the Amazon region have also intensified Amazon research in recent years.[366]

366 In this context, there are a number of academic activities, of which PROCAD (Programa de Cooperação Acadêmica em Defesa Nacional – National Programme for Academic Cooperation) will be mentioned here as an example. PROCAD is an initiative launched under the responsibility of CAPES (Coordenação de Aperfeiçoamento de Pessoal de Nível Superior – Coordination for the Improvement of Higher Education Personnel) and is primarily intended to promote academic cooperation. PROCAD-Amazônia is explicitly targeted at the North of Brazil and the state of Maranhão in order to reduce interregional imbalances (Filocreão, Pizzio, and Theis 2022, 21 f.). The programme aims to strengthen postgraduate studies in the northern region and Maranhão state by supporting joint research projects that build academic networks and make it possible to use the human resources and infrastructures available at the different participating institutions. New research topics will be taken up to create the conditions for increased research in Brazilian Amazonia and to improve the quality of courses offered by higher education institutions (Insti-

Findings of research projects have been successfully incorporated into the environmental policy of Amazonian states. Unfortunately, the environmental policy of the Brazilian federal government frequently did not consider essential research results because they did not correspond to the political objectives of various governments.

At this point it is only possible to briefly introduce some of the most important research centres.

The **National Institute of Amazonian Research (INPA)** is an internationally highly regarded public research and educational institution, headquartered in Manaus. It was founded in 1952 and implemented in 1954, with the purpose of furthering scientific knowledge of the Brazilian Amazon region. Most of INPA's research focuses on tropical forest management, ecology, molecular ecology, zoology, botany, tropical agriculture and tropical pisciculture. INPA offers graduate masters and doctorate programmes in the mentioned scientific fields.

In its early years, INPA did pioneering work on surveys and inventories of fauna and flora. In 1969, the cooperation with the Max Planck Institute for Limnology in Plön (Germany) in the field of tropical ecology was the first of many other international agreements of bilateral cooperation.[367] INPA has been carrying out scientific studies of the physical environment and living conditions in the Amazon region to promote human well-being and social development in regional economy. The Institute also is a cooperation partner in the German-Brazilian ATTO (Amazon Tall Tower Observatory) programme.[368]

Today, the challenge is to sustainably expand the use of the Amazon's natural resources. INPA has the general coordination of research in the following focuses: Environmental dynamics; society, environment and health; technology and innovation; and biodiversity. With its outstanding research results, INPA is a world reference in tropical biology.[369]

Since 1971, INPA publishes the multidisciplinary scientific journal *Acta Amazônica* with research results in and about the Amazonian region in a broad range of disciplines.[370]

The **Museu Paraense Emilio Goeldi**[371] is a renowned research institution linked to the Ministry of Science. It conducts research on the Amazonian flora and operates in the areas of taxonomy and biosystematics, ethnobotany and economic botany, anatomy of wood and vegetative organs and in studies of biodiversity.

---

tuto de Ensino Superior, IES) in this region (https://www.gov.br/capes/pt-br/acesso-a-informacao/acoes-e-programas/bolsas/programas-estrategicos/desenvolvimento-regional/procad-amazonia) (accessed September 10, 2023).

367 See chapter II.8.2.

368 Cf. chapter II.8.2.

369 https://www.developmentaid.org/organisations/view/246143/inpa (accessed 15.01.2023).

370 Agronomy and forestry, animal sciences and fisheries, biodiversity and conservation, biotechnology, chemistry and pharmacology, environmental sciences, food sciences, geosciences, health sciences, human and social sciences, and materials technology.

371 The Goeldi Museum was founded in Belém/Pará in 1866 and later named in honour of the Swiss naturalist Emil Goeldi, who reorganised the institution and was its director from 1894 to 1905. He was a zoologist and was commissioned to turn the Museum into an important research centre on the Amazon (https://www.museu-goeldi.br [accessed January 15, 2023]).

The studies in zoology have the objective of building an inventory of the Amazonian fauna, the analysis of its geographic distribution, behaviour, and relationship with the environment. The aim is to prepare plans for the conservation of the environment and management of fauna. Research is realised in all major groups of vertebrates (*avifauna, herpetofauna, ichthyofauna* and *mastofauna*) and several groups of invertebrates.

The Goeldi Museum has also the aim of increasing public awareness of science in the Amazon by means of its museums, botanical garden and zoological park.

The archaeology area develops research on human societies through material remains and landscapes modified by human populations that occupied the Amazon from the pre-colonial past to the present day. The institution is probably the largest repository of Amazonian collections in the world.[372]

Research in geosciences and ecology is developed on the evolution and functioning of ecosystems (including palaeontology, palynology, stratigraphy, and ecology) at different spatial and temporal scales, and on land use and sustainability with studies on land and soil use and their effects on biota as well as the conservation and use of Amazonian environments and species.

The Museu Paraense Emílio Goeldi offers graduate and postgraduate courses in biodiversity and in sociocultural diversity. In addition to these, there are masters' and doctorate' courses in zoology, sociology, anthropology, tropical botany and in environmental sciences.[373] Scientific publications, such as the *Boletim do Museu Paraense Emílio Goeldi* in Human and Natural Sciences, among others, are highly regarded.

The Museum maintains a scientific research station in the Amazonian rain forest (Estação Científica Ferreira Penna), inaugurated in 1993, with 330 km^2 in the Caxiuanã National Forest, (municipality of Melgaço, Pará).

The **Nucleus of High Amazonian Studies (NAEA)** is one of the academic units of the Federal University of Pará (UFPA) in Belém. It was created in 1973, with the aim of producing knowledge about the Pan-Amazon and forming professionals specialised in regional development planning. The Nucleus stands out for being the first in Amazonia to dedicate itself to the development of the Amazonian region based on paradigms of social and environmental sustainability in an interdisciplinary way (Castro and Campos 2015).[374] As a central theme, regional development began to incorporate interconnected themes, such as the study of the state, policies, and public management.

The NAEA has become a national and international reference, cooperating with research centres in many countries, in addition to being one of the most important producers of research results and scientific discourses on the region. Many foreign researchers worked in collaboration with NAEA. Its actions are concentrated in its numerous research groups of the most varied themes. The scientific productions come from the Graduate Programme in Sustainable Development of the Humid Tropics and the Graduate Programme in Public Management.

---

372 The Museu Goeldi offers more than 120 000 pieces in the archaeological collection, including ceramic artifacts, and more than 14 000 pieces in the ethnographic collection, including Indigenous cultures.

373 https://www.museu-goeldi.br (accessed January 15, 2023).

374 http://www.naea.ufpa.br/ (accessed January 17, 2023).

The *Revista Novos Cadernos NAEA* is an interdisciplinary journal, dedicated to the scientific publications on topics relevant to the areas of development, planning and the environment. There is a large number of book publications on Amazonian topics.

Research groups of different Amazonian universities have intensified their scientific programmes on Amazonian themes. Some contributed to research programmes with foreign countries and research centres, such as the Federal University of Mato Grosso in Cuiabá, founded in 1970, in the SHIFT programme and in the Carbiocial project with Germany,[375] to give just an example of the manifold activities.

8.2. German-Brazilian research programmes

After decades of personal collaboration between Brazilian and international scientists in individual research projects, larger projects of institutional collaboration had been established.[376] Of Brazil's bilateral research programmes at government level, only the German-Brazilian research cooperation in Amazonia may be mentioned here as an example. In addition to development cooperation at the political level (Fatheuer 2019), some of the most important German-Brazilian research programmes have been cofinanced by the German Ministry of Education and Research (BMBF) and the Ministry of Economic Cooperation (BMZ). Traditionally, German-Brazilian scientific cooperation has always been very active in many scientific disciplines.[377] In the Amazon region, the National Institute of Amazonian Research (INPA) in Manaus had established cooperation with the Max Planck Institute for Limnology in Plön (Germany) in 1969 in the field of tropical ecology,[378] whereby the experience of Harald Sioli – he did research and lived from 1938 to 1956 in Amazonia – played an important role on both sides.

In the 1990s, projects of the German-Brazilian scientific and technical cooperation within the framework of the SHIFT programme (1990–2002: Studies on Human Im-

375 See chapter II.8.2. In the SHIFT programme, a research group of the UFMT (Núcleo de Estudos Rurais e Urbanos, NERU) worked in close cooperation with the Centre of Latin American Studies (FLA) of the Institute of Geography, University of Tübingen (Research group of Gerd Kohlhepp).

376 Some projects fell victim to the political circumstances during the military dictatorship. An example is the initiative of Orlando Valverde, who, together with his colleagues from the Instituto Brasileiro de Geografia (IBG) of the IBGE and the Department of Geography of the University of Heidelberg, Germany (research group of Gottfried Pfeifer, Gerd Kohlhepp, Gisbert Glaser and Hanna Bremer), wanted to carry out a research project in Amazonia with a small research vessel in the early 1970s. Although an agreement had been concluded between the two institutions in 1971, and financing was secured on the German side, the project failed due to political, administrative, and financial problems of the Brazilian counterpart (cf. Kohlhepp 2017b, 15).

377 Scientific and technological relations have been a central element of cooperation and are highlighted by the German-Brazilian Strategic Partnership Action Plan. The Brazilian Ministries of Science and Education and the German BMBF identified in regular meetings the thematic priorities of their cooperation. Cf. https://www.bmbf.de/bmbf/en/international-affairs/worldwide-networking/the-americas-and-canada/brazil-research-partner-for-sustainability-and-innovation.html#-searchFacets (accessed January 14, 2023).

378 The agreement signed in 1969 between the German Max Planck Society and the Brazilian National Research Council (CNPq) opened up new possibilities for bilateral cooperation in tropical ecology research in the Amazon region. As early as 1965, Harald Sioli and his Brazilian colleague Djalma Batista founded the journal *Amazoniana*, a renowned publication in which landscape-ecological and limnological research results have been published (cf. Sioli 1968; 2007).

pact on Tropical Forests and Floodplains in the Brazilian Tropics) provided an excellent opportunity to intensify research on the Amazonian issue creating opportunities for scientists in both countries for basic and applied research, as was already mentioned before.[379] The aim of the multidisciplinary programme, with the focus on life and earth sciences of Brazilian and German university institutes and research centres, was to analyse the impact of human activities on tropical ecosystems, especially in the rain forest regions of Central and Eastern Amazonia, the *várzea* areas, the floodplain of the Pantanal and the catchment area of the Upper Rio Paraguai in Mato Grosso. Different projects contributed to the development of sustainable land use systems in tropical regions.

Another bilateral research programme, the MADAM programme (1995-2005: Mangrove Dynamics and Management) focused on the study of sustainable management of mangrove forests and its resources in the Belém coastal region.

The CarBioCial project (Carbon sequestration, biodiversity and social structures in Southern Amazonia: models and implementation of carbon-optimised land management strategies, 2011–2016), in close cooperation with its Brazilian partner project Carbioma,[380] investigated viable carbon-optimised land management strategies maintaining ecosystem services under changing climate conditions in southern Amazonia. The project was funded by the German Ministry of Education and Research (BMBF), the Carbioma project by the Brazilian National Council for Scientific and Technological Development (CNPq).

The multi- and interdisciplinary Carbiocial project "aims at understanding the vital natural processes and socio-economic driving forces in the region and develops strategies to enhance and protect carbon stocks in the recently deforested agro landscapes of central/northern Mato Grosso and southern Pará" (Gerold *et al.* 2014, 4).[381] Analysing the fundamental factors soil, water, and climate in this "hotspot of global change," the agrarian structures and production models, social and political transformations, it is the goal to find the starting points for a necessary change of local and regional production patterns, considering the local livelihoods as well as the current national and global conditions (Gerold *et al.* 2014; Mello-Théry and Cunha, 2014; Schönenberg *et al.* 2017). The research supported the goals set by the Brazilian ABC programme[382] and international treaties such as REDD and the Kyoto protocol. Brazil is responsible for about 20 % of worldwide carbon emissions caused by tropical deforestation. Drivers of this process are the international agricultural markets, where there is high demand for soybean products, palm oil, and sugar cane for biofuels.

The land use frontier of southern Amazonia with its extremely dynamic processes of land use change was frequently struck by land conflicts. In parts of this region, most of the farmers had no regular land title. As deforestation was accelerating along

379 See chapter II.3.2.2.

380 Scientific programme coordinators were: Gerhard Gerold (University of Göttingen, Germany) and Eduardo Guimarães Couto (Federal University of Mato Grosso, Cuiabá).

381 www.carbiocial.de.

382 In 2010, the Brazilian Government designed the Low-Carbon Agriculture Plan (ABC Plan) to provide resources and incentives for farmers to adopt sustainable agricultural techniques. The objective is to reduce emissions of carbon dioxide (CO_2), methane (CH_4), and nitrous oxide (N_2O) from agriculture. (https://www.climatepolicydatabase.org/) (accessed 13.01.2023); cf. chapter II.6.3.1.

the Cuiabá–Santarém highway, associated with major carbon losses and greenhouse gas releases, global interest in mitigating these emissions is high. The relevance of the affected ecosystems (rain forest, *cerradão* and *cerrado*) for carbon storage and GHG cycling is of global importance (Gerold and Hohnwald 2012).

Three regions were selected: Novo Progresso (southern Pará) with the most active deforestation; Sinop (northern Mato Grosso): centre of young soybean production; Cuiabá (central Mato Grosso): established agrarian cultivation (>20 years) and adapted mechanised cropping (e.g., no till).

The research project connected working groups from 17 universities and research centres in Brazil, Germany, and Austria, including the Brazilian agricultural research corporation Embrapa.

The joint main goals of the research cluster were (Gerold *et al.* 2014):

- to perform region-specific analyses in order to improve and apply interdisciplinary sets of models of land use impacts on carbon-stocks, water and GHG balances,
- to develop and optimise viable land management strategies that minimise carbon losses and GHG emission and maximise carbon sequestration,
- to assess the trade-offs between land management options and socio-economic impacts in terms of GHG reduction, profitability, and ecological sustainability,
- to elaborate regionally specified models which are essential and the key target of the project as model calculations of carbon and GHG fluxes from the respective ecosystems for different land use scenarios are still highly uncertain,
- to support the Brazilian partners to implement the optimised techniques in practice, considering the soybean value chain and overall carbon balance.

All research and implementation activities included direct involvement of the stakeholders, such as state environmental agencies, planning authorities and municipal administration, private organisations of farmers, and the agricultural research corporation Embrapa. Joint field experiments for improving carbon storage and ecosystem functions were performed in cooperation with an NGO founded by the farmers' organisation of Mato Grosso.

For the farmers of the region and for the state planning and environmental authorities, this applied research was of great importance as the farmers are increasingly suffering the effects of climate change with longer dry periods, a delayed rainy season, and greater variability in precipitation levels (Mello-Théry *et al.* 2020).

As the region's agriculture is very export-oriented and highly important for Brazilian export revenues, as well as globally relevant in economic and climate policy terms, the findings of this research can certainly offer positive results with far-reaching perspectives.

The ATTO project (Amazon Tall Tower Observatory) is an ongoing bilateral research project since 2009 in the Amazon rain forest to analyse the relationship between climate, atmospheric chemistry, and the rain forest, using highly sensitive instruments. Scientists from Brazil and Germany continuously record meteorological, chemical, and biological data, such as the concentration of greenhouses gases. Because the Amazon region is of such importance to the global climate, it is of vital importance to get a better understanding of these complex processes. The findings will enable to better predict developments of the climate and more accurate climate predictions in the future.

The research site is located in a largely untouched nature reserve in the Amazon rain forest to the exclusion of direct anthropogenic impacts, about 150 km north of Manaus. The German Ministry of Education and Research (BMBF) had provided financial means for the construction of a 325 m high measuring steel tower (Tall Tower, inaugurated in 2015), built under difficult conditions, with smaller towers (80 m) and a base camp site with air-conditioned laboratory containers in the rain forest. Since 2011, measuring equipment for atmosphere, biosphere, and climate research (carbon dioxide, ozone, volatile organic compounds, nitrogen-containing trace gases, aerosols, meteorology, clouds, weather data and micrometeorology, among others) has been set up. Satellite connection for data transmission and device control exists since 2013.[383] Brazilian funding is realised by Financiadora de Estudos e Projetos (FINEP-MCTI). In addition, six other subprojects are funded by CNPq.

The main research objectives are:[384]

- collecting data on the influence of the vast, largely untouched rain forest on the climate,
- understanding sources and sinks of greenhouse gases such as CO_2, methane and N_2O,
- investigating the formation of aerosols which is important for cloud formation,
- investigating the transport processes of air masses and their alteration through the forest over a distance of several hundred kilometres.

The ATTO data can also serve as a basis for environmental regulations for the sustainable development of the Amazon region.

The German-Brazilian research project Chemistry of the Atmosphere: Field Experiment in Brazil (CAFE Brazil) started in December 2022 and is an extension to the ATTO project. An international research team led by the Max Planck Institute for Chemistry began collecting data on the chemical processes in Brazil's largely clean atmosphere above the Amazonian rain forest. 20 measurement flights with the High Altitude and Long Range (HALO) research aircraft from DLR, the German aeronautics and space research centre, are planned. The flights over the rain forest will follow set patterns to measure vertical and horizontal profiles. The plan also includes "helix" flights, in which HALO spirals up from low altitudes to an altitude of 15 kilometres.[385]

---

383 Main partners of this German-Brazilian joint project are: Max-Planck-Institute (MPI) for Chemistry, Mainz, Germany; Max-Planck-Institute for Biogeochemistry, Jena, Germany; Instituto Nacional de Pesquisas da Amazônia (INPA), Manaus, Brazil; Universidade do Estado de Amazonas (UEA), Manaus, Brazil. Information about this project was provided by https://www.mpg.de; www.bgc-jena.mpg.de; www.mpic.de; www.bmbf.de; www.inpa.gov.br; www.attoproject.org (accessed January 14, 2023).

384 www.attoproject.org (accessed January 14, 2023).

385 Information about this project was provided by https://www.mpic.de; www.dlr.de (accessed January 14, 2023). Cooperation partners in CAFE-Brazil: Germany: Max-Planck-Institute (MPI) for Chemistry; Frankfurt University; Brazil: Universidade de São Paulo (USP) and Instituto Nacional de Pesquisas Espaciais (INPE). HALO: German aeronautics and space research centre (DLR).

The Amazonian rain forest is of global ecological importance, producing oxygen, stabilising the global climate, and influencing the water and carbon cycles. Dozens of parameters are measured, including aerosols, volatile organic compounds, sulphur and nitrogen oxides, carbon monoxide, methane, ozone, free radicals, and water. In addition to the measurements using the aircraft, data are collected with the help of balloons and drones from the ground at the ATTO research station. Studies conducted at the ATTO station will complement the HALO data. In addition to climate observations at different heights in the atmosphere, ATTO will enable research into the rain forest biosphere. This is a unique opportunity to link measurements in and directly above the rain forest.

Research objectives are to find out how atmospheric oxidation processes take place in the troposphere above the Amazonian rain forest and how they influence the formation and growth of aerosol particles, which are of central importance for the formation of clouds and precipitation. New insights into the interactions between the biosphere and the atmosphere are expected to better explain the fundamental role of the rain forest in the terrestrial system.[386]

8.3. National and international NGOs' research activities in the Amazon region

8.3.1. National NGOs with research activities in Amazonia

In Brazilian Amazonia, a number of regional non-profit and impartial NGOs have played an important role since the 1990s as key actors in the socio-environmental movements together with environmental activists and grassroots organisations in critical monitoring of state regional policy, with special efforts to prevent and control deforestation (Barbosa 2015). This applies in particular to organisations that did not only provide the public discussion with press reports about failed state activities, but which increasingly had scientifically trained staff members, who clearly analysed socio-environmental problems from the point of view of bio-, geo- and social sciences and were therefore able to make specific proposals for solutions to state agencies.

Although these solutions were initially rarely taken up,[387] they have been increasingly considered in project-related implementation in recent years. In some cases, NGOs have also been consulted in the formulation of environmental requirements, especially since public authorities often did not have suitably qualified experts in their ranks.

386 https://www.mpic.de; www.dlr.de (see footnote 384).

387 Some early foundations of NGOs, especially during the military dictatorship, had great difficulty in publishing their analyses when they criticised state decisions and projects. This was the case, for example, for the NGO CNDDA (National Campaign of Defence and Development of Amazonia), founded in 1967 by the renowned geographer Orlando Valverde and some colleagues, with the critical journal *A Amazônia Brasileira em Foco*. Members were renowned scientists as Aziz Nacib Ab'Sáber, Darcy Ribeiro, Warwick E. Kerr, Harald Sioli, Philip M. Fearnside and Irene Garrido Filha (General Secretary), among others. The journal was supported by contributions from members and donations from national and foreign environmentalists and sponsors, as well as congresses of CNDDA (cf. Kohlhepp 2017a, footnote 41).See also chapter I.6.2. for other examples.

National environmentalists and NGOs have made an important contribution to the implementation of environmental issues in the new Constitution of 1988.[388] NGOs have also contributed to the realisation of public policies through participatory processes and incorporation of local communities in environmental management. They often carry out their activities in a conflictual and sometimes hostile "social climate" and have to assert themselves against numerous opponents and strong resistance. NGOs can also act as intermediaries between governments, rural communities and the private sector to implement socio-environmental development programmes and strengthen good governance processes. They have analysed environmental impact assessments of infrastructure projects, such as dams, to support local organisations and communities affected by them (Jordão 2022, 97 f.).[389]

On the other hand, NGOs advocate for the government to change and implement its policies to protect land rights. They induce social pressure through information disclosure in the media and serve as intermediaries between transnational environmental NGOs and communities in campaigns to pressure decision-makers.

The involvement of NGOs in the preparation of expert reports in an advisory capacity for government agencies or also for private donors can of course also lead to the danger of donors exerting too much influence on the independence of NGOs. This is especially challenging, as smaller NGOs often find it difficult to secure their existence on the disputed project market.

All NGOs are of course dependent on donations which are either provided by official authorities, by environmentally or philanthropically oriented foundations, but mostly by private inland and international donors (industrial companies, banks, journals, NGOs, individual donors) either as permanent donations or as one-time transfers. There is an increasing competition on the environmental project market for these donations – there are hundreds of funding organisations with different cultures of action – so that special efforts are required in public appearance, media access and especially on the internet for appropriate self-presentation and explanation of the desired objectives. Success in fundraising depends on public recognition, credibility, reliable management systems (external auditing, accountability, transparency, compliance), profound expertise and reputation related to their professionalism, technical capacity, and permanence in the territory. Open dialogue with all stakeholders, especially at the local level, continuity of leadership and the collaborative presentation of results are especially important (Jordão 2022, 168 f., Table 2-2; 259, Table 3-1).

A big challenge for NGOs is the establishment of a network with partners which can support certain campaigns but of course can also arouse fears about the limited autonomy and competitive thinking. Since international NGOs are usually larger, very well-organised, and globally well-known institutions with a much higher budget, national NGOs also need to cooperate with experienced international partners, which is not always welcome in Brazil.

According to a recent survey, there are 73 environmental NGOs working in Amazônia Legal (Jordão 2022, 168, Table 2-1). In the following, only a few national NGOs can be mentioned that have distinguished themselves through their work and publications around Amazonia.

388 See chapters I.6.1, 6.2.

389 See examples in chapters II.5.2 and II.6.1, 6.2 of this volume.

ISA (Instituto SocioAmbiental/Socio-Environmental Institute) was established in 1994 to work on integrated solutions to social and environmental problems of Indigenous, *quilombola* and extractivist communities. ISA aims to protect their territories, strengthen their culture and traditional knowledge, raise their political profile, and develop sustainable economies. ISA has pioneered the concept of integrating environmental protection and sustainable development and the important cooperation with Indigenous groups in various Amazonian regions.[390] The Institute seeks to strengthen the role of partner communities by promoting forest restoration actions in the basins of the Rio Negro in Amazonas and Roraima and the Rio Xingu in Mato Grosso and Pará.

ISA's work has achieved significant impact by influencing public policies.

> ISA has introduced integrated programmes from satellite mapping and monitoring against land invasions, to sustainable income-generation, to extending formal citizenship. These initiatives have become models for Indigenous socio-environmental development in Brazil and around Latin America.[391]

ISA serves as a national reference for the production, analysis and quality of data on Indigenous peoples in Brazil. Furthermore, in terms of monitoring of protected areas, the organisation produces a wide variety of information which influences public policy decisions and government actions concerning "the defence of collective rights and the protection and conservation of Brazil's environmental heritage."[392] Monitoring programmes are based on Indigenous territories and federal and state conservation units, as well as other public lands. The monitoring follows the processes of demarcation of protected areas and the threats of deforestation, infrastructure impacts, fires, mining, and *grilagem*, providing information to the public debate.

Imazon (Amazon Institute of People and the Environment) is a Brazilian research institution, founded in 1990 in Belém, with studies on conservation and sustainable development in Amazonia. Imazon proposes solutions to problems with the use and conservation of natural resources in the Amazon region. Numerous technical papers have been published in international scientific journals and a large number of books and brochures have been released to support decision-making in the public sector and to communicate expertise to the general public. Since 2008, Imazon has been releasing a monthly "Deforestation Bulletin" with data on deforestation and degradation in the Brazilian Amazonia.[393]

Ipam (Amazon Environmental Research Institute) is a scientific NGO that has worked for the sustainable development of the Amazon since 1995. Its purpose is to consolidate the Amazonian tropical development model by 2035, by producing knowledge, implementing local initiatives, and directing public policies in a way that influences economic development, social equality, and environmental preservation. The aim is to promote science and innovation for an environmentally sound, economically prosperous, and socially just Amazonia, testing the application and viability of public

---

390 http://www.socioambiental.org/pt-br (accessed January 20, 2023). See chapter II.7.2.

391 Self-declaration of ISA, http://www.socioambiental.org/pt-br (accessed 20.01.2023)..

392 Idem.

393 Self-declaration of Imazon, https://imazon.org.br/en/ (accessed January 20, 2023)..

policies. Extensive data on biophysical factors (topography, soil types, and hydrology) and factors of human influence (critical infrastructure, major protected areas) have been collected to make maps on areas of high and low suitability for agriculture and large mammal habitat. Ipam has an extensive international cooperation and a large network of funding agencies and partners.[394]

The **Instituto Centro de Vida** (ICV),[395] founded in Mato Grosso in 1991, is a non-profit civil society organization of public interest. ICV is an NGO that works to build shared sustainability solutions that reconcile agricultural and forestry production with the conservation and restoration of natural ecosystems and their services (ICV 2022). Its actions reach state, national and international levels in terms of transparency, environmental governance, and public policies, as well as the municipal level through practical experiences. Partnerships exist with various sectors, such as governments, organisations, networks, collectives, companies, and media.

Fase (Federation of Organisations for Social and Educational Assistance), founded in 1961, is a non-profit, non-governmental organisation dedicated to popular education and the defence of human rights, with national operations and regional units in the Amazon region in Mato Grosso and Pará.[396] It operates in the municipalities of the metropolitan region of Belém, Baixo Tocantins and Baixo Amazonas, aiming at regional development and alternatives such as agro-extractivism and cooperativism. It defends the socio-environmental sustainability of territories and supports women's groups encouraging economic and political autonomy.

A number of NGOs also work together with foreign institutions and colleagues in the field of research. This applies – as one example among others – to the NGO Instituto Araguaia and the Frankfurt Zoological Society. There is a cooperation to protect the biodiversity of the Araguaia River Basin and its ecological processes in the Cantão State Park in the state of Tocantins, a "hot spot" for the conservation of biodiversity in the border area of the *cerrado* and the tropical rain forest.

The source and amount of funding will ultimately limit and influence the range of activities of Brazilian NGOs, seeking cooperation with more well-funded international NGOs as far as possible.

8.3.2. The role of international NGOs

International NGOs have contributed to slow down deforestation and reverse environmental degradation in Brazilian Amazonia. Brazilian and international NGOs participated in planning the National Programme for the Protection of the Environment (PNMA).[397] Pressure from international conservation NGOs has mediated government policies (Barbosa 2015).[398]

---

394 Self-declaration of Ipam, https://ipam.org.br; https://www.devex.com (accessed January 20, 2023).. With 76 partners, Ipam has the most extensive network of partners (cf. Jordão 2022, 355).

395 Self-declaration of ICV, https://www.icv.org.br (accessed January 28, 2023)..

396 Self-declaration of Fase, https://fase.org.br/pt/onde-atuamos/fase-amazonia/ (accessed January 28, 2023)..

397 See chapter II.1.5.

398 Valuable basic information in Mongabay Series: Amazon infrastructure, Amazon conservation. Mongabay is a US-based non-profit conservation and environmental science news platform. Its ex-

In conservative and nationalist circles within Brazilian society, but also among the various governments after the military dictatorship, the socio-ecological activities of international NGOs were and are viewed with a certain degree of suspicion. Not surprisingly, their activities criticising the government's agenda are often interpreted as direct or indirect interference by foreign organisations in Brazil's internal affairs. This is especially the case when pressure of large transnational NGOs has influenced the environmental and climate policy decisions in Brazil with strong effects, such as changes in legal requirements. International NGOs are sometimes in an ambiguous position because their parent countries, the industrialised nations, have incorporated Amazonia into the international commodity chains which to a large extent have caused problems of increasing deforestation.

But their financial resources and cooperation with national NGOs are of great importance for both sides to be able to implement well-prepared and really necessary projects with the appropriate perseverance. International NGOs that want to work in Amazonia need – except permission to work in the country – mainly Brazilian partners and collaborators with a specific local, regional and cultural knowledge as well as political contacts at all levels in the country.

At this point, it is only possible to mention a few transnational NGOs with Brazilian branches that played an essential role in the discussion about an environmentally friendly and more sustainable regional policy in Amazonia and contributed to important decisions.

Greenpeace

Greenpeace is a transnational non-profit organisation which is committed to environmental nature and climate protection as well as peace and, according to its own statements, "fights with direct non-violent actions for the protection of the natural livelihoods of man and nature and justice for all living beings."[399]

Greenpeace has been working in Brazil for 30 years denouncing and confronting governments, companies and projects that encourage the destruction of the Amazon region and threaten the global climate. Greenpeace Brazil investigates the impact of global supply chains in Amazonia, emphasises the problems involved and tries to influence federal, state, and local governments to bring about change by innovative methods of proceeding. The work in Amazonia has included the Amazon soybean moratorium that bans felling native forests for the purpose of establishing soybean plantations to meet EU requirements of responsible soybean production. This agreement happened also due to a large-scale Greenpeace campaign (Nepstad *et al.* 2014; Nepstad and Shimada 2018).[400]

Since 2006, many companies have agreed to stop buying soybeans from Brazilian farmers that destroy the Amazon rain forest. Soybean-financing institutions have also adhered to the compliance of the zero-deforestation policy as a requirement for loans. Greenpeace and other international NGOs continue to pressure national and re-

---

pertise is respected among science journalism and researchers due to the critical analysis of environmentally relevant state decisions in Amazonia and their effects. https://rainforests.mongabay.com/amazon/ (accessed January 28, 2023).

399 https://www.greenpeace.org/international (accessed January 23, 2023).

400 Cf. chapter II.4.3.

gional institutions into adapting to higher environmental standards to continue being competitive in international markets. Politicisation of commodity chains has brought awareness and positive results for the conservation of the region (Barbosa 2015). This has significantly reduced deforestation for soybean fields in Brazilian Amazonia. Greenpeace investigated the international market's role in cattle-driven deforestation in Amazonia and in protecting critical forest areas from problematic infrastructure expansion. A Greenpeace report gained visibility internationally and propelled the Brazilian government to exert stricter controls on cattle farming and leather operations in Amazônia Legal (Greenpeace 1997; 2009a). The Greenpeace International Amazon campaign includes the adjacent biome *cerrado* which is under serious threat from the same drivers that are devastating the Amazonian rain forests.

Greenpeace commissioned leading researchers from various fields to provide critical and independent analyses of the Tapajos project's "Environmental Impact Study" and "Environmental Impact Report" (EIA/RIMA). The scientists concluded that the EIA/RIMA submitted to IBAMA should be rejected by the licensing agency, because it does not fulfil its purpose of analysing the environmental viability of the project.

Reports prepared by the international NGO Greenpeace have encouraged changes in policies and financing requirements that propelled stricter controls on activities causing deforestation in the Brazilian Amazônia Legal.

WWF (World Wide Fund for Nature)

The WWF, founded in 1961, is one of the largest international nature and environmental organisations. It has worked in Brazil since 1971, but officially opened its office there in 1996. WWF runs dozens of projects in Brazil in partnership with regional NGOs, universities and government agencies. It develops activities in support of research, environmental legislation, public policy, environmental education and communication. In particular, many conservation projects are aimed at stimulating sustainable economic alternatives that both involve and benefit local communities.

> WWF-Brazil is part of the WWF network and currently is working in more than 90 projects in the Amazon, *cerrado*, Atlantic Forest, Pantanal, and marine ecosystems on the Brazilian coast. The aim is to protect and restore biodiversity, strengthen family farming and local production, as well as generate studies on the impact of deforestation and fires. WWF has a strong presence in the climate and energy debate, defending and creating solutions for a future of climate security.[401]

In 2002, Brazil had established the Amazon Region Protected Areas (ARPA) programme, implemented in partnership with federal, state, and municipal governments and the support of the World Bank, the German Government Cooperation Bank (KfW) and WWF Brazil. The programme was the world's largest initiative for the conservation of tropical forests, protecting 60 million hectares (Kohlhepp 2007a).[402]

In 2014, WWF helped launch ARPA for Life (ARPA-phase III), "an initiative securing long-term funding for the programme through an innovative conservation finance approach known as Project Finance for Permanence" (Foster 2022, n. p.). These pro-

401 Self-declaration of WWF, https://wwf.org/international (accessed January 23,2023).

402 See chapter II.5.1; https://www.kfw-entwicklungsbank.de (accessed January 23, 2023).

jects secure necessary policy changes and funding of multiple stakeholders to ensure that large-scale systems of conservation areas are well managed, sustainably financed, and benefit the communities that depend on them. Two decades after its first creation, ARPA continues to play an essential role in the conservation of the rain forest, preserving biodiversity, reducing deforestation and supporting local livelihoods (Foster 2022).

"It is one of WWF's great successes: the world's largest tropical forest conservation area programme has been secured in the long term."[403] Deforestation has been greatly reduced in the Amazonian rain forest, an important carbon reservoir, what is essential for mitigating climate change. Between 2008 and 2020, the protected areas supported by ARPA reduced deforestation by approximately 260 000 km², corresponding to an estimated 104 million tons of avoided CO_2 emissions. ARPA's effectiveness with a reinforced balance of protection and sustainable use can be partly attributed to the programme's management and governance.[404] ARPA has become an icon of conservation efforts in the Amazon biome due to impressive results (Barbosa 2015). The programme currently supports 114 federal and state protected areas distributed throughout the nine states of Amazônia Legal.

A large number of other international NGOs work in the Brazilian Amazonia:[405]

Friends of the Earth is a civil society organisation dedicated to protecting the environment and promoting development with sustainability and social justice. The entity *Amigos da Terra/Brasil* is a member of the International Federation Friends of the Earth, the largest network of grassroots environmental groups. It develops programmes, campaigns and projects that combine resistance, mobilisation, and transformation actions. *Amigos da Terra (Amazônia Brasileira)* defend the compatibility of production with goals of zero deforestation for the two main agricultural commodities, soybeans, and cattle, by 2030.[406]

International Rivers works with threatened communities, Indigenous peoples, social movements, and NGOs to fight destructive dams planned for the Amazon, while supporting alternative strategies to meet legitimate energy needs and promoting the permanent protection of the region's rivers, communities, and livelihoods.[407]

Amazon Watch fights the destruction of the Amazon, supports Indigenous rights and finds climate justice solutions.

The **Amazon Conservation Team** works hand-in-hand with Indigenous leaders to ensure the long-term welfare of the Amazon rain forest.

The **Amazon Conservation Association** has trained hundreds of conservationists who work to support the restoration of the Amazonian rain forest and sustainable Indigenous-led economies.

---

403 https://wwf.org/international; https://www.wwf.de; https://www.worldwildlife.org (accessed January 23, 2023).

404 "half of the areas ARPA supports are 'integral protection areas,' which strictly limit resource use. The other half are 'sustainable use areas,' which seek to balance conservation with the sustainable use of natural resources by local populations" (Foster 2022, n. p.).

405 The following statements are self-determined statements of the NGOs.

406 http://www.amigosdaterrabrasil.org.br/ (accessed January 27, 2023).

407 https://www.internationalrivers.org/ (accessed January 27, 2023).

Survival International recognises that there is no protecting Amazonia without Indigenous communities leading the way and works to amplify the voices of Indigenous leaders.

The **International Working Group for Indigenous Affairs** focuses on protecting Indigenous cultures, which always includes an environment-first approach.

The **Rainforest Action Network** preserves forests, protects the climate and upholds human rights by challenging corporate power and systemic injustice through frontline partnerships and strategic campaigns.

The **Rainforest Trust** has saved more than 23 million acres of the Amazonian rain forest since 1988 by funding projects that restore and protect ecosystems.

The NGOs mentioned here are only some of the active organisations.

International NGO interactions with economic interest groups included the wood (mahogany), food (soybean and beef), leather, and power (hydroelectric dams) industries. But there are critical opinions as well: "It would not be difficult to find examples of big NGOs proposing sustainable development projects in the Amazon that lack a nuanced understanding of traditional peoples' culture and livelihoods and their environmental impacts" (Barbosa 2015, n. p.).

Without underestimating the achievements of national and international NGOs, however, it must be emphasised that the real guardians of the rain forest are the Indigenous peoples or traditional peasant communities native to Amazonian territories. In recent years, they have organised a considerable number of their own NGOs.[408]

408 Cf. chapter II.7.2.

III Devastation and environmental degradation policies in Amazônia Legal during the Bolsonaro Government (2019–2022)

1. Chaotic activities of a decided enemy of sustainability in Amazonia[409]

The extremely right-wing populist President Jair Bolsonaro, a former low-ranking officer in the Brazilian Armed Forces, took office in 2019. He came to power with the support of large sections of the corporate elite, a combination of right-wing and conservative circles, which shared his distrust of previous governments discredited by corruption scandals. Bolsonaro's radical discourse was accepted by these groups as necessary. The rapidly increasing number of evangelicals in Brazil (about one-third of the population), among which are also ultra-conservatives groups ("with God to power"), supported his aims to play a decisive role in domestic politics, to strengthen internal security in the country and to conquer the rural area in a biblical sense.

Bolsonaro had no international experience. With his seizure of power, Brazilian democracy felt strongly endangered (Stuenkel 2021; Birle and Speck 2022). Due to his right-wing extremist views[410] and his gruff appearance, the tabloid press called him "tropical Trump" in a comparison to the US ex-president, who was a kind of role model for Bolsonaro.

His plan to abolish the Ministry of the Environment as an independent ministry was widely met with incomprehension by the Brazilian public and was not realised due to considerable protests. In addition, leaders of large landowners had convinced the president not to extinguish the ministry because this could cause restrictions on Brazilian exports. Nevertheless, the environmental portfolio lost the Brazilian Forest Service to the Ministry of Agriculture, led from 2019 to March 2022 by the well-known hardliner Tereza Cristina Dias, representative of the agribusiness lobby.

Bolsonaro's strategy was to weaken environmental licensing. He appointed Ricardo Salles as Minister of the Environment, a "ruralist" and ex-environment secretary of the state of São Paulo, where he radically dismantled the agency. Salles announced the revision of all conservation units in the country. It was apparently his strategy to threaten experienced managers in the environmental sector who represented other views of the problems. He did this with inspectors of the Chico Mendes Institute for Biodiversity Conservation (ICMBio)[411] and administrative officials. Environmentalist

409 This chapter is based on Kohlhepp (2020a; 2021b).

410 The "bbb-slogans" ("boi, bala e biblia": beef, bullet and bible) of Bolsonaro and his supporters were frequently cited (cf. Lapper 2021).

411 The Chico Mendes Institute for Biodiversity Conservation is named after the environmental activist Chico Mendes from Acre, a rubber tapper and trade union leader. His aim was to preserve the Amazonian rain forest and he advocated for the human rights of Brazilian peasants and Indigenous

Adalberto Eberhard resigned as president of the institute. Salles appointed police officers from São Paulo in place of biodiversity experts. None of the substitutes had the level of expertise of the predecessors. ICMBio managed almost 10 % of the Brazilian territory (Trigueiro 2019).

It was absolutely scandalous that the Minister of the Environment used the distraction of the press during the catastrophic consequences of the completely neglected organisation of measures against Covid-19 in Brazil (lacking vaccine import etc.) in order to pass "infralegal reforms" to push ahead with the deregulation of environmental legislation – in a way hidden from the public (he himself mentioned it during the infamous cabinet meeting of April 22, 2020 that reverberated around the world). With this attitude, he disqualified himself (Kohlhepp 2020a; 2021b).

Salles' idea, "adopt a Park," was aimed at private investors, funds, banks, and large corporations who had expressed their criticism of the government's Amazonian policy, which so much undermined the image of Brazil. They should compensate for the lack of state resources. This was reminiscent of corresponding roll calls for "financing for the conservation of tropical rain forests" during the military dictatorship. Financing of projects already happened indirectly – with constraints – within the Amazon Fund. However, neither domestic investors nor foreigners – discredited by the president – thought of abundant investments in the current precarious Amazonian environmental policy.[412] 132 protected areas in Amazonia for which the costs were to be covered were offered by Salles without asking the inhabitants of these mostly inhabited areas.

According to Brazilian environmental experts and former heads of IBAMA, President Bolsonaro was waging an "ideological war" against all those engaged in trying to prevent the destruction of Amazonia.[413] By request from the president, Salles publicly criticised inspectors who destroyed equipment used by criminals to remove illegal wood from a conservation unit in Pará, despite a federal decree authorising this procedure in certain situations (Trigueiro 2019). Later, the president prohibited the destruction of machines for illegal deforestation of the timber mafia.

Some of Brazil's former ministers of the environment, who were taking a stand against the Bolsonaro government's environmental policies, had held intensive discussions with PPG7's International Advisory Group (IAG) in the 1990s on the emerging problems of implementing projects under the programme. Now, former Minister Marina Silva called Bolsonaro's environment minister an "environmental opponent."[414]

---

peoples. Chico Mendes was assassinated by a rancher in 1988 (cf. MMA 2017). The mission of the Chico Mendes Institute is to protect the Brazilian natural heritage and promote the environmental development. The ICMBio is an autarchy under a special scheme. It was created in 2007 and is linked to the Ministry of Environment and member of the National Environmental System (SISNAMA).The institute is in charge of performing the action of the National System of Protected Areas.

412 Only a few large companies, such as Coca Cola, Carrefour, and Heineken, hoping for favourable market conditions, offered to take over the environmental costs of some territories.

413 The expression "ideological war" was employed by Adriana Ramos, advisor to the Socio-Environmental Institute (ISA), in 2019 (cf. Kohlhepp 2020a, 432).

414 Marina Silva had resigned in 2008 during Lula da Silva's presidency under pressure from agribusiness, construction companies and power plant lobby. In the new government of Lula da Silva, in office since January 2023, she accepted again the appointment as Minister of the Environment. Cf. chapter IV.2.

The protests of former Brazilian environment ministers,[415] belonging to different governments and political parties with different ideological currents, against the counterproductive activities of the new government in environmental policy, were accompanied by a multitude of other protests, such as

- protests of the Academia Brasileira de Ciências (ABC) against discrediting science and scientists and the cutdown of CNPq, CAPES and university budgets,
- protests of the governors of Amazonian States against refusal of EU help,
- protests of Indigenous groups against invasions of mining and timber companies into Indigenous territories,
- protests of NGOs and other members of the civil society against denial of climate change, accelerating deforestation, and the irresponsible regional policy in Amazonia,
- protests of donors against the highly problematic action of environment minister Salles concerning administration and reorganisation of the Amazon Fund.

In some European countries (France, Ireland, Austria, etc.) there were protests against the ratification of the EU-Mercosur agreement in view of the radical environmental policies of the Bolsonaro government.

In a way, fire clearance in Amazonia has been officially supported by promoting aggressive agribusiness, logging and cattle ranching activities.

Pronouncements[416] and actions of President Bolsonaro and ministers of his government resulted in a long list of superficial and irresponsible comments, such as statements

- against rain forest protection and implementation of Indigenous territories,
- against national and international NGOs ("communist infiltration"),
- against environmentalists by mentioning strange conspiration theories,
- against the movement of the landless (MST),
- against scientific evaluation of deforestation by the prestigious INPE,
- against activities of the National Indian Foundation (FUNAI) and the Brazilian Institute of Environment and Renewable Natural Resources (IBAMA) with the consequence of budget cutdown and dismissal of controllers,
- against punishment of illegal activities at the pioneer front and against fines for environmental crimes,
- against proposals of support for fire control by EU member countries,
- against previous administration of the Amazon Fund and against use of donations of Norway and Germany for rain forest protection projects of NGOs and local communities.

---

415 José Sarney Filho, Carlos Minc, Izabella Teixeira, Marina Silva, Rubens Ricúpero and José Carlos Carvalho participated in a special meeting and formulated a protest note: "social and environmental governance in Brazil is being dismantled in an affront to the Constitution" and "is the real risk of uncontrolled increase in deforestation of the Amazon" (Trigueiro 2019).

416 Ferrante and Fearnside (2019), especially supplementary material.

Politically, the ministry of environment had lost strength, power, and prestige (Trigueiro 2019).

During the Covid-19 pandemic, President Bolsonaro gave useless advice on dubious drugs and exercised a disastrous crisis management, even calling Covid-19 a "small flu" (*gripezinha*). By the end of 2022, over 700 000 people have died of Covid-19 in Brazil.

National and international criticism of the environment and Amazonia policies of the Bolsonaro government increased the aggressiveness of the political actors and the far-right party members. A new dimension of emotion had reached politics. Bolsonaro "strongly embodies the phenomenon of wrath" and "voters who hope for an improvement in economic and security policy, got attracted to this rage" (Maihold 2019a, n. p.).

Members of the Brazilian Academy of Sciences (ABC), including former Science Minister José Israel Vargas, and hundreds of other researchers had vehemently opposed President Bolsonaro's statements and insinuations by various ministers toward science and scientists, as well as the funding cuts, and had sharply criticised the lack of environmental and human rights policies of the federal government in Amazonia. Due to the hyper-critical attitude of the Bolsonaro government to science and its analytical findings, multi- and interdisciplinary bilateral research collaborations and the internationally recognised high qualification of Brazilian scientists were obviously negated in Brasília. NGOs, some of which played an essential role in the development of guidelines for environmental protection and the safeguarding of the Indigenous habitat with scientifically sound analyses, were regarded as an "enemy image" and as "politically infiltrated" by members of the government. International NGOs were discriminated against as "foreign agents."

Supervisors of IBAMA and FUNAI were impeded in their activities or even bribed. Environmental licensing should be weakened or even be carried out without any impact analysis. This would further marginalise environmental impact assessment, which is already damaged by the lack of adequate participation of civil society (Ruaro *et al.* 2022).

NGOs or other members of the civil society (small farmers, priests, Indigenous people) were threatened by armed private militia (*pistoleiros*) of large-scale farmers and quite often their life was in danger.

President Bolsonaro's sharp reaction to the offer of help formulated by French President Macron on the occasion of the huge forest fires showed incomprehension and mistrust ("No one donates without consideration"). With PPG7, Brazil's reservation about its national sovereignty in Amazonia had been eliminated by explicitly not calling the Amazonian rain forests a "global good" at the time.[417] Macron had underestimated the traditional sensitivity of Brazilian governments to Amazonia with the phrase "our house is burning".

The new National Council of Amazônia Legal, led by Vice President Hamilton Mourão, a retired general, and composed of ministers of the federal government but not by the governors of the Amazonian states and by no member of the civil society, assumed the coordination of government activities in "defence, protection and sustainable development of the Amazon."

Since the beginning of his term, Bolsonaro had relied heavily on military personnel in his cabinet. At times, six ministers were former high-ranking military officers.

---

417 See chapter II.2.1.

More than 6000 officers occupied positions within the state apparatus during Bolsonaro's government. The army became increasingly politicised.

The National Environmental Force formed alongside the "elite force" for "environmental disasters" – which, according to critics from Amazonia, represented a veritable "militarisation" – certainly could not, from a socio-ecological point of view and for the benefit of the regional population, take on all those tasks that were neglected or "forgotten" by Minister Salles.

For President Bolsonaro, man-made climate change does not exist, and he detested the international discussion on this subject. He appointed Ernesto Araújo as Minister of Foreign Affairs (from January 2019 up to his resignation in March 2021) who considered global warming an "invention of Marxist ideology" (Fearnside 2019; Ferrante and Fearnside 2019; Maihold 2019a). Araújo was a career diplomat who did not have the experience to lead the prestigious Brazilian Foreign Ministry. He "belonged to the ideological, anti-globalist camp within Bolsonaro's cabinet" (Weiffen 2022, 56) and was an ardent supporter of Trump and, most problematically for Brazil, a fierce critic of China, making it difficult to import vaccines from there. Contrary to the diplomatic tradition of the Ministry of Foreign Affairs, the Itamaraty, Araújo liked to attack all supposed opponents severely with obscure and insulting arguments. Multilateralism, regional integration projects and, above all, environmental protection were put on the back burner. In the spirit of the president, Araújo emphasised that international institutions use climate change as an excuse to restrict Brazil's sovereignty through regulations, thus endangering Brazil's international relations.

Brazil's commitments under the 2015 Paris Climate Agreement[418] were not taken seriously and had completely disappeared from the official environmental policy discussion in Brazil. Bolsonaro refused to host the 2019 Climate Change Conference (COP 25), the largest climate meeting in the world, in Brazil, which was eventually held in Chile. During the COP 26 in Glasgow (2021), Bolsonaro stressed in his official statement that Brazil would end illegal deforestation by 2030. However, he did not tell the truth by withholding the newest deforestation rates.

The question of securing the country's borders in Amazonia has been important since 2015 with the increasing migratory pressure from Venezuela, especially for the border state of Roraima, which had already declared a state of emergency at the end of 2017 in view of up to 2000 refugees per day. Bolsonaro has "inherited" this problem and openly expressed his opposition to the Maduro government, with which the Workers' Party of Brazil (PT) had sympathised. In 2018, Bolsonaro had been voted by 72 % of the electorate in Roraima and the population expected the problem to be dealt severely by the president. In any case, the state of Roraima had major border problems due to the cross-border habitat of the Yanomami, which was difficult to secure throughout the north of the country due to expanding gold mining by *garimpeiros* and drug trafficking routes. However, a closure of the border to Venezuela was rejected by the Supreme Court. The refugees against whom there were violent protests in Roraima (Maihold 2019a) were also distributed outside Amazonia in the country.

---

418 In 2015, negotiated by 196 countries (parties) under the aegis of the UN, the Paris Agreement is a legally binding international treaty on climate change. The Paris Agreement (COP 21) aimed to hold the increase in the global average temperature to "well below" 2°C, preferably to 1.5°C, compared to pre-industrial levels. The Agreement underpinned the COP 26 climate talks in Glasgow.

The president has spoken out decisively for the "valorisation" of the natural resources of Amazonia and against tropical forest protection and the area size of Indigenous territories. Fires in Amazonia seemed to promote Bolsonaro's "economic development model" for the rain forest region. However, Brazilian entrepreneurs have publicly complained that the government's initial lack of response to the countless fires in Amazonia damaged Brazil's image. Only international pressure led to the use of the military to fight fires, after Bolsonaro's long hesitation and the claim that this problem could be solved without foreign help. The next fire season will threaten the Amazonian rain forest and the crucial question is how to deal with this challenge. Obviously, this did not worry President Bolsonaro.

2. Destruction of tropical forest ecosystems due to logging and slash-and-burn activities

The tropical rain forests of Amazonia are not the "lungs of the world" and they do not produce 20 % of the oxygen needed by mankind, as parts of the press, news channels and politicians repeat like a prayer wheel.

The Amazon rain forest is not a big source of oxygen since the trees consume almost all the oxygen they produce through photosynthesis. Amazonian rain forests produce only about 6 % of the planet's oxygen[420] and the forest ecosystems have hardly any effect on the oxygen content in the atmosphere.

But the extremely important function of intact rain forests is the storage of large amounts of carbon with their biomass. 150–200 billion tons of carbon are stored in vegetation and soils. Production of woody biomass accounts for 8–13 % of the photosynthetic carbon uptake. "The ability of ecosystems to capture, process, and store carbon and other nutrients is determined by climatic, edaphic, hydrological, and biological factors" (Nobre *et al.* 2021, Message 4). Tropical forest ecosystems are a huge CO_2 reservoir that binds greenhouse gases that are responsible for climate change, among other trace gases. In 2022, global CO_2 emissions amounted to about 37 billion tons. The Amazonian ecosystems absorb 2 billion tons of CO_2 per year or 5 % of global annual emissions (Nobre *et al.* 2016).[421]

In 2021, total Brazilian CO_2 emissions amounted to 1.48 billion tons, i.e., a share of 3.6 % on global CO_2 emissions. CO_2 emissions from land-use change in Brazil reached 993 million tons, i.e., 67 % of Brazil's total emissions or a share of 25.2 % on global CO_2 emissions from land-use change.[422]

The tropical forests are biodiversity hotspots. Slash-and-burn not only releases enormous amounts of CO_2 but also destroys the high biodiversity, reduces evaporation and regional precipitation, and damages the water balance. Increased forest fragmentation leaves areas of the remaining rain forests more vulnerable (Laurance *et al.* 2001).

Data of deforestation, based on satellite image evaluations and published by the internationally renowned INPE, show, that in the Brazilian Amazon region from 1975 (only 0.6 %) to 2021 19.9 % of the original rain forest area (4.1 million km^2: nearly the total area of the European Union) were devastated. This means that smaller fires close

419 Cf. chapters I.3.3; I.4.5.1; II.2.2.2; II.6.3.1.

420 According to Jonathan Foley, Climate and environmental scientist, Executive Director of Project Drawdown (Zimmer 2019).

421 Emissions are measured in CO_2 equivalents (CO_2 eq).

422 Source: https://ourworldindata.org/carbon-deforestation-trade (accessed April 22, 2023).

to the ground, which lead to dehydration and greatly promote the subsequent risk of fire, are not yet covered. All the data were disputed by Bolsonaro and led to the unjust dismissal of INPE's director.

Figure 38. Deforestation in Amazônia Legal (1988–2021) (by area and share of states)[423]

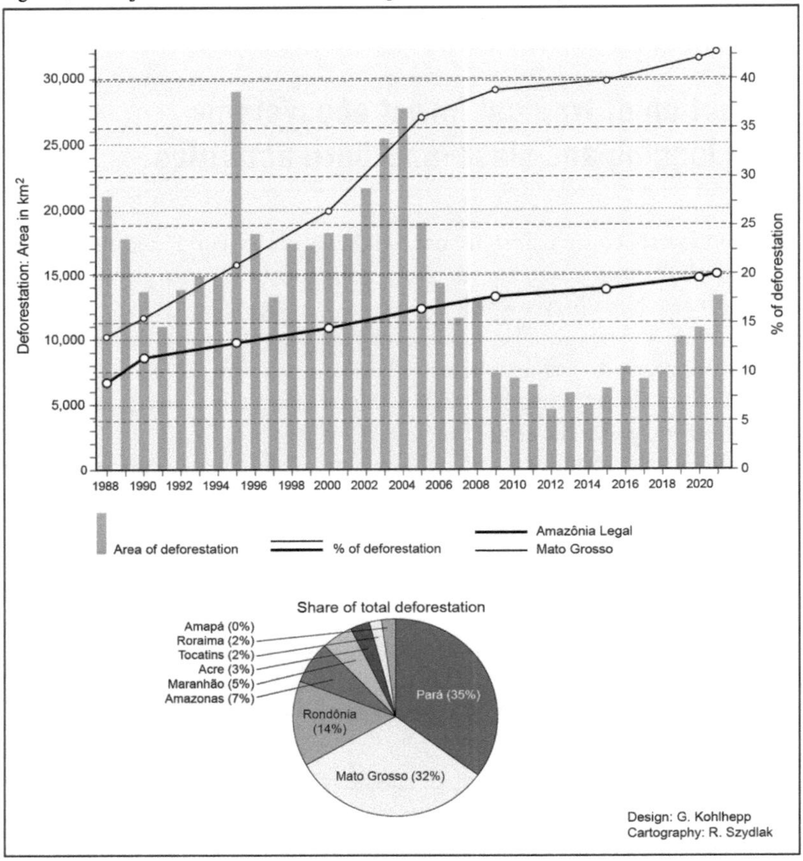

Source: Data INPE/PRODES. Design: G. Kohlhepp.

n some years, deforestation had reached extremely high levels, corresponding to the extent of some countries. For example, 29 059 km² (about the size of Belgium) of rain forest was cleared in 1995 and 27 772 km² (about the size of Haiti) in 2004. Slash-and-burn, having decreased from 2004 to 2012 by more than 84 % – caused by the soybean moratorium, blacklists, and CAR registry – during the phases I and II of the Action Plan for the Prevention and Control of Deforestation in the Legal Amazon (PPCDAm), launched in 2004, increased again in recent years but has continued to increase very quickly since 2019 (Fig. 38).

This was also due to illegal clearing in Indigenous territories and protected areas, which amounted to 14 % of total deforestation in the last two decades. The total area de-

423 Annual deforestation is calculated from August 1 to July 31 of the following year.

forested in Indigenous territories during Bolsonaro's first three years was 138 % higher than in the previous three years (2016–2018), according to the Socio-Environmental Institute (ISA). Under Bolsonaro, deforestation in the Amazon region increased by 73 % between 2019 and 2021, reaching its highest level in 15 years. More than 13 000 km^2 of rain forest were destroyed in 2021, the highest figure reported since 2006. The area deforested in the first half of 2022 (nearly 4000 km^2) was 80 % larger than in the same period in 2018, the year before Bolsonaro took office. This shows that even in the main rainy season (until April) more clearing was done than usual, especially as the passability of unpaved paths and roads is very limited during this time.

Table 18. Deforestation in Amazônia Legal 1975–2021 (in % of the original rain forest area and total deforestation area)

Federal states	**Original rain forest area (in 1000 km^2)**	**% of state area**	**Deforestation 1975–2021**			
			1975–1987 in %	1988–2021 in %	Total in km^2	Total in %
Acre	163.7	99.4	4.9	10.2	24 652	15.1
Amapá	113.3	79.5	1.3	1.5	3155	2.8
Amazonas	1449.7	93.0	1.0	2.1	44 910	3.1
Maranhão	97.4	37.3	55.1	22.8	75 924	77,9
Mato Grosso	473.9	52.5	10.8	31.7	201 649	42.5
Pará	1112.2	89.3	10.7	14.6	281 011	25.3
Rondônia	212.7	89.5	14.9	30.4	96 282	45.3
Roraima	182.8	81.8	1.6	4.9	11 886	6.5
Tocantins	23.5	8.5	52.8	37.3	21 183	90.1
Amazônia Legal	**3829.2**	**76.3**	**7.6**	**12.3**	**760 652**	**19.9**

Source: Own elaboration, based on deforestation data INPE/PRODES; IMAZON (2021,Table 5, original rain forest area); Percentages: own calculations.

In a detailed overview between 1975 and 2021, the dynamism of deforestation in the various phases is becoming abundantly clear. From 1975 to 1987, in the initial phase of modern exploitation of Amazonia, only 7.6 % of the Brazilian Amazon rain forest area were cleared, from 1988 to 2021 12.3 % more, so that in 2021 a total area of 760 652 km^2 or 19.9 % of the rain forest area of Amazônia Legal were devastated (Fig. 38). This corresponds to the size of Turkey. It is important to remember that at least the same area, but probably almost one million km^2 of rain forest, has been additionally degraded. This means that about 45 % of the original tropical rain forest area has already been affected to various degrees by deforestation and its side effects.

In the individual federal states of Amazônia Legal, deforestation developed very differently. In the states of Maranhão and Tocantins, which have a considerable share of *campos cerrados*, a high proportion of the existing forest area was cleared very quickly with over 50 %. In Rondônia, Pará and Mato Grosso large areas were cleared by agrarian colonisation projects, cattle ranching, and timber industry. Only during the second phase of exploitation, soybean cultivation expanded especially in Mato Grosso.

While in Amazonas, Amapá and Roraima only relatively low percentages of deforestation have been recorded so far, this nevertheless affects relatively large areas. Apart from Tocantins and Maranhão, having only a relatively small original rain forest area in Amazonian relations, which were already deforested by 90 respectively 78 %, the states of Rondônia (45.3 %) and Mato Grosso (42.5 %) account for the largest proportion of deforestation with significantly over 40 %. In these states, the increase in the period between 1988 and today was particularly large (Table 18). In Fig. 38, in addition to the curve for the whole area of Amazônia Legal, the curve for the state of Mato Grosso is shown, which had a very rapid rise until 2005 and has since flattened out somewhat but rose sharply again in the last four years. In terms of the share of total deforestation area, Pará (35 %) and Mato Grosso (32 %) are in the leading position. The area deforested in both states in four and a half decades is almost the size of Spain.

About 80 % of the deforestation in Amazonia, accounting for two-thirds of the Brazilian CO_2-emissions, were due to large-scale cattle farms. Only 6 % of the area deforested is used by farming, among others for soybean cultivation, which has so far penetrated mainly into the southern and eastern areas due to the generally low soil fertility of Amazonia. Despite of obscure conspiracy theories of the Bolsonaro government relating to probable arsonists – the government even accused NGOs – cattle farmers were also responsible for the majority of the 2019 large-scale fires. A "day of fire" had been proclaimed by ranchers in the state of Pará on August 10, 2019 (Fig. 39).

Figure 39. Forest fires in Amazônia Legal, August 12–25, 2019

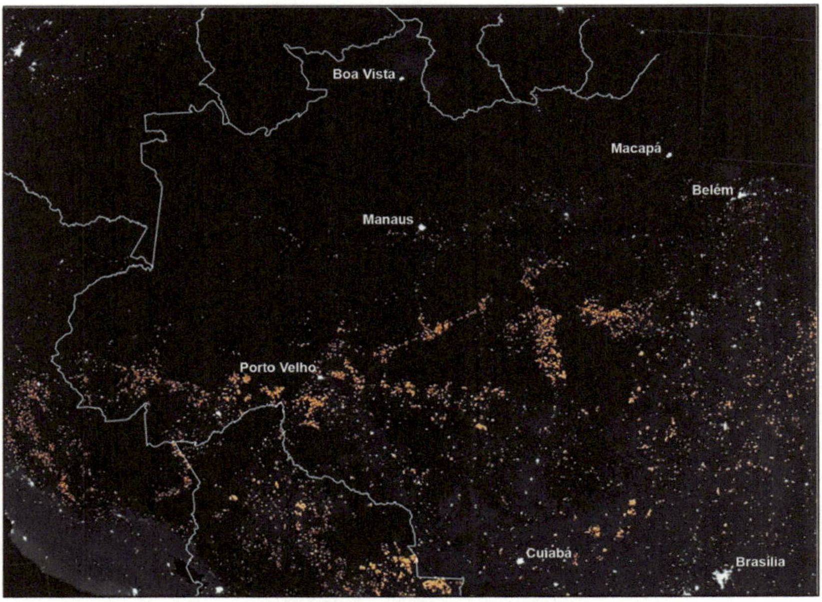

Source: MODIS/NASA Earth Observatory/ Joshua Stevens.

It is obvious that the larger forest fires occurred along the main axes of the road connections BR-163 (northern section in Pará) (Klingler 2022), BR-230 (central section of the Transamazônica in Pará and Amazonas), and BR-364 (in Rondônia and especially in Acre). Furthermore, forest fires raged in North Mato Grosso and in the Terra do Meio,[424] a region located in the central portion of southern Pará, in the interfluves of the Xingu and Iriri rivers.

Frequently, land speculation was and still is the background of deforestation because deforesting for cattle pasture is the practical way to secure land holdings. Money from drug trafficking, corruption and fiscally undisclosed income sources can be converted by "money laundering" to "legal" money and invested in Amazonian deforestation with minimal risk (Fearnside 2017c).[425] Especially in the 1970s and 1980s, the first phase of large-scale exploitation of Amazonia, land speculation often was one of the main factors. In these cases, officially approved cattle grazing projects after a few years were abandoned.[426] In some regions, the increase in land prices and land speculation made more profit than raising cattle (Kohlhepp 1979; Hecht 1985 and 1993; Hecht *et al.* 1988).[427]

The cattle herd in Amazônia Legal has increased from 8 million in the early 1960s to 93 million animals in 2021, i.e., 43 % of Brazil's cattle (224.6 million) graze in Amazonia. The largest cattle population per state in Brazil is in Mato Grosso (32.7 million = 14.4 % of Brazil's total) (InfoAmazonia, 09.11.2021; Greenpeace 2009a). Cattle ranching is expanding in Amazônia Legal despite all attempts to tackle this major problem of deforestation. The "success" of cattle farming in Amazonia with low stocking density (1–1.3 animals/ha) is only ensured by the expansion of clearing new pastures with a very low average productivity at 70–80 kg meat/ha/year. Pasture expansion for cattle production is the main driver of deforestation with about 80% of clearing (Skidmore *et al.* 2021; Global Forest Atlas 2019; Fatheuer 2017).[428] The substitution of ranching by more profitable agricultural land use (soybean, sugarcane, etc.) in South and South-

424 Terra do Meio is a region with a rich biodiversity, formed by a mosaic of natural conservation units, including state and federal units, and Indigenous territories. It is a vast area, which is approximately twice the size of the state of Rio de Janeiro. The region is suffering from three major fronts of anthropic pressure: the Altamira-Itaituba section of the Transamazônica to the north, the BR-163 to the west and the most exposed agricultural frontier of the Amazon biome, to the southeast. The mosaic is part of a territory of contiguous protected areas, which covers 28 million ha, and which makes the region the second largest biodiversity corridor in Brazil (https://www.funbio.org.br [accessed February 12, 2023]) (Schmink et al. 2019). Terra do Meio, especially the region of São Félix do Xingu and Tucumã, was one of the most deforested regions in the Amazon in recent years. The Apyterewa Indigenous Territory (Parakanã people) has lost nearly 30 % of its forest cover, with some 5 % cleared in 2019 alone (https://news.mongabay.com/2023/02/in-brazil-criminals-dismantle-one-of-the-best-preserved-swaths-of-the-amazon/ [accessed September 23, 2023]).

425 The Terra do Meio in Pará, for many years has been dominated by drug traffickers (cf. Schönenberg 2002a, 2002b; Machado 2002; 2009), *grileiros* and other illegal actors.

426 Cf. chapter I.1.1.2, Fig. 1.

427 In the late 1950s and 1960s, along the Belém–Brasília highway, first settlers were squatters who were later expelled, often violently, and replaced by large ranchers (Fearnside 2017c; cf. Valverde and Dias 1967; Glaser, 1971; Schmink and Wood 1992).

428 Almost 20 % of the land that had been cleared for new pastureland was abandoned and not put to any other productive use (Hirota *et al.* 2022).

east Brazil, and the cheap land prices in Amazonia contributed to a progressive transference of cattle herds to the North (Smeraldi and May 2008).[429]

Deforestation for cattle pastures even occur in Indigenous territories, conservation units and extractive reserves. Sown pasture with *Brachiaria brizantha* – allowing a reasonable forage production during the dry season – has become the major forage species in Amazônia Legal today, in contrast to *Panicum maximum* in the beginning of cattle breeding in the 1960s and 1970s (Veiga *et al.* 2002),[430] which has a higher nutritive value. The main ecological consequences of deforestation are chemical and physical soil depletion as well as weed encroachment. The main technological reasons of pasture degradation are insufficient pasture establishment, neglected management, lack of investments, technology and know-how (P and N fertiliser) (Hohnwald *et al.* 2010; Serrão and Nepstad 1996).

After beef exports had been barred from international markets for some time due to the foot-and-mouth disease, since 2015 no cases of this disease were stated in all states of Brazilian Amazonia. In 2015 and 2016, negotiations with Russia and China have opened these markets to Brazilian beef. The Chinese market is extremely important since its potential scale is infinite from the perspective of Brazilian producers (Fearnside 2017c). Brazil is also China's main supplier of leather.

The cattle industry in Amazônia Legal is dominated by large exporting meatpacking companies that supply the domestic and the international markets. In 2009, Greenpeace (2009b) published a report linking the cattle industry to the deforestation of Amazonia, which caused uproar of the international press. Because this was threatening their export strategies, major meatpackers signed a "cattle agreement" with Greenpeace to block deforestation from their supply chains (Skidmore *et al.* 2021).

Four of the world's largest cattle producers and traders[431] have agreed to stop buying cattle from newly deforested areas in the Amazon rain forest. In this "cattle moratorium," they will implement certification and monitoring systems to ensure that beef and leather in their supply chains is not a result of new forest clearings. Cattle and by-products shall only be supplied by farms who have formally committed to adopting a verifiable tracking system. However, some years later, many still have no monitoring systems.

Besides meat processing, JBS also operates in the leather segment and has 15 tannery units, with the capacity to process nearly 50 000 hides per day in Brazil. As the world's largest leather processor, it produces for the automotive, furniture, footwear and leather goods sectors. The non-transparent leather supply chain in Amazonia runs from the cattle ranches via JBS slaughterhouses and tanneries, frequently to the Lear Corporation in Atlanta/USA, one of the world's leading automotive technology companies in the seating sector with its high-quality leather production for car seats for the most important European manufacturers of high-priced cars.

429 In 2007, the number of cattle slaughtered in Amazônia Legal exceeded 10 million, which represented 41 % of the total slaughtered in Brazil that year.

430 Cf. chapter I.1.1.2; Kohlhepp (1979).

431 JBS-Friboi is the world's largest beef producer and global exporter of processed beef. JBS produces and sells beef through two business units: Friboi, in Brazil, and JBS USA Beef, present in the United States, Canada and Australia.

There were actually two agreements: in July 2009 a "term of adjustment of conduct" was signed, and in October 2009 a "zero deforestation agreement" (Fearnside 2017c). The companies also agreed not to buy cattle from ranches using slave labour or illegally occupying protected areas and Indigenous reserves. Land grabbing and land conflicts had to be rejected by the participants.

The agreements had a positive effect, despite problems with "laundering" cattle. "'Laundering' cattle occurs when a non-participating ranch moves its cattle to a participating ranch, from which the cattle are sold to one of the signatory slaughterhouses" (Gibbs *et al.* 2016, 39).

Under the "cattle agreement," "progress has been made on monitoring direct suppliers for deforestation, but broader impacts on forest conservation have lagged behind" (Skidmore *et al.* 2021, n. p.).

With less than one head per ha, cattle ranching has low productivity and, overall, a small local benefit. However, very low production costs and low variability in prices seems to guarantee safe returns in cattle ranching for smallholders to large farmers and agribusiness companies (Skidmore *et al.* 2021).[432] Success of cattle farming in Amazonia is only ensured by the expansion of forest clearing for pastures. This makes it difficult to convince cattle ranchers of zero-deforestation, especially those who do not comply with the cattle moratorium and engage in "cattle laundering."

There were significant shortcomings to the existing cattle agreements. Hundreds of thousands of cattle continue grazing on areas which should have been excluded from the cattle supply chain in Amazônia Legal. This demonstrated the importance of organising new systems for monitoring cattle supply chains in remote areas of the Amazon region (Klingler *et al.* 2018).

The failure of the "cattle agreement" motivated Greenpeace to withdraw from the agreement in 2017 and to renew its campaign to boycott Brazilian beef. This was a challenge for the three largest packaging companies to move their self-imposed deadline for eliminating illegal deforestation back from 2035 to 2025.

Nearly 90 % of the timber industry in the Amazon region had been illegal already under previous governments. Questionable statements by top Bolsonaro government officials on environmental issues, budget and job cuts at IBAMA leading to a decrease in regulatory inspections and reduced or no longer imposed penalties for environmental crimes characterised the situation. Thus, IBAMA, which had previously struggled with a shortage of funds, was almost completely deprived of its function. For example, the forest law that stipulates the preservation of 80 % of the forest area per plot in Amazonia was on the brink of collapse because it could not be implemented.

The state of Mato Grosso, where agribusiness with soybean cultivation and huge cattle ranches dominate the economy, wanted to escape the Forest Code, which requires a "legal reserve" of native forests of 80 % for any private property with forest in Amazônia Legal. A bill introduced in the National Congress in 2022 provided that Mato Grosso would leave the Amazônia Legal planning region and thus only need to

432 Small farmers are increasingly opting for livestock farming. This is profitable due to the low-interest loans granted for dairy farming and the transfer payments from the bolsa-família programme (Pereira, R. *et al.* 2016). In areas with rising land prices, smallholders often sell their land to land speculators or larger landowners and move to new forest frontiers, where they acquire larger plots and restart the land rotation system.

maintain a legal reserve of 20 % as is fixed in forest and *cerrado* areas outside Amazônia Legal (Ribeiro *et al.* 2022). This would then allow huge areas to be legally cleared. The bill prepared under the Bolsonaro government will certainly also cause problems for the government of its successor.

The very well-located mafia-like criminal networks that dominate illegal logging and timber trade could violently secure their influence with their own militias almost undisturbed. Cattle ranchers realised illegal deforestation to a very high degree. Violence and death threats prevented complaints from civil society or posed a very high risk. Even state employees were often openly threatened. The selective logging of hardwood, very sought after on the international markets, is not only lucrative (1 m^3: about US$ 500 in 2019) but a very small, sometimes punctual clearing is unfortunately hardly visible and detectable even by satellite images.

Figure 40. Total deforestation in the Brazilian Amazônia Legal until 2021

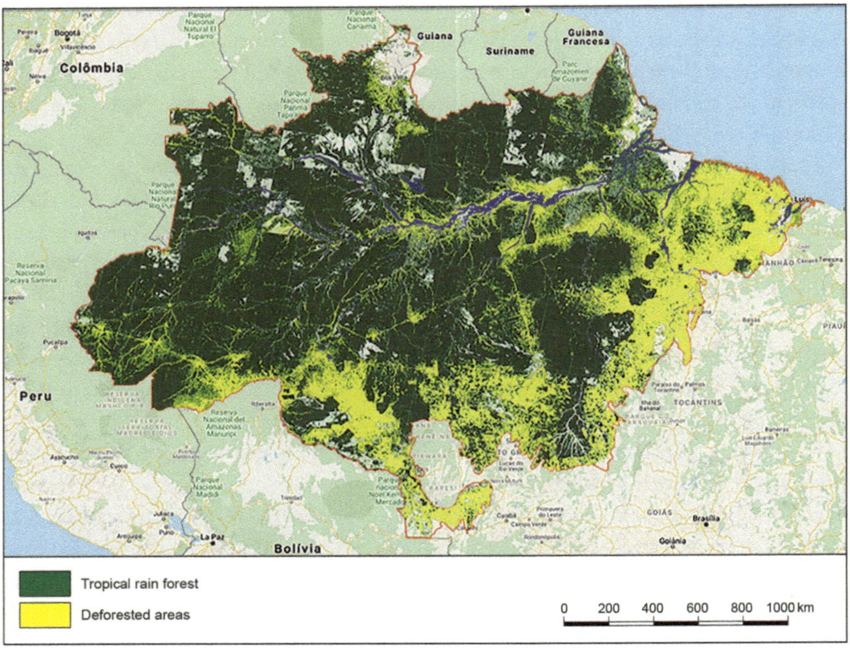

Source: Terra Brasilis/PRODES/INPE.

By bribery and falsification of documents, logging and slash-and-burn activities for cattle ranches were "legalised" as well as – unfortunately almost traditionally – land titles illegally acquired (*grilagem*) (Torres *et al.* 2017). These crimes, which lead to social tensions and violent conflicts over land and natural resources, and which had recently increased considerably, can only be combated with improved governance and legal presence on the ground. However, this was hardly or only inadmissibly taking place during the Bolsonaro government. Affected residents even spoke of a *carte blanche* for forest destruction. Uncontrolled activities of several hundred thousand gold and diamond prospectors (*garimpeiros*) contributed in large parts of Amazônia Legal to environmental damage and violation of legally defined boundaries of Indigenous territories, of ecological corridors or other protected areas. All this led to the fact that earlier positive results under the Pilot Programme (PPG7)[433] were not continued accordingly. Since the 1990s, very many so-called sustainable experiments could not be implemented for the benefit of the local population and their vision of a sustainable regional development of Amazonia. However, in the 2010s, Mato Grosso was a pioneer in testing innovative governance models to promote an integrated model characterised by a better balance between environmental protection and social and economic considerations (Mello-Théry 2016; Arvor *et al.* 2018).

The overall picture of deforestation in Amazônia Legal highlights the problem of the destruction of large parts of the Amazon ecosystems. The eastern areas of the planning region, especially in Maranhão and Pará, are largely deforested. Very clearly, the deforested areas along the eastern section of the Transamazônica and in the Terra do Meio stand out. Forest destruction in North Mato Grosso is very advanced and the development axis of BR-163 shows a strong expansion of economic activities.[434]

The central section of the Transamazônica is not yet strongly integrated into the economic process of large-scale deforestation. On the other hand, the huge deforestation in Rondônia shows economic activities of agrarian colonisation and expanding ranching that increasingly affect the state of Acre.

The tropical rain forest areas west of the Rio Madeira must be preserved at all costs. This will be a task for future governments. So far, north of the Rio Solimões/Amazonas mainly mining companies have acted selectively but the massively occurring *garimpeiros* are responsible in the state of Roraima for widespread deforestation and destruction of the habitat of the Yanomami.

433 Cf. chapter II.2.

434 See chapters II.4.2; II.4.4; II.5.2. Scholz *et al.* (2003); Scholz (2005); IAG (2004a); UNEP (2006); Fearnside (2007); Passos (2007; 2019; 2022); Coy and Neuburger (2008); Kohlhepp and Coy (2010); Coy and Klingler (2014); Klingler and Mack (2020); Klingler (2022).

3. The ecological impacts of deforestation and problems of climate change

Forests act as a carbon sink because trees absorb CO_2 from the atmosphere through the process of photosynthesis. CO_2 is stored in the rain forest trees' trunks, leaves, and roots. The Amazonian ecosystems store an estimated 150 to 200 billion tons of carbon. From 2003 to 2019, gross carbon loss from Brazilian Amazonia totalled 3.04 billion tons of carbon. A high amount of these CO_2 emissions is attributed to deforestation (56 %), the rest of 44 % due to forest degradation and other human-based activities (Kruid *et al.* 2021; Nobre *et al.* 2016).

Recent scientific studies reveal that parts of the Amazon region now emit more CO_2 into the atmosphere than they absorb (Gatti *et al.* 2021; Harris *et al.* 2021). The Brazilian Amazonia has been transformed from a CO_2 sink to a source for new emissions over the past two decades, whereas the total Amazon biome is still a net carbon sink. It removed about 1.7 billion metric tons of CO_2 equivalent (eq.) more than it emitted. But the Brazilian portion of the Amazonian rain forests, which covers about 60 % of the total Amazonian biome, emitted 3.6 billion metric tons of CO_2 eq. more than it sequestered (Gatti *et al.* 2021; Kruid *et al.* 2021). This means, that Brazilian Amazônia Legal has been transformed by deforestation into a net emitter of carbon dioxide with dangerous implications for regional climate change and global warming.

Protected areas and Indigenous territories are the exception and have been especially effective carbon sinks. They have proved their importance for overall conservation in the Amazon region as a bulwark against climate change (Kruid *et al.* 2021; Hirota *et al.* 2022). Unfortunately, deforestation in Indigenous territories and in conservation units of sustainable use increased in recent years (Santos *et al.*2021).

Cattle ranching is Brazil's largest source of greenhouse gas (GHG) emissions. Cattle methane (CH_4) emissions account for 17 % of all greenhouse gases released in the country (InfoAmazonia, 09.11.2021).

One source of GHG emissions are the numerous reservoirs of hydroelectric power plants in the Amazon region, which are often neglected in the calculation. Hydroelectric plants are often presented as "green energy," which means an energy source without GHG emissions. However, reservoirs emit GHG in various forms by decay of forest biomass. The emissions vary according to the geographical location, and the characteristics of the reservoir, such as flow, water replacement time, area, and water level fluctuations. Methane emissions of hydroelectric reservoirs contribute to global warming. Methane is formed when organic matter decomposes without oxygen present, for example, at the bottom of a reservoir.[435] Furthermore, Amazonian wetlands release 6–8 % of global methane emissions (Nobre *et al.* 2021, Message 4).[436]

Brazil's commitment in Paris 2015 (COP 21[437]) referred to zero "illegal" deforestation by 2030 and to the goal of bringing global warming below the 2°C mark and down to 1.5°C if possible.

However, forest clearing can continue as long as it is "legal". The Rural Environmental Register (CAR) makes it easy to obtain permission for "legal" deforestation up to the limits of Brazil's current Forest Code (20 % in Amazonia). Since many properties still have little clearing, large amounts of "legal" deforestation can continue (Fearnside 2017c).

In 2018, Lovejoy and Nobre (2018; 2019) had already analysed two "tipping points" (deforestation with conversion of the rain forest into drier savannahs and global warming), which will be discussed later.[438] Finer[439] recently emphasised that another "tipping point" is the transformation of Brazilian Amazonia from carbon sink to carbon source of CO_2 emissions (Finer and Mamani 2021). This, of course, concerns Amazônia Legal as a whole, while there is a regional differentiation as mentioned above (Fig. 40) due to the strong spatial differences in deforestation.

For decades, scientists have pointed out the consequences of deforestation in the Amazon region.[440] In recent publications, the alarming situation of climate change has been repeatedly stated, to which deforestation contributes significantly. Trade winds from the Atlantic Ocean with high water temperatures are transporting enormous quantities of water vapour to Amazonia. The humidity falls back onto the forest as rain. The forest returns rainwater to the atmosphere in the form of water vapour. A single tree is capable of sending in the atmosphere up to 1000 liters a day. Antônio Nobre (INPE) has calculated the total amount of water released into the atmosphere every day by the rain forest at around 20 billion tonnes. Air currents at an altitude of approximately 3 km carry the humidity across Amazonia and toward the Andes, which act as a natural barrier with high precipitation rates on the eastern slopes, but redirect the huge vapour masses southwards toward the Midwest, south Brazil and Argentina.

These air currents are popularly known as "flying rivers", i.e. they are "atmospheric waterways" consisting of air masses filled with water vapour. Without "flying rivers,"

---

435 Fearnside (1997b; 2002; 2005; 2013a; 2016, among others) has been studying this issue intensively for many years.

436 In 2021, according to ourworldindata.org the share of total Brazilian methane emissions (588.7 million tons; 57 % from agriculture) amounted to 5.7 % on global methane emissions (https://ourworldindata.org/carbon-deforestation-trade; accessed April 22, 2023).

437 COP is the acronym for "Conference of the Parties" to the United Nations Framework Convention on Climate Change (UNFCCC).

438 "A 'tipping point' is the point at which a small change to a stressor or ecosystem state causes the whole ecosystem to shift abruptly to an alternative state, accelerated by amplifying (or self-reinforcing) feedback mechanisms." This may cause systemic collapse (Hirota *et al.* 2022, n. p.).

439 The study was published by the Monitoring of the Andean Amazon Project (MAAP), an initiative of the US-based non-profit Amazon Conservation Association.

440 Among the early publications are: Sioli (1956; 1968; 1973; 1984; 1985); Goodland and Irwin (1975); Nobre *et al.* (1991); Fearnside (1982; 1990; 1997a), among others. In 2021, during COP 26 in Glasgow, renowned scientists launched a new initiative, the *Amazon Assessment Report 2021* (Nobre *et al.* 2021), which emphasised the importance of the Amazon region as a key element of the Earth's climate system and the risk of environmental collapse for the region (Hirota *et al.* 2022).

much of southern Brazil would be a dry zone or even a desert as in comparable latitudes worldwide. Deforestation and expansion of agriculture and cattle farming in the Amazon region will cause loss of ecoservices and negative impacts with reduced rainfall for agribusiness in the South. The hydrological cycle of the Amazon region depends on the transpiration of the forest's biomass and on the evaporation from the surfaces of the rain forest.

> When it rains on the Amazonian forest landscape, at least 75% of the moisture is returned to the westward-moving air mass. The rainforest recycles the moisture five to six times before it turns southward, feeling the proximity of the high wall of the Andes. Over the whole basin, the air rises, cools, and precipitates out close to 20% of the world's river water in the Amazon river system (Lovejoy and Nobre 2019, n. p.).[441]

Since more than 50% of rainwater runs off after deforestation and is no longer available for recycling, this leads to the basic question of how much deforestation rain forests can tolerate, until too little moisture not only threatens their existence but turns large parts of the rain forests into tropical savannahs?

The first model to analyse the "tipping point" for deforestation-generated degradation of the hydrological cycle (Sampaio *et al.* 2007) showed "that at about 40% deforestation, central, southern and eastern Amazonia would experience diminished rainfall and a lengthier dry season, predicting a shift to savannah vegetation to the east" (Lovejoy and Nobre 2018; 2019, n. p.).

Lovejoy and Nobre "believe that negative synergies between deforestation, climate change and widespread use of fire indicate a tipping point for the Amazon system to flip to non-forest ecosystems in eastern, southern and central Amazonia at 20–25% deforestation. [...] Today, we stand exactly in a moment of destiny: The tipping point is here, it is now" (Lovejoy and Nobre 2018, n.p.).

Since 19.9% of the original rain forest area in Amazonia has already been cleared by 2021 (Table 18; Fig. 38), this means that – if the research calculations of 20–25% are taken as a basis – a tipping point ("point of no return") from rain forest to degraded savannah is imminent or at least looms in the next few years. This would have serious negative consequences for climate and biodiversity throughout the region, which would be self-reinforcing and also have global climatic impacts.

Another tipping point is global warming.[442] Climate change has an impact on the hydrological cycle. In the absence of other contributing factors, 4°C of temperature increase in the Amazon region would be the tipping point to degraded savannahs in most of central, southern, and eastern Amazonia (Nobre *et al.* 2016).[443] Exceptional

---

441 Up to 50% of the precipitation within the Amazon basin is regionally recycled. The discharge of the Amazon river supplies 16 to 22% of the world's total river input into the oceans (Nobre *et al.* 2021, Message 3). https://www.environment.co.za/world-environmental-issues-news/a-flying-river-how-the-amazon-forest-produces-the-largest-flying-river-in-the-world.html (accessed May 23, 2024).

442 The Intergovernmental Panel on Climate Change (IPCC) 2022 report "leaves no doubt about the urgency to dramatically cut emissions; to stay on track to limit earth's warming to 1.5°C. GHG emissions need to be cut by 45% by 2030, compared to 2019 levels" (IPCC 2022).

443 In the last 60 years, warming in the Amazon region was about 1°C. Temperature increase was more pronounced in the last three decades and in deforested areas, such as pastures, during the dry season with up to 1.5°C.

heat waves in Amazonia are becoming more frequent. The number of days with temperatures above 35°C will increase, climate models show between 60 and 150 days more per year by the end of the century. Heat stress increases bacterial infestation and degrades water quality, threatening Amazonian fish, whose existence requires rain forest protection.[444]

Forests maintain an evapotranspiration[445] rate year-round, whereas evapotranspiration in pastures is dramatically lower in the dry season. The contribution of dry season evapotranspiration to rainfall in south-eastern South America is important. When evapotranspiration exceeds precipitation, the result is a water deficit in the forests. (Lovejoy and Nobre 2018). Large-scale forest fires lead to drying of surrounding forest and cause a greater vulnerability to fire in the following year.

The hope for a continuation of the strong decline in deforestation between 2005 and 2019 (-84 %) has unfortunately not been fulfilled and has even turned into a very strong increase in forest destruction under the Bolsonaro government. All security and protection criteria such as better satellite monitoring, stricter laws and controls, moratoria on value chains (soybeans, meat), credit freezes in deforestation regions and the expansion of protected areas and Indigenous territories have been disregarded or deliberately not implemented.

When considering the climatic consequences of deforestation in Amazonia, climate variability, the intensity of extreme events such as droughts and floods and the length of the dry season are crucial factors. The average annual precipitation in Brazilian Amazonia is between more than 3000 mm in the west/northwest (absence of a dry season) and about 1700 mm in the south-eastern region, known as "arc of deforestation". In the south-east and south of Amazonia there is a distinct dry season with more than 4 months (monthly <100 mm) (Nobre *et al.* 2016). Large-scale deforestation could lead to a reduction in regional precipitation.

The variability of precipitation is influenced by fluctuations in sea surface temperatures of the tropical Pacific Ocean (El Niño Southern Oscillation, ENSO) and tropical Atlantic Ocean, which are higher than ever before. Severe droughts in the context of El Niño events have been known in Amazonia for a very long time and occurred in modern times e.g., in 1926, 1983, 1992, 1998, 2005, 2010 and 2015 especially in the central and eastern part (Meggers 1994).[446] Human-induced climate change is expected to make them even more common in the future.

A nine months' rainfall deficit during an El Niño event was reported in 1997/1998 (July/August 1997 to April/May 1998), ranging from 500 mm in Belém, 900 mm in Marabá to 1200 mm in Belterra on the Rio Tapajós in Central Amazonia (Nepstad *et al.* 1999; Kohlhepp 2001b, 172, and Fig. 4 and 6), compared with the cumulative amount of rainfall in "average" years. In Roraima, this drought was associated with huge forest and *campo cerrado* fires (Fig. 25). Temperature fluctuations in the Atlantic Ocean (warmer tropical North, cooler tropical South Atlantic) affect west and northwest

444 Webinário da Academia Brasileira de Ciências, Ed.42: Brasil e as mudanças climáticas: Novo relatório do IPCC; August 10, 2021 (www.abc.org.br/transmissão (PT).

445 Evapotranspiration is the sum of transpiration and evaporation, i.e., the evaporation of water from plant and animal life and from soil and water surfaces.

446 Cf. chapter II.3.2.

Amazonia and caused severe droughts. In 2010, about 3 million km^2 were affected (Nobre *et al.* 2016).

Extreme droughts (2005, 2010, 2015) and floods (2009, 2012, 2014) in the last two decades indicate that extreme events are becoming more frequent and are clear signs of climate change and "could well represent the first flickers of this ecological tipping point" (Lovejoy and Nobre 2018, n. p.).

This has now come true. Since May 2023, with the development of a strong El Niño, an unusually strong warming has been observed in the tropical Pacific as well as in the North Atlantic (2–4°C above average). The months of August, September and October are traditionally dry, with lows occurring in mid-October, but this year the situation has become much more severe. Apparently, cold fronts were prevented from arriving by a dry air bubble.[447]

At the beginning of October 2023, the level of the Solimões river dropped by 30 cm per day; the level of the Rio Negro, which is about 21 m in Manaus at this time, dropped to less than 15 m. This has severely affected shipping, especially regarding supplies to small towns and settlements in the tributary area. Supply to the Manaus Free Trade Zone was also affected. The drought impacted 500 000 people in the state of Amazonas. Many people had difficulties accessing food, drinking water and other important products. Nearly all municipalities depend on water transport. Most rural communities are highly dependent on navigation for their daily lives, to access urban centres and to transport agricultural production to the markets. Health and education services depend on navigation.[448]

Scheduled services on the Rio Solimoes/Amazonas were also affected. At least 90 % of the vessels operating on the state's 116 shipping lines were restricted in their activities. 50 % of the cargo capacity was affected and only 45 % of the total passenger numbers could be served.

This extreme drought was associated with a tremendous fish kill this year. Whether this is solely related to the high water temperature has not yet been clarified. Hundreds of dolphins also died. In Lake Tefé, 550 km above Manaus on the Solimões river in the western state of Amazonas, a water temperature of 39°C was measured, which exceeded the long-term average by approx. 8°C according to the Mamirauá Institute for Sustainable Development.[449]

Manaus has been suffering from another problem associated with the drought: smoke from forest fires. In September 2023, the state of Amazonas had the second highest number of fire outbreaks for the month.

The heavy rainfall in southern Brazil and the increasing drought in the Northeast are further consequences of El Niño.

Lengthening of the dry season (about one week per decade so far) is associated with a later onset of the rainy season in southern Amazonia. This of course also lengthens the duration of the fire season with the corresponding forest losses and is increasing the risk of wildfires. This is particularly the case in southern and south-eastern Ama-

447 https://apublica.org/2023/10/aquecimento-anormal-do-atlantico-agrava-seca-na-amazonia-e-traz--riscos-imprevisiveis/ (accessed October 4, 2023).

448 https://g1.globo.com/meio-ambiente/noticia/2023/10/03/seca-extrema-pode-ter-agravado-desmoronamento-que-engoliu-vila-no-interior-do-amazonas-entenda.ghtml (accessed October 4, 2023).

449 See footnote 447.

zonia, where the intensity of human activities and their impacts is particularly high in the "arc of deforestation" in the border region of rain forest, the transition forest *cerradão* and the *campos cerrados*. Here, "savannisation," i.e., the transition from rain forest to savannah, is particularly to be expected in 30 to 50 % of the Amazon basin, as tropical forests cannot tolerate a dry season longer than 4 months and rainfall below 1800 mm/year (Nobre *et al.* 2016; Hirota *et al.* 2022).[450]

Regional climate change due to large-scale deforestation and the effects of forest fires make tropical rain forests more vulnerable. A substantial reduction of over 60 % in the Amazonian forest area by 2050 must be expected according to all new model calculations (Nobre *et al.* 2021, chapter 23).

The ever-increasing penetration of the Amazon rain forests by human-induced economic activities is leading to a relatively little-discussed topic, which was surprising in times of the Covid-19 pandemic. Increased human interaction with animals (bats, monkeys, mosquitoes) in newly incorporated forest areas increases the chances of a "virulent virus" or bacteria that jumps from one species to another.[451] According to the Instituto Evandro Chagas (Belém), of the 220 different types of viruses in the Amazon region, 15 have the potential to cause epidemics.

Reducing deforestation mitigates emissions of greenhouse gases. At the 2015 COP 21 in Paris, Brazil committed to 12 million ha of reforestation by 2030. This commitment, which would mean a protective wall against the Amazon tipping point (Lovejoy and Nobre 2018), has not yet been fulfilled.

---

450 According to Hirota *et al.* (2021, n. p.), there are four potential tipping points that Amazonian forests could shift to: "1) a closed-canopy seasonally dry tropical forest state; 2) a native savannah state; 3) an open-canopy degraded state; 4) a closed-canopy secondary forest state." Hirota *et al.* (2021) consider the occurrence of numbers 3 and 4 more likely over large areas, particularly in the "arc of deforestation."

451 Kohlhepp (2020a): Scientific research results of Adalberto Luís Val, INPA. Cf. Ferrante *et al.* (2021).

4. Threats to the Indigenous population and their habitats in Amazonia

According to the Brazilian Constitution, the government is obliged to establish and protect Indigenous territories in which the Indigenous population traditionally lives. The demarcation of Indigenous territories (TI: formerly called "reservations") was always controversially discussed in Brazil but was successfully promoted above all by the PPG7 programme, which supported the difficult work of FUNAI. This agency is responsible for the Indigenous population, identifying settlement areas, defining the boundaries of protected areas, and even legal registering. As already mentioned, the Indigenous territories amount to 22.3 % of the 5.2 million km^2 of the area of the planning region Amazônia Legal.

President Bolsonaro stated that not a single inch of land will be demarcated for Indigenous peoples and that both the protected areas for natural ecosystems as well as Indigenous lands should be open to agriculture and mining. "The 'agenda of death' included the abolition of legal reserves and the opening of conservation units and Indigenous lands to mining, agriculture, and livestock" (Ferrante and Fearnside 2019, n. p.; Rorato *et al.* 2020).[452] Bolsonaro fulfilled his commitment made during the 2018 election campaign: not to demarcate or homologate land for Indigenous peoples. No demarcation process – of the 248 underway at FUNAI – had been completed.

The Bolsonaro government that saw the Indigenous population as an obstacle to economic growth – this was last heard during the military dictatorship in the 1970s – has allowed the use of these Indigenous lands by timber trade and mining companies (Vilani *et al.* 2022; Ferrante and Fearnside 2022). The responsibility of demarcation of Indigenous territories was transferred to the Ministry of Agriculture, in favour of agribusiness. The withdrawal of the jurisdiction of the Ministry of Justice for FUNAI was reversed by the Congress in May 2019, but the FUNAI president had been dismissed.

Boundary definitions of the protected areas are not only called into question, but the well-known argumentation of the "zoo effect of reservations" was cleverly advanced in order to discredit secure borders. Invasions of Indigenous territories, death threats and violence in the face of resistance from those affected were increasing considerably, especially in the "arc of deforestation" and in the state of Roraima.

The Indigenous peoples were afflicted by many threats and attacks which, in various intensities, make their daily lives a major struggle for survival: Deforestation, forest degradation, fires, gold mining, expansion of croplands, pastures, and the

452 Cf. chapter II.7.2, Table 17 in this volume: Approved Indigenous territories: Bolsonaro government (2019–2022): 0.

excessive advancing of infrastructural projects, particularly new roads. The threats related to forest loss were more intense in the buffer zones of the Indigenous territories than within, proving that these territories effectively promote environmental preservation.

There were no surveillance actions for combating illegal deforestation or removing invaders. During the pandemic, the government had cut the budgets of the environmental control agency to such an extent that the 250 employees were unable to monitor many thousands of mostly illegal mining sites. The environmental budget amounted to less than 1% of the state budget. Illegal mining has exploded in the Amazon region in recent decades. Between 1985 and 2020 the area mined in Brazil grew six times to a total of 206 000 ha, more than 70% of it in the Amazonian rain forests. *Garimpeiro* activities in gold mining (94% in Amazonia) surpassed the area associated with industrial mining in 2020.[453]

The Indigenous peoples rights were deliberately not guaranteed. In the future, only areas where Indigenous peoples already lived in 1988 can be declared Indigenous territories.[454] Indigenous lands are key factors in conservation because they protect more than 22% of the Brazilian Amazônia Legal (Ferrante and Fearnside 2019). The transfer of the responsibility of demarcation from the Ministry of Justice to a new Ministry of Women, Family and Human Rights, headed by another controversial minister, left a weak FUNAI.

In the twisted logic of the president and his advisers, all the activities to establish Indigenous territories have been attributed to the influence of international NGOs which, as the spearhead of foreign governments, are only out to harm the export success of Brazilian agribusiness for competitive reasons. Even at his speech at the United Nations, Bolsonaro stated that "some people, from inside and outside Brazil, supported by NGOs, insist on treating and maintaining our Indians as true cavemen" (Phillips 2021, n. p.).

There was a clear strategy of Bolsonaro's government to convince society of the absence of isolated peoples and denouncing their existence as an invention of anthropologists. The dismantled FUNAI was an accomplice. This legitimised the final opening of traditional Indigenous territories to squatters, landowners and loggers (Verdum 2022).

All these problems also occurred with homologated territories, e.g., in the case of the Yanomami whose territory was already attacked in the late 1980s by gold seekers who settled in numerous places for prospecting and also created their own landing sites for small aircraft.[455] During the Bolsonaro government, *garimpeiros* had free access to these territories where more than 20 000 gold prospectors with armed militia worked with the support of the federal and the state governments. Many gold miners work as loggers when the price of gold drops but will shift to gold mining when prices rise. Illegal clearing of forests, contamination of water courses with mercury, toxic to fish and affecting the health of Indigenous peoples severely, and increase of malnutrition were registered by NGOs. The mercury used to leach the gold causes water pollution, accumulates in the food chain and causes serious neurological damage.

---

453 https://mapbiomas.org/ (accessed February 28, 2023).

454 Cf. chapters I.6.1 and IV.2.

455 Cf. chapter I.3.2.2 and Fig. 10 in this volume.

In some Yanomami villages, 92 % of the inhabitants are contaminated with mercury (Prinz 2021; Wenzel 2021).

The *garimpeiros* moved there violently without any concern for the Indigenous inhabitants, who were not only threatened, but also chased away and, in a direct confrontation, killed. Diseases from outside and sexual abuse of Indigenous women were other main problems. The Covid-19 pandemic facilitated invasions into Indigenous territories; illegal miners penetrated unhindered during the lockdown. "They dragged the virus to the furthest corners of the forest. At the same time used their gold to buy the vaccinations intended for the Indigenous people" (Prinz 2021, n. p.). The infection and mortality rate among the Indigenous population was far higher than in the rest of Brazil. The Covid-19 pandemic is a devastating zoonosis that shows that biodiversity must be preserved at all costs (Nobre 2020). "[T]he pandemic and the militarisation of Brazil's environmental protection have served as smokescreens to weaken environmental protections and have also put Brazil's Indigenous people at risk and violated their rights" (Ferrante and Fearnside 2020, 258). The vulnerability of Indigenous groups has increased sharply because of failing provisions against Covid-19, such as vaccination.

Garimpeiros leave behind a crater landscape, in recent years they acquired suction dredgers and other heavy machinery, speedboats, small aircraft, and recently automatic weapons.

Meanwhile, with the appearance of the drug mafia,[456] gold exploitation has reached a new dimension. Lack of inspections, impunity and links with politics were attracting organised crime.[457] The PCC (First Command of the Capital) is a dreaded drug mafia from São Paulo, now apparently operating in the area of the Alto Parima in Roraima and tyrannising the Yanomami villages. They threaten not only the Indigenous population, but also the *garimpeiros*: For about three years, the PCC has now dominated gold production in Roraima. They even control access to the rivers and charge fees. Since "the government doesn't regulate the purchase of gold, the *garimpeiros* have no one to sell it to and end up being lured by these criminals and traffickers" (Prinz 2021, n. p.).

The fact that organised crime is now also involved in gold mining makes the problems all the bigger (Reuters, 18.08.2022). Gold is attractive to the mafia mainly because it allows to launder money from drug or arms deals. The gold illegally mined on Yanomami territory reaches the global gold market without major problems. It is sold in the neighbouring countries of Venezuela, Suriname and French Guiana or in the small shops of the Rua do Oro, the "Gold Street", in Boa Vista, the capital of Roraima, without authorisation from the Central Bank (Prinz 2021). In 2020, almost 30 % of the 174 tons of gold production in Brazil was sold irregularly. This amounts to US$ 1.8 billion of potentially illegal gold, more than three times the Ministry of Environment's 2020 budget (Wenzel 2021).

There is alarming concern about increasing violence and links between drug traffickers and environmental crimes such as illegal logging, fishing and mining in the rain forest. Obviously, ties are existing between the major cocaine trafficking organisation

---

456 On drug trafficking in Amazonia see also: Machado (2002; 2007; 2009); Schönenberg (2002a; 2002b; 2010); among others.

457 Informations based on the network Amazônia Real. The independent and investigative journalism agency Amazônia Real is part of a global network of more than 200 news outlets.

PCC and wildcat gold miners. Less stringent controls make criminal environmental activities attractive for drug gangs as a means of laundering drug money. Cross-border criminal groups in the Javari region are buying up local river fish to launder drug funds. Visitors travelling in this region are at high risk, some have been killed. The homicide rate in the Brazilian Amazon region rose by 62 % in 2021, whereas the overall rate for Brazil fell by 9 % (Fabio 2022).

Since the mid-1990s, transport routes of drug trafficking have increasingly spread from the cocaine production areas in Colombia, Peru, and Bolivia to the southern route via Paraguay or via the Brazilian Amazon region. According to Europol, 45 tons of cocaine from Brazil worth more than € 1 billion were seized in Europe in 2020.[458] In recent times, drug smugglers have switched to transport by small aircraft, using numerous hidden landing sites in the rain forest on the way to Europe via Guyana and Suriname, without being detected by radar. However, the small unpaved runways are visible in aerial photographs and satellite imagery. Sometimes, however, this was "overlooked" by the control bodies.

In addition to the Yanomami in Roraima, the Mundurukú and Kayapó in Pará, the Karipuna and Uru-Eu-Wau-Wau in Rondônia and the Guajajára in Maranhão are affected by the new gold rush. The Munduruku Indigenous territory has been under intense attack, when heavily armed *garimpeiros* with air support from helicopters invaded the territory, attacked the houses of Indigenous leaders and a federal security force base that had been established there to fight the criminals (Wenzel 2021). Some of the Munduruku people have been recruited as paid workers by the *garimpeiros*.

Hundreds of illegal mining dredges are concentrated on the Rio Madeira, creating a floating city. The miners count on the support of businessmen and politicians who have been promoting this illegal activity for many years and illegal miners feel empowered to carry on with little concern. At times, the Federal Police and IBAMA destroyed some rafts located in the Rio Madeira, but many miners escaped with their equipment.

In general, in Amazônia Legal, the official control and security measures on site have been greatly reduced through job cuts. Indigenous leaders took a stand against the invasions of Indigenous territories and called the government's projects as "genocide, ethnocide, and ecocide" and an "open declaration of war against the native population."[459]

The repeatedly cited comparison of the population density between Indigenous territories – 520 000 people living there in 2012[460] – and regions of the rest of Brazil is nonsensical. The demand for land of groups operating in shifting cultivation which, however, only create small areas of deforestation for self-sufficiency and after a few years migrate on to an ecologically more favourable location, is much higher than in other regions of the country. The protection of rain forests by Indigenous peoples is of paramount importance.

The Amazon Synod, which met in Rome in October 2019 under the leadership of Pope Francis, dealt not only with central ecclesiastical topics but also with "holistic ecology." The environmental problems in the Amazon region, their social consequences as well as the protection of the habitat of Indigenous peoples were discussed in partic-

458 David Klaubert, *FAZ*, March 11, 2023.

459 Documents of ISA (Instituto SocioAmbiental) and *The Guardian*; Kohlhepp (2021b).

460 Information of ISA in 2019.

ular. In view of the conflict-laden situation in Amazonia, which also threatens church representatives – the case of Bishop Kraeutler of the diocese of Xingu,[461] threatened with death, went through the world press – the Indigenous population hoped for support and pragmatic help from the Catholic Church.

The Intergovernmental Panel on Climate Change (IPCC) and the Intergovernmental Platform on Biodiversity and Ecosystem Services (IPBES) agree unequivocally that the climate crisis and the loss of biodiversity are problems of the highest order. According to the IPBES, the sustainable use of wild plants and animals and the preservation of stable ecosystems are the most important factors to stop species extinction and the loss of natural habitats (IPBES 2019).

Indigenous peoples are the guardians of ecosystems that store large amounts of carbon. At the UN Climate Summit in Glasgow 2021 (COP 26), the Indigenous were the focus of a UN environment conference for the first time. Tropical rain forests protected by Indigenous groups are very strong carbon sinks, crucial for climate protection, with 80 % of the remaining biodiversity worldwide. In Glasgow, public and private sectors pledged US$ 19 billion to stop tropical deforestation to fight climate change and protect biodiversity. 141 countries, including Brazil, have signed a declaration to respect the land rights of Indigenous peoples. However, the wording "in accordance with national legislation" raised many doubts about the practical implementation of these proposals (Seligmann 2021).

461 Cf. chapter II.6.1.

5. Disagreements between donor countries and the Bolsonaro government regarding the Amazon Fund

Governors of Amazonian states, who also informed the Amazon Synod about the current situation, had spoken out against the Amazonian policy of the Brazilian federal government and its rejection of offered foreign financial aid, which was urgently needed in the region. The governors were prepared to negotiate direct aid with international donors. This would be complicated but could offer new opportunities through a regional bank independent of the central government.

Objectives of the Amazon Fund are the reduction of CO_2 emissions caused by slash-and-burn agriculture, reforestation, promotion of sustainable agroforestry, environmental management and safeguarding of human rights in Indigenous protected areas as well as financial support of the important environmental register. The Amazon Fund is the largest financial instrument to support REDD+ actions in the tropics. Since 2008, it has raised around US$ 1.3 billion in promised donations from bilateral agreements. The situation was good as long as the projects approved under the Amazon Fund were aligned with national policies to reduce deforestation and emissions, such as PPCDAm, and ENREDD+ (Jordão 2022, 204; van der Hoff *et al.* 2018).

From a geopolitical perspective, the Amazon Fund's creation and consolidation strengthened Brazil's international position as a country with political leadership and technical ability to control deforestation and promote sustainable land use. The Fund's resources allocated to government agencies became one of the only sources of financing strategies to control deforestation.[462]

Environment Minister Salles caused great embarrassment to the backers of the Amazon Fund (Norway contributes 94 %, Germany 5 % of the funds) by criticising the project's management model. "Without filing any complaints or irregularities, Salles ended up triggering a diplomatic incident" (Trigueiro 2019, n. p.). Norway and Germany considered the governance of the Amazon Fund exemplary and also praised the BNDES mediation, transparency and the concrete results of the 103 projects funded so far. Salles wanted to change the Amazon Fund Advisory Committee by raising government participation and using part of the funds given to pay compensation to landowners located illegally within conservation units, which is contrary to the Fund's rules. In order to change the composition of the decision-making body for the allocation of funds at the National Development Bank (BNDES) to the detriment of NGOs, Salles

462 It was mentioned by NGOs that it could take a long time to get a project approved and accessing funds could be quite bureaucratic and required more organised administrative and accountability systems (Jordão 2022, 205).

had dissolved the body. The Bolsonaro government definitely wanted to change the objectives of the Fund. Of course, the donor countries did not agree to changing the committee and misappropriating the Fund.

The main donor countries of the Amazon Fund, Norway and Germany, had pledged funds due to the deforestation situation – the German Ministry of the Environment has also frozen funds for other forest protection projects for the time being. Bolsonaro responded with sarcastic formulations: "We don't need German funding" and "Germany wants to buy Amazonia," among others.

The Amazon Fund is regarded as the world's most successful financing initiative for rain forest conservation to date. Government projects (federal, state, environmental agencies, municipalities) received 60 % of the financial means. Important projects of non-governmental organisations of Indigenous people and scientific research were supported by the other funds, as well as the manifold advisory services of the German GIZ.[463]

Therefore, no projects could be approved under the Bolsonaro government. Even after talks between the German Minister for Economic Cooperation and Development (BMZ), Müller, and the Brazilian Environment Minister Salles, no solution was on the horizon. After numerous scandalous actions and statements by Salles and his statement in a cabinet meeting on how to circumvent the environmental laws in Amazonia, Salles disappeared from the scene.[464] From the point of view of the donor countries and the affected population, however, it is essential to continue promoting projects of the civil society that the Bolsonaro government wanted to marginalise.

463 GIZ (German Agency for International Cooperation). The main commissioning party is the German Federal Ministry for Economic Cooperation and Development (BMZ).

464 The head of the investigation of the Federal Police against illegal timber trade had reported Minister of Environment Salles, a hardliner in implementing Bolsonaro's anti-ecological strategies, for obstruction of environmental investigations, abuse of office and participation in a criminal organisation of illegal timber exports. Salles resigned in June 2021 (Compilation of press information).

6. The EU-Mercosur agreement failed under Bolsonaro's presidency

It was the aim of the free trade agreement between the EU and the Mercosur (Brazil, Argentina, Uruguay, Paraguay) to create a common market with more than 720 million people, 20% of the global gross domestic product and 17% of the worldwide exports. Internal trade barriers should be largely abolished, and extensive labour and environmental legislation implemented. The agreement signed in 2019 could not be ratified during Bolsonaro's government. In Europe, Bolsonaro's irresponsible environmental policy with the destruction of Amazonian rain forests after 2019 raised concerns that demand for soybeans and meat could encourage increased deforestation and invasions into Indigenous territories to expand the catchment area for logging and grazing pastures for cattle. The European opponents of the agreement were made up of the agricultural lobby, anti-globalisation and environmental activists and green parties (Nolte 2023). On the other hand, Brazilian farmers feared that European countries were pushing environmental criteria to protect their farmers from importing cheaper Brazilian agricultural products. The questioning of the ratification of the free trade agreement between the EU and the Mercosur confederation, in which Brazil is the largest player, was discussed by various EU states, including France, as a possible sanction.

The original goal of Mercosur as the most ambitious integration project in Latin America went far beyond mere trade policy, but also envisaged the creation of common institutions. The EU-Mercosur agreement had been negotiated for more than two decades without participation of large parts of the civil society in South America and Europe. The rivalry between the two major Mercosur partners Brazil and Argentina often played a slowing down, so that even after 30 years of existence, not even a full customs union has been achieved.

With the EU-Mercosur agreement, which was also likely to face coordination difficulties with Brazil within Mercosur due to the left-wing government in Argentina at the time, both sides saw great export opportunities for their different product range in view of the customs disputes between the US and China and in the future perhaps also with the EU. It became abundantly clear that possible economic sanctions against Brazil would not make the government's stance more environmentally friendly, but could at most strengthen its course domestically, although former Brazilian Environment Minister Ricúpero saw continued international pressure as effective for environmental policy changes.

Boycott threats against Brazilian products, which were hastily expressed in Europe, would not contribute to a change in the Amazonian policy of the government and were no stable solution to the problem (Kohlhepp 2021b). Measures that promote the preservation of biological diversity in the Amazonian rain forest and the safeguarding of the protected areas are needed. This requires environmental funds and financial instruments that make such a policy attractive for Brazilian politics and society (Maihold 2019b). However, a large northern Europe asset manager had withdrawn JBS, the largest exporter of meat operating supply chains in the Amazon region, from its investment portfolio. Probably, the boycott threats may have better contributed to Bolsonaro's fire brigade actions with the help of the army in the delayed firefighting.

Since China has been leading the Brazilian export statistics since 2009 (2021: China: 31.3 %; EU: 11.7 %; US: 11.2 %),[465] Brazil has safe alternatives for the purchase of its agricultural products and mineral raw materials.

In the case of the EU-Mercosur agreement, all parties involved had reservations and legitimate self-interests. Ecological reservations of the EU, especially against imports of Brazilian agricultural and livestock products, produced in areas of Amazonian rain forest destruction, were absolutely justified. About 20 % of Brazilian beef and soybean exports to the EU are related with illegal deforestation in the Amazon region and importers should be obliged to ensure that these products do not originate from these areas. To do this, the EU needs a supply chain law for meat and soybean from Brazil.[466] However, exaggerated EU expectations should not be used as a pretext to protect European agriculture.

The agreement could be of great geopolitical importance for both sides, especially since China is gaining more and more influence, and the EU is also dependent on the Mercosur states – the fifth largest economic area in the world – as democratic partners, and should take their specific problems into account. However, it was clear that there can be no trade agreement without binding human rights and environmental standards. Compliance to sustainable development, the participation of civil society and the implementation of the Paris Agreement were not guaranteed. Unfortunately, this was not possible in the desired sense under Bolsonaro. The agreement was virtually put on hold and threatened to disappear from the common agenda, but at least had a completely uncertain future (Grundberger *et al.* 2021; Wollrad and Barreto 2021; Maihold 2019a; 2020).

In a completely deadlocked and almost hopeless situation, it should be important to cultivate a multilateral culture of discussion on environmental issues between politicians and representatives of civil society, especially with the scientific community, which in many areas in Brazil is highly relevant to the tropical ecological problems on the ground.

In the discussion about the appropriate environmental policy for rain forest protection, it must be remembered that project offers for sustainable development have nothing to do with the "internationalisation of Amazonia" or interference in the internal affairs of the country, repeatedly conjured up by nationalists in Brazil.

Brazil's national sovereignty with regard to the Amazon region is beyond question. The projects are based on financial and technical assistance from donor countries

465 Quoted from de.statista.com 2023.

466 Interview with Delara Burkhardt and Nilto Tatto, IPG, July 30, 2020. https://www.ipg-journal.de/interviews/artikel/kein-handelsabkommen-ohne-umweltschutz-und-menschenrechte-4547/ (accessed October 22, 2023).

– without any required "consideration" – for the regional population and the preservation of their habitat, with additional global significance. The integration of neighbouring countries with an Amazon share in promoting mechanisms for rain forest protection within the framework of the long passive Amazon Pact, had been revived with the meeting of the heads of government of Bolivia, Brazil, Ecuador, Guyana, Colombia, Peru, and Surinam in September 2019 in Letícia, Colombia. However, the call for increased cooperation in combating illegal practices in mining, drug trafficking, logging and in the expansion of crops and pastures (Maihold 2019b) could put Bolsonaro's Amazon policy under pressure.

Bolsonaro's quest for a second term led many to fear that this could lead to a further erosion of democracy in Brazil. On the other hand, ex-President Lula da Silva was expected to return as a candidate in the 2022 election, after his conviction was legally overturned. For a "third way," which many Brazilians in this polarised country would have liked as a counterpoint to the two extremes, no promising candidate was recognisable (Czymmeck and Garcia 2022).

7. The situation of Amazônia Legal during the Bolsonaro Government and possible future perspectives

In Amazonia, there was a climate of violence and a weakening or absence of judiciary power. Ethical principles and environmental justice were ignored by the Bolsonaro government. There was no liability to protect this region and its Indigenous and neo-Brazilian rural populations. His mindless rejection of all major issues of climate change and the importance of tropical rain forests of Amazonia as greenhouse gas storage was not only internationally problematic for Brazil, but also contributed to squandering Brazil's ecological capital. Negative consequences of large-scale deforestation have been denied, important climate data withheld or ridiculed as an invention by misguided scientists who were against national progress. The manner in which Bolsonaro led the government divided the Brazilian society and radicalised supporters who were spurred on in their illegal actions in Amazonia. On social media, his clientele spread the crudest conspiracy theories and fake news.

The Brazilian government remained increasingly isolated internationally. The deliberately unsolved Amazon issue hampered international communication and Brazil's potential in the field of renewable energies and green hydrogen, which could open up close cooperation opportunities with the EU, remained untapped during his term of office. Even political relations with China – after all Brazil's main trading partner – were threatened by the activities of members of the government.

Bolsonaro's four-year term ended with a 60 % increase in Amazonian deforestation rates, the highest in a presidential term since 1988, when measurements by satellite imagery began. Intensification of agricultural and ranching activities in non-forest regions of the country could have prevented destruction of biodiversity in rain forests and the living space of native populations. However, Bolsonaro gave free access to all interested in ranching, crop cultivation, logging, and gold mining in Amazonia.

Amazonia had become a free space for all kinds of economic exploitation. All previous attempts to contribute to sustainable development in Amazonia through specific projects with participation of regional and local groups and communities have been negated and mostly discredited at national level during the Bolsonaro government. Even numerous cabinet reshuffles and significant concessions to the *Centrão*[467] have not helped Bolsonaro to secure his re-election.

467 In Brazilian politics, the *Centrão* ("big centre") refers to political parties that do not have a consistent ideological orientation and aim at ensuring proximity to the executive in order to guarantee advantages and allow them to distribute privileges through clientelist networks.

The lessons learned of the former rain forest protection programme PPG7 and other projects had not yet reached the responsible politicians of the central government in Brasília or were not used for ideological reasons. However, Brazil will continue to depend on international cooperation in the future and certainly does not want to endanger its image as a global player. The ecosystems of Amazonia, the regional and the global climate in the long term won't forgive a lack of understanding of the ecological and socio-economic necessities, a lack of environmental awareness and misguided action of politicians under the pressure of agribusiness and timber lobbies.

IV Epilogue

1. Hopes after the change of government in 2023: Lula da Silva as game changer?

1.1. Uncertainty and violence during run-off elections and change of government

With 49.1 % of the valid votes, Bolsonaro lost very narrowly against the former President Lula da Silva[468] (50.9 %) from the left workers' party and won far more votes (58.3 million) than had been predicted. In addition to the strong evangelical, fundamentally Christian electorate, the majority of which is devoted to Bolsonaro, people from the middle of society gave him their votes. In the rural South and Southeast and in southern Amazonia, the economically successful landowners, often descendants of former European immigrants, and the urban elite voted for Bolsonaro,[469] who was strongly supported by the military and police forces. In the narrow-minded mental map of the extended South, Bolsonaro represents the successful, manufacturing Brazil against Lula da Silva's "underdeveloped" Northeast, which depends on support from the rest of Brazil. A "third way" with other candidates, hoped for by many, proved unsuccessful.

The rainbow press described the election campaign of the two controversial main candidates as "plague against cholera." Thousands of radicalised supporters of the deselected President Bolsonaro demonstrated since the election against the result of the run-off election of October 30, 2022. Road blockades and truck drivers' strikes hampered long-distance traffic. In front of the military facilities, Bolsonaro's followers set up veritable camps in the vein hope of military intervention in their favour. As a former military officer, Bolsonaro as President had always praised the military dictatorship and filled many positions, even in the cabinet, with military personnel. The triple alliance of his followers of military, evangelical churches and neoliberal technocrats had a high mobilising capacity (Maihold 2022).

His supporters believed – and still believe – it was a stolen election without being able to present any evidence. They felt they were victims of a conspiracy since the release of Lula da Silva, who was originally convicted of corruption, and the annulment

468 The 77-year-old Lula da Silva, who was president from 2003 to 2010, also wanted to run against Bolsonaro in 2018, but was barred from the 2018 campaign by his conviction on corruption charges.

469 Presidential election results of October 30, 2022: Bolsonaro: South Brazil (58.9 %; Santa Catarina 69.3 %, Paraná 62.4 %); Mid-West (60.2 %; Mato Grosso 65.1 %); Amazônia Legal: Rondônia 70.7 %; Special situation in Roraima: 76.1 % (Venezuelan immigration problems; gold boom).

of the trials against him by the Supreme Court. The judge Sérgio Moro in the Lula da Silva trial, who had become Bolsonaro's justice minister, was declared biased.

Bolsonaro had systematically undermined confidence in the electoral process. Now he questioned his election defeat but there was no evidence of manipulation of the electronic voting system (Heuser 2022). The myth of electoral fraud persisted above all in the digital networks with fake news, conspiracy theories and taboo breaks. Mudslinging and vulgar insults characterised the election campaign. Bolsonaro refused to be present at the official change of office of the presidents on January 1, 2023, and travelled to Florida early. Since the change of government at the beginning of January, Bolsonaro no longer has political immunity.

After the official assumption of office by President Lula da Silva, radical and violent right-wing extremists among Bolsonaro's supporters devastated the Congress and the Supreme Court in Brasília on January 8, 2023. The security forces, whose chiefs stood by Bolsonaro, were conspicuously restrained.

Brazil's Supreme Electoral Court has barred Bolsonaro from holding public office until 2030 for his attacks on the electoral system. This means that he will not be able to run in the next presidential election in 2026.

Bolsonaro's government has caused an epochal break in Brazil's domestic and foreign policy, which will complicate the initial situation of President Lula da Silva (Maihold 2022; Winter 2022).

1.2. Lula da Silva's restart: Establishment of new ministries, environmental and Indigenous agencies, and reorganisation of Amazonian issues

For Lula da Silva, the renewed assumption of the presidency basically offers a favourable starting point: all decisions that are now taken, especially the revitalisation in the environmental policy and in the Amazonian issue, will now differ positively from the irresponsible policy of his predecessor. After four years of presidency under right-wing populist Bolsonaro, Lula da Silva promised a fundamental turnaround. Bolsonaro had dismantled environmental regulations and Indigenous rights during his term of office.

The new decisions, decrees, direct measures, and laws in preparation were welcomed not only by Lula da Silva's followers in Brazil but also by the international press and many governments worldwide. Some of these governments offered financial support for carrying out the new tasks. At the UN biodiversity conference in Montreal in December 2022, the governments agreed on ambitious new targets to protect nature. The European Union approved its strongest regulations on deforestation-free trade (Watts 2022).

However, it also immediately became clear that Lula da Silva would find a very difficult political situation in the Chamber of Deputies and especially in the Senate, with a strong faction of the agribusiness lobby trying to torpedo his plans. Hostility in Congress and from extractive industries will be permanent problems, as well as the very difficult budgetary situation. At the state level, only 10 of the 27 governors belong to the Lula camp. Even the governor of São Paulo, by far the most important state economically, is a former minister from Bolsonaro's cabinet. In addition, the splitting up of the Brazilian society is extremely problematic for the objectives of the new government, as a significant part of the Brazilian population continues to associate the current president with earlier allegations of corruption and, above all, with reservations about former high-ranking staff members of Lula da Silva.

The first weeks of his presidency show that Lula da Silva made some well-considered and politically extremely clever decisions. This applies in particular to the environment policy and the Amazon region, where he was able to rely on former ministers, advisors and NGOs experienced in the Amazonian issue, who did essential preparatory work for future decisions.

He devoted himself in particular to the strengthening of socio-environmental public policies and decided changes in the structure of government, the creation or recreation of new ministries, internal reorganisations, and redistribution of competences. It was his commitment to strengthen the protection of traditional peoples and combat deforestation and climate change.[470]

In forming a government, Lula da Silva is dependent on a many-party coalition and an alliance with parties of the centre. The 37 ministries of the new government (11 female ministers), 14 more than the government of his predecessor Bolsonaro, will further increase the existing budget deficit and limit the financial room for manoeuvre of the various departments.

As in his first two terms, Lula da Silva relies on his former Environment Minister Marina Silva, a Pentecostal evangelical. She had resigned during his government in 2008,[471] had later even put herself up as a presidential candidate of the Green Party, but – for some people surprisingly – she then was ready to take over this office again. She accepted the appointment as a minister, as the president stressed that he considers environmental and climate policy to be one of the most important priorities of his government. Together with Marina Silva, he participated in the Climate Change Conference COP 27 in Sharm El Sheikh in Egypt in November 2022, shortly after his victory in the run-off election.

Marina Silva is not only experienced in office and one of the internationally respected voices in the fight for environmental protection but has always represented her concerns with great perseverance and is well networked, especially in the NGO sector. However, as can be seen from the Brazilian press, she obviously has secured numerous promises from the president for her ministry. Just as between 2003 and 2008, she appointed João Paulo Capobianco, a renowned biologist and environmentalist, experienced in many environmental policy functions, as executive secretary of the Ministry.

Marina Silva's getting back to Lula da Silva in the last election was due to her strong opposition to the Bolsonaro government. As new Minister of the Environment and Climate Change, Marina Silva revoked acts of the previous government that placed obstacles in the judgement of environmental infractions assessed by IBAMA. She determined that the infraction notices must be public and made available on the internet. 50 % of the amounts collected in fines must be reverted to the National Environmental Fund (FNMA).[472]

She returned to the Ministry of the Environment with the mission of guaranteeing zero illegal deforestation in the Amazon by 2030 and recovering Brazil's leading role

---

470 https://www.socioambiental.org, February 1, 2023 (accessed March 4, 2023).

471 Cf. chapter II.5.1.

472 https://www.socioambiental.org, February 1, 2023 (accessed March 4, 2023).

in the environmental agenda. It is a challenge for her, recovering and reorganising IBAMA and ICMBio. "The reality is much worse than we expected, because we had a blackout," said Marina Silva in an interview with AFP[473] and stressed that the state was weakened and criminal groups had taken control in many places. It will thus be necessary to invest in sustainable public activities such as low-carbon agriculture, reforestation, the creation of protected areas, Indigenous lands and the establishment of a national climate risk authority.

Illegal deforestation must be punished more quickly and more severely. Marina Silva had already carried out punishments with business embargoes, credit withdrawal, blacklisting and fines during her first term of office.[474] The detection of illegal logging activities is much easier now because high-tech satellite monitoring can accurately identify where land is being cleared and who is the owner. There is less need to field visits on the ground. It is particularly important today to punish environmental offences quickly and without exceptions and to really collect the penalties.

The Brazilian Forestry Service is structurally reinserted and assumes the management of the Rural Environmental Registry (CAR), an adequate instrument for environmental planning and combating deforestation in rural properties. In addition, the ministry will deal with key agendas for the environmental issue, such as bioeconomy and sustainable use of ecosystems.

With the multitude of tasks facing Marina Silva and the pressure of the agricultural lobby being hostile to her, it is to be hoped that she will be able to reorganise this office with her earlier determination and implement her goals politically and in practice. She can be sure of international support. COP 30 in 2025 will be held in the Amazon region, in Belém.

With the creation of a new Ministry for Indigenous Peoples, President Lula da Silva has landed another surprise coup. He sent a special signal to the national and international public and, of course, especially to the Indigenous population of Brazil with the creation of the ministry led by an Indigenous woman, the federal deputy Sônia Guajajara (PSOL-SP),[475] an environmentalist and human rights activist. The milestone in national politics is Indigenous policy, instead of Indigenist policy. The appointment of Indigenous people to lead the policies of their interest demonstrates that "interests in the territories and other Indigenous rights will have to be dealt with directly, and not through agents or supposed guardians" (Santilli 2023, n.p.).

The ministry will resume the implementation of policies paralysed in the last four years by the Bolsonaro administration, such as the demarcation and protection of Indigenous lands and the National Policy for Territorial and Environmental Management of Indigenous Lands (PNGATI).[476] It was established in 2012, with the objective of ensuring and promoting the protection, recovery, conservation, and sustainable use of

473 *Agence France-Presse*, January 24, 2023.

474 See chapter II.5.1.; Nepstad *et al.* (2014); Nepstad and Shimada (2018).

475 She is a leader of the Guajajara Indigenous people in Maranhão, one of the largest Indigenous groups in Brazil. With the support of FUNAI she attended an agricultural boarding school, obtained a degree in literature, followed by postgraduate studies in special education. She is the coordinator of APIB (Articulation of the Indigenous peoples of Brazil), the national reference of the Indigenous movement in Brazil.

476 "PNGATI is one of the greatest advances in the autonomous and sustainable management of Indigenous territories" (Santilli 2023, n. p.).

natural resources in Indigenous territories to ensure the integrity of Indigenous assets and respecting their socio-cultural autonomy.

However, the new competences of the ministry are already being questioned in the majority conservative National Congress. For example, the designation of Indigenous territories will again be carried out by the Ministry of Justice. A bill that has now been resubmitted stipulates that the designation of new Indigenous territories will only take into account those areas that were demonstrably inhabited by Indigenous peoples when the new Constitution came into force in October 1988.[477] The law, formulated in 2007, is about the time framework (*marco temporal*) of territorial allocations to Indigenous peoples. The vehement protests of Indigenous peoples in May 2023 reject this, arguing that many Indigenous groups were driven from their ancestral lands and that the Constitution guarantees them the right to their ancestral territories. The law does not affect the territories currently recognised by law, but it does affect many territories still awaiting registration.

In September 2023, Brazil's Supreme Court voted against agribusiness-backed "marco temporal" (time marker) thesis, an attempt to prevent Indigenous communities from claiming land they did not physically occupy in 1988. The Court has rejected efforts to restrict native peoples' rights to reservations on their ancestral lands. In a specific case, the Brazilian Supreme Court ruled in favour of restoring territory to the Xokleng people in Santa Catarina/South Brazil, from which they were evicted. The ruling sets a precedent for hundreds of Indigenous land claims especially in the Amazon region and is expected to have widespread consequences for Indigenous land rights.[478]

Lula da Silva and the new Minister for Indigenous Peoples Guajajara already made an emergency visit to the Yanomami territory in the state of Roraima, to lead the government's response to the violence and the high level of Indigenous malnutrition. At the same time, it was urgently necessary to give a clear signal to the powerful miners' mafia that the current government will ensure the security of the Yanomami. The violent events in Roraima during Bolsonaro's presidency, which also had been observed in recent decades, were described by Lula da Silva as "genocide." The Brazilian government has launched – with the environmental protection agency IBAMA, the newly created Ministry for Indigenous Peoples and FUNAI – the long-awaited operation to drive tens of thousands of illegal miners from the country's largest Indigenous reserve, with special-forces, destroying machinery, small aircraft, generators and seizing weapons and boats, establishing a base along the Uraricoera river.

Illegal mining had been encouraged by the Bolsonaro government, even in Indigenous and other protected areas. Lula da Silva revoked the pro-mining decree of the previous government which had enabled connections of gold mining with organised crime.

The initial raids, arrests, and expulsions of *garimpeiros* sent a strong signal, but a long-term solution of these fundamental problems be necessary. This will take years and is much more complex because hundreds of illegal mining camps are scattered all over Amazonia and sometimes include co-opted Indigenous people (Watts 2022). Thousands of poor, unskilled people who were driven out of these lands now will need

477 Cf. chapters I.6.1. and III.4.

478 https://www.theguardian.com/world/2023/sep/21/brazil-supreme-court-Indigenous-land-rights-win (accessed September 23, 2023).

relocation and organised substantial support for starting a different life (Phillips 2023). But the main problem is that the *garimpeiros* expelled by the federal police and the military often return after a relatively short period of time.

Authorities extinct by the Bolsonaro government will be recreated, such as the National Council for Indigenous Policy (CNPI), a collegiate body that guarantees social participation in the formulation of public policies for Indigenous peoples (Pereira and Mortari 2022).

FUNAI, subordinated to the new Ministry of Indigenous Peoples, will now be called the National Foundation for Indigenous Peoples, a request from native peoples leaders (Mendes 2023), and will be chaired for the first time by an Indigenous woman, former federal deputy of Roraima and lawyer Joênia Wapichana.[479] This is a major change in Brazilian indigenist policy. The last four years of FUNAI – led by military personnel and managers with no experience in public policies for Indigenous peoples – have been marked by setbacks for the Indigenous peoples and their territories. FUNAI had faced lacking resources, disorganization, and the complete absence of demarcations of Indigenous lands. In addition, FUNAI employees were often threatened with death by *pistoleiros* of large landowners.

Ordinances for the creation of work groups for the demarcation of territories, a work group to monitor the situation of the Yanomami people and restriction ordinances of two Indigenous lands with the presence of isolated peoples have already been signed (Pereira and Mortari 2022). The director of the Indigenous Health Secretariat of the Ministry of Health will be the Indigenous leader Weibe Tapeba.

The Action Plan for the Prevention and Control of Deforestation in Amazônia Legal (PPCDAm), created in 2004, was primarily responsible for reducing deforestation in this biome by more than 80 % between 2004 and 2012. The new government is planning to expand deforestation control policy even to other Brazilian biomes such as the *cerrado*. In the Permanent Interministerial Commission for the Prevention and Control of Deforestation, 17 ministries – under the command of the Civil House – will participate in the implementation of the action plans.[480]

The president determined the reestablishment of the National Council for the Environment (CONAMA). Created in 1981 and dismantled during the Bolsonaro government, CONAMA is responsible for advising and proposing environmental priority policies to the government, with the participation of federal, state, and municipal agencies, the private sector and civil society.

The creation of the Directorate for the Amazon and Environment at the Federal Police is responsible for directing, controlling, and executing activities for the prevention and repression of criminal offenses against the environment, the Indigenous peoples, and traditional communities, as well as the public safety in Amazônia Legal.

The new Ministry of Racial Equality will be responsible for dealing with policies related to *quilombolas* and other traditional peoples, with the National Institute of Col-

---

479 She is a member of the Wapixana tribe in Roraima, was the first ever Indigenous woman elected to Brazil's Congress and became the first Indigenous lawyer to argue before the Supreme Court. Wapichana is the current president of the National Commission for the Defence of the Rights of Indigenous Peoples.

480 https://acervo.socioambiental.org/acervo/noticias/no-primeiro-dia-do-ano-governo-lula-garante-novo-folego-ao-meio-ambiente (accessed March 6, 2023).

onisation and Agrarian Reform (INCRA) reorganising the recognition of *quilombos* and other traditional territories.[481]

The National Attorney for the Defence of Climate and Environment at the Advocacy-General of the Union is created to enable the transformations necessary for an effective ecological transition. As with other newly established functions, here we have to wait and see whether this function will be equipped with the appropriate prerequisites to be successful in the implementation of the tasks.

1.3. Revitalization of the Amazon Fund, the free trade agreement EU-Mercosur and BRICS geopolitics

When the main donors of the Amazon Fund, Norway and Germany, signalled that they intend to continue financing it, President Lula da Silva reestablished the Amazon Fund. Created in 2008 to finance projects reducing deforestation, the Fund had been paralysed since April 2019, when the Bolsonaro government extinguished collegiate bodies that were part of the Amazon Fund. Now the groups have been reestablished with the participation of representatives from ten ministries and state governments in Amazônia Legal, which have plans to prevent and combat deforestation. The Fund's steering committee will also include civil society entities, such as the Coordination of Indigenous Organizations of the Brazilian Amazon (COIAB) and the National Confederation of Industry.[482] The money sent by European countries will be raised by the National Bank for Economic and Social Development (BNDES).

The Norwegian Ministry of Climate and Environment informed that Brazil can already apply about R$ 3 billion donated by the country to the Amazon Fund and still available. Scandinavian asset managers attach great importance to avoiding the suspicion of greenwashing.[483] The BNDES announced an agreement with the German Development Bank KfW for a donation of € 35 million to the Fund.

With the political decision of the Lula da Silva government to primarily fight deforestation and to manage lower deforestation rates quickly, the Amazon Fund will again be the right place for the international community to remunerate the country for services to reduce deforestation and emissions. In the opinion of Adriana Ramos, advisor to the Instituto SocioAmbiental (ISA), without the Fund's resources, the government is unable to adequately finance projects aimed at preserving the forest and the sustainable development of the region.[484] After Norway and Germany, which previously financed the Amazon Fund, now also the European Union, France and the United Kingdom are planning to participate in the financing.

---

481 A *quilombo* is a settlement founded by people of African origin who resisted the slavery regime in Brazil, abolished in 1888. Most of the inhabitants of *quilombos*, called *quilombolas*, were maroons, a term for escaped slaves. According to IBGE (2023), 1.3 million *quilombola* people live in Brazil. In Amazônia Legal, the 2022 Census found 426 449 *quilombola* persons (1.6 % of the population in this area and almost one third of the *quilombolas* in Brazil).

482 https://g1.globo.com/politica/noticia/2023/01/01/lula-assina-decreto-que-retoma-fundo-amazonia-e-outras-medidas-ambientais.ghtml (accessed March 6, 2023).

483 "Greenwashing" is a term for public relation methods that aim to give a company an environmentally friendly and responsible image in public without a sufficient basis for proving this.

484 See footnote 480.

In the case of the National Environmental Fund, social participation was contemplated again with the return of representatives of civil society to the deliberative council of this fund since it had been eliminated by the Bolsonaro government.

Another major challenge for all parties involved will be the European Union (EU)-Mercosur free trade agreement. In January 2023, during the visit of the German Chancellor Scholz to Brasília, President Lula da Silva said he hoped to conclude the trade agreement by mid-2023 (Fontes 2023).[485] The agreement would create the largest free trade area in the world. The treaty, proposed more than 20 years ago, was only signed in June 2019, during the Bolsonaro government, but it was never ratified, due to a series of obstacles, in particular Brazil's setbacks in the socio-environmental agenda and a strong EU opposition against the lacking environmental policy of the Brazilian government.

The EU legislation has the potential to deny exports – meat, leather, soybean, wood pulp, timber, rubber, cocoa, palm oil and biofuel – from Brazilian areas that have been deforested, even with legal permission, after December 31, 2020. Particular attention will be paid to beef imports from Mercosur, which are subject to a quota system, also applied to poultry and sugar (Maihold 2019b). The European Parliament agreed to the project of sustainability-related binding reciprocal accompanying measures. EU member states will not rely on voluntary actions and had adopted new regulations "to impose strict traceability-requirements on forest products, and punishments for companies and countries that fail to halt unsustainable deforestation or degradation" (Watts 2022).[486]

According to the EU Parliament, about 10 % of deforestation between 1990 and 2020 was caused by consumers in the EU. The EU would like to address the issue of embodied deforestation consumption by placing deforestation-free supply chains at the centre of negotiations surrounding the EU-Mercosur Association Agreement (Müller 2020) as a safety net against deforestation. The EU adopted a regulation on supply chains and will prohibit imports of goods from deforested areas in Amazonia, however, without distinguishing between legal and illegal deforestation. In the future, companies will have to make a due diligence declaration that the product has not caused damage to the forest anywhere. However, from an economic point of view, there are concerns as to whether this effort, which has a strong financial impact, will also be possible for medium-sized enterprises. In any case, the regulation of supply chains in Amazonia is an extremely complex process. If the entire supply chain is properly checked, the suppliers of the suppliers and their suppliers would also have to be recorded and checked. As already mentioned, this can be circumvented relatively easily by fraudulent false reports and therefore casts doubt on the success of practical implementation in certain regions and conditions that are difficult to control.

The European Parliament's Delegation for relations with Brazil stressed that the Brazilian government must reinstate all the environmental laws and institutions that were dismantled by Bolsonaro. It will need a revision that guarantees stricter commit-

485 In an interview, the Minister of Foreign Affairs Vieira stressed that the agreement will be treated as a priority by Brazil (*Veja* 6, January 15, 2023).

486 However, producers in Brazil have many well-known tricks to get around the regulations. An example is "cattle laundering" (see chapter III.2).

ments with the environmental actions aligned with the reduction of deforestation.[487] The EU will put sustainability and the fight against deforestation in the core of the agreement (Fontes 2023). It is hoped that China and the United States will adopt similar measures.

In the EU, a coalition of opponents against the agreement had formed from the agricultural lobby, the centre-right as well as green parties, anti-globalisation and environmental activists. In particular, the French government had opposed the agreement to protect domestic agriculture, which was facilitated by the inadequate environmental policies of the Bolsonaro government. "Certain key actors within the EU pursued a morally dressed up protectionism" (Nolte 2023).

The EU had neglected relations with Latin America for almost a decade. With the victory of Lula da Silva, the member states of the EU will now have to be clear about a future strategy in trade relations with the Mercosur. In June 2023, the President of the European Commission, Ursula von der Leyen, during her visit in Brazil underlined the ambition to conclude the EU-Mercosur agreement, the latest by the end of the year. The agreement will also support the reindustrialisation of Brazil. The Mercosur states must also agree on a strategic line. The La Plata states will not let Brazil's Amazonian problems spoil their trade interests with European partners. The run-off elections in Argentina in November 2023 with the clear victory of the eccentric ultra-right-wing Javier Milei will lead to maximum incompatibilities between Brazil's and Argentina's strategies. Milei has already labelled Brazilian President Lula da Silva as "corrupt and communist," making cooperation between the two difficult to imagine, even though Brazil is Argentina's main trading partner. The new political situation in Argentina with an elected president who, like Bolsonaro in Brazil in the past, denies climate change, detests China – Argentina's second largest trading partner – and wants to reduce state funding for science and culture will make negotiations with the EU already on the Mercosur side extremely difficult, if not altogether almost impossible.

On the other hand, Brazil will play a decisive role in the Mercosur and at the same time show the Europeans that it will now build its own agenda of international relations as a global player in the interest of the Global South. Lula da Silva had made it clear immediately after his election: "We are not interested in trade agreements that condemn our country to the eternal role of exporter of commodities and raw materials."[488] He could probably have added that this also applies – from the point of view of many Brazilians – to the "exaggerated problematisation" of the Amazonian deforestation among the European countries in negotiating the trade agreement. However, since this issue is the source of support payments from European states and the United

487 This also applies to Brazil's admission to the Organization for Economic Co-operation and Development (OECD). In June 2022, the OECD emphasised that "Brazil must adopt and fully implement policies in line with its climate goals, including combating forest loss, before considering the country's accession to the organisation". This request includes "strengthening environmental agencies, protecting the rights of Indigenous peoples and local communities, and addressing impunity of violence and intimidation against environmental defenders" (https://www.hrw.org/the-day-in-human-rights/2022/11/04) (accessed March 6, 2023).

488 https://g1.globo.com/politica/noticia/2023/01/01/lula-assina-decreto-que-retoma-fundo-amazonia-e-outras-medidas-ambientais.ghtml (accessed March 6, 2023). Lula da Silva: "The additional instrument presented by the European Union in March of this year is unacceptable" (https://www.gov.br/planalto/en/follow-the-government/speeches-statements/2023/speech-by-president-lula-on-the-occasion-of-the-62nd-mercosur-summit [accessed October 20, 2023]).

States to Brazil, this criticism will be strictly omitted. For Lula da Silva, according to the high economic potential of the country – in 2021, Brazil concentrated 74.1% of the total export value of the Mercosur states[489] – the agreement must go far beyond the Amazonian environmental issues. Brazil's hope is to provide good export opportunities not only for a wide range of agricultural products but also for the country's mineral and industrial production as well as the renewable energies for producing green hydrogen.

In the opinion of many Brazilian and international observers, "the fate of the rain forest is not decided in the Amazon, but in the overseas markets that buy its beef, wood, soybean, and iron ore. In this regard, the European Union, which is the world's biggest consumer of forest products, is indirectly, the world's biggest deforester" (Watts 2022).

At the international level, President Lula da Silva, like other leaders of emerging economies, has his own global political agenda, as was demonstrated in his recent dubious assessment of the war in Ukraine, for whose emergence he holds not only Russia but also Ukraine equally responsible. Brazil is a member of the BRICS group[490] and therefore Lula da Silva is not willing to oppose Russia, with which it holds intensive trade relations, in particular regarding Russian fertiliser imports urgently needed in Brazil. Sanctions of the western coalition against Moscow because of the Russian war of aggression against Ukraine are strictly rejected by the Lula da Silva government, just as the supply of ammunition for Ukraine, as the president stated during the visit of German Chancellor Scholz.

In Latin American left parties, the anti-American narrative sees the United States as an imperialist and Russia always on the side of the revolutionaries. There is still a solidarity with the Cuban revolution. This is underlined by the success of Russian propaganda channels that can be received everywhere on cable TV in Latin America.[491]

Brazil wants to deliver its exports to Russia and China as well as to the US and Europe. Lula da Silva is not interested in taking sides in the conflict between the great powers. According to the Brazilian tradition, Lula da Silva wants to adopt a non-aligned position. He had spoken of a "peace club" of interested states and indicated in the case of the war in Ukraine, that he could act as a mediator. This is probably an overestimation of his influence. However, Brazil will host the G20 summit in 2024. Western countries desperately want to avoid the BRICS group becoming an anti-western trading bloc. China and the New Development Bank (NDB) of the BRICS states, which is headed by the former Brazilian President and successor to Lula da Silva, Dilma Rousseff, profile themselves as important donors.

Even before the BRICS summit in Johannesburg in August 2023, it became known that about two dozen countries had formally applied to join the BRICS grouping, which accounts for 26% of the world economy. China, which today generates about 70% of the GDP of the BRICS states, had been advocating BRICS membership expansion for years (Maihold and Müller 2023, 2). Brazil, like India and South Africa, had been rather

---

489 Mercosur: Total export value in 2021: US$ 378.7 billion; Argentina: 20.6%; Paraguay 2.8%; Uruguay 2.5% (data from de.statista.com, 2022).

490 BRICS is an acronym for the emerging nations of Brazil, Russia, India, China and South Africa (member since 2010). They believe to be the dominant suppliers of manufactured goods, services (China, India), and raw materials (Brazil, Russia) by 2050.

491 Tjerk Brühwiller, *FAZ*, February 7, 2023.

reluctant to expand the number of members, as this would weaken their influence in the alliance. Since all decisions have to be unanimous, the question of selecting new candidates for membership is not easy. During the BRICS summit in South Africa, it was decided that Argentina, Egypt, Ethiopia, Iran, Saudi Arabia and the United Arab Emirates would first be invited as permanent members.

The selection of these six states may be considered quite surprising. The long-standing political tensions between China and India, which is opposed to ever greater Chinese influence in the Asian region, will also play a role in the future enlargement issue. With three oil-exporting states – despite the previous political conflicts between Iran and Saudi Arabia – this economic sector in the Middle East marked by political tensions is strongly emphasised. In Argentina, the new president Javier Milei – after the change of government in the run-off election in November 2023 – already declared that he will not join the BRICS group. Before the BRICS summit and the Argentinian elections, Brazil had recommended Argentina as a candidate for admission.

For China and Russia, which will take over the BRICS presidency in 2024, the creation of a counterweight to the hitherto Western-dominated global order is of particular importance. On the other hand, Brazil, India and South Africa are still interested in good trade relations on both sides.

China sees the BRICS group as creation of a new multipolar world order and – with the New Development Bank – as an alternative to the World Bank and the IMF. Chinese investment in this context will be a decisive factor for further Chinese influence in Brazil. It is not yet possible to predict how the role of China and the BRICS development bank will affect the EU-Mercosur negotiations. After the EU-Mercosur agreement, Brazil will try to start free trade negotiations with China, the most important export destination for its products. During his state visit to China in April 2023, Lula da Silva was accompanied by a large group of Brazilian entrepreneurs. Chinese leader Xi Jinping stressed that relations with Brazil are a "high priority" for China. Numerous bilateral agreements were signed, some refer to infrastructural investments and could be of major importance for projects in Amazonia.

There is a growing realisation in the Global South that de-dollarisation is an important step towards a multipolar world and that a multi-currency trading system will gradually emerge. Against the backdrop of the current tensions between the major powers and membership in BRICS, Brazil wants to be the independent voice of the Global South. However, this position is very much sought by India, which hosted the G20 summit in September 2023 and whose economic power is growing very strongly. India will be supported by the Global Gateway Initiative of the EU, Gulf States and the USA, which are striving for an alternative to China's new "Belt and Road" initiative.

For Brazil, de-dollarisation is part of its foreign policy strategy to challenge the dominance of the dollar in international trade and finance. Transactions with China are to be conducted directly in Chinese *renminbi* and Brazilian *reais* within the framework of the New Development Bank of the BRICS countries. Brazil's trade volume with China reached the record value of US$ 150.5 billion in 2022 (Hirst and Tokatlian 2023). However, at the same time, Brazil has the presidency of the Inter-American Development Bank (IDB) since December 2022, so it remains present in both systems.

In the negotiations on the EU-Mercosur agreement, it will be of decisive importance for Brazil whether China, by far the most important trading partner, will continue to be an environmentally less critical importer and thus an "attractive" alternative to Europe and the United States, which insist on socio-ecological sustainability. If China were to switch to the global line of climate and forest protection, however, this possibility would no longer exist.

Lula da Silva is in an ideal position to push his agenda and persuade wealthy nations to pay more for stewardship of rain forest protection and mitigation of climate change. Through his stance on the Russian war of aggression against Ukraine, this support could be seriously jeopardised. The hope that he will keep his promise to get deforestation under control quickly is still high in Europe and the United States. However, it must be stated that the environmental policy of Lula da Silva in his first term was mixed and economic growth at all costs had absolute priority. The environmental success at that time was very much due to the Minister of the Environment Marina Silva whose resignation in 2008 was justified by the giving in of the president to the economic lobbies. From the point of view of his critics, Lula da Silva "used his previous presidency to promote a 20th century national development programme of roads, dams, increased consumption, higher credit and massive state subsidies for the oil, beef, soy, mining, and construction industries" (Watts 2022, n. p.).

It is to be hoped that this time it will be different. In view of the numerous announcements of the new government in the environmental sector, the domestic political situation – no majority of environmentally conscious politicians in Congress and financial scarcity – and the lack of Brazil's export boom today raise doubts about its feasibility, especially considering the political and social tensions in the country. For the vast majority of the Brazilian population, climate protection and deforestation in the Amazonian region are only marginal phenomena against the background of social disparities and the need to create jobs to save parts of the population from extreme poverty.

Strong support from Europe and the United States will be particularly important for Brazil. Germany has a strategic partnership with Brazil on environment, climate, and energy issues since 2008. After the elections in Brazil, the German government believed that the window has opened for the protection of the Amazon rain forest. Above all, the German Social Democratic governing party (SPD) has a long special connection to Lula da Silva. The German government provided a large amount of emergency aid to give Lula da Silva the best possible start. Germany was supporting the new Brazilian government with € 200 million in the first 100 days of its term of office.

After the presence of Germany's President Steinmeier at the inauguration of Lula da Silva in Brasília,[492] the visit of the German Chancellor Scholz followed in January 2023 – with the Minister of Economic Cooperation and Development. The desire to finally conclude the EU-Mercosur trade agreement, which is underlined by the negotiations planned with the president of the European Commission, was also a topic of the visit of the German minister for Economic Affairs and Climate Protection and the minister of Agriculture in March 2023.[493] However, German expectations in the Lula da Silva government may be too optimistic.

492 On the occasion of his trip to Brazil, the German president visited the German-Brazilian research project ATTO (cf. chapter II.8.2) in Amazonia together with the German Minister of Environment.

493 Above all, however, this visit was about the possibilities of using Brazil's huge potential in wind and solar energy for the production of green hydrogen as a future replacement for Russian natural gas in Germany.

When Lula da Silva took office, he was given great advance praise internationally. However, the President is under a great deal of domestic and foreign environmental pressure. NGOs in Europe and Brazil reject the EU-Mercosur agreement as totally inadequate in terms of content. International NGOs such as Human Rights Watch (HRW), Survival International, WWF and Greenpeace urged the rapid implementation of promised environmental measures.

HRW asked the Lula da Silva government to develop a plan for the protection of the Amazonian region, which aims at a joint action by federal bodies, police forces, public ministries, and state governments "for the prevention and accountability for environmental crimes and violence, including dismantling the criminal networks" operating in the region. HRW also referred to the promise of Lula da Silva

> strengthening the capacity of agencies that protect the environment and Indigenous rights, and institute mechanisms for controlling and monitoring the productive chain of gold, meat and other agricultural products in order to guarantee that it is not linked to deforestation.[494]

The plan includes the resumption of the demarcation of Indigenous lands and the fight against land grabbing. All this is urgently needed, but it is not feasible to this extent in the near future and under the current political circumstances in the Brazilian Congress.

In the first weeks of his new term, the president tried sending a strong signal to the public, especially to the international press, that he immediately addresses the fundamental problems caused during the Bolsonaro period. However, one thing must be clear: it will take much more time than the government admits and critics think to reorganise ministries, agencies, etc. and implement appropriate sustainable measures. This requires not only a highly unlikely budget increase for the different ministries that were starved under Bolsonaro, but also many vacancies have to be filled, which means difficult selection criteria and training time. The government must realise a reliable selection of experts, which has been depressed in recent years. Some NGOs have done a lot of preparatory work for the individual measures announced by Lula da Silva. Now, the president must decide what is of priority for the well-being of Amazonia without getting lost in regional and local details or in NGOs' competitive actions.

It came as a shock when the figures for deforestation in the first quarter of 2023 exceeded even those of the Bolsonaro period, amounting to 867 km^2, the second highest figure for this period since 2008. In February/March at the peak of the rainy season, high levels of deforestation are unusual. One explanation for this, however, could be that logging activities were quickly increased for fear of tightening controls under the new government immediately before and directly after President Lula da Silva took office. That means: before the reorganisation of IBAMA is working. A similar situation arose before and immediately after President Cardoso took office in 1995, when record levels of deforestation were reached.[495]

494 https://www.hrw.org/pt/content/383849; https://www.dw.com/pt-br/um-pa%C3%ADs-de-muitas-urg%C3%AAncias/a-64518010 (accessed March 8, 2023).

495 Cf. chapter II.2.2.2.

After a deforestation of 13 038 km² (August 1, 2020–July 31, 2021) and 11 594 km² (August 2021–July 2022), a deforestation of 9001 km² was recorded in the observation period 2022–2023 with 7 months under the Lula da Silva government. This represents an overall decrease of deforestation of 22 % compared to 2021–2022. The highest deforestation in the period 2022–2023 occurred in Pará (36 %) and Mato Grosso (23 %). Compared to the previous year, there was a slight absolute increase (5–8 %) in deforestation in Mato Grosso, Roraima and Maranhão.

According to the new preliminary INPE data, deforestation in Amazônia Legal decreased by 50 % in the calendar year 2023 compared to the previous year and reached its lowest level since 2018, albeit still at 5153 km².[496] The comparison with the Bolsonaro government is favourable, although deforestation in 2023 continued into November due to an unusual drought. Deforestation in Indigenous Territories decreased by 27 % between 2022 and 2023 (RAD 2024).

However, it must be emphasised that deforestation in the cerrado increased by 68 % to 11 103 km² in 2023 compared to 2022 (RAD 2024) and was thus greater than forest destruction in Amazônia Legal for the first time in 2023. This occurred primarily in MATOPIBA (2022–2023: + 59 %).

All those who are in favour of measures against deforestation and finance corresponding activities will take a close look at the results of new INPE evaluations.

As for the new government's tasks for Amazonia, there are a number of pressing and long-standing issues that need to be addressed and resolved. Some of these tasks have already been determined by the president as follows:

- the National Policy for the Territorial and Ecological Management of Indigenous Lands (designated),
- a Directorate for the Amazon and the environment within the Federal Police to control activities to prevent and repress crimes against the environment, Indigenous peoples and traditional communities, and public security in Amazônia Legal (designated),
- environmental institutions closed under Bolsonaro were reactivated (designated),
- IBAMA and FUNAI resume their original tasks in a restructured form (designated),
- establishment of a national authority for climate risks (planned).

At this point, only some of the most important points that still need to be carried out or improved in Amazônia Legal may be mentioned:

- the state monopoly on the use of force in Amazônia Legal must be imposed or restored,
- the judiciary needs to be present on the ground,
- environmental justice has to be ensured,
- corruption must be fought and punished at all levels,

496 https://www.gov.br/inpe/pt-br/assuntos/ultimas-noticias/estimativa-de-desmatamento-na-amazonia-legal-para-2023-e-de-9-001-km2/2023_1020_Nota_tecnica_Estimativa_Taxa_2023_SEI.pdf (accessed September 4, 2024). See also Butler (2024), cf. RAD (2024).

- activities of criminal organisations must be identified, prevented and severely punished,
- environmental violations have to be punished quickly and without exceptions, and the fines collected,
- environmental impact assessment and environmental licensing must be placed under special supervision to avoid any collusion, influence or other irregularities. Well-organised public hearings must be held before the real decisions are made,
- good local forest governance and legal presence on the ground have to be realised,
- borders of Indigenous territories, conservation units and protected areas must be better secured. Projects in progress should be completed more quickly,
- land titles in Amazonia must be granted on the basis of secure documentation by the Rural Environmental Registry,
- peasants without land title (*posseiros*) need a clear perspective on obtaining a title of ownership,
- the needs of the majority of the poor rural population should be taken into account to a greater extent,
- illegal occupation of land (*grilagem*) must be identified and the unlawfully acquired land expropriated,
- landscape-destroying activities and contamination of water courses with mercury by gold prospectors (*garimpeiros*) will have to be severely restricted and strictly controlled,
- illegal forest clearing can be safely recorded and punished with high-tech satellite monitoring. Punishment can be fines, blacklisting, and credit withdrawal, as has been done in the past,
- illegal clearing of primary forest for the production of charcoal must be prevented,
- tax relief could be offered to avoid legal clearing on the basis of the Forest Code,
- mega-projects, especially hydroelectric power plants with large reservoirs, must be avoided at all costs due to past experience with negative socio-ecological and environmental impacts and excessive financial burdens,
- renewable solar and wind energy generation or small-scale run-of-river power stations are ecologically efficient alternatives,
- promotion of innovations in agricultural management and developing a local forest economy
- small projects of the riverine and Indigenous population for sustainable development should be particularly promoted (e.g., agroforestry, cooperative management),
- intensification of scientific research in Brazil on Amazonia and its biological potential is essential as well as further promotion of regional scientists and research institutions,
- ecologically and economically sustainable alternatives in agroforestry are urgently needed to strengthen regional social actors and promote the empowerment of local communities and Indigenous groups,
- incentives for ecologically oriented actions must be promoted and sustainability has to be the long-term economic and social goal,
- low-carbon agriculture and reforestation are sustainable goals that deserve extraordinary support,

- in view of globalisation, rapid urbanisation and increasing urban-rural interactions, special programmes for sustainable urban development in the Amazon are urgently needed.

All this must be realised in Amazonia beyond party political considerations and covert government propaganda. It is only possible through the fair participation of the local and regional population in environmental assessment and democratic decision-making on government plans and strategies (Science Panel for the Amazon 2021). Environmental justice is one of the key elements for peaceful coexistence (Fearnside 2020).

The necessary measures must be combined with the process of insight in industrialised countries that Amazonia is no longer a mere reference area for supply of cheap raw material and agricultural commodities. To this end, this applies to the environmental performance of financial investments and transactions in the international engagement in fighting deforestation in Amazonia (Barroso and Mello 2021).[497]

Carlos Nobre pointed out that the discussion so far on the Amazonian development ranges only between the environmentalist approach of maximisation of protected areas and the conservative economic modernisation approach of intensification of agriculture and livestock farming as well as the expansion of hydropower capacities. He proposes in the short term and with a low-tech approach a third way as a paradigm for sustainable development (Nobre *et al.* 2016; Nobre and Nobre 2019; 2020) that also enables the zero-deforestation strategy to reduce CO_2 emissions and to slow down climate change.

A number of Amazonian products, such as the *babaçu* palm (*Attalea speciosa*), *cupuaçu* (*Theobroma grandiflorum*), and the Brazil nut tree (*Bertholletia excelsa*) have already impacted the local economies. The market for fruits of the *acaí* palm (*Euterpe oleracea*) has developed particularly strongly. Thus, these economic alternatives of biodiversity-based product value chains could also reach the global markets. Amazonia "as a global public good of biological assets and biomimetic designs that can enable the creation of innovative, high-value products [...]" (Nobre *et al.* 2016, 10764) also means, of course, that products, which could be important for the cosmetic and pharmaceutical industry worldwide, must under no circumstances lead to a new process of exploitation. However, the term "global public good", which was intentionally avoided in the international PPG7 programme, could also be misunderstood in Brazil in a global discussion about the "general valorisation" of these Brazilian products.

The problem of biopiracy, i.e., the unauthorised taking and smuggling of animal and plant species, must be ruled out in Amazonia – not only for historical reasons of the smuggling of *hevea brasiliensis* out of the country. The non-consensual appropriation of traditional knowledge of Indigenous peoples for the acquisition of patent rights on biological or chemical substances must also be excluded (Barroso and Mello 2021). In particular, the Indigenous people's knowledge of how to obtain medicinal plants to treat a wide variety of diseases must be safeguarded for their survival.

In order to show the basic problem of unequal valorisation of natural resources in a comparison, Nobre has contrasted the commodities currently in demand based on deforestation and Amazonian biodiversity. Soybean cultivation and cattle breeding

497 Financial flows that connect "actors engaged in deforestation-related activities to government actors and decisions" must be identified and quantified (Garrett *et al.* 2021, 645).

in Amazonia yielded US$ 14 billion in 2017 from a deforested area of 240 000 km². In contrast, Brazil nuts, cocoa and *açaí* palm in agroforestry on an area of only 4000 km² without deforestation brought a return of US$ 2 billion and generated income for over 300 000 people in the region A comparison of the yield of 1 ha of a well-run agroforestry farm (US$ 1000–1200/year) with 1 ha of a cattle farm (US$ 100/year) and 1 ha of a well-organised soybean cultivation (US$ 200/year) shows the enormous potential of sustainable economy (Nobre and Nobre 2020).[498] This is the sustainable alternative with low impact on the environment excluding the agribusiness profits and concentrating on regional social actors.

1.4. A new impetus for the Amazon Cooperation Treaty?

Given the importance of Amazonia for biodiversity, rain forest protection, the preservation of the culturally diverse regional population and its decisive role for the global climate, regionally coordinated cross-border policies for sustainable development would be a fundamental strategy to meet the demands of its population and member countries.[499]

With regard to international cooperation in Amazonia, it will be of interest whether the government of Lula da Silva will give new impetus to the Amazon Cooperation Treaty (ACT). The ACT, signed in 1978, gave rise to the Amazon Cooperation Treaty Organization (ACTO/OTCA, Organización del Tratado de Cooperación Amazónica) formed by the eight Amazonian countries: Bolivia, Brazil, Colombia, Ecuador, Guyana, Peru, Surinam, and Venezuela.[500] The conclusion of the treaty was extremely general, and the development objective was "harmonious and in mutual cooperation," an agreement on a minimum consensus. Since the beginning, Brazil had tried to dispel the concerns of neighbouring countries about its possible dominance in this region and proposed coordinated development measures in the economic, social, and ecological fields in the same way for all areas. For Brazil, the establishment of the Amazon Pact was not only a counterpoint to the Andean Pact, but also offered an opportunity to encourage the Andean countries to cooperate economically more closely with Brazil in an agreement in which Brazil was a part (Kohlhepp 1983a). Today, apart from a broad vision of south-south cooperation, ACT is still without any specific geopolitical strategy but oriented to "promote the harmonious development of the Amazonian territories in such a way that the joint actions of the Amazonian countries produce equitable and mutually beneficial results in achieving the sustainable development of the Amazon region."[501]

498 In 2020, socio-biodiverse products by Indigenous people and riverine communities from Amazônia Legal totalled R$ (Brazilian Real) 11 billion (US$ 2.15 billion), with 50 % of the products destined for the local market, 41 % for the rest of Brazil and 3 % for the global market (Hirota *et al.* 2022). Carlos Nobre in: "Amazônia entre a vida e a morte", Jornalismo TV Cultura, episódio 2, https://www.youtube.com/watch?v=Zlwf8nSXJmo (accessed September 4, 2024).

499 http://otca.org/en/ (accessed 16.03.2023).

500 Ferris (1981), among others; cf. Kohlhepp (1983a, footnote 60).

501 https://otca.org/en/about-us/ (accessed 16.03.2023).

It will only be possible to achieve an economically, socially, and ecologically sustainable policy on natural resources management in the Amazonian region if the relevant actors agree on common goals and new rules. Since the majority of the participating states have left-wing governments, at least for the time being, it may well be possible for Lula da Silva to establish more intensive contacts for a coordinated regional development in Amazonia, even with the Maduro government in Venezuela. This is particularly true, because the Amazon region is of major importance for mitigation of CO_2 emissions and slowdown of global climate change. In addition, cross-border migration, goods trade, and the ubiquitous drug trafficking give rise to greater surveillance of the region and border areas.

All states bordering the Amazon region have control stations to monitor deforestation with the help of satellite images. Since 2002, the eight ACTO member states have had access to a Permanent Technical Secretariat in Brasília with the aim to organise regional development measures and cooperation programmes between the participating countries. Nevertheless, little effort has been made in supranational cooperation in recent decades.

In early August 2023, Lula da Silva has invited the eight ACTO states, which last met 14 years ago, to a summit in Belém. For the Brazilian president, this was an attempt to stimulate new activities among the neighbouring countries regarding the protection of the Amazonian forests and at the same time to underline Brazil's leadership role in environmental issues. This, especially against the background of the World Climate Summit (COP 30) to be held at the same location in 2025.

In the run-up to the event, Indigenous and environmental organisations held large protest demonstrations to highlight what they saw as the major problems of deforestation and the lack of respect for human rights. The main proposals of civil society were formulated for the meeting, including the protection of territories. The internationally known charismatic Kayapó leader Raoni Metuktire ("I will talk to the governments to keep the forest standing") also tried to talk to Lula da Silva about banning the oil drilling planned by the state-run Brazilian oil giant Petrobras in the Amazon estuary (Watso 2023).

The results of the "Belém Declaration" were disappointing. The participating states were able to agree on increased cooperation in sustainable development and to strengthen combating deforestation but could not agree jointly on the Brazilian proposal to end illegal deforestation by 2030. Bolivia and Venezuela stood by their refusal to name this date. However, there was agreement on combating organised crime, which is growing very rapidly in the Amazon region. Brazil offered a Centre for International Police Cooperation in Manaus for collaborative efforts between the police forces of the eight countries and the establishment of an Air Traffic Control System to combat illicit air traffic and drug trafficking.[502]

Large parts of Amazonia have long been in the hands of organised crime. Criminal networks dominate land speculation, gold mining, logging in all parts of Amazonia.

---

502 G1.globo.com/meio-ambiente, August 6, 23 (accessed August 8, 2023). In addition, the establishment of a number of entities within the ambit of the ACTO was announced, such as the Forum of Amazonian Cities, among others (Agência Brasil, August 9, 2023, https://agenciabrasil.ebc.com.br/en/geral/noticia/2023-08/presidents-eight-amazon-countries-sign-belem-declaration [accessed August 8, 2023]).

Coca cultivation in Peru, Colombia, Bolivia and Venezuela also affects tropical forest areas. Smuggling routes for cocaine also use the Amazonian rain forest areas, which are difficult to control.

At the Amazon summit, Lula da Silva criticised "green neo-colonialism"[503] and defended facilitated funding for sustainable projects. However, Lula da Silva could not avoid a very critical discussion point. The oil issue became an important topic of this summit. The President of Colombia, Gustavo Petro, criticised during the plenary of presidents that the issue of fossil fuels is not treated with due attention by politics. He tried to put pressure on his neighbouring states and asked for an end to oil and gas extraction in Amazonia. This exploration forms the economic basis for some states with lowlands in western Amazonia, such as Ecuador, Peru and Bolivia, as well as in Venezuela.

The Brazilian government is divided over oil exploration in the Amazon biome. The Minister of Mines and Energy defends research of Petrobras to assess the viability of oil at the mouth of the Amazon river. On the other hand, the Minister of the Environment, Marina Silva, calls for detailed scientific data for decision-making. In May 2023, the Brazilian environmental authority IBAMA denied the drilling request of Petrobras. Eighty civil society and environmental organisations, WWF Brasil and Greenpeace, protested against a fast-track approval and have called for an in-depth study.[504] A permit would certainly lead to further drilling in the entire region.

It can be assumed that Lula da Silva is in favour of the economic potential of this project, which would fit in with the president's positive attitude towards large-scale projects in the Amazon region, however, seriously affect his new image as a defender of the environment if the mega-projects proceed. In view of the interests of the aforementioned oil-producing states and in consideration of the unresolved Brazilian situation, the ban on oil exploration in Amazonia was not included in the document of the ACTO summit.[505]

Lula da Silva's credibility on environmental protection in Amazonia has been damaged by his continued advocacy for large infrastructure projects. While environmental organisations describe these projects as disastrous for the Amazon region, members of Lula da Silva's Workers' Party emphasise their economic importance. The president advocates the reconstruction of the BR-319 (Fig. 3: Porto Velho–Manaus), which was abandoned in the 1980s and is now to be repaved. The construction of the Rio Negro Bridge – a 3.6 km long cable-stayed bridge near Manaus, which crosses the Rio Negro just before it flows into the Amazon and was opened to traffic in 2011 – has led to controversy over the possible repaving of the BR-319, which connects the region with Porto Velho in Rondônia. As this road is on the south side of the Amazon, traffic from Manaus would still have to cross the main branch of the river by ferry despite the bridge. The recommissioning for the transport of commodities would lead to uncontrolled deforestation in the region by increasing land speculation and giving easy access to *grileiros*.

---

503 https://www1.folha.uol.com.br/ambiente/2023/08/brasil-nao-pode-aceitar-neocolonialismo-verde-diz-lula.shtml (accessed August 24, 23).

504 Petrobras has reserved almost half of its 5-year exploration budget for this area (Biller 2023).

505 G1.globo.com/meio-ambiente, August 6, 23 (accessed August 9, 2023).

Another difficult problem is related to the planned *Ferrogrão* railway line in Mato Grosso and Pará (Sinop–Miritituba) (Fig. 34)[506] – a top priority project for the Minister of Transport – that would move grains from the main soybean producing region towards the Tapajos river for shipping abroad. The construction of the railway depends on a court decision on the permissibility of clearing in the Jamanxim National Park, which would be affected by the route. One of the Kayapó chiefs called it "the railway of Indigenous genocide."

Belo Monte[507] is also back on Lula da Silva's agenda, as the renewal of IBAMA's operating licence is under review, as the operator Norte Energia is said to have failed to meet many of the conditions of the original licence – issued under heavy pressure from Rousseff's government – according to a letter from the environmental journalism website *Sumauma* (Biller 2023).

As a result of the Amazon summit, it can be stated that the Amazonian countries are not willing to give up economic progress for measures against climate change, especially since these countries are only responsible for a small part of global greenhouse gas emissions. Brazil had already made clear its reservations about environmental protection requirements during the preliminary talks on the upcoming EU-Mercosur negotiations. These requirements, which are perceived as excessive, such as the example of the EU's new supply chain law, would mean trade disruptions.

Many of the Amazonian states are facing major domestic political and socio-economic problems, which ultimately push rain forest protection into the background. To prevent this, the Amazonian countries will make financial demands on the industrialised nations to carry out environmentally protective sustainable development projects. Whether this will lead to an overarching cooperation of the ACTO members in the Amazon region remains to be seen.

Since Brazil has so far used the majority of international support for Amazonian issues for its own programmes, the beginning of coordinated regional sustainable development in this area will be a new challenge. In any case, it is certain that in the overall region of Amazonia, rain forest protection will not be available for free. The international community will have to offer suitable compensation mechanisms for all countries involved (Maihold 2019b).

Lula da Silva has repeatedly demanded that the promised US$ 100 billion be made available to developing countries so that they can use it for climate and forest protection. Marina Silva stressed that Brazil, which during Lula da Silva's first two terms in office (2003–2010) would have avoided the release of around 5 billion tons of CO_2 by reducing deforestation,[508] must play a leadership role in international climate and forest protection. . In November 2024, Brazil will chair the G20 Summit in Rio de Janeiro and host the World Climate Change Conference in Belém in 2025. Brazil will then also have to convince the international public of what the current Lula da Silva government has done for Amazonia in social and ecological terms, especially with regard to the planned oil production in the Amazon river estuary.

---

506 cf. chapter II.4.4

507 cf. chapter II.6.1; II.6.2.

508 Interview with Marina Silva by Tjerk Brühwiller, *FAZ*, September 11, 2023. https://www.faz.net/aktuell/politik/ausland/regenwald-abholzung-im-amazonas-der-stopp-reicht-nicht-fuer-die-rettung-19164270.html (accessed September 4, 2024).

2. Concluding remarks

A little more than 50 years ago, the Brazilian Military Government decided to grant private capital almost unlimited access to the largest tropical rain forest area in Amazonia with generous tax incentives after the failure of the widely announced state-led agricultural colonisation of small farmers. The exploitation of the complex Amazonian ecosystems has been carried out against the warnings of scientists, without regard for the Indigenous as well as the regional rural population and the ecological fragility of the natural conditions. Scientific preliminary studies and the necessary management control were largely lacking. Infrastructure projects, large-scale cattle grazing, extensive slash-and-burn agriculture and mining dominated the Polamazônia programme.

The military's economic development model was based on an "El Dorado" mentality of unlimited economic growth. Hasty, inadequately prepared project planning of conservative modernisation "from above" without consideration of social and ecological consequences characterised the state's approach. Tropical ecosystems and the regional population were seen more as obstacles to economic "progress." The lack of understanding for sustainable regional development, the deficient coordination of state and private projects at the federal, regional and above all local level resulted in high follow-up costs and social burdens. This continued to be the case frequently after the end of the military dictatorship in 1985.

Land speculation and conflicts with the regional Indigenous population and with squatters led to serious problems. Some national and international investors were more interested in increasing the value of their estates than in cattle breeding, favoured by nearby road building and other investments in infrastructure. A highly speculative land market emerged, and cattle grazing projects served as a suitable means to acquire land using the tax breaks.

Pioneer front areas in Amazônia Legal are characterised by clashes between different social actors in a permanent struggle for land access and spatial domination of rain forest areas and their natural resources. Land grabbing at the Amazonian frontier is associated with ubiquitous illegal procedures (*grilagem*), corruption and violence. The untrustworthiness of land titles, sometimes based on dubious or falsified historical documents or by forging of the land register through bribery was one of the basic problems. For a long time, the riverine population was not supported by targeted government programmes, so that, like the Indigenous population, they suffered most from illegal and often violent land grabbing, displacement and forced migration to the poverty-stricken neighbourhoods of large cities.

It is most regrettable that the state monopoly of violence is rarely existing in peripheral frontier regions, or the official institutions were weakened – sometimes intentionally – or frequently corruptible. Violation of law plays a key role in most conflicts of interest. Indirect "structural violence" is the result of unequal power relations and unequal distribution of natural resources or even leads to direct violent activities between persons or groups involved.

Most democratic governments that followed the military dictatorship were also unwilling to invest in Indigenous affairs and often did not admit their indifference, lack of appreciation and little understanding for Indigenous people. The responsible authority for Indigenous affairs, FUNAI, has not been able to adequately address the problems of the Indigenous population. This agency was dependent on changing government strategies, worked with small financial resources, and suffered from persistent corruption, lack of qualified anthropologists and administrative ambiguities. Only recently this has changed among some decision-makers in Amazonian states, as it has become clear that preserving biodiversity through reduced deforestation will have positive effects.

In their regionally dispersed territories, the Indigenous population was frequently seen as an obstacle to the economic exploitation of Amazonia. Amazonian states saw the establishment and registration of Indigenous territories by the federal government as a negative influence on their economic development opportunities. Although more than 22 % of the area of Amazônia Legal are Indigenous territories and mostly legally recognised, they suffer from the pressure of advancing pioneer fronts, constant border violations for illegal exploitation of natural resources. They are jeopardised by the lack of state presence and administrative weakness. However, it is generally recognised that the real guardians of the rain forest are the Indigenous peoples or traditional peasant communities native to some Amazonian regions.

Due to modern infrastructure, expansion of cattle breeding and agribusiness, mining activities, wood extraction, drug trafficking, biopiracy and environmental degradation, the physical, economic and especially the socio-cultural vulnerability of Indigenous societies in Amazonia is highly endangered.

In general, Indigenous peoples are still the losers of the regional policy for Amazonia. There was a fundamental conflict at the moral-ethical level in addressing Indigenous problems within regional development programmes: granting financial compensation for the deprivation of habitat, the destruction of the cultural identity and self-determined economic existence of a minority that was the government's protégé under the Brazilian Constitution.

In the smallholder sector, the Polonoroeste programme, with financial support from the World Bank, attempted to implement "development from below" based on credit for small-scale farmers, cooperative organisation and agricultural extension services. The positive impulse of the programme suffered from an overly optimistic timetable and was hampered by grossly underestimated immigration and conflicts on the pioneering front, as well as by the weakness of regional institutions.

However, the almost simultaneous establishment of the mega-project Programa Grande Carajás (PGC), whose planning concept originates from the authoritarian military regime, completely ignored the positive approaches to integrated rural development of *Polonororeste*. The PGC was announced to be the world's major integrated regional development project. The new democratic governments after 1985 were confronted with a development programme that proved to be a model of "development from above," placing the Amazonian periphery entirely under the control of Brasília without taking into account the basic needs of the marginalised rural poor or ecological and environmental issues.

Unchanged authoritarian decision-making structures, confusion of competence in planning or even unrealistic solutions of project implementation prevailed in the PGC administration. SUDAM, which never had a sound regional development strategy, was deprived of its former status. An unclear situation with dubious land titles, invasions and land conflicts of all kinds dominated the scenario. The destruction of tropical rain forests' biodiversity by huge fires and the unimaginable deforestation rates alarmed the international public.

The iron ore project in Serra dos Carajás, organised by Cia Vale do Rio Doce (CVRD), was the core project of the PGC, which made Brazil the largest iron ore producer and exporter next to Australia. In contrast to the well thought-out environmental planning in the CVRD concession area, obliged to comply with the conditions of the World Bank loans, the directly related projects such as the railway construction and the other PGC large-scale projects (Tucuruí hydropower plant, alumina and aluminium industry, charcoal-based pig iron production) led to mass migration and a chaotic and violent situation in the surrounding PGC region. In addition, the gold rush at Serra Pelada increased social tensions and demonstrated the lack of state control over regional development.

The PGC didn't have a clearly defined regional planning strategy that included all social actors. It was a development programme without a budget of its own, living of state subsidies and financing projects to integrate Amazonia's natural resources into the world market. Unfortunately, the "sell-out" of Amazonia did not bring sufficient financial resources back into the region to enable ecologically and socially sustainable development for the benefit of the majority of the population. In PGC, the living conditions and protection of Indigenous territories in East Amazonia were not given special consideration. The landless rural population of the PGC region had very difficult access to land and remained marginalised. There was a lack of political will to implement communal programmes for integrated development to achieve sustainable forms of agroforestry and agricultural production to meet the social needs and a socially balanced regional development.

The socio-economic and environmental impacts of large-scale projects and the related social and ecological costs were not duly considered. There was a lack of assessment of the environmental impact of projects during preparation and monitoring of ongoing projects. Reasonable doubts arose about the seriousness of the environmental impact assessments, as the side effects associated with the implementation of the projects that caused environmental damage were not taken into account. In many cases, consulting companies prepared reports favourable to the approved projects, because they were contracted by the proponents of the projects, interested in the positive assessment.

These projects directly interfered with the municipal development in the affected areas and were by no means coordinated with municipal necessities. Large-scale projects often lead to spatially isolated enclaves, polarisation effects prevail, and intra-regional disparities steadily increase. Information of the population affected by such projects – if available at all – was inadequate and delayed. Follow-up costs and the financial burdens for the protection against environmental damage remained with the regional or municipal administration which were neither prepared nor financially able to cope with this. Tax breaks for large projects resulted in low tax revenues in the municipalities.

Large hydroelectric power plants like Tucuruí were considered to produce "green" energy but the process of anaerobic decomposition of biomass in the huge, flooded area of the reservoir caused emissions of toxic greenhouse gases such as CO_2, H_2S and methane. Resettlement projects were not planned in advance and had disastrous social and economic effects on the population. The already low compensation payments were often deliberately delayed and devalued by inflation. Retention and dumping of red mud produced in the refining process of alumina caused lasting dangerous environmental problems and were the reason for severe groundwater pollution. Large-scale projects attracted tens of thousands of construction workers. After the end of construction only few permanent positions remained, which were filled by well-trained technicians. Unskilled workers were dismissed but remained living near the project in precarious conditions.

The Grande Carajás programme must be evaluated as an administratively and functionally inefficient, institutionally uncoordinated and vertically incoherent mega-programme. The objective of decentralising spatial planning decisions and involving the affected regional population was not achieved. By far the majority of the regional population judged PGC to be an "attack on the heart of Amazonia."

The new Brazilian Constitution of 1988 created the basis for a legally regulated environmental policy with a separate chapter on environment protection. However, the establishment of environmental agencies was no guarantee for the practical implementation of the new regulations, as the control of compliance with the legal provisions in a frontier region remained difficult. On the basis of the Constitution, numerous NGOs were founded which, together with environmental activists and grassroots organisations, were important actors in the socio-ecological movements in the 1990s. Environmentalists campaigned with great commitment for the anchoring of environmental protection in the Constitution of the federal states. NGOs, which increasingly had scientifically trained staff members, have also contributed to the realisation of public policies through participatory processes and incorporation of local communities in environmental management and monitoring of state regional policy. NGOs strengthened good governance processes.

Pressure from international environmental NGOs has mediated government policy and – two decades later – led to important agreements, such as the soybean moratorium and the cattle agreement. However, in conservative and nationalist circles in Brazil, the socio-ecological activities of international NGOs are viewed with some suspicion.

As deforestation increased rapidly, the G7 proposal to financially support the Brazilian review of new regional development models for the Amazon region was accepted by the Brazilian government. The aim of the International Pilot Programme to Conserve the Brazilian Rain Forests (PPG7), with Germany as its main donor, was the implementation of a sustainable development approach. It was a unique opportunity to realise the principles of the Agenda 21 of the 1992 UNCED summit in Rio de Janeiro.

PPG7 was the starting point for some significant environmental and regional policy improvements for Amazonia. One of the main contributions was the elaboration of joint management in strengthening federal government entities in the implementation of sustainable environmental policies, with public-private-partnership integrating the different groups of civil society, such as active networks of NGOs. On the other hand, decentralisation of environmental management in priority areas of Amazonian states was strongly supported, improving state-controlled environmental policies with the management of natural resources and of protected areas.

The implementation of so-called demonstration projects gave a very important impetus to small-scale projects by regional groups and NGOs. The aim of this "development from below" was to generate income and strengthen the livelihoods of local communities, which had been completely forgotten by the government for a long time. Improving the security of the Indigenous population, demarcating and protecting their territories and disseminating the traditional knowledge of these groups also received international attention.

Unfortunately, some relevant ministries did not participate in PPG7, and thus many problems of small farmers, tenants, and *posseiros* were not considered. Problems of urban development also remained excluded.

However, despite deficits or organisational and implementation obstacles, PPG7 was the most comprehensive example of an international environmental cooperation programme realised in the Brazilian Amazon with the explicit participation of the Brazilian government and the civil society.

All the more incomprehensible was the implementation of extensive infrastructure programmes almost simultaneously, which aimed at a conservative modernisation and were without any environmental component or social relevance for the mass of the Amazonian population. These programmes, counterproductive to previous environmental goals and with determined private economic interests, had far-reaching negative consequences and were associated with enormous deforestation.

In the first government of Lula da Silva, the Minister of Environment, Marina Silva, succeeded in reducing deforestation very significantly. Prevention and control of deforestation were at the centre of the measures. The strict application of environmental laws successfully tried to detect illegal deforestation activities. Blacklists of municipalities with high deforestation were established, and farmers involved in illegal deforestation were not admitted to public agricultural credit programmes.

The highly controversial Forest Code had been increased to a legal forest protection of 80 % for private property in the Amazon rain forest biome under the Cardoso government, amidst great protest from the agribusiness sector. Under the Rousseff government, Lula da Silva's successor, forest protection in Amazonia was reduced from 80 % to 50 % under pressure from the agribusiness lobby. In 2018, the Supreme Court revised the amendment.

Clear title deeds existed for only 10 % of the private land in Amazônia Legal. In 2010, the federal government made it mandatory to map all private rural land and register it in the Rural Environmental Registry, an important component in keeping deforestation under control. Protected areas and conservation units were created with the aim of protecting biodiversity in the ecosystems of the Amazon region and promoting sustainable development. The combination of deforestation control and the establishment of the Amazon Fund enabled state governments to elaborate own plans for prevention and control of deforestation with projects relevant to smallholders.

Lula da Silva's Plan of Sustainable Amazonia could not resolve the severe conflicts between the powerful supporters of infrastructure development and the engaged, well-prepared environmental groups with the aim of regional sustainability. Agribusiness was specially supported, and the extensive activities of cattle ranching could not be reduced. Environmental policies were frequently realised without consideration of important environmental issues. The government was unwilling or unable to implement the sustainability approach in its programmes after the departure of Marina Silva, provoked in 2008 by the president's caving in to pressure from agribusiness and the hydroelectric power plant lobby. This was a setback for Brazil's ambitions to become a major voice in global environmental debates.

Towards the end of the second term of Lula da Silva's government, Brazil had started actions in collaborating with the global programmes to combat climate change and implemented the National Plan of Climate Change and the Low-Carbon Agriculture Plan.

Some years later, REDD+ projects provided financial incentives for the results achieved in combating deforestation and forest degradation. Forest-related greenhouse gas emission reductions and enhancement of forest carbon stocks were rewarded with results-based payments from various international sources. These projects promoted changes in the political articulation, funding possibilities and mobilisation of civil society and led to the conservation of biodiversity and social benefits to the region. Lack of political commitment and inefficient local governance questioned the success of these projects.

Already in the late 1980s, the availability of large land reserves had caused migration of southern Brazilian farmers to the *cerrados* of the Planalto Central and the adjacent Amazonian region. Decisive for these activities were the significantly lower land prices compared to southern Brazil and the favourable natural conditions for mechanised agriculture, especially in the *cerrado*. The process of globalisation and world market integration of the *cerrado* and Amazon rain forest areas developed on the basis of rapidly expanding soybean monocultures in the 1990s onwards. Agro industrialisation was supported by agricultural research, technical assistance, a high degree of mechanisation and specific pricing and credit policies. Agribusiness was integrated into global value chains with agricultural production, marketing, logistics, financing, agricultural machinery and trade strategies.

The expansion of soybean cultivation first transformed northern Mato Grosso, introducing large-scale, modernised and export-oriented agriculture with new no-till methods, but with high pesticide use and genetically modified seeds. In addition to increasing economic power in rural and urban areas and socio-cultural conflicts with the traditional population, the farmers from South Brazil have also significantly expanded their political influence in the region at all levels.

Concentration of ownership of large soybean entrepreneurs led to the displacement of smallholders who had been traditionally engaged in subsistence agriculture in this region. The "winners" still cling to the frontier myth that they have successfully achieved their goal of setting up farms with government approval, but now complain about the rapidly changing laws and the new environmental and climate dialogue and its direct and indirect impact on their life and prosperity. They were now confronted with the soybean moratorium, which banned the sale of soybean from areas deforested in Amazonia after 2008. However, soybean expansion has not been suppressed because of the abundance of cattle pastures for conversion to soybean.

The most diverse conflicts of interest between the social actors led to a constantly escalating competition in land acquisition and land use combined with illegal actions and often also violence. This is how the idea of an important cross-problem regional planning came into being. The Sustainable Regional Development Plan for the BR-163 area provided for land title regularisation along the Cuiabá–Santarém road and the delimitation of conservation units and extractive reserves, was not implemented properly by the Lula da Silva and the following governments. Provision of few financial resources, lack of trained personnel, insufficient monitoring, improper implementation of the protected areas were the most important failures which resulted in the advance of the agricultural frontier opening new areas for forest devastation.

The crucial issue for regional development and the question of asphalting BR-163 was either an export corridor for world market-oriented agricultural products or socio-ecologically based sustainable development to protect vulnerable populations. Finally, asphalting was completed in 2019. The expansion of transport infrastructure for commodity export, which significantly reduces transport costs, took precedence over poverty-oriented regional sustainability strategies.

The highway was the backbone of one of the most important export corridors in Brazilian Amazonia. Some federal ministries, the governments of the affected federal states and transnational agribusiness exerted strong pressure on the decision-making process. They were backed by soybean farmers, sawmill owners, timber trade, transport companies, representatives of the municipalities concerned and urban businessmen. On the other hand, a broad mobilisation of social organisations, small farmers' unions, rubber tappers, and Indigenous groups supported by national and international NGOs tried in vain to secure their livelihoods. The new highway benefited the economic elite of Mato Grosso and, to a certain extent, of the southwest of Pará. Former pioneer towns changed very strongly into globalised trading centres for commodities and very soon showed an alarming socio-spatial fragmentation.

Lula de Silva's government stuck to large infrastructure projects and hydroelectric power plants in Amazônia Legal. In 2007, the Growth Acceleration Programme was introduced with huge investments. The Belo Monte power plant mega-project, whose construction had not been approved in the late 1980s, now appeared revived as a renamed run-of-river power plant depending on the flow of the river and was considered an anchor project of the new investment plans. However, it was known that the Xingu river has one of the greatest annual variations in water flow of all Amazon tributaries. Belo Monte was met with great resistance from the riverine population and Indigenous peoples and triggered strong protests from NGOs. The project was also strongly questioned due to bureaucratic and insufficient public hearings and the lack of a qualified environmental impact assessment. Despite numerous lawsuits against the construction of Belo Monte and rulings to stop the project, as well as all environmental, hydrological, social, financial and economic counterarguments, Belo Monte was built with partial permits until its completion in 2019.

Belo Monte is a prime example of the lack of environmental justice in large hydroelectric projects. Common problems include the violation of basic human rights, measures that completely ignore environmental concerns, loss of biodiversity, landscape degradation, destruction of the livelihoods of people who depend on fishing or hunting, involuntary resettlement and lack of resettlement management.

The electric energy produced in Belo Monte is used for the electro-intensive alumina, aluminium, iron, and other smelting industries in Pará and Maranhão, predominantly owned by global players. Belo Monte is one of the most inefficient hydro-power plants in Brazil, generating only 10 % of its potential capacity of 11 233 MW for four months and only 39 % on average for the year. The need for more dams upstream, officially denied by the government, threatens to ensure sufficient water flow.

Political pressure on technical staff in the approval process was omnipresent. Top managers testified in court that bribes paid by large construction companies to the petroleum sector also applied to the electrical sector and contracts for Belo Monte. The leading political parties obtained substantial financial contributions to election campaigns from construction enterprises. Brazilian prosecutors uncovered a system of corruption and massive fraud in the construction of mega-projects in Amazonia involving a kind of criminal association of Brazil's biggest construction companies, influential government officials and highest-ranking politicians. This has severely damaged the country's intentions for sustainable planning in Amazonia and Brazil's reputation internationally.

Despite serious problems with mega-projects in Amazonia, official measures for sustainable regional development have been attempted from time to time since the 1990s and some have also been implemented with varying success. Indigenous territories were approved, but unfortunately not always sufficiently secured. At least temporarily, government measures have been able to greatly reduce deforestation. The *ribeirinhos'* own initiatives for small-scale agricultural and agroforestry projects (e.g., honey production, use of fruits and vegetable cultivation, partly with a cooperative structure), which were not financed by the government, increasingly received support from local and regional NGOs.

When the far-right populist Bolsonaro came to power in 2019, all previous achievements were abruptly abolished, and the democratic constitution was endangered. Deforestation in Amazonia had already been on the rise since 2013, but the rates of increase were particularly high during his four years in office. Bolsonaro dismantled environmental licences and regulations as well as Indigenous rights. No new Indigenous territories were created, mining and timber companies could now operate in these areas with official approval. The president denied climate change, was an opponent of forest protection, disregarded scientific findings, was an enemy of NGOs and did not attach any importance to Brazil's commitment under the Paris Climate Agreement of 2015. With his aggressive and insulting behaviour, Bolsonaro attracted negative attention both nationally and internationally.

Under his presidency, Amazonia experienced a new phase of absolute exploitation without regard for social inequalities and environmental concerns. Deforestation for cattle pastures even occurred in Indigenous territories, conservation units and extractive reserves. Uncontrolled deforestation, excessive forest fires, gold mining, expansion of croplands and pastures and the advancing of infrastructural projects marked this phase. Land was illegally acquired and "legalised" by falsifying documents. Criminal networks also dominated illegal logging and timber trade undisturbed. Budget and staff cuts weakened the environmental authorities. Opponents of his extermination strategies were violently attacked or received death threats. The state's monopoly on the use of force disappeared in large parts of Amazonia and was replaced by violent actions of private criminal unscrupulous social actors.

In Amazônia Legal, there was a climate of violence, fear, despair and a weakening or absence of judiciary power. Ethical principles and environmental justice were intentionally ignored by the Bolsonaro government. The way he ran the government contributed to squandering Brazil's ecological capital, dividing Brazilian society and radicalising his supporters.

Bolsonaro's government demonstrated how quickly environmental measures to protect Amazonia can be overturned in domestic political struggles and a change of political orientation. Environmental institutions were brought to a virtual standstill, and violence and chaos became omnipresent.

At this point, at the latest, it became clear to most that Amazônia Legal had become a scene of environmental destruction and crime in recent decades. To date, about 20% of tropical rain forests have been cleared, mostly illegally, and another 20% are severely degraded. Tropical forest ecosystems are a huge CO_2 reservoir. The Amazonian ecosystems store about 150 to 200 billion tons of carbon.

The main cause of deforestation continues to be expanding large-scale cattle ranches, which account for about 80% of deforestation in Amazonia and are responsible for two-thirds of Brazil's CO_2 emissions. Slash-and-burn releases enormous amounts of carbon dioxide emissions, destroys the high biodiversity and thus the habitat of Indigenous and riverine populations. Excessive emission of greenhouse gases cause dangerous impacts on regional climate change and global warming. Tropical rain forests protected by Indigenous groups, on the other hand, are very strong carbon sinks. Threatening problems of deforestation are destruction of the closed nutrient cycle of ecosystems, increasing temperature, regional instability of rainfall, reduced evaporation, severe soil degradation and erosion, changes in the hydrological cycle and problems of dryness, reinforced by El Niño effects. The intensity of extreme events such as droughts, the length of the dry season and floods is increasing. Regional climate change due to large-scale deforestation and the effects of forest fires make remaining tropical rain forests more vulnerable. The immense scale of CO_2 emissions in Amazonia is having an ever-increasing impact on the global climate.

The most alarming news is that Brazilian Amazônia Legal has changed from a CO_2 sink to a source of new CO_2 emissions in the last two decades. This means that deforestation, climate change and widespread forest fires at a total deforestation rate of 20-25% mark a tipping point where the Amazonian rain forests turn into non-forest ecosystems (savannahs), especially in eastern, southern and central Amazonia. This "point of no return" could be imminent.

After four years of presidency under the right-wing populist Bolsonaro, the new leftist government of Lula da Silva, in office since the beginning of 2023, has a great opportunity for a fundamental turnaround with the final reversal of destructive activities in the Amazon region and the aim of sound sustainable development. The new decisions to revitalise the environmental institutions, to strengthen their functions and to rapidly reduce deforestation rates were welcomed not only by Lula da Silva's supporters in Brazil, but also by many governments worldwide. However, it must be borne in mind that there is still scope for legal logging in many regions due to the existing Forest Code with a maximum logging rate of 20% for private property in rain forests.

The Lula da Silva government established a separate Ministry of Indigenous Affairs and the appointment of Indigenous persons to high-level positions in an attempt to increase the involvement of the Indigenous population. Due to the evolved self-confidence in parts of the Indigenous people, who know how to articulate themselves in defence of their rights, participation in sustainable solutions is now possible. However, the promised improved participation of members of the Afro-Brazilian population in high-ranking positions has not yet been met.

The Amazon Fund, which was stopped under Bolsonaro, will once again provide the international community with the opportunity to compensate Brazil for environmental services in reducing deforestation and emissions and promoting sustainable land use. The Fund's resources allocated to government agencies have been one of the few sources of funding to control deforestation. Some foreign governments offered more financial support for conducting the new tasks.

Lula da Silva trusts the Minister of Environment Marina Silva and former staff members, advisors and some NGOs on Amazonian environmental issues. The country's economic situation - far from the times of an export boom during Lula da Silva's first term and high unemployment of more than 13 million people (2021) - and the political and social tensions raise doubts about the feasibility of all announced projects.

The Lula da Silva government is under environmental pressure at home and abroad. NGOs in Brazil and Europe reject the EU-Mercosur agreement as completely inadequate in content. The EU, whose residents as consumers of Amazonian goods were responsible for about 10% of deforestation between 1990 and 2020, has issued a new regulation on supply chains and will ban the import of goods from deforested areas in Amazônia Legal. In Brazil, agribusiness fears that the EU's prohibitive environmental standards are a deliberate pretence to make exports to Europe more difficult. In the EU, a complex coalition of opponents against the agreement had formed from the agricultural lobby to environmental activists.

Today, Lula da Silva has an autonomous foreign policy agenda, in which both the global supply of Brazilian agricultural and mineral commodities and Brazil's membership in the BRICS alliance together with China and Russia are particularly important. Brazil wants to be the independent voice of the Global South. This explains why Lula da Silva strongly opposes Western coalition sanctions against Moscow, despite Russia's war of aggression against Ukraine. China and the new BRICS Development Bank will play an even greater role in future investments in Brazil and the Amazon region.

For Brazil, China is – if necessary – always a "worthwhile" export alternative to Europe and the United States, which are strongly focused on environmental protection. The hosting of the G20 summit in Brazil in 2024 and the UN Conference on Climate Change (COP 30), which will take place in 2025 in Belém in the Amazon region, naturally strengthen Lula da Silva's international role.

Amazônia Legal is still heavily marked by economic exploitation, a region where the invaders ruthlessly threaten and curtail the rights of the Indigenous population. Until then it has not been possible to eliminate speculation, illegality and corruption. The importance of the Amazonian ecosystems as a hotspot of biodiversity has been sacrificed to short-term economic success.

Brazil "is a territory geographically fragmented into regions that continuously reproduce a socioeconomically unequal and environmentally predatory development" (Theis 2019, 356). Amazônia Legal is one of these "regions that escape the needs and interests of the subalternate classes" and deprives the majority of the human beings of their means of living. The regional development strategies adopted in Amazonia are part of the problem, not of the solution (Theis 2022, 88 and 92).

The El Dorado mentality of exploitation and mere extraction of natural resources must belong to the past. Actually, this would now be the big chance for the new government to address and improve the core problems. In the Amazon region, this would contribute to greater resilience among Indigenous and smallholder societies. However, this must be actively promoted by the government at all levels with clear strategies and without reservations (Hecht *et al.* 2021). Ecological, social and economic improvements brought about by political measures were mostly short-term, regionally limited or insufficient and difficult to reverse. However, "expectations on ongoing initiatives for sustainable development, zero deforestation, and environmental recuperation should not be too high" (Pokorny *et al.* 2021; Pokorny 2013).

In summary, it is realistic not to overestimate the possibilities of President Lula da Silva to act as a "game changer", as he and his supporters have in mind. As is to be expected and can already be seen, the National Congress, especially the Senate, will oppose the reorganised environmental protection and Indigenous policy of the Lula da Silva government with all conceivable resistance and will prevent or at least try to severely weaken corresponding bills.

The political split in the country prevents a political consensus, which is needed to guide the activities of the various social groups towards a regional development that meets the claim to sustainability and the socio-economic needs of the population concerned. Today, more than 28 million people live in Amazônia Legal. Since 1970, the Amazonian population has quadrupled, more than 80% are urban people. This means that one in eight Brazilians lives in Amazonia. About 3.3 % of the Amazonian population is Indigenous.

Amazonian rain forests must no longer serve as a field of experience for so-called conservative development models and must not be a space of action for conflicts of interest on the globalised periphery. Direct and indirect ecological and social costs as well as the follow-up costs must be calculated precisely before projects begin and the follow-up costs must be estimated in detail. Fearnside points out that "the intrinsic value of Amazon biodiversity is a key to maintaining Amazonian ecosystems with all their environmental functions" (Fearnside 2021b). In projects, understood as economically necessary, there must be a totally new classification scale in environmental impact assessments, on what "development" means, for whom this development serves and with which specific measures resilience of the population affected almost without warning by the economic and social changes can be achieved.

The realisation that a living forest is worth more than a cut-down forest leads to a new paradigm of sustainable development. This well-founded discussion, which is being conducted in the scientific field, could be taken up by politics for a new appreciation of the Amazonian region. New bioeconomic innovations open the way to a third path of development.

Brazil has the capacity in science, environmental knowledge and technology to analyse the pressing problems of Amazônia Legal and find sustainable solutions that will convince serious governments to put them into practice. To this end, Brazil welcomes multinational technical-scientific funds and environmentally oriented financial investments as part of the international commitment to combat deforestation in Amazonia and strengthen its population.

Brazil does not need lectures from outside, but the return to successful environmental initiatives for Amazonia in international scientific and financial cooperation could contribute in the best sense to overcoming the problems of implementing sustainable regional development. Environmental programmes like PPG7 could help to find new ways.

The Brazilian government and appropriate critical actors from the ranks of Brazilian civil society must work together to avoid fundamental undesirable developments in Amazonia. The ecologically and socially vulnerable region must be protected from further questionable large-scale projects that are associated with serious social disadvantages for the majority of the regional population, far-reaching social conflicts and lasting ecological damage, and that overburden the state financially.

Protecting biodiversity in Amazônia Legal will have a positive impact on the living conditions of the Amazonian population and on global impacts related to slowing climate change and global warming. This would further strengthen Brazil's national prestige and international reputation.

Appendix

List of Figures

List of Tables

Acronyms

ABC	Brazilian Academy of Sciences
ACT	Amazon Cooperation Treaty
ACTO	Amazon Cooperation Treaty Organisation
ADA	Agency of Development of Amazonia
AMZA	Amazon Mining Co.
ARPA	Amazon Protected Areas Programme
ATIX	Xingu Lands Indigenous Association
ATTO	Amazon Tall Tower Observatory
BFC	Brazilian Forest Code
BMBF	German Ministry of Education and Research
BMFT	German Ministry of Research and Technology
BMZ	German Ministry for Economic Cooperation and Development
BNDES	Brazilian National Bank for Economic and Social Development
BR	Brazilian Federal Roads
BRICS	Group of emerging states: Brazil, Russia, India, China, South Africa
BSM	Brazilian Soybean Moratorium
CAPES	Coordination for the Improvement of Higher Education
CAPOIB	Articulation Council of Indigenous Peoples and Organisations of Brazil
CAR	Rural Environmental Registry
CDM	Clean Development Mechanism
CHESF	Hydroelectric Company of the São Francisco River
CIMI	Indigenous Missionary Council
CIPGC	Interministerial Council for the Grande Carajás Programme
CNDDA	National Campaign of the Defence and Development of Amazonia
CNPq	National Council for Scientific and Technological Development
CNPI	National Council of Indigenous Policy
COIAB	Coordination of the Indigenous Organisations of the Brazilian Amazon
CONAB	National Supply Company
CONAMA	National Council for the Environment
CONAMAZ	National Council for the Legal Amazon
COP	Conference of the Parties
CPATU	Agricultural Research Centre of the Humid Tropics
CPT	Rural Pastoral Commission
CVRD	Cia. Vale do Rio Doce
DETER	Deforestation Detection System
DNER	National Department of Highways

DNPM	National Department of Mineral Production
EC	European Community
EdIGUT	Editor Institute of Geography University of Tübingen
EEC	European Economic Community
EFC	Carajás railroad
EIA/RIMA	Environmental Impact Assessment/Report of Environmental Impact
EMATER	Agricultural Extension Service
EMBRAPA	Brazilian Agricultural Research Cooperation
ENREDD	National strategy for reducing emissions from deforestation and forest degradation
EU	European Union
FAB	Brazilian Air Force
FAO	Food and Agricultural Organisation of the UN
FINAME	Special Agency for Industrial Financing
FNMA	National Environmental Fund
FSC	Forest Stewardship Council
FUNAI	National Indigenous People Foundation
GDP	Gross Domestic Product
GEAMAM	CVRD's Environmental Study and Advisory Group
GETAT	Executive Group of Araguaia-Tocantins Lands
GHG	Greenhouse gases
GIZ	German Agency of International Cooperation
GTA	Amazonian Working Group
GTZ	German Technical Cooperation Agency
IAG	International Advisory Group
IBAMA	Brazilian Institute of Environment and Renewable Natural Resources
IBDF	Brazilian Institute of Forest Development
IBGE	Brazilian Institute of Geography and Statistics
ICMBio	Chico Mendes Institute for Biodiversity Conservation
IDB	Inter-American Development Bank
IDCJ	National Development Centre of Japan
IDESP	Institute for Economic and Social Development of Pará
IEA	Institute of Amazonian and Environmental Studies
IMAZON	Amazon Institute of People and the Environment
INCRA	National Institute for Colonisation and Agrarian Reform
INPA	National Institute for Amazonian Research
INPE	National Space Research Institute
IPAM	Amazon Environmental Research Institute

IPBES	Intergovernmental Platform on Biodiversity and Ecosystem Services
IPCC	Intergovernmental Panel on Climate Change
IPEA	Institute of Applied Economic Research
ISA	Socio-Environmental Institute
ITTA	International Tropical Timber Agreement
IWGIA	International World Group for Indigenous Affairs
JICA	Japanese International Cooperation Agency
KAS	Konrad Adenauer Foundation
KfW	German Government Development Bank
MAB	Man and the Biosphere
MATOPIBA	Maranhão, Tocantins, Piauí, Bahia
MIRAD	Ministry of Agrarian Reform and Agrarian Development
MMA	Ministry of the Environment
MME	Ministry of Mining and Energy
MRN	Mining Company Rio do Norte
MST	Movement of the Landless
mt	million tons
mtpy	million tons per year
NGO	Non-Governmental Organisation
NUAR	Urban Nucleus of Rural Support
OAS	Organisation of American States
PAC	Growth Acceleration Programme
PAS	Plan of Sustainable Amazonia
PCC	First Command of the Capital
PDRI	Integrated Rural Development Project
PGC	Grande Carajás Programme
PIN	National Programme of Integration
PMDB	Brazilian Democratic Movement Party
PNMA	National Environmental Programme
PNMC	National Plan on Climate Change
PPCDAm	Plan for the Prevention and Control Programme for Deforestation in Amazonia
PPG7	Pilot Programme to conserve the Brazilian tropical rain forests (of the G7 states)
PPTAL	Integrated Project for the Protection of Indigenous Peoples and Lands in the Legal Amazon
PROBOR	Programme for Rubber Production
PRODES	Satellite Monitoring of Deforestation in the Legal Amazon
PRODESQUE	Fire and Deforestation Control Project

RADAM	Radar in the Amazon
REDD	Reducing Emissions from Deforestation and Forest Degradation
REM	REDD Early Movers
RESEX	Extractive Reserve
RFT	Rain Forest Trust Fund
SBPC	Brazilian Society for the Advancement of Science
SCA	Secretariat of Coordination of Amazonia
SEDEC-MT	Secretary of Economic Development of the State of Mato Grosso
SEMA	Environmental Protection Agency
SEPLAN	Secretariat of Planning of the Presidency of the Republic
SHIFT	Studies on Human Impact on Tropical Forests and Floodplains in Brazil
SISNAMA	National System for the Environment
SIVAM	System of Vigilance over the Amazon
SNI	National Information Service
SNUC	National System of Conservation Units
SOPREN	Society of Amazonia's Natural and Cultural Resources Preservation
SPI	Indian Protection Service
SPU	Union Heritage Secretariat
SPVEA	Superintendency of Amazon Economic Development
SUDAM	Superintendency of Development for the Amazon
SUDECO	Superintendency of Central-West Development
SUDENE	Superintendency of Northeast Development
SUDEPE	Superintendency for Fishery Development
SUDHEVEA	Superintendency of Rubber
SUFRAMA	Superintendency of the Manaus Free Trade Zone
TBGL	Tübinger Beiträge zur Geographischen Lateinamerikaforschung (Tübingen Contributions to Geographical Research on Latin America)
TFAP	Tropical Forestry Action Plan
tpy	tons per year
UDR	Democratic Association of Ruralists
UNCED	United Nations Conference on Environment and Development
UNCTAD	United Nations Conference on Trade and Development
UNEP	United Nations Environmental Programme
UNFCCC	United Nations Framework Convention on Climate Change
WWF	World Wide Fund for Nature

Glossary

barrageiros	power plant workers
boias frias	migrant workers
cacique	chief
empreiteiro	subcontractor
favela	slum, shantytown
fazenda	farm
fazendeiro	farmer
garimpo	gold mine
garimpeiro	gold digger
grilo	grabbed land
grileiro	land grabber
grilagem	land grabbing
latifundio	big estate
minifundio	small plot of land
minifundista	smallholder
pistoleiro	gunman
posseiro	squatter, settler without land title
prefeitura	mayor's office
ribeirinhos	riverside population
ruralista	large landholder
seringal	rubber plantation
seringalista	owner of a rubber plantation
seringueiro	rubber tapper
várzea	floodplain

References

Abdenur, Adriana E., Maurício Santoro, and Maiara Folly. 2021. *What railway deals taught Chinese and Brazilians in the Amazon.* Washington, D.C.: Carnegie Endowment for International Peace.

Ab'Sáber, Aziz Nacib. 1987. "Gênese de uma nova região siderúrgica: acertos e distorções de uma nova origem na faixa Carajás/São Luís." *Pará Desenvolvimento* 22: 3–15.

Ab'Sáber, Aziz Nacib. 1989. "Zoneamento ecológico e econômico da Amazônia. Questões de escala e método." *Estudos Avançados* 3, no. 5: 4–20.

Ab'Sáber, Aziz Nacib. 1995. "Elements for a strategy for territorial settlement and ecodevelopment in the Amazon." In *Brazilian perspectives on sustainable development of the Amazon region,* edited by Miguel Clüsener-Godt and Ignacy Sachs, 287–303. Paris: UNESCO/Parthenon.

Ab'Sáber, Aziz Nacib. 1996a. *Amazônia: Do discurso à praxis.* São Paulo: EDUSP.

Ab'Sáber, Aziz Nacib. 1996b. "Aspectos ambientais na faixa Carajás-São Luís." In *Amazônia: Do discurso à praxis,* 91–112. São Paulo: EDUSP.

Ab'Sáber, Aziz Nacib. 1996c. "Da Serra Pelada à Serra dos Carajás. A rebelião (im) prevista dos garimpeiros." In *Amazônia: Do discurso à praxis,* 238–286. São Paulo: EDUSP.

Ab'Sáber, Aziz Nacib. 2005. "Problemas da Amazônia Brasileira." Entrevista. Dossiê Amazônia Brasileira I. *Estudos Avançados* 19, no. 53: 7–34.

Acker, Antoine. 2017. *Volkswagen in the Amazon: The tragedy of global development in modern Brazil.* Cambridge: Cambridge University Press.

Adams, William M. 1991. *Green development. Environment and sustainability in the Third World.* London/New York: Routledge.

Alencar, Ane A. C. 2005. *A rodovia BR-163 e o desafio da sustentabilidade.* Belém: IPAM.

Allegretti, Mary H. 1990. "Extractive reserves: An alternative for reconciling development and environmental conservation in Amazonia." In *Alternatives to deforestation: steps toward sustainable use of the Amazon rain forest,* edited by Anthony B. Anderson, 252–264. New York: Columbia University Press.

Allegretti, Mary H. 1994. "Policies of the use of renewable natural resources: The Amazon region and extractive activities." In *Extractivism in the Brazilian Amazon: perspectives on regional development,* edited by Miguel Clüsener-Godt and Ignacy Sachs, 14–33. Paris: UNESCO.

Almeida, Alfredo Wagner B. de. 1982. *Conflitos de terra no Maranhão.* São Luís: IPES.

Almeida, Alfredo Wagner B. de. 1986. "Estrutura fundiária e expansão camponesa." In *Carajás: desafio político, ecologia e desenvolvimento,* organised by J. M.Goncalves de Almeida Jr., 265–293. São Paulo: Brasiliense/Conselho Nacional de Desenvolvimento Científico e Tecnológico.

Almeida Jr., José Maria Gonçalves de, org. 1986. *Carajás: desafio político, ecologia e desenvolvimento.* São Paulo: Brasiliense/Conselho Nacional de Desenvolvimento Científico e Tecnológico.

Anderson, Maximo. 2017. "Displaced by Brazil's giant Belo Monte hydroelectric dam, 'river people' reoccupy reservoir." Mongabay Series Amazon Infrastructure, March 13, https://news.mongabay.com/2017/03/displaced-by-brazils-giant-belo-monte-hydroelectric-dam-river-people-reoccupy-reservoir/ (accessed November 23, 2022).

Altvater, Elmar. 1987a. *Sachzwang Weltmarkt. Verschuldungskrise, blockierte Industrialisierung und ökologische Gefährdung; der Fall Brasilien.* Hamburg: VSA-Verlag.

Altvater, Elmar. 1987b. "Consequências regionais da crise do endividamento global. No exemplo do Pará." In *Homem e natureza na Amazônia,* TBGL 3, edited by Gerd Kohlhepp and Achim Schrader, 169–187. Tübingen: EdIGUT.

Amigos da Terra (Programa Amazônia). 1997. *Garimpagem florestal. Relatório atualizado sobre extração ilegal de madeira na Amazônia Brasileira.* São Paulo: Amigos da Terra.

Anderson, Anthony B., ed. 1990. *Alternatives to deforestation: Steps toward sustainable use of the Amazon rain forest.* New York: Columbia University Press.

Andrade, Maristela de Paula *et al.* 1995. *Carajás: destruição ou desenvolvimento?* São Luís: CPT.

Anhuf, Dieter. 2008. "Der Amazonas-Regenwald im zukünftigen Treibhausklima – Perspektiven eines bedrohlichen Szenariums." In *Entwicklungskontraste in den Americas,* Passauer Kontaktstudium Erdkunde 9, edited by Eberhard Rothfuss, 51–61. Passau: Selbstverlag Fach Geographie der Universität Passau.

Anhuf, Dieter. 2010. "Brasilien. Naturräumliche Grundlagen." In *Brasilien heute,* edited by Sérgio Costa, Gerd Kohlhepp, Horst Nitschack, and Hartmut Sangmeister, 15–31. Frankfurt a. M.: Vervuert.

Antunes, Walter Coronado. 2010. "Crítica ao aproveitamento hidrelétrico Belo Monte." *Jornal do Instituto de Engenharia* 59: 8–9.

Arvor Damien *et al.* 2018. "Combining socioeconomic development with environmental governance in the Brazilian Amazon: the Mato Grosso agricultural frontier at a tipping point." *Environment, Development and Sustainability* 20, no. 1: 1–22. https://doi.org/10.1007/s10668-016-9889-1

Asselin, Victor. 1982. *Grilagem. Corrupção e violência em terras do Carajás.* Petrópolis: Vozes.

Assies, Willem. 1997. "The extraction of non-timber products as a conservation strategy in Amazonia." *European Review of Latin American and Caribbean Studies* 62: 33–53.

Azevedo, Marta M. 2011. "O Censo 2010 e os povos indígenas." In *Povos indígenas no Brasil: 2006-2010,* edited by Beto Ricardo, and Fany Ricardo, 45–48. São Paulo: Instituto SocioAmbiental.

Barbira-Scazzocchio, Françoise, ed. 1980. *Land, people, and planning in contemporary Amazonia.* Cambridge: Cambridge University Press.

Barbosa, Luiz C. 2015. *Guardians of the Brazilian Amazon Rainforest: Environmental Organizations and Development.* London/New York: Routledge.

Barros, Ana C., Daniel Nepstad, Capobianco, João P. Ribeiro *et al.* 2001. "Os custos ambientais do programa Avança Brasil." In *Amazônia: Avança o Brasil?*, edited by Wilhelm Hofmeister, 51–78. São Paulo: Fundação Konrad Adenauer.

Barroso, Luís R. and Patrícia Perrone Campos Mello. 2021. *How to save the Amazon: The reasons why a living forest is worth more than a cut-down one.* Cambridge: Harvard Kennedy School, Carr Center for Human Rights Policy.

Becker, Bertha K. 1982. *Geopolítica da Amazônia, a nova fronteira de recursos.* Rio de Janeiro: Zahar.

Becker, Bertha K. 1985. "Fronteira e urbanização repensadas." *Revista Brasileira de Geografia* 47: 257–371.

Becker, Bertha K. 1988. "Carajás: gestão do território e territorialidade na Amazônia." *Espaço & Debates: Revista de Estudos Regionais e Urbanos* 8, no. 25: 77–89.

Becker, Bertha K. 1994. "Gestão do território e territorialidade na Amazônia: A CVRD e os garimpeiros em Carajás." In *Amazônia: A fronteira agrícola 20 anos depois*, edited by Philippe Léna and Adélia E. de Oliveira, 333–350. Belém: Museu Paraense Emílio Goeldi.

Becker, Bertha K. 1995. "Undoing myths: The Amazon – an urbanized forest." In *Brazilian perspectives on sustainable development of the Amazon region*, edited by Miguel Clüsener-Godt and Ignacy Sachs, 53–89. Paris: UNESCO/Parthenon.

Becker, Bertha K. 1999. *Cenários de curto prazo para o desenvovimento da Amazônia.* Cadernos do NAPIAm 6. Brasília: MMA/SCA.

Becker, Bertha K. 2001. "Construindo a política brasileira de meio ambiente para a Amazonia: Atores, estratégias e práticas." In *Brasil – modernização e globalização*, coordinated by Gerd Kohlhepp, 197–207. Madrid/Frankfurt a. M.: Iberoamericana/Vervuert.

Becker, Bertha K. 2005. "Geopolítica da Amazônia." *Estudos Avançados* 19, no. 53: 71–86.

Becker, Bertha K. 2010. "Novas territorialidades na Amazônia: Desafio às políticas públicas." *Boletim do Museu Paraense Emílio Goeldi, Ciências Humanas* 5, no. 1: 17–23.

Becker, Bertha K. and Claudio A. G. Egler. 1992. *Brazil: a new regional power in the world economy.* Cambridge: Cambridge University Press.

Becker, Bertha K. and Claudio A. G. Egler. 1997. *Details of the methodology for execution of ecological-economical zoning by the states of the Legal Amazon Region.* Brasília: SAE/MMA.

Bertrand, Jean-Pierre, Neli Aparecida de Mello, and Hervé Théry. 2007. "Le contexte agricole des biocarburants au Brésil." http://www.univ-tlse2.fr/amlat/gral/index.htm (accessed March 12, 2020).

Biller, David. 2023. "Oil drilling project near mouth of Amazon River rejected by Brazil's environmental regulator." *The Associated Press*, July 5. https://apnews.com/article/brazil-amazon-oil-drilling-9bff80ae2d9318024cb4a297d0392500 (accessed August 9, 2023).

Binswanger, Hans. 1987. *Fiscal and legal incentives with environmental effects on the Brazilian Amazon.* Washington, D.C.: The World Bank.

Birle, Peter and Bruno Speck, eds. 2022. *Brazil under Bolsonaro. How endangered is democracy?* Ibero Online 14. Berlin: Ibero-Amerikanisches Institut. https://publications.iai.spk-berlin.de/receive/iai_mods_00000128 (accessed February 23, 2023).

Blumenschein, Markus. 1995. “Die modernisierte Landwirtschaft des Cerrado und ihre Bedeutung für eine nachhaltige Entwicklung der Pantanal-Region.” In *Mensch-Umwelt-Beziehungen in der Pantanal-Region von Mato Grosso,* edited by Gerd Kohlhepp, 221–246. Tübingen: EdIGUT.

Blumenschein, Markus. 2001. *Landnutzungsveränderungen in der modernisierten Landwirtschaft in Mato Grosso, Brasilien. Die Rolle von Netzwerken, institutionellen und ökonomischen Faktoren für agrarwirtschaftliche Innovationen auf der Chapada dos Parecis.* TBGL 12. Tübingen: EdIGUT.

Blumenschein, Markus. 2004. “Deregulierung in der brasilianischen Sojawirtschaft: Innovation oder Stagnation?” *Geographische Rundschau* 56, no. 11: 34–40.

BMBF, ed. 1995. *Forschung für den Tropenwald.* Bonn: BMBF.

BMBF, ed. 1998. *Proceedings at the Third SHIFT-Workshop Manaus.* Hamburg: BMBF.

BMZ, ed. 1998. *Das Internationale Pilotprogramm zur Bewahrung der tropischen Regenwälder in Brasilien (PPG7).* Bonn: BMZ.

BNDES. 1998. *Programa Amazônia Integrada.* Rio de Janeiro.

BNDES. 2000. *Programa Brasil em Ação. Estudo dos eixos nacionais de integração e desenvolvimento.* Relatório Síntese, 2 vols. Brasília: BNDES.

Boadle, Anthony. 2023. “Brazil’s Indigenous population double the size previously recorded – census.” Reuters, August 7. https://www.reuters.com/world/americas/brazils-indigenous-population-double-size-previously-recorded-census-2023-08-07/ (accessed September 4, 2024).

Borges, André. 2021. “Portos amazônicos vão desbancar os do restante do país no transporte de grãos.” *Estadão Conteúdo,* April 11.

Boudeville, Jacques-R. 1968. *L’espace et les pôles de croissance.* Paris: Presses Univ. de France.

Branford, Sue and Oriel Glock. 1985. *The last frontier. Fighting over land in the Amazon.* London: Zed Books.

Branford, Sue and Maurício Torres. 2018. “China increasingly involved in Brazil’s ambitious Amazon rail network.” *Mongabay Series: Amazon Agribusiness, Amazon Infrastructure,* https://news.mongabay.com/2018/11/china-increasingly-involved-in-brazils-ambitious-amazon-rail-network/ (accessed August 20, 2023).

Bratman, Eve Z. 2014. “Contradictions of Green Development: Human rights and environmental Norms in light of Belo Monte Dam activism.” *Journal of Latin American Studies* 46, no. 2: 261–289. https://doi.org/10.1017/S0022216X14000042.

Bratman, Eve Z. 2015. “Passive revolution in the green economy: activism and the Belo Monte dam.” *International Environmental Agreements: Politics, Law and Economics* 15: 61–77. https://doi.org/10.1007/s10784-014-9268-z.

Bremer, Hanna. 1999. *Die Tropen.* Berlin/Stuttgart: Gebr. Bornträger.

Brooks, Edwin. 1974. “Frontiers of ethnic conflict in the Brazilian Amazon.” *International Journal of Environmental Studies* 7: 63–74.

Brooks, Edwin, René Fuerst, John Hemming, and Francis Huxley. 1973. *Tribes of the Amazon Basin in Brazil 1972.* London/Tonbridge: Ch. Knight & Co.

Browder, John O., ed. 1989. *Fragile lands of Latin America. Strategies for sustainable development.* Boulder etc.: Avalon.

Browder, John O. and Brian J. Godfrey. 1997. *Rainforest cities: Urbanization, development and globalization of the Brazilian Amazon.* New York: Columbia University Press.

Brünig, Eberhard F. 1989. "Use and misuse of tropical rain forests." In *Tropical rain forest ecosystems*, edited by Helmut Lieth and Marinus J. A. Werger, 611–636. Amsterdam: Elsevier.

Brünig, Eberhard F. and J. Poker. 1991. "Is sustainable utilization of the tropical evergreen moist forest possible?" In *Tropical ecosystems*, edited by Walter Erdelen, Natarajan Ishwaran, and Paul Müller, 91–106. Saarbrücken: Josef Margraf.

Brum, Eliane. 2018. "They owned an island, now they are urban poor: the tragedy of Altamira." *The Guardian*, February 6, 2018. https://www.theguardian.com/cities/2018/feb/06/ (accessed November 12, 2021).

Bundesregierung Deutschland, Bundespresseamt. 1990. *Schutz und Bewirtschaftung der Tropenwälder. Tropenwaldbericht der Bundesregierung*. Bonn: n. p.

Bunker, Stephen G. 1985. *Underdeveloping the Amazon: Extraction, unequal exchange, and the failure of modern State*. Chicago: University of Chicago Press.

Burger, Dietrich. 1991. "Nutzungsformen des Amazonaswaldes: ökologische kontra institutionelle Rahmenbedingungen." *Nord-Süd aktuell* 3: 376–386.

Butler, Tina. 2005. "Pre-Columbian Amazon supported millions of people." Mongabay, October 18. https://news.mongabay.com/2005/10/pre-columbian-amazon-supported-millions-of-people/ (accessed December 12, 2022).

Butler, Stuart. 2024. "Deforestation declines in Brazilian Amazon". Geographical, January 22. https://geographical.co.uk/news/deforestation-declines-in-brazilian-amazon (accessed April 17, 2024).

Cabral, Umberlândia, and Irene Gomes. 2023. "Brasil tem 1,7 milhão de indígenas e mais da metade deles vive na Amazônia Legal." https://agenciadenoticias.ibge.gov.br/agencia-noticias/2012-agencia-de-noticias/noticias/37565-brasil-tem-1-7-milhao-de-indigenas-e-mais-da-metade-deles-vive-na-amazonia-legal (accessed August 8, 2023).

Calcagnotto, Gilberto. 1990. "Umweltpolitik und nachholende Industrialisierung: Das Beispiel Brasilien." In *Nord-Süd aktuell* 1: 86–92.

Canto, Ana C. Barbosa do, Renato Marques, Fernanda Figueiredo G. D. Leite, *et al.* 2020. "Land use and cover maps for Mato Grosso from 1985 to 2019." https://youtu.be/7k311ZwsRbA (accessed November 21, 2022).

Capobianco, João P. Ribeiro. 2001. "Representatividade das unidades de conservação e terras indígenas em relação às fitofisionomias na Amazônia Legal." In *Biodiversidade na Amazônia Brasileira: avaliação e ações prioritárias para a conservação, uso sustentável e repartição dos benefícios*, organised by João P. Ribeiro Capobianco *et al.*, 263–267. São Paulo: ISA.

Capobianco, João P. Ribeiro. 2017. *Governança socioambiental na Amazônia brasileira na década de 2000*. PhD thesis, Universidade de São Paulo. https://doi.org/10.11606/T.106.2018.tde-10122018-095025

Cardoso, Fernando H. 1998. *Avança, Brasil: proposta de Governo*. Rio de Janeiro: Saraiva.

Carvalho, R. 1999. *A Amazônia rumo ao "ciclo da soja."* Amazônia Papers no. 2, Programa Amazônia. São Paulo: Amigos da Terra.

Cassol, Henrique L. Godinho *et al.* 2020. "Maximum fraction images derived from year-based project for on-board autonomy-vegetation (PROBA-V) data for the rapid assessment of land use and land cover areas in Mato Grosso state, Brazil." *Land* 9, no. 139: n. p. https://doi.org/10.3390/land9050139

Castro, Edna M. Ramos de, org. 1989. *Amazônias em tempo de transição*. Belém: UFPA/NAEA.

Castro, Edna M.Ramos de and Jean Hébette, org. 1989. *Na trilha dos grandes projetos: modernização e conflito na Amazônia*. Belém: UFPA/NAEA.

Castro, Edna M. Ramos de, and Florence Pinton, ed. 1997. *Faces do trópico úmido: conceitos e novas questões sobre desenvolvimento e meio ambiente*. Belém: UFPA/NAEA.

Castro, Edna M. Ramos de, and Índio Campos, org. 2015. *Formação socioeconômica da Amazônia*. Col. Formação Regional da Amazônia, vol. 2. Belém: UFPA/NAEA.

Castro, Edna M. Ramos de, and Eunápio D. Carmo, org. 2019. *Dossiê desastres e crimes da mineração em Barcarena*. Belém: UFPA/NAEA.

Celentano, Danielle, and Adalberto Veríssimo, eds. 2007. *The State of the Amazon Indicators. The Brazilian Amazon and the Millennium Development Goals*. Belém: Imazon.

CIPGC. 1981. *Greater Carajás Program. A challenge for all segments of Brazilian society*. Brasília: CIPGC.

CIPGC. 1985. *Programa Grande Carajás. Análise da situação atual e novas diretrizes*. Brasília: CIPGC.

CIPGC. 1986. *Plano operativo do Programa Grande Carajás para 1986*. Brasília: CIPGC.

Cleary, David. 1990. *Anatomy of the Amazon goldrush*. Houndsville/Basingstoke/London: The Macmillan Press Ltd.

Clüsener-Godt, Miguel, and Ignacy Sachs, eds. 1994. *Extractivism in the Brazilian Amazon: perspectives on regional development*. Paris: UNESCO.

Clüsener-Godt, Miguel, and Ignacy Sachs, eds. 1995. *Brazilian perspectives on sustainable development of the Amazon region*. Paris/Carnforth: UNESCO.

CODEBAR/SUDAM. 1986. *Problemática do carvão vegetal na área do Programa Grande Carajás*. Belém.

Coffey, Peter. 1985. *A case study – the Carajás project*. Amsterdam: Europa Instituut Univ. of Amsterdam.

Comissão Pro-Indio de São Paulo, ed. 1988. *As hidrelétricas do Xingu e os povos indígenas*. São Paulo.

Commission on Environment and Development. 1987. *Our Common Future*. Brundtland Report. Oxford: Oxford University Press.

Conroy, Michael E. 1973. "Rejection of growth center strategy in Latin American regional development planning." *Land Economics* 49, no. 4: 371–380.

Constituinte. 1989. *Programa "Nossa Natureza": GTI – VI – Proteção do meio ambiente, das comunidades indígenas e das populações envolvidas no processo extrativista*. Relatório final. Brasília.

Constitution. 1988. *Constitution of the Federal Republic of Brazil*. Brasília.

Cotton, C., and T. Romine. 1999. *Facing destruction. A Greenpeace briefing on the timber industry in the Brazilian Amazon*. Amsterdam: Greenpeace International Publications.

Coy, Martin. 1986. "Regionalentwicklung in Rondônia. Integrierte ländliche Entwicklung und politische Rahmenbedingungen." *Geographische Zeitschrift* 74, no. 3: 177–185.

Coy, Martin. 1988. *Regionalentwicklung und regionale Entwicklungsplanung an der Peripherie in Amazonien. Probleme und Interessenkonflikte bei der Erschließung einer jungen Pionierfront am Beispiel des brasilianischen Bundesstaates Rondônia*. TBGL 5. Tübingen: EdIGUT.

Coy, Martin. 1991. "The frontier of North Mato Grosso between soybean production, timber extraction and gold mining. Incorporation and differentiation of new social spaces by private colonization and spontaneous processes." In *The incorporative drive. Examples from Latin America*, edited by Jan M.G. Kleinpenning, 50–58. Saarbrücken: Breitenbach.

Coy, Martin. 1992. "Pioneer front and urban development. Social and economic differentiation of pioneer towns in Northern Mato Grosso, Brazil." *Applied Geography and Development* 39: 7–29.

Coy, Martin. 1995. "Von der Interiorstadt zur Regionalmetropole. Stadtverfall, Stadterweiterung und Konzepte einer Stadterneuerung in Cuiabá." In *Mensch-Umwelt-Beziehungen im Einzugsgebiet des Oberen Rio Paraguai*, TBGL12, organised by Gerd Kohlhepp, 279–314. Tübingen: Selbstverl. des Geographischen Instituts der Universität Tübingen.

Coy, Martin. 2001. "Entre a globalização e a regionalização. Efeitos da modernização, conflitos de interesse e fatores determinantes do desenvolvimento regional sustentável no espaço rural brasileiro." In *Brasil - modernização e globalização*, edited by Gerd Kohlhepp, 259–273. Madrid/Frankfurt a. M.: Iberoamericana/Vervuert.

Coy, Martin. 2005. "Between globalization and regionalization. The political ecology of pioneer fronts in the South-West of the Amazon." In *Global impact, local action: New environmental policy in Latin America*, edited by Anthony Hall, 13–35. London: University of London.

Coy, Martin, and Reinhold Lücker. 1993. *Der brasilianische Mittelwesten. Wirtschafts- und sozialgeographischer Wandel eines peripheren Agrarraumes*. TBGL 9. Tübingen: EdIGUT.

Coy, Martin, Martin Friedrich, and Reinhold Lücker. 1997. "Town and countryside in the Brazilian midwest. Modernization and urbanization of a pioneer region." In *Small towns and beyond. Rural transformation and small urban centres in Latin America*, edited by Paul van Lindert, and Otto Verkoren, 31–52. Amsterdam: Thela.

Coy, Martin, and Martina Neuburger. 2002. "Brasilianisches Amazonien. Chancen und Grenzen nachhaltiger Regionalentwicklung." *Geographische Rundschau* 54, no. 11: 12–20.

Coy, Martin, and Gerd Kohlhepp, coords. 2005. *Amazônia sustentável. Desenvolvimento sustentável entre políticas, estratégias inovadoras e experiências locais.* Rio de Janeiro/Tübingen: Garamond/TBGL 28/EdIGUT.

Coy, Martin, and Martina Neuburger. 2008. "Amazonien: Straße Cuiabá–Santarém. Ein Großprojekt im politisch-ökologischen Kontext." *Geographische Rundschau* 60, no. 12: 10–17.

Coy, Martin, and Martin Klingler. 2014. "Frentes pioneiras em transformação: o eixo da BR-163 e os desafios socioambientais." *Territórios e Fronteiras* 7, no. 1: 1–26. https://doi.org/10.22228/rt-f.v7i0.282

Coy, Martin, Martin Klingler, and Gerd Kohlhepp. 2017. "De frontier até pós-frontier: regiões pioneiras no Brasil dentro do processo de transformação espaço-temporal e sócio-ecológico." *Confins (Revista Franco-Brasileira de Geografia)* 30: 1–48. https://doi.org/10.4000/confins.11683

Coy, Martin, Tobias Töpfer, and Frank Zirkl. 2020. "Relações campo-cidade e funções urbanas em regiões do agronegócio: o caso de Sinop (Mato Grosso)." In *Estratégias de expansão do agronegócio em Mato Grosso. Os eixos da BR-163 e da BR-158 em perspectiva comparativa*, organised by Martin Coy, João C. Barrozo, and Edison A. de Souza, 33–69. Brasília: Ed.IABS.

Coy, Martin, and Christoph Huber. 2020."Der Sojakomplex in Nord-Mato Grosso. Eine politisch-ökologische Perspektive." *Geo-Öko* 41, no. 1–2: 128–155.

Coy, Martin, Christoph Huber, and Felix M. Dorn. 2021. "Soja für den Weltmarkt. Wie das globale Produktionsnetzwerk des Agrobusiness die brasilianische Peripherie durchdringt." *Geographische Rundschau* 73, no. 12: 4–9.

Coy, Martin, Felix M. Dorn, Christoph Huber, and Tobias Töpfer. 2022. "Regional and urban development under the signs of globalization: The soybean complex and the city of agribusiness in Mato Grosso." *Journal of Latin American Geography* 21, no. 2: 86–111.

CVRD. 1981. *Projeto Ferro Carajás*. Rio de Janeiro: CVRD.

CVRD. 1985. *Projeto Ferro Carajás. Fator de desenvolvimento e integração*. Rio de Janeiro: CVRD.

CVRD. 1986. *Annual report 1985*. Rio de Janeiro: CVRD.

CVRD. 1974–2009. *Jornal da Vale* (monthly publication). Rio de Janeiro.

Czymmeck, Anja, and Luiz Eduardo Garcia. 2022. "Wahljahr in Brasilien: zwischen Ungewissheit und Unentschlossenheit." *KAS-Auslandsbüro Brasilien*. https://www.kas.de/de/laenderberichte/detail/-/content/wahljahr-in-brasilien-zwischen-ungewissheit-und-unentschlossenheit (accessed April 9, 2022).

Davis, Shelton H. 1977. *Victims of the miracle. Development and the Indians of Brazil*. Cambridge: Cambridge University Press.

Dean, Warren. 1997. *A ferro e fogo. A historia e a devastação da Mata Atlântica Brasileira*. São Paulo: Companhia das Letras.

Denevan, William M. 1966. "A cultural ecological view of the former aboriginal settlement in the Amazon Basin." *The Professional Geographer* 18, no. 6: 346–351.

Denevan, William M. 2014. "Estimating Amazonian indian numbers in 1492." *Journal of Latin American Geography* 13, no. 2: 207–221. https://doi:10.1353/lag.2014.0036

Deutscher Bundestag, ed. 1990. *Protecting the tropical forests: a high-priority international task*. 2nd Report of the Enquete Commission. Bonn: Deutscher Bundestag.

DNPM (Departamento Nacional de Produção Mineral). 1974–1982. *Projeto RADAMBRASIL. Levantamento de Recursos Naturais*, vol. 4–20, 22, 26. Rio de Janeiro: MME.

Dória, Carlos Alberto, and Carlos Alberto Ricardo. 1972. "Populations indigènes du Brésil: Perspectives de survie dans la région dite "Amazonie légale." *Bulletin de la Societé Suisse des Américanistes* 36: 19–35.

Dostal, Walter, ed. 1972. *The situation of the Indian in South America*. Genève: World Council of Churches.

Dubreuil, Vincent, Robert Bariou, and Messias M. dos Passos. 2004. *Environnement et télédétection au Brésil - Meio ambiente e teledetecção no Brasil: Mato Grosso, Paraná, São Paulo*. Rennes: Presses Universitaires de Rennes.

Durigan, Giselda, Natalia Guerin, and José N. Martorano Neves da Costa. 2013. "Ecological restoration of Xingu Basin headwaters: motivations, engagement, challenges and perspectives." *Phil. Trans. R. Soc.* B368: n p. https://doi.org/10.1098/rstb.2012.0165

Dutra e Silva, Sandro. 2020. "Challenging the environmental history of the Cerrado: Science, biodiversity and politics on the Brazilian agricultural frontier." *Historia Ambiental Latinoamericana y Caribeña (HALAC)* 10, no. 1: 82–116. https://doi.org/10.32991/2237-2717.2020v10i1.p82-116

Eletrobras. 1987a. *Plano Nacional de Energia Eletrica 2010: Relatorio Executivo.* Rio de Janeiro: Eletrobras.

Eletrobras. 1987b. *Plano diretor para conservação e recuperação do meio ambiente nas obras e serviços do setor elétrico.* Brasília: Eletrobras.

Eletronorte. 1986. *UHE Tucuruí.* Junho 86. Brasília: Eletronorte.

Emperaire, Laure, ed. 1996. *La forêt en jeu. L'extractivisme en Amazonie Centrale.* Collection Latitudes 23. Paris: ORSTOM/UNESCO.

Estado de Roraima/SEPLAN. 1998. *Roraima. Seca-incêndios. Síntese da situação em 7.4.1998.* Boa Vista.

Fabio, Andre C. 2022. "Death and deforestation: Cocaine trade adds to Amazon's woes." https://www.context.news/nature/death-and-deforestation-cocaine-trade-adds-to-amazons-woes (accessed March 2, 2023).

FASE/IBASE, eds. 1993. *Anais do seminário sobre o Programa Piloto para a Amazônia.* Rio de Janeiro: Federacao de Orgaos para Assistencia Social e Educacional/Instituto Brasileiro de Análises Sociais e Econômicas.

Fatheuer, Thomas. 1993. *Hoffnung für den Regenwald? Das Pilotprogramm der G-7 und Ansätze für eine neue Politik in Amazonien.* Rio de Janeiro: Federacao de Orgaos para Assistencia Social e Educacional.

Fatheuer, Thomas. 2017. *Amazonien: Entwaldung, "Entwicklung" und Widerstand. Der Kampf um den größten Regenwald der Welt. Dossier.* Berlin: FDCL.

Fatheuer, Thomas. 2019. *Deutsche Entwicklungszusammenarbeit im brasilianischen Amazonasgebiet: Erfolge und Herausforderungen von 1992 bis heute.* Berlin: Heinrich-Böll-Stiftung.

Fearnside, Philip M. 1982. "Deforestation in the Brazilian Amazon: How fast is it occurring?" *Interciência* 7, no. 2: 82–88.

Fearnside, Philip M. 1985. "Environmental change and deforestation in the Brazilian Amazon." In *Change in the Amazon Basin. Vol. 1: Man's impact on forests and rivers,* edited by John Hemming, 70–89. Manchester: Manchester University Press.

Fearnside, Philip M. 1986a. "Spatial concentration of deforestation in the Brazilian Amazon." *Ambio* 15, no. 2: 74–81.

Fearnside, Philip M. 1986b. "Os planos agrícolas: desenvolvimento para quem e para quanto tempo?" In *Carajás: desafio político, ecologia e desenvolvimento,* organised by J. M. Gonçalves de Almeida Jr., 362–418. São Paulo: Brasiliense/Conselho Nacional de Desenvolvimento Científico e Tecnológico.

Fearnside, Philip M. 1988. "Jarí at age 19: Lessons for Brazil's silvicultural plans at Carajás." *Interciência* 13, no. 1: 12-24.

Fearnside, Philip M. 1989a. "Brazil's Balbina dam: Environment versus the legacy of the Pharaohs in Amazonia." *Environmental Management* 13, no. 3: 401–423.

Fearnside, Philip M. 1989b. "Deforestion in Brazilian Amazonia." In *The earth in transition: Patterns and processes of biotic impoverishment,* edited by George M. Woodwell, 1–19. New York: Cambridge University Press.

Fearnside, Philip M. 1989c. "The charcoal of Carajás: a threat to the forests of Brazil's Eastern Amazon region." *Ambio* 18, no. 2: 141–143.

Fearnside, Philip M. 1989d. "Processos predatórios na floresta tropical úmida da Amazônia Brasileira." *Estudos Avançados* 3, no. 5: 21–35.
Fearnside, Philip M. 1989e. "Extractive Reserves in Brazilian Amazonia. An opportunity to maintain tropical rain forest under sustainable use." *BioScience* 39, no. 6: 387–393.
Fearnside, Philip M. 1990. "The rate and extent of deforestation in Brazilian Amazonia." *Environmental Conservation* 17, no. 3: 213–226.
Fearnside, Philip M. 1997a. "Greenhouse gases from deforestation in Brazilian Amazonia. Net committed emissions." *Climate Change* 35, no. 3: 321–360.
Fearnside, Philip M. 1997b. "Greenhouse-gas emissions from Amazonian hydroelectric reservoirs: The example of Brazil's Tucuruí Dam as compared to fossil fuel alternatives." *Environmental Conservation* 24, no. 1: 64–75. https://doi.org/10.1017/S0376892997000118
Fearnside Philip M. 1999. "Social impacts of Brazil's Tucuruí Dam." *Environmental Management* 24, no. 4: 485–495.
Fearnside, Philip M. 2000. "Deforestation impacts, environmental services and the international community." In *Amazonia at the crossroads: the challenge of sustainable development*, edited by Anthony Hall, 11–24. London: University of London Press.
Fearnside, Philip M. 2001a. "Environmental impacts of Brazil's Tucuruí dam: Unlearned Lessons for Hydroelectric Development in Amazonia." *Environmental Management* 27, no. 3: 377–396.
Fearnside, Philip M. 2001b. "Avança Brasil: conseqüências ambientais e sociais na Amazônia." In *Amazônia: Avança o Brasil?*, edited by Wilhelm Hofmeister, 101–124. São Paulo: Fundação Konrad Adenauer.
Fearnside, Philip M. 2001c. "Soybean cultivation as a threat to the environment in Brazil." *Environmental Conservation* 28, no. 1: 23–38.
Fearnside, Philip M. 2001d. "Effects of land use and forest management on the carbon cycle in the Brazilian Amazon." *Journal of Sustainable Forestry* 12, no. 1/2: 79–97.
Fearnside, Philip M. 2002. "Greenhouse gas emissions from a hydroelectric reservoir (Brazil's Tucuruí Dam) and the energy policy implications." *Water, Air and Soil Pollution* 133, no. 1–4: 69–96. https://doi.org/10.1023/A:1012971715668
Fearnside, Philip M. 2005. "Do hydroelectric dams mitigate global warming? The case of Brazil's Curuá-Una Dam." *Mitigation and Adaptation Strategies for Global Change* 10, no. 4: 675–691. https://doi.org/10.1007/s11027-005-7303-7
Fearnside, Philip M. 2006. "Dams in the Amazon: Belo Monte and Brazil's hydroelectric development of the Xingu River Basin." *Environmental Management* 38, no. 1: 16–27. http://www.springerlink.com/content/65j70r74581gl231 (accessed May 21, 2022).
Fearnside, Philip M. 2007. "Brazil's Cuiabá-Santarém (BR-163) highway: The environmental cost of paving a soybean corridor through the Amazon." *Environmental Management* 39, no. 5: 601–614.
Fearnside, Philip M. 2008. "The roles and movements of actors in the deforestation of Brazilian Amazonia." *Ecology and Society* 13, no. 1, article 23: n. p. http://www.ecologyandsociety.org/vol13/iss1/art23/ (accessed October 23, 2022).
Fearnside, Philip M. 2013a. "Carbon credit for hydroelectric dams as a source of greenhouse-gas emissions: The example of Brazil's Teles Pires Dam." *Mitigation and Adaptation Strategies for Global Change* 18, no. 5: 691–699. https://doi.org/10.1007/s11027-012-9382-6

Fearnside, Philip M. 2013b. "Credit for climate mitigation by Amazonian dams: loopholes and impacts illustrated by Brazil's Jirau Hydroelectric Project." *Carbon Management* 4, no. 6: 681–696. https://doi.org/10.4155/cmt.13.57

Fearnside, Philip M. 2015a. "Amazon dams and waterways: Brazil's Tapajós Basin plans." *Ambio* 44: 426–439.

Fearnside, Philip M. 2015b. *Hidrelétricas na Amazônia: impactos ambientais e sociais na tomada de decisões sobre grandes obras*. Vol. 1. Manaus: Editora do INPA.

Fearnside, Philip M. 2016. "Environmental and Social Impacts of Hydroelectric Dams in Brazilian Amazonia: Implications for the Aluminum Industry." *World Development* 77: 48–65. https://doi.org/10.1016/j.worlddev.2015.08.015

Fearnside, Philip M. 2017a. "Belo Monte: Actors and arguments in the struggle over Brazil's most controversial Amazonian dam." *Die Erde – Journal of the Geographical Society of Berlin* 148, no. 1: 14–26.

Fearnside, Philip M. 2017b. "Brazil's Belo Monte dam: Lessons of an Amazonian resource struggle." *Die Erde – Journal of the Geographical Society of Berlin* 148, no. 2–3: 167–184.

Fearnside, Philip M. 2017c. "Deforestation of the Brazilian Amazon." *Environmental Science*, n. n.: n. p. https://doi.org/10.1093/acrefore/9780199389414.013.102

Fearnside, Philip M. 2019. "Will President Bolsonaro withdraw Brazil from the Paris Agreement?" *Mongabay*, January 31. https://news.mongabay.com/2019/01/commentary-will-president-bolsonaro-withdraw-brazil-from-the-paris-agreement/ (accessed October 16, 2022).

Fearnside, Philip M. 2020. "Environmental justice and Brazil's Amazonian dams." In *Landscapes of Inequity: The Quest for Environmental Justice in the Andes/Amazon Region*, edited by Nicholas A. Robins, and Barbara Fraser, 85–126. Lincoln: University of Nebraska Press.

Fearnside, Philip M. 2021a. "Brazil's Belo Monte Dam: Greenwashing contested (commentary)." *Mongabay*, February 1. https://news.mongabay.com/2021/02/brazils-belo-monte-dam-greenwashing-contested-commentary/ (accessed November 25, 2022).

Fearnside, Philip M. 2021b. "The intrinsic value of Amazon biodiversity." *Biodiversity and Conservation* 30: 1199–1202. https://doi.org/10.1007/s10531-021-02133-7

Fearnside, Philip M., and Judy M. Rankin. 1980. "Jarí and development in the Brazilian Amazon." *Interciência* 5, no. 3: 146–156.

Fearnside, Philip M., and Judy M. Rankin. 1985. "Jarí revisited: Changes and the outlook for sustainability in Amazonia's largest silvicultural estate." *Interciência* 10, no. 3: 121–129.

Ferrante, Lucas, and Philip M. Fearnside. 2019. "Brazil's new president and 'ruralists' threaten Amazonia's environment, traditional peoples, and the global climate." *Environmental Conservation* 46, no. 4: 261–263. https://doi.org/10.1017/S0376892919000213 [Supplementary material: https://static.cambridge.org/resource/id/urn:cambridge.org:id:binary:20190724051006906-0823:sup-mat:20190724051006906-0823:S0376892919000213sup001.pdf (accessed November 25, 2022)].

Ferrante, Lucas, and Philip M. Fearnside. 2020. "Military forces and Covid-19 as smokescreens for Amazon destruction and violation of indigenous rights." *Die Erde – Journal of the Geographical Society of Berlin* 151, no. 4: 258–263. https://doi.org/10.12854/erde-2020-542

Ferrante, Lucas, and Philip M. Fearnside. 2022. “Mining and Brazil’s indigenous peoples.” *Science* 375, no. 6578: 276. https://doi.org/10.1126/science.abn6753

Ferrante, Lucas, Reinaldo I. Barbosa, Luiz Duczmal, and Philip M. Fearnside. 2021. “Brazil’s planned exploitation of Amazonian indigenous lands for commercial agriculture increases risk of new pandemics.” *Regional Environmental Change* 21, no. 81: n p. https://doi.org/10.1007/s10113-021-01819-6

Ferris, Elisabeth G. 1981. “The Andean Pact and the Amazon treaty.” *Journal of Inter-american Studies and World Affairs* 23: 147–175.

Filocreão, Antonio S. Monteiro, Alex Pizzio, and Ivo M. Theis, org. 2022. *Contradições do desenvolvimento regional na Amazônia brasileira*. Florianópolis: Nave.

Finer, Matt, and N. Mamani. 2021. “The Amazon & climate change: Carbon sink vs carbon source. *MAAP* 144: n. p. https://maaproject.org/2021/amazon-carbon-flux/ (accessed March 29, 2023).

Finer, Matt, and A. Ariñez. 2022. “Soy deforestation in the Brazilian Amazon”. *MAAP* 161: n. p.

Fontes, Cristiane. 2023. “European Union-Mercosur Trade Agreement Depends on Environmental Commitments and Stricter Text, Says MEP”. *Folha de S.Paulo*, March 3. https://www1.folha.uol.com.br/internacional/en/scienceandhealth/2023/03/european-union-mercosur-trade-agreement-depends-on-environmental-commitments-and-stricter-text-says-mep.shtml (accessed March 6, 2023).

Foster, Nina. 2022.“Celebrating 20 years of protecting the Brazilian Amazon.” https://www.worldwildlife.org/stories/celebrating-20-years-of-protecting-the-brazilian-amazon (accessed January 23, 2023).

Foweraker, Joe. 1982. *A luta pela terra: A economia política da fronteira pioneira no Brasil de 1930 aos dias atuais*. Rio de Janeiro: Zahar.

Freitas, Maria de L. Davies de. 1986. “Metodologia de avaliação ambiental aplicada para um caso de enfoque preventivo Projeto Ferro Carajás.” *Espaço, Ambiente e Planejamento* 1, no. 1: 5–26.

Freitas, Maria de L. Davies de. 1987. “Projeto Ferro Carajás, Refexoes ambientais.” In *Homem e natureza na Amazônia*, TBGL 3, edited by Gerd Kohlhepp, and Achim Schrader, 347–352. Tübingen: EdIGUT.

Freitas, Maria de L. Davies de, and C. S. Shluger. 1983. *Brazil’s Carajás iron ore project. Environmental aspects*. Presented at the Commission of the European communities, Brussels and Luxembourg. Brussels: n. p.

Friedmann, John. 1972. “A general theory of polarized development.” In *Growth centers in regional economic development*, edited by Niles Hansen, 82–107. New York: The Free Press.

Friedrich, Martin. 1999. *Stadtentwicklung und Planungsprobleme von Regionalzentren in Brasilien. Cáceres und Rondonópolis/ Mato Grosso: ein Vergleich*. TBGL 18. Tübingen: EdIGUT.

Gall, Norman. 1979. “Ludwig’s Amazon empire.” *Forbes*, May 14: 127–144.

Gallo, Patrícia, Alice Brites, and Tatiane Micheletti. 2020. “REDD+ achievements and challenges in Brazil. Perceptions over time (2015–2019).” *CIFOR infobriefs* 288, 1–8. https://doi.org/10.17528/cifor/007628

Galtung, Johan. 1972. “Eine strukturelle Theorie des Imperialismus.” In *Imperialismus und strukturelle Gewalt: Analysen über abhängige Reproduktion*, edited by Dieter Senghaas, 29–104. Frankfurt a. M.: Suhrkamp.

Garcia, Ana, Maria E. Rodriguez, Cleiton M. Brito, and Cândido Grinsztejn. 2023. *Chinese investments in Brazil: Investment data, public policies for investment facilitation and the case of the Manaus industrial pole.* Rio de Janeiro: PUC/BRICS Policy Center. https://www.researchgate.net/publication/372816884_CHINESE_INVESTMENTS_IN_BRAZIL_INVESTMENT_DATA_PUBLIC_POLICIES_FOR_INVESTMENT_FACILITATION_AND_THE_CASE_OF_THE_MANAUS_INDUSTRIAL_POLE (accessed August 29, 2023).

Garrett, Rachael D. *et al.* 2021. "Forests and sustainable development in the Brazilian Amazon: History, trends, and future prospects." *The Annual Review of Environment and Resources* 46: 625–652. https://doi.org/10.1146/annurev-environ-012220-010228

Garrido Filha, Irene. 1980. *O Projeto Jarí e os capitais estrangeiras na Amazônia.* Petrópolis: Vozes.

Garrido Filha, Irene *et al.* 1988. "Estudo da área mineradora de Carajás." *Revista Brasileira de Geografia* 50, no. 4: 105–163.

Gatti, Luciana V. *et al.* 2021. "Amazonia as a carbon source linked to deforestation and climate change." *Nature* 595: 388–393. https://doi.org/10.1038/s41586-021-03629-6

Gebara, Maria F. 2017. "Can REDD+ help Brazil roll back rising deforestation rates?" *Forest News.* https://forestsnews.cifor.org/50288/ (accessed December 2, 2022).

Gerold, Gerhard, and Stefan Hohnwald. 2012. "Models and implementation of carbon-optimised land management strategies in Southern Amazonia: Carbiocial. Abstract." Tropentag 2012, Göttingen. https://www.tropentag.de/2012/abstracts/links/Gerold_2aqryLAZ.pdf (accessed 14.01.2023).

Gerold, Gerhard, Hermann F. Jungkunst, Karl M. Wantzen, Regine Schönenberg, Ricardo S. Amorim, Eduardo G. Couto, Beata Madari, and Stefan Hohnwald, eds. 2014. *Interdisciplinary analysis and modelling of carbon-optimized land management strategies for Southern Amazonia.* Göttingen: Universitätsverlag.

Gibbs, Holly K. *et al.* 2014. "Brazil's soy moratorium. Supplementary text." *Science* 347, no. 6220: 377–378. https://doi.org/10.1126/science.aaa0181

Gibbs, Holly K. *et al.* 2016. "Did ranchers and slaughterhouses respond to zero-deforestation agreements in the Brazilian Amazon?" *Conservation Letters* 9: 32–42. https://doi.org/10.1111/conl.12175

Gistelinck, Frans. 1988. *Carajás, usinas e favelas.* São Luís: Minerva.

Glaeser, Bernhard, ed. 1984. *Ecodevelopment. Concepts, projects, strategies.* Oxford: Pergamon Press.

Glaser, Gisbert. 1969. "Der Zinnstein-Abbau in Rondônia." *Geographische Zeitschrift* 57, no. 4: 241–267.

Glaser, Gisbert. 1971. "Neue Aspekte der Rinderweidewirtschaft in Zentralbrasilien." In *Beiträge zur Geographie Brasiliens,* edited by Gisbert Glaser, 19–42. Heidelberg: Selbstverlag Geogr. Inst. Univ. Heidelberg.

Global Forest Atlas. 2019. *Cattle ranching in the Amazon region.* Yale School of Forestry and Environmental Studies.

Golińska, Beata. 2014. "Amazonian Dark Earths in the context of pre-Columbian settlements." *Geology, Geophysics & Environment* 40, no. 2: 219–232. https://doi.org/10.7494/geol.2014.40.2.219

Goodland, Robert J. A. 1978. *Environmental assessment of the Tucuruí Hydroproject, Rio Tocantins, Amazonia., Brazil.* Brasília: Eletronorte.

Goodland, Robert J. A. 1985. “Brazil’s environmental progress in Amazonian development.” In *Change in the Amazon Basin*, vol. 1: *Man’s impact on forests and rivers*, edited by John Hemming, 5–35. Manchester: Manchester University Press.

Goodland. Robert J.A. 1989. *The World Bank’s new policy on the environmental aspects of dams and reservoirs*. Washington, D.C.: The World Bank.

Goodland, Robert J. A. 1990a. “Environmental aspects of dam and reservoir projects – the World Bank’s new policy.” *Waterlines* 8, no. 4: 7–10.

Goodland, Robert J. A. 1990b. “Tropical moist forest management: The urgency of transition to sustainability.” *Environmental Conservation* 17, no. 4: 303–318.

Goodland, Robert J. A., and Howard S. Irwin. 1975. *Amazon jungle: green hell to red desert? An ecological discussion of the environment impact of the highway construction program in the Amazon Basin*. Amsterdam/Oxford/New York: Elsevier Scientific Publ. Co.

Goodman, David, and Anthony Hall, eds. 1990. *The future of Amazonia: Destruction or sustainable development*. New York: St. Martin’s Press.

Goodman, David, and Michael Redclift, eds. 1991. *Environment and development in Latin America. The politics of sustainability*. Manchester/New York: Manchester University Press.

Gramkow, Márcia M., org. 2002. *Demarcando terras indígenas II: experiências e desafios de um projeto de parceria*. Brasília: PPTAL/PPG7.

Greenpeace, ed. 1997. *Logging the planet. Asian companies marching across our last forest frontiers*. Greenpeace International, Asian Companies Report.

Greenpeace, ed. 2009a. *Wie Rinder den Regenwald fressen. Mato Grosso in Amazonien, ein Gebiet der Zerstörung*. Hamburg: Greenpeace.

Greenpeace, ed. 2009b. *Slaughtering the Amazon*. Amsterdam. https://www.greenpeace.org/usa/research/slaughtering-the-amazon/ (accessed November 12, 2022).

Greenpeace, ed. 2013. *Driving destruction in the Amazon. How steel production is throwing the forest in the furnace*. Amsterdam. https://www.greenpeace.org/usa/wp-content/uploads/2015/05/423-Driving-Destruction-in-the-Amazon.pdf (accessed May 20, 2023).

Grundberger, Sebastian *et al.* 2021. “Mercosur: Familienkrach zum Jubiläum.” *KAS Länderbericht*, https://www.kas.de/de/laenderberichte/detail/-/content/mercosur-familienkrach-zum-jubilaeum (accessed October 22, 2022).

GTA (Grupo de Trabalho Amazônico)/FOE (Friends of the Earth). 1994. *Políticas públicas coerentes para a região amazônica*. São Paulo: FOE.

GTA/FOE. 1996. *Políticas públicas coerentes para uma Amazônia sustentável. O desafio da inovação e o Programa Piloto*. São Paulo: FOE.

GTI (Grupo de Trabalho Interministerial). 2006. *Plano de desenvolvimento regional sustentável para a área de influência da rodovia BR-163 Cuiabá-Santarém*. Brasília: GTI.

Guerreiro, Manoel G. 1984. “Desenvolvimento e perspectiva do setor mineral na Amazônia. Perigo estratégico da desnacionalização.” *A Amazônia Brasileira em Foco* 14: 51–81.

Guimarães, Roberto Pereira. 1986. *Ecopolitics in the Third World: an institutional analysis of environmental management in Brazil*. Ph.D. thesis, Univ. of Connecticut/UMI, Ann Arbor.

Guimarães, Roberto Pereira. 1989. “La ecopolítica en el desarrollo del Brasil.” *Revista de la CEPAL* 38, 89–104.

Haddad, Paulo, and Fernando Resende. 2002. *Instrumentos econômicos para o desenvolvimento sustentável da Amazônia*. Brasília: MMA/SCA.

Haesbaert, Rogério. 1994. *Território e identidade: o encontro entre "gaúchos" e nordestinos no Brasil*. Niterói: EDUFF.

Haesbaert, Rogério. 1997. *Des-territorialização e identidade: a rede gaúcha no Nordeste*. Niterói: EDUFF.

Hagemann, Helmut. 1994. *Not out of the woods yet. The scope of the G-7 initiative for a Pilot Program for the Conservation of the Brazilian rain forests*. Saarbrücken: Breitenbach.

Hall, Anthony. 1987. "Agrarian crisis in Brazilian Amazonia. The Grande Carajás Program." *Journal of Development Studies* 23, no. 4: 522–552.

Hall, Anthony. 1989. *Developing Amazonia: Deforestation and Social Conflict in Brazil's Carajas Programme*. Manchester/New York: Manchester University Press.

Hall, Anthony. 1997a. *Sustaining Amazonia: grassroots action for productive conservation*. Manchester/New York: Manchester University Press.

Hall, Anthony. 1997b. "Peopling the environment: A new agenda for research, policy and action in Brazilian Amazonia." *European Review of Latin American and Caribbean Studies* 62: 5–31.

Hall, Anthony, ed. 2000. *Amazonia at the crossroads: The challenge of sustainable development*. London: University of London Press.

Hall, Anthony, and Sue Branford. 2012. "Development, dams and Dilma: the saga of Belo Monte." *Critical Sociology* 38, no. 6: 851–862. https://doi.org/10.1177/0896920512440712

Hanbury-Tenison, Robin. 1973. *A question of survival for the Indians of Brazil*. New York: Charles Scribner's Sons.

Hansen, Niles. 1967. "Development pole theory in a regional context." *Kyklos* 20, no. 3: 709–727.

Harris, Nancy L. *et al*. 2021. "Global maps of twenty-first century forest carbon fluxes." *Nature Climate Change* 11, no. 3: 234–240. https://doi.org/10.1038/s41558-020-00976-6

Hartmann, Günther, ed. 1989. *Amazonien im Umbruch*. Berlin Dietrich Reimer Verlag.

Hébette, Jean. 1985. "Grandes projetos e transformações na fronteira." *Espaco e Debates* 5, no. 15: 75–85.

Hébette, Jean. 1986. "The posseiros' resistance in the region of the Greater Carajás Program (Brazil)." In *Competition for rural and urban space in Latin America. Its consequences for low income groups*, edited by Jan M. G. Kleinpenning, 28–42. Amsterdam/Nijmegen: Koninklijk Nederlands Aardrijkskundig Genootschap.

Hébette, Jean. 1991. *O cerco está se fechando*. Rio de Janeiro: Vozes.

Hecht, Susanna B. 1983. "Cattle ranching in the Eastern Amazon: environmental and social implications." In *The dilemma of Amazonian development*, edited by Emílio F. Morán, 155–188. Boulder: Westview Press.

Hecht, Susanna B. 1984. "Cattle ranching in Amazonia: Political and ecological considerations." In *Frontier expansion in Amazonia*, edited by Marianne Schmink, and Charles H. Wood, 366–398. Gainesville: University of Florida Press.

Hecht, Susanna B. 1985. "Environment, development and politics: Capital accumulation and the livestock sector in Eastern Amazonia." *World Development* 13, no. 6: 663–684.

Hecht, Susanna B. 1993. "The logic of livestock and deforestation in Amazonia." *Bioscience* 43, no. 10: 687–695. https://doi.org/10.2307/1312340

Hecht, Susanna B. 2003. "Indigenous management and the creation of Amazonian Dark Earths: Implications of Kayapó practices." In *Amazonian Dark Earths. Origin, properties, and management,* edited by Johannes Lehmann, Dirse C. Kern, Bruno Glaser, and William I. Woods, 355–372. Dordrecht: Kluwer Academic Publishers.

Hecht, Susanna B., Richard B. Norgaard, and Giorgio Possio. 1988. "The economics of cattle ranching in eastern Amazonia." *Interciência* 13: 233–240.

Hecht, Susanna B., and Alexander Cockburn. 1990. *The fate of the forest: Developers, destroyers, and defenders of the Amazon.* Chicago/London: The University of Chicago Press.

Hecht, Susanna B. *et al.* 2021. "The Amazon in motion: Changing politics, development strategies, peoples, landscapes, and livelihoods." In *Amazon Assessment Report 2021. Science Panel for the Amazon,* edited by Carlos Nobre *et al.*, chapter 14. New York: United Nations Sustainable Development Solutions Network. https://doi.org/10.55161/RWSX6527

Heck, Egon *et al.* 2005. "Amazônia indígena: conquistas e desafios." *Estudos Avançados* 19, no. 53: 237–255.

Hemming, John, ed. 1985. *Change in the Amazon Basin.* Vol. 1: *Man's impact on forests and rivers*; vol. 2: *The frontier after a decade of colonization.* Manchester: Manchester University Press.

Hemming, John. 2019. *People of the Rainforest: The Villas Boas Brothers, explorers and humanitarians of the Amazon.* London: C. Hurst & Comp. Ltd.

Heurich, Guilherme Orlandini. 2013. "A barragem e a canoa de Jawitï." https://pib.socioambiental.org/files/file/PIB_verbetes/arawete/osaraweteeoplanoemergencial.pdf (accessed October 29, 2022).

Heuser, Christoph. 2022. "Duell des Jahres." https://www.ipg-journal.de/regionen/lateinamerika/artikel/duell-des-jahres-6215/ (accessed October 10, 2022).

Higgins, Tiffany. 2020. "Belo Monte boondoggle: Brazil's biggest, costliest dam may be unviable." *Mongabay series: Amazon infrastructure,* January 17, https://news.mongabay.com/2020/01/belo-monte-boondoggle-brazils-biggest-costliest-dam-may-be-unviable/ (accessed October 30, 2022).

Hiratuka, Célio. 2022. "Why Brazil Sought Chinese Investments to Diversify Its Manufacturing Economy." Carnegie Endowment for International Peace, https://carnegie-production-assets.s3.amazonaws.com/static/files/Hiratuka-China-Brazil-Economy_final_1.pdf (accessed August 30, 2023).

Hirota, Marina *et al.* 2021. "Resilience of the Amazon Forest to Global Changes: Assessing the risk of tipping points". In *Amazon Assessment Report 2021. Science Panel for the Amazon,* edited by Carlos A. Nobre *et al.*, chapter 24. New York: United Nations Sustainable Development Solutions Network. https://doi.org/10.55161/RWSX6527

Hirota, Marina *et al.* 2022. "Policy brief: A call for global action to move the Amazon forest system away from tipping points (extended version)". *Science Panel for the Amazon.* https://doi.org/10.55161/VYKJ5240

Hirschman, Albert O. 1958. *The strategy of economic development.* New Haven/London: Yale University Press.

Hirst, Monica, and Juan G. Tokatlian. 2023. "Das Ende der Dollar-Vorherrschaft." *IPG- Wirtschaft und Ökologie.* https://www.ipg-journal.de/rubriken/wirtschaft-und-oekologie/artikel/das-ende-der-dollar-vorherrschaft-1-6688/?tx_web2pdf_pi1%5Baction%5D&tx_web2pdf_pi1%5Bargument%5D=printPage&tx_web2pdf_pi1%5Bcontroller%5D=Pdf (accessed September 4, 2024).

Hohnwald, Stephan *et al.* 2010. "Degraded pasture distribution and woody enrichment strategies for pasture fertility preservation in the Bragantina region, north-eastern Amazon." *Erdkunde* 64, no. 1: 17–31.

Homma, A. K. O. 1994. "Plant extractivism in the Amazon: Limitations and possibilities." In *Extractivism in the Brazilian Amazon: Perspectives on regional development*, edited by Miguel Clüsener-Godt, and Ignacy Sachs, 34–57. Paris: UNESCO.

Hopper, Janice H., ed. 1967. *Indians of Brazil in the Twentieth Century*. Washington, D.C.: Institute for Cross Cultural Research.

Hurwitz, Zachary. 2010. "Brazil: Don't Shove Belo Monte Down Our Throats!" International Rivers, September 2. https://riverresourcehub.org/resources/brazil-don-t-shove-belo-monte-down-our-throats/ (accessed September 4, 2024).

Hurwitz, Zachary. 2012. "Dirty Business in Brazil: Rousseff backslides on the environment." *NACLA Report on the Americas* 45, no. 1: 17–22. https://doi.org/10.1080/10714839.2012.11722107

IAG (International Advisory Group). 2003. *O Plano Amazônia Sustentável (PAS) e a segunda fase do Programa Piloto*. Relatório da XX reunião. Brasília.

IAG. 2004a. *O Plano BR-163 Sustentável no quadro das políticas governamentais para Amazônia*. Relatório da XXI reunião. Brasília.

IAG. 2004b. *O Plano BR-163 Sustentável no quadro das políticas governamentais para Amazônia: Evolução e tendências*. Relatório da XXII reunião. Brasília.

Ianni, Octávio. 1979a. *Colonização e reforma agrária na Amazônia*. Petrópolis: Vozes.

Ianni, Octávio. 1979b. *Ditadura e agricultura. O desenvolvimento do capitalismo na Amazônia: 1964-1978*. Rio de Janeiro: Civilização Brasileira.

Ianni, Octávio. 1981. *A luta pela terra. História social da terra e da luta pela terra numa área da Amazônia*. Petrópolis: Vozes.

IBASE. 1983. *Carajás: O Brasil hipoteca seu futuro*. Rio de Janeiro: Achiamé.

IBGE. 1984. *Anuário Estatístico do Brasil*. Rio de Janeiro: IBGE.

IBGE. 2001. *Censo Demográfico do Brasil de 2000*. Rio de Janeiro: IBGE

IBGE. 2011a. *Censo Demográfico do Brasil de 2010*. Rio de Janeiro: IBGE. https://www.ibge.gov.br/estatisticas/sociais/populacao/9662-censo-demografico-2010.html?=&t=resultados (accessed December 10, 2022).

IBGE. 2011b. *2010 Census*: indigenous population. https://www.ibge.gov.br/estatisticas/sociais/trabalho/9662-censo-demografico-2010.html?edicao=9677&t=destaques (accessed December 10, 2022).

IBGE. 2022. *Anuário Estatístico do Brasil de 2020*. Rio de Janeiro: IBGE. https://biblioteca.ibge.gov.br/visualizacao/periodicos/20/aeb_2020.pdf (accessed December 10, 2022).

IBGE. 2023. *Censo Demográfico 2022*. População e domicílios : primeiros resultados. Rio de Janeiro: IBGE. https://www.ibge.gov.br/estatisticas/sociais/trabalho/22827-censo-demografico-2022.html?edicao=37225 (accessed 08.08.2023).

ICV (Instituto Centro de Vida). 2022. *Características do desmatamento na Amazônia Mato Grossense em 2022*. Cuiabá: ICV. https://www.icv.org.br/publicacao/caracteristicas-do-desmatamento-na-amazonia-mato-grossense-em-2022/ (accessed 20.03.2023).
IDCJ. 1980. *A preliminary study on regional development of the Carajás corridor in Brazil*. Tokyo.
IDESP, ed. 1987. *O cavão vegetal e a indústria siderúrgica na Amazônia*. Pará Desenvolvimento 22. Belém: IDESP.
IDESP, ed. 1988. *O impacto da implantação do pólo siderúrgico na estrutura produtiva e no movimento migratório em Marabá*. Relatório de Pesquisa 12. Belém: IDESP.
IEA/USP. 1990. "Projeto Floram – uma plataforma." *Estudos Avançados* 4, no. 9: 63–119.
IMAZON. 2021. *Fatos da Amazônia 2021*. https://imazon.org.br/publicacoes/fatos-da-amazonia-2021/ (accessed Feburary 4, 2023).
INESC. 2021. *Enquanto a soja passa: Impactos da empresa Hidrovias do Brasil em Itaituba, Pará*. : Flint Charles S. Mott Foundation.
INPE (Instituto Nacional de Pesquisas Espaciais). 1998. *Amazonia – deforestation 1995–1997*. São José dos Campos: INPE.
INPE. 2000. *Monitoramento da floresta amazônica brasileira por satélite 1998–1999*. Funcate/São José dos Campos: INPE.
IPAM *et al*. 1998. *Risque 98. Mapa de risco de incêndios florestais e queimadas agrícolas na Amazônia Brasileira para o segundo semestre de 1998*. Belém: Instituto de Pesquisa Ambiental da Amazônia.
IPBES (Intergovernmental Science-Policy Platform on Biodiversity and Ecosystem Services). 2019. *Global assessment report on biodiversity and ecosystem services*. Bonn: IPBES. https://doi.org/10.5281/zenodo.3831673
IPCC. 2022. *Climate Change 2022: Impacts, Adaptation, and Vulnerability*. Contribution of Working Group II to the Sixth Assessment Report of the Intergovernmental Panel on Climate Change. Cambridge/New York: Cambridge University Press. https://doi.org/10.1017/9781009325844
IPEA/IPLAN. 1973. *Projeto Aripuanã*. Brasília: IPEA.
ISA (Instituto SocioAmbiental). 2004. *Amazônia Brasileira 2004*. São Paulo: ISA.
ISA (Instituto SocioAmbiental). 2012. "Y Ikatu Xingu – salve a agua boa do Xingu." https://acervo.socioambiental.org/acervo/documentos/y-ikatu-xingu-salve-agua-boa-do-xingu (accessed December 28, 2022).
ISA (Instituto SocioAmbiental). 2013. *Relatório de atividades 2012*. https://www.socioambiental.org/sites/default/files/2021-05/rel2012_jul01.pdf (accessed January 5, 2023).
ISA (Instituto SocioAmbiental). 2020. *Áreas Protegidas* [shapefile].
IWGIA. 2022. *Indigenous world 2020: Brazil*. https://www.iwgia.org/en/brazil/3616-iw-2020-brazil.html (accessed 29.12.2022).
JICA/PGC. 1985. *The study related to the regional development plan of the Greater Carajás Program of the Federative Republic of Brazil. Phase II. Final Report*. Tokyo: JICA/PGC.
Jordão, Carolina de Oliveira. 2022. *Saving the rainforest? Experiences of being and acting as NGOs in the Amazon*. PhD thesis, University of Florida, Gainesville.
Junk, Wolfgang J. 1989. "The use of Amazonian floodplains under an ecological perspective." *Interciência* 14, no. 6: 317–322.

Junk, Wolfgang J., and J. A. S. Nunes de Mello. 1987. "Impactos ecológicos das represas hidrelétricas na Bacia Amazônica Brasileira." In *Homem e natureza na Amazônia. Hombre y Naturaleza en la Amazonía*, edited by Gerd Kohlhepp, and Achim Schrader, 367–385. Tübingen: EdIGUT.

Junk, Wolfgang J. *et al.* 2000. *The Central Amazonian floodplaIn Actual use and options for a sustainable management.* Leiden: Backhuys.

Junk, Wolfgang J. 2003. "Ökologische Grundlagen zur Bewertung der Nutzungsmöglichkeiten zentralamazonischer Ökosysteme – eine Bestandsaufnahme." In *Brasilien. Entwicklungsland oder tropische Großmacht des 21. Jahrhunderts?*, edited by Gerd Kohlhepp, 187–214. Tübingen: Attempto.

Junqueira, Carmen. 1973. *The Brazilian indigenous problem and policy: The example of the Xingu National Park.* Copenhagen/Genève: IWGIA.

Kaiser, Anna Jean. 2019. "Brazil's former president Michel Temer arrested in corruption investigation." *The Guardian*, March 21. https://www.theguardian.com/world/2019/mar/21/brazils-former-president-michel-temer-arrested-in-corruption-investigation (accessed September 4, 2024).

Karp, Bernd. 1986. "Das agrare Genossenschaftswesen als raumgestaltender Faktor. Zur Ambivalenz gelenkter Modernisierung am Beispiel von West-Paraná." *Geographische Zeitschrift* 74, no. 4: 241–250.

Karp, Bernd. 1987. "Agrarkolonisation, Landkonflikte und disparitäre Regionalentwicklung im Spannungsfeld ethno-sozialer Gruppen und externer Einflussfaktoren in West-Paraná." In *Brasilien. Beiträge zur regionalen Struktur- und Entwicklungsforschung*, TBGL 1, edited by Gerd Kohlhepp, 39–69. Tübingen: EdIGUT.

Kasburg, Carola, and Márcia M. Gramkow, org. 1999. *Demarcando terras indígenas: experiências e desafios de um projeto de parceria.* Brasília: FUNAI/PPTAL/GTZ.

KfW. 2017. "REDD+ in the State of Acre, Brazil: Rewarding a pioneer in forest protection and sustainable livelihood development." https://www.kfw-entwicklungsbank.de/PDF/Entwicklungsfinanzierung/Themen-NEU/REDD-Early-Movers-Acre-Fact-Sheet.pdf (accessed December 3, 2022).

Kirchhoff, Volker Walter Johann Heinrich. 1992. *Queimadas na Amazônia e efeito estufa.* São José dos Campos: Contexto.

Kitamura, Paulo C., and Carlos H. Müller. 1984. *Castanhais nativos de Marabá, Pa: Fatores de depredação e bases para a sua preservação.* Belém: EMBRAPA/CPATU.

Kleinpenning, Jan M. G. 1975. *The Integration and Colonisation of the Brazilian Portion of the Amazon Basin.* Nijmegen: Geografisch en Planologisch Instituut, Katholieke Universiteit Nijmegen.

Kleinpenning, Jan M. G. 1979. *An Evaluation of the Brazilian Policy for the Integration of the Amazon Basin. 1964–1976.* Nijmegen: Geografisch & Planologisch Instituut.

Kleinpenning, Jan M. G., ed. 1986. *Competition for rural and urban space in Latin America. Its consequences for low-income groups.* Amsterdam/Nijmegen: Koninklijk Nederlands Aardrijkskundig Genootschap.

Kleinpenning, Jan M. G., ed. 1991. *The incorporation drive. Examples from Latin America.* Saarbrücken/Fort Lauderdale: Breitenbach.

Klingler, Michael. 2022. *Die politische Ökologie der Null-Entwaldung. Amazonien zwischen (Neo-)Extraktivismus und post-frontier-governance.* Stuttgart: Franz Steiner Verlag.

Klingler, Michael, Peter D. Richards, and Roman Ossner. 2018. "Cattle vaccination records question the impact of recent zero-deforestation agreements in the Amazon." *Regional Environmental Change* 18, no. 1: 33–46. https://doi.org/10.1007/s10113-017-1234-1

Klingler, Michael, and Philipp Mack. 2020. "Post-frontier governance up in smoke? Free-for-all frontier imaginations encourage illegal deforestation and appropriation of public lands in the Brazilian Amazon." *Journal of Land Use Science* 15, no. 2–3: 424–438. https://doi.org/10.1080/1747423X.2020.1739765

Kohlhepp, Gerd: Author's publications on Amazonia cited in this volume; see Appendix of the bibliography.

Kolk, Ans. 1998. "From Conflict to Cooperation. International policies to protect the Brazilian Amazon." *World Development* 26, no. 8: 1481–1493.

Kopper, Christopher. 2017. *VW do Brasil in the modern military dictatorship 1964–1985. A historical study.* Wolfsburg: Quensen.

Kosinski, Leszek A., ed. 1991. *Ecological disorder and Amazonia.* Rio de Janeiro: EDUCAM.

Kostcho, Ricardo. 1984. *Serra Pelada: uma ferida aberta na Selva.* São Paulo: Brasiliense.

Krug, Telma *et al.* 1997. *Incidência de queimadas no período de junho a novembro de 1995 e 1996 detectadas pelo sensor AVHRR de satélite NOAA.* São José dos Campos: INPE.

Kruid, Sanne *et al.* 2021. "Beyond deforestation: Carbon emissions from land grabbing and forest degradation in the Brazilian Amazon." *Frontiers in Forests and Global Change. Sec. Tropical Forests* 4: n. p. https://doi.org/10.3389/ffgc.2021.645282

Lapper, Richard. 2021. *Beef, bible, and bullets. Brazil in the age of Bolsonaro.* Manchester: Manchester University Press.

Laurance, William F. 1998. "Fragments of the forest." *Natural History* 107, no. 6: 34–39.

Laurance, William F. *et al.* 2001. "The future of the Brazilian Amazon." *Science,* 291: 438–439. (Supplementary material. *Science Online,* 2001). https://www.science.org/doi/10.1126/science.291.5503.438 (accessed 12.09.2022).

Lehmann, Johannes, Dirse C. Kern, Bruno Glaser, and William I. Woods, eds. 2003. *Amazonian Dark Earths. Origin, properties, and management.* Dordrecht: Kluwer Academic Publishers.

Lévi-Strauss, Claude. 1963. *Tristes tropiques: An anthropological study of primitive societies in Brazil.* New York: Atheneum.

Lieberei, Reinhard, Christoph Reisdorff, and Antônio Dantas Machado, eds. 1996. *Interdisciplinary research on the conservation and sustainable use of the Amazonian rain forest and its information requirements.* Geesthacht: GKSS.

Lieberei, Reinhard, and Eneas F. Salati. 1998. "SHIFT – concept, achievements, and perspectives for sustainable management." In *Proceedings of the Third SHIFT Workshop. A German-Brazilian Research Program,* 3–7. Manaus: BMBF.

Lima, Ronei Coelho de, and Nelba Azevedo Penna. 2016. "A logística de transportes do agronegócio em Mato Grosso, Brasil." *Confins* 26: n. p. https://doi.org/10.4000/confins.10707

Lombardo, Umberto, C. H. McMichael, and E. Kazuo Tamanaha. 2018. "Mapping pre-Columbian land use in Amazonia." *Past Global Changes Magazine* 26, no. 1: 14–15. https://doi.org/10.22498/pages.26.1.14

Lourenço, José Seixas. 1995. "Organizing research for the development of the Amazon region." In *Brazilian perspectives on sustainable development of the Amazon region,* edited by Miguel Clüsener-Godt, and Ignacy Sachs, 237–257. Paris: UNESCO.

Lovejoy, Thomas E., and Carlos A. Nobre. 2018. "Amazon tipping point." *Science Advances* 4, no. 2: n. p. https://doi.org/10.1126/sciadv.aat2340
Lovejoy, Thomas E., and Carlos A. Nobre. 2019. "Amazon tipping point: Last chance for action." *Science Advances* 5, no. 12: n. p. https://doi.org/10.1126/sciadv.aba2949
Lücker, Reinhold. 1986. *Agrarräumliche Entwicklungsprozesse im Alto Uruguai-Gebiet (Südbrasilien)*. TBGL 2. Tübingen: EdIGUT.
Lutzenberger, José. 1977. *Fim do futuro? Manifesto ecológico brasileiro*. Porto Alegre: Movimento.
Machado, Lia Osório. 1982. "Urbanização e migração na Amazônia Legal: Sugestão para uma abordagem geopolítica." *Boletim Carioca de Geografia* 32: 2–10.
Machado, Lia Osório. 1996. "O comércio ilícito de drogas e a geografia da integração financeira: uma símbiose?" In *Brasil. Questões atuais da reorganização do território*, orgnised by Iná Elias de Castro *et al.*, 15–64. Rio de Janeiro: Bertrand Brasil.
Machado, Lia Osório. 2002. "Drug trafficking and money laundering in the Amazon region. Geoeconomic and geopolitical effects." In *Globalisation, drugs, and criminalisation*. Final Report MOST-UNESCO International Research Project, organised by Christian Geffray *et al.*, 151–171. https://unesdoc.unesco.org/ark:/48223/pf0000127644 (accessed March 2, 2023).
Machado, Lia Osório. 2007. "Medidas institucionais para o controle do tráfico de drogas e da lavagem de dinheiro e seus efeitos geoestratégicos na região Amazônica brasileira." *Cadernos IPPUR/UFRJ* 21, no. 1: 9–31.
Machado, Lia Osório. 2009. "Ambiguity between the legal and the illegal: Trafficking networks of illicit drugs and territory." https://www.academia.edu/29983331/_2009 (accessed March 7, 2023).
Mahar, Dennis J. 1979. *Frontier development policy in Brazil: A study of Amazonia*. New York: Praeger.
Mahar, Dennis J. 1982. "Instituições internacionais de empréstimo público e o desenvolvimento da Amazônia Brasileira: A experiência do Banco Mundial." *Revista de Administração Pública* 16, no. 4: 23–38.
Mahar, Dennis J. 1989. *Government policies and deforestation in Brazil's Amazon region*. Washington, D.C.: The World Bank.
Mahar, Dennis J. 2000. *Land use zoning in the Amazon region: The experience of Rondônia, Acre and Tocantins* (mimeo).
Mahar, Dennis, and Céline E.H. Ducrot. 1998. *Land-use zoning on tropical frontiers: Emerging lessons from the Brazilian Amazon*. Washington, D.C.: The World Bank.
Maihold, Günther. 2019a. "Der Zorn des Jair Bolsonaro: Brasiliens Rückfall aus der Zukunft." *ZFAS (Z. f. Außen- und Sicherheitspolitik)* 12: 301–319. https://doi.org/10.1007/s12399-019-00775-8
Maihold, Günther. 2019b. "Amazonas Schutz und Freihandel. Das EU-Mercosur-Abkommen steht auf der Kippe." *SWP-Aktuell* 51, n. p. https://doi.org/10.18449/2019A51
Maihold, Günther. 2020. "Frühtod eines Abkommens? Das EU-Mercosur-Abkommen droht an fehlendem Vertrauen zu scheitern." *SWP Kurz gesagt*, https://www.swp-berlin.org/publikation/das-eu-mercosur-abkommen-droht-an-fehlendem-vertrauen-zu-scheitern (accessed August 12, 2022).
Maihold, Günther. 2022. "Lulas Rückkehr an die Macht in Brasilien." *SWP-Aktuell* 81, n. p. https://www.swp-berlin.org/10.18449/2022A81/ (accessed March 7, 2023).

Maihold, Günther, and Melanie Müller. 2023. "Eine neue Entwicklungsphase der BRICS. Erweiterung und neue Identität." *SWP-Aktuell* 52, n. p. https://doi.org/10.18449/2023A52

Margulis, Sérgio. 2004. *Causes of Deforestation of the Brazilian Amazon.* Washington, D.C.: The World Bank.

Martins, Edilson. 1982. *Amazônia, a última fronteira.* Rio de Janeiro: Codecri.

Martins, José de Souza. 1982. *Expropriação e violência: a questão política no campo.* São Paulo: HUCITEC.

Martins, José de Souza. 1983. *Os camponeses e a política no Brasil. As lutas ssociais no campo e seu lugar no processo político.* Petrópolis: Vozes.

Martins, José de Souza. 1987. "O poder de decidir no desenvolvimento da Amazônia – conflitos de interesse entre planejadores e suas vitimas." In *Homem e natureza na Amazônia*, TBGL 3, edited by Gerd Kohlhepp, and Achim Schrader, 407–414. Tübingen: EdIGUT.

Mattos, Marli M., and Christopher Uhl. 1994. "Economic and ecological perspectives on ranching in the Eastern Amazon." *World Development* 22, no. 2: 145–158. https://doi.org/10.1016/0305-750X(94)90066-3

McIntyre, Loren. 1980. "Jarí: "A massive technology transplant takes root in the Amazon jungle." *National Geographic* 157, no. 5: 693–711.

Meggers, Betty J., and Clifford Evans. 1957. "Archeological investigations at the mouth of the Amazon." *Bureau of American Ethnology Bulletin* 167: 1–664.

Meggers, Betty J. 1971. *Amazonia: Man, and culture in a counterfeit paradise.* Chicago: Aldine Atherton Inc.

Meggers, Betty J. 1994. "Archeological evidence for the impact of Mega-Niño events of Amazonia during the past two millennia." *Climate change* 28: 321–338.

Mello, Neli Aparecida de. 1997. "Um modelo para gestão ambiental integrada e zoneamento ecológico-econômico." In *Programa Piloto para Proteção das Florestas Tropicais do Brasil.* Livro das Secretarias Técnicas. Brasília: MMA.

Mello, Neli Aparecida de. 2000. *Trinta anos de políticas amazônicas.* Nogent sur Marne: Centre de Coopération Internationale en Recherche Agronomique pour le Développement.

Mello, Neli Aparecida de, and Hervé Théry. 2001. "A armadura do espaço amazônico: eixos e zoneamentos." *Alceu* 1, no. 2: 181–214.

Mello, Neli Aparecida de, Richard Pasquis, and Hervé Théry. 2004. "L'Amazonie 'durable' de Marina Silva." In *Pour comprendre le Brésil de Lula,*coordinated by Denis Rolland, and Joëlle Chassin, 169–186. Paris: L'Harmattan.

Mello, Neli Aparecida de, Richard Pasquis, and Hervé Théry. 2005. "A Amazônia 'sustentável' de Marina e Lula." In *Amazônia sustentável. Desenvolvimento sustentável entre políticas, estratégias inovadoras e experiências locais*, TBGL 28, coordinated by Martin Coy, and Gerd Kohlhepp, 45–62. Rio de Janeiro/Tübingen: Garamond/EdIGUT.

Mello-Théry, Neli Aparecida de. 2006. *Políticas territoriais na Amazônia.* São Paulo: Annablume.

Mello-Théry, Neli Aparecida de. 2016. "L'Amazonie entre les myriades d'expériences et les politiques publiques dominantes." *Confins* 26: n. p. https://doi.org/10.4000/confins.10749

Mello-Théry, Neli Aparecida de, and Paulo R. Cunha. 2014. "Environmental policies and forest code: Changes and repercussions on the agriculture in Mato Grosso." In *Interdisciplinary analysis and modelling of carbon-optimized land management strategies for Southern Amazonia*, edited by Gerhard Gerold *et al.*, 137–147. Göttingen: Universitätsverlag.

Mello-Théry, Neli Aparecida de, Eduardo de Lima Caldas, Beatriz M. Funatsu, Damien Arvor, and Vincent Dubreuil. 2020. "Climate change and public policies in the Brazilian Amazon State of Mato Grosso: Perceptions and challenges." *Sustainability* 12, no. 12, 5093: n. p. https://doi.org/10.3390/su12125093

Melo-Reiners, Irma Silvana de. 2009. *Regenwaldschutz in Brasilien und das Umweltvölkerrecht. Die Amazonasfrage als internationaler Streitfall*. Aachen: Shaker.

Mendes, Karla. 2023. "'Funai is ours': Brazil's indigenous affairs agency is reclaimed under Lula." *Mongabay Series: Indigenous Peoples and Conservation*. https://news.mongabay.com/2023/01/funai-is-ours-brazils-indigenous-affairs-agency-is-reclaimed-under-lula/ (accessed March 22, 2023).

Millikan, Brent, and Zachary Hurwitz. 2011. "Landmark vote in Brazil upholds indigenous rights on Belo Monte." *Upside Down World* , October 19.

Millikan, Brent, and Christian Poirier. 2015. "Mounting evidence of corruption in the Brazilian dam industry." https://amazonwatch.org/news/2015/0319-corruption-scandal-deepens-in-brazil (accessed December 11, 2022).

Ministério da Agricultura. 1983. *Programa Grande Carajás Agrícola. Versão preliminar*. 6 vol. Brasília: Ministério da Agricultura.

Ministério das Minas e Energia. 1981. *Programa Grande Carajás*. Brasília: Ministério das Minas e Energia.

MIN (Ministério da Integração Nacional). 2003. *Política nacional de desenvolvimento regional*. Brasília: MIN.

MIN/MMA (Ministério do Meio Ambiente). 2004. *Plano Amazônia Sustentável – PAS. Vol. 1: Diagnóstico e Estratégia*. Brasília: MIN/MMA.

MIRAD (Ministry of Agrarian Reform and Agrarian Development). 1985. *Plano Nacional de Reforma Agrária – PNRA*. Brasília: MIRAD.

MIRAD. 1986. *Conflitos de terra, vol. 1*. Brasília: MIRAD.

Miranda, E.E. de *et al.* 1994. *Monitoramento orbital das queimadas no Brasil*. Campinas: ECOFORCA.

MMA. 2017. *National biodiversity strategy and action plan*. Brasília: MMA.

MMA/CONAMAZ. 1998. *Síntese das ações para a implementação da política nacional integrada para a Amazônia Legal. Período de 1995 a 1997*. Brasília: MMA/CONAMAZ.

MMA/SCA. 1995. *Política nacional integrada para a Amazônia Legal*. Brasília: MMA/SCA.

MMA/SCA. 1996. *Programa Piloto para a proteção das florestas tropicais do Brasil*. Brasília: MMA/SCA.

MMA/SCA. 1997. *Subprograma de política de recursos naturais – SPRN*. Brasília: MMA/SCA.

MMA/World Bank. 1998. *Pilot program to conserve the Brazilian rain forest*. Brasília: MMA/World Bank.

MMA/PPG7. 2009. *Caminhos para a sustentabilidade. As contribuições do maior programa ambiental do país para o uso e a proteção das florestas tropicais brasileiras*. Brasília: MMA/PPG7.

Monteiro, Maurílio de Abreu. 1998. *Siderurgia e carvoejamento na Amazônia: drenagem energético-material e pauperização regional*. Belém: UFPA/ETFPA.

Monteiro, Maurílio de Abreu. 2003. "ICOMI in Amapá: half a century of mining." *Novos Cadernos NAEA* 6, no. 2: 113–168.

Monteiro, Maurílio de Abreu. 2005. "Industrial mining in the Amazon and its implications for regional development." *Novos Cadernos NAEA* 8, no. 1: 141–187.

Morán, Emílio F. 1983. *The dilemma of Amazonian development.* Boulder: Westview Press.

Morán, Emílio F. 1987. "A produção agrícola em um projeto da colonização em Carajás." In *Homem e natureza na Amazônia*, TBGL 3, edited by Gerd Kohlhepp, and Achim Schrader, 387–406. Tübingen: EdIGUT.

Morán, Emílio F. 1990. *A ecologia humana das populações da Amazônia*. Petrópolis: Vozes.

Morán, Emílio F. 1993. "Deforestation and land use in the Brazilian Amazon." *Human Ecology* 21: 1–21.

Mougeot, Luc J. A. 1986. River impoundment related population displacement in Brazilian Amazonia: The Tucuruí resettlement program (TRP), 1976–84." In *Competition for rural and urban space in Latin America*, edited by Jan M. G. Kleinpenning, 43–60. Amsterdam/Nijmegen: Koninklijk Nederlands Aardrijkskundig Genootschap.

MPBM (Ministry of Planning, Budget and Management). 1999. *Avança Brasil. Development structures for investment.* Brasília: MPBM.

MPOG (Ministry of Planning, Budget and Management). 2000. *Brasil em Ação. Relatório final 1996–1999.* Brasília: MPOG.

Müller, Cristina. 2020. *Brazil and the Amazon Rainforest. Deforestation, Biodiversity and Cooperation with the EU and International Forums.* Luxembourg: European Parliament. https://www.europarl.europa.eu/thinktank/en/document/IPOL_IDA(2020)648792 (accessed March 12, 2023).

Muntingh, H. 1988. *Draft report on the environmental problems of the Amazon region.* Bruxelles: European Parliament.

Nepstad, Daniel C. 1999. "Large-scale impoverishment of Amazon forests by logging and fire." *Nature* 398: 505–508.

Nepstad, Daniel C. *et al.* 2000. *Avança Brasil: os custos ambientais para a Amazônia.* Belém: Alves.

Nepstad, Daniel *et al.* 2014. "Slowing Amazon deforestation through public policy and interventions in beef and soy supply chains." *Science* 344, 1118–1123. https://www.science.org/doi/10.1126/science.1248525 (accessed September 4, 2024).

Nepstad, Daniel C., and Stephan Schwartzman. 1993. "Extractive Reserves examined: non-timber products from tropical forests, evaluation of a conservation and development strategy." *Bioscience* 43, no. 9: 644–646.

Nepstad, Daniel C., Adriana G. Moreira, and Ane A. Alencar. 1999. *Flames in the rain forest: origins, impacts and alternatives to Amazonian fires.* Brasília: World Bank/MMA/SCA.

Nepstad, Daniel C., David McGrath, Ane A. Alencar, A. C. Barros, G. Carvalho, M. Santilli, and Maria del C. Vera-Diaz. 2002. "Frontier governance in Amazonia." *Science* 295, 629–631. https://doi.org/10.1126/science.1067053

Nepstad, Daniel, and João Shimada. 2018. *Soybeans in the Brazilian Amazon and the case of the Brazilian soy moratorium.* Washington, D.C.: The World Bank.

Neuburger, Martina. 2002. *Pionierfrontentwicklung im Hinterland von Cáceres (Mato Grosso). Ökologische Degradierung, Verwundbarkeit und kleinbäuerliche Überlebensstrategien.* TBGL 23. Tübingen: EdIGUT.

Neuburger, Martina. 2008. "Global discourses and the local impacts in Amazonia. Inclusion and exclusion processes in the Rio Negro region." *Erdkunde* 62, no. 4: 339–356.

Neves, Eduardo G. *et al.* 2021. "Peoples of the Amazon before European colonization." In *Amazon Assessment Report 2021. Science Panel for the Amazon,* edited by Carlos Nobre *et al.*, chapter 8, 1–40. New York: United Nations Sustainable Development Solutions Network. https://doi.org/10.55161/LXIT5573

Nitsch, Manfred. 1989. "Die Rolle der internen politisch-administrativen Strukturen und der externen Geldgeber bei der Zerstörung tropischer Wälder – der Fall des brasilianischen Amazoniens." In *Die Bedrohung tropischer Wälder,* edited by Jürgen Bähr *et al.*, 63–85. Kiel: Geographisches Institut der Universität Kiel.

Nitsch, Manfred. 1996. "Aktuelle Strategien zur Verteidigung des Regenwaldes und zur Sicherung einer umweltverträglichen Entwicklung in Amazonien. Zur Problematik des 'zoneamento ecológico-econmico'." In *Brasilien im Umbruch,* edited by Dietrich Briesemeister, and Sérgio P. Rouanet, 115–140. Berlin: TFM.

Nobre, Carlos A. 2020. "Quo vadis humanitas?" In *FAZ*, June 17.

Nobre, Carlos A. *et al.* 1991. "Amazonian deforestation and regional climate change." *Journal of climate* 4: 957–988.

Nobre, Carlos A., Gilvan Sampaio, Laura S. Borma, and Manoel Cardoso. 2016. "Land-use and climate change risks in the Amazon and the need of a novel sustainable development paradigm." *Proceedings of the National Academy of Sciences (PNAS)* 113, no. 39: 10759–10768. https://doi.org/10.1073/pnas.1605516113

Nobre, Carlos A., and Ismael Nobre. 2020. "The need of a novel sustainable development paradigm for the Amazon." *IPEA. Boletim Regional, Urbano e Ambiental* 22: 159–170. https://doi.org/10.38116/brua22art12

Nobre, Carlos A. *et al.*, eds. 2021. *Amazon Assessment Report 2021. Science Panel for the Amazon.* Chapters 1–34. New York: United Nations Sustainable Development Solutions Network. https://doi.org/10.55161/RWSX6527

Nobre, Ismael, and Carlos Nobre. 2019. "Amazonia 4.0: defining a third way for the Amazon." *Revista Futuribles* 2: 7–20. https://medium.com/fundação-fhc/amazon-4-0-project-defining-a-third-path-for-the-amazon-f0412305f066 (accessed May 12, 2023).

Nolte, Detlef. 2023. "The European Union and Latin America: Renewing the partnership after drifting apart." *GIGA Focus Lateinamerika* 2: 1–12. https://doi.org/10.57671/gfla-23022

Oliveira, Ariovaldo U. de. 2016. *A fronteira amazônica Mato-Grossense: Grilagem, Corrupção e Violência.* São Paulo: Iãnde.

Oliveira, Marília Silva. 2015. "Capacidade estatal e implementação de política de desenvolvimento regional sustentável na Amazônia." *Novos Cadernos NAEA* 18, no. 3: 271–291. https://doi.org/10.5801/ncn.v18i3.1931

Oliveira, Marcos A. de, and Marcio Sepulvia de Oliveira. 2021. "Operational characterization of Luis Eduardo Magalhães hydroelectric power plant and the use of water resources of the Tocantins river for energy generation." *Brazilian Journal of Development* 7: 44952–44964. https://doi.org/10.34117/bjdv7n5-085

Pandolfo, Clara. 1974. *Estudos básicos para o estabelecimento de uma política de desenvolvimento dos recursos florestais e de uso racional das terras da Amazônia.* Belém: SUDAM.

Pasca, Dan. 2002. "Indigene Völker in Brasilien – von der Bevormundung zur Selbstbestimmung." *Petermanns Geographische Mitteilungen* 146, no 1: 22–33.

Pasca, Dan. 2004. *Ressourcennutzungskonflikte und Strategien zur Sicherung indigener Räume an der brasilianischen Peripherie.* TBGL 24. Tübingen: EdIGUT.

Pasca, Dan. 2005. "Lokal bekämpft, weltweit unterstützt. Die indigenen Völker Brasiliens im Fangnetz des neuen Entwicklungsdiskurses." In *Wirtschafts- und sozialräumliche Strukturwandlungen und Interessenkonflikte in Lateinamerika,* edited by Gerd Kohlhepp, 103–145. Tübingen: EdIGUT.

Passos, Messias M. dos. 2007. *BR-163 – De estrada dos colonos a corredor de exportação.* Maringá: Massoni.

Passos, Messias M. dos. 2015. *Colonização agrícola e povoamento na Amazônia Matogrossense.* Maringá: EDUEM.

Passos, Messias M. dos. 2019. "BR-163: from 'landless men' to 'manless land'." *Cadernos de Geografia* 39, 41–53. Coimbra: FLUC.

Passos, Messias M. dos. 2022. *BR-163 em 5 tempos: uma abordagem geo-foto-gráfica.* Maringá: EDUEM.

Paul, Wolf. 1990. "Rechtsschutz für den Amazonas-Regenwald: Brasiliens Antwort auf die internationale Tropenwaldkampagne." *DBJV-Mitteilung* 1/90: 2–11.

Paul, Wolf. 1994. "Verfassungsgebung und Verfassung." In *Brasilien heute. Politik, Wirtschaft, Kultur,* edited by Dietrich Briesemeister, Gerd Kohlhepp, Ray-Güde Mertin, Hartmut Sangmeister, and Achim Schrader, 197–206. Frankfurt a. M.: Vervuert.

Paul, Wolf, and R. dos Santos Vieira, eds. 1993. *Amazônia – Realität und Recht; umwelt- und arbeitsrechtliche Fragestellungen.* Frankfurt a. M. *et al.*: Peter Lang.

Pereira, Ana K., Alexandre de Ávila Gomide, Rafael Machado, and Marcela Ibiapino. 2022. "Governance arrangements for socio-environmental sustainability in the implementation of large infrastructure projects in the Brazilian Amazon." https://doi.org/10.1590/1679-395120210073x

Pereira, Luis Filipe, and Marco Mortari. 2022. "Lula terá 37 ministros; conheça quem comandará cada pasta do novo governo." InfoMoney, December 30. https://www.infomoney.com.br/politica/lista-ministros-lula/ (accessed March 4, 2023).

Pereira, Ritaumaria, Cynthia S. Simmons, and Robert Walker. 2016. "Smallholders, agrarian reform, and globalization in the Brazilian Amazon: Cattle versus the environment." *Land* 5, no. 24: n. p. https://doi.org/10.3390/land5030024

Perroux, François. 1950. "Economic space: theory and applications." *The Quarterly Journal of Economics* 64: 90–97.

Perroux, François. 1955. "Note sur la notion de 'pôle de croissance'." *Économie Appliquée* 8, no. 1–2: 307–320.

Pfeifer, Gottfried. 1966. "Observaciones a largo de las nuevas fronteras de colonización en Paraná y Mato Grosso." In *UGI-Conf. Regional Latino-Americana. Vol. 1: La geografia y los problemas de población,* 314–328. México.

Pfeifer, Gottfried, and Gerd Kohlhepp. 1967. "Kontraste in Rio Grande do Sul: Campanha und Alto Uruguai." *Geographische Zeitschrift* 55, no. 3: 163–206.

Phillips, Tom. 2021. "Bolsonaro vowed to show a new Brazil but 'lie-filled' UN speech cuts little ice." *The Guardian,* September 21. https://www.theguardian.com/world/2021/sep/21/jair-bolsonaro-brazil-un-speech (accessed February 22, 2023).

Phillips, Tom. 2023. "Brazil launches operation to drive illegal miners from Yanomami lands." *The Guardian*, February 8. https://www.theguardian.com/world/2023/feb/08/brazil-illegal-mining-indigenous-lula?emci=ddc638c4-7ca8-ed11-994d-00224832eb73&emdi=32fc3598-7da8-ed11-994d-00224832eb73&ceid=4606001 (accessed March 7, 2023).

Pilot Programme. 1993. *Quarterly Newsletter of the Pilot Programme*. The World Bank.

Pinto, Lúcio Flávio. 1982. *Carajás, o ataque ao coração da Amazônia*. Rio de Janeiro: Marco Zero.

Pinto, Lúcio Flávio. 1984. "O império de D. K. Ludwig: um mistério de 15 anos." *O Liberal*, 3° Caderno, November 15.

Pinto, Lúcio Flávio. 1986. *Jarí: Toda a verdade sobre o projeto de Ludwig*. São Paulo: Marco Zero.

Pivetta, Marcos. 2018. "More people in the rainforest." https://revistapesquisa.fapesp.br/en/more-people-in-the-rainforest/ (accessed December 22, 2022).

POEMA (Poverty and Environment in Amazonia). 1994. *Trópico em movimento. Alternativas contra a pobreza e a destruição ambiental no trópico úmido*. Série POEMA 2. Belém: POEMA.

Poirier, Christian, and Brent Millikan. 2017. "Desperate to save his job, Brazil's President Temer escalates assault on indigenous peoples and Amazonian forests." https://amazonwatch.org/news/2017/0721-desperate-to-save-his-job-brazils-president-temer-escalates-assault (accessed December 12, 2022).

Pokorny, Benno. 2013. *Smallholders, forest management and rural development in the Amazon*. London/New York: Routledge. https://doi.org/10.4324/9780203073919

Pokorny, Benno, Pablo Pacheco, Wil de Jong, and Steffen K. Entenmann. 2021. "Forest frontiers out of control: The long-term effects of discourses, policies, and markets on conservation and development of the Brazilian Amazon." *Ambio* 50, no. 46: 2199–2223. https://doi.org/10.1007/s13280-021-01637-4

Pokorny, Benno, Imme Scholz, and Wil de Jong. 2013. "REDD+ for the poor or the poor for REDD+? About the limitations of environmental policies in the Amazon and the potential of achieving environmental goals through pro-poor policies." *Ecology and Society* 18, no. 2, Art. 3: n. p. https://dx.doi.org/10.5751/ES-05458-180203

Posey, Darrell A. 1982. "Indigenous ecological knowledge and development of the Amazon." In *The dilemma of Amazonian development*, edited by Emílio F. Morán, 225–257. Boulder: Westview Press.

Posey, Darrell A. 1985a. "Indigenous management of tropical forest ecosystems: the case of the Kayapó indians of the Brazilian Amazon." *Agroforestry Systems* 3: 139–158.

Posey, Darrell A. 1985b. "Native and indigenous guidelines for new Amazonian development strategies: understanding biological diversity through ethnobiology." In *Change in the Amazon Basin*. Vol. 1: *Man's impact on forests and rivers*, edited by John Hemming, 156–181. Manchester: Manchester University Press.

Posey, Darrell A. 1987. "Etnobiologia e ciência de folk: Sua importância para Amazônia." In *Homem e natureza na Amazônia*, TBGL 3, edited by Gerd Kohlhepp, and Achim Schrader, 95–108. Tübingen: EdIGUT.

Posey, Darrell A. 2000. "Biodiversity, genetic resources, and indigenous people in Amazonia: (Re)discovering the wealth of traditional resources of native Amazonians." In *Amazonia at the crossroads*, edited by Anthony Hall, 188–204. London: Institute of Latin American Studies.

Prien, Hans-Jürgen. 1989. "Mission und Indianer in ihrer gegenwärtigen Problematik." In *Amazonien im Umbruch*, edited by Günther Hartmann, 371–387. Hamburg: Dietrich Reimer Verlag.

Prinz, Ulrike. 2021. "Goldrausch am Amazonas: Der wahre Preis des Goldes." https://www.spektrum.de/news/goldrausch-am-amazonas-der-wahre-preis-des-goldes/1923763 (accessed February 28, 2023).

Rabben, Linda. 2010. "Demarcation – and then what? Brazil takes a step, but its commitment to protecting indigenous lands is not proven." *Cultural survival*, https://www.culturalsurvival.org/publications/cultural-survival-quarterly/demarcation-and-then-what-brazil-takes-step-its-commitment (accessed December 29, 2022).

RAD. 2024. "Relatório Annual de Desmatamento no Brasil 2023". São Paulo: MapBiomas. https://alerta.mapbiomas.org (accessed June 7, 2024).

Redwood III, John. 2002. *World Bank approaches to the Brazilian Amazon: The bumpy road toward sustainable development*. Sustainable Development Working Paper No. 13. Washington, D.C.: The World Bank.

Ribeiro, Darcy. 1957. "Culturas e línguas indígenas do Brasil." *Educação e Ciências Sociais* 6, 1–102.

Ribeiro, Darcy. 1962. *A política indigenista Brasileira*. Rio de Janeiro: Ministerio da Agricultura.

Ribeiro, Darcy. 1970. *Os índios e a civilização: A integração das populações indígenas no Brasil moderno*. Rio de Janeiro: Global.

Ribeiro, Ricardo da Silva, Ricardo E. Vicente, Solange Arrolho, and Philip M. Fearnside. 2022. "Amazon deforestation restrictions likely to be circumvented." *Die Erde – Journal of the Geographical Society of Berlin* 153, no. 3: 216–217. https://doi.org/10.12854/erde-2022-621

Ricardo, Beto, and Fany Ricardo. 2011. *Povos indígenas no Brasil: 2006–2010*. São Paulo: Instituto SocioAmbiental.

Rocha, Bolivar Moura. 1989. "The Brazilian Constitution of 1988." *MPI für ausländisches öffentliches Recht und Völkerrecht* 49: 61–88.

Rodrigues, Jondison Cardoso, and João Santos Nahum. 2023. "The concession of the BR-163 highway in the Brazilian Amazon: Corporatization of territory and conflicts." *Die Erde – Journal of the Geographical Society of Berlin* 154, no. 1–2: 42–48. https://www.die-erde.org/index.php/die-erde/article/view/624/464 (July 24, 2024).

Röper, Monika. 2001. *Planung und Einrichtung von Naturschutzgebieten aus sozialgeographischer Perspektive. Fallbeispiele aus der Pantanal-Region (Brasilien)*. TBGL 22. Tübingen: EdIGUT.

Rorato, Ana C. *et al*. 2020. "Brazilian Amazon indigenous peoples threatened by mining bill." *Environmental Research Letters* 15, no. 10: n. p. https://doi.org/10.1088/1748-9326/abb428

Ruaro, Renata, Gustavo H. Zaia Alves, Lívia Tonella, Lucas Ferrante, and Philip M. Fearnside. 2022. "Loosening of environmental licensing threatens Brazilian biodiversity and sustainability." *Die Erde – Journal of the Geographical Society of Berlin* 153, no. 1: 60–64. https://www.die-erde.de/index.php/die-erde/article/download/614/408 (accessed September 4, 2024).

Russo, Tatiana O., Marcus P. C. Rocha, Maisa S. G. Tobias, Matheus M. Souza, and Neydson M. S. Silva. 2022. "Analysis model of the corridor of the Arco Norte of the Amazon for the soybean of Mato Grosso." *International Journal for Innovation Education and Research* 10, no. 3: 84–104.

Sachs, Ignacy. 1980. *Stratégies de l'écodéveloppement.* Paris: Les Éditions Ouvrières.

Sachs, Ignacy. 1992. "Lost paradise or promised land: An ecodevelopment perspective on the Amazon region." In *Amazonia: Ecology and sustainable development,* edited by Wil Pansters, 147–160. Utrecht: ISOR/Rijksuniversiteit te Utrecht.

SAE (Secretaria de Assuntos Estratégicos). 1991. *Programa de zoneamento ecológico-econômico da Amazônia Legal.* Brasília: SAE.

Salati, Eneas. 1979. *Floresta amazônica e a concentração de gaz carbônico na atmosfera.* Suplemento Cultural do Estado de São Paulo 130.

Sampaio, Gilvan *et al.* 2007. "Regional climate change over eastern Amazonia caused by pasture and soybean cropland expansion." *Geophysical Research Letters* 34, no. L17709: n. p. https://doi.org/10.1029/2007GL030612

Sandner, Gerhard. 1971. "Die Hauptphasen der wirtschaftlichen Entwicklung in Lateinamerika in ihrer Beziehung zur Raumerschließung." *Hamburger Geogr. Studien* 24: 311–334.

Sandner, Gerhard. 1975. "Wachstumspole und regionale Polarisierung der Entwicklung im Wirtschaftsraum. Ein Bericht über lateinamerikanische Erfahrungen." *Erdkundliches Wissen* 41: 78–90.

Santilli, Márcio. 2023. "Indigenous policy: Ministry of Indigenous Peoples, Funai and the Indigenats Health Secretariat will be led by indigenous leaders." https://www.socioambiental.org/en/socio-environmental-news/indigenous-policy (accessed March 4, 2023).

Santos, Breno Augusto dos. 1986. "Recursos minerais." In *Carajás: Desafio político, ecologia e desemvolvimento,* organised by J. M. Gonçalves de Almeida Jr., 294–361. São Paulo.

Santos, Milton. 1974. "Sous-développement et pôles de croissance économique et sociale." *Revue Tiers-Monde* 15, no. 58: 271–286.

Santos, Ricardo Ventura *et al.* 2019. "The identification of the indigenous population in Brazil's official statistics, with an emphasis on demographic censuses." *Statistical Journal of the IAOS* 35, no. 1: 29–46. https://doi.org/10.3233/SJI-180471

Santos, Daniel, Rodney Salomão, and Adalberto Veríssimo. 2021. *Fatos da Amazônia 2021.* IMAZON/Centro de Empreendedorismo da Amazônia. https://doi.org/10.59346/report.amazonia2030.202103.ed3

Sautchuk, Jaime, Horácio Martins de Carvalho, and Sérgio Buarque de Gusmão. 1980. *Projeto Jarí. A invasão Americana.* São Paulo: Ed. Brasil Debates Ltda.

Schipulle, Hans-Peter. 1989. "Nossa Natureza: Chance für Neuorientierung der brasilianischen Amazonaspolitik." *Entwicklung und Zusammenarbeit* 8/9: 25–29.

Schipulle, Hans-Peter. 1992. "Einbeziehung der Umweltdimension in die Entwicklungspolitik der Bundesregierung." In *Umweltorientierte Entwicklungspolitik,* edited by Wolfgang Hein, 151–163. Hamburg: Deutsches Übersee-Institut.

Schmink, Marianne. 1982. "Land conflicts in Amazonia." *American Ethnologist* 9, no. 2: 341–357.

Schmink, Marianne, and Charles H. Wood, eds. 1984. *Frontier expansion in Amazonia.* Gainesville: University of Florida Press.

Schmink, Marianne, and Charles H. Wood. 1992. *Contested Frontiers in Amazonia.* New York: Columbia University Press.

Schmink, Marianne, Jeffrey Hoelle, Carlos V.A. Gomes, and Gregory M. Thaler. 2019. "From contested to 'green' frontiers in the Amazon? A long-term analysis of São Félix do Xingu, Brazil." *The Journal of Peasant Studies* 46, no. 2: 377–399. https://doi.org/10.1080/03066150.2017.1381841

Schneider, Robert R. *et al.* 2000a. *Amazônia sustentável: limitantes e oportunidades para o desenvolvimento rural.* Brasília/Belém: IMAZON/World Bank.

Schneider, Robert R. *et al.* 2000b. *Sustainable forestry and the changing economics of land: The implications for public policy in the Amazon.* Brasília: The World Bank.

Schneider, Martina *et al.* 2021. "The commodity report: Soy production's impact on forests in South America." https://www.globalforestwatch.org/blog/commodities/soy-production-forests-south-america/ (accessed February 5, 2023).

Schönenberg, Regine. 1993. *Konflikte und Konfliktregulation in Amazonien. Ursachen, Formen und Folgen ländlicher Konflikte in Süd-Pará.* Bonn: Holos.

Schönenberg, Regine. 2002a. *Die Kriminalisierung gesellschaftlicher Transformationsprozesse. Der Fall des brasilianischen Amazonasgebiets.* Frankfurt a.M.: Hessische Stiftung Friedens- und Konfliktforschung.

Schönenberg, Regine. 2002b. "Drug trafficking in the Brazilian Amazon." In *Globalisation, drugs, and criminalisation.* Final Report MOST-UNESC International Research Project, organised by Christian Geffray, *et al.*, 151–171. https://unesdoc.unesco.org/ark:/48223/pf0000127644 (accessed October 21, 2022).

Schönenberg, Regine. 2010. "Gewalt, Kriminalität und Drogenhandel. In *Brasilien heute. Geographischer Raum, Politik, Wirtschaft, Kultur,* edited by Sérgio Costa *et al.*, 265–281. Frankfurt a. M.: Vervuert.

Schönenberg, Regine, Rüdiger Schaldach, Tobia Lakes, Jan Göpel, and Florian Gollnow. 2017. "Inter- and transdisciplinary scenario construction to explore future land-use options in southern Amazonia." *Ecology and Society* 22, no. 3: n. p. https://www.jstor.org/stable/26270154 (accessed October 20, 2022).

Scholz, Imme. 1999. *Nutzung natürlicher Ressourcen zwischen Raubbau und Nachhaltigkeit. Sozioökonomische Bedingungen und unternehmerische Handlungsmuster. Das Beispiel der Tropenholzindustrie in Pará (Brasilien) 1960–1997.* Köln: Weltforum.

Scholz, Imme. 2002. *Entwaldung und Entwicklung umweltpolitischer Institutionen in Amazonien: ein Wettlauf zwischen Hase und Igel? Der Beitrag des PPG7.* Bonn: Deutsches Institut für Entwicklungspolitik.

Scholz, Imme. 2005. "Environmental policy cooperation among organised civil society, national public actors and international actors in the Brazilian Amazon." *European Journal of Development Research* 17, no. 4: 681–705. http://dx.doi.org/10.1080/09578810500367466

Scholz, Imme. 2007. "Entre compromissos globais e interesses nacionais: elementos definidores da agenda da cooperação internacional na Amazônia brasileira." In *O Brasil na América Latina. Interações, percepções, interdependências,* edited by Sérgio Costa, Hartmut Sangmeister, and Sonja Steckbauer, 177–200. São Paulo: Annablume/ADLAF/Fundação Heinrich Böll.

Scholz, Imme, Daniel Dräger, Isabela Floer, Constanze Nehr, and Julia Unger. 2003. *Handlungsspielräume zivilgesellschaftlicher Gruppen und Chancen für eine kooperative Umweltpolitik in Amazonien*. Berichte und Gutachten 12/2003. Bonn: Deutsches Institut für Entwicklungspolitik.

Scholz, Imme, and Regine Schönenberg. 2007. "The Pilot Programme to conserve the Brazilian rainforests." In *From project to policy reform: experiences of German development cooperation*, edited by Tilman Altenburg, 97–122. Bonn: Deutsches Institut für Entwicklungspolitik (DIE). https://nbn-resolving.org/urn:nbn:de:0168-ssoar-109895 (accessed October 22, 2022).

Schubart, Herbert O. R. 1994. "O zoneamento ecológico-econômico como instrumento para o desenvolvimento sustantável." In *Amazônia e a crise da modernização*, organised by Maria A. D'Incão, and Isolda Maciel de Silveira, 490–500. Belém: Museu Paraense Emílio Goeldi.

Schwantes, Norberto. 1989. *Uma cruz em terra nova*. São Paulo: Scritta Oficina.

Schwartzman, Stephan, and Barbara Zimmerman. 2005. "Conservation alliances with indigenous peoples of the Amazon." *Conservation Biology* 19, no. 3: 721–727. https://doi.org/10.1111/j.1523-1739.2005.00695.x

Science Panel for the Amazon. 2021. *Executive Summary of the Amazon Assessment Report 2021*. United Nations Sustainable Development Solutions Network. New York: UN.

Segebart, Dörte. 2007. *Partizipatives Monitoring als Instrument zur Umsetzung von Good Local Governance. Eine Aktionsforschung im östlichen Amazonien/Brasilien*. TBGL 30. Tübingen: EdIGUT.

Seligmann, Peter. 2021. "Hoffnungsträger im Kampf gegen den Klimawandel." *FAZ*, December 1.

SEPLAN. 1974. *Programa de pôlos agropecuários e agrominerais da Amazônia. Polamazônia*. Brasília: SEPLAN.

SEPLAN. 1985. *Programa Grande Carajás. Legislação e normas*. Brasília: SEPLAN.

SEPLAN. 1986. *Programa Grande Carajás. Plano operativo para 1986*. Brasília: SEPLAN.

SEPLAN. 1989. *Programa Grande Carajás. Plano-diretor do corredor da Estrada de Ferro Carajás*. Brasília: Natron.

SEPLAN-RO/NURE. 1984. *5 anos de migração em Rondônia*. Porto Velho: SEPLAN-RO/NURE.

SEPLAN-RO/NURE. 1985. *Projeção populacional*. Porto Velho: SEPLAN-RO/NURE.

Serrão, E. Adilson, and Daniel C. Nepstad. 1996. "Pastures on Amazonian forestlands: A review of environmental and economic performance." In *Interdisciplinary research on the conservation and sustainable use of the Amazonian rain forest and its information requirements*, edited by Reinhard Lieberei, Christoph Reisdorff, and Antônio Dantas Machado, 221–234. Geesthacht: GKSS.

Silva, Marina. 2005. "The Brazilian protected areas program." *Conservation Biology* 19, no. 3: 608–611. https://doi.org/10.1111/j.1523-1739.2005.00707.x

Silva, Bruna Alves da, Cassiano de Brito Rocha, Maria de Fátima Oliveira, and Sandro Dutra e Silva. 2022. "A colonização gaúcha no vale do Araguaia: discursos de modernização da agricultura em Barra do Garças – Mato Grosso." *Revista Notas Históricas y Geográficas* 28: 197–222.

Silva, Pablo A. J., and Cintia Garabini Lages. 2020. "From forestry law to environmental law: A historical rescue of juridical protection of the environment." *E-legis* 31: 12–31.

Silveira, Semida. 1993. *Transformations in Amazonia. The spatial reconfirmation of systems.* PhD thesis, Tekniska högskolan, Stockholm.

Simões, Rolf *et al.* 2020. "Land use and cover maps for Mato Grosso State in Brazil from 2001 to 2017." *Sci Data* 7, Article 34: n. p. https://doi.org/10.1038/s41597-020-0371-4

Sioli, Harald. 1956. "Über Natur und Mensch im brasilianischen Amazonasgebiet." *Erdkunde* 10, no. 2: 89–109.

Sioli, Harald. 1968. "Zur Ökologie des Amazonasgebietes." In *Biogeography and ecology in South America,* edited by Ernst J. Fittkau *et al.*, 137–170. Den Haag: Junk Publ.

Sioli, Harald. 1973. "Recent human activities in the Brazilian Amazon region and their ecological effects." In *Tropical forest ecosystems in Africa and South America. A comparative review,* edited by Betty J. Meggers, Edward S. Ayensu, and W. Donald Duckworth, 321–334. Washington, D.C.: Smithsonian Institution Press.

Sioli, Harald. 1983. *Amazonien. Grundlagen der Ökologie des größten tropischen Waldlandes.* Stuttgart: Wiss. Verlagsgesellschaft.

Sioli, Harald, ed. 1984. *The Amazon. Limnology and landscape ecology of a mighty tropical river and its basin.* Dordrecht: Junk.

Sioli, Harald. 1985. "The effects of deforestation in Amazonia." *The Geographical Journal* 151, no. 2: 197–203.

Sioli, Harald. 2007. *Gelebtes, geliebtes Amazonien. Forschungsreisen im brasilianischen Regenwald zwischen 1940 und 1962,* edited and arranged by Gerd Kohlhepp. München: Verlag Dr. Friedrich Pfeil.

Skidmore, Marin E. *et al.* 2021. "Cattle ranchers and deforestation in the Brazilian Amazon: Production, location, and policies." *Global Environmental Change* 68: n. p. https://doi.org/10.1016/j.gloenvcha.2021.102280

Skillings, Robert F. 1985. "Economic development of the Brazilian Amazon: Opportunities and constraints." In *Change in the Amazon Basin.* Vol. 1: *Man's impact on forests and rivers,* edited by John Hemming, 36–57. Manchester: Manchester University Press.

Skole, David, and Compton J. Tucker. 1993. "Tropical deforestation and habitat fragmentation in the Amazon: Satellite data from 1978 to 1988." *Science* 260: 1905–1910.

Smeraldi, Robert, and Adalberto Veríssimo. 1999. *Hitting the target. Timber consumption in the Brazilian domestic market and promotion of forest certification.* São Paulo: Amigos da Terra/Imaflora/Imazon.

Smeraldi, Roberto, and Peter H. May. 2008. *The cattle realm: A new phase in the livestock colonization of Brazilian Amazonia.* São Paulo: Amigos da Terra.

Smith, Nigel J. H. *et al.* 1996. "Agroforestry trajectories among smallholders in the Brazilian Amazon: innovation and resiliency in pioneer and other settled areas." *Ecological Economics* 18: 15–27.

Smith, Nigel J. H. *et al.* 1998. *Agroforestry experiences in the Brazilian Amazon: Constraints and opportunities.* Brasília: PPG7.

Souza, Úrsula Gonçalves Theodoro de Faria. 2023. *'Beiradeiros' no complexo Rio Madeira: (In)sustentabilidades e (in)visibilidades de identidades coletivas ribeirinhas no planejamento e implantação nas usinas hidrelétricas.* PhD thesis, Universidade do Vale do Itajaí. http://bit.ly/3AMkpUe (accessed November 20, 2023).

Souza-Higa, Tereza C. Cardoso de, and Flávio Gatti. 2020. "Logística de escoamento da agroprodução Mato-Grossense e seus impactos na rede urbana regional." In *Estratégias de expansão do agronegócio em Mato Grosso. Os eixos da BR-163 e da BR-158 em perspectiva comparativa*, organised by Martin Coy, João C. Barrozo, and Edison A. de Souza, 89–107. Brasília: IABS.

Steinen, Karl von den. 1886. *Durch Central-Brasilien: Expedition zur Erforschung des Schingú im Jahre 1884*. Leipzig: Brockhaus.

Steinen, Karl von den. 1894. *Unter den Naturvölkern Zentral-Brasiliens. Reiseschilderungen und Ergebnisse der zweiten Schingú-Expedition 1887–1888*. Berlin: Verlag Dietrich Reimer.

Sternberg, Hilgard O'Reilly. 1981. "Frentes pioneiras contemporâneas na Amazônia Brasileira: Alguns aspectos ecológicos." *Espaço e conjuntura* 6: 1–38.

Sternberg, Hilgard O'Reilly. 1988. "Gegenwärtige Siedlungsfronten im brasilianischen Amazonien. Gedanken zur Umweltzerstörung." *Geographische Rundschau* 40, no. 11: 42–49.

Sternberg, Hilgard O'Reilly. 1998 [1956]. *A água e o homem na várzea do Careiro*, 2 vols. Belém: Museu Paraense Emilio Goeldi.

Stuenkel, Oliver. 2021. "Democracy is dying in Brazil. To stop Bolsonaro, the opposition must unite." *Foreign Affairs*, November 1. https://www.foreignaffairs.com/articles/brazil/2021-11-01/democracy-dying-brazil (accessed Feburary 25, 2023).

SUDAM. 1975. *II Plano de desenvolvimento da Amazônia (1975–1979)*. Belém: SUDAM.

SUDAM. 1983. *Relação dos projetos aprovados*. Belém: SUDAM.

SUDAM. 1984. *Relação dos projetos aprovados*. Belém: SUDAM.

SUDAM/SUDECO. 1975. *Programa de polos agropecuários e agrominerais da Amazônia. Polamazônia*. Síntese. Belém: SUDAM/SUDECO.

Tagliani, Paulo R., Roberta Pohren, and Luís F. Carvalho Perello. 2020. "Brazilian environmental impact assessment system: A critical analysis." *WIT Transactions on Ecology and the Environment* 245: 1–8. https://doi.org/10.2495/EID200011

Theis, Ivo M. 2019. "O que é desenvolvimento regional? Uma aproximação a partir da realidade brasileira." *Redes* 24, no. 3: 334–360. https://doi.org/10.17058/redes.v24i3.13670

Theis, Ivo M. 2022. "The imperial mode of living in a semi-peripheral social formation: notes on the case of Brazil." *Die Erde – Journal of the Geographical Society of Berlin* 153, no. 2: 84–96. https://doi.org/10.12854/erde-2022-615

Théry, Hervé. 1981. "Routes transamazoniennes et réorganisation de l'espace, le cas de Rondônia." *Cahiers d'Outre Mer* 133: 5–22.

Théry, Hervé. 1997a. *Configurações territoriais na Amazônia*. Paris: CNRS.

Théry, Hervé, ed. 1997b. *Environnement et développement en Amazonie Brésilienne*. Paris: Belin.

Théry, Hervé. 2005. "Situações da Amazônia no Brasil e no continente." *Estudos Avançados* 19, no. 53: 37–49.

Théry, Hervé, and Hélène Rivière d'Arc. 1980. "State and entrepreneurs in the development of Brazilian Amazonia." In *Land, people, and planning in contemporary Amazonia*, edited by Françoise Barbira-Scazzocchio, 72–79. Cambridge: Cambridge University Press.

Tófoli, Raffael M. *et al.* 2017. "Gold at what cost? Another megaproject threatens biodiversity in the Amazon." *Perspectives in Ecology and Conservation* 15, no. 2: 129–131. https://doi.org/10.1016/j.pecon.2017.06.003

Tollefson, Jeff. 2015. "Stopping deforestation: Battle for the Amazon." *Nature* 520: 20–23.

Torres, Mauricio, Juan Doblas, and Daniela Fernandes Alarcon. 2017. *Dono é quem desmata: conexões entre grilagem e desmatamento no sudoeste paraense.* São Paulo/Altamira: Urutu-branco/Instituto Agronômico da Amazônia.

Trigueiro, André. 2019. "15 points to understand the directions of disastrous environmental policy in the Bolsonaro government." https://g1.globo.com/natureza/blog/andre-trigueiro/post/2019/06/03/15-pontos-para-entender-os-rumos-da-desastrosa-politica-ambiental-no-governo-bolsonaro.ghtml (accessed January 28, 2023).

UFMA. 1986. *Jornada de trabalho: Perspectivas das atividades minero-industriais e agro-pastoris no desenvolvimento regional do Sudeste a Amazônia.* São Luís.

UNEP. 1989. *Report on new projects 1988.* Nairobi: UNEP.

UNEP. 2006. *Brazil: Integrated assessment and planning in the context of the sustainable Amazon Plan: With focus on the BR-163 Highway area of influence and the soybean sector.* Genève: UNEP.

Vale. 2012. *Carajás S11D iron project: a new impetus to Brazil's sustainable development.* Rio de Janeiro: Vale.

Valverde, Orlando. 1981. "Ecologia e desenvolvimento da Amazônia." *Revista Brasileira de Tecnologia* 12, no. 4: 3–16.

Valverde, Orlando. 1987. *Impactos ecológicos e econômico-sociais na área de influência de E. F. Carajás.* Rio de Janeiro (manuscript).

Valverde, Orlando. 1989. *Grande Carajás: planejamento da destruição.* Rio de Janeiro: Forense Universitária.

Valverde, Orlando, and Catharina Vergolino Dias. 1967. *A Rodovia Belém–Brasília: estudo de geografia regional.* Rio de Janeiro: IBGE.

Valverde, Orlando, and Tácito L. Reis de Freitas. 1980. *O problema florestal da Amazônia Brasileira.* Petrópolis: Vozes.

Vandergeest, Peter, and Nancy Lee Peluso. 2015. "Political forests." In *The International Handbook of Political Ecology*, edited by Raymond L. Bryant, 162–175. Cheltenham/Northampton: Edward Elgar Publishing.

Van der Hoff, Richard, Raoni Rajão, and Pieter Leroy. 2018. "Clashing interpretations of REDD+ 'results' in the Amazon Fund." *Climatic Change* 150, no. 3–4: 433–445.

Vaz de Melo, M. T. 1985. *The CVRD iron ore deposits, Brazil. A general view.* Belo Horizonte: CVRD.

Veiga, Jonas Bastos da *et al.* 2002. "Cattle ranching in the Amazon rainforest." *Animal Production in Australia* 24: 253–256.

Veja. 1982. "O país afinal comprou o sonho do Jarí." January 13: 68–73.

Vera-Diaz, Maria del C., Robert K. Kaufmann, and Daniel C. Nepstad. 2009. *The environmental impacts of soybean expansion and infrastructure development in Brazil's Amazon Basin.* Medford: Tufts University.

Verdum, Ricardo. 2022. "Bolsonaro's strategy to make indigenous peoples disappear in Brazil." IWGIA, June 14. https://www.iwgia.org/en/brazil/4838-bolsonaro-s-strategy-to-make-indigenous-peoples-disappear-in-brazil.html (accessed Feburary 16, 2023).

Veríssimo, Adalberto *et al.* 1998. "Zoning of timber extraction in the Brazilian Amazon." *Conservation Biology* 12, no. 1: 128–136.

Vidal, Lux Boelitz. 1986. "A questão indígena." In *Carajás: desafio político, ecologia e desenvolvimento*,organised by J. M. Gonçalves de Almeida Jr., 222–264. São Paulo: Brasiliense/Conselho Nacional de Desenvolvimento Científico e Tecnológico.

Vieira, Roberto dos Santos. 1988. "Desenvolvimenrto da Amazônia: A questão da ecologia versus economia e direito ambiental." In *Umweltrecht in Deutschland und Brasilien*, edited by Michael Bothe, 41–74. Frankfurt a. M./Bern/New York/Paris: Peter Lang.

Vieira, Roberto dos Santos. 1993. "Das brasilianische Umweltrecht und seine Wirkung in Amazonien." In *Amazônia - Realität und Recht; umwelt- und arbeitsrechtliche Fragestellungen*, edited by Wolf Paul, and Roberto dos Santos Vieira, 91–128. Frankfurt a. M.: Peter Lang.

Vilani, Rodrigo Machado, Lucas Ferrante, and Philip M. Fearnside. 2022."Amazonia threatened by Brazilian President Bolsonaro's mining agenda." *Die Erde – Journal of the Geographical Society of Berlin* 153, no. 4: 254–258. https://doi.org/10.12854/erde-2022-622.

Villas Bôas, Orlando, and Cláudio Villas Bôas. 1973. *Xingu. The Indians, their myths*. New York: Farrar, Straus, and Giroux.

Villas Bôas, Orlando, and Cláudio Villas Bôas. 1994. *A Marcha para o Oeste: a epopeia da Expedição Roncador-Xingu*. São Paulo: Globo.

Viola, Eduardo J. 1988. "The ecologist movement in Brazil (1974–1986) from environmentalism to ecopolitics." *International Journal of Regional and Urban Research* 12, no. 2: 211–227.

Volbeda, Sjoukje. 1986. "Pioneer towns in the jungle. Urbanization at an agricultural colonization frontier in the Brazilian Amazon." *Revista Geográfica* 104, 15–140.

Waibel, Leo. 1948. "A vegetação e o uso da terra no Planalto Central." *Revista Brasileira de Geografia* 10, no. 3: 335–380.

Waibel, Leo. 1950. "European colonization in Southern Brazil." *The Geographical Review* 40, no. 4: 529–547.

Watson, Katy. 2023. "Carbon credits – land grab or the Amazon's future?" BBC News Brazil, August 8. https://www.bbc.com/news/world-latin-america-66435166 (accessed August 8, 2023).

Watts, Jonathan. 2017. "Operation car wash: Is this the biggest corruption scandal in history?" *The Guardian*, June 1. https://www.theguardian.com/world/2017/jun/01/brazil-operation-car-wash-is-this-the-biggest-corruption-scandal-in-history?cmpid=BBD060117_MKT&utm_medium=email&utm_source=newsletter&utm_term=170601&utm_campaign=markets (accessed December 3, 2022).

Watts, Jonathan. 2019. "Poorly planned Amazon dam project poses serious threat to life." *The Guardian*, November 9.

Watts, Jonathan. 2022. "The New Year resolutions Lula should make for the Amazon." SUMAÚMA, December 21. https://sumauma.com/en/sete-resolucoes-de-ano-novo-para-lula-e-a-favor-da-amazonia/ (accessed March 3, 2023).

Weiffen, Brigitte. 2022. "Foreign policy and international relations: Taking stock after two years of the Bolsonaro administration." In *Brazil under Bolsonaro. How endangered is democracy?* Ibero Online 14, edited by Peter Birle, and Bruno Speck, 55–66. https://publications.iai.spk-berlin.de/receive/iai_mods_00000128 (accessed February 23, 2023.)

Weischet, Wolfgang. 1980. *Die ökologische Benachteiligung der Tropen.* Stuttgart: B. G. Teubner.

Weischet, Wolfgang. 1981. "Ackerland aus Tropenwald – eine verhängnisvolle Illusion." *Holz Aktuell* 3: 14–33.

Weißermel, Sören. 2019. *Die Aushandlung von Enteignung. Der Kampf um Anerkennung und Öffentlichkeit im Rahmen des Staudammbaus Belo Monte, Brasilien.* Stuttgart: Franz Steiner.

Weißermel, Sören. 2020. "Towards a conceptual understanding of dispossession – Belo Monte and the precarization of the riverine people." *Novos Cadernos NAEA* 23, no. 1: 11–34. https://www.periodicos.ufpa.br/index.php/ncn/article/view/7498 (accessed December 8, 2022).

Wenzel, Fernanda. 2021. "Brazil prosecutors seek ban on all gold mining in hard-hit Amazonian region." *Mongabay Series: Amazon Conservation, Land rights and extractives.* https://news.mongabay.com/2021/07/brazil-prosecutors-seek-ban-on-all-gold-mining-in-hard-hit-amazonian-region/ (accessed February 28, 2023).

Winter, Brian. 2022. "Can Brazil turn back the clock? Latin America's nostalgia trap and the return of Lula." *Foreign Affairs,* June 21. https://www.foreignaffairs.com/articles/brazil/2022-06-21/brazil-turn-back-clock (accessed February 25, 2023).

Wollrad Dörte, and Viviana Barreto. 2021. "In der politischen Gefriertruhe." IPG, Lateinamerika, August, 20. https://www.ipg-journal.de/regionen/lateinamerika/artikel/in-der-politischen-gefriertruhe-5372/ (accessed October 22, 2022).

Woods, William I. *et al.*, eds. 2009. *Amazonian Dark Earths: Wim Sombroek's Vision.* Berlin: Springer.

World Bank. 1990. *The World Bank and the environment. First annual report Fiscal 1990.* Washington, D.C.: The World Bank.

World Bank. 1993. *Rain Forest Pilot Program Update.* Quarterly Newsletter of the Pilot Program to conserve the Brazilian rain forest. Brasília: The World Bank.

World Bank. 1994. *Pilot Program to conserve the Brazilian rain forests.* Washington, D.C: The World Bank.

Xingu Vivo. 2012. "Tucuruí: Mesmo depois de 30 anos continuamos sem receber indenização." https://xinguvivo.org.br/2011/04/tucurui-mesmo-depois-de-30-anos-continuamos-sem-receber-indenizacao/ (accessed August 12, 2022).

Zimmer, Katarina. 2019. "Why the Amazon doesn't really produce 20% of the world's oxygen". *National Geogrpahic,* https://www.nationalgeographic.com/environment/article/why-amazon-doesnt-produce-20-percent-worlds-oxygen (accessed September 23, 2022).

Author's publications on Amazonia cited in this volume

Kohlhepp, Gerd. 1976a."Planung und heutige Situation staatlicher kleinbäuerlicher Kolonisationsprojekte an der Transamazônica." *Geographische Zeitschrift* 64, no. 3: 171–211.

Kohlhepp, Gerd. 1976b. "Stand und Problematik der brasilianischen Entwicklungsplanung in Amazonien." *Amazoniana* 6, no. 1: 87–104.

Kohlhepp, Gerd. 1977a. "Zum Problem von Interessenkonflikten bei der Neulanderschliessung in Ländern der Dritten Welt. Am Beispiel des brasilianischen Amazonasgebietes." In *Die Geographie und ihre Didaktik*, edited by Karl Heinz Reinhardt, 15–31. Frankfurt a. M.: Johann-Wolfgang-Goethe-Universität.

Kohlhepp, Gerd. 1977b. "Bergbaustandorte im östlichen Amazonasgebiet. Entwicklungspole oder Orte temporärer Extraktion mineralischer Rohstoffe?" In *Studien zur allgemeinen und regionalen Geographie*, edited by Gerald Gruber *et al.*, 239–273. Frankfurt a. M.: Johann-Wolfgang-Goethe-Universität.

Kohlhepp, Gerd. 1978a. "Erschließung und wirtschaftliche Inwertsetzung Amazoniens. Entwicklungsstrategien brasilianischer Planungspolitik und privater Unternehmen." *Geographische Rundschau* 30, no. 1: 2–13; no. 6: 252.

Kohlhepp, Gerd. 1978b. "Wirtschafts- und sozialgeographische Aspekte des brasilianischen Entwicklungsmodells und dessen Eingliederung in die Weltwirtschaftsordnung." *Die Erde – Journal of the Geographical Society of Berlin* 109, no. 3–4: 353–375.

Kohlhepp, Gerd. 1978c. "Siedlungsentwicklung und Siedlungsplanung im zentralen Amazonien. Gedanken zum zentralörtlichen System 'Agrovila, Agrópolis, Rurópolis'." *Frankfurter Wirtschafts- und Sozialgeographische Schriften* 28: 171–191.

Kohlhepp, Gerd. 1979. "Brasiliens problematische Antithese zur Agrarreform: Agrarkolonisation in Amazonien. Evaluierung wirtschafts- und sozialgeographischer Prozessabläufe an der Peripherie im Lichte wechselnder agrarpolitischer Strategien." In *Agrarreform in der Dritten Welt*, edited by Hartmut Elsenhans, 471–504. Frankfurt a. M./New York: Campus.

Kohlhepp, Gerd. 1983a. "Strategien zur Raumerschließung und Regionalentwicklung im Amazonasgebiet. Zur Analyse ihrer entwicklungspolitischen Auswirkungen." In *Entwicklungsstrategien in Lateinamerika in Vergangenheit und Gegenwart*, edited by Inge Buisson, and Manfred Mols, 175–193. Paderborn/München/Wien/Zürich: Ferdinand Schöningh.

Kohlhepp, Gerd. 1983b. "Amazonien: Entwicklung wohin? Zur Problematik regionaler Entwicklungsstrategien und räumlicher Erschließungsprozesse." *Spixiana* 9: 179–196.

Kohlhepp, Gerd. 1984a. "Development planning and practices of economic exploitation in Amazonia. Recent trends in spatial organization of a tropical frontier region in Brazil (1966–1981)." In *The Amazon. Limnology and landscape ecology of a mighty tropical river and its basin*, edited by Harald Sioli, 649–674. Dordrecht/Boston/Lancaster: Dr. W. Junk Publishers.

Kohlhepp, Gerd. 1984b. "Der tropische Regenwald als Siedlungs- und Wirtschaftsraum. Am Beispiel jüngster Entwicklungsprozesse im brasilianischen Amazonasgebiet." In *Tropische Regenwälder: eine globale Herausforderung*, edited by Wolfgang Engelhardt, and Ernst J. Fittkau, 131–157.

Kohlhepp, Gerd. 1984c. "Colonización y desarrollo dependiente en el oriente Paraguayo." *Revista Geográfica* 99: 5–33.

Kohlhepp, Gerd. 1985. *Regionalentwicklungsprogramm "Grande Carajás"* (Ost-Amazonien). Expert assessment (Short report). Tübingen (unpublished).

Kohlhepp, Gerd. 1986. "Der Einbruch der modernen Zivilisation in Amazonien." In *Umwelt, Kultur und Entwicklung in der Dritten Welt*. Tübinger Gespräche zu Entwicklungsfragen 1986. Materialien zum Internationalen Kulturaustausch 27, 162–189, Stuttgart: IfA.

Kohlhepp, Gerd. 1987a. *Amazonien. Regionalentwicklung im Spannungsfeld ökonomischer Interessen sowie sozialer und ökologischer Notwendigkeiten*. Köln: Aulis.

Kohlhepp, Gerd. 1987b. "Wirtschafts- und sozialgeographische Auswirkungen der Weltmarktintegration Ost-Amazoniens. Zur Bewertung der regionalen Entwicklungsplanung im Grande Carajás-Programm in Pará und Maranhão." In *Brasilien. Beiträge zur regionalem Struktur- und Entwicklungsforschung*, TBGL 1, edited by Gerd Kohlhepp, 213–254. Tübingen: EdIGUT.

Kohlhepp, Gerd. 1987c. "Problemas do planejamento regional e do desenvolvimento regional na área do Programa Carajás no Leste da Amazônia." In *Homem e natureza na Amazônia*, TBGL 3, edited by Gerd Kohlhepp, and Achim Schrader, 313–345. Tübingen: EdIGUT.

Kohlhepp, Gerd. 1987d. *Itaipú. Basic geopolitical and energy situation – socio economic and ecological consequences of the Itaipú dam and reservoir on the Rio Paraná (Brazil/Paraguay)*. GATE-GTZ Division, 21, Ecology and Environmental Protection. Braunschweig/Wiesbaden: Vieweg & Sohn.

Kohlhepp, Gerd. 1987e. "Desafios à ciência e às políticas de desenvolvimento regional. Reflexões e recomendações sobre o futuro desenvolvimento da Amazônia." In *Homem e natureza na Amazônia*, TBGL 3, edited by Gerd Kohlhepp, and Achim Schrader, 485–499. Tübingen: EdIGUT.

Kohlhepp, Gerd. 1989a. "Ursachen und aktuelle Situation der Vernichtung tropischer Regenwälder im brasilianischen Amazonien." In *Die Bedrohung tropischer Wälder. Ursachen, Auswirkungen, Schutzkonzepte*, edited by Jürgen Bähr *et al.*, 87–110. Kiel: Geographisches Institut der Universität Kiel.

Kohlhepp, Gerd. 1989b. "Die Vernichtung der tropischen Regenwälder Amazoniens. Zur Problematik von Regionalentwicklung und Umweltpolitik in der Dritten Welt." *Eichholzbrief* 1: 36–53.

Kohlhepp, Gerd. 1989c. "Schutz tropischer Wälder." Statement to the "Enquete Commission for the protection of tropical forests" of the German Bundestag. In *EK-Drucksache* 11/78, 1–12. Bonn: Deutscher Bundestag.

Kohlhepp, Gerd. 1989d. "Raumwirksame Tätigkeit ethnosozialer Gruppen in Brasilien. Am Beispiel donauschwäbischer Siedler in Entre Rios/Paraná." In *Europäische Ethnien im ländlichen Raum der Neuen Welt*, edited by Klaus Rother, 31–46. Passau: Passavia Universitätsverlag.

Kohlhepp, Gerd. 1990. "Desafios à ciência e às políticas de desenvolvimento regional. Reflexões e recomendações sobre o futuro desenvolvimento da Amazônia." *Estudos Avançados* 3, no. 7: 183–199.

Kohlhepp, Gerd. 1991a. "The destruction of the tropical rain forests in the Amazon region of Brazil. An analysis of the causes and the current situation." *Applied Geography and Development* 38: 87–109.

Kohlhepp, Gerd. 1991b. "Mudanças estruturais na agropecuária e mobilidade da população rural no Norte do Paraná (Brasil)." *Revista Brasileira de Geografia* 53, no. 2: 79–94.

Kohlhepp, Gerd. 1991c. "Impactos regionais de 'grandes projetos' e as possibilidades de reorganização do espaço na periferia amazônica." In *A desordem ecológica na Amazônia*, organised by Luís E. Aragón, 253–269. Belém: UNAMAZ/UFPA.

Kohlhepp, Gerd. 1991d. "Umweltpolitik zum Schutz tropischer Regenwälder in Brasilien. Rahmenbedingungen und umweltpolitische Aktivitäten." *KAS – Auslandsinformationen* 7: 1–23.

Kohlhepp, Gerd. 1991e. "The regional impact of major projects and possible spatial reorganization on the Amazon periphery." In *Ecological disorder and Amazonia*, edited by Leszek A. Kosinski, 147–167. Rio de Janeiro: International Social Science Council.

Kohlhepp, Gerd. 1992. "Problems of regional development in the Brazilian Amazon area." In *Amazonia: Ecology and sustainable development*, edited by Wil Pansters, 131–146. Utrecht: ISOR/Rijksuniversiteit te Utrecht.

Kohlhepp, Gerd. 1995. "The International Pilot Programme for Amazonia: An approach to sustainable regional development." *International Geographical Union, Bulletin* 45: 17–30. Bonn: IGU/UNESCO.

Kohlhepp, Gerd. 1997a. "Die deutsch-brasilianische wissenschaftliche Zusammenarbeit, unter besonderer Berücksichtigung der Umweltforschung." In *Bestandsaufnahme und Perspektiven der deutsch-brasilianischen Beziehungen*, edited by Andreas Boeckh, and Rafael Sevilla, 183–207. Frankfurt a. M.: Vervuert.

Kohlhepp, Gerd. 1997b. "Regional policies in Brazil: the spatial impact of state activity in Amazonia." In *The diversity of development: Essays in honour of Jan Kleinpenning*, edited by T. van Naersson, 231–240. Assen: Van Gorcum.

Kohlhepp, Gerd. 1998a. "Das Internationale Pilotprogramm zum Schutz der tropischen Regenwälder Brasiliens. Globale, nationale, regionale und lokale Akteure auf dem Weg zu einer Strategie der nachhaltigen Entwicklung?" In *Mensch-Umwelt-Beziehungen und nachhaltige Entwicklung in der Dritten Welt*, TBGL 15, edited by Gerd Kohlhepp, and Martin Coy, 51–86. Tübingen: EdIGUT.

Kohlhepp, Gerd. 1998b. "O problema do espaço vital dos povos indígenas e os conflitos de interesse na demarcação das Áreas Indígenas na Amazônia Brasileira." In *El indio como sujeto y objeto de la historia latinoamericana. Pasado y presente.* Americana eystettensia. Publikationen des Zentralinstituts für Lateinamerika-Studien der Kath. Universität Eichstätt, Serie A: Kongressakten 18, edited by Hans-Joachim König, 109–120. Madrid/Frankfurt a. M.: Iberoamericana/Vervuert.

Kohlhepp, Gerd. 1998c. "Große Staudammprojekte in Brasilien. Ökologische und sozioökonomische Probleme." *Geographische Rundschau* 50, no. 7–8: 428–436.

Kohlhepp, Gerd. 1999. "Incorporação do espaço fronteiriço do leste do Paraguai na esfera de influência brasileira." In *El espacio interior de América del Sur*, edited by Barbara Potthast, Karl Kohut, and Gerd Kohlhepp, 205–225. Madrid/Frankfurt a. M.: Iberoamericana/Vervuert.

Kohlhepp, Gerd. 2001a."Estratégias da política ambiental e regional para a proteção das florestas tropicais no Brasil. O Programa Piloto Internacional e seus atores em direção ao desenvolvimento sustentável?" In *Brasil – modernização e globalização*, coordinated by Gerd Kohlhepp, 209–234. Madrid/Frankfurt a. M.: Iberoamericana/Vervuert.

Kohlhepp, Gerd. 2001b. "Amazonia 2000: An evaluation of three decades of regional planning and development programmes in the Brazilian Amazon Region." *Amazoniana* 16, no. 3/4: 363–395.

Kohlhepp, Gerd. 2001c. "A Amazônia frente a um novo desafio: o desenvolvimento sustentável e o Programa Avança Brasil." In *Amazônia: Avança o Brasil?*, edited by Wilhelm Hofmeister. Cadernos Adenauer 2, no. 4: 9–38. São Paulo: Fundação Konrad Adenauer.

Kohlhepp, Gerd. 2005. "Desenvolvimento sustentável na Amazônia? Dúvidas na consolidação do Programa Piloto, as recentes estratégias e a realidade amazônica." In *Amazônia sustentável, Desenvolvimento sustentável entre políticas, estratégias inovadoras e experiências locais*, TBGL 28, coordinated by Martin Coy, and Kohlhepp, 75–96. Rio de Janeiro/Tübingen: Garamond/EdIGUT.

Kohlhepp, Gerd. 2007a. "Desenvolvimento regional na Amazônia Brasileira. Estratégias de ordenamento territorial e conflitos entre interesses econômicos e uso sustentável dos recursos naturais nas florestas tropicais." In *BR-163 – De estrada dos colonos a corredor de exportação*, edited by Messias M. dos Passos, 15–62. Maringá: Massoni.

Kohlhepp, Gerd. 2007b. "Die lebensräumliche Situation der indigenen Bevölkerung Amazoniens vor dem Hintergrund der brasilianischen Regionalpolitik und raumwirtschaftlicher Interessenkonflikte." In *Curt Unckel Nimuendajú – ein Jenenser als Pionier im brasilianischen Nord(ost)en*, edited by Joachim Born, 195–221. Wien: Praesens.

Kohlhepp, Gerd. 2010a. "Strukturprobleme der Agrarwirtschaft und Entwicklungsdynamik des Agrobusiness." In *Brasilien heute. Geographischer Raum, Politik, Wirtschaft, Kultur*, edited by Sérgio Costa, Gerd Kohlhepp, Horst Nitschack, and Hartmut Sangmeister, 349–367. Frankfurt a. M.: Vervuert.

Kohlhepp, Gerd. 2010b. "Regionale Disparitäten und Regionalplanung." In *Brasilien heute. Geographischer Raum, Politik, Wirtschaft, Kultur*, edited by Sérgio Costa, Gerd Kohlhepp, Horst Nitschack, and Hartmut Sangmeister, 91-109. Frankfurt a. M.: Vervuert.

Kohlhepp, Gerd. 2010c. "Energiewirtschaft im Umbruch." In *Brasilien heute. Geographischer Raum, Politik, Wirtschaft, Kultur*, edited by Sérgio Costa, Gerd Kohlhepp, Horst Nitschack, and Hartmut Sangmeister, 369–381. Frankfurt a. M.: Vervuert.

Kohlhepp, Gerd. 2014. *Colonização agrária no Norte do Paraná. Processos geoeconômicos e sociogeográficos de desenvolvimento de uma zona pioneira tropical do Brasil sob a influência da plantação do café.* Maringá: Ed. da Universidade do Maringá. [Original publication: *Agrarkolonisation in Nord-Paraná. Wirtschafts- und sozialgeographische Entwicklungsprozesse einer randtropischen Pionierzone Brasiliens unter dem Einfluss des Kaffeeanbaus*. Wiesbaden: Franz Steiner-Verlag, 1975].

Kohlhepp, Gerd. 2017a. "Orlando Valverde (1917–2006). Um geógrafo brasileiro de renome internacional – entusiasta e entusiasmante." In *Orlando Valverde. O geógrafo e sua obra*, organised by Dirce M. Antunes Suertegaray *et al.*, 157–188. Porto Alegre: Geociências/UFRGS.

Kohlhepp, Gerd. 2017b. "Nas trilhas de Leo Waibel: Pesquisas alemãs de Geografia Humana do Brasil – de Heidelberg à Tübingen (1950–2005)." *Revista Brasileira de Geografia* 62, no. 2: 7–24.

Kohlhepp, Gerd. 2018. "O Programa Piloto Internacional de Proteção das Florestas Tropicais no Brasil (1993–2009). As primeiras estratégias da política ambiental e de desenvolvimento regional para a Amazônia Brasileira." *Revista NERA*, Dossiê Amazônia, 21, no. 42: 308–331.

Kohlhepp, Gerd. 2020a. "O Brasil sofre com uma "guerra ideológica" contra todos os que estão comprometidos contra a destruição da Amazônia." Interview by Marcelo Lopes de Souza. *Ambientes. Revista de Geografia e Ecologia Política* 2, no. 2: 398–437.

Kohlhepp, Gerd. 2020b. "Transformações da paisagem natural no Norte do Paraná entre as décadas de 1930 e 1980: Da monocultura do café à modernização agrária e suas consequências ecológicas, econômicas e sociais." *HALAC* 10, no. 2: 255–283.

Kohlhepp, Gerd. 2021a. "A contribuição de Leo Waibel para o conhecimento da colonizacão agrária no Brasil do séc. XX." In *Cooperação Acadêmica para Estudos Ambientais do Cerrado.* Vol. I: Novas Fronteiras no Oeste: relação entre Sociedade e Natureza na Microrregião de Ceres em Goiás (1940–2013), organised by Cezar A. Leal *et al.*, 53-78. Goiânia: Kelps.

Kohlhepp, Gerd. 2021b. "Umwelt- und Amazonienpolitik der Regierung Bolsonaro." *eTópicos* 1/2021: 14–15.

Kohlhepp, Gerd, and Martin Coy. 1985. *Regional development in Southwestern Amazonia. The Polonoroeste-Programme in Rondônia and the state of colonization in Acre.* Evaluation by order of GTZ, 99 pp. Tübingen: unpublished.

Kohlhepp, Gerd, and Martin Coy. 1986. "Conflicts of interests and regional development planning in colonizing the Brazilian Amazon: The case of Rondônia." In *Competition for rural and urban space in Latin America, its consequences for low-income groups,* edited by Jan M. G. Kleinpenning, 61–75. Amsterdam/Nijmegen: Koninklijk Nederlands Aardrijkskundig Genootschap.

Kohlhepp, Gerd, and Martin Coy. 2010. "Amazonien. Vernichtung durch Regionalentwicklung oder Schutz zur nachhaltigen Nutzung?" In *Brasilien heute,* edited by Sérgio Costa, Gerd Kohlhepp, Horst Nitschack, and Hartmut Sangmeister, 111–134. Frankfurt a. M.: Vervuert.

Kohlhepp, Gerd, and Bernd Karp. 1987. "Itaipú. Raumwirksame sozioökonomische Probleme hydroelektrischer Inwertsetzung des Rio Paraná im brasilianisch-paraguayischen Grenzraum." In *Brasilien. Beiträge zur regionalen Struktur- und Entwicklungsforschung,* TBGL 1, edited by Gerd Kohlhepp, 71–116. Tübingen: EdIGUT.

Kohlhepp, Gerd, and Achim Schrader, eds. 1987. *Homem e natureza na Amazônia. Hombre y Naturaleza en la Amazonía.* TBGL 3. Tübingen: EdIGUT.

Kohlhepp, Gerd, Reinhold Lücker, and Irene Garrido Filha. 1987. *Programa Grande Carajás. An evaluation of the Regional Development Programme in Brazilian Eastern Amazonia.* Evaluation for the German Agency of Technical Cooperation (GTZ), 221 pp. Tübingen: unpublished.

Kohlhepp, Gerd, and Markus Blumenschein. 2000. "Brasileiros sulistas como atores da transformação rural no Centro-Oeste brasileiro: O caso de Mato Grosso." *Território* 8: 47–66.

Kohlhepp, Gerd, and Sandro Dutra e Silva. 2022. "Colonização no Brasil Central: a fronteira agrícola em Mato Grosso entre as décadas de 1950 e 1970." *Fronteiras. Revista Catarinense de História* 39: 50–81.